D1713622

THE DEMOGRAPHY
OF TROPICAL AFRICA

UNDER THE EDITORIAL SPONSORSHIP
OF THE OFFICE OF POPULATION RESEARCH
PRINCETON UNIVERSITY

THE DEMOGRAPHY OF
TROPICAL AFRICA

WILLIAM BRASS, ANSLEY J. COALE,

PAUL DEMENY, DON F. HEISEL,

FRANK LORIMER, ANATOLE ROMANIUK,

AND ETIENNE VAN DE WALLE

PRINCETON, NEW JERSEY

PRINCETON UNIVERSITY PRESS

1968

Preface

This book weaves together strands of interest in African demography on the part of many persons and several institutions—strands that in some instances extend back for many years. The Office of Population Research has a tradition that began with its founding in 1936 of special attention to international demography, consistently emphasizing population trends in the less developed areas of the world and the significance of these trends. Another persistent theme in the Office's research interests has been the development and application of techniques of estimation of such important variables as birth rates and death rates from the incomplete or inaccurate data that exist in these areas. When censuses and special surveys providing quantitative information about a substantial fraction of the population of tropical Africa began to appear for the first time in the years after World War II, there was a natural interest at Princeton in seeing what could be learned from a systematic analysis of these data. In 1958 Karol J. Krótki, who as Census Controller in the Sudan had played a major part in the planning and execution of the sample census of population in that country in 1956, completed a doctoral dissertation at Princeton entitled *Estimating Vital Rates from Peculiar and Inadequate Age Distribution (Sudanese Experience)*.

In the fall of 1960 Frank Lorimer accepted a part-time research position at Princeton to conduct a reconnoitering survey of the extent and quality of population data on tropical Africa. Lorimer's active work on African population had begun in 1952 when he went on a mission for UNESCO that included making arrangements for field studies of fertility at the East African Institute of Social Research and at the University of Ghana. In 1957 he undertook a survey of existing information on African population at Boston University in collaboration with members of the Africa Studies Program and published a report as a result of this survey entitled "Demographic Information on Tropical Africa." It was on Lorimer's initiative that the International Union for the Scientific Study of Population held a colloquium in Paris in 1959 which brought together demographers and statisticians who had a working knowledge of African population statistics. He also spent half a year at the University of Ghana in 1960 helping to inaugurate a program of population studies. As part of his exploratory work at the Office of Population Research in 1960-1962, Lorimer visited research centers and statistical offices in various African countries to complete the acquisition of basic data and related material.

During 1961-1962 the Office decided to launch a full-scale research program. William Brass and Don Heisel were added to the full-time professional staff for that year, and Paul Demeny devoted a substantial fraction of his research time to the project. Brass came to Princeton on leave of absence from Aberdeen University, where he was professor of statistics. Before assuming this post he had spent several years in the East African Statistical Office where he had had extensive first-hand experience with population censuses, demographic surveys, and vital statistics. In Africa and in Aberdeen he had begun to invent and apply the methods of estimation that in a more developed form have been heavily utilized in this book and that indeed represent perhaps the most valuable single contribution of this project. The Director of the Office had, since the early 1940's, studied age patterns of mortality and their use in the construction of model life tables, and the use of age distributions in conjunction with model life tables to estimate the fertility and mortality of a population. In collaboration with Paul Demeny, he developed four families of "regional" model life tables and stable populations that form another principal basis of estimation used in this project, in addition to the techniques of Brass.

Don Heisel had been trained in statistics and in techniques of demographic analysis at the University of Wisconsin. Anatole Romaniuk and Etienne van de Walle came to Princeton in the fall of 1960 as visiting students in the special training program at the Office of Population Research. Romaniuk had a background of extensive experience and responsibility in a demographic survey of the Congo in 1956-1957 and van de Walle had been employed for four years by the Institut pour la Recherche Scientifique en Afrique Centrale in Ruanda-Urundi. During their year as visiting students both participated in the research project in addition to taking part in graduate seminars, and in the summer of 1962 they joined the project on a full-time basis. Most of the substantive analysis of demographic data from Africa was carried out by Brass, Demeny, Heisel, Lorimer, Romaniuk, and van de Walle. Coale contributed to the development of methods and constructed estimates for some of the regions for which an intensive case study was not attempted. It was Frank Lorimer's wide personal knowledge of African statistics and of knowledgeable statisticians that made it possible to assemble this group, and it was his energy and enthusiasm that supplied the impetus needed to launch the project. His advice and ideas contributed to almost every chapter, not merely those where he is listed as an author. An indispensable contributor to the completion of this volume was Marion O'Connor, who collected the data and made the calculations underlying the density map, made or supervised many of the computations throughout the volume, and patiently attempted to impose more consistency and uniformity on material prepared by different authors who often employed different statistical techniques. Mrs. O'Connor made a number of the estimates for territories that had not been the subject of intensive case studies and had a hand in drafting parts of the summary chapters. She assisted Lorimer in the collection of data and was responsible for putting and keeping the large body of statistical material amassed by the project in order. Rémy Clairin spent three months on leave from the Institut National de la Statistique et des Etudes Economiques at Princeton and provided valuable first-hand knowledge and able technical assistance to William Brass in his case studies of areas where statistical inquiries had been made with INSEE assistance. Andrews Aryee, then with the Central Bureau of Statistics in Ghana, and Father Joseph Boute were also visiting students in the special training program in demography at Princeton during the period when this research was conducted and contributed from their special knowledge and experience.

Hazel Chafey, who was secretary to the staff of the project, successfully handled an unusually difficult typing job. Most of the charts were drawn by Lynn Demeny, and the others by Joan Westoff. We cannot mention all of the persons who have given advice or statistical material to the project, but wish to acknowledge the generosity of the Statistical Offices of many countries in tropical Africa for providing us with special material often unpublished. Special acknowledgement is due Mr. Robert Blanc at INSEE for giving free access to the data compiled at his organization, and to Mr. John Blacker and Mr. A. T. Brough, respectively former demographer and chief statistician of the Ministry of Economic Development and Planning of Kenya for making available unpublished material from the sample census of Kenya in 1962. This project enjoyed financial support of special grants from The Population Council, largely from funds originating in the Carnegie Corporation. In addition, this project as well as other work at the Office of Population Research was sustained by general support provided by the Rockefeller Foundation, the Ford Foundation, and the Milbank Memorial Fund. The computer facilities of Princeton University by which some of the tables were calculated are supported in part by the National Science Foundation (NSF-GP579). The editor of *Population Studies* generously gave permission to reproduce material that had been published in that journal.

Ansley J. Coale

The Authors

All of the authors were members of the professional staff at the Office of Population Research, Princeton University, when the manuscript was written. Their more recent affiliations are as follows:

WILLIAM BRASS

Reader in Medical Demography, London School of Hygiene and Tropical Medicine.

ANSLEY J. COALE

Director, Office of Population Research, Princeton University.

PAUL DEMENY

Associate Professor of Economics, and Research Associate at Population Studies Center, University of Michigan.

DON F. HEISEL

Field Associate, The Population Council, Inc., at the University College, Nairobi.

FRANK LORIMER

Visiting Professor of Demography, University of the Philippines.

ANATOLE ROMANIUK

Associate Professor of Demography, Department of Social Sciences, University of Ottawa.

ETIENNE VAN DE WALLE

Research Demographer, Office of Population Research, Princeton University.

Contents

PART II: CASE STUDIES OF THE DEMOGRAPHY OF AREAS COVERED BY PARTICULAR KINDS OF CENSUSES OR SURVEYS

List of Tables

List of Figures

PART I.

FERTILITY, MORTALITY, AND NUPTIALITY IN TROPICAL AFRICA: DATA, METHODS OF ANALYSIS, AND SUMMARY OF ESTIMATES

||||| 1 |||||

Introduction

BY FRANK LORIMER

The Present Situation of Demography
in Africa South of the Sahara

The information on the population of sub-Saharan Africa has undergone marked improvement in recent years. The results of systematic inquiries (complete censuses or national sampling surveys) are now replacing cruder sources of demographic information (tax registers, opinions of local officials, etc.) in most countries. These modern inquiries generally include specific information on the characteristics of the persons concerned, and frequently on previous vital events, in place of simple counts of persons with distinction only between males and females and perhaps between "children" and "adults." The transition has been spectacular.

The first critical investigation of information on the population of Africa was carried out by R. R. Kuczynski. His study on the Cameroons and Togoland, published in 1939, was followed by *A Demographic Survey of the British Colonial Empire*, of which Volumes I and II dealing with British Africa were published in 1948 and 1949. Kuczynski's conclusions with respect to the possibility of substantial knowledge on the basis of the information then available were largely negative.

Prior to the late nineteenth century, any interest in the population of tropical Africa was largely romantic. African chiefs had no occasion to conduct inquiries into the numbers of their subjects. Neither did the European powers so long as Africa was for them essentially a "continent of outposts."[1] There were, of course, sporadic counts of colonists and of the total population in certain trading centers and special colonies. There was, for example, a remarkable series of annual enumerations of the Sierra Leone Crown Colony from 1833 through 1851, to check on the alleged kidnapping and re-enslavement of Africans. But there was little interest in, and no real knowledge of, the population in the interior zones of the continent.

The situation changed with the division of all Africa into spheres of European influence. Investment in mines, railways, and plantations gave rise to labor supply problems. The extension of metropolitan rule

---

[1] Lord Hailey, *An African Survey*, Revised 1956, p. 1264.

[3]

into the hinterland required an administrative apparatus with some adaptation to the numbers and characteristics of the indigenous population in different parts of each country. This included the establishment of local rolls of adult males subject to taxation and the initiation of economic schemes and medical programs necessitating records of population. It now became the practice of the administering powers (including, in some cases, commercial corporations, such as the Companhia de Moçambique which assumed responsibility for census operations in Manica and Sofala through 1940) to prepare periodic estimates of the indigenous population based on tax registers and impressionistic surveys by local officials. The so-called censuses of the native population of South Africa, prior to 1936, as well as the official statistics on the population of most countries in tropical Africa prior to World War II were of this type. These surveys did provide a more systematic basis for estimates of the numbers of inhabitants than earlier purely speculative figures, but their apparent precision (often complete to the last digit) was misleading. The first international compilations of population estimates by the League of Nations and a large but decreasing proportion of the population estimates for African countries summarized by the United Nations in successive *Demographic Yearbooks* are of this character.

A 1933 compilation by the League of Nations of official country-by-country estimates for Africa gave a summary figure of 145 million. About 15 years later, the United Nations in a retrospective estimate of the growth of the world's population put the figure for Africa in 1930 at 155 million (in a series rising from 136 million in 1920 to 198 million in 1949). The authors of this series provide the following comments:

> The estimated population of Africa increases with every new estimate as more adequate counts and estimates for many African territories come to hand. The estimate of 198 million for 1949 is no more than a rough approximation and may well be an understatement. With the exception of the white population of the Union of South Africa and of some of the countries on the North African coast, census figures and vital statistics are almost entirely lacking. Estimates vary from fairly reliable head counts and "group enumerations," to those based on the number of taxpayers or huts and some that are hardly more than guesses." (United Nations *Demographic Yearbook*, 1949-50, p. 11.)

It is quite true that the results of census-type inquiries have often led to drastic upward revisions of current estimates previously based on population registration systems or incomplete surveys. On the other hand, the comment cited above from the 1949-50 *Demographic Yearbook* is unduly pessimistic, even with respect to the situation at that time in Africa south of the Sahara. Complete house-to-house censuses had already been carried out (1948) in British East Africa, i.e., Kenya, Tanganyika, Uganda, and Zanzibar, and in the Gold Coast (later Ghana). Moreover, a revolutionary technique which was to prove of great importance in the development of demographic statistics in Africa, namely the sampling survey, had been introduced during the same year (1948) by J. R. H. Shaul in Southern Rhodesia. Also, two or more periodic enumerations of the African populations (involving village-to-village, though not house-to-house, inquiries) had already been carried out in the Union of South Africa and the High Commission territories (1936, 1946) and were soon to be completed in Angola and Mozambique (1940, 1950).

The new trend in the collection of demographic statistics in Africa was carried further during the 1950's. A major development of this period was the initiation of nationwide demographic inquiries on a sampling basis in Guinea (1954-55), in the Congo (1955-57), and in the Sudan (1955-56). Subsequently most African countries of French expression followed the Guinea lead, at least on part of their territory. Most of these sampling inquiries were designed to yield rather detailed information on various aspects of the dynamics of population: age and sex composition, fertility, and mortality. Moreover in Ghana, East Africa, and Gabon sampling inquiries were used to complement the results of complete enumerations.

Progress in the systematic collection of demographic statistics through field surveys in Africa is the result of new national and international interest in all aspects of economic and social development. It is an indication of the rise in statistical standards throughout the world—a trend in which the United Nations and other international agencies and organizations have played a leading role. It was made possible by the gradual acquisition in Africa of the resources, equipment, and skills required for carrying out such operations—though these are still in very short supply. Finally, advance along this line has been due also to advances in statistical techniques and in the definition of statistical needs and possibilities.

There are, then, many positive aspects in the recent development of demographic statistics in Africa, but very serious limitations and problems remain. There still is almost no information on the size of the population of a few regions of tropical Africa. The *terra incognita*, in the sense of areas never surveyed, is being rapidly diminished. The only large country in that category today is Ethiopia. Where official estimates are available, they are often the results of administrative counts without great statistical value; thus official estimates for large areas of Africa are of dubious validity. Even where complete censuses have been taken, it is at times difficult to interpret their figures on population size. In Nigeria, a new problem has emerged from the confusion of political with statistical issues. A comparison of the 1952-53 and the 1963 censuses

—a census taken in 1962 was officially repudiated as in part fraudulent —reveals an impossibly large increase of population. On the basis of the magnitude of the increase, it is clear that either the first figure (30 million, 1953) was grossly deficient, or the second (55.7 million) was grossly inflated, or both, and it seems impossible to determine the objective situation on the basis of the evidence now available. However, the consensus of informed opinion is that the 1952-53 count was a substantial understatement and that the count in 1963 was at least 10 percent too large.

There is even less positive knowledge concerning vital rates and trends in tropical Africa. Reliable information on births and deaths from civil registers in a nation requires an elaborate administrative structure in effective relationship with the individual members of a nation, dispersed through its towns, villages, and hamlets. No such system is in effect in most African countries, nor can such a system be expected within the near future. Most countries of tropical Africa have some sort of vital registration, but it usually has very limited coverage.

An attempt was made more than half a century ago (1904) to establish a vital registration system in Uganda, and this is still in operation in some parts of the country, but the system has never been really effective and it is unlikely that more than half of the births or deaths in recent years have been recorded. An interesting experiment was inaugurated about a decade ago in Katsina District of Northern Nigeria, with the approval and support of the Emir. In spite of a serious and sustained effort, the indicated frequencies of birth and death are so low as to be obviously incomplete. Registration systems are maintained with efficiency in certain African cities, e.g., in Lagos and in 12 urban centers in Ghana. But the population represented in these records cannot be precisely defined and is not representative of any larger population. The nearest approach to completeness in the registration of vital events in any tropical African country was that effected in the Congo in the 1950's under Belgian administration. These registration data, though incomplete in themselves, proved valuable in the control of data obtained through a nationwide sampling survey in 1955 to 1957.

For the most part, demographic studies in tropical Africa, now and in the near future, must be developed without any dependence on current vital statistics. It follows that estimates of vital trends in tropical Africa must be based on cross-sectional reports on *population status* (e.g., age and sex composition, family composition, marital status, etc.) at a particular time, or at several specified times, and/or *retrospective reports* on vital events during a specified period, or during the whole previous experience of individuals (e.g., children ever born to women). This, indeed, is a serious limitation, especially in view of the fact that the information obtained in successive censuses has as yet rarely been sufficiently detailed or reliable to permit any inferences concerning changes from two or more observations on the same cohorts. The efficacy of various analytic methods for developing incomplete demographic data along the lines suggested here is dependent on the scope and specificity of available information. If data are sufficiently bad, they cannot be evaluated except to note that they lack creditability. And if they are extremely crude, they cannot be intensively developed.

Officials responsible for the design of demographic surveys in some African countries during the last two decades have given special attention to framing of questions intended to elicit information, not otherwise available, on the dynamics of population. The need for detailed information by age has been more widely recognized. There has, furthermore, been some recognition in the design of demographic inquiries of the need to obtain similar information in several different ways in order to obviate complete dependence on a single set of data of unknown reliability.

An encouraging aspect of the present situation is that, for the first time, sets of demographic data for some African countries are emerging above the threshold of completeness and specificity required for critical evaluation and analysis.

Aim and Coverage of the Present Study

It is to this critical evaluation and analysis that the present book is devoted. The main body of this volume consists of a series of case studies, each study (or group of studies) being concerned with comparable data, collected by similar methods. Thus, discussion of data on the countries of French expression constitutes a separate chapter. Many of these countries have organized national or regional sample inquiries, and in this they have received technical assistance in collection and analysis of data and publication of results from the French government.[2] Similar methods and questionnaires and standardized form of publication have resulted in readily comparable sets of data. Similarly, homogeneous materials permitting systematic development exist for the Congo (Leopoldville), for the Portuguese territories, and for the Sudan. The quality of the various sets of data and the methods required to analyze them, however, vary greatly among sets.

In each of these studies, the respective author has weighed whatever forms of evidence he could find, seeking confirmation of estimates of fertility or mortality derived from one set of data in estimates based on independent information and has adapted general procedures to the spe-

---

[2] The sponsoring agencies have changed with time. The most recent reports are published by the French Ministère de la Coopération and the Institut National de la Statistique et des Etudes Economiques (INSEE), Service de Coopération, jointly with the Statistical Service of the country involved. We shall henceforth refer to them as INSEE inquiries.

cial circumstances in the area. Because of variations in completeness and quality of information, the reliability of estimation differs from one case study to another, but in each study the evidence is described in critical detail, methods of analysis are presented in full, and the reader is given the basis for judging the quality of the estimates.

Because of the variety of circumstances under which data were collected, each system of data required analysis that was typically either a modification of procedures used in other instances or an *ad hoc* procedure not applicable elsewhere.

In addition to the case studies, this book contains chapters with a broader territorial focus. The first of these chapters (Chapter 2) is devoted to a systematic description of various systems of data collecting in tropical Africa and of how these influence the data collected. This chapter incorporates statistical tables with crude data laid out for comparison, but with very few substantial results. It is followed by a discussion (Chapter 3) of the most widely applicable methods of estimation, perfected in large part for this research project, but useful in many countries with incomplete and inaccurate demographic data, whether in Africa or elsewhere. Chapter 4 is a summary of estimates of fertility and mortality. It brings together results from the various case studies, supplemented by estimates for other areas of tropical Africa made by the application of the standard methods described in Chapter 3, usually without extended critical examination of the basic data characteristic of the case studies. An additional chapter (Chapter 5) contains the study of a special demographic subject—nuptiality—across boundaries. We had first intended another special study—of migration—but migration data in their present state are too monographic and circumscribed to fit in our frame; migration studies have usually been written by anthropologists or urban sociologists concerned only with a limited area. The inclusion of migration questions in demographic sample surveys (mostly unpublished as yet) foreshadows more importance for the subject in the future. The main conclusions reached from our preliminary survey of African migrations are published elsewhere.[3]

Despite the improvement in demographic information in Africa described in the first part of this introduction, only a fraction of the population of tropical Africa has been submitted to surveys that permit even the approximate direct estimation of vital rates. Table 1.1 shows estimates of population as of 1960 taken from the *Demographic Yearbook* of the United Nations (1964) for the countries that we have for our purposes included in tropical Africa. The Republic of South Africa, Basutoland, Swaziland, and the area north of the Sahara were some-

[3] Frank Lorimer, William Brass, and Etienne van de Walle, "Demography," in Robert A. Lystad, ed., *The African World: A Survey of Social Research*, Praeger, 1965.

what arbitrarily excluded. The remainder of Africa—the part considered eligible for study in this book—had a population around 1960 that totaled about 185 million. However, this total includes virtually baseless estimates for Ethiopia, Somalia, and French Somaliland (estimated total about 23 million) and a figure for Nigeria derived from the census of 1952-53, which is generally considered a substantial undercount. Acceptance of a figure of 50 million or more for Nigeria in 1960 (the 1963 census, generally considered inflated, gave 55.7 million) would increase the 1960 estimate for tropical Africa to about 200 million.

Table 1.1 also shows the coverage of the tropical African population by censuses and surveys that permit various kinds of estimates of fertil-

Table 1.1. Estimated 1960 population of countries in tropical Africa, and nature of data supporting fertility or mortality estimates

Region	Country	1960 Estimate of Population (thousands)	Nature of Population Data Supporting Fertility or Mortality Estimates (see Table 1.2 for explanation of codes)
Northeast		34,400	
	Ethiopia	20,600	D
	French Somaliland	67	D
	Somalia	2,010[1]	D
	Sudan	11,770	A.3
West		70,900	
	Dahomey	1,944	A.1
	Gambia	284	B.2
	Ghana	*6,777	B.2
	Guinea	3,072	A.1
	Ivory Coast[2]	3,230[3]	C
	Liberia	1,000	B.2
	Mali[2]	*4,100	C
	Mauritania[2]	750[4]	C
	Niger	2,823	B.1
	Nigeria	35,091	B.2
	Portuguese Guinea	* 521	A.2
	Senegal[2]	3,110	B.2
	Sierra Leone	2,450	C
	Togo	1,440	B.2
	Upper Volta	*4,300	A.1
Central		50,200	
	Angola	4,642	A.2
	Cameroon[2]	4,600[4]	C
	Central African Republic[2]	1,210	C
	Chad	2,660	C
	Congo (Brazzaville)	760	C
	Congo, Democratic Rep. of	14,139	A.1
	Equatorial Guinea		
	Fernando Po	62	C
	Rio Muni	182	C
	Gabon	440	B.1
	Madagascar	5,393	C
	Malawi	2,830	C
	Mozambique	6,495	A.2
	Rhodesia	3,640	B.2
	Zambia	3,210	B.2

Table 1.1 (continued)

Region	Country	1960 Estimate of Population (thousands)	Nature of Population Data Supporting Fertility or Mortality Estimates
East		29,200	
	Burundi	2,224	B.2
	Kenya	8,115	B.1
	Rwanda	2,665	B.2
	Tanzania		
	Tanganyika	9,237	B.1
	Zanzibar	309	C
	Uganda	6,677	B.1
South	Bechuanaland	330	C
	South West Africa	*522	C
Total		185,700	

Note: unless stated otherwise, 1960 estimates of population are those
      reported in Table 4 of the United Nations, Demographic Yearbook 1964.

*Provisional

[1]Average of the 1959 and 1961 estimate.

[2]Component areas were the subject of case studies and should be classed
as A.1: the 1st Agricultural Sector of Ivory Coast, the Mopti area of
Mali, the Senegal River Valley with a population of 267 thousand most of
whom reside in Senegal and the remainder in Mauritania, some tribal groups
in Upper Volta and North Cameroon, and Oubangui Center in the Central
African Republic. The population coverage achieved by each of the above
studies is cited in Table 4.2.

[3]An estimate, not given by the Demographic Yearbook, but based on the census
of 1962.

[4]For 1959.

ity and mortality. The same data are assembled in different form in Table 1.2. Note that the estimates provided in the detailed case studies cover only about 26 percent of the population of tropical Africa and that more cursory estimates were made for an additional 46 percent.

Table 1.2. Coverage of population data from censuses and surveys after 1950
permitting the estimation of fertility and mortality in tropical Africa

Description of data	Population Covered (millions)
A. Data subjected to detailed analysis in Chapters 6 through 10, summarized in Chapter 4.	48
1. Information on detailed age distribution; births last year, children ever born and surviving children by age of mother, and deaths last year by age of decedent.	25
2. Information on detailed age distribution, children ever born and surviving by age of mother and inter-censal growth.	12
3. Information on numbers in a few approximate age categories, births and deaths last year, children ever born to women past menopause.	12
B. Data subjected to more cursory analysis to provide estimates in Chapter 4.	86
1. Information on detailed age distribution, births last year, children ever born and surviving children by age of mother, and deaths last year by age of decedent.	27
2. Information primarily on age distribution, with varying supplementary data.	59
C. Some population data from censuses or surveys published, no estimates of fertility and mortality prepared because of inadequate age-data or other insufficiency.	28
D. No recent valid censuses or general population surveys.	23

Characteristics of African Demographic Data

BY ETIENNE VAN DE WALLE

Demographic data are necessarily influenced by psychological and administrative processes involved in their collection and organization. They are therefore subject to various kinds of systematic errors. Some types of error seem to be almost universal, as, for example, a tendency in case of doubt to report ages at the pivotal digits of the decimal system. Other patterns of distortion are limited to specific cultural or administrative conditions, as, for example, a tendency to report infants of one sex more completely than those of the other, or to classify as lacking a given characteristic persons from whom no answer was obtained.

The people described in African inquiries and censuses differ widely in cultural characteristics. Their customs, taboos, and attitudes toward birth and death and toward census taking present an extraordinary diversity. The demographic surveys have also been organized along quite different lines in various countries with tremendous differences in climate and natural conditions. It would, therefore, be naive to suppose that African demographic data are always closely similar or always subject to particular kinds of errors, or that these errors are only encountered in tropical Africa. On the other hand, some conditions are more widely prevalent in African than in most other world regions, and the state of administrative resources has led to the adoption of several rather special systems of data collection. It may, therefore, be expected that some patterns of distortion and bias in African data differ to some extent from those generally found in other countries.

The development of methods of measuring errors and making adjustments to eliminate their effects and of ways of combining independent data of dubious validity to eliminate biases is an important aspect of the development of demography as a science. The analytical procedures used in the studies reported in this volume are, in large part, methods particularly designed to these ends in dealing with available sets of African demographic data. A general discussion of African data collection procedures and their results, however, is in order before specific cases are considered.

Our aim in this chapter is to present in a comparative, standardized manner both the methods by which African demographic data were collected and the resulting data. We will attempt—

(a) to discover patterns in African demographic data that reflect particular kinds of bias, or systematic error, and conversely find to what extent data are free from such distortions;

(b) to investigate the extent to which particular types of bias may be associated with particular systems of data collection; and

(c) to investigate the extent to which the methods used in the gathering and in the treatment of these data have been effective in obviating the effects of bias or, on the contrary, may have given birth to other errors.

We can hardly expect to achieve fully any of these objectives, but we hope to make some contributions along these lines.

Our approach here is in a sense opposite to the procedures followed in the studies of particular populations. Similar problems are encountered, but they are treated in a different way. The case studies attempt to treat each statistic in its context, within a set of data collected in the same survey; consistency and inconsistency appear from the analysis of various aspects of the same data. In contrast, the treatment here is mainly comparative without regard to the individual context of the statistics. The data on a particular topic obtained in different inquiries are examined in juxtaposition.

The scope of our observations in this chapter will be extended by examining the results of several censuses and inquiries not subjected to intensive investigation elsewhere in this volume. In this connection, it is sometimes as instructive to scrutinize very poor data whose quality did not warrant inclusion in the case studies, as it is to look at very careful inquiries with multiple built-in checks.

Attention will be directed primarily to data on the distribution of populations by age classes, and on fertility and mortality. First, sets of data on each of these topics will be examined with respect to the methods by which they were obtained. Then, their types of biases will be analyzed. And finally the respective merits of various methods of data collection will be discussed, and further possibilities of improvement and avenues of study examined.

Age Reporting in Tropical Africa

All African demographic surveys share the problem of trying to record the ages of people who do not know their exact ages and are not fundamentally interested in knowing them. Headway has lately been made in this respect in several countries where vital registration was instituted, but vital registration improves the accuracy of age reporting only for certain young ages.

Age Classification
in Broad Groupings

The problems of estimating age have discouraged many census takers. Only minimum information has been collected in several censuses and inquiries, including most of those taken under British supervisors or with British technical assistance. These surveys have usually resorted to age classifications based on physiological characteristics or to broad, unstandardized age classes.

The first of these approaches consists in distinguishing children from adults by the criterion of puberty and has been used in early sample inquiries in the Rhodesias, Ruanda-Urundi, and the Sudan. Old women are often identified as those having passed menopause. For males, the criterion of "taxpaying ages" is sometimes used instead of fecund ages. Whichever category is used, male and female classes are not comparable. All the inquiries include a class of children under age 1. Table 2.1 gives proportions of females at various "ages" in the relevant inquiries.

Table 2.1. Classification of females into "physiological" age intervals—selected censuses and surveys

Area and date of inquiry		a) Per cent of females in each age category			
		Under 1	1 - Puberty	Puberty to Menopause	After Menopause
†Rhodesia	1948	3.6	47.2		
†Rhodesia	1953-55	3.9	41.7	41.0	13.4
*Zambia	1950-51	4.7	35.8		
Rwanda	1952	4.8	40.9	43.4	11.0
Rwanda	1953-57	4.4	41.3	42.3	12.0
Burundi	1952	4.4	35.9	48.2	11.6
Burundi	1953-57	4.0	38.0	45.8	12.3
Sudan	1956	4.8	36.1	44.6	14.4

Area and date of inquiry		b) Per cent cumulated to specified ages			
		1	Puberty	Menopause	Total
†Rhodesia	1948	3.6	50.8		
†Rhodesia	1953-55	3.9	45.6	86.6	100.0
*Zambia	1950-51	4.7	40.4		
Rwanda	1952	4.8	45.7	89.1	100.1
Rwanda	1953-57	4.4	45.7	88.0	100.0
Burundi	1952	4.4	40.3	88.5	100.1
Burundi	1953-57	4.0	42.0	87.8	100.1
Sudan	1956	4.8	41.0	85.6	100.0

† Formerly Southern Rhodesia
* Formerly Northern Rhodesia

Provided the word "puberty" refers to a physiological event—menarche—presumably occurring roughly at the same average age in the countries considered, the proportion of the population under puberty depends on the steepness of the age distribution and therefore reflects mainly the level of fertility. There should be a direct correlation between the proportion under age 1 and the proportion under puberty. This is not so in Table 2.1. The recording of the proportion under 1 is unreliable in most of the inquiries discussed in this chapter. Furthermore, as stated by the census officials of Rhodesia, the age of puberty refers probably "to the age of social maturity rather than the age of biological maturity."[1]

The "broad-age-group" system is exemplified by the following age categories in Nigeria (1952-53) and Tanganyika (1957):[2]

Nigeria: 0-1; 2-6; 7-14; 15-49; 50 and over
Tanganyika: Less than 1; 1-5; 6-15; 16-45; 46 and over.

It is not clear why, in either case, these and not other age classes were used. In particular, the adoption of age classes ending in 5 in Tanganyika (e.g., 16 to 45 instead of 15 to 44 years) is unfortunate for comparisons with other areas. But this has been standard practice in East Africa at least since the 1948 round of censuses, with the exception of Zanzibar in 1958, where five-year age classes were used under age 20, followed by an age class 20-45. The broad central group 15-49, or 16-45, or whatever it may be, fulfills really the same function as a physiological grouping of adults and has some of the same defects. The comparison of East African censuses and post-enumeration sample surveys at different dates (see Table 2.2) suggests that estimates of vital trends derived from such distributions considered separately may be false. In particular, it shows how sensitive the reporting of ages is to the quality of enumeration. In all cases where parallel information exists, the proportions under 1 and under 6 are significantly smaller in the presumably more accurate sample census.

Conventional Age Distribution

Age distributions by smaller age groups offer a number of advantages for analytical purposes, even if the inaccuracy of age reporting introduces important biases:

(1) Biases appear more clearly in a detailed distribution.

(2) A detailed age distribution provides an approximate ranking of people by ages, even if the scale is grossly defective. In other words, persons reported in an age group generally have a mean age greater than

---

[1] Mimeographed report on the Southern Rhodesia 1953 Demographic Inquiry, no title, no date, p. 4.

[2] As elsewhere in this chapter, age at last birthday is always implied.

Table 2.2. Age distribution into broad age groupings (both sexes)—East African
censuses and sample censuses in special areas

a) Per cent of population in each age category

		Under 1	1 - 5	6 -15	16-45	46 and over
Kenya	1948			Not published		
Sample		4.5	19.0	24.6	43.2	8.7
†Tanganyika	1948	5.2	17.4	22.3	42.6	12.5
Sample		3.6	15.2	23.4	47.8	10.0
Uganda	1948			Not published		
Sample		2.8	14.3	23.8	47.5	11.6
†Tanganyika	1957	6.1	17.7	20.6	44.1	11.5
Sample		3.8	17.2	22.6	44.5	11.9
Uganda	1959	5.7	18.2	19.6	43.8	12.7
Sample		3.8	16.6	22.8	44.0	12.8

b) Per cent cumulated to specified age

		1	6	16	46	Total
Kenya	1948			Not published		
Sample		4.5	23.5	48.1	91.3	100.0
†Tanganyika	1948	5.2	22.6	44.9	87.5	100.0
Sample		3.6	18.8	42.2	90.0	100.0
Uganda	1948			Not published		
Sample		2.8	17.1	40.9	88.4	100.0
†Tanganyika	1957	6.1	23.8	44.4	88.5	100.0
Sample		3.8	21.0	43.6	88.1	100.0
Uganda	1959	5.7	23.9	43.5	87.3	100.0
Sample		3.8	20.4	43.2	87.2	100.0

† Tanganyika is the mainland area of Tanzania (established
26 April, 1964) which includes, as well, the off-shore
islands formerly known as the Zanzibar Protectorate.

that in the preceding one and less than that in the following one even though all three mean ages may be in error. This is invaluable, for instance, in the analysis of fertility.

(3) Successive cumulation of small segments of the age distribution tends to smooth out errors to an extent impossible in broad categories with poorly defined edges. In particular, estimating fertility from the detailed ages successively cumulated from birth is a convenient method used at several points in the case studies of this volume.

An argument in favor of broad age groups in a census is economy in conducting and tabulating the census or survey. In post-enumeration surveys, and in demographic sample inquiries, where accuracy is a more important factor than time, detailed tabulations of age seem to be well worth while because of the more meaningful demographic analysis that they permit.

Most demographic inquiries have in fact collected detailed information on age. This was also the case in some full censuses, notably those in South Africa, the Portuguese territories, Ghana in 1960, Togo, and Gabon. Thus there are a number of distributions that can be presented in standardized form. This is the purpose of Tables 2.3 (males) and 2.4 (females). Cumulated distributions are given in Tables 2.5 and 2.6.

Table 2.3. Male percent age distribution—selected regions of Africa

	Year of Census or Survey	0-1	1-4	5-9	10-14	Ages 15-19	20-24	25-29	30-34
West Africa									
Dahomey	1961	5.29	14.84	17.84	10.49	6.76	5.87	6.98	5.52
Ghana	1960	3.99	14.81	15.11	10.52	8.15	7.89	8.25	7.14
Guinea	1954-55	5.16	13.87	17.22	9.40	8.27	6.12	7.01	5.23
Forest	1954-55	5.02	12.42	15.47	7.94	8.92	6.40	8.05	5.26
Fouta-Djallon	1954-55	5.50	15.04	18.31	10.51	7.74	5.90	5.77	4.95
Maritime	1954-55	4.74	13.52	17.66	9.01	7.77	6.04	7.45	5.91
Upper	1954-55	5.17	14.50	17.54	10.27	8.98	6.21	7.28	4.91
Konkouré (de facto)	1957	4.03	13.98	19.52	10.56	7.22	5.04	6.84	5.33
Konkouré (de jure)	1957	17.34		18.85	10.18	8.15	6.02	7.28	5.39
Ivory Coast									
1st Agricultural Sector	1957-58	4.42	16.26	16.92	12.99		17.53		13.66
Mali									
Central Niger Delta	1956-58	14.98		14.92	8.93	7.79	6.92	7.61	6.52
Niger	1960	19.50		18.43	9.04	8.30	6.48	8.58	5.57
Portuguese Guinea	1950	4.09	8.93	15.11	11.01	8.03	7.24	8.29	6.95
Senegal	1961	3.81	15.04	16.34	9.04	6.84	6.79	7.95	6.80
Middle Senegal Valley	1957	3.92	14.58	16.80	8.85	7.34	6.41	6.89	6.26
Togo	1958-60	5.04	17.79	20.06	8.26	5.70	5.76	7.15	5.12
Kabré Country	1957	4.73	14.63	14.41	19.11		15.35		11.32
Upper Volta	1960-61	4.18	14.14	16.14	9.96	8.17	6.97	7.77	5.78
Central Africa									
Angola	1940	2.87	12.68	15.70	12.43	7.97	7.70	8.71	6.95
Angola	1950	2.51	12.75	14.53	11.50	8.69	9.39	8.88	6.74
Benguela	1940	2.87	13.49	15.22	12.49	8.65	8.83	9.35	6.93
Benguela	1950	2.37	13.65	13.61	11.05	9.14	9.43	9.66	7.35
Bié	1940	2.70	9.99	14.20	12.83	8.44	6.21	7.39	6.75
Bié	1950	1.75	11.78	14.75	10.19	7.37	7.70	8.46	6.64
Huíla	1940	2.86	12.43	16.54	15.04	9.19	6.31	6.07	5.06
Huíla	1950	2.92	12.45	15.10	12.89	8.59	9.63	8.55	5.66

Table 2.3 (continued)

	Year of Census or Survey	Ages							
		0-1	1-4	5-9	10-14	15-19	20-24	25-29	30-34
Central Africa (cont'd)									
Angola (cont'd)									
Luanda	1940	3.14	14.01	16.37	11.33	7.50	8.69	9.78	7.91
Luanda	1950	3.09	12.82	14.82	12.61	9.23	9.76	8.60	6.60
Malange	1940	2.74	12.80	16.72	11.42	6.11	7.19	9.56	7.38
Malange	1950	2.51	12.32	15.10	11.13	8.63	10.36	8.57	6.74
Cameroon									
North Cameroon	1960	3.87	11.69	15.00	8.92	7.01	6.09	7.20	6.25
Hill Pagans	1960	5.18	13.61	16.45	8.29	6.08	4.77	6.36	5.74
Moslems	1960	2.55	8.36	11.61	8.93	7.34	6.70	8.04	7.34
Plains Pagans	1960	4.03	15.03	16.92	9.63	7.64	6.38	6.83	5.56
Mbalmayo	1956	1.67	8.77	8.35	8.47	8.48	9.18	9.41	8.84
Congo(Leopoldville)	1955-57	4.06	12.94	13.00	11.02	6.52	7.07	8.53	8.07
Equateur	1955-57	3.63	11.61	12.00	10.09	6.45	7.46	8.38	8.27
Katanga	1955-57	4.85	15.02	13.13	10.12	4.75	6.32	8.82	8.63
Kasaï	1955-57	4.44	12.74	13.16	11.74	6.31	5.58	8.39	8.18
Kivu	1955-57	4.37	14.90	14.35	11.28	6.47	7.79	8.41	7.72
Leopoldville	1955-57	4.36	14.25	13.79	12.14	8.61	7.73	8.57	7.02
Orientale	1955-57	2.89	9.51	11.34	9.96	5.17	7.09	8.63	9.14
East Africa									
Madagascar									
Majunga	1962	15.87		14.43	9.56	5.93	6.62	7.25	7.71
Tananarive	1962	20.38		14.31	8.59	8.78	8.11	7.25	6.63
Mozambique	1950	15.63		15.92	12.77	7.35	7.66	8.01	7.21
Central	1950	16.92		16.45	13.47	7.94	7.92	7.47	6.72
North	1950	15.38		16.52	10.96	5.54	6.70	8.32	7.85
South	1950	13.93		14.16	14.36	9.13	8.67	8.42	7.07
Tanzania									
Zanzibar	1948		11.75	12.79	7.42	6.07	6.57	8.62	9.87
Zanzibar	1958	3.38	9.98	13.95	7.50	7.24			
Uganda									
Kyaddondo	1959	4.60	14.07	12.01	7.83	8.59	7.68	9.62	8.00
South Africa									
Rep. of South Africa	1936	2.40	11.34	13.86	12.70	10.38	8.15	8.80	7.14
Rep. of South Africa	1946	1.89	10.97	13.02	12.14	10.57	8.41	9.31	7.38
Rep. of South Africa	1951	2.49	11.28	12.66	11.83	10.28	8.84	8.67	7.77
Rep. of South Africa	1960		15.17	14.05	11.72	9.52	8.67	8.16	6.83

Table 2.3 (continued)

	Year of Census or Survey	35-39	40-44	45-49	50-54	55-59	60-64	65+	Not Declared
West Africa									
Dahomey	1961	6.13	4.23	4.20	3.00	2.62	1.99	4.25	0
Ghana	1960	5.76	4.90	3.63	2.86	1.77	1.87	3.33	0.04
Guinea	1954-55	6.36	4.82	4.76	3.15	3.07	1.80	3.72	0.04
Forest	1954-55	7.45	5.25	5.68	3.22	3.51	1.72	3.64	0.04
Fouta-Djallon	1954-55	5.50	4.41	4.21	3.12	3.06	2.00	3.98	0.01
Maritime	1954-55	6.29	5.00	4.60	3.18	2.87	1.69	4.17	0.08
Upper	1954-55	6.34	4.75	4.43	3.03	2.43	1.57	2.52	0.06
Konkouré (de facto)	1957	5.69	3.71	4.92	3.17	3.00	2.08	4.91	0.01
Konkouré (de Jure)	1957	5.59	3.66	4.82	3.07	2.89	1.99	4.77	0
Ivory Coast									
1st Agricultural Sector	1957-58	13.66		8.17		5.07		4.98	0
Mali									
Central Niger									
Delta	1956-58	7.03	5.57	4.89	3.27	3.44	3.33	4.63	0.16
Niger	1960	6.34	3.56	4.41	2.58	2.40	1.54	3.25	0.01
Portuguese Guinea	1950	6.70	6.39	5.12	4.04	2.39	2.41	3.30	0
Senegal	1961	5.90	4.60	4.70	3.40	2.84	2.07	3.89	0
Middle Senegal Valley	1957	6.11	4.63	5.14	3.68	3.10	1.96	4.33	0
Togo	1958-60	5.71	4.08	4.10	2.74	2.00	1.75	4.72	0
Kabré Country	1957	11.32		8.68	5.13		6.65		0
Upper Volta	1960-61	6.37	4.58	4.58	2.99	2.59	1.99	3.78	0
Central Africa									
Angola	1940	7.22	5.44	3.80	2.25	1.50	1.59	2.90	0.30
Angola	1950	6.64	5.03	4.16	2.59	1.85	1.63	2.95	0.16
Benguela	1940	6.83	4.64	3.03	1.94	1.38	1.51	2.61	0.22
Benguela	1950	7.03	4.87	3.81	2.22	1.52	1.45	2.68	0.17
Bie	1940	7.60	7.05	5.22	3.20	2.16	2.07	4.06	0.14
Bie	1950	7.62	6.19	5.60	3.61	2.58	2.14	3.60	0.02
Huila	1940	6.39	5.11	4.64	2.68	1.67	1.83	4.06	0.12
Huila	1950	5.32	3.89	3.80	2.82	2.14	1.86	4.37	0.02

Table 2.3 (continued)

	Year of Census or Survey	35-39	40-44	45-49	50-54	55-59	60-64	65+	Not Declared
Central Africa (cont'd)									
Angola (cont'd)									
Luanda	1940	6.66	4.93	3.06	1.81	1.14	1.33	2.19	0.16
Luanda	1950	6.18	4.80	3.48	2.11	1.54	1.43	2.49	0.43
Malange	1940	8.66	5.86	3.86	1.96	1.31	1.38	2.21	0.85
Malange	1950	6.53	5.30	4.46	2.66	1.86	1.54	2.26	0.02
Cameroon									
North Cameroon	1960	7.72	5.46	6.11	3.98	4.00	2.13	4.46	0.13
Hill Pagans	1960	8.22	4.42	6.91	3.87	4.44	1.87	3.80	0
Moslems	1960	7.59	6.13	6.45	5.04	4.40	3.06	6.32	0.13
Plains Pagans	1960	7.37	5.29	5.29	3.35	3.39	1.67	3.53	0.09
Mbalmayo	1956	9.43	9.76	5.60	4.19	4.25	0.94	1.65	1.01
Congo(Leopoldville)	1955-57	12.71		10.06			6.02		0
Equateur	1955-57	14.79		11.20			6.11		0
Katanga	1955-57	11.78		10.29			6.29		0
Kasai	1955-57	12.01		11.53			5.92		0
Kivu	1955-57	10.79		7.19			6.73		0
Leopoldville	1955-57	11.11		8.27			4.14		0
Orientale	1955-57	16.05		12.56			7.67		0
East Africa									
Madagascar									
Majunga	1962	7.06	6.25	5.00	4.34	3.78	2.37	3.84	0
Tananarive	1962	5.98	5.08	4.26	3.42	2.54	1.81	2.84	0
Mozambique	1950	7.28	5.80	4.65	2.28	1.43	1.69	2.31	0
Central	1950	6.61	5.17	4.15	1.93	1.26	1.71	2.28	0
North	1950	7.96	6.33	5.01	2.63	1.76	2.12	2.92	0
South	1950	7.36	6.01	4.91	2.33	1.19	1.01	1.44	0
Tanzania									
Zanzibar	1948	6.55	7.69	4.11	5.98	1.76	4.85	5.59	0.39
Zanzibar	1958		57.85						0.11
Uganda									
Kyaddondo	1959	6.63	4.99	4.27	3.84	2.05	2.31	3.51	0
South Africa									
Rep. of South Africa	1936	6.59	4.98	3.88	2.84	1.96	1.71	3.22	0.05
Rep. of South Africa	1946	6.64	5.26	4.51	2.87	1.89	1.74	3.27	0.34
Rep. of South Africa	1951	6.54	5.30	4.23	3.42	1.81	1.63	3.16	0.10
Rep. of South Africa	1960	6.11	5.30	4.36	3.12	2.23	1.76	2.88	0.13

Table 2.4. Female percent age distribution—selected regions of Africa

	Year of Census or Survey	Ages							
		0-1	1-4	5-9	10-14	15-19	20-24	25-29	30-34
West Africa									
Dahomey	1961	5.35	14.11	15.80	8.41	7.08	9.27	9.20	6.92
Ghana	1960	4.27	15.41	15.21	9.77	7.93	9.58	9.26	7.42
Guinea	1954-55	4.91	12.63	14.53	6.81	9.49	9.19	9.92	6.74
Forest	1954-55	5.02	11.78	13.20	5.67	9.26	9.16	10.54	6.77
Fouta Djallon	1954-55	4.85	12.67	14.91	7.38	9.96	9.16	9.41	6.61
Maritime	1954-55	4.94	12.64	14.95	6.71	9.26	9.50	10.01	7.41
Upper	1954-55	4.82	14.35	15.69	7.76	8.94	8.95	9.98	6.13
Konkouré (de facto)	1957	3.81	12.81	15.74	6.63	9.20	8.78	10.41	6.92
Konkouré (de jure)	1957	16.75		15.95	6.71	9.08	8.82	10.46	6.85
Ivory Coast									
1st Agricultural Sector	1957-58	5.52	18.68	16.28	5.17	8.90	9.99	10.57	6.48
Bongouanou	1955-56		39.84			13.65	14.39	7.86	4.89
Mali									
Central Niger									
Delta	1956-58		14.69	13.72	8.51	8.27	9.06	9.54	6.74
Niger	1960		19.41	15.56	5.68	10.67	9.78	11.73	5.28
Portuguese Guinea	1950	4.32	8.88	13.01	7.98	6.78	9.28	11.66	9.43
Senegal	1961	4.06	14.61	14.88	7.41	8.35	9.04	10.42	7.07
Middle Senegal Valley									
Togo	1957	3.80	13.59	13.84	6.68	7.55	8.23	10.00	6.61
	1958-60	4.72	16.29	16.22	6.18	5.76	9.39	10.64	6.46
Kabré Country	1957	4.05	13.24	13.74	8.74	7.41	7.62	7.78	7.09
Upper Volta	1960	4.22	12.85	14.26	7.43	7.43	9.64	9.64	7.43
Central Africa									
Angola	1940	2.87	11.94	13.13	9.41	7.74	8.47	10.06	8.26
Angola	1950	2.60	12.56	12.77	9.42	8.09	9.77	9.55	8.16
Benguela	1940	2.88	13.09	13.49	10.21	8.13	9.32	9.82	7.75
Benguela	1950	2.62	14.21	12.95	10.05	8.21	9.42	9.93	8.27
Bié	1940	2.65	9.21	11.30	9.11	7.49	7.73	9.78	8.62
Bié	1950	1.71	11.03	11.85	7.89	6.93	8.91	9.91	9.19
Huíla	1940	2.75	10.94	13.12	11.36	7.96	7.16	8.10	6.97
Huíla	1950	2.70	11.46	12.77	10.29	7.68	9.44	9.35	7.15
Luanda	1940	3.20	13.42	14.02	8.77	7.15	8.37	9.89	9.02
Luanda	1950	3.21	12.76	13.45	10.23	8.30	9.30	8.40	7.68
Malange	1940	2.79	11.98	13.48	7.85	7.92	8.93	12.30	8.76
Malange	1950	2.60	11.95	12.52	8.25	9.05	12.05	10.16	8.29

Table 2.4 (continued)

	Year of Census or Survey	0-1	1-4	5-9	10-14	15-19	20-24	25-29	30-34
Central Africa (cont'd)									
Cameroon									
North Cameroon	1960	5.34	10.98	13.32	6.57	8.01	9.50	9.81	8.82
Hill Pagans	1960	4.57	12.35	14.95	6.69	7.78	9.69	10.44	9.35
Moslems	1960	2.40	7.76	10.10	6.05	7.88	9.82	9.65	8.90
Plains Pagan	1960	3.40	12.68	15.08	7.06	8.32	8.90	9.20	8.27
Mbalmayo	1956	1.67	8.54	7.96	7.42	9.48	9.48	9.57	8.19
Congo (Brazzaville)	1960-61	3.95	57.17			4.61	6.77	6.53	8.71
Congo (Leopoldville)	1955-57	3.55	12.72	12.81	8.23	7.20	8.30	9.22	10.59
Equateur	1955-57	4.58	11.09	11.82	7.04	6.27	7.87	9.67	9.82
Katanga	1955-57	3.98	14.90	13.04	7.36	6.93	8.14	9.05	11.19
Kasai	1955-57	4.39	12.54	12.44	7.63	5.44	7.38	9.67	12.53
Kivu	1955-57	4.23	14.94	14.29	8.79	8.73	9.28	8.68	9.31
Leopoldville	1955-57		13.83	13.62	9.91	8.10	8.64	9.32	9.16
Orientale	1955-57	3.02	10.00	11.27	7.44	7.14	8.21	8.85	11.94
East Africa									
Madagascar									
Majunga	1961		15.88	14.02	8.48	5.92	9.20	8.64	9.96
Tananarive	1956		20.20	14.11	7.79	8.43	8.75	8.04	7.14
Mozambique	1950		14.94	13.15	9.12	6.37	8.13	9.06	9.06
Central	1950		16.57	14.34	10.24	7.02	8.03	8.97	8.55
North	1950		14.71	13.15	7.39	5.00	8.25	9.83	10.40
South	1950		12.80	11.34	9.93	7.36	8.10	8.10	7.89
Tanzania									
Zanzibar	1948	3.59	13.13	14.57	5.68	8.54	10.21	9.43	9.98
Zanzibar	1958		11.25	15.08	6.28	11.90			
Uganda									
Kyaddondo	1959	4.53	13.94	11.14	6.31	8.08	11.63	11.38	8.21
South Africa									
Rep. of South Africa	1936	2.68	12.47	15.91	11.74	9.75	8.64	7.73	7.24
Rep. of South Africa	1946	2.11	11.99	13.41	12.03	10.20	8.66	8.06	7.08
Rep. of South Africa	1951	2.74	12.19	13.05	11.88	10.12	8.92	7.70	7.45
Rep. of South Africa	1960		15.99	14.11	11.75	9.46	8.86	7.83	6.71

Table 2.4 (continued)

	Year of Census or Survey	35-39	40-44	45-49	50-54	55-59	60-64	65+	Not Declared
West Africa									
Dahomey	1961	5.91	4.23	3.76	2.66	2.34	1.70	3.26	0
Ghana	1960	5.32	4.36	2.86	2.48	1.48	1.66	2.99	0
Guinea	1954-55	7.29	4.68	4.44	2.59	2.29	1.44	2.95	0.09
Forest	1954-55	8.74	4.90	5.29	2.63	2.51	1.43	3.04	0.06
Fouta Djallon	1954-55	6.51	4.75	4.00	2.66	2.17	1.64	3.30	0.01
Maritime	1954-55	7.61	4.63	3.81	2.21	2.10	1.26	2.66	0.30
Upper	1954-55	6.00	4.05	4.72	2.80	2.44	1.14	2.16	0.06
Konkouré (de facto)	1957	6.61	4.73	3.96	2.56	1.76	1.92	4.14	0.01
Konkouré (de jure)	1957	6.59	4.75	3.94	2.49	1.68	1.87	4.06	0
Ivory Coast									
1st Agricultural Sector	1957-58	5.69	3.27	3.47		3.22		2.76	0
Bongouanou	1955-56	5.61	3.13	2.08	2.14	2.39		4.02	0
Mali									
Central Niger Delta	1956-58	5.70	4.80	4.89	3.57	3.01	2.74	4.65	0.11
Niger	1960	6.45	3.03	3.82	1.97	2.10	1.28	3.22	0.02
Portuguese Guinea	1950	7.92	6.89	4.27	3.10	1.63	1.94	2.90	0
Senegal	1961	6.08	4.20	3.87	2.72	1.99	1.64	3.65	0
Middle Senegal Valley	1957	6.77	4.61	4.38	3.80	3.09	2.27	4.76	0
Togo	1958-60	6.18	4.21	4.05	2.58	1.92	1.62	3.78	0
Kabré Country	1957	6.84	5.18	4.32	3.66	3.04	2.39	4.90	0
Upper Volta	1960	7.43	4.82	4.62	2.81	2.61	2.01	2.81	0
Central Africa									
Angola	1940	7.88	6.49	4.04	2.69	1.74	2.03	3.01	0.22
Angola	1950	7.16	5.66	4.28	3.00	1.92	2.15	2.84	0.08
Benguela	1940	7.04	5.75	3.67	2.60	1.64	1.79	2.62	0.21
Benguela	1950	6.90	5.17	3.84	2.67	1.69	1.84	2.19	0.05
Bie	1940	8.91	8.01	4.82	3.17	2.16	2.55	4.30	0.20
Bie	1950	8.72	6.68	5.14	3.52	2.25	2.56	3.67	0.02
Hufla	1940	7.63	6.63	4.87	3.16	2.02	2.68	4.54	0.12
Hufla	1950	6.41	5.04	4.50	3.58	2.31	2.80	4.48	0.03
Luanda	1940	7.67	6.20	3.87	2.65	1.56	1.80	2.23	0.18
Luanda	1950	6.93	5.93	4.21	2.98	1.85	2.10	2.43	0.24
Malange	1940	8.55	6.31	3.42	2.06	1.45	1.70	2.12	0.37
Malange	1950	6.88	5.59	4.07	2.63	1.75	1.85	2.35	0.01

Table 2.4 (continued)

	Year of Census or Survey	35-39	40-44	45-49	50-54	55-59	60-64	65+	Not Declared
Central Africa (cont'd)									
Cameroon									
North Cameroon	1960	7.62	5.46	5.15	3.36	2.64	1.88	3.43	0.10
Hill Pagans	1960	6.69	4.57	4.30	3.00	1.91	1.37	2.32	0
Moslems	1960	8.22	6.45	6.45	4.51	3.48	2.63	5.54	0.17
Plains Pagans	1960	7.64	5.25	4.75	2.77	2.48	1.55	2.52	0.13
Mbalmayo	1956	10.09	9.39	4.89	3.30	4.09	1.28	3.20	1.44
Congo(Brazzaville)	1960-61	7.96		15.09		13.15			
Congo(Leopoldville)	1955-57	13.61		8.17		5.21			
Equateur	1955-57	16.23		9.85		6.81			
Katanga	1955-57	12.37		7.43		5.01			
Kasai	1955-57	14.61		9.19		4.60			
Kivu	1955-57	10.41		6.22		4.97			
Leopoldville	1955-57	11.41		7.30		4.48			
Orientale	1955-57	17.10		9.17		5.84			
East Africa									
Madagascar									
Majunga	1961	6.68	6.62	4.10	3.78	2.62	1.61	2.49	0
Tananarive	1956	6.15	5.13	4.20	3.22	2.40	1.72	2.72	0
Mozambique									
Central	1950	7.93	6.46	4.66	2.98	2.11	2.90	3.14	0
North	1950	7.68	5.65	4.25	2.46	1.85	2.27	2.11	0
South	1950	8.34	7.27	4.79	3.07	1.91	3.14	2.75	0
	1950	7.70	6.52	5.08	3.64	2.78	3.52	5.25	0
Tanzania									
Zanzibar	1948	4.68	6.81	2.67	4.75	1.04	3.76	4.40	0.34
Zanzibar	1958			51.80					0.09
Uganda									
Kyaddondo	1959	5.83	5.25	3.42	3.07	1.53	2.60	3.08	0
South Africa									
Rep. of South Africa	1936	5.77	5.04	3.43	3.30	2.09	2.37	3.80	0.04
Rep. of South Africa	1946	5.57	5.10	3.87	3.17	1.90	2.34	4.15	0.34
Rep. of South Africa	1951	5.63	4.97	3.78	3.50	1.87	2.17	3.96	0.07
Rep. of South Africa	1960	5.50	5.02	3.68	3.10	2.09	2.12	3.69	0.09

Table 2.5. Cumulated male percent age distribution—selected regions of Africa

	Year of Census or Survey	1	5	10	15	20	25	30	35
West Africa									
Dahomey	1961	5.29	20.13	37.97	48.45	55.21	61.08	68.06	73.58
Ghana	1960	3.99	18.80	33.91	44.43	52.58	60.48	68.73	75.87
Guinea	1954–55	5.16	19.03	36.25	45.66	53.92	60.04	67.05	72.28
Forest	1954–55	5.02	17.44	32.91	40.85	49.77	56.18	64.23	69.49
Fouta Djallon	1954–55	5.50	20.54	38.85	49.36	57.09	62.99	68.77	73.72
Maritime	1954–55	4.74	18.26	35.93	44.94	52.71	58.75	66.20	72.11
Upper	1954–55	5.17	19.67	37.21	47.48	56.47	62.68	69.96	74.87
Konkouré(de facto)	1957	4.03	18.01	37.53	48.09	55.31	60.35	67.19	72.52
Konkouré(de jure)	1957	–	17.34	36.20	46.37	54.52	60.54	67.82	73.21
Ivory Coast 1st Agricultural Sector	1957–58	4.42	20.68	37.61	–	50.60	–	68.12	–
Mali									
Central Niger Delta	1956–58	–	14.98	29.90	38.83	46.61	53.54	61.15	67.67
Niger	1960	–	19.50	37.93	46.97	55.27	61.75	70.33	75.90
Portuguese Guinea	1950	4.09	13.02	28.13	39.14	47.17	54.41	62.70	69.66
Senegal	1961	3.81	18.85	35.19	44.23	51.07	57.85	65.80	72.60
Middle Senegal Valley	1957	3.92	18.50	35.30	44.15	51.49	57.90	64.80	71.06
Togo	1958–60	5.04	22.83	42.90	51.16	56.86	62.62	69.78	74.90
Kabré Country	1957	4.73	19.36	33.77	–	52.87	–	68.22	–
Upper Volta	1960	4.18	18.33	34.46	44.42	52.59	59.56	67.33	73.11
Central Africa									
Angola	1940	2.87	15.55	31.25	43.68	51.65	59.35	68.06	75.01
Angola	1950	2.51	15.27	29.80	41.30	49.99	59.38	68.26	74.99
Benguela	1940	2.87	16.36	31.59	44.07	52.73	61.56	70.90	77.83
Benguela	1950	2.37	16.01	29.62	40.67	49.82	59.25	68.91	76.26
Bie	1940	2.70	12.69	26.89	39.73	48.17	54.37	61.76	68.51
Bie	1950	1.75	13.35	28.28	38.48	45.85	53.55	62.01	68.65
Huíla	1940	2.86	15.29	31.83	46.87	56.06	62.36	68.43	73.49
Huíla	1950	2.92	15.36	30.46	43.35	51.95	61.57	70.12	75.78
Luanda	1940	3.14	17.14	33.51	44.84	52.34	61.02	70.81	78.72
Luanda	1950	3.09	15.91	30.73	43.34	52.58	62.34	70.94	77.55

Table 2.5 (continued)

	Year of Census or Survey	1	5	10	15	20	25	30	35
Central Africa (cont'd)									
Angola (cont'd)									
Malange	1940	2.74	15.54	32.26	43.67	49.79	56.97	66.53	73.92
Malange	1950	2.51	14.83	29.93	41.07	49.70	60.06	68.63	75.37
Cameroon									
North Cameroon	1960	3.87	15.56	30.56	39.48	46.49	52.58	59.78	66.03
Hill Pagans	1960	5.18	18.80	35.25	43.54	49.62	54.39	60.75	66.48
Moslems	1960	2.55	10.91	22.53	31.46	38.80	45.50	53.54	60.88
Plains Pagans	1960	4.03	17.05	35.97	43.60	51.24	57.62	64.45	70.01
Mbalmayo	1956	1.67	10.44	18.78	27.26	35.74	44.92	54.33	63.17
Congo(Leopoldville)	1955-57	4.06	17.00	29.99	41.01	47.53	54.60	63.13	71.20
Equateur	1955-57	3.63	15.24	27.24	37.33	47.79	51.25	59.63	67.90
Katanga	1955-57	4.85	19.87	33.00	43.12	47.87	54.19	63.01	71.64
Kasaï	1955-57	4.44	17.18	30.34	42.08	48.39	53.96	62.35	70.53
Kivu	1955-57	4.37	19.27	33.61	44.89	51.36	59.15	67.57	75.29
Leopoldville	1955-57	4.36	18.61	32.40	44.54	53.15	60.88	69.45	76.48
Orientale	1955-57	2.89	12.39	23.73	33.69	38.86	45.95	54.58	63.71
East Africa									
Madagascar									
Majunga	1961	-	15.87	30.29	39.85	45.78	52.40	59.65	67.36
Tananarive	1956	-	20.38	34.70	43.29	52.07	60.18	67.43	74.07
Mozambique	1950	-	15.63	31.56	44.33	51.68	59.34	67.35	74.56
Central	1950	-	16.92	33.37	46.84	54.78	62.70	70.17	76.89
North	1950	-	15.38	31.90	42.86	48.40	55.10	63.41	71.26
South	1950	-	13.93	28.09	42.45	51.59	60.26	68.68	75.75
Tanzania									
Zanzibar	1948	-	11.75	24.53	31.95	38.02	44.59	53.21	63.08
Zanzibar	1958	3.38	13.36	27.31	34.81	42.04	-	-	-
Uganda									
Kyaddondo	1959	4.60	18.68	30.69	38.51	47.11	54.79	64.40	72.40
South Africa									
Rep. of South Africa	1936	2.40	13.74	27.60	40.30	50.68	58.83	67.63	74.76
Rep. of South Africa	1946	1.89	12.87	25.88	38.02	48.39	56.80	66.11	73.49
Rep. of South Africa	1951	2.49	13.76	26.43	38.25	48.53	57.37	66.04	73.81
Rep. of South Africa	1960	-	15.17	29.21	40.93	50.45	59.12	67.28	74.11

Table 2.5 (continued)

	Year of Census or Survey	40	45	50	55	60	65	Total*
West Africa								
Dahomey	1961	79.70	83.94	88.14	91.14	93.76	95.75	100.00
Ghana	1960	81.63	86.53	90.16	93.02	94.80	96.67	100.00
Guinea	1954–55	78.64	83.46	88.22	91.37	94.44	96.24	99.96
Forest	1954–55	76.94	82.18	87.86	91.08	94.59	96.32	99.96
Fouta Djallon	1954–55	79.22	83.63	87.84	90.96	94.02	96.02	99.99
Maritime	1954–55	78.40	83.40	88.01	91.18	94.06	95.75	99.92
Upper	1954–55	81.20	85.95	90.39	93.42	95.84	97.41	99.94
Konkouré (de facto)	1957	78.20	81.92	86.84	90.01	93.01	95.09	99.99
Konkouré (de jure)	1957	78.80	82.46	87.28	90.35	93.24	95.23	100.00
Ivory Coast 1st Agricultural Sector	1957–58	81.78	-	89.95	-	95.02	-	100.00
Mali								
Central Niger Delta	1956–58	74.70	80.28	85.16	88.43	91.88	95.21	99.84
Niger	1960	82.24	85.80	90.21	92.79	95.19	96.73	99.99
Portuguese Guinea	1950	76.36	82.74	87.87	91.90	94.29	96.70	100.00
Senegal	1961	78.50	83.09	87.79	91.19	94.04	96.11	100.00
Middle Senegal Valley	1957	77.17	81.79	86.93	90.61	93.71	95.67	100.00
Togo	1958–60	80.61	84.68	88.79	91.52	93.53	95.28	100.00
Kabré Country	1957	79.54	-	88.22	-	93.35	-	100.00
Upper Volta	1960–61	79.48	84.06	88.65	91.63	94.22	96.22	100.00
Central Africa								
Angola	1940	82.23	87.67	91.47	93.71	95.21	96.81	99.70
Angola	1950	81.63	86.66	90.82	93.41	95.26	96.90	99.84
Benguela	1940	84.67	89.31	92.34	94.28	95.65	97.16	99.78
Benguela	1950	83.29	88.15	91.96	94.18	95.70	97.15	99.83
Bié	1940	76.10	83.16	88.38	91.58	93.73	95.81	99.86
Bié	1950	76.27	82.46	88.06	91.67	94.25	96.38	99.98
Huíla	1940	79.88	84.99	89.63	92.31	93.99	95.82	99.88
Huíla	1950	81.10	84.98	88.79	91.60	93.75	95.61	99.98
Luanda	1940	85.38	90.31	93.37	95.18	96.32	97.65	99.84
Luanda	1950	83.73	88.52	92.00	94.11	95.65	97.08	99.57

* Differs from 100 because of those not declared.

Table 2.5 (continued)

	Year of Census or Survey	40	45	50	55	60	65	Total*
Central Africa (cont'd)								
Angola (cont'd)								
Malange	1940	82.57	88.43	92.30	94.26	95.57	96.95	99.15
Malange	1950	81.90	87.20	91.66	94.32	96.18	97.72	99.98
Cameroon								
North Cameroon	1960	73.75	79.20	85.31	89.29	95.28	95.41	99.87
Hill Pagans	1960	74.71	79.13	86.04	89.91	94.33	96.20	100.00
Moslems	1960	68.47	74.60	81.05	86.06	90.49	95.55	99.87
Plains Pagans	1960	77.39	82.68	87.98	91.32	94.71	96.38	99.91
Mbalmayo	1956	72.60	82.36	87.96	92.16	96.41	97.35	98.99
Congo(Leopoldville)	1955-57	–	83.92	–	92.98	–	–	100.00
Equateur	1955-57	–	82.69	–	93.89	–	–	100.00
Katanga	1955-57	–	83.42	–	93.71	–	–	100.00
Kasaï	1955-57	–	82.55	–	94.08	–	–	100.00
Kivu	1955-57	–	86.08	–	93.27	–	–	100.00
Leopoldville	1955-57	–	87.58	–	95.86	–	–	100.00
Orientale	1955-57	–	79.77	–	92.33	–	–	100.00
East Africa								
Madagascar								
Majunga	1961	74.42	80.67	85.67	90.01	93.79	96.16	100.00
Tananarive	1956	80.04	85.13	89.39	92.81	95.35	97.16	100.00
Mozambique	1950	81.85	87.64	92.29	94.57	96.00	97.69	100.00
Central	1950	83.49	88.67	92.81	94.75	96.01	97.72	100.00
North	1950	79.23	85.55	90.56	93.20	94.96	97.08	100.00
South	1950	83.11	89.12	94.04	96.36	97.56	98.56	100.00
Tanzania								
Zanzibar	1948	69.63	77.32	81.43	87.41	89.17	94.02	99.61
Zanzibar	1958	–	–	–	–	–	–	99.89
Uganda								
Kyaddondo	1959	79.03	84.02	88.29	92.13	94.18	96.49	100.00
South Africa								
Rep. of South Africa	1936	81.35	86.33	90.21	93.05	95.01	96.73	99.95
Rep. of South Africa	1946	80.13	85.39	89.90	92.77	94.66	96.39	99.66
Rep. of South Africa	1951	80.35	85.65	89.89	93.30	95.11	96.74	99.90
Rep. of South Africa	1960	80.22	85.52	89.88	93.00	95.23	96.99	99.87

* Differs from 100 because of those not declared.

Table 2.6. Cumulated female percent age distribution—selected regions of Africa

	Year of Census or Survey	Ages							
		1	5	10	15	20	25	30	35
West Africa									
Dahomey	1961	5.35	19.45	35.25	43.66	50.74	60.01	69.21	76.13
Ghana	1960	4.27	19.67	34.88	44.65	52.58	62.16	71.43	78.85
Guinea	1954-55	4.91	17.54	32.07	38.88	48.37	57.56	67.49	74.23
Forest	1954-55	5.02	16.79	29.99	35.66	44.92	54.08	64.62	71.39
Fouta Djallon	1954-55	4.85	17.52	32.43	39.81	49.77	58.93	68.34	74.95
Maritime	1954-55	4.94	17.58	32.54	39.25	48.51	58.00	68.01	75.42
Upper	1954-55	4.82	19.17	34.85	42.61	51.55	60.50	70.49	76.62
Konkouré(de facto)	1957	3.81	16.62	32.36	38.99	48.19	56.97	67.38	74.30
Konkouré(de jure)	1957	–	16.75	32.70	39.41	48.49	57.30	67.77	74.62
Ivory Coast									
1st Agricultural Sector	1957-58	5.52	24.20	40.47	45.65	54.54	64.54	75.11	81.59
Bongouanou	1955-56	–	–	–	39.84	53.50	67.88	75.75	80.64
Mali									
Central Niger Delta	1956-58	–	14.69	28.41	36.92	45.19	54.26	63.80	70.53
Niger	1960	–	19.41	34.97	40.65	51.32	61.10	72.82	78.11
Portuguese Guinea	1950	4.32	13.20	26.21	34.18	40.96	50.25	61.91	71.34
Senegal	1961	4.06	18.67	33.55	40.96	49.31	58.35	68.77	75.84
Middle Senegal Valley	1957	3.80	17.39	31.23	37.92	45.47	53.70	63.70	70.31
Togo	1958-60	4.72	21.01	37.23	43.42	49.18	58.57	69.20	75.66
Kabré Country	1957	4.05	17.29	31.03	39.76	47.17	54.79	62.57	69.66
Upper Volta	1960-61	4.22	17.07	31.33	38.76	46.18	55.82	65.46	72.89
Central Africa									
Angola	1940	2.87	14.81	27.94	37.35	45.10	53.57	63.63	71.90
Angola	1950	2.60	15.16	27.93	37.35	45.44	55.21	64.76	72.91
Benguela	1940	2.88	15.97	29.46	39.67	47.80	57.12	66.94	74.68
Benguela	1950	2.65	16.83	29.78	39.81	48.02	57.44	67.37	75.64
Bie	1940	2.65	11.85	23.15	32.26	39.74	47.48	57.26	65.88
Bie	1950	1.71	12.74	24.59	32.48	39.41	48.32	58.23	67.42
Hufla	1940	2.75	13.69	26.81	38.17	46.13	53.29	61.39	68.36
Hufla	1950	2.70	14.16	26.94	37.23	44.91	54.35	63.70	70.85
Luanda	1940	3.20	16.62	30.63	39.41	46.56	54.93	64.82	73.84
Luanda	1950	3.21	15.97	29.42	39.65	47.95	57.25	65.65	73.33

Table 2.6 (continued)

	Year of Census or Survey	1	5	10	15	20	25	30	35
Central Africa (cont'd)									
Angola (cont'd)									
Malange	1940	2.79	14.77	28.25	36.10	44.02	52.96	65.26	74.02
Malange	1950	2.60	14.55	27.08	35.33	44.38	56.42	66.58	74.87
Cameroon									
North Cameroon	1960	3.34	14.32	27.65	34.21	42.23	51.72	61.53	70.36
Hill Pagans	1960	4.57	16.93	31.88	38.57	46.35	56.04	66.48	75.84
Moslems	1960	2.40	10.16	20.26	26.31	34.19	44.01	53.65	62.56
Plains Pagans	1960	3.40	16.09	31.16	38.22	46.54	55.44	64.64	72.91
Mbalmayo	1956	1.67	10.21	18.16	25.59	35.07	44.55	54.11	62.30
Congo (Brazzaville)	1960-61	-			37.17	41.79	48.55	55.08	63.79
Congo (Leopoldville)	1955-57	3.95	16.66	29.47	37.70	44.90	53.20	62.42	73.01
Equateur	1955-57	3.55	14.63	26.45	33.49	39.75	47.63	57.30	67.11
Katanga	1955-57	4.58	19.48	32.53	39.89	46.82	54.96	64.00	75.19
Kasai	1955-57	3.98	16.51	28.95	36.59	42.03	49.41	59.07	71.61
Kivu	1955-57	4.39	19.33	33.62	42.41	51.13	60.41	69.09	78.40
Leopoldville	1955-57	4.23	18.06	31.68	41.59	49.69	58.33	67.65	76.81
Orientale	1955-57	3.02	13.03	24.30	31.74	38.88	47.09	55.95	67.89
East Africa									
Madagascar									
Majunga	1961	-	15.88	29.91	38.39	44.31	53.51	62.15	72.11
Tananarive	1956	-	20.20	34.31	42.10	50.53	59.28	67.32	74.46
Mozambique	1950	-	14.94	28.08	37.20	43.57	51.69	60.76	69.82
Central	1950	-	16.57	30.90	41.14	48.17	56.20	65.17	73.72
North	1950	-	14.71	27.86	35.26	40.26	48.51	58.34	68.73
South	1950		12.80	24.15	34.07	41.43	49.53	57.63	65.52
Tanzania									
Zanzibar	1948	3.59	13.13	27.71	33.39	41.93	52.14	61.57	71.55
Zanzibar	1958	-	14.84	29.92	36.20	48.10	-	-	-
Uganda									
Kyaddondo	1959	4.53	18.47	29.61	35.92	44.00	55.63	67.01	75.21
South Africa									
Rep. of South Africa	1936	2.68	15.15	29.06	40.80	50.55	59.18	66.92	74.15
Rep. of South Africa	1946	2.11	14.10	27.51	39.54	49.74	58.40	66.47	73.55
Rep. of South Africa	1951	2.74	14.93	27.98	39.86	49.97	58.89	66.60	73.05
Rep. of South Africa	1960	-	15.99	30.10	41.85	51.31	60.18	68.01	74.72

Table 2.6 (continued)

	Year of Census or Survey	40	45	50	55	60	65	Total*
West Africa								
Dahomey	1961	82.04	86.27	90.03	92.69	95.04	96.74	100.00
Ghana	1960	84.17	88.53	91.40	93.87	95.35	97.01	100.00
Guinea	1954-55	81.52	86.20	90.64	93.22	95.51	96.96	99.91
Forest	1954-55	80.14	85.03	90.33	92.96	95.47	96.90	99.94
Fouta Djallon	1954-55	81.45	86.21	90.21	92.87	95.04	96.69	99.99
Maritime	1954-55	83.03	87.66	91.47	93.68	95.78	97.04	99.70
Upper	1954-55	82.62	86.66	91.39	94.19	96.63	97.77	99.94
Konkouré(de facto)	1957	80.91	85.64	89.61	92.17	93.93	95.85	99.99
Konkouré(de jure)	1957	81.21	85.96	89.90	92.39	94.07	95.94	100.00
Ivory Coast								
1st Agricultural Sector	1957-58	87.28	90.55	94.02	–	97.24	–	100.00
Bongouanou	1955-56	86.25	89.38	91.46	93.59	95.98	–	100.00
Mali								
Central Niger Delta	1956-58	76.24	81.04	85.92	89.49	92.50	95.24	99.89
Niger	1960	84.56	87.59	91.41	93.38	95.48	96.76	99.98
Portuguese Guinea	1950	79.26	86.16	90.43	93.53	95.16	97.10	100.00
Senegal	1961	81.92	86.12	90.00	92.72	94.71	96.35	100.00
Middle Senegal Valley	1957	77.08	81.69	86.07	89.87	92.96	95.24	100.00
Togo	1958-60	81.84	86.05	90.10	92.69	94.60	96.22	100.00
Kabré Country	1957	76.51	81.69	86.01	89.67	92.71	95.10	100.00
Upper Volta	1960-61	80.32	85.14	89.76	92.57	95.18	97.19	100.00
Central Africa								
Angola	1940	79.78	86.27	90.31	93.00	94.74	96.77	99.78
Angola	1950	80.07	85.73	90.01	93.01	94.93	97.08	99.92
Benguela	1940	81.72	87.47	91.14	93.74	95.38	97.17	99.79
Benguela	1950	82.55	87.72	91.56	94.23	95.92	97.76	99.95
Bie	1940	74.78	82.80	87.62	90.79	92.95	95.50	99.80
Bie	1950	76.14	82.82	87.97	91.49	93.74	96.30	99.98
Huila	1940	75.99	82.62	87.49	90.65	92.67	95.35	99.88
Huila	1950	77.26	82.30	86.80	90.38	92.69	95.49	99.97
Luanda	1940	81.51	87.72	91.59	94.24	95.80	97.60	99.82
Luanda	1950	80.25	86.19	90.39	93.38	95.23	97.33	99.76

* Differs from 100 because of those not declared.

Table 2.6 (continued)

	Year of Census or Survey	40	45	50	55	60	65	Total*
Central Africa (cont'd)								
Angola (cont'd)								
Malange	1940	82.57	88.88	92.30	94.36	95.91	97.50	99.63
Malange	1950	81.75	87.53	91.41	94.04	95.79	97.64	99.99
Cameroon								
North Cameroon	1960	77.97	83.44	88.59	91.95	94.59	96.47	99.90
Hill Pagans	1960	82.53	87.10	91.40	94.40	96.31	97.68	100.00
Moslems	1960	70.78	77.23	83.68	88.18	91.67	94.29	99.83
Plains Pagans	1960	80.55	85.80	90.55	93.32	95.80	97.35	99.87
Mbalmayo	1956	72.39	81.79	86.68	89.98	94.08	95.36	98.56
Congo(Brazzaville)	1960-61	71.76	–	86.85	–	–	–	100.00
Congo (Leopoldville)	1955-57	–	86.63	–	94.79	–	–	100.00
Equateur	1955-57	–	83.34	–	93.19	–	–	100.00
Katanga	1955-57	–	87.56	–	94.99	–	–	100.00
Kasaï	1955-57	–	86.21	–	95.40	–	–	100.00
Kivu	1955-57	–	88.81	–	95.03	–	–	100.00
Leopoldville	1955-57	–	88.22	–	95.52	–	–	100.00
Orientale	1955-57	–	84.99	–	94.16	–	–	100.00
East Africa								
Madagascar	1961	78.79	85.41	89.51	93.29	95.90	97.51	100.00
Majunga	1956	80.61	85.74	89.94	93.16	95.56	97.28	100.00
Tananarive	1950	77.75	84.21	88.87	91.85	93.96	96.86	100.00
Mozambique								
Central	1950	81.40	87.06	91.31	93.77	95.61	97.89	100.00
North	1950	77.07	84.34	89.13	92.20	94.11	97.25	100.00
South	1950	73.22	79.74	84.82	88.45	91.24	94.75	100.00
Tanzania								
Zanzibar	1948	76.23	83.05	85.72	90.47	91.50	95.26	99.66
Zanzibar	1958	–						99.91
Uganda								
Kyaddondo	1959	81.05	86.29	89.72	92.79	94.32	96.92	100.00
South Africa								
Rep. of South Africa	1936	79.93	84.95	88.39	91.69	93.79	96.16	99.96
Rep. of South Africa	1946	79.12	84.22	88.09	91.27	93.17	95.52	99.66
Rep. of South Africa	1951	79.68	84.65	88.43	91.93	93.80	95.97	99.93
Rep. of South Africa	1960	80.22	85.23	88.91	92.01	94.10	96.21	99.91

* Differs from 100 because of those not declared.

Data are usually presented in five-year age groups, except for children under 1 year of age often tabulated separately. But the similar tabulations are based on heterogeneous ways of recording age on the original data sheets of the interviewers. Age was originally recorded by individual years of age in the French-oriented demographic inquiries and in the Ghana, South African, and Portuguese censuses; by individual years of birth in Mbalmayo and the Southern Rhodesian census of 1962 (for persons born after 1945); by five-year age groups in the Congo up to age 34, followed by ten-year age groups to age 54, with a residual group of 55 and over.

Biases in the data are related to collection procedures. Very few inquiries publish age distributions the way ages were originally recorded —by individual years. Indeed, such distributions are usually so conspicuously distorted that they appear to serve only as demonstrations of inaccurate age reporting and patterns of biases. They undoubtedly deserve to be published for this purpose, and to permit adjustment of the original data in various ways.

Figures 2.1 and 2.2 (demographic inquiries of Niger and Guinea, census of Ghana) and Figures 2.3 and 2.4 (censuses of Angola, Por-

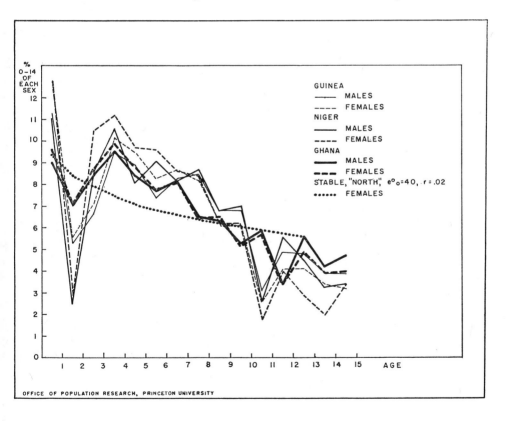

2.1. Children by single years in percent of all children under age 15, for Ghana, 1960; Guinea, 1954-55, and Niger, 1960.

tuguese Guinea, South Africa, and Ghana) exemplify the pattern of bias for single-year age distributions. The graphs present ages in percent of children and adults of each sex respectively. The censuses (as opposed to the two demographic inquiries) all exhibit the same traits, including age heaping on even ages and multiples of five. The age group 0-1 is clearly underreported in the censuses by assembly in South Africa and Angola. The two demographic inquiries (Guinea and Niger) and the Ghana census up to age 10, have in turn similar features: underreporting of age 1 (or misreporting with transfer to adjoining ages), overreporting between 3 and 9 years. The French inquiries, where interviewers have been cautioned against figures ending in 0, exhibit a characteristic age "avoidance" at these ages; the interviewers in Guinea shun also ages ending in 5, but the interviewers in Niger heap on them.

It is hard to tell whether an instruction to avoid multiples of five or ten makes the data more reliable. At any rate, it affects the distortions in tabulations by larger age intervals. As indicated by Table 2.7, age classes including a multiple of ten (20 to 24 years, 30 to 34, etc.) are usually smaller than the mean of the two adjacent age groups (15 to 19 + 25 to 29, etc.) in the INSEE inquiries. Age ratios obtained by relating these two values are significantly under 1.00, although they are

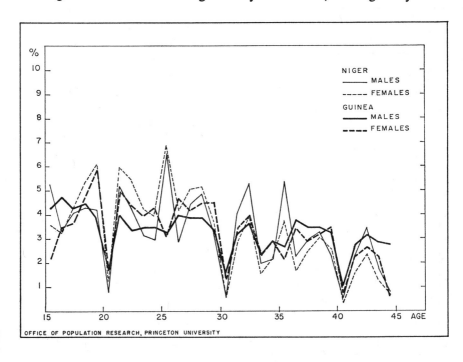

2.2. Adults by single years (15 to 44) in percent of all adults
aged 15 to 44, for Guinea, 1954-55, and Niger, 1960.

Table 2.7. Number of cases of age ratios* above unity, and percentage of the total number of observations, by age and sex—INSEE inquiries and censuses of the Portuguese and English traditions

Age ratios above unity

Age group	INSEE Inquiries				Portuguese and English Censuses			
	MALES		FEMALES		MALES		FEMALES	
	Number	% of observations	Number	% of observations	Number	% of observations	Number	% of observations
15-19	6	40	10	56	1	5	1	5
20-24	0	0	10	56	6	29	15	71
25-29	15	100	17	94	21	100	16	76
30-34	0	0	1	6	3	14	10	48
35-39	15	100	16	89	18	86	11	52
40-44	0	0	0	0	7	33	17	81
45-49	15	100	15	83	12	57	3	14
50-54	0	0	1	6	5	24	9	43
55-59	14	93	10	56	0	0	0	0
Number of observations	15	–	18	–	21	–	21	–

Note: Based on information in Tables 2.3 and 2.4. Total country not included in number of observations when subdivisions are included. The normal expectation, in the absence of distortion, is that the age ratio would be close to unity.

* Age ratio: ratio of age group to the mean of the two adjacent age groups.

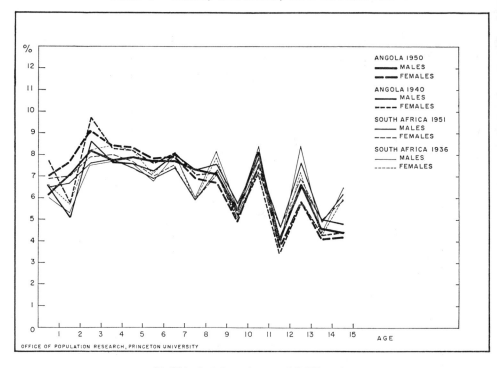

2.3. Children by single years in percent of all children under age 15, for Angola, 1940 and 1950, and South Africa, 1936 and 1951.

expected to be very close to 1.00 in the absence of distortions. The pattern is not so clear among countries when age heaping occurs on multiples of ten, i.e., the Portuguese and English-oriented censuses. Figure 2.5 shows the average value of the age ratios in the two series of censuses and inquiries. There is a very distinct cyclical pattern for the INSEE inquiries, and the opposite pattern for females in Portuguese and English-oriented censuses; age heaping is very marked on age 60 for the males. On this score, the traditional methods where interviewers are not cautioned against age heaping seem to fare better. But there is need for experimenting on the subject.

Age was directly reported in classes of five and ten years in the Congo, so that heaping effects were largely eliminated. Classifying a person within a group requires different mental processes and presumably involves other biases than filling in an estimated age in digits, especially for age groups as large as ten years.

Despite different collection procedures, African age distributions show interesting consistencies when juxtaposed in a table or a graph. It has often been asserted by writers discussing individual inquiries that some peculiarities of the data (e.g., deficit of persons in their teens) might be

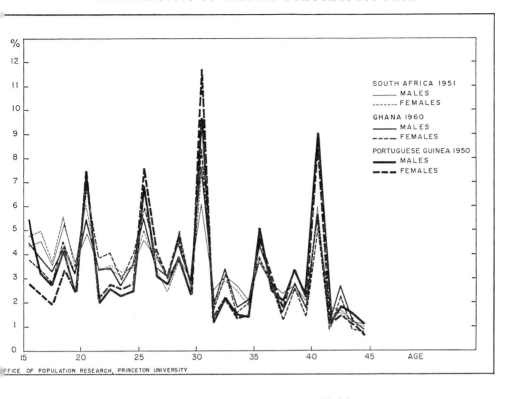

2.4. Adults by single years (15 to 44) in percent of all adults
aged 15 to 44, for Ghana, 1960; Portuguese Guinea, 1950;
and South Africa, 1951.

genuine and due to some past event such as the Second World War, bad
crops, or epidemics. Although such disturbances have doubtless affected
some age distributions, there is a very strong presumption that no past
events would have had the same kind of effect on age distributions collected at different dates in areas far apart. The validity of this argument
is confirmed in Figure 2.1. Guinea in 1955 exhibits the same deficiency
at ages 10 to 14 as Niger and Ghana five years later.

Of the age groups listed in Tables 2.3 and 2.4, 33 percent of the
entries in male age group 20-24 and 88 percent of the entries in female
age group 20-24 either equaled or were greater than entries for age group
10-14 or 15-19; while 74 percent of the entries in male age group 25-29
and 86 percent of the entries in female age group 25-29 either equaled
or were greater than entries for age group 15-19 or 20-24. Male age
groups show somewhat different patterns of relationship than the female, but both indicate the general tendency to exaggerate the proportion in the center of the adult period. The normal expectation, in the absence of distortion or anomaly would preclude any such patterns.

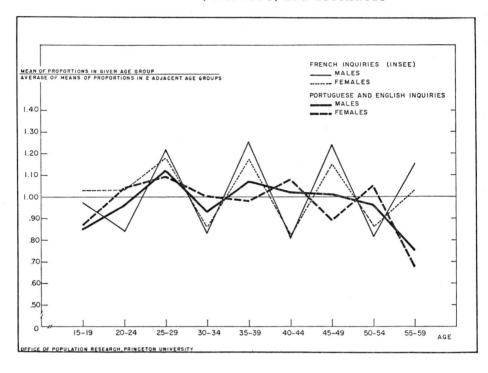

2.5. Average value of age ratios, or the mean of proportions
in any given age group divided by the average of means of
the proportions in two adjacent age groups, for the French
inquiries by INSEE and for the Portuguese and English
inquiries combined.

Sex ratios (males per female) further caution against putting too much
emphasis on the influence of past events on the age distribution (see
Table 2.8). Past history of fertility and mortality would have affected
both sexes in approximately the same way, but age misreporting is known
to be sex-selective. Figure 2.6 (French inquiries) and Figure 2.7 (other
regions) in general show, when plotted by age, that sex ratios under age
5 are smaller than unity; that they rise above unity between 5 and 15
years; that they drop under 1.00 between ages 15 and 40; and that they
remain above unity over 40 years. Variants to this pattern can be traced
back in certain cases to a history of migration, as in Mozambique, a
country of outmigration, or as in Ghana, where there is a continuous
influx of foreigners.

The actual trend of sex ratios by age cannot be deduced precisely from
available data. Sex ratios at birth in tropical Africa may be markedly
below those in countries with reliable statistics. Almost all areas with
a majority of African Negroes in the population have a sex ratio at birth
below the world average. In the United States, the sex ratio at birth
of Negroes has been consistently below that of whites.[3] Sex ratios at

[3] Parvin Visaria, "The Sex Ratio of the Population of India," unpublished Ph.D.
Dissertation, Princeton University, 1963.

Table 2.8. Sex ratio of population (males per female)—selected regions of Africa

	Year of Census or Survey	Ages								
		0-1	1-4	5-9	10-14	15-19	20-24	25-29	30-34	35-39
West Africa										
Dahomey	1961	0.95	1.01	1.08	1.20	0.92	0.61	0.73	0.77	1.00
Ghana	1960	0.96	0.98	1.02	1.10	1.05	0.84	0.91	0.98	1.11
Guinea	1954-55	0.95	1.00	1.08	1.25	0.79	0.60	0.64	0.70	0.79
Forest	1954-55	0.95	1.01	1.11	1.32	0.91	0.66	0.72	0.73	0.81
Fouta Djallon	1954-55	0.97	1.03	1.05	1.21	0.66	0.55	0.52	0.64	0.72
Maritime	1954-55	0.92	0.92	1.14	1.29	0.81	0.61	0.72	0.77	0.80
Upper	1954-55	0.98	1.01	1.02	1.20	0.91	0.63	0.66	0.73	0.96
Konkouré (de facto)	1957	0.98	1.01	1.15	1.48	0.73	0.53	0.61	0.72	0.80
Konkouré (de jure)	1957		1.00	1.14	1.46	0.86	0.66	0.67	0.76	0.82
Ivory Coast										
1st Agricultural Sector	1957-58	0.87	0.94	1.12	1.00	1.00	0.92		1.21	
Mali										
Central Niger Delta	1956-58		0.99	1.05	1.02	0.91	0.74	0.77	0.94	1.20
Niger	1960		0.99	1.17	1.57	0.77	0.65	0.72	1.04	0.97
Portuguese Guinea	1950	0.93	0.98	1.13	1.35	1.16	0.76	0.69	0.72	0.83
Senegal	1961	0.91	1.00	1.06	1.18	0.79	0.73	0.74	0.93	0.94
Middle Senegal Valley	1957	1.00	1.04	1.18	1.29	0.94	0.76	0.67	0.92	0.88
Togo	1958-60	0.98	1.00	1.14	1.23	0.91	0.56	0.62	0.73	0.85
Kabré Country	1957	1.04	0.99	0.94	1.06	1.06	0.89	0.89	0.73	
Upper Volta	1960-61	1.00	1.11	1.14	1.35	1.11	0.73	0.81	0.78	0.86
Central Africa										
Angola	1940	0.90	0.95	1.07	1.18	0.92	0.81	0.78	0.75	0.82
Angola	1950	0.92	0.97	1.09	1.16	1.03	0.92	0.89	0.79	0.89
Benguela	1940	0.92	0.95	1.04	1.13	0.98	0.88	0.88	0.83	0.90
Benguela	1950	0.89	0.95	1.04	1.09	1.10	0.99	0.96	0.88	1.00
Bie	1940	0.90	0.96	1.11	1.25	1.00	0.71	0.67	0.69	0.75
Bie	1950	0.98	1.02	1.19	1.23	1.02	0.83	0.82	0.69	0.84
Huila	1940	0.89	0.97	1.08	1.13	0.99	0.75	0.64	0.62	0.71
Huila	1950	1.01	1.01	1.10	1.17	1.04	0.95	0.85	0.74	0.77
Luanda	1940	0.88	0.94	1.05	1.16	0.94	0.93	0.89	0.79	0.78
Luanda	1950	0.91	0.95	1.05	1.17	1.06	1.00	0.97	0.82	0.85

Table 2.8 (continued)

	Year of Census or Survey	0-1	1-4	5-9	10-14	15-19	20-24	25-29	30-34	35-39
Central Africa (cont'd)										
Angola (cont'd)										
Malange	1940	0.88	0.96	1.11	1.30	0.69	0.72	0.70	0.75	0.91
Malange	1950	0.89	0.95	1.11	1.24	0.88	0.79	0.78	0.75	0.88
Cameroon										
North Cameroon	1960	1.08	0.99	1.05	1.27	0.82	0.60	0.68	0.66	0.94
Hill Pagans	1960	1.12	1.09	1.09	1.22	0.77	0.49	0.60	0.61	1.21
Moslems	1960	0.95	0.96	1.03	1.32	0.83	0.61	0.75	0.74	0.83
Plains Pagans	1960	1.10	0.95	1.04	1.27	0.85	0.67	0.69	0.62	0.90
Mbalmayo	1956	0.96	0.98	1.00	1.09	0.86	0.93	0.94	1.03	0.89
Congo (Leopoldville)	1955-57	0.97	0.96	0.96	1.27	0.86	0.81	0.87	0.72	0.88
Equateur	1955-57	0.97	0.99	0.96	1.36	0.98	0.90	0.82	0.80	0.87
Katanga	1955-57	1.00	0.95	0.95	1.30	0.65	0.74	0.92	0.73	0.90
Kasai	1955-57	1.01	0.92	0.96	1.39	1.05	0.68	0.79	0.59	0.74
Kivu	1955-57	0.95	0.96	0.96	1.23	0.71	0.81	0.93	0.80	0.99
Leopoldville	1955-57	0.96	0.96	0.94	1.14	0.99	0.84	0.86	0.72	0.91
Orientale	1955-57	0.93	0.93	0.98	1.31	0.71	0.84	0.95	0.75	0.92
East Africa										
Madagascar										
Majunga	1961	1.01		1.04	1.14	1.01	0.73	0.85	0.78	1.07
Tananarive	1956	1.01		1.02	1.11	1.04	0.93	0.90	0.93	0.98
Mozambique	1950	0.95		1.10	1.28	1.05	0.86	0.81	0.73	0.84
Central	1950	0.96		1.08	1.24	1.07	0.93	0.79	0.74	0.81
North	1950	0.95		1.14	1.34	1.00	0.74	0.77	0.68	0.86
South	1950	0.95		1.09	1.26	1.08	0.93	0.91	0.78	0.83
Tanzania										
Zanzibar	1948	1.05	0.99	0.97	1.44	0.78	0.71	1.01	1.09	1.54
Zanzibar	1958			1.03	1.33	0.68	-	-	-	-
Uganda										
Kyaddondo	1959	0.98	0.97	1.04	1.19	1.02	0.64	0.81	0.94	1.09
South Africa										
Rep. of South Africa	1936	0.90	0.92	1.01	1.09	1.07	0.95	1.15	0.99	1.15
Rep. of South Africa	1946	0.94	0.95	1.01	1.05	1.06	1.01	1.20	1.09	1.24
Rep. of South Africa	1951	0.95	0.96	1.01	1.04	1.06	1.03	1.17	1.09	1.21
Rep. of South Africa	1960		0.97	1.01	1.02	1.02	1.00	1.06	1.04	1.13

Table 2.8 (continued)

	Year of Census or Survey	Ages 40-44	45-49	50-54	55-59	60-64	65+	Total Population	Not Declared	Births
West Africa										
Dahomey	1961	0.96	1.08	1.08	1.07	1.12	1.25	0.96	–	–
Ghana	1960	1.15	1.30	1.18	1.23	1.15	1.14	1.02	–	–
Guinea	1954-55	0.94	0.97	1.11	1.22	1.13	1.14	0.91	0.42	1.00
Forest	1954-55	1.01	1.01	1.16	1.32	1.14	1.13	0.95	0.64	1.01
Fouta Djallon	1954-55	0.79	0.90	1.00	1.20	1.04	1.03	0.85	0.62	1.00
Maritime	1954-55	1.04	1.16	1.38	1.32	1.29	1.51	0.96	0.25	0.96
Upper	1954-55	1.07	0.85	0.99	0.90	1.25	1.06	0.91	0.91	1.03
Konkouré(de facto)	1957	0.73	1.15	1.15	1.58	1.00	1.10	0.93	1.00	0.99
Konkouré(de jure)	1957	0.74	1.18	1.19	1.65	1.02	1.13	0.96	–	0.98
Ivory Coast 1st Agricultural Sector	1957-58	–	1.31	–	1.70	–	1.95	1.08	–	0.90
Mali Central Niger Delta	1956-58	1.13	0.97	0.89	1.11	1.18	0.97	0.96	1.46	1.01
Niger	1960	1.16	1.14	1.29	1.13	1.19	1.00	0.99	0.70	1.01
Portuguese Guinea	1950	0.90	1.17	1.27	1.43	1.21	1.11	0.98	–	–
Senegal	1961	1.06	1.17	1.21	1.38	1.22	1.03	0.97	–	–
Middle Senegal Valley	1957	0.97	1.14	0.94	0.97	0.84	0.88	0.98	–	–
	1958-60	0.89	0.93	0.98	0.96	1.00	1.15	0.92	–	–
Togo Kabré Country	1957		0.82		0.68	0.82		0.89		1.08
Upper Volta	1960-61	0.96	1.00	1.07	1.00	1.00	1.36	1.01	–	–
Central Africa										
Angola	1940	0.75	0.84	0.75	0.77	0.70	0.86	0.90	1.21	–
Angola	1950	0.85	0.93	0.82	0.92	0.72	0.99	0.95	1.88	–
Benguela	1940	0.75	0.76	0.69	0.77	0.78	0.92	0.92	0.98	–
Benguela	1950	0.93	0.98	0.82	0.89	0.78	1.21	0.99	3.09	–
Bie	1940	0.78	0.96	0.89	0.88	0.72	0.83	0.88	0.61	–
Bie	1950	0.89	1.04	0.98	1.09	0.80	0.94	0.96	0.96	–
Huila	1940	0.66	0.81	0.72	0.71	0.58	0.76	0.85	0.87	–
Huila	1950	0.72	0.79	0.73	0.86	0.62	0.91	0.93	0.73	–
Luanda	1940	0.71	0.71	0.62	0.65	0.67	0.88	0.90	0.80	–
Luanda	1950	0.77	0.78	0.67	0.79	0.64	0.97	0.95	1.70	–

Table 2.8 (continued)

	Year of Census or Survey	Ages						Total Population	Not Declared	Births
		40-44	45-49	50-54	55-59	60-64	65+			
Central Africa (cont'd)										
Angola (cont'd)										
Malange	1940	0.83	1.01	0.85	0.81	0.73	0.93	0.89	2.02	--
Malange	1950	0.88	1.01	0.93	0.98	0.77	0.89	0.92	1.25	--
Cameroon										
North Cameroon	1960	0.93	1.10	1.10	1.41	1.06	1.21	1.01	1.17	--
Hill Pagans	1960	0.96	1.59	1.27	2.29	1.35	1.62	1.04	--	--
Moslems	1960	0.85	0.89	1.00	1.13	1.04	1.02	0.99	--	--
Plains Pagans	1960	0.94	1.04	1.12	1.27	1.00	1.30	0.98	0.67	--
Mbalmayo	1956	0.99	1.10	1.22	0.99	0.70	0.49	0.97	0.67	--
Congo (Leopoldville)	1955-57	--	1.16	--	1.09	--	--	0.94	--	0.98
Equateur	1955-57	--	1.08	--	0.85	--	--	0.95	--	0.97
Katanga	1955-57	--	1.31	--	1.19	--	--	0.95	--	0.99
Kasai	1955-57	--	1.13	--	1.17	--	--	0.90	--	1.02
Kivu	1955-57	--	1.11	--	1.30	--	--	0.96	--	0.98
Leopoldville	1955-57	--	1.06	--	0.86	--	--	0.93	--	0.96
Orientale	1955-57	--	1.34	--	1.28	--	--	0.98	--	0.95
East Africa										
Madagascar										
Majunga	1961	0.95	1.23	1.16	1.46	1.49	1.56	1.01	--	--
Tananarive	1956	0.99	1.02	1.06	1.06	1.05	1.05	1.00	--	--
Mozambique	1950	0.82	0.91	0.70	0.62	0.53	0.67	0.91	--	--
Central	1950	0.86	0.92	0.74	0.64	0.71	1.02	0.94	--	--
North	1950	0.79	0.95	0.78	0.84	0.61	0.96	0.91	--	--
South	1950	0.81	0.84	0.56	0.37	0.25	0.24	0.87	--	--
Tanzania										
Zanzibar	1948	1.25	1.70	1.39	1.87	1.42	1.40	1.11	1.25	--
Zanzibar	1958	--	1.24	--	--	--	--	1.10	1.26	--
Uganda										
Kyaddondo	1959	0.92	1.20	1.20	1.29	0.86	1.09	--	--	--
South Africa										
Rep. of South Africa	1936	1.00	1.14	0.87	0.95	0.73	0.85	1.01	1.52	--
Rep. of South Africa	1946	1.07	1.21	0.94	1.03	0.77	0.82	1.04	1.04	--
Rep. of South Africa	1951	1.11	1.17	1.02	1.01	0.78	0.83	1.04	1.44	--
Rep. of South Africa	1960	1.08	1.21	1.03	1.09	0.85	0.79	1.02	1.36	--

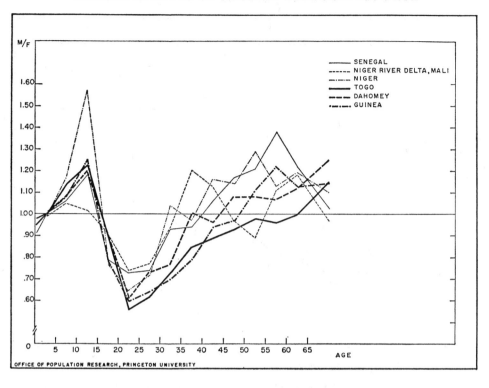

2.6. Sex ratios (males per female) by age group for selected areas of French expression: Senegal, 1960-61; Niger River Delta (Mali), 1956-58; Niger, 1960; Togo, 1958-60; Dahomey, 1961; and Guinea, 1954-55.

birth recorded in tropical African surveys are under unity as often as above. In a large majority of cases, girls under age 1, or aged 1 to 4 years, are reported as more numerous than boys of the same age (see Table 2.9). The reported age group 5 to 9 presents everywhere a sex ratio above unity except in the Congo and in its provinces, which are the only areas for which a large majority of the children had been registered at birth. Underreporting of boys or differential misreporting which would produce a sex ratio under unity at birth or under age 5 cannot be ruled out. Sex ratios of children ever born, discussed at a later point, are usually above unity.

Whatever the sex ratio at birth in tropical African regions, and whatever the pattern of mortality by sex, only differential age misreporting and omissions can explain the standard pattern of sex ratios after early childhood. The biases for either sex separately are best investigated by relating males and females to appropriate stable populations derived from information concerning mortality and fertility. If the information is sufficiently complete and accurate, the model will better describe the

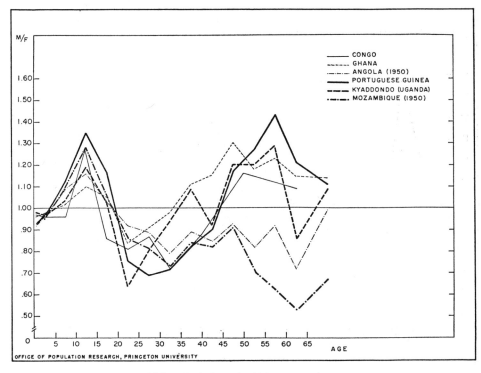

2.7. Sex ratios (males per female) by age groups for: the
Democratic Republic of the Congo, 1955-57; Ghana, 1960;
Angola, 1950; Portuguese Guinea, 1950; Kyaddondo (Ugan-
da), 1959; Mozambique, 1950.

actual age distribution than the recorded data. Within reasonable limits,
a number of stable populations can be used as meters against which
biases can be measured.

Ratios of female age distributions recorded in territories formerly under French administration to stable populations calculated by Brass are
shown in Figure 2.8. They are essentially consistent with underestima-

Table 2.9. Sex ratios (males per female) under or equal to
unity at birth, under 1 year, and between age 1 and 4—
selected regions of Africa

	Number of sex ratios under unity	Number of observations
At birth	8	15
Under one year	30	33
1 - 4 years	33	40

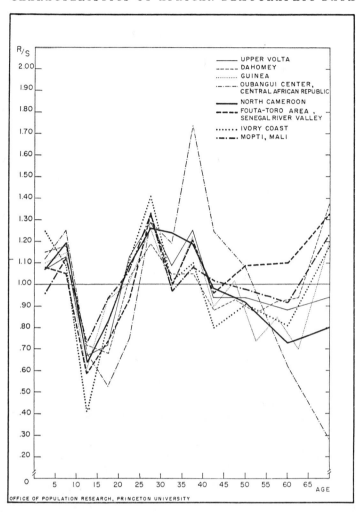

2.8: Ratios of reported age distribution to Brass's African
stable age distribution for selected surveys in countries and
regions of French expression.

tion of ages of some women aged 10-14, while the age of some others
may have been overstated. There is an excess of women reported as
aged between 20 and 40 years. Women are apparently transferred to
the childbearing period from both under and above this range. More
often than not, there are too many women assigned to the group over
age 65.

A comparison with the ratio of reported to stable population distributions for males is provided in Figure 2.9 for two representative INSEE
countries.[4] Males in their teens are apparently rejuvenated to an even

[4] Since Brass has restricted the analysis to the females, model North stable

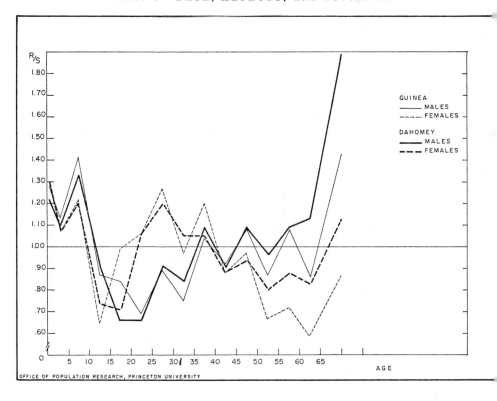

2.9. Ratios of reported age distribution to North model stable age distribution, by age group and sex, for Dahomey, 1961, and Guinea, 1954-55.

larger extent than females. Adult males are underreported, or reported as either younger or older (while females in their childbearing years were too numerous compared with the stable population). Ages after 35 seem better reported, and there is some concentration of males after 65. Avoidance of figures ending in 0 gives to both distributions the familiar sawtoothed look.

Despite the familiar shortage of women aged between 10 and 20 years and the plethora reported between 20 and 35, the Congo and Kyaddondo (Buganda) present altogether different characteristics (Figure 2.10).[5]

populations were used for this purpose. Compared to the set of stable populations calculated by Brass, the North model tends for Guinea and Dahomey to enlarge the ratios reported population to stable population before age 25, and to diminish them later, for the same crude birth and death rates. (For North stable populations, see Chapter 3 and Ansley J. Coale and Paul Demeny, *Regional Model Life Tables and Stable Populations*, Princeton University Press, 1966.)

[5] The Congo stable population has been calculated by Romaniuk by reference to the reported age class 0 to 5, which is trustworthy in that country, thanks to vital registration. Kyaddondo's is a North stable population with mortality and fertility computed by Brass.

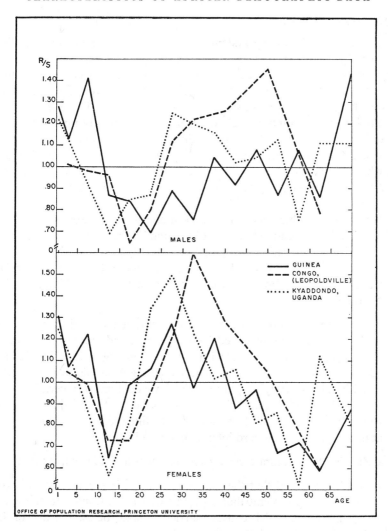

2.10. Ratios of reported age distribution to North model
stable age distribution, by age group and sex, for the Democratic Republic of the Congo, 1955-57; Guinea, 1954-55;
and Kyaddondo (Uganda), 1959.

In contrast with the French inquiries, the data indicate upward rather
than downward transfer of girls aged 10 to 14 years, and there is a
marked tendency to report persons of both sexes in the middle of the
age distribution. The 5-9 age class is understated in Kyaddondo. Age
heaping on multiples of ten is clearly recognizable here, but not in the
Congo, thanks to the recording in broad age groups instead of individual
ages.

Causes of Distortion

There are undoubtedly systematic patterns of error in the recording of ages in the absence of birth registration when interviewers have to rely on their judgment to evaluate ages. Characteristics of an individual are associated, unavoidably, with certain ages: the weaning of a child, his walking, the first payment of taxes, marital status. There is some indication that the number of children of age 1 is usually underestimated (see Figure 2.1), and this may be due to an assumption that children who are not yet weaned (or walking, or talking . . .) are aged under 1, while other children are over 2. Widows may be considered older than married women, etc. . . . The exact genesis of error is obviously difficult to trace.

Is there a plausible reason for the most consistent pattern of bias noted above, i.e., for the understatement of the number of females in their teens and for the concentration at the middle of the fecund period? The question has often been answered by authors in connection with particular censuses or surveys. For instance, a report on the Upper Volta inquiry states the following:

> There is an important underestimation (between 15 and 25 per cent) of the number of women aged 10 to 14 years, and to a lesser extent of those aged 15 to 19 years with a corresponding over-estimation of adult age groups (20 to 40). The explanation of this bias, common to all inquiries, would require special investigation; it is certainly due to a tendency of the interviewers systematically to age those women who are already married or mothers, starting from a "supposed" age at marriage and a standard interval between births.[6]

The Zanzibar Protectorate census report offers a similar explanation:

> It will be observed that the deficit of females is greater than that of males, and it is thought that this may well be attributed to the early age at marriage, which causes married females below the age of 15 to be placed in the adult age groups.[7]

Similar statements are found in other inquiries:

> If in the minds of the interviewers, it is deemed normal for a woman to have her first child after 15, presumed age of menarche, and for a mother of three to be near thirty . . . such a tendency on the part of interviewers would result in aging the women in the age group 10 to 30, proportionately to their number of children . . . etc.[8]

[6] Upper Volta, Service de Statistique, *La situation démographique en Haute-Volta, Résultats partiels de l'Enquête Démographique 1960-1961.* Ministère de la Coopération, INSEE, Service de Coopération, République Française, Paris, 1962, p. 29.

[7] Zanzibar Protectorate, *Report on the* [1958] *Census of the Population of Zanzibar Protectorate,* Government Printer, Zanzibar, 1960, p. 27.

[8] J. L. Boutillier *et al., La Moyenne Vallée du Sénégal,* Paris, 1962, p. 26.

The reference to past events for estimating a person's approximate date of birth (the so-called historical calendar method) is lengthy and difficult. As far as young adults are concerned, the single versus married dichotomy is bound to be important for estimating ages because of its simplicity. Some kind of normative age of marriage usually exists, at least in the minds of census takers. In most cases, censuses and inquiries have themselves set such norms, by setting a minimum age under which girls should not be interviewed regarding their marital status—such as 15 years in the Congo, or 14 years in the French inquiries.

Estimation of age by reference to an assumed "normal" age at marriage can produce several varieties of error in the age distribution. The assumption of a "normal" age quite different from the true mean age at marriage, for example, would result in a net upward or downward bias in the reported age of young married women. Another effect may be to "evacuate" the age interval at which the normal age at marriage is assumed to occur. Unmarried girls may be assigned to a younger interval, and married girls to an older.

A plausible explanation of some of the patterns of age misreporting of women most frequently encountered in tropical Africa is that there is a quasi-universal tendency to assume a higher "typical" age of marriage than actually prevails. Teenage single girls are graded downward from this reference point, perhaps in terms of their physical appearance, and the 5-9 age group may be accordingly inflated. Married women's ages are scaled upward from the reference point, by successive transfers. This may happen by applying the "mere arithmetic" criticized in one of the French reports, according to which the age of a mother is computed from the "normal" age of marriage by adding the number of children times a standard interval between births.[9]

The relationship between parity and the misreporting of ages is entirely plausible, but it is difficult to document because parity and age progress together anyway, at least until the end of the fecund period. The number of children ever born to women past age 50 should normally level off, provided (1) there has been no marked systematic change of fertility in the past and (2) the survival of old women is not connected with fertility. Since older women may be increasingly prone to lapses of recall, sets of parities increasing with age after the end of the childbearing period suggest errors in age reporting in function of parity, unless there was a genuine past trend of declining fertility. Guinea shows a smooth pattern of increase (see Table 2.10) but this is far from universal. Women aged 50 and over (55 and over in the Congo) have higher parity than women aged 45-49 (45-54 in the Congo) in about half the cases for which we possess data. The part played by bias is difficult to measure, but data classified by age always have to be used with caution.

[9] Central African Republic, *Enquête démographique Centre-Oubangui 1959, Méthodologie—Résultats provisoires*, Paris, May 1960, p. 13.

Table 2.10. Average parity, and percent distribution of women aged 40 and over
by number of children—Guinea 1954-55

Number of children	Ages of women						
	40–44	45–49	50–54	55–59	60–64	65–69	70 and over
Average number of children	5.01	5.29	5.33	5.39	5.53	5.54	5.64
Percent of women with:							
0–4	43.1	40.8	39.9	39.1	38.1	37.8	34.7
5–9	51.6	51.4	50.9	51.4	52.4	51.5	53.9
10 and over	5.3	7.8	9.2	9.4	9.5	10.7	11.4

This predicament cannot be avoided in tropical Africa. One has to recognize the presence of biases, and the potential distortion of various measurements.

The Improvement of Statistics on Age

Many countries of Africa have some form of vital registration. In Uganda, where vital registration has existed since 1904, Kuczynski's evaluation of the system was as follows:

An experience of thirty years has shown that native birth and death records are obtainable in Uganda, and the available vital statistics suggest that the records are fairly complete in a number of sazas but quite inadequate in others.[10]

But according to Martin at a later date, ". . . the standard of recording has possibly declined over the years."[11]

An effort was made from 1950 on in former French Africa to improve vital registration. Forty-six thousand births were declared in Guinea in 1954. The 1954-55 demographic inquiry enumerated 129,000 children under 1 year, of whom 19,000 had a birth certificate. Apart from loss of cases due to infant mortality, ". . . the discrepancy (between 46 and 19 thousand) corresponds either to omissions on the part of the census takers, or to certificates that had been lost or were not, at the time of the Census, in the enumerated persons' hands."[12]

[10] R. Kuczynski, *Demographic Survey of the British Colonial Empire*, Volume II, Oxford University Press, 1949, p. 272.

[11] C. J. Martin, "A method of measuring fertility in underdeveloped countries where birth registration is non-existent or defective," in *Proceedings of the World Population Conference* [Rome] *1954*, Papers Volume IV, p. 384, U.N., New York, 1955.

[12] *Etude démographique par Sondage en Guinée 1954-55, Résultats définitifs,* I, p. 13. The number of children under age 1 was clearly overestimated in Guinea.

The vital registration system was fairly efficient at the time of the 1955-57 Congo demographic inquiry. According to the official report, ". . . 83 per cent of the births enumerated in the inquiry had been declared in the prescribed manner to the Vital Registrar's Offices."[13]

The list could be expanded. Compulsory registration areas cover about 12 percent of the population of Ghana. Mission records often contain dates of births for church members. Almost nowhere is the information on age complete or accurate, even for the younger ages, but census agencies should seek to take maximum advantage of all the available information on age. A vital registration system, however belated or incomplete, constitutes a great asset in the taking of a census. Even when a person has not been registered at birth, his age can be compared with that of registered persons with whom he has been associated since birth or who show comparable development. In cases of the recent introduction of birth registration, the accurate knowledge of age among young children can be put to good use in quasi-stable population analysis. These facts are illustrated in Romaniuk's chapter about the Congo.

The demographic boon of identity booklets with information on vital events in every man's family is not likely to befall census takers elsewhere in Africa for some time. However, even when birth registration cannot be systematically used to improve census returns, it can provide opportunities for careful studies aimed either at controlling the information of the main inquiry or at analyzing the nature of biases affecting the reporting.

Improved knowledge of the distribution by age and its biases should rank high in the order of priorities in African demography, since no thorough demographic analysis is possible without it. Special investigations of the biases in reporting should be attempted in the wake of every survey. A statement made with registration of vital events in mind may be extended to the study of age misreporting:

> . . . there seems little doubt that an event-by-event matching of two independent systems represents the most promising technique for assessing the accuracy of any system of recording.[14]

Matching ages recorded by conventional census methods with birth registration where it has existed for some time affords an interesting method of studying biases in relation to marital status, parity, physical development (e.g., puberty), the paying of taxes, etc. As noted by Coale, independence of the two systems is required, but it could be realized for in-

[13] République du Congo, Bureau de la Démographie, *Tableau général de la démographie congolaise,* Leopoldville, 1961, p. 47.
[14] Ansley J. Coale, "The design of an experimental procedure for obtaining accurate vital statistics," in *Proceedings of the International Population Conference, New York 1961,* Vol. II, p. 373, London, 1963.

stance in parts of Uganda, where fairly complete birth registration has existed for a long time.

Other ways of improving the recording of ages than vital registration must also be investigated. In small studies the investment of considerable time might produce at least a satisfactory ranking of all inhabitants by age; each person would be defined as "older than X" or "younger than Y." Some individuals in the ranking would know their ages precisely, and this would afford landmarks permitting definition of the whole age pyramid in a more satisfactory fashion.

Information on Fertility

First, we shall review the various procedures used to collect data on fertility, and we shall examine the following topics: nature of information, identity of respondent, unit of observation, time period covered, and phrasing of questions. At a second stage, we shall investigate the effects of collection procedures on the data themselves.

Data Collection Procedures

Nature of information. Direct information on fertility relates either to current fertility, i.e., to children born during a definite, recent period of time, or is of retrospective nature and concerns all children born during the interviewed woman's life. Data on current fertility only was collected in the Togo census; retrospective data on parity only in some of the East African post-enumeration surveys and the Portuguese censuses. Both sets of data have been assembled in most French demographic inquiries, in the Congo and in the Ghana post-enumeration survey. Tables 2.11 and 2.12, respectively, show age-specific fertility rates and parity ratios.

Identity of respondents. The informant is either the head of the unit of observation (family, household, etc.) or the woman whose fertility is reported. In most cases, both the information on current and on retrospective fertility is collected from women; in French inquiries and in Ruanda-Urundi, current fertility is asked twice. Usually, only certain categories of women are interviewed:

"adult" women (East Africa);
women over puberty (Zambia and Rhodesia,[15] Ruanda-Urundi, Sudan);
15 and over (Ghana, Dahomey, Congo-Leopoldville);
15 and over and married women under 15 (Congo-Brazzaville);
14 and over (all the other French inquiries).

[15] Formerly Northern and Southern Rhodesia, respectively.

Table 2.11. Age-specific fertility rates of women—selected regions of Africa

	Year of Census or Survey	15-19	20-24	25-29	30-34	35-39	40-44	45-49	50-54	Not Declared
West Africa										
Dahomey	1961	0.207	0.339	0.311	0.250	0.167	0.085	0.027	–	–
Guinea	1954-55	0.238	0.334	0.311	0.246	0.171	0.069	0.028	–	–
Forest	1954-55	0.212	0.334	0.320	0.271	0.181	0.076	0.034	–	–
Fouta Djallon	1954-55	0.251	0.341	0.304	0.251	0.166	0.060	0.022	–	–
Maritime	1954-55	0.274	0.321	0.295	0.201	0.157	0.076	0.027	–	–
Upper	1954-55	0.202	0.333	0.328	0.244	0.181	0.068	0.025	–	–
Konkouré (de jure)	1957	0.171	0.216	0.199	0.136	0.039	0.031	–	–	–
Ivory Coast										
1st Agricul-tural sector	1957-58	0.239	0.353	0.338	0.224	0.177	0.092	0.057	–	0.007
Bongouanou	1955-56	0.185	0.279	0.284	0.222	0.107	0.056	0.019	–	–
Mali										
Central Niger Delta	1956-58	0.196	0.313	0.259	0.275	0.164	0.098	0.031	–	–
Niger	1960	0.197	0.341	0.306	0.260	0.191	0.099	0.047	–	–
Senegal	1961	0.158	0.242	0.243	0.204	0.153	0.047	0.026	–	0.007
Middle Senegal Valley	1957	0.169	0.262	0.275	0.240	0.173	0.088	0.037	–	–
Togo										
Kabré Country	1957	0.198	0.430	0.396	0.391	0.297	0.138	0.052	–	–
Upper Volta	1960-61	0.169	0.308	0.265	0.220	0.154	0.084	0.021	–	–
Central Africa										
Cameroon										
Mbalmayo	1956	0.103	0.150	0.114	0.090	0.050	0.020	0.006	0.002	0.033
Congo (Leopold-ville)	1955-57	0.136	0.265	0.231	0.168	0.080	0.080	0.016	–	–
Equateur	1955-57	0.089	0.249	0.219	0.160		0.072	0.011	–	–
Katanga	1955-57	0.210	0.306	0.251	0.186		0.106	0.022	–	–
Kasai	1955-57	0.144	0.268	0.234	0.170		0.080	0.015	–	–
Kivu	1955-57	0.182	0.290	0.261	0.182		0.086	0.018	–	–
Leopoldville	1955-57	0.094	0.280	0.270	0.213		0.107	0.019	–	–
Orientale	1955-57	0.134	0.201	0.147	0.103		0.048	0.012	–	–
East Africa										
Madagascar										
Majunga	1961	0.208	0.259	0.249	0.128	0.104	0.030	0.011	–	–
Tananarive	1956	0.205	0.333	0.301	0.227	0.146	0.066	0.018	–	–

Table 2.12. Parity by age of mother—selected regions of Africa

	Year of Census or Survey	Children ever born to women aged					
		15-19	20-24	25-29	30-34	35-39	40-44
West Africa							
Dahomey	1961	0.490	1.890	3.280	4.490	5.110	5.730
Guinea							
Forest	1954-55	0.539	1.745	2.862	3.889	4.477	5.021
Fouta Djallon	1954-55	0.427	1.528	2.602	3.649	4.364	4.980
Maritime	1954-55	0.598	1.856	2.970	3.929	4.446	4.783
Upper	1954-55	0.627	1.791	2.828	3.809	4.341	5.070
Konkouré (de jure)	1954-55	0.474	1.822	3.205	4.481	5.098	5.876
Ivory Coast	1957	0.579	1.575	2.416	3.011	3.864	4.100
1st Agricultural Sector	1957-58	0.640	2.100	3.280	4.350	5.010	6.090
Bongouanou	1955-56	0.422	2.026	3.617	4.984	6.121	6.652
Mali							
Central Niger Delta	1956-58	0.500	1.800	3.150	4.310	4.980	5.360
Niger	1960	0.462	1.790	2.926	4.167	4.718	5.161
Senegal							
Middle Senegal Valley	1957	0.396	1.677	2.860	3.831	4.540	5.046
Togo							
Kabre Country	1957	0.360	1.976	3.236	4.429	5.242	5.983
Upper Volta	1960	0.320	1.660	3.130	4.110	4.810	5.140
Central Africa							
Angola							
Angola	1940	0.072	1.054	2.017	2.719	3.341	3.738
Angola	1950	0.176	1.069	2.123	2.858	3.612	3.826
Benguela	1940	0.059	1.128	2.319	3.180	4.013	4.546
Benguela	1950	0.146	1.153	2.237	3.191	3.959	4.179
Bie	1940	0.065	0.857	1.546	1.997	2.491	2.698
Bie	1950	0.193	0.843	1.711	2.144	2.771	2.769
Huila	1940	0.044	0.798	1.718	2.329	2.957	3.384
Huila	1950	0.093	0.834	1.944	2.578	3.341	3.550
Luanda	1940	0.124	1.288	2.398	3.203	3.987	4.558
Luanda	1950	0.203	1.239	2.486	3.428	4.123	4.685
Malange	1940	0.065	1.006	1.821	2.470	2.975	3.302
Malange	1950	0.228	1.094	1.969	2.615	3.321	3.583

Table 2.12 (continued)

	Year of Census or Survey	Children ever born to women aged					
		15-19	20-24	25-29	30-34	35-39	40-44
Central Africa (cont'd)							
Cameroon							
Mbalmayo	1956	0.331	1.022	1.500	2.023	2.535	3.112
Congo (Brazzaville)	1960-61	0.399	1.571	2.270	2.984	3.369	3.703
Cnngo (Leopoldville)	1955-57	0.345	1.450	2.387	3.252	3.850	
Equateur	1955-57	0.169	1.055	1.885	2.665	3.265	
Katanga	1955-57	0.542	1.657	2.460	3.292	3.829	
Kasaï	1955-57	0.364	1.440	2.316	3.237	3.984	
Kivu	1955-57	0.522	2.019	3.315	4.330	4.878	
Leopoldville	1955-57	0.206	1.331	2.671	4.041	5.066	
Orientale	1955-57	0.352	1.228	1.638	2.068	2.540	
East Africa							
Mozambique	1950	0.147	0.905	1.842	2.605	3.334	3.760
Central	1950	0.174	1.039	2.188	3.221	4.104	4.848
North	1950	0.146	0.794	1.565	2.092	2.659	2.975
South	1950	0.109	0.870	1.750	2.580	3.237	3.607

Table 2.12 (continued)

	Year of Census or Survey	Children ever born to women aged					Not Declared
		45-49	50-54	55-59	60-64	65+	
West Africa							
Dahomey	1961	5.810	5.770				–
Guinea	1954-55	5.276	5.329	5.380	5.512	5.593	3.529
Forest	1954-55	5.159	5.554	5.493	5.575	5.561	2.800
Fouta Djallon	1954-55	4.959	4.912	5.014	5.253	5.295	1.923
Maritime	1954-55	5.360	5.036	5.366	5.477	5.801	3.867
Upper	1954-55	6.265	6.347	6.423	6.488	6.710	4.348
Konkouré (de jure)	1957	4.593	3.942	4.706	4.007	4.876	–
Ivory Coast							
1st Agricultural Sector	1957-58	5.911	5.837		5.825		–
Bongouanou	1955-56	6.421	6.382	6.667	6.599		–
Mali							
Central Niger Delta	1956-58	5.470	5.410	5.430	5.230	5.370	2.250
Niger	1960	5.817	5.729	5.561	5.474	5.493	–
Senegal							
Middle Senegal Valley	1957	5.295	5.054	5.315	5.312	5.248	–
Togo							
Kabré Country	1957	5.916		6.244			–
Upper Volta	1960	5.340	5.350	5.370	5.270	5.435	–
Central Africa							
Angola	1940	3.989	4.072	4.068			1.858
Angola	1950	4.216	4.125	3.885		3.856	–
Benguela	1940	4.680	4.407	4.634			2.495
Benguela	1950	4.549	4.538	4.363		4.407	–
Bie	1940	2.919	3.069	3.113			2.028
Bie	1950	3.247	3.079	2.817		2.816	–
Huíla	1940	3.619	3.704	3.722			2.731
Huíla	1950	3.975	3.734	3.588		3.538	–
Luanda	1940	4.833	4.967	5.114			2.543
Luanda	1950	5.178	5.059	4.692		5.792	–
Malange	1940	3.678	3.942	3.753			0.652
Malange	1950	3.866	3.951	3.757		3.725	–

Table 2.12 (continued)

	Year of Census or Survey	Children ever born to women aged					
		45-49	50-54	55-59	60-64	65+	Not Declared
Central Africa (cont'd)							
Cameroon							
Mbalmayo	1956	2.956	3.288	3.436	3.895		2.130
Congo (Brazzaville)	1960-61	3.703					—
Congo (Leopoldville)	1955-57						—
Equateur	1955-57	3.968		3.908			—
Katanga	1955-57	3.506		3.748			—
Kasaï	1955-57	3.702		3.754			—
Kivu	1955-57	4.163		3.385			—
Leopoldville	1955-57	4.423		4.186			—
Orientale	1955-57	5.192		3.226			—
	1955-57	2.722		4.895			—
				2.818			
East Africa							
Mozambique	1950	4.008	3.892	3.892	3.365	3.256	—
Central	1950	5.075	5.165	4.987	4.618	4.596	—
North	1950	3.236	3.113	3.112	2.702	2.716	—
South	1950	3.721	3.553	3.571	3.004	2.855	—

[57]

Unit of observation. The question on current births has been directed to various aggregates:

births in the family (e.g., Guinea, First Agricultural Sector of the Ivory Coast, Senegal Valley, Central Nigerian Delta, Centre-Oubangui, Senegal, Niger, Upper Volta);
in the household (Gabon, Congo-Brazzaville);
among the inhabitants of a dwelling unit (Ruanda-Urundi);
in the dwelling unit (Kabré Country, Dahomey).

Whenever a question was asked of women only, the unit of observation was these women, wherever they were at the time of birth and to whatever family they may have belonged.

Period of time. The period covered by the question concerning current fertility was usually twelve calendar months, except in

Kabré Country: 13 lunar months;
Ruanda-Urundi: since last annual inquiry;
Tanganyika 1957: since last dry season;
Uganda 1959: since 1st September 1958;
Zanzibar: since previous Ramadhan (i.e., 1st May 1957; the census was taken on the night of the 19th and 20th March, 1958).

Phrasing of questions. The presentation of the fertility question ranges for a single space on the form without comment in the instructions (e.g., the Portuguese censuses) to an elaborate wording regarding a precise order and designed to elicit as complete results as possible. For instance, French inquiries take special care to ensure the reporting of a birth even in the case of death of the child, and usually combine information relative to fertility and mortality.[16]

Thus, although all surveys ultimately seek identical information, there is a surprising variety for each item. Some of the differences are admittedly due to local conditions. An obvious example is the reference to Ramadhan in Moslem Zanzibar to help in determining the observation period. Of the procedures just enumerated, one would nevertheless expect some to be more appropriate than others. We will review each of the five topics and scrutinize the collected data in order to see if we can relate some of their characteristics to collection procedures.

[16] The general instructions elaborated by INSEE fix the following order of questions concerning the total number of children ever born: "Once you have asked: How many live-born children did you have? How many boys, how many girls? you will ask: how many have survived? How many boys, how many girls. . . . Finally, you will inscribe the number of dead children after having checked with the women that for either sex and both sexes together, the sum: *Still alive + Deceased* is equal to: *Born alive." Enquête démographique par sondage—Manuel d'enquêteur et de controleur,* INSEE, Paris, 1961, pp. 37, 38.

Biases Due to Respondent, Unit, or Time of Observation

As noted previously, questions relating to the identity of the informant and to the unit or the time period for which fertility was reported do not arise in connection with parity information. The question on current fertility however can be addressed to various persons. Mothers may or may not be better informants than heads of family. They may be more reluctant to mention a dead child; on the other hand, they may remember more vividly whether the child was a boy or a girl, whether he was still- or live-born. Wherever the double battery of questions has been included, it would be instructive to compare answers concerning current fertility (a) from mothers and (b) from heads of household or family. The comparison is only possible for one inquiry, that of the Central Niger Delta in Mali:

	Last year's births	
	in the family	to women
Boys	6,055	5,905
Girls	5,845	5,840
Total	11,900	11,745

Some discrepancy between the two figures is to be expected as a result of mobility, divorces and deaths of women, and disruptions of families. While the balance of these factors would seem to incline towards a larger understatement of births to women, the difference is likely to be small. Any large discrepancy would probably indicate some bias related to the type of informant.

Births to women represent a clear and manageable *de facto* concept. Alternative units of reference could obviously cause biases of predictable kinds. For instance, if births *in* the dwelling unit are considered, as the phrasing of some questionnaires suggests,[17] births in a neighboring hospital would legitimately be left out. If the household is the unit, events in dissolved households risk being omitted or counted twice.

Since the results of consumer surveys in industrially developed areas seem to indicate memory differences with regard to a fixed period of reference, the problem can only be greater in a society where people are not accustomed to calendars. Various inquiries have attempted to delimit the observation period in a less abstract fashion than by merely saying "within 12 months." The trouble is that there are few alternative phrasings of the question. There is no indication that people are more

[17] Detailed instructions were not available for the Kabré Country (where the unit of observation was the *vestibule*, or cluster of huts) nor for Dahomey (where the related concept of *concession* was used). These instructions may conceivably have insisted on usual dwelling place of the parents rather than on physical occurrence of the birth.

at ease with lunar months than with calendar months.[18] The Tanganyika post-enumeration sample tried to enumerate births "since the last dry season," but this was abandoned as unsatisfactory in later East African censuses: "It should be observed that the dry season is an ill-defined period of time lasting in some areas for several months."[19] Furthermore, in any particular year, there are differences in the timing of the rains among regions. The number of arid months per year in Tanganyika may vary, according to the region, between zero to three and eight to eleven months.[20] The question used in Zanzibar and referring to Ramadhan was apparently not successful, even after adjustment for the fact that Ramadhan had been celebrated less than one year before.[21]

Responses on births in a recent interval are highly vulnerable to period errors and should always be collected in conjunction with retrospective information on the total number of previous births to women, which is not subject to the same defects. The use of independent data for cross-checking is almost a prerequisite to meaningful results under African conditions, and it is likely that sample demographic inquiries which devote much of their questionnaire space to assessing fertility, both current and retrospective, fare better with respect to completeness and accuracy than censuses (such as the Portuguese ones) covering the total population and including perfunctorily an isolated question on the number of children ever born. The care taken in devising and administering the questionnaire and the actual wording of the questions are significant variables in the study of fertility in tropical Africa.

Current and Retrospective Fertility in Conjunction

Figure 2.11 shows ratios of parity to current fertility cumulated to comparable ages of women, for selected regions (see also Table 2.13). Taken at an appropriate age, these ratios (called for simplicity P/F ratios) indicate whether there has been an over- or underestimation of the reference period during which recorded births had occurred. If the ratios were consistently under unity, it would suggest that births occurred during a longer period than 12 months. The latter case seems to hold in most of the large-scale inquiries for which the two sets of information exist. Only in Mbalmayo, Konkouré, and Bongouanou, three

---

[18] The Kabré Country, where 13 lunar months was used instead of 12 calendar months, is on record as the place where the period of reference seems to have been the most exaggerated.

[19] Tanganyika, *African Census Report, 1957*, Dar es Salaam, 1963, p. 81.

[20] According to a map (after W. Lauer) included in G.H.T. Kimble, *Tropical Africa*, Vol. I, The Twentieth Century Fund, New York, 1960, p. 47.

[21] ". . . there is some evidence that there was an understatement of births since the previous Ramadhan. These birth rates are incompatible with those based on the numbers of children under one year . . . they are appreciably lower than those obtained from the statistics of total fertility." (Zanzibar Protectorate, *Report on the Census . . .* , Zanzibar, 1960, p. 49.)

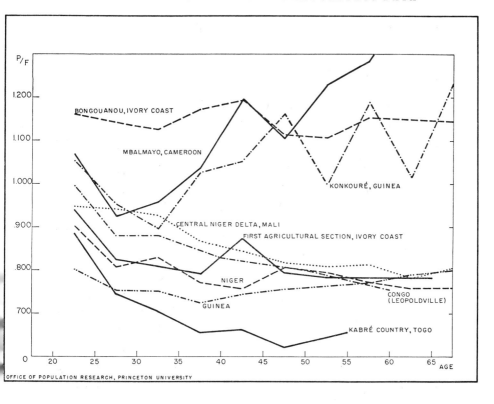

2.11. Ratios of parity to current fertility (*P/F*), by age
groups of women, for selected regions of Africa.

small areas covered without sampling, were fewer current births reported
at most ages than implied in the retrospective information.

It seems reasonable enough to use the *P/F* ratio at an appropriate age
as correction coefficient for the current fertility estimates, but the choice
of a particular ratio at a particular age is difficult. There is good ground
to adopt the youngest possible age (20 to 24 years for instance) because
retrospective reporting at older ages of women is probably affected increasingly by recall lapses and counting problems.

Unfortunately, the *P/F* ratios are almost certainly affected by other
factors than forgetting. Lapses of recall fail to account for the shape of
P/F curves in Figure 2.11. There is a universal tendency for the ratios
to decrease between ages 20-24 and 25-29, and this decline is often
steeper than at any other age. Surely, young women in the second of
these age classes should not be so much more inclined to forget their
children than those in the first. Furthermore, the subsequent shape of the
curve may vary a great deal. Often, after a trough in middle age, there
is a recovery of the ratio up into ages where the presumed poor recol-

[61]

Table 2.13. Ratios of parity to current fertility (P/F)—selected regions of Africa

	Year of Census or Survey	Ages									
		20-24	25-29	30-34	35-39	40-44	45-49	50-54	55-59	60-64	65+
West Africa											
Dahomey	1961	0.932	0.893	0.888	0.842	0.861	0.838	0.763	0.833	0.789	-
Guinea	1954-55	0.802	0.752	0.751	0.724	0.744	0.756				0.801
Forest	1954-55	0.749	0.704	0.706	0.696	0.726	0.722	0.777	0.771	0.780	0.778
Fouta Djallon	1954-55	0.820	0.764	0.747	0.709	0.704	0.710	0.704	0.769	0.753	0.759
Maritime	1954-55	0.771	0.730	0.748	0.730	0.780	0.793	0.745	0.794	0.810	0.858
Upper	1954-55	0.917	0.874	0.881	0.835	0.878	0.906	0.918	0.929	0.938	0.971
Konkouré (de jure)	1957	1.056	0.953	0.896	1.027	1.052	1.162	0.997	1.190	1.014	1.233
Ivory Coast											
1st Agricultural Sector	1957-58	0.941	0.824	0.810	0.792	0.874	0.794	0.785		0.783	
Bongouanou	1955-56	1.161	1.141	1.125	1.173	1.193	1.114	1.108	1.157		1.145
Mali											
Central Niger Delta	1956-58	0.948	0.942	0.925	0.866	0.844	0.819	0.810	0.813	0.783	0.804
Niger											
Niger	1960	0.903	0.807	0.830	0.770	0.757	0.806	0.794	0.771	0.759	0.761
Senegal											
Middle Senegal Valley	1957	1.040	0.961	0.899	0.861	0.856	0.851	0.813	0.855	0.854	0.844
Togo											
Kabré country	1957	0.885	0.745	0.704	0.655	0.662	0.622			0.657	
Upper Volta	1960-61	0.953	0.979	0.937	0.908	0.877	0.875	0.876	0.880	0.863	0.890
Central Africa											
Cameroon											
Mbalmayo	1956	1.070	0.925	0.958	1.036	1.195	1.105	1.230	1.285		1.457
Congo (Leopoldville)	1955-57	0.999	0.880	0.881	0.829		0.800			0.755	
Equateur	1955-57	0.913	0.799	0.811	0.784		0.793			0.850	
Katanga	1955-57	0.850	0.733	0.745	0.682		0.612			0.560	
Kasaï	1955-57	0.961	0.835	0.860	0.845		0.828			0.833	
Kivu	1955-57	1.147	1.050	1.020	0.927		0.788			0.575	
Leopoldville	1955-57	1.050	0.995	1.041	0.984		0.935			0.882	
Orientale	1955-57	0.974	0.766	0.755	0.768		0.773			0.800	

lections of old women would have it go down. These irregularities have to be accounted for by other explanations, such as genuine past trends in fertility, selective survival of women in function of parity, or mere random fluctuations. Finally, it appears that influence of age misreporting is perceptible in certain features of the curves, such as the characteristic decline in the two first considered age groups. It would deflect us from our argument to study here in detail the influence of age misreporting. We discuss it more lengthily in an appendix to Chapter 3 and illustrate the reasoning by a model based primarily on Congolese data. The general relevance of the model does not depend for its use upon any particular body of data. Any distortion in the age distribution will somewhat affect the P/F ratios, and the effect of shifting women from one age group to the next (downward as well as upward) may be accentuated if the shifts take place in function of fertility and parity.

Although the decline of the P/F ratios with age is not systematic enough to lead to definitive conclusions about a general forgetting pattern, there are other indications that forgetting exists. Increasing recall lapses are documented in other preliterate societies, and they are often sex- and parity-specific.

In tropical Africa, the question on children ever born has usually been asked by sex, but it has rarely been tabulated in that way. And indeed sex ratios show a marked trend with age of mother in three of the four surveys for which the information has been published.[22] (See Table 2.14 and Figure 2.12.) Barring an impossible time trend of sex ratios at birth, the anomaly must originate in one of the following biases:

Table 2.14. Sex ratios (males per 100 females) of children ever born, by age of mother—selected regions of Africa

Age[*]	Mozambique 1940	Mozambique 1950	Niger 1960	Guinea 1954-55
14-19	103.3	99.1	100.8	103.2
20-24	101.3	101.5	103.5	102.1
25-29	103.7	102.8	105.4	103.5
30-34	105.8	104.7	107.7	106.4
35-39	108.1	104.5	103.1	103.7
40-44	109.1	105.9	108.3	102.2
45-49	111.6	106.5	111.8	102.5
50-54	111.4	107.4	118.3	100.6
55-59	118.5	107.6	119.1	103.2
60-64	117.8	108.9	109.8	99.8
65+	119.0	109.3	122.1	102.9

[*]In Mozambique (1940): 16-20, 21-25, 26-30 ... 66 and over.

[22] Even in Guinea, where no such trend is discernible, the overall sex ratio of children ever born, at 103 males per 100 females, is higher than the sex ratio of births reported the last 12 months (100) and than the sex ratio of children aged under 1 year (95).

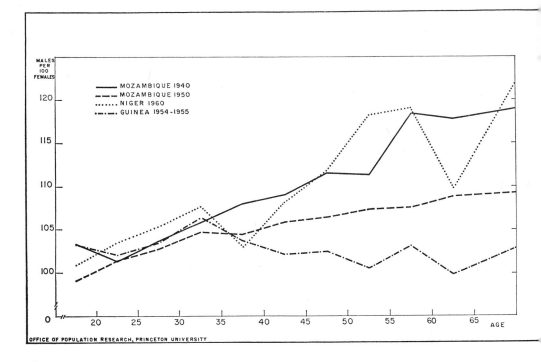

MALES
PER
100
FEMALES

——— MOZAMBIQUE 1940
— — — MOZAMBIQUE 1950
· · · · · · · NIGER 1960
·—·—·— GUINEA 1954-1955

OFFICE OF POPULATION RESEARCH, PRINCETON UNIVERSITY

2.12. Sex ratios of children born during the lifetime of
mothers, by the age group of mothers, according to the
Mozambique censuses of 1940 and 1950 and the sample
surveys taken in Niger in 1960 and in Guinea in 1954-55.

fictitious boys are added;

girls are reported as boys; or

boys are "remembered" better than girls;

and even more so with older mothers. The two first hypotheses are included for completeness, but the third seems the most likely. The words
forgetting and *remember*, however, have to be qualified.

Omissions in the Reporting of Parity

Omissions may, for example, imply taboos against mentioning dead
people. There is some likelihood that misreporting is of absent or dead
children, since checking is easy on the part of enumerators in the case
of live, present children. To make this hypothesis fit sex ratios increasing
with age of mothers in Niger and Mozambique, one would have to assume that dead or absent girls are more frequently omitted than dead
or absent boys. Another kind of "forgetting" would result from illiterate
respondents' difficulties in handling high numbers; high parities could
systematically be underestimated.

A priori, the proportions of women having borne zero, one, or two children after having been subjected to a long period of pregnancy risks (say after 35 years of age) should be good indices of subfecundity and should be highly intercorrelated. Furthermore, there should be an inverse correlation between each of these three indices and the proportion of prolific women, for instance those having had more than seven children during their life.

These *a priori* expectations are to a large extent vindicated by actual African data (Tables 2.15 and 2.16). There are significant positive correlations between proportions of women with no children and with one or two children. The correlations between zero- and one-child women drops however after 50 years and ceases to be significant at 65 years and over. This drop is paralleled at the same ages by an increase of the negative correlation between women with zero children and with seven or more children. The latter correlation is finally very high ($r = .9$ at 60 to 64 years and at 65 and over).

Table 2.15. Correlations between proportions of women with zero children and with one and two children, and between proportions with one child and with two children—selected regions of Africa

Age	0 children vs. 1 child r	0 children vs. 2 children r	1 child vs. 2 children r
35–39	.70	.21	.73
40–44	.71	.50	.79
45–49	.81	.50	.77
50–54	.76	.67	.77
55–59	.71	.73	.70
60–64	.59	.76	.74
65+	.39	.67	.78

Table 2.16. Correlations between proportions of women with seven or more children and with zero, one, or two children—selected regions of Africa

Age	7 + vs. 0 r	7+ vs. 1 r	7+ vs. 2 r
35–39	-.46	-.72	-.79
40–44	-.59	-.72	-.94
45–49	-.66	-.77	-.89
50–54	-.76	-.68	-.91
55–59	-.79	-.60	-.88
60–64	-.91	-.72	-.88
65+	-.92	-.61	-.82

The detailed data on childlessness by country and region (in Table 2.17) make it apparent that the increasing correlations are the result of opposite trends associated with the origin (Portuguese or French-language) of the data. Within French-language territories, there is a tendency for proportions of childless women to drop with increasing age after the childbearing years;[23] the reverse is true of the Portuguese territories. The proportions of women with seven children and over follow opposite trends: decrease in the Portuguese, increase in the French-speaking territories. The systematic association of either characteristic with a system of data collection makes it suspect. Furthermore, the Portuguese territories in general have higher proportions of childless women and lower recorded fertility. One suspects that the more detailed demographic inquiries of the French tradition simply have elicited more complete answers.

Heisel (in Chapter 8) suggests that the obvious underreporting of children ever born in the Portuguese territories is associated with characteristics of a census by assembly, and specifically with the need to resort to the help of local headmen in order to gain information on absent women. He argues that this explains both the slow start of the Portuguese parity distribution and the rise of childlessness by age, for a headman would not be up to date on recent births, and he would omit absent or dead children from the count for absent women.[24] No information would often be mistaken for no children.

Evaluation of the Fertility Questions

If carefully administered, the standard sets of questions on fertility including information on birth during the last 12 months and on total number of births addressed partly to the head of family and partly to women appears to be an appropriate way of studying fertility. The interpretation of answers still presents many problems, originating in the imprecision of the reference period, in the uncertainty concerning ages, and in the possible omission of children who died in infancy. Since most sets of questions on fertility are well developed, better phrasing is not likely to enhance much further the quality of the data. If, as is plausible, the deficient report by older women of children ever born is caused partly by the omission of persons who have left the household, separate questions on (a) surviving children still in the household, (b) surviving children who have left, and (c) children who have died might yield

[23] This may be spurious, and related to an association of age reporting with parities. Cf. supra.

[24] This would provide a plausible explanation for two mystifying features of the Portuguese parities, namely the increasing sex ratio (as exogamy moves girls away from the chief's jurisdiction) and age heaping of the distribution of childless women on age 60 (as absent women are reported disproportionately both as ages 60 and as without children).

Table 2.17. Percent childless women by age—selected regions of Africa

	Year of Census or Survey	Ages					
		15–19	20–24	25–29	30–34	35–39	40–44
West Africa							
Guinea							
Forest	1954–55	56.0	15.0	9.2	7.3	6.7	6.4
Fouta Djallon	1954–55	62.4	16.2	10.0	6.8	5.7	4.6
Maritime	1954–55	53.3	14.6	7.8	7.1	7.0	7.8
Upper	1954–55	50.0	15.4	11.0	10.0	8.8	7.7
Konkouré (de jure)	1957	59.3	13.1	8.4	4.5	5.3	4.3
		50.3	20.1	13.8	12.6	8.7	10.1
Ivory Coast							
Bongounou	1955–56	68.4	16.6	6.4	9.9	4.2	3.7
Niger	1960	77.4	19.8	12.8	10.9	9.9	9.9
Senegal							
Middle Senegal Valley	1957	68.7	23.7	12.0	11.0	8.2	7.7
Upper Volta	1960	73.5	15.7	7.2	6.8	6.4	7.0
Central Africa							
Angola	1940	94.4	38.8	19.6	15.2	11.1	9.6
Angola	1950	86.5	41.1	18.4	15.4	11.8	13.5
Benguela	1940	95.6	39.5	16.1	11.4	4.9	2.3
Benguela	1950	89.1	37.5	16.3	11.8	9.2	12.5
Bie	1940	94.6	45.3	29.3	23.9	19.3	17.3
Bie	1950	84.4	47.9	27.3	25.8	21.5	22.9
Huila	1940	96.5	48.0	22.9	17.8	14.4	12.7
Huila	1950	92.5	46.9	15.1	11.5	9.9	10.4
Luanda	1940	90.7	29.3	14.4	12.0	7.9	8.3
Luanda	1950	85.4	40.0	16.7	12.3	7.7	10.1
Malange	1940	94.6	36.6	19.1	14.0	11.7	9.3
Malange	1950	78.5	38.4	17.4	16.2	10.4	10.5
Cameroon							
Mbalmayo	1956	75.4	47.5	46.4	43.4	40.0	34.8
Congo (Brazzaville)	1960–61	67.2	24.5	23.9	20.4	22.8	20.5

Table 2.17 (continued)

	Year of Census or Survey	15-19	20-24	25-29	30-34	35-39	40-44
Central Africa (cont'd)							
Congo (Leopoldville)	1955-57	74.0	28.1	22.1	22.4	22.3	
Equateur	1955-57	84.8	37.2	29.7	29.2	29.8	
Kasai	1955-57	71.4	28.8	22.8	22.2	20.9	
Katanga	1955-57	60.9	23.3	20.1	22.1	21.4	
Kivu	1955-57	65.9	15.6	12.0	11.3	11.5	
Leopoldville	1955-57	82.6	26.2	12.5	10.5	9.6	
Orientale	1955-57	72.1	38.9	38.9	38.1	35.3	
East Africa							
Mozambique	1950	88.7	45.2	23.5	18.3	14.4	13.7
Central	1950	86.9	39.8	17.3	12.3	9.1	7.9
North	1950	88.8	50.3	29.0	23.8	18.8	18.0
South	1950	91.3	45.8	24.3	17.8	15.2	14.5

Table 2.17 (continued)

	Year of Census or Survey	45-49	50-54	55-59	60-64	65+	Not Declared
West Africa							
Guinea							
Forest	1954-55	5.7	5.7	6.1	5.1	4.0	5.0
Fouta Djallon	1954-55	4.7	3.6	5.0	3.0	2.0	4.0
Maritime	1954-55	7.1	7.2	7.8	6.9	5.1	25.0
Upper	1954-55	7.8	9.7	6.8	6.4	6.2	4.7
Konkouré	1957	2.1	1.5	3.5	1.5	1.7	-
Konkouré (de jure)	1957	8.2	14.6	10.2	13.8	6.8	-
Ivory Coast							
Bongounou	1955-66	4.7	8.2	4.1	5.8		-
Niger	1960	7.2	6.3	6.4	6.5	3.4	-
Senegal							
Middle Senegal Valley	1957	6.1	7.4	6.9	3.9	5.1	-
Upper Volta	1960	5.9			6.2		-
Central Africa							
Angola	1940	10.2		13.5			52.1
Angola	1950	11.9	15.6	16.0	18.3	18.7	-
Benguela	1940	8.9		14.5			40.4
Benguela	1950	10.1	14.7	12.8	16.6	16.6	-
Bie	1940	15.1		16.4			40.8
Bie	1950	21.4	22.7	25.2	23.3	24.3	-
Huila	1940	11.2		15.2			23.7
Huila	1950	9.6	13.6	14.7	16.1	15.6	-
Luanda	1940	6.1		7.4			42.6
Luanda	1950	7.6	12.4	11.0	15.6	14.3	-
Malange	1940	9.2		12.1			79.8
Malange	1950	10.1	14.1	17.2	20.5	23.0	-
Cameroon							
Mbalmayo	1956	34.8	31.9	29.5	22.4	22.4	-
Congo (Brazzaville)	1960-61	20.5		17.1			41.2

Table 2.17 (continued)

	Year of Census or Survey	45-49	50-54	55-59	60-64	65+	Not Declared
Central Africa (cont'd)							
Congo (Leopoldville)							
Equateur	1955-57	20.5			17.6		-
Kasaï	1955-57	28.6			20.7		-
Katanga	1955-57	20.0			16.9		-
Kivu	1955-57	23.2			21.8		-
Leopoldville	1955-57	11.3			14.7		-
Orientale	1955-57	9.5			8.7		-
	1955-57	30.3			24.2		-
East Africa							
Mozambique	1950	13.8	15.6	15.7	23.2	25.8	-
Central	1950	8.3	9.2	11.0	17.3	16.5	-
North	1950	18.0	20.3	21.4	28.4	28.6	-
South	1950	15.0	16.2	14.8	22.2	29.3	-

better data. However, it would seem that the most progress can be made by combined tabulation and publication of the data already collected. Only a small part of such tabulation has been made available. The data as they stand, are to some extent the product of numerous cross-checks in the questionnaire, and the complementary information would not be independent, but could illuminate sources of bias. Some inquiries have included questions on stillbirths and illegitimate births, and on month of occurrence. The latter question and the parallel one on age in months of infants might afford insights into the reference period bias.

A procedure similar to that adopted in the Congo as a preliminary to the interviews, and reported in Romaniuk's chapter, may improve the reporting with respect to reference period accuracy and to completeness. The Congo enumerators had to compile a list of births during the last year and a half in the village by date of occurrence; they were instructed for that purpose to use vital registration, reports by village elders, and other sources. The list was later matched against individual interviews.

Ultimately, a better knowledge of fertility levels and patterns depends largely on improved reporting of ages. The age distribution provides alternative indices of fertility ranging from gross measures, such as the child-woman ratio or the Bourgeois-Pichat index,[25] to intrinsic birth rates derived from quasi-stable population theory. The precision of the latter depends to a large extent on the accuracy of age estimates. The child-woman ratios are vulnerable to bad reporting of the 0 to 5 and of the 15 to 44 age classes. The division separating those who are 14 from those 15 years of age as required for the Bourgeois-Pichat index is notoriously unreliable under African conditions. Table 2.18 relates some of the fertility measures obtained directly from reported data with the corresponding measure in the stable population derived from a full analysis in the case studies. Period error, largely avoided in the Congo, tends to push upward the former French territories' estimates of the birth rate. In the Congo, the recorded birth rate tends to be an understatement because of the omission of births followed by death in early infancy (according to Romaniuk's diagnosis). The total fertility ratio is affected by age distribution biases, as are age-specific fertility rates.[26]

Evidence of overestimation of the proportion of females reported as aged 15 to 44 is shown in Table 2.18, where the ratios of reported to stable proportions in that age group are usually greater than 1.00; this particular tendency to age misstatement has a depressing effect on the general fertility rate.

---

[25] The child-woman ratio is the ratio of children of both sexes aged under 5 years, to women aged between 15 and 44 years. The Bourgeois-Pichat index relates ages 5 to 14 years to ages 5 and over either for males or females.

[26] Some possible effects of age misstatement on age-specific fertility rates and total fertility ratios are analyzed in an appendix to Chapter 3.

Table 2.18. Ratio of reported indices of fertility and of the proportion females
aged 15-44 to corresponding indices in a stable population—
selected regions of Africa

Regions	Ratio of Reported to Stable				
	Child-Women ratio	Bourgeois-Pichat Index	Proportion 15 to 44 females	Birth Rate	Total Fertility Ratio
Cameroon: North	.98	.93	1.09	1.11	.96
Central African Republic: Central Oubangui	1.04	1.00	1.07	1.11	.91
Congo (Leopoldville)	.88	.86	1.13	.96	.85
Dahomey	1.20	1.00	.97	1.12	1.08
Guinea	1.05	.92	1.05	1.35	1.21
Mali: Mopti	.90	.93	1.05	1.06	.97
Ivory Coast: 1st Agricultural Sector	1.19	.83	1.05	1.07	1.01
Senegal: Middle Senegal Valley	1.07	.85	1.01	1.04	.98
Upper Volta	1.02	.92	1.05	1.00	.94

Information on Mortality

The topics discussed in the treatment of fertility are relevant to mortality information as well. The nature of the collected information, the identity of the informants, the unit of observation and the time period covered, as well as the phrasing of questions, are equally or perhaps even more important in the case of mortality. However it is possible to refer the reader to the previous discussion, because questions on both subjects are closely related. Questions on births during the last 12 months are usually accompanied by questions on deaths during the same period, and each woman is asked about the number of her *surviving* children just before or after she is asked about her total births (both survivors and nonsurvivors).

Data Collection Procedures

There are, however, two exceptions to the symmetry. First, cross-checks concerning mortality are usually more numerous than those concerning fertility, and second, the unit of observation is sometimes different.

Schedules used in a typical former French territory include three questions relating to fertility: questions on the total number of births during the last 12 months, both in the family and to every woman of the family; and children ever born to women. The same typical schedules include up to six questions on mortality:

(a) To the head of family concerning the members of the family:
(1) deaths during the last 12 months by age;

(2) number of children surviving and/or dead among those born during the last 12 months; and

(3) last death in the family, by age.

(b) To women concerning their offspring:

(1) total surviving and/or dead;

(2) dead during the last 12 months; and

(3) dead or surviving children among those born during the last 12 months.

The possibilities of cross-checks are thus greater than for fertility information, a tacit acknowledgment that it is more difficult to obtain complete coverage of mortality in an African survey.

Questions in (a) usually include a specific reference to date and place of death as well as to age and sex of the deceased. If the unit of observation is the family or the household, deaths are treated on a *de jure* basis. Even if they occurred far away, for example in a hospital, or out of the country, all deaths of members have to be included. In fact, the choice of a *de jure* concept for the publication of most data on population numbers appears in the INSEE inquiries to be largely motivated by the need of a base for the computation of vital rates corresponding to the way births and deaths were collected.[27]

The Congo (Leopoldville) inquiry was in direct contrast with that procedure. Deaths were enumerated on a *de facto* basis. Interviewers were instructed to count all deaths in the sample units, that is, in the villages for the rural strata or in compounds for the mixed and urban strata. Their first step in the unit was to establish a basic list of deaths during the preceding 18 months based on registers and other written sources and on the reports of village headmen and elders. The list was a hedge against omission of deaths outside households existing at the time of survey, and against omission or double count of deaths outside the usual place of residence.[28]

Both the *de facto* and the *de jure* systems have their advantages and disadvantages. The Congolese system seems excellent when sampling units in rural areas are villages, but the compound was used as the sample unit in towns. In these mobile urban populations, interviewers often had to ask tenants about events that occurred before they occupied their

---

[27] "Although data pertaining to the *de facto* (present) population are in general more satisfactory than those concerning the *de jure* (legal) population, the latter has nevertheless been used here in order to be able to relate directly to it the birth and death figures collected during the interviews." Mission Socio-Economique de la Basse Vallée du Sénégal, *Enquête Démographique 1957*, Résultats Provisoires, Paris, 1957, p. 5. It is not clear whether only the *de facto* reporting of deaths in the dwelling units was really intended in the Kabré Country of Togo and in Dahomey, as implied in the questionnaire.

[28] There was a special provision for the inclusion of deaths in hospitals or institutions not covered by the sample.

present dwelling. The help of chiefs, elders, or neighbors was less of an asset in poorly structured communities. Romaniuk shows that the reporting of mortality was less complete in urban strata of the Congo.

In the *de jure* system (INSEE inquiries), any dead person belonging to the interviewed family or household is to be reported without consideration of place of death. The trouble here is that some families or households may cease to exist between a death and the survey and that they often do so precisely at the occasion of the death of a member— usually the head—of the enumeration unit. Surviving members are then redistributed among other relatives' households or families, and responsibility for the reporting of the death rests with no one. The influence of this factor on actual reporting is difficult to evaluate. The effect may be different in areas with different customs governing the extent of the family. Deaths of adult males are liable to special underreporting as a result of this procedure, because they are usually the heads of family. In this as in other matters, we are reduced to conjecture. Age-specific death rates for males and females are shown in Table 2.19.

Cross-checks on Infant Mortality

French inquiries usually included a question on the children born during the last 12 months and deceased before the time of the inquiry. This information was collected from heads of family and from women.[29] Even in the absence of such a question, a simple comparison between reported births and children under 1 year of age must yield essentially the same information on infant mortality if recording is accurate and complete. The covered population differs slightly, but the three figures should be essentially similar in a large sample. These indices have the advantage of simplicity as compared to the standard measure of infant mortality which incorporates all deaths of children under age 1 (even if born more than one year ago, provided they died before their first birthday). The three first estimates, however, represent an underestimate of infant mortality; by how much, is not known *a priori*. Empirical studies outside of Africa suggest that deaths of children born in the last year account for about two-thirds to 70 percent of the infant mortality during the entire first year of life.[30]

A conventional infant mortality rate can be computed from deaths of children under 1 year of age, reported together with persons of other ages as dead during the last 12 months. Furthermore, an approximation is given by the proportion of dead children among the total born to women aged 15-19.[31]

[29] In the Congo it was asked of women only.

[30] See, for instance, Robert Blanc, *Manuel de recherche démographique en pays sous-développé*, CCTA, 1959, p. 127, and INSEE: *Perspectives de population dans les pays africains et malgaches d'expression française*, Paris, 1963, p. 22.

[31] The average proportion of dead children among those ever born to mothers

Table 2.19. Age-specific death rates by sex (per thousand)—selected regions of Africa

	Year of Census or Survey	Males: Ages							
		0-1	1-4	5-9	10-14	15-19	20-24	25-29	30-34
Congo (Leopoldville)	1955-57	110.0	32.0	11.0	6.0	6.0	8.0	8.0	11.0
Kasai	1955-57	129.0	33.2	17.1	10.9	10.3	10.4	11.7	16.0
Dahomey	1961	-	-	-	-	-	-	-	-
Guinea									
Forest	1954-55	293.5	59.6	15.6	12.9	25.7	24.2	21.6	23.7
Fouta Djallon	1954-55	348.0	65.6	21.0	16.9	21.0	18.1	17.0	17.6
Maritime	1954-55	272.3	52.8	13.9	10.1	28.6	28.8	23.6	23.4
Upper	1954-55	293.0	67.7	14.1	14.1	17.9	13.6	21.2	25.0
Konkouré (de facto)	1957	236.2	56.3	12.1	12.0	39.6	42.0	29.5	36.9
		128.9	42.9	9.7	14.5	14.2	14.5	5.3	4.1
Ivory Coast 1st Agricultural Sector	1957-58	187.4	43.3	11.3	11.9	11.9	13.4		11.3
Madagascar									
Majunga	1961		28.2	5.3	3.5	7.2	5.6	7.4	7.9
Tananarive	1956		34.7	3.2	3.0	3.5	4.1	4.5	4.6
Mali Central Niger Delta	1956-58	216.4		19.0	7.0	7.0	5.8		4.1
Senegal									
Middle Senegal	1961	114.0	44.8	5.5	1.8	5.1	3.1	9.1	6.1
Valley	1957	191.1	46.0	12.0		7.0	8.0		9.0
Togo Kabré Country	1957	339.8	86.3	14.1	10.6		11.0		22.3

Table 2.19 (continued)

	Year of Census or Survey	Females: Ages							
		0-1	1-4	5-9	10-14	15-19	20-24	25-29	30-34
Congo (Leopoldville)	1955-57	98.0	28.0	9.0	5.0	6.0	9.0	9.0	12.0
Kasai	1955-57	117.5	30.4	13.2	6.6	10.3	11.4	12.3	13.5
Dahomey	1961	-	-	-	-	-	-	-	-
Guinea	1954-55	239.1	50.1	13.0	21.6	21.5	17.4	23.1	24.7
Forest	1954-55	297.4	49.2	15.3	38.9	26.6	22.1	29.7	28.0
Fouta Djallon	1954-55	215.5	45.3	12.8	16.4	17.7	15.0	21.1	24.3
Maritime	1954-55	230.3	62.6	12.7	17.3	20.3	14.8	21.3	17.0
Upper	1954-55	189.5	48.2	9.8	13.7	24.7	18.4	15.9	31.0
Konkouré (de facto)	1957	117.9	33.4	10.8	19.5	3.7	3.9	5.9	11.8
Ivory Coast									
1st Agricultural Sector	1957-58	143.7	31.0	6.3		11.3		12.7	13.0
Madagascar									
Majunga	1961		28.1	4.9	3.2	6.2	5.3	7.4	6.6
Tananarive	1956		31.4	3.1	3.0	3.8	4.4	4.9	5.4
Mali									
Central Niger Delta	1956-58	186.2		20.1		4.8		7.8	8.3
Senegal	1961	96.9	39.0	7.7	1.7	4.0	3.1	4.2	3.7
Middle Senegal Valley	1957	188.0	46.0	14.0	7.0	7.0	5.0	5.0	7.0
Togo									
Kabré Country	1957	291.0	66.7	21.0		7.0		13.4	12.6

Table 2.19 (continued)

	Year of Census or Survey	Males: Ages							
		35-39	40-44	45-49	50-54	55-59	60-64	65+	Not Declared
Congo (Leopoldville)	1955-57	15.0			27.0			51.0	–
Kasaï	1955-57	18.4			34.3			68.2	–
Dahomey	1961							26.4	–
Guinea									
Forest	1954-55	23.7	27.8	30.2	37.8	42.1	67.5	106.7	
Futa Djallon	1954-55	26.0	24.5	29.3	33.6	34.9	63.8	109.8	10.3
Maritime	1954-55	17.8	27.1	33.8	42.3	41.7	74.1	106.7	0
Upper	1954-55	25.1	27.0	24.9	27.1	45.6	62.9	98.3	0
Konkouré	1957	29.6	38.8	31.9	51.7	60.7	60.7	116.8	0
Konkouré(de facto)	1957	5.1	19.7	17.8	9.2	7.3	17.6	41.7	47.6 *
Ivory Coast									
1st Agricultural Sector	1957-58	11.3		24.3	31.8		83.9		–
Madagascar									
Majunga	1961	8.5	10.3	14.3	20.5	14.3	38.8	76.3	–
Tananarive	1956	5.3	6.6	8.6	11.2	15.4	21.1	53.9	–
Mali									
Central Niger Delta	1956-58	4.1		11.1		14.6	42.6		228.6
Senegal	1961	9.3	7.5	11.1	15.7	21.1	27.1	31.9	–
Middle Senegal Valley	1957	9.0	12.0		20.0		49.2		–
Togo									
Kabré Country	1957	22.3	29.1		47.9			77.0	–

* Rates for Konkouré (de facto population) are based on 20 male deaths and 5 female deaths within the twelve months preceding the survey and applied to 1 person each of the male and female population who did not give their ages when interviewed.

Table 2.19 (continued)

	Year of Census or Survey	Females: Ages							
		35-39	40-44	45-49	50-54	55-59	60-64	65+	Not Declared
Congo (Léopoldville)	1955-57		16.0	24.0				43.0	–
Kasaï	1955-57		18.7	26.6				60.5	–
Dahomey	1961								–
Guinea									
Forest	1954-55	23.7	25.2	29.2	31.9	43.9	65.1	25.6	8.6
Fouta Djallon	1954-55	31.0	26.8	46.3	33.7	58.0	51.3	99.0	40.0
Maritime	1954-55	14.4	25.3	19.6	26.7	29.2	64.4	92.9	0
Upper	1954-55	21.0	14.9	20.2	33.0	34.7	65.7	97.8	0
Konkouré	1954-55	34.9	37.2	20.7	41.9	61.7	104.9	129.0	0
Konkouré (de facto)	1957	14.4	8.6	10.3	2.7	3.9	24.7	34.5	*
Ivory Coast									
1st Agricultural Sector	1957-58	13.0		28.2	32.0		100.6		–
Madagascar									
Majunga	1961	8.5	9.1	10.9	15.9	12.0	41.8	84.3	–
Tananarive	1956	5.9	6.6	7.6	9.6	14.5	22.3	74.5	–
Mali									
Central Niger Delta	1956-58	8.3		6.5	22.6		41.5		708.3
Senegal	1961	5.7	7.1	6.0	22.3	12.3	15.7	51.7	–
Middle Senegal Valley	1957	7.0	13.0		16.0		33.8		◄
Togo									
Kabré Country		12.6	19.1		15.0		60.2		–

* Rates for Konkouré (de facto population) are based on 20 male deaths and 5 female deaths within the twelve months preceding the survey and applied to 1 person each of the male and female population who did not give their ages when interviewed.

Here are thus a total of five possible measures of infant mortality. They are not perfectly independent one from another, but they are sufficiently independent to afford meaningful comparisons. Although all the information is usually collected, it has never been fully tabulated in comparative fashion. Table 2.20 attempts that tabulation whenever information is available for more than one index.

Although all the estimates in Table 2.20 are reasonably consistent for certain countries (Guinea, for example), there are discrepancies that cannot easily be explained. Leaving aside some as yet very incompletely published data (such as for Senegal and Dahomey), one is left with inconsistent results in the Kabré Country, in the First Agricultural Sector of the Ivory Coast, and in the Middle Senegal River region. In these three cases, the difference between reported births and children under 1 year is larger than the reported deaths—it is more than twice as large in the Kabré Country. On the other side of the range (notably the Congo), the ratio of living infants to births seems too large. In all cases, the infant mortality rate (estimate A) is smaller than the proportion of children dead to women aged 15-19 (estimate D).

In Table 2.21 we present the available information on the proportion dead of children ever born. Analysis by Brass and Romaniuk indicates that retrospective reports on dead children by age of mother (one example of which—at age 15-19—is our estimate D) give a more complete coverage of the mortality of children than current reports. There is no wholly satisfactory explanation of this empirical finding. Incomplete reporting of dead infants may affect various indices in different ways. Omission is sometimes the result of taboos; also, omitted children may be those who died before having left their mark and before they were considered members of the family. After some time, there may be doubt as to whether they ever lived at all.[32] But it is unlikely that women would omit these deaths more frequently when reporting current deaths than in retrospective reports. The former should be less subject to forgetting to the extent that they occurred more recently. A set of high negative correlations between number of children ever born and proportion of children surviving suggests that the forgetting of dead infants acts to depress the first and to inflate the second at least in certain areas; low parities and high proportions surviving are associated chiefly in inquiries of more doubtful accuracy such as the Portuguese censuses, where more forgetting should be expected (see Table 2.22).

---

aged 15 to 19 years is very close to the proportion dying under 1 year. We neglect here any adjustment to account for the shape of the fertility curve.

[32] The distinction between a stillbirth and a death after having breathed is a narrow one at best, and is difficult for others as well as for statisticians.

Table 2.20. Infant mortality measures: (A) deaths under 1 year to 1,000 births of the year; (B) difference between births of year and children under 1, per 1,000 births; (C) dead children per 1,000 born during year; (D) proportion dead children per 1,000 children born to women aged 15-19

	Year of Census or Survey	A	B	C	D
Cameroon					
Mbalmayo	1956		358		170
Congo	1955-57	104	65		159
Equateur	1955-57	100	66		127
Katanga	1955-57	98	62		134
Kasai	1955-57	117	55		227
Kivu	1955-57	105	72		168
Leopoldville	1955-57	103	79		151
Orientale	1955-57	86	39		133
Dahomey	1961	110	15		
Guinea	1954-55	216	185	192	253
Forest	1954-55	254	211	218	325
Fouta Djallon	1954-55	200	179	181	249
Maritime	1954-55	212	187	202	224
Upper	1954-55	183	139	148	197
Konkouré (de jure)	1957	114	73		175
Ivory Coast					
1st Agricul- tural Sector	1957-58	138	157		237
Bongouanou	1955-56	157			192
Mali					
Central Niger Delta	1956-58	288		236	388
Senegal					
Lower Senegal Valley	1957	167			200
Middle Senegal Valley	1957	152	200		200
Togo					
Kabré Country	1957	193	390	196	

Notes to Table 2.20:
   Estimates are computed as follows: (per 1,000)
   (A) Deaths of year in unit of observation to births to women during past year.
   (B) Births to women minus children under one, divided by births to women in past year.
   (C) Children born during last 12 months, but not surviving, divided by births during last 12 months.
   (D) Children dead among children ever born to women aged 15 to 19 except in the following cases:
Senegal and Dahomey: not clear whether data was collected from women or in the unit of observations
Central Niger Delta: (A) Deaths of year in family to births of year in family.
Bongouanou: (A) Deaths and births to women.

Table 2.21. Proportion dead of children ever born—selected regions of Africa

	Year of Census or Survey	15-19	20-24	Ages 25-29	30-34	35-39	40-44
West Africa							
Dahomey	1961	.189	.275	.319	.358	.377	.422
Guinea							
Forest	1954-55	.253	.316	.364	.385	.410	.430
Fouta Djallon	1954-55	.325	.350	.414	.424	.449	.472
Maritime	1954-55	.249	.311	.335	.349	.378	.399
Upper	1954-55	.224	.299	.350	.397	.401	.420
Konkouré(de jure)	1954-55	.197	.284	.361	.392	.398	.439
Ivory Coast	1957	.175	.267	.269	.305	.310	.343
1st Agricultural Sector	1957-58	.237	.239	.290	.333	.342	.350
Bongouanou	1955-56	.192	.247	.235	.295	.340	.378
Mali							
Central Niger Delta	1956-58	.388	.440	.454	.483	.483	.511
Niger	1960	.219	.269	.281	.307	.329	.339
Portuguese Guinea	1950	.237	.273	.272	.290	.298	.320
Senegal							
Middle Senegal Valley	1957	.200	.277	.314	.356	.392	.422
Upper Volta	1960	.231	.317	.396	.412	.452	.478
Central Africa							
Angola	1940	.304	.312	.341	.366	.380	.417
Benguela	1940	.299	.309	.359	.380	.403	.445
Bie	1940	.217	.265	.291	.306	.325	.357
Huila	1940	.215	.191	.207	.246	.261	.284
Luanda	1940	.370	.380	.404	.428	.442	.491
Malange	1940	.314	.315	.329	.363	.377	.412
Cameroon							
Mbalmayo	1956	.170	.205	.253	.285	.312	.348

Table 2.21 (continued)

	Year of Census or Survey	Ages					
		15-19	20-24	25-29	30-34	35-39	40-44
Central Africa (cont'd)							
Congo (Leopoldville)	1955-57	.159	.206	.252	.293		.330
Equateur	1955-57	.127	.192	.238	.272		.305
Katanga	1955-57	.134	.166	.193	.236		.268
Kasai	1955-57	.227	.260	.300	.344		.398
Kivu	1955-57	.168	.230	.291	.334		.367
Leopoldville	1955-57	.151	.192	.253	.302		.345
Orientale	1955-57	.133	.174	.188	.210		.245
East Africa							
Mozambique	1950	.258	.262	.264	.264	.271	.284
Central	1950	.272	.312	.313	.320	.316	.341
North	1950	.238	.210	.204	.195	.206	.214
South	1950	.253	.244	.257	.257	.267	.278

Table 2.21 (continued)

	Year of Census or Survey	Ages					Not Declared
		45-49	50-54	55-59	60-64	65+	
West Africa							
Dahomey	1961	.442		.454	-	-	-
Guinea		.444	.471	.479	.498	.523	-
Forest	1954-55	.480	.490	.521	.547	.573	.417
Fouta Djallon	1954-55	.404	.435	.446	.467	.493	.429
Maritime	1954-55	.449	.482	.476	.497	.517	.000
Upper	1954-55	.447	.503	.495	.481	.519	.414
Konkouré (de jure)	1957	.334	.344	.318	.360	.393	.400
Ivory Coast							
1st Agricultural Sector	1957-58	.360		.410	.451		
Bongouanou	1955-56	.384	.459	.474	.586		
Mali							
Central Niger Delta	1956-58	.510	.484	.502	.491	.545	.519
Niger	1960	.351	.361	.342	.342	.385	-
Portuguese Guinea	1950	.321	.341	.349	.355	.387	-
Senegal							
Middle Senegal Valley	1957	.433	.458	.424	.456	.496	-
Upper Volta	1960	.494	.522	.513	.521	-	-
Central Africa							
Angola	1940	.441		.506			.431
Benguela	1940	.471		.521			.428
Bie	1940	.370		.442			.389
Huila	1940	.305		.399			.272
Luanda	1940	.525		.605			.525
Malange	1940	.453		.521			.458
Cameroon							
Mbalmayo	1956	.382	.413	.433	.498		.370

Table 2.21 (continued)

	Year of Census or Survey	Ages 45-49	50-54	55-59	60-64	65+	Not Declared
Central Africa (cont'd)							
Congo (Leopoldville)	1955-57	.382			.441		—
Equateur	1955-57	.345			.434		—
Katanga	1955-57	.318			.362		—
Kasai	1955-57	.447			.502		—
Kivu	1955-57	.406			.453		—
Leopoldville	1955-57	.408			.484		—
Orientale	1955-57	.295			.343		—
East Africa							
Mozambique	1950	.315	.338	.372	.390	.430	—
Central	1950	.364	.399	.426	.448	.477	—
North	1950	.254	.275	.314	.330	.364	—
South	1950	.303	.316	.347	.373	.431	—

Table 2.22. Correlation coefficient, by age of mother, of
parity with proportion of children surviving—
selected regions of Africa

Age of mother	r	Number of observations
15-19	.24	31
20-24	-.20	31
25-29	-.41	31
30-34	-.53	31
35-39	-.54	24
40-44	-.50	24
45-49	-.44	24
50-54	-.77	17
55-59	-.68	17
60-64	-.75	15
65 and over	-.68	15

A more satisfactory explanation of the discrepancy between retrospective and current indices of mortality may be found in the possibility of a mistaken perception of the reference period. Survivorship ratios are immune to this type of bias. Questions concerning births during the last 12 months and concerning deaths of children less than 12 months old during the last 12 months leaves room for period error at more than one step in the calculation. Estimate C of Table 2.20 offers only one possibility of erring on this score, and the ratio of estimate C to estimate A is larger, wherever it can be computed, than was assumed *a priori* from European experience.[33] (See Table 2.23.)

Table 2.23. Ratio of mortality of children born during the
last 12 months (estimate C) to infant mortality
(estimate A)*—selected French inquiries

Guinea	.89
Maritime	.95
Fouta Djallon	.91
Upper Guinea	.81
Forest	.86
Mali	
Central Niger Delta	.82
Togo	
Kabré Country	1.02

*
Infant mortality rates are the number of
deaths of children under one year per
1,000 live births.

[33] As stated earlier, French-oriented inquiries assumed estimate C to represent about two-thirds or seven-tenths of infant mortality rate.

Evaluation of the Information Concerning Mortality

New tabulations could shed light on whether underreporting of infant mortality is due to omission of early deaths or to period error. The information necessary to establish a distribution of deaths by months of age is usually available but not tabulated. Rather independent information immune from period error would result from a tabulation of last deaths in the family, a standard question in French-oriented inquiries. This would provide an interesting age distribution of deaths.

Mortality is the underdeveloped subject in African demography, despite great efforts in the questionnaires and the survey procedures. A full publication of results concerning mortality would considerably enhance the knowledge of possible bias and specific underenumerations.

One reason for cursory publication only has been, no doubt, that detailed tabulation would be repetitive and wasteful in a summary document if selected partial information yielded satisfactory results. It is understandable that administrative reports shy away from disseminating obviously biased information. The authors of the report on the Niger inquiry invoke that very argument in order to justify the absence of direct mortality information:

> . . . unfortunately for various reasons: reluctance of people to declare deaths, bad estimation of the 12 last months' period, etc. . . . it clearly appears that deaths have been underestimated. . . . It is thus necessary to investigate the level of mortality in Niger by other means, that is, from survival ratios of children born by age of their mothers.[34]

The layman would be misled by biased data, but research workers are entitled to all the available information. Although these tabulations would be onerous, a close scrutiny on a sample basis would be justified, perhaps in special reports devoted to analysis. A synthetic report on all inquiries to date in French-language countries[35] uses for its estimates of mortality the dead children among those born in the last 12 months, indicating thus that the tabulations have been made and that they may be made available in future INSEE publications.

Conclusion on African Demographic Data

This chapter has been devoted to a description of systems of data collection in tropical Africa and to an inquiry into their effect on collected data. The following conclusions seem important:

[34] Niger, *Étude démographique du Niger, Données individuelles, Résultats définitifs*, 2me Fascicule, Paris, 1963.

[35] INSEE: *Perspectives de population dans les pays africains et malgaches d'expression française: Étude de synthèse des enquêtes démographiques récentes*, Paris, 1964.

1. *Concerning questionnaires and methods of inquiry.* Questionnaires should be detailed and should involve many cross-checks. Whenever possible, references to outside sources of information such as vital registration should be incorporated.

2. *Concerning the questions asked.* Minimum information collected in all demographic inquiries should include a complete age distribution for both sexes (at least in five-year age classes), questions on mortality by age and on fertility by age of mother during a period of one year, and questions on children ever born and surviving, for each sex of children.

3. *Concerning publication of results.* Detailed publication of nonadjusted figures, even when they reflect obvious biases, should be made available. At present, a greater breakthrough in demographic knowledge would probably result from tabulation of already collected data than from new inquiries.

There are clearly many biases involved at various stages of collection and analysis, and users of the data need to exercise caution when they interpret results. The present volume offers a number of new estimates of vital rates for various areas of tropical Africa which differ in some cases quite radically from the original estimates. In particular, the overreporting of births and underreporting of deaths may result in overestimating the growth rate. Combined with reported age distributions—also subject to distortion—growth rates may give misleading indications for economic and social planning.

The next chapter reviews methodology designed to cope with characteristics of biased and incomplete data.

Methods of Analysis and Estimation

BY WILLIAM BRASS

AND ANSLEY J. COALE

The necessity for a long book that in the end presents little more than estimates of fertility and mortality for various areas in tropical Africa originates in the nature of the statistical information about African populations. The conventional source of accurate knowledge about births and deaths—the continuous and complete registration of those events—is simply not found in Africa, and there is no choice but to try to estimate the number of events (and their incidence by age of mother and by age and sex of decedent) from less direct evidence. The indirect evidence is of two principal sorts: (1) evidence about the age and sex composition of the population from a census or a demographic survey sometimes supplemented by an indication of the rate of natural increase from two enumerations of the same population and (2) evidence about fertility and mortality from responses to questions about children ever born to women plus the number of those surviving and from responses to questions about births and deaths occurring in the year before the census or survey.

Even when this evidence apparently provides the desired data, i.e. when the surveys give births and deaths during the previous year by age, it cannot be accepted at face value without a critical appraisal. Respondents usually make mistakes about the duration of the year (or other reference period) for which events are to be reported, and among the largely illiterate populations of tropical Africa it has usually been impossible to obtain an accurate record of age. Thus the major research effort that underlies this book is the invention, adaptation, and application of methods for extracting the best attainable estimates of fertility and mortality from data that are indirect, inaccurate, or both. The procedures employed were different from population to population because of differences in the nature of the censuses and surveys in various areas. The particular methods of analysis employed in each area are described in the chapters giving the detailed results for the area, but three principal methods of analysis and estimation were employed widely enough in this project to warrant this separate chapter for their description.

The three widely used methods are (1) the estimation of fertility from the combined analysis of data on births in the pre-survey year and on children ever born to women of childbearing age; (2) the estimation of mortality in infancy and childhood from data on children ever born and surviving children; and (3) the estimation of fertility, mortality, and adjusted age distributions from a variety of data through the use of model life tables and stable populations. The first two of these methods were derived by William Brass. Brass's methods described in this chapter (and in further detail in the chapter on the areas analyzed by Brass) were developed at the Office of Population Research for specific application to the African populations, although they represent the culmination of earlier work.[1] The model life tables and stable populations devised by Ansley J. Coale and Paul Demeny are the outcome of preliminary work over several years by Coale with the assistance of Erna Harm; the mass electronic calculations of model tables by Paul Demeny were carried out to make possible the ready use of model life table population techniques with African data. For nearly two years this extensive collection of model tables was devoted almost solely to this research project; the tables existed in only two copies of a machine print-out. However, these tables (nearly 5,000 in number) have now been published separately, and their discussion later in this chapter is therefore not very detailed.[2]

A final comment is in order before we begin a description of the Brass methods of analyzing fertility and mortality. A consistently maintained objective in the analysis of data for the various areas was to compare wherever possible estimates obtained from independent kinds of evidence, and our confidence in the estimates hinged on agreement. Thus the most reassuring feature of estimates derived from reported births plus reported numbers of children ever born is that they are usually consistent, both with respect to level for whole populations and with respect to variation for different sub-groups, with estimates derived from age composition.

Estimates of Fertility
from Survey Data on Births and
Children Ever Born

In many censuses and surveys in Africa and other underdeveloped areas, fertility data of two kinds have been collected. The two types of data,

[1] William Brass, "The derivation of fertility and reproduction rates from restricted data on reproductive histories," *Population Studies*, Vol. 7, No. 2, November 1953.

Brass, "The estimation of fertility rates from ratios of total to first births," *Population Studies*, Vol. 8, No. 1, July 1954.

Brass, "The estimation of total fertility rates from data for primitive communities," *World Population Conference* [Rome], 1954.

Brass, "The graduation of fertility distributions by polynomial functions," *Population Studies*, Vol. 14, No. 2, November 1960.

[2] Ansley J. Coale and Paul Demeny, *Regional Model Life Tables and Stable Populations*, Princeton University Press, 1966.

both recorded by age of mother, are births in a current period and the number of children ever born to each woman. In this section we will discuss methods of analyzing such records to obtain plausible estimates of the level of fertility even when both sets of data are subject to error.

The information on current births is obtained by questioning the women about whether they have borne children in a short period preceding the census. For definiteness it will be assumed that the period is the most usual one of a year. The methods can be extended to other intervals of time without difficulty. Age-specific fertility rates can be derived by division of the number of births to mothers by the corresponding total women in the population for each age group. Measures based on such specific rates will be referred to as "current," and the indices of fertility obtained from the mean number of children ever born to women of each age will be called "retrospective."

The two types of measure can be used to detect and allow for errors in the data because of the logical relationship between them. As a cohort of women moves through life the mean number of children ever born at each exact age equals the cumulative total of age-specific fertility rates to that age, if it can be assumed that the women dying have the same fertility as those surviving. If the fertility of the population is constant, the age-specific rates of each cohort will be the same as the "current" ones and the relationship will hold for all ages of women. These theoretical results will apply approximately to an actual population if fertility rates have not been subject to a marked trend.

The mean number of children ever born per woman at each age calculated from the current data can be compared with the corresponding retrospective data. If the two sets of indices agree at every age the evidence for accuracy is strong. Applications of the procedure to records for many African populations have revealed systematic discrepancies. These have a pattern that is consistent with what is known about errors in survey reports of vital events. A fertility rate based on responses to a question about births occurring during the year preceding a census or survey is frequently so clearly wrong as to be unusable, mostly because the level is far too low, but sometimes because it is grossly inflated. On the other hand, the reported mean numbers of children ever born often increase too gradually with age of woman, especially above 30 or 35 years, and decline at ages beyond the reproductive period; there is a very strong probability that this is due to the omission of an increasing proportion of the children born from the reports as women become older.

Each of the two forms of data may be clearly deficient, but the natures of the errors are different. Because of this a technique can be developed for estimating total fertility from those parts of the two sets of measurements which are likely to be most reliable. The technique depends on the following propositions:

1. The most important source of error in the recalled number of births in the year preceding the census is imprecision in the *reference period*. The respondents may report events which occurred, on average, in the past 8 months or (with a different culture or framing of questions) in the past 15 months. Similar difficulties about time intervals in which purchases have been made have occurred in retrospective surveys of consumption in developed countries such as the United States. The same average reference period, however, can be expected to hold for each age of mother, particularly in surveys of illiterate populations, where the interviewer tries to check the consistency of the responses. He will often see the infants whose births are recorded and judge the validity of the reports from his estimates of their ages. Any bias in his judgment (e.g., because of a tendency to equate the age of weaning with 1 year although it is usually much later in African societies) is not likely to be influenced by the mother's age. The shape of the distribution of current specific fertilities, i.e., the relations between the rates at different ages, can plausibly be accepted as approximately correct, although the level may not be.

2. The number of children ever born is reported with good accuracy by younger women. The events which the young women are asked to recall have happened recently; the total births to each are typically not more than two or three so that the difficulties of counting large numbers in a non-numerate society do not arise; living children (and a higher proportion of children ever born to younger mothers will survive to the time of the census) will often be present at the interviews, and few will be omitted because they have grown up and left the household.

On the basis of these propositions a technique for estimating fertility has been developed. The *age pattern* of fertility rates obtained from the reports of current births is accepted, but the *level* of fertility is estimated from the mean number of children ever born reported by the younger women. In the application of the procedure the number of children ever born implied by the current rates is compared at each age with the observed retrospective value. The ratios of the retrospective to the cumulated current measures for the young women give a factor which is applied to the current fertility rates at all ages to adjust the fertility to the required level. It is also possible to derive age-specific fertility rates from the retrospective data on children ever born and compare them with the corresponding current values, but the procedure of converting current fertility to mean number of children ever born is preferred because cumulation tends to reduce the effects of small errors and irregularities in the observations.

The Comparison of Average Parity
(Mean Number of Children Ever Born)
and Average Value
of Cumulated Current Fertility

If consistent data on births by individual years of age were available the calculations for making the comparisons would be straightforward. Usually, however, the tabulations are by five-year groups of women, typically 15-20, 20-25, etc., either because the records were collected in this form or because grouping has been used to reduce the effects of age errors, due to digit preference, etc., and chance fluctuations of small numbers. It must also be noted that the current fertility experience is for ages about six months less than the tabulated ones. This displacement arises because the births reported occurred over the preceding year; on average the mothers were half a year younger when giving birth than at the time of the census.

The fertility rate for an age interval is an average value per year. These average fertility rates for the seven five-year groups that effectively cover the reproductive period will be denoted f_i (where $i = 1, 2, \ldots,$ 7). Multiplication by the number of years in the interval gives the mean number of births which would occur to women passing through the interval. The cumulation of the f values (multiplied by 5) from the lowest age group gives the mean number of children ever born at the upper boundaries of the intervals. Thus, if the tabulated age groups are 15-20, 20-25 years, etc., the cumulated f's give the mean number of children ever born at exact ages 20, 25 years, etc., if a correction has been made for the half-year displacement but, in the more usual situation where this has not been done, at exact ages 19½, 24½ years, etc.

The retrospective reports of mean number of children ever born per woman for the same five-year age groups will be denoted by P_1, P_2 (or P_i where $i = 1, 2, \ldots, 7$) and so on. The letter P is chosen because demographers refer to the number of children a woman has borne as her "parity." Thus P_1 is the average parity of women 15-20, P_2 of women 20-25, etc. These are not measures at exact ages, but averages over the age group. With constant fertility, the mean number of children ever born must increase with age; the P value for an age interval will therefore lie between the mean number of children ever born at the exact ages which form the lower and upper boundaries of the interval. It is, therefore, necessary to devise some procedure for calculating from the f values the corresponding average values of cumulated fertility for each of the age intervals. The calculated ratios will be referred to as F values—F_1 being the estimated average value of cumulated fertility for women 15-20, F_2 for women 20-25, etc. (or F_i where $i = 1, 2, \ldots,$ 7).

If age-specific fertility is constant in an interval, cumulative fertility will increase linearly with age and the average for the interval will be midway between the cumulated f values at the lower and upper boundaries. The estimated mean cumulated fertility would then be obtained by adding two and one-half times the fertility for the interval to the cumulated fertility up to the lower age boundary. If there is a half-year displacement in the age groups for current rates it can be allowed for by adding the number of children who would be born in the half year. Thus for the ith age interval, where ϕ_i is the cumulated total of $5f_1 + 5f_2$, etc. up to $5f_{i-1}$, the estimate of the mean cumulative fertility in the interval would be $\phi_i + 3.0f_i$.

The multiplier of f_i in this formula is accurate over the middle range of the reproductive period, where the specific rates vary little with age, but has a much greater error at the extremes of the childbearing range, where fertility is changing rapidly. The inaccuracy at the upper ages is not important for our purpose since f_i is then much smaller than the ϕ_i component, which is known exactly. The estimate for the first age group will usually be badly in error, and there is often an appreciable bias in the derived value for the second group also. Nevertheless, this simple formula gives estimated average values of cumulated fertility which can be satisfactorily compared with the observed average parities to obtain an approximate impression, at least, of errors.

A more complicated estimation procedure, which can however be applied very easily, has been developed. The basis for the procedure is a model distribution of age-specific fertilities in which the shape is fixed but the location may vary; i.e., the curve describing the shape can move along the age axis so that the lower and upper ages of childbearing and the mean of the distribution are displaced by the same amount. For evenly spaced locations of the model the following values were calculated: (1) the mean age of the fertility distribution; (2) the ratio of f_1 to f_2, i.e., of the fertility rate in the first age interval to that in the second; (3) for each age group, the factor k_i by which the f_i value had to be multiplied in order that the formula $\phi_i + k_i f_i$ should give exactly F_i (a) when there was no age displacement in the reported current fertility rates and (b) when there was a half-year displacement in the current rates. No allowance was made in the calculations for possible effects of the variation in the number of women at individual years in an age interval because it can be shown that these would be very small. The mathematical form of the model and the methods of calculation are described in Appendix A to this chapter. Also shown there are the calculated values of k_i which apply when there is no age displacement of the current rates. The values for the more usual case of a half-year displacement are given in Table 3.1.

The k factors in the table are close to 3.0 for the third and fourth

Table 3.1. Multiplying factors for estimating the average value over five-year age groups of cumulated fertility (F_i) according to the formula $F_i = .\phi_i + k_i f_i$ (when f_i is for ages 14.5 to 19.5, 19.5 to 24.5, etc.)

Exact limits of age interval								
15–20	1.120	1.310	1.615	1.950	2.305	2.640	2.925	3.170
20–25	2.555	2.690	2.780	2.840	2.890	2.925	2.960	2.985
25–30	2.925	2.960	2.985	3.010	3.035	3.055	3.075	3.095
30–35	3.055	3.075	3.095	3.120	3.140	3.165	3.190	3.215
35–40	3.165	3.190	3.215	3.245	3.285	3.325	3.375	3.435
40–45	3.325	3.375	3.435	3.510	3.610	3.740	3.915	4.150
45–50	3.640	3.895	4.150	4.395	4.630	4.840	4.985	5.000
f_1/f_2	.036	.113	.213	.330	.460	.605	.764	.939
$\bar{m}$ (years)	31.7	30.7	29.7	28.7	27.7	26.7	25.7	24.7

age groups for all locations of the model distribution, and the divergence for the second age group is also small when childbearing starts early. These results are consistent with the comments on the accuracy of the linear approximation for determining the F's from the current fertility rates. The routine for using the factors in the table is the following: From the age-specific fertility rates derived from births reported in the year before the survey calculate the mean age $\bar{m}$ of the schedule, the ratio f_1/f_2, and the values of ϕ_i, the cumulated fertility to the lower boundary of the ith age interval ($\phi_i = 5 [f_1 + f_2 + \ldots + f_{i-1}]$). Calculate a column of k factors by linear interpolation between the columns of Table 3.1. Interpolation is guided by the observed f_1/f_2 for the first three k_i's, and by the observed $\bar{m}$ for the remaining age groups. Then estimate F_i from the expression $\phi_i + k_i f_i$.

In effect, by this procedure, the observed age-specific fertility distribution is fitted first by the model with the same f_1/f_2 ratio and second by the one with the same mean. The k factors precisely appropriate for the model fertility schedule are taken as the estimates for the observed data. Selecting the model fertility by an f_1/f_2 ratio ensures that the observed and model distributions are in good agreement at the younger ages, and equality of means leads to a similar outcome over the middle range of reproduction. For the reasons discussed above, accuracy at the higher ages is less important. The transition from one method of fitting to the other can take place smoothly between the third and fourth age groups because in this region age-specific fertility rates are nearly constant, and variations in f_1/f_2 and $\bar{m}$ have little effect on the k factors.

[94]

The table has been constructed on the assumption that the records are given for the standard five-year age groups of women, 15-20, 20-25, etc., and that births in the year preceding the census were reported. It is easy, however, to modify the method for other conditions. The only index in the table which depends on the age taken as the lower boundary of the reproductive period is the mean. If this is reduced by one year for all columns, the table will relate to records for the age groups 14-19, 19-24 years, etc. Thus the factors can be used for data in any set of seven five-year groups if the means are changed appropriately.

If the recording period for current births is not one year but some other short interval so that the displacement is different, the appropriate set of k factors can be constructed by interpolation from Table 3.1. and Appendix Table 3.A.2, which is for a zero displacement. The f_1/f_2 ratios are not changed, but the displacement must be subtracted from the means in Appendix Table 3.A.2 to give the correct values.

In the technique described, the f values cumulated to the lower boundaries of the age intervals are accepted as correct, and only the additional average number of births to women still in the age group are estimated. Methods for deriving the mean number of children ever born from age-specific rates for five-year intervals and vice versa, in which the whole distribution of observations is smoothed by the use of fertility models, are given by Brass.[3] These more complicated procedures are particularly suitable for analyzing observations from small surveys in which sampling errors are large.

The Accuracy of the Procedure for Estimating F_i

The accuracy of the estimated values of F_i can be tested by applying the method of estimating to accurate data consisting of fertility rates by single years of age as well as by five-year intervals. To assemble data of this sort, the average number of children ever born per woman in five-year age groups was constructed from the single-year age-specific fertility rates for four populations. Details of the data are given in the paper by Brass[4] referred to above.

The exact values constructed from single-year rates are compared in Table 3.2 with those estimated by the k factor procedure. The constructed values are assumed to correspond to the average parity (P_i) that would be reported in an accurate survey, and the estimated F_i values, calculated by our procedure, can be compared for each age group to these constructed P_i's.

All the P/F ratios except those for the first age group are close to 1.00, the value for perfect agreement. The P/F ratio for the first group is very sensitive to the exact shape of the specific fertility distribution

[3] Brass, "The graduation of fertility distributions by polynomial functions."
[4] Ibid.

Table 3.2. Comparison of estimated average cumulative fertility (F) and
constructed numbers of children ever born per woman (P)

Exact limits of age interval	Ukraine 1926-27			Slovenia 1948-52			England & Wales 1951			Australia 1932-34		
	F	P	P/F	F	P	P/F	F	P	P/F	F	P	P/F
15-20	0.040	0.038	0.95	0.019	0.024	1.26	0.018	0.024	1.33	0.029	0.033	1.14
20-25	0.747	0.778	1.04	0.398	0.399	1.00	0.385	0.389	1.01	0.353	0.352	1.00
25-30	2.045	2.057	1.01	1.157	1.166	1.01	1.067	1.087	1.02	0.925	0.929	1.00
30-35	3.280	3.277	1.00	1.916	1.919	1.00	1.643	1.650	1.00	1.481	1.479	1.00
35-40	4.244	4.238	1.00	2.491	2.488	1.00	1.980	1.981	1.00	1.876	1.872	1.00
40-45	4.845	4.835	1.00	2.822	2.826	1.00	2.122	2.123	1.00	2.086	2.086	1.00
45-50	5.104	5.090	1.00	2.920	2.920	1.00	2.151	2.151	1.00	2.144	2.144	1.00
50+	5.135	5.135	1.00	2.926	2.926	1.00	2.152	2.152	1.00	2.147	2.147	1.00

in the first few years of reproduction. It might be suspected that in populations where childbearing starts early, as in most African communities, the P/F ratio for the youngest age group would be more consistent, but there are no satisfactory records of African age-specific fertilities by individual years to allow examination of the possibility. In deriving a correction factor for the reported current fertility rates, little weight can be given to the P/F ratio for the youngest age group. There are other reasons besides the difficulty of accurate estimation for this conclusion; because of the small number of births the sampling error of the measurements for the earliest group may be high, and they are also particularly vulnerable to the effects of age misstatement. The level of fertility is best judged by the mean number of children ever born reported by the youngest group of women for which the results have acceptable accuracy to reduce the effect of memory failures. As a rule, therefore, the P/F ratio for the age group 20-25 years will be used to adjust the level of reported current fertility rates unless there is evidence that the ratio at 20-25 is distorted or inconsistent with the trend of the values at later ages. The accuracy of the method is not such that adjustments of a few percent are justified; much larger corrections are necessary in many of the analyses of census records. Sets of P/F ratios from fertility data for a number of the African communities studied are shown for illustration in Table 3.3.

Illustrative Calculation of Fertility with Synthetic Data

Before we consider the characteristics and problems of the method in applications to African census records which may be very deficient, the calculations for a hypothetical set of observations will be outlined. The example was constructed from the fertility data for the Ukraine,

Table 3.3. Examples of P/F ratios computed from African census records

Exact limits of age interval	Dahomey	Guinea	Territory Fouta–Toro (Senegal Valley)	Buganda (Uganda)
15–20	0.89	0.78	0.87	1.36
20–25	0.93	0.80	1.04	1.13
25–30	0.89	0.75	0.95	0.89
30–35	0.89	0.75	0.89	0.79
35–40	0.84	0.72	0.86	0.74
40–45	0.86	0.74	0.86	0.71
45–50	0.84	0.76	0.86	0.72
50–60	0.83	0.76	0.84	--

1926-27, already used in Table 3.2 for the verification of the technique, by making the following changes: (a) the age-specific fertilities were adjusted to what the observed rates would have been if recording was of births in the year preceding a census, and if 25 percent of "current" births were not reported at all ages of mothers; (b) a proportion of the children, varying linearly from zero in the age group 15-20 years to 24 percent for the group 45-50 years, was omitted from the constructed retrospective values of children ever born.

Table 3.4 shows how the computations are made. The fertility rates for five-year age groups, calculated from the reported births in the year preceding the census of the hypothetical population, are multiplied by five and cumulated to give the ϕ column. The mean number of children ever born per woman, recorded for this population, are in the column headed P_i; f_1/f_2 and $\bar{m}$, calculated from the fertility schedule, are shown at the foot of the table.

Reference is then made to Table 3.1. The observed f_1/f_2 ratio of 0.124 lies between the second and third column of factors, and is a proportion $0.011/0.100 = 0.11$ of the column interval from the first of these; linear interpolation between the k factors, using this proportion, gives the values for the first three age groups in Table 3.4. Similarly the mean 30.22 is 0.48 of the interval along from the second to the third column, and the k values for the fourth to the seventh age groups are obtained by interpolation. When the estimated k factors are entered in the expression $\phi_i + k_i f_i$ the F_i values are derived.

The P/F ratios fall consistently with age, with a value of 1.33 for the age group 20-25. The level of fertility implied by the retrospective reports of children ever born to this age group is, therefore, 33 percent higher than that indicated by the current rates. Multiplication of the

Table 3.4. Example to illustrate the P/F ratio method of estimating the level of fertility

Exact limits of age interval	i	f_i*	ϕ_i	k_i	$\phi_i + k_i f_i = F_i$	P_i	P_i/F_i	Adjusted f_i*
15-20	1	0.021		1.345	0.028	0.038	1.36	.028
20-25	2	0.170	0.105	2.695	0.563	0.747	1.33	.226
25-30	3	0.195	0.955	2.865	1.533	1.892	1.23	.260
30-35	4	0.172	1.930	3.085	2.459	2.884	1.17	.228
35-40	5	0.124	2.788	3.200	3.184	3.560	1.12	.164
40-45	6	0.067	3.406	3.405	3.634	3.868	1.06	.089
45-50	7	0.022	3.741	4.020	3.829	3.868	1.01	.029
Total fertility		3.851	3.851	-	3.851	3.868	1.00	5.122

$$f_1/f_2 = 0.124; \quad \bar{m} = 30.22$$

* For age intervals half a year younger than shown.

recorded f values and total fertility by 1.33 leads to the adjusted measures of the final column.

The estimate of total fertility is 5.122, compared with the true level in the hypothetical population of 5.135. The accuracy achieved by the method for this example is rather better than we have a right to expect; the 4 percent omissions assumed in the reporting of children ever born by the women aged 20-25 years was largely offset by a compensating error in the estimate of k_2. It is worth noting that the derived total fertility rate is about one-third higher than the values obtained from either the observed current rates or the mean number of children ever born to women of completed fertility. The near equality of these two values, which occurs because the proportion of births in the preceding year not reported was made about the same as the omissions of children borne by the older women, is no evidence of accuracy. A coincidence of error of this kind has occurred in some census records of African populations.

Since the estimated total fertility is near to the hypothetical value, the adjusted f measures are also in close agreement with those postulated. For comparisons with other populations, it is a nuisance to have f measures, and the corresponding specific rates, for age groups which are six months displaced from the standard system. An elaborate procedure for making the translation is not justified because, in the records analyzed, age-specific rates are erratic because of sampling errors, age misstatements, etc. Simple adjustments are made by assuming that at the boundaries the specific fertility rate is equal to the mean of the values in the adjacent age groups. If δf_i is the quantity which has to be added to f_i to correct for the half-year displacement the adjustments are:

$$\delta f_1 = (f_1 + f_2)/20 \qquad\qquad \delta f_5 = (f_6 - f_4)/20$$
$$\delta f_2 = (f_3 - f_1)/20 \qquad\qquad \delta f_6 = (f_7 - f_5)/20$$
$$\delta f_3 = (f_4 - f_2)/20 \qquad\qquad \delta f_7 = (-f_6 - f_7)/20$$
$$\delta f_4 = (f_5 - f_3)/20$$

These corrections were made to the f values estimated for the hypothetical population in Table 3.4. The resulting measurements are compared below with the observed age-specific fertility rates for the standard age groups calculated from the original specific rates at single years.

	Age							Total fertility
	15-20	20-25	25-30	30-35	35-40	40-45	45-50	
Observed	0.043	0.238	0.259	0.223	0.157	0.082	0.024	5.135
Estimated	0.041	0.238	0.259	0.223	0.157	0.082	0.023	5.122

Effects of Errors in the Data or in the Assumptions

The procedure for estimating fertility gives good results if the assumptions about the relations between cohort and current rates and the propositions about the nature of reporting errors hold. It is also robust, i.e., insensitive to the types of variation from the assumptions which are to be expected in the records for underdeveloped communities. The adjustment factor for the level of fertility is derived from the mean number of children ever born to women aged 20-25 years. In this age group only a small proportion of the women who entered the reproductive period have died, and the possible effects of a differential fertility of the dead is slight. Since the great majority of the births to women aged 20-25 years will have taken place within a few years of the census, the estimate of fertility level will apply to a very recent experience, even when there is a trend in rates. The P/F ratios for the older women may be distorted by the differential fertility of survivors and time trends in the birth rates as well as by omissions of children because of memory failures. Although the precise interpretation of the pattern of P/F ratios may thus be complicated, the estimate of fertility level is hardly affected.

There are some errors in reporting which are not allowed for by the analysis. No correction is made for any class of births which is omitted equally by women of all ages both in current and retrospective records. Such a class may be the children who die very young, in the first few days or weeks of life. It is also possible that the omissions or time errors in the reporting of current births are not completely independent of age of mother; a plausible suggestion is that the necessary correction may increase with age. Both these categories of error would lead to underestimates of fertility. Some checks on both these possibilities can be made by the examination of census data on mortality and age distributions, as is explained later.

One of the major difficulties in censuses or surveys of African populations is the measurement of age. The problem is not simply one of vagueness, digit preference, etc., by the respondent, but more commonly of complete ignorance. The enumerator frequently has to make an estimate from appearance, memories of events, status in the family, etc. Examination of age distributions obtained in African censuses reveals great and, as is shown in Chapter 2, systematic distortions. We must consider carefully therefore the sensitivity of the method of estimating fertility to age misstatements. In fact, a great advantage of the method is that the age measurements, including the errors, are the same for the two sets of observations, namely current and retrospective, compared. If the fertility records were from two different sources, e.g., registration and census, with different age distortions, the conclusions to be drawn from comparisons would be much more doubtful.

A constant bias in all ages of women would only affect the estimation of the total fertility (although the age-specific rates would be wrong) because the correction factor for level would be taken from a slightly different age group. Otherwise the procedure, which depends on the relation of current and retrospective observations, is not modified by labeling the age groups which should have been (say) 13-18, 18-23, and so on, as 15-20, 20-25, etc. Now consider what would happen if data for two communities with roughly the same age distribution but *different* constant biases in the recording were combined. The correction factors for fertility level would be about right for both communities, separately, and also for the combined observations. By extending this idea to many communities with different constant biases we can see that certain kinds of age misstatement have little effect on the estimate of total fertility. Broadly, these are errors whose distribution is the same at each age in the reproductive range. It is not necessary for the errors to be independent of fertility, but the relation must again be the same at each age in the range; e.g., the distribution of misstatements by women a fixed percentage above the average in fertility must be independent of age. We can see this by considering the amalgamation of data for populations with different fertility levels and age biases.

To illustrate these ideas, calculations were made for a simple example, again using the specific fertility rates at single years for the Ukraine, 1926-27, as a basis. A rectangular distribution of age errors with an upwards bias of one year and a range of ten was applied; i.e., it was taken that women whose ages were reported as x were distributed evenly from six years below to four years above the nominal value. Table 3.5

Table 3.5. Illustration of the effect of age errors on P/F ratios

Exact limits of age interval	i	f_i*	$\varnothing_i$	k_i	$\varnothing_i+kf_i$ $=F_i$	P_i	P_i/F_i
15-20	1	0.045	-	1.780	0.080	0.095	1.19
20-25	2	0.166	0.225	2.810	0.693	0.672	0.97
25-30	3	0.249	1.057	2.995	1.802	1.795	1.00
30-35	4	0.232	2.300	3.065	3.011	3.012	1.00
35-40	5	0.176	3.460	3.180	4.021	4.016	1.00
40-45	6	0.106	4.342	3.350	4.696	4.688	1.00
45-50	7	0.053	4.871	3.775	5.070	5.022	0.99
Total fertility		5.135	5.135	-	5.135	5.123	1.00

$$f_1/f_2 = 0.270; \; \overline{m} = 31.17$$

* For age intervals half a year younger than shown.

shows the current age-specific fertilities (with half-year displacement), the constructed average number of children ever born per woman, and the calculation of the P/F ratios for the hypothetical census records with these age errors. The ratios are not far from 1.00, except for the youngest age group. When reported ages are spread about the correct value the resulting specific fertility distribution is "wider," i.e., has a larger variance and range, than the true one. This influences the accuracy of the factors for deriving the mean number of children ever born per woman from the current age-specific fertility rates. That the inaccuracy introduced is small, even where the spread of error is large, is illustrated by the example.

Although P/F ratios are insensitive to some forms of age misstatement, extreme age misreporting in the childbearing interval may result in an erratic sequence of ratios. In some African censuses and surveys, extensive systematic misreporting of age is evident in seriously distorted age distributions—not only single-year distributions but also those distributed in five-year intervals. A characteristic form of distortion in female distributions is deficient numbers reported in the age intervals near the beginning and end of childbearing and excessive numbers reported in intervals near the central childbearing ages. The usual net effect is an overstatement of the proportion of females in the span 15-49, so that even when births are correctly estimated, the general fertility rate, total fertility, and the age-specific fertility rates are understated by the inclusion in the denominator of women from outside the fertile ages.

In Appendix B to this chapter, there is a description of an experiment with the effects on the P/F ratios of hypothetical age misstatements that would produce the extensively distorted age distribution in the Congo. Large proportions of the women in certain age intervals must have been reported in adjacent intervals to account for the reported age distribution, and no matter what assumption is made about current fertility and parity of the women reported in the wrong age interval, a substantial effect on the sequence of P/F ratios is unavoidable.

The distortion evident in other African age distributions is often less than in the Congo (at least with regard to the ages of childbearing), and the P/F sequences in other areas may not have been greatly affected by age errors.

So far we have considered primarily how age errors may modify the P/F ratios. As noted above, they can also lead to inaccuracy in the estimated total fertility even if the number of births recorded is correct. (This happens primarily when too many women are reported to be in the reproductive period. Reported ages of women in many African censuses show a tendency toward overstatement in the years near the beginning of the reproductive period and understatement at the end, with a characteristic crowding toward the center.) If women who are really below and above the childbearing range are wrongly included, the computed age-specific birth rates and the total fertility rate are lower than they should be. The wrong inclusion of adolescents with no births tends to lower both the calculated current specific rates and the retrospective mean number of children ever born for the younger women, and the P/F ratios in this region will therefore be less affected. At the upper ages the opposite occurs, since the F_i estimates from the current rates are reduced but the retrospective mean number of children increased by the inclusion of women past the reproductive period.

When the number of women 15-49 has been obviously inflated by age misreporting, the P/F ratio for the age group 20-24 should be used to adjust the reported *total number of births* for the preceding year, rather than the age-specific fertility rates, or their sum, the total fertility rate. The number of female births can be taken as one-half the number of all births, since what evidence there is concerning the sex ratio at birth in Africa indicates a value close to 100. The female birth rate (female births/female population) can thus be estimated, and the gross reproduction rate can be approximated by assuming the population to be stable and by accepting the estimate of the female birth rate and the mean age of the fertility function from the reported current fertility rates. Such estimation of the GRR is readily accomplished by interpolation in tabulated model stable populations.[5]

[5] Coale and Demeny, *Regional Model Life Tables and Stable Populations.*

Further powerful checks on the accuracy of fertility reports can be made if the current and retrospective data are tabulated by birth order. The tables required are the distribution in age groups by the number of children ever born of all women and of those who have had a child in the preceding year. Just as, under constant conditions, the cumulated current age-specific fertilities give the mean number of children ever born, the sums of the age-specific rates for first, second, third births, etc., to each age give the proportion of women who have borne at least one, two, and three children, etc., by that point respectively. The methods described for comparing current and retrospective observations of births without regard to order can be applied to the component birth orders to extract further information on the patterns of error. To obtain the most accurate results the factors for calculating the average cumulative fertility in five-year age groups from the current rates would have to be modified to allow for the different shapes of the age-specific fertility distributions of births of individual orders.

The most illuminating comparisons are likely to be of cumulated first-birth rates with the proportion of women who are mothers. The reporting of first births in a year will be affected by time scale errors, but it is reasonable to expect that, because of the importance of a first birth and the youth of most of the mothers, omissions and age differentials in the reference period will have little influence. Again, the classification of a woman as a mother will be less subject to error than the determination of the number of children born to her. For these reasons, and because the proportion of women who become mothers after the age of 30 years is small in most African populations, the ratio of ever-fertile women to cumulated first-birth rates at ages 30-34 years should be a useful index of the time scale error. The denominator of this ratio is, effectively, the sum of the current age-specific rates for first births at all ages, which we will call F_c.

Unfortunately the required tabulations (particularly of current births) are available for few populations, although they can be prepared whenever the census form records age, the number of children ever born, and the occurrence or non-occurrence of a birth in the past year for each woman. For only one of the censuses analyzed are there data on the order of current births and then not by age of mother. However, F_c can still be estimated with little error if the mean age $\bar{m}_c$ of the fertility schedule of first births can be calculated. The estimate is made by dividing the first births by the average number of women per year of age in an interval centered on $\bar{m}_c$ and effectively covering the range within which these births occur. Why this gives a good approximation can be seen by considering a population with a constant number of women at each age in the range. The first births to mothers of each age are then divided by this constant number, which is also the average, to give the age-specific rates; division of the total first births by the constant gives the sum of the rates. In general, the number of women per year falls with age, but the average in a range centered on $\bar{m}_c$, can be used as a divisor, because for fixed rates the extra births due to the larger number of younger women are closely compensated by the missing births because of the fewer older ones. A more mathematical examination of this result is given by Brass.[6] More details of the application of the procedure and the estimation of $\bar{m}_c$ are given in the case study of the Republic of Guinea.

Estimates of Infant and Child Mortality from Survey Data on the Survival of Children Ever Born

Records of mortality in African communities are even more scanty and unreliable than those of fertility. Deaths are registered in only a few countries and regions, and in most of these very incompletely. Data are better for a few towns, but the inhabitants of these are not representative of the general population in sex and age distributions, economic and social conditions, supply of medical services, etc. There have been important studies of the mortality of special groups, e.g., children born to mothers attending a clinic, mining workers. In all these surveys high death rates have been found, but the levels and patterns by sex and age have been quite variable. It is not possible, therefore, to generalize this evidence, with any pretense of accuracy, to provide a basis for checking observations on a particular African community, although it has to be taken into account in the assessment.

We will be concerned in this section with the extraction of information on the incidence of deaths from data obtained at a single census or survey. In particular, a method is developed for the estimation of mortality in childhood from reports by mothers of the number of their children who have died.

Age-specific death rates for all ages (including childhood) can be calculated from the deaths in each age interval reported as occurring in the preceding year and from the population by age as recorded in the census or survey. Such death rates are "current" death rates, while the childhood mortality rates derived from the reported number of children who have died among those ever born are "cumulative" rates (cumulated from the birth of the children). The cumulated rates are free of errors of the "reference period"—errors that affect the validity of death rates calculated for the period just before the census. Superficially, it appears that these cumulative childhood rates could be compared with the current rates for childhood to derive a correction factor for current mortality rates at all ages, in a manner analogous to the procedure used

---

[6] "The estimation of fertility rates from ratios of total to first births."

in estimating fertility. However, the crucial assumption that errors in reporting current fertility are not markedly age-selective is not transferable
to errors in reporting current mortality. The accuracy of reported mortality, affected by a combination of omission and reference period error,
is quite likely to depend on the importance of the decedent in the eyes
of the community in general and of the respondent in particular and
hence to vary with age and sex. In the fertility estimates described earlier
it was assumed that a correction factor applicable to the reported current fertility of women 20-25 could be applied to the reported fertility
of all women, but there is no warrant for assuming that a correction
factor applicable to the reported current mortality of children could
be applied to the reported mortality of adults.

Although errors in reporting current mortality appear to be quite different at different ages, the mortality rates themselves at different age
intervals are strongly interrelated in populations having reliable data, and
inferentially in African populations as well. Heavy reliance is therefore
placed on model life tables that express typical age patterns of mortality
at different mortality levels. After all the available data and evidence
have been surveyed, the most convincing mortality estimates are often
the childhood rates derived by the method described in the immediately
following pages. Although the estimates are scarcely precise, they appear
to establish a value of childhood mortality acceptable as a valid lower
bound of the true rate, and this provides a very useful parameter—
useful in estimating fertility from age distribution data, for example.

The Estimation of
Childhood Mortality

In the estimation of mortality from reports of the number of children
ever born who had died previous to the census, it will be assumed that
age-specific fertility and mortality rates have remained constant for
the required age range and time period; the experience of the surviving
women will also be taken to be effectively that of the total numbers exposed to the risk of births and deaths of children. The consequences of
deviations from these assumptions will be examined later. Throughout
the presentation the description will be in terms of vital events for children of both sexes, but the results hold if observations for males and
females are treated separately.

Suppose that there has been an unchanging schedule of mortality,
such that the proportion surviving to age a (l_a/l_0 in life table terminology) is $p(a)$, and the proportion dying before age a ($_aq_0$ in life table
notation) is $q(a)$. Suppose the proportion of women at age x bearing a
child is $f(x)$, in a fertility schedule that has been constant in recent
years. The proportion dead among children ever born depends on their
age distribution and on $q(a)$. Consider the age distribution there would

be among children ever born to women of a particular age, say 25, if none of the children had died. This age distribution is:

$$c_{25}(a) = \frac{f(25 - a)}{\int_0^{25} f(x)dx} \qquad (1)$$

The proportion of these children who would have died is:

$$d_{25} = \int_0^{25-\alpha} c_{25}(a)q(a)da \qquad (2)$$

where d_{25} is the proportion dead among the children ever born to women at age 25 and α is the earliest age of childbearing.

Now examine the two functions that determine d_{25}. The first, $c_{25}(a)$, is simply the proportionate fertility schedule up to age 25, *written backward*, and the second, $q(a)$, is the cumulative proportion dying up to age a under the specified mortality conditions (see Figure 3.1). In

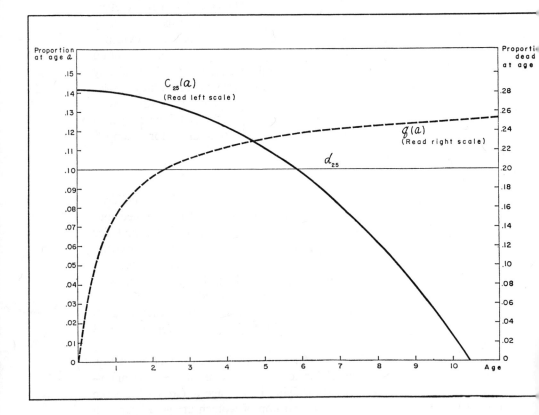

3.1. Factors determining d_{25}, the proportion dead among children ever born to women at exact age 25: $c_{25}(a)$, the age distribution of children ever born to women aged 25, and $q(a)$, the proportion dead by age a under prevalent mortality risks.

other words, d_{25} is the weighted average of the proportions dying, the weight being the age distribution that children ever born to 25-year old women would have if all of the children had survived. There is an age $(\bar{a}_{25})$ between zero and 25—a such that $q(\bar{a}_{25}) = d_{25}$. Because $q(a)$ rises sharply during the first year of life, and very gradually after age 5, and because $c_{25}(a)$ falls to low values at ages above 5, $\bar{a}_{25}$ is surprisingly small (2.5 years in the example shown in Figure 3.1).

For specified fertility and mortality functions, $\bar{a}_x$ can be calculated for every age x from the lower limit of childbearing to the highest age for which data about children ever born (living and dead) are available. Under conditions of unchanging fertility and mortality, such an exercise would establish a relation between $q(a)$ (a life table function pertaining to the children women have borne) and d_x (the proportion who have died among the children ever born to women at age x).

Brass's estimation procedure makes it possible to use this kind of relationship to estimate $q(1)$, $q(2)$, $q(3)$, $q(5)$, $q(10)$, . . . , etc.— up to $q(35)$ under optimum circumstances—from D_1, D_2, D_3, . . . , D_{10} (where D_i is the proportion dead among children born to women in the ith five-year age interval, the first interval being 15-20).

The procedure depends on the approximate equality of $q(1)$ and D_1, $q(2)$ and D_2, . . . , $q(35)$ and D_{10}, when the fertility and mortality schedules are "standard" ones with age patterns roughly like those found in African populations. These approximate equalities are affected by variations that occur in the age pattern of fertility more strongly than by variations occurring in the age pattern of mortality. Brass has calculated a set of multipliers (see Table 3.6) by which values of D_i can be converted into estimates of $q(a)$—the multipliers differing for different fertility functions but not differing for different "shapes" of mortality. The idea underlying the multipliers can be illustrated by an example. A fertility schedule can be chosen so that with a typical age pattern of mortality D_2 is identical with $q(2)$. Now consider a population that has an earlier start of childbearing. On the average, the children ever born to women 20-25 in this population are older than in the population where D_2 equals $q(2)$. In the population with the earlier start of fertility, D_2 thus equals $q(2+)$, and hence in this population $q(2) < D_2$. Brass's table of multipliers gives values ranging from about 0.94 (very early childbearing) to 1.19 (very late childbearing) to convert D_2 into an estimate of $q(2)$. There are three indexes of early versus late childbearing in Table 3.6: (a) the ratio of the average parity of women 15-20 to the average parity of women 20-25 (P_1/P_2); (b) the mean age of the fertility schedule $(\bar{m})$; (c) the median age of the fertility schedule $(\bar{m}')$. The first index is a measure of when fertility starts and how fast it rises with age and is therefore a guide to the multipliers needed to convert D_1 into $q(1)$, D_2 into q(2), and D_3 into $q(3)$. The other two

Table 3.6. Multiplying factors for estimating the proportion of children born alive
who die by age a, $q(a)$, from the proportion dead among children
ever born to women 15-20, 20-25, etc.

15-20	q(1)	0.859	0.890	0.928	0.977	1.041	1.129	1.254	1.425
20-25	q(2)	0.938	0.959	0.983	1.010	1.043	1.082	1.129	1.188
25-30	q(3)	0.948	0.962	0.978	0.994	1.012	1.033	1.055	1.081
30-35	q(5)	0.961	0.975	0.988	1.002	1.016	1.031	1.046	1.063
35-40	q(10)	0.966	0.982	0.996	1.011	1.026	1.040	1.054	1.069
40-45	q(15)	0.938	0.955	0.971	0.988	1.004	1.021	1.037	1.052
45-50	q(20)	0.937	0.953	0.969	0.986	1.003	1.021	1.039	1.057
50-55	q(25)	0.949	0.966	0.983	1.001	1.019	1.036	1.054	1.072
55-60	q(30)	0.951	0.968	0.985	1.002	1.020	1.039	1.058	1.076
60-65	q(35)	0.949	0.965	0.982	0.999	1.016	1.034	1.052	1.070

Guide to
selection of
multiplier

P_1/P_2	0.387	0.330	0.268	0.205	0.143	0.090	0.045	0.014
$\bar{m}$	24.7	25.7	26.7	27.7	28.7	29.7	30.7	31.7
$\bar{m}'$	24.2	25.2	26.2	27.2	28.2	29.2	30.2	31.2

B. Ten-year age intervals of women.

15-25	q(2)	0.982	1.000	1.021	1.045	1.072	1.105	1.144	1.193
25-35	q(5)	0.990	1.004	1.018	1.033	1.048	1.064	1.081	1.099
35-45	q(15)	0.977	0.993	1.009	1.024	1.040	1.056	1.071	1.086
45-55	q(25)	0.990	1.008	1.025	1.043	1.062	1.080	1.099	1.118
55-65	q(35)	0.990	1.007	1.025	1.043	1.061	1.080	1.099	1.119

indexes are measures of the age around which childbearing centers. At
ages much above the mean of the fertility function, the proportion surviving is very nearly the same as if all births occurred at the mean age
of childbearing. Hence, $\bar{m}$ or $\bar{m}'$ are the relevant parameters of the fertility schedule for selecting the multiplier to use with D_4 to D_{10}.[7]

[7] There is no strong reason for preferring $\bar{m}$ or $\bar{m}'$. If the fertility schedule is
recorded, $\bar{m}$ is easily calculated; otherwise, $\bar{m}'$ is estimated as the age x at which
$P_x = \frac{1}{2}P_{50}$.

How the Multipliers for Estimating q(a) *Were Developed*

We shall examine the relationship between D_2 and $q(2)$ to illustrate the method by which the multipliers in Table 3.6 were obtained. The multipliers are based on the same model fertility functions used earlier:

$$f(x) = k(x\text{-}s) \, (s + 33 - x)^2$$
$$\text{(for } s \leq x \leq s + 33\text{).}$$ (3)

s is the earliest age of childbearing, and *k* is a "scale" factor that determines the total number of children ever born by the end of child-bearing (at age $s + 33$). *k* does not affect the relation of D_2 to $q(2)$. In the absence of mortality, the age distribution of the children ever born to women 20 to 25 would be[8]

$$C_2(a) = \frac{\int_{20}^{25} f(x - a)dx}{\int_{0}^{25-s} \int_{20}^{25} f(x - a)dxda}$$ (4)

where $C_i(a)$ is the age distribution (in the absence of mortality) of the children ever born to women in the *i*th age interval, $C_1(a)$ pertains to children born to women 15-20, $C_2(a)$ to women 20-25, etc. Figure 3.2 shows $C_2, C_3, \ldots, C_7$ for $s = 14.5$ years.

The proportion dead among children ever born to women 20-25 is[9]

$$D_2 = \int_{0}^{25-s} C_2(a)q(a)da$$ (5)

It is a laborious, but not intrinsically difficult, process to calculate $C_2(a)$ from equation (4), for a given value of *s*, and then to calculate D_2 from this age distribution, and values of $q(a)$ from a specified life table. When $s = 14.5$, and $q(a)$ is taken from a "standard" life table,[10] D_2 is found very nearly equal to $q(2)$—equal to 0.990 $q(2)$, in fact. A multi-plier of 1.010 is therefore needed to convert D_2 into $q(2)$. P_1 and P_2 (average parity for women 15-20 and 20-25) can be obtained by twice integrating $f(x)$ in equation (3). When *s* is 14.5, P_1/P_2 is 0.205. Note that 0.205 is one of the values entered in Table 3.6. The calculation of other entries was by a parallel procedure. The tabulated adjustment factors are valid for a "standard" mortality schedule, and for fertility schedules defined by equation (3) for different values of *s*, the earliest age of childbearing. Their usefulness for practical application depends on these considerations: (1) whether (with "standard" mortality) the

---

[8] Cf. equation (1).
[9] Cf. equation (2).
[10] The "standard" life table was obtained by averaging the $q(a)$ values from a number of high-mortality tables. It is almost identical to a model table from the West family.

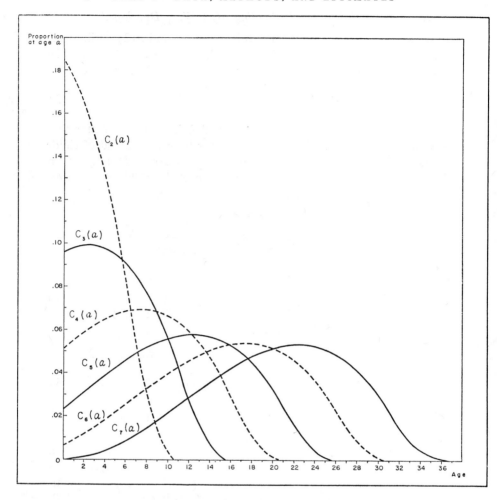

3.2. Age distributions of children ever born to women, for
mothers 20-25 $[C_2(a)]$ to 45-50 $[C_7(a)]$.

multipliers appropriate for fertility schedules defined by equation (3)
are also appropriate for actual fertility schedules with the same values
of P_2/P_1, $\bar{m}$, or $\bar{m}'$; (2) whether correction factors appropriate for a
"standard" life table are valid for other age patterns of mortality.

Extensive numerical calculations are reassuring with regard to both
considerations. Insensitivity of the multipliers to the detailed shape of
the fertility function is suggested by the small range of correction factors
even with quite different values of P_1/P_2, $\bar{m}$, or $\bar{m}'$. For example, a value
of $\bar{m}$, (or $\bar{m}'$) two years higher, or a value of P_1/P_2 54 percent as great,
is associated with a multiplier for D_2 only 6 percent higher, and for D_3
only 2.5 percent higher, although the multiplier of D_1 is 11 percent

higher. Observed fertility schedules for single years of age, when combined with the standard mortality schedule in equation (5), give calculated values of D_i usually differing by less than 2 percent from the values calculated with a fertility function defined by equation (3), having the same value of P_1/P_2. Exceptions—larger differences—occur at the youngest ages in the relation of D_1 to $q(1)$ in different fertility schedules with a given value of P_1/P_2. As equation (5) shows, the relation of D_i to $q(a)$ depends on how the age composition of children ever born affects the proportion dead. A given ratio of P_1/P_2 leaves little room for variation in the division into younger and older children of those ever born to women 20-25 or 25-30; but even with a given value of P_1/P_2, there can be significantly different age distributions of children born to women 15-20. Thus estimates of $q(1)$ based on D_1 are subject to large errors.[11]

To illustrate the effect of the detailed shape of the fertility function, values of D_i were calculated from the age-specific fertility schedule (in single years of age) for England and Wales, 1951, in conjunction with the "standard" mortality schedule. Then multiplying factors were computed that would convert these values of D_i into $q(1), q(2), \ldots, q(20)$ —computed by dividing $q(1)$ by the calculated D_1, $q(2)$ by the calculated D_2, and finally $q(20)$ by the calculated D_{20}. Note that the fertility schedule is not in good agreement with the model, since as is typical of fertility in highly modernized countries, the variance is much less than in the model. The accurate multiplying factors calculated for this fertility schedule are compared here with the factors taken from Table 3.6 for model schedules with the same mean age (28.16 years) and the same P_1/P_2 (0.062) as the schedule for England and Wales.

Comparison of Accurate and Estimated Multiplying Factors

	Age group of mothers in years						
	15-20	20-25	25-30	30-35	35-40	40-45	45-50
Accurate	1.119	1.121	1.037	1.017	1.021	0.998	0.996
Estimated: $\bar{m}$	1.006	1.025	1.002	1.008	1.018	0.995	0.994
P_1/P_2	1.207	1.111	1.047	1.040	1.049	1.031	1.032

These comparisons show neatly the characteristics of the approximations introduced by the application of the fertility model. At ages above 30 years the estimates from the location index $\bar{m}$ are better than those obtained from the P_1/P_2 measure and are very close to the accurate fac-

---

[11] There are other reasons for mistrusting the proportion dead reported among children born to women under 20. In a sample survey, or the census of a small population, the total number of dead children for this age group is apt to be small and subject to large sampling variability. Secondly, in some populations (if not in all) infant mortality among children born to very young mothers is not representative of general infant mortality.

tors. For the age groups 20-25 and 25-30 years, reliance on the observed P_1/P_2 gives much the more satisfactory results. The rule proposed (the use of the index P_1/P_2 for the first three groups and $\bar{m}$ subsequently) leads to an error in the estimated factors of less than 1 percent except for the youngest mothers. For this first age group of women neither of the location measures provides estimates which are very close to the accurate value. The error from the use of P_1/P_2 (about 8 percent) would not lead to a grossly inaccurate $q(1)$. The reasons for the inadequacy of the model in the early years of the reproductive period have already been discussed in relation to the estimation of the mean number of children ever born per woman from current fertility rates. The limitations are imposed by the nature of the evidence and the observations; they could not be overcome simply by the modification of calculating techniques.

In the derivation of the multiplying factors a fixed standard life table was used. It is easy to see that exactly the same results would have been obtained from another life table in which the probability of dying before any age was some constant C times the corresponding standard measure. All proportions of children dead by age of mother, and hence the D values, would be multiplied by C; the ratios of the q probabilities to the D proportions, which give the multiplying factors, would be unaltered.

The multipliers appropriate for a "standard" mortality table, $q_s(a)$ are also appropriate for any mortality table where the proportion dying at each age follows the same pattern as in the standard table; i.e., where $q(a) = V \cdot q_s(a)$, V being any constant. For life tables conforming to the West model tables and $e°_0$ between 30 and 50 years, the proportion surviving to young adult ages is very nearly a constant multiplier of values in the standard, as Table 3.7 shows.

Table 3.7. $q(a)$ in four West model life tables as multiple of $q_s(a)$

Age a	$e°_0 = 20.0$	$e°_0 = 30.0$	$e°_0 = 40.0$	$e°_0 = 50.0$
1	2.44	1.71	1.19	.79
5	2.31	1.68	1.19	.79
10	2.27	1.68	1.20	.80
15	2.24	1.68	1.21	.81
20	2.17	1.64	1.19	.81

Other model tables do not conform as well in mortality patterns to the standard. Among the Coale-Demeny model tables, the least conforming are the South tables (see Table 3.8). For a typical life table with the

Table 3.8. $q(a)$ in four South model life tables as multiple of $q_s(a)$

Age a	$e_o^o = 20$	$e_o^o = 30$	$e_o^o = 40$	$e_o^o = 50$
1	2.06	1.53	1.15	.86
5	2.44	1.83	1.38	.95
10	2.41	1.83	1.35	.95
15	2.36	1.80	1.34	.94
20	2.25	1.74	1.30	.91

South pattern (Spain 1930), the correction factor for estimating $q(2)$ is only 2 percent in error where P_1/P_2 is 0.205, and the error for $q(3)$, $q(5)$, and older ages is even less. However, if fertility has an unusually young pattern, the error in estimating $q(2)$ is larger, as is the error in estimates of $q(1)$ with mortality schedules that "deviate" from the standard.

There are indications (not wholly conclusive) that the pattern of mortality in infancy and childhood in the North family of model life tables fits African experience better than does that of the West family. The relevant distinctive feature of North mortality is that infant mortality is relatively low and childhood mortality (above age 1) relatively high. This characteristic matches what many observers (and some special studies) have reported about African populations. Therefore an "African standard" life table,[12] based in infancy on the North family, was constructed, and an alternative set of factors for converting D_i into $q(a)$ calculated on the basis of this somewhat different mortality pattern. These alternative multipliers are compared in Table 3.9 with the multipliers based on a standard life table that conforms to the West pattern.

Although the pattern of differences between the two sets of factors is complex, the main features are clear. The largest deviations occur when the factors are furthest away from the value 1.00. The errors are greatest for the youngest age groups of mothers and tend to decrease for the older women. Except for the first age group and, in some instances, extreme locations of the fertility distribution, the maximum difference in the factors is about 3.5 percent. In addition the direction of the difference is not the same in all age groups.

These differences indicate that in the presence of uncertainty about the shape of the mortality schedule precise estimates cannot be expected. On the other hand, other sources of error and bias are known to exist,

[12] See p. 132, below.

Table 3.9. Comparison of multiplying factors derived from standard (S) and African (A) mortality patterns

Age interval	S	A	S	A	S	A	S	A
15–20	0.890	0.831	0.977	0.936	1.129	1.124	1.425	1.530
20–25	0.959	0.916	1.010	0.983	1.082	1.076	1.188	1.212
25–30	0.962	0.917	0.994	0.960	1.033	1.013	1.081	1.081
30–35	0.975	0.937	1.002	0.972	1.031	1.010	1.063	1.055
35–40	0.982	1.001	1.011	1.038	1.040	1.075	1.069	1.115
40–45	0.955	0.962	0.988	0.999	1.021	1.037	1.052	1.076
45–50	0.953	0.954	0.986	0.989	1.021	1.026	1.057	1.067
$\bar{m}$	25.7		27.7		29.7		31.7	

and the imprecision resulting from the age pattern of mortality does not appear important.[13]

What has been said so far about the Brass method of estimating mortality can be summarized in three statements:

(1) The proportion dead among children ever born to women 15-20, 20-25, 25-30, . . . , 60-65 is approximately equal to $q(1)$, $q(2)$, $q(3)$, $q(5)$, $q(10)$, . . . , $q(35)$, provided the fertility schedule has a mean age of about 28 years.

(2) Table 3.6 makes it possible to estimate $q(1)$, $q(2)$, etc. from D_1, D_2, . . . , etc., for fertility schedules with early or late childbearing as well as with a mean age of 28 years.

(3) Variations of pattern among fertility schedules with the same P_1/P_2 (or the same $\bar{m}$) and variations in age pattern of mortality cause errors in estimating $q(2)$, $q(3)$, $q(5)$, etc. but only of a few percent; however, those variations can cause larger errors in estimates of $q(1)$.

It has been implicitly assumed in this discussion that the estimates are made from accurate data about a population with unchanging fertility and mortality rates. We shall now consider how estimates of $q(1)$, $q(2)$, . . . are affected by changes in fertility or mortality rates, by the inaccuracies found in African censuses or surveys, and by selective forces tending to make reported survival rates nonrepresentative.

[13] The multiplying factors based on the North pattern were developed and compared with those based on a West pattern only after the population analysis reported in other chapters had been completed. Because the true pattern of mortality is a matter of conjecture and because the differences are small for all except young ages and extreme fertility patterns, the calculations based on the original "standard" life were retained.

Changing Fertility and
Brass Estimates of Infant
and Child Mortality

The Brass estimates of child mortality are affected by—and allow for —the age pattern of fertility but are not affected by the *level* of fertility. Hence, the inaccuracy introduced by changing fertility arises from differences in age pattern between the fertility of a given *cohort* (say the women now 25-30) and of the given *cross section* of the population. Imagine that fertility at all ages has been falling. The age distribution estimated for children ever born to women 25-30 is based on the assumption that when these women were 15-20 and 20-25 they had the same fertility as women now at those ages. But when fertility has fallen, women now 25-30 had *higher* fertility when 15-20 or 20-25 than that now reported by the younger women. Hence the age distribution of children ever born contains more older children than is implicitly assumed in selecting the multiplier for estimating $q(3)$. The value of P_1/P_2 for the *cohort* is higher than in the *cross section* covered by the census. Hence the multiplier selected from Table 3.6 is too large, and the estimate of $q(3)$ too big. However, the effect is not likely to be important, because with few exceptions any fertility trends experienced in Africa are gradual, and because the factors in Table 3.6 are not sensitive to small differences in P_1/P_2.

Changing Death Rates
and Brass Estimates of
Child Mortality

The conversion of D_i into $q(a)$ is derived by use of values from a life table expressing the mortality risks young children are exposed to. However, $q(a)$ can be identified with the life table prevailing at the time of the survey only if mortality has been constant during the years preceding the survey. In fact, $q(a)$ in equation (5) is the proportion of deaths by age a among persons born a years before the survey or census; it expresses *cohort* mortality rather than the mortality of the period of the survey. When mortality is changing, the biggest change is usually in infant mortality. Therefore, the infant mortality experienced by 9- or 10-year olds may have been very different from that experienced by children now under 1. Figure 3.3 shows a $q(a)$ that expresses the cumulative mortality experienced by each of the cohorts born in the preceding 15 years, on the assumption that expectation of life at birth has risen from 38.5, in the 15-year interval, to 52.4. For comparison, the curve representing mortality $[q'(a)]$ in the *current* life table is also shown. Under these circumstances, D_3 is about 1.25 times $q'(3)$—and about 1.15 times $q(3)$—if the mean age of the fertility schedules is 27.7 years. The multiplier in Table 3.6 is 0.994; the appropriate multiplier to ob-

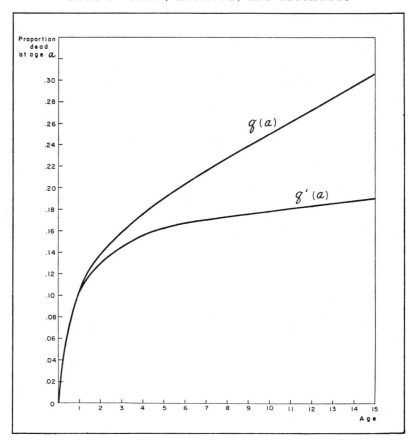

3.3. Proportion dead by age *a* according to current life table,
$q(a)$ (West model, females, $e°_0 = 52.5$), and according to
the risks experienced by each cohort when $e°_0$ has been rising
by 0.92 years per year, $q'(a)$.

tain the *current* value of $q(3)$ from D_3 would be only about 0.80. When
mortality rates fall rapidly, the succession of estimates $q(1)$, $q(2)$, $q(3)$,
$q(5)$ . . . tends to increase more rapidly with age than *either* $q'(a)$,
expressing current mortality, or $q(a)$, expressing the cumulative deaths
of children aged *a* at the time of the survey. Nevertheless, the estimates
of $q(2)$ and $q(3)$ would be representative of the average mortality for
a short period (less than a decade) before the census or survey.

Brass Estimates of Mortality
and the Tendency to Understate
the Number of Children Ever Born

Earlier in this chapter (in the discussion of fertility estimation) a
tendency was noted for older women (or women with many children)
to understate the number of children they have borne. It seems plausible

that women would tend to omit a higher proportion of children who have died than of those who have survived. The National Sample Survey in India found lower reported infant mortality among children born in the remote past than among children born in the years just before the survey,[14] although mortality undoubtedly declined rather than increased during the years in question. There is no secure warrant for asserting that biases found in Indian surveys are duplicated in Africa, but experience in India buttresses the natural skepticism about the accuracy of proportions reported dead by older women. The form of bias to be expected from this possible effect is an estimated $q(a)$ that increases too slowly with age—or, if the effect were large enough, falls off with age. This bias would, of course, be least in the estimates of $q(1)$, $q(2)$, and $q(3)$.

Another kind of omission that is expected in survey data on child survival is the omission of children who died shortly after birth. Respondents may not realize the need to report the birth of a child who did not survive long enough to have a place in the household. The bias caused by such omissions would presumably reduce the estimates of $q(a)$ at all ages by about the same amount, but the bias would not be revealed by any visible distortion in the form of $q(a)$.

Brass Estimates of Mortality
and Age Misstatement

The age distribution recorded in most African censuses or surveys is clearly inaccurate, so that a carefully phrased definition of D_2 should read, "the reported proportion dead of children ever born by women whose *recorded age* is 20-25." The true ages of such women include some that are truly 20-25 and many that are not. A general discussion of the effects of age misreporting cannot be attempted here because the effects depend in a complex way on the relations there may be between parity of the mother and the survival of her young children on the one hand, and misreporting of age on the other. D_2 is (to repeat) really a statement of proportions dead among children ever born for women whose average parity is that of women *reported* to be 20-25. The age distribution of the children ever born is judged by P_1/P_2. But if, for example, two-parity teenagers were typically reported as over 20, the recorded value of P_1/P_2 would be too small, and the multiplier applied to D_2 to estimate $q(2)$ would tend to be too large. Other distortions could result if age estimates for women whose child (or children) had died were systematically different from estimates for women whose children had survived.

The fact that the age indices used to calculate the adjustment factors

[14] Ajit Das Gupta *et al.*, *Couple Fertility. The National Sample Survey*, Number 7, India, Department of Economic Affairs, 1955, pp. 59-61.

in Table 3.6 are based on reported fertility or reported parity by age means that the age errors affecting D_1, D_2, etc., are the same as those that affect the estimated adjustment factors. If age errors had no systematic relation with parity, fertility, or proportions of children surviving, inaccurate reporting of age would not in consequence have a major effect on the estimates of $q(a)$.

Brass Estimates of Mortality
and Selective Forces Affecting
the Proportion Dead
among Children Ever Born.

The proportions dead among children ever born to women in a given age interval—say 30 to 35—is not necessarily representative of the proportion dead among *all* children born at the same time theirs were born. There may be, in fact it seems there probably is, lower mortality among children born to women who have themselves survived than among children born to women who subsequently died. A number of factors tend to cause such a correlation: contagion within households, higher mortality environments affecting both mother and children, and the direct influence of the mother's death itself in making the mortality of her children more probable. This association implies that estimates of $q(a)$ based on proportions dead among their offspring reported by living women are downward biased. The possible bias is less important for younger women (under 30) because of the relatively small cumulative effect of mortality at the younger maternal ages.

Another source of bias is the association between infant mortality on the one hand and age and parity of the mother on the other. In many populations having reliable records the mortality of the first born, and of children born to teen-age women, is substantially higher than the mortality of other children. This difference, if also prevalent in Africa, would tend to make the $q(1)$ estimated from D_1 unrepresentatively high.

Overall Bias in Estimates of
Mortality by the Brass Method

It is not possible to come to a final conclusion valid for all African data about the net bias arising in estimates of $q(a)$ from proportions dead among children ever born. Incomplete reports of past events would almost certainly cause an understatement of mortality, because the omission of a higher proportion of living than of dead offspring is scarcely likely. Similarly, biases from differential mortality among children with surviving or non-surviving mothers cause an underestimate of $q(a)$. Memory lapses increasing with age and higher mortality among orphans both tend to cause $q(a)$ to fall increasingly below the appropriate values as a increases, while the omission of children who died soon after birth lowers the estimates of $q(a)$ at all ages. A declining trend in mortality tends to make the estimates of $q(a)$ too high if they are interpreted as mortality at the time of the census or survey—increasingly too high as a increases. However, when mortality has been declining, the estimates would not tend to be too large if interpreted as average rates prevailing in pre-censal years—the past two or three years for $q(1)$, the past five or six for $q(2)$, the past eight or nine for $q(3)$.

Age misreporting can either increase or decrease the estimates of mortality at a given age, perhaps producing an irregular sequence of $q(a)$ estimates, but not leading to any generally predictable upward or downward bias.

The omission of dead children in retrospective surveys has been noted in non-African countries, and reports on deaths among children under age 1 relative to reported births indicate unacceptably low infant mortality rates. These facts lend substance to the intrinsically plausible hypothesis that African respondents tend to omit a higher proportion of dead than surviving children. This likelihood, combined with a possible downward bias resulting from selective forces, leads to the conclusion that estimates of $q(a)$ by the Brass methods should usually be viewed as lower limits.

The exact sequence of $q(1)$, $q(2)$, $q(3)$, $q(5)$, etc. cannot be taken seriously as precise figures. Omissions, age misstatements, and the effect of trends in fertility and mortality are too widely prevalent. $q(1)$ is an especially untrustworthy figure, and $q(10)$, $q(15)$, etc. are based on the memory of remote events by women whose responses are likely unrepresentative, especially of current mortality experience. The estimates $q(2)$, $q(3)$, and $q(5)$ can often be accepted as minimum indications of the level of recent infant and child mortality.

It is surprising and reassuring with regard to the usefulness of the method that the level of infant and child mortality inferred from proportions dead among children ever born is almost always higher than the level reported by women when asked about events *last year*. Why respondents should report dead children more completely when asked about their total experience than when asked about experience in a recent specified period is puzzling. Perhaps a reluctance to report dead children is more readily expressed in a reference period error than in outright suppression of the event. Whatever the explanation, the Brass estimates of $q(a)$ appear to give more valid indications of mortality early in life than direct inquiries about mortality.

An Example of the
Use of the Tables

The proportions of female children who died previous to the sample census of French Guinea in 1954-55 were:

Age of mother in years

15-20	20-25	25-30	30-35	35-40	40-45	45-50	50-55	55-60	60-65

Proportion of female children dead

.224	.299	.354	.379	.401	.429	.448	.478	.484	.505

From retrospective reports on children born, P_1 is 0.54 and P_2 is 1.75, giving 0.309 for P_1/P_2. The mean age of the specific fertility distribution, calculated directly from the rates found from births in the year preceding the survey, is 27.32. From Table 3.6 the multiplying factors corresponding to 0.309 for P_1/P_2 are found by interpolating between the second and third columns of factors, and those corresponding to the mean of 27.32 by interpolation between the third and fourth columns with the following results:

Age group of mothers

15-20	20-25	25-30	30-35	35-40	40-45	45-50	50-55	55-60	60-65

Factors from P_1/P_2

0.903	0.967	0.967	0.979	0.987	0.960	0.958	0.972	0.974	0.971

Factors from $\bar{m}$

0.957	1.000	0.988	0.997	1.005	0.981	0.979	0.994	0.995	0.992

The use of the first three factors from the P_1/P_2 row and the remainder from the $\bar{m}$ row for multiplying the corresponding proportions of children died gives the q values below:

$q(1)$	$q(2)$	$q(3)$	$q(5)$	$q(10)$	$q(15)$	$q(20)$	$q(25)$	$q(30)$	$q(35)$
.202	.289	.342	.378	.403	.421	.439	.475	.482	.501

The first eight values show a normal mortality pattern with little irregularity, but the last two are too low to be consistent with the others.

Estimation by Model Life Tables and Stable Populations

In recent years, model life tables and stable populations have been used with increasing frequency in estimating the characteristics of populations having only meager records of births and deaths and only incomplete or inaccurate data on age and sex distributions. Information about African populations is meager, incomplete, and often inaccurate; and the circumstances of African life indicate that most African age distributions are probably not widely different from stable distributions. In consequence, life tables and stable population techniques have been the principal means of estimation used in this book.

A model life table is an estimated mortality schedule based on (1) patterns of mortality observed in the recorded experience of various populations other than the one in question and (2) some clue about or recorded aspect of the mortality of the latter. The logical justification for estimation by means of model life tables is that age patterns of mortality vary only within restricted limits. Death rates for one age group are highly correlated with death rates for other groups; model life tables are an expression of this interrelationship.

Many alternative methods could be devised to summarize possible mortality schedules in the form of model tables.[15] Two kinds of model tables were used at the Office of Population Research in analyzing African data—one kind is here designated Coale-Demeny model life tables and the other Brass model life tables. Associated with any life table is a set of stable age distributions incorporating the life table and alternative rates of increase determined by the specified mortality and various possible fertility schedules. Each form of model life tables thus implies its accompanying model stable populations.

Coale-Demeny life tables and stable populations were used to estimate birth rates, death rates, and adjusted age composition in the Congo, the Sudan, Kenya, Tanganyika, Niger, Senegal, Liberia, Gambia, Ghana, Togo, Zambia, Rhodesia, Nigeria, and the Portuguese territories.[16] The method of estimation was to choose a stable population sharing a selected feature of the recorded age distribution, and some other observed or estimated property of the population, such as the intercensal rate of increase or the childhood mortality rates. It was then assumed that the birth rate, death rate, and age composition by five-year intervals of the stable population served as approximations of actual population parameters. In many instances, the estimates obtained by this method could be confronted with estimates from essentially independent sources; e.g., the birth rate could be compared with estimates obtained from the Brass method of calculating fertility. Where comparisons of this sort were possible, the agreement was gratifyingly close.

The Brass model life tables and stable populations were used in a somewhat different way. Fertility estimates in the areas that Brass analyzed were obtained by the methods described earlier in this chapter. A model life table was selected that was consistent with estimates of child mortality obtained by methods already described, and also consistent (where possible) with reported information on deaths last year of the non-child population. A stable population was then chosen that had the estimated levels of fertility and mortality, and the stable age distribution was compared with the recorded distribution. Again the model-life-table–stable-population device served as a means of checking the consistency of the recorded age distribution and estimates of fertility and mortality derived from other kinds of data, and again the stable

[15] Several different methods already used by demographers are cited in Coale and Demeny, *Regional Model Life Tables and Stable Populations.*
[16] See Chapters 4, 6, and 8-10.

population provided the basis for an adjusted age distribution; but the form of the check of consistency was different. The Brass model life tables and stable populations were used in this way in Dahomey, Guinea, the Central African Republic, Upper Volta, North Cameroon, the Senegal Valley, the Ivory Coast, and Mali.[17]

The Two Kinds of Model Life Tables

A set of model life tables presents the age-specific death rates or the number of survivors to each age to be expected under varying mortality conditions. If it is assumed that mortality experience can be closely represented by variation in the value of one parameter, a single "family" of model life tables can be calculated. In these circumstances, the number of survivors to every age, or mortality rates at all ages, are estimated from a single index of the mortality experience of a population, such as expectation of life at birth, or the proportion surviving to age 2. The United Nations model life tables are an example. Examination of recorded life tables reveals instances of mortality schedules diverging markedly from the U.N. model tables, and it is clear that no single-parameter family of tables would produce a good fit to the observed diverse patterns of mortality.

Two methods of accommodating the model-life-table device to the diversity of mortality patterns have been used. One (employed in the Coale-Demeny models) is to locate several individual "families" of life tables that are more uniform in pattern than the totality of observed life tables, and then to construct several one-parameter collections of model life tables, each representing a cluster of similar mortality patterns. The other approach (exemplified by the Brass model tables and also by model life tables based on factor analysis) is to employ two or more parameters to form model life tables that exhibit some of the variety of age patterns found in observed life tables.

The Coale-Demeny model life tables were deliberately based on a preselected group of recorded life tables known to be derived from relatively reliable data; i.e., life tables derived from data with extreme age-misreporting, or major omissions of deaths, or extensive underenumeration of the base population were discarded. Life tables derived from poor-quality data often have strongly individual age patterns of mortality, and in the Coale-Demeny view it is uncertain whether such divergence results from genuine differences in mortality pattern or is produced by errors in age reporting, in death registration, or in enumeration of the base population. It cannot be assumed that the life tables of *every* population are approximated by one of the four families. Three of the families are derived wholly from European life tables, and 60

---

[17] See Chapter 7.

percent of the tables underlying the fourth family are European; it is improbable that the variety of European patterns of mortality exhausts the variety to be found in the world.

If precise African life tables existed they might well conform loosely, at best, to any one pattern of mortality in the experience of the limited number of populations that have accurate vital statistics and censuses. There is no reason to expect that the life tables for every African population, if known, would conform at all well to tables found in the Coale-Demeny families. However, one of these families (the West family) is close to the central pattern shown by all good-quality life tables considered together; it incorporates experience of more tables than any of the other families; and life tables from Taiwan, Japan, and Singapore have been found to conform as well as European tables with the West models. Hence there is some rationale for accepting the West as a best guess of the prevalent pattern of mortality for any population in the absence of contrary evidence. On the other hand, at moderate to high levels of mortality (such as is found in African populations), estimates of birth and death rates based on North model tables are little different from those obtained from the West family, and the North family of life tables has one feature—low infant mortality relative to mortality from 1 to 5—that observers have often ascribed to African populations. Hence the North tables were sometimes chosen in preference to the West ones in making estimates for Africa.

Brass has constructed a two-parameter system of model life tables that has a basic age pattern expressing certain features apparently common in African mortality experience: the low infant mortality relative to mortality at 1 to 5 mentioned in the preceding paragraph, and mortality rates that increase rapidly from age 20 to 50. His simple two-parameter model of mortality permits the use of clues about certain features of the age pattern of deaths experienced by a particular population. In fact, a Brass model table can be constructed to yield a pre-assigned proportion surviving to each of two arbitrarily chosen ages. Thus if there are trustworthy indications of the relative levels of child mortality and adult mortality, the Brass system of model life tables permits the selection of a life table incorporating such a relationship.

The Coale-Demeny approach would accept as correct the most soundly based mortality rates—for example, estimates of the proportions surviving to age 2 or 3 derived from reports of survival among children ever born—and then choose the corresponding model life table from the West or the North family. Typically the adult mortality rates in a model table selected in this way differ from the adult mortality rates reported for the preceding year in the censuses or demographic survey. The Coale-Demeny approach accepts the adult mortality that would accompany the given estimated child mortality in the experience of populations with accurate data, and gives no weight to the reports of last year's adult deaths that on various grounds appear untrustworthy. The Brass approach also accepts the relatively convincing estimates of child mortality from data on children ever born, and then seeks clues (in the reported adult mortality rates) about how mortality varies with age.

Coale-Demeny Model Life Tables
and Stable Populations—
Calculation and Use

Regional Model Life Tables and Stable Populations[18] contains several hundred pages of tables; the reader who wishes to base estimates on the model tables must refer to this volume and can consult the description and instructions in the introduction. The discussion in this chapter is therefore limited to a brief statement of how the model tables were constructed, and a description of their use in making estimates for African populations.

Each of the four families of model life tables expresses the pattern of mortality rates by age found in a group of populations characterized by homogeneity of mortality pattern. The homogeneity was detected when the mortality rates in every reliable life table were compared with a preliminary one-parameter set of model tables expressing average world experience. A group of Scandinavian life tables showed a consistent tendency toward low old-age mortality, and also low infant mortality relative to rates at ages 1 to 4; another group of tables from central Europe had a characteristic pattern that included high rates in infancy and old age; and a third group from Southern Europe showed high rates at 1-4 and low rates in late middle age. A large residual group, encompassing experience in much of Western Europe, plus the United States, Canada, Australia and New Zealand, Taiwan, and Japan, showed no consistent distinctive deviations from the average world age pattern of mortality. The Scandinavian tables were used as the basis for the North model life tables; central European tables were the basis for the East; southern European for the South; and the residual life tables, relatively close to average experience, were the basis for the West. The correlations between mortality rates at different ages were very high (almost always above .90, and usually above .95) within each family, and in each family higher than in the four families considered together.

Each set of model tables was calculated by first computing the linear regression of $_1q_0$, $_4q_1$, $_5q_5$, . . . , $_5q_{75}$ on $e°_{10}$ for males and females within the selected family of life tables, and then permitting the index ($e°_{10}$) to take on values that would generate model tables at levels ranging from an expectation of life at birth (for females) of 20 years to a life ex-

[18] Coale and Demeny.

pectancy higher than experienced by any African population. At higher expectations of life a transition was made to the regression of the logarithm of the mortality rates on $e°_{10}$ to avoid absurd mortality rates at certain ages. However, this feature of the model tables is not relevant for most of the estimations in this book.

For each model life table, 26 stable populations were calculated, at growth rates ranging from –0.010 to 0.050 and gross reproduction rates from 0.800 to 6.00. Various parameters—the birth rate, the death rate, rate of increase, gross and net reproduction rates, mean age, etc. —were calculated and printed for each stable population.

A stable population has the age distribution, rate of increase, and many other properties that would characterize a closed population subject for many years to specified schedules of fertility and mortality. Hence, if fertility and mortality have not changed markedly in a population's recent history, and if the impact of migration on age composition has been minor, the population will have the essential characteristics of a stable population. Moreover, if the age pattern of mortality conforms approximately to one of the model life tables, the characteristics of the population in question will be very close to the characteristics of one of the model stable populations.

If there has been no strong recent trend in fertility and mortality, the birth rate, the death rate, and a smooth age distribution can be found in a model stable population that presumably duplicates more or less closely the population in question. If the West or the North pattern of mortality can be accepted, the problem of estimation reduces to that of locating (by interpolation) the model stable population that best fits the given one from among the 624 stable populations tabulated for each sex within each family. The "best fit" is determined by comparing certain recorded or estimated features of the actual population with the tabulated values of the stable populations.

Since an entire family of stable populations is generated by variations in the level of mortality and in the rate of natural increase (jointly determined in turn by mortality and fertility), each family of stable populations is a two-parameter system. In general, then, two features of an actual population are sufficient to locate a stable population within one of the families. Among the characteristics used to select a model stable population are the following: the proportions of the population in certain age intervals, notably under 5 and under 15; the intercensal rate of increase; the proportion estimated to survive to ages 2, 3, and 5; and the death rate among non-infants, or persons having passed the first birthday.

The choice of clues by which stable populations were selected was guided by (1) the apparent quality of different forms of data about the population and (2) the sensitivity of estimates to flaws in the assumptions underlying the estimation procedure. For example, there are certain almost universal tendencies toward age misreporting in African censuses and surveys; underreporting of females 10-14, and rising proportions with increasing age from 10-14 to 25-29 or even 30-34; understatements of the proportion of males 15-19, etc. Some of the missing females at 10-14 appear, in some censuses or surveys, as girls under 10, and often the proportion of the population under 10 appears higher than is consistent with other evidence about fertility and mortality. The selection of a female stable population having the observed proportion under age 15 appears to be a conservative basis for estimating the birth rate.

In the demographic survey of the Congo in 1956, enumerators were instructed to verify the age of young children by asking respondents for documentary evidence in the form of birth certificates or entries in the parent's identification booklet. Such verification was made for about 80 percent of children under 5, and the age of other children was often ascertained in comparison with the verified age of one or more of his siblings. There is therefore a strong reason for special confidence in the reported age of young children in the Congo, and stable populations were selected having the recorded proportions under age 5.

Consideration of the sensitivity of the estimates to questionable or at least unverifiable assumptions led to certain preferences among the possible methods of selecting model stable populations. For example, when the stable population is used to estimate the birth rate, preference was given to the selection by means of the proportions in the younger age groups (i.e., at ages less than 20, if possible), combined with estimated levels of infant and child mortality. The reason for preferring this combination can be seen by examining the relation between the birth rate and the proportion at some young age in the population. The average birth rate in the five years preceding a census could be determined by a reverse projection of the population under five to estimate how many births were required to provide the given survivors in this age group, and by projecting the whole population two and a half years back to estimate the denominator of the birth rate.

$$ b = \frac{{}_5P_0 \left(\dfrac{l_0}{{}_5L_0} \right)}{Pe^{-2.5r}} \tag{6} $$

In equation (6), b is estimated as the population under age 5, times a reverse survival factor from the life table, divided by the total population times a factor allowing for 2.5 years of growth. The birth rate in a stable population is related to the proportion under 5 by the following relation:

$$b = \frac{\int_0^5 c(a)da}{\int_0^5 e^{-ra}p(a)da} \qquad (7)$$

Since

$$\frac{{}_5P_0}{P} = \int_0^5 c(a)da$$

and

$$\frac{{}_5L_0}{l_0} e^{-2.5r} = \int_0^5 e^{-ra}p(a)da$$

equations (6) and (7) are essentially identical. To estimate the birth rate by reverse projection of the proportion under 5 using a model life table chosen to have a known value of ${}_5L_0$ is equivalent to estimation through a model stable population based on this life table. But the only use made of the assumption of stability in this instance is in determining the average rate of increase of the population during the preceding 2½ years—not an important source of inaccuracy in estimating the birth rate. Furthermore, only slightly variant values of ${}_5L_0$ are consistent with a given value of l_2 or l_3. Thus the birth rate in a model stable population identified by the proportion of the population under 5 and the proportion of children surviving to age 2 or 3 is essentially the same as in *any* population (whether stable or not) with the same proportion of young children and the same childhood survival rate (whether mortality at adult ages conforms to the model pattern or not). This argument favors staying as much as possible with proportions at younger ages and survival rates in childhood in making estimates of the birth rate; however, when the Brass method of estimating mortality cannot be used, infant and child mortality may be harder to ascertain or estimate than mortality at other ages, and because of age misreporting and sometimes differential omission, the proportion of children under some early age—1, 5, or even 10—may be quite unreliably recorded. In these instances the stable population method of estimation yields less trustworthy approximations to the birth rate.

The Brass Model Life Tables and Stable Populations

The Brass method of constructing model life tables is to subject the survivor function in a life table chosen as a "standard" to the so-called *logit* transformation, and then to consider the life tables generated by assuming that their logits are linearly related to the logit of the standard table. In this way, a two-parameter set of model life tables can be constructed.

The logit function is as follows:

$$\text{logit}(x) = \frac{1}{2}\log_e \frac{1-x}{x} \qquad (8)$$

[127]

For x in equation (8), Brass substitutes $p(a)$ (or l_a/l_0 in life-table nota-tion). He then selects a standard table, $p_s(a)$, and constructs his model life tables by assigning different values to α and β in

$$\text{logit } p(a) = \alpha + \beta \text{ logit } p_s(a) \tag{9}$$

This transformation implies that:

$$\frac{q(a)}{p(a)} = A\left(\frac{q_s(a)}{p_s(a)}\right)^\beta \tag{10}$$

where $A = e^{2\alpha}$.

The Nature of the Linear Logit Transformation of a Standard Life Table

The logit transformation can generate a survivor function $p(a)$ that passes through arbitrarily preassigned values at any two ages a_1 and a_2, by the selection of α and β.[19] The life table thus generated has the pre-assigned values of $p(a)$ at the selected ages and shares the shape, in a generalized sense, of the "standard" life table.

Figure 3.4 illustrates the effect of different values of α and β on the standard life table that Brass has constructed for Africa. The survival curves include: (a) the standard ($\alpha = 0$, $\beta = 1.00$); (b) a curve that differs from the standard by having a β of 1.20 instead of 1.00; (c) a curve that has the same value of $p(2)$ as the standard, but a β of 1.20, and (d) a curve that differs from the standard by having a value of α of 0.30 instead of zero. Note that the curve with $\alpha = 0$ and $\beta = 1.20$ intersects the standard at an age where $p_s(a) = 0.50$. This is a general relation: all curves with the same α and different β's intersect at $\bar{a}$ de-termined by $p_s(\bar{a}) = 0.500$, because logit $0.5 = 0$. Hence variation of β produces a sub-family of survival curves, fixed at age 0 and ω, and with a node at $\bar{a}$ (about age 51 in the standard table). At ages below this node or intersection, the life table based on the larger β has higher values of $p(a)$, and at higher ages the opposite relation holds. As a result the area under these two curves (which in each instance is the expectation of life at birth) is very nearly the same.[20] However, this near constancy

---

[19] Given any preassigned $p(a_1)$ and $p(a_2)$, we obtain two equations:
$$\alpha + \beta \text{ logit } p_s(a_1) = \text{logit } p(a_1)$$
$$\alpha + \beta \text{ logit } p_s(a_2) = \text{logit } p(a_2)$$
The known values of $p_s(a_1)$ and $p_s(a_2)$ together with the preassigned values of $p(a_1)$ and $p(a_2)$ provide a unique determination of α and β, and hence a com-plete life table.
$$\text{logit } p(a) = \alpha + \beta \text{ logit } p_s(a).$$
[20] For the standard life table, $e°_0 = 43.6$, and for $\beta = 1.2$, $e°_0 = 44.1$. There is a kind of symmetry among curves with different values of β, and $\alpha = 0$. The difference in p for each young age such that $p_s(a') > 0.5$ is matched by an equal (and opposite) difference in p for the older age a'' such that $p_s(a'') = 1 - p_s(a')$. Thus when $p_s(a) = 0.50$ occurs near the middle of the range zero to ω, life tables with $\alpha = 0$ and different values of β have nearly the same $e°_0$.

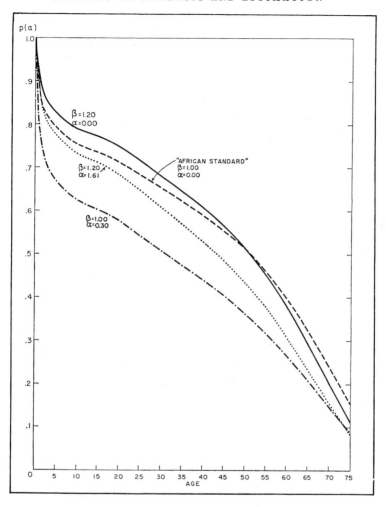

3.4. Proportion surviving to age a, $p(a)$, obtained from the
transformation $p(a) = \alpha + \beta \; \text{logit} \; p_s(a)$ for various values
of α and β.

of e°_0 for different values of β is *not* a general relationship, but is the result of the selection of a standard life table with $p(51) = 0.50$. If a higher-mortality standard life table had been chosen, tables with the same a would intersect at a younger age (say 25) and higher values of β would lower the expectation of life at birth.

Note that the logit transformation permits the acceptance of a trustworthy estimate of childhood survival—e.g., an estimate of $p(2)$—and then the selection of some overall estimate of adult mortality, in the form of a choice of $p(30)$ or $p(50)$ given the accepted value of $p(2)$. The transformation of the standard table (with a and β chosen in this manner) then provides a whole model life table.

The Importance of the Standard Life Table
in the Linear Logit Transformation

The logit transformation will generate life tables having any preassigned level of childhood mortality—expressed, for example, by a value of $q(2)$—and of adult mortality—expressed, for example, by $_{48}q_2$, or $p(50)/p(2)$. How well do such life tables conform to the observed age pattern of mortality in empirical populations? The Coale-Demeny families of model tables provide an interesting test. Each family of these tables expresses the particular age pattern of mortality found in the well-recorded experience of a group of populations. The groups of life tables underlying each family were assembled because of noticeable similarities in age patterns. Figure 3.5 shows the typical result of trying to express a model table within one of the families (a) as the linear logit transformation of another table in the same family, and (b) as the logit transformation of a table from a different family. Note that logit $p(a)$

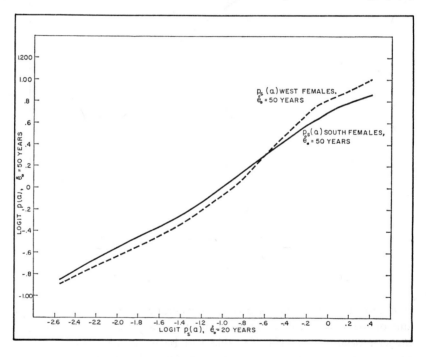

3.5. Logit $p(a)$ plotted against logit $p_s(a)$, when $p(a)$ is South model life table, females, $e°_0 = 20$ years, and $p_s(a)$ is alternatively West model and South model table, $e°_0 = 50$ years.

for the South model life table (females) with $e°_0 = 20$ has a very nearly linear relation to logit $p(a)$ for the South model table where $e°_0 = 50$

years, but that the relation to logit $p(a)$ for the *West* model table with $e°_0 = 50$ is by no means linear. Figure 3.6 shows the result of attempting to approximate the South model table with $e°_0 = 30$ years by a logit transformation of the South model table with $e°_0 = 50$, and the West model table with $e°_0 = 50$. Calculations of the same sort with the

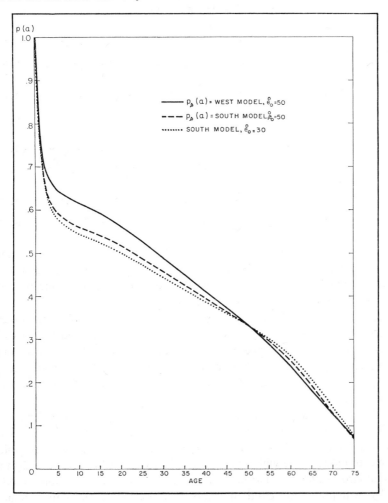

3.6. South model life table, females, $e°_0 = 30$ years compared with life tables obtained by linear logit transformation of South and West model tables, $e°_0 = 50$ years.

other Coale-Demeny families of model tables led to a similar result: linear logit transformations reproduce the model life tables *within* a family very closely, but between families not nearly so well. Table 3.10 shows the values of a and β needed to transform the female table with

Table 3.10. Values of α and β in logit $p(a) = \alpha + \beta$ logit $p_s(a)$ for North, South, East, and West model life tables (female), various levels of e°_0, life table with $e^{\circ}_0 = 50$ serving as $p_s(a)$

		$e^{\circ}_0 = 20$	$e^{\circ}_0 = 30$	$e^{\circ}_0 = 40$	$e^{\circ}_0 = 50$	$e^{\circ}_0 = 60$	$e^{\circ}_0 = 70$
North	α	1.008	0.612	0.295	0.000	−0.316	−0.734
	β	1.296	1.154	1.064	1.000	0.950	0.900
West	α	1.036	0.632	0.307	0.000	−0.339	−0.819
	β	1.306	1.161	1.068	1.000	0.944	0.893
South	α	1.057	0.650	0.318	0.000	−0.356	−0.803
	β	1.533	1.318	1.155	1.000	0.810	0.599
East	α	1.000	0.618	0.302	0.000	0.338	0.813
	β	1.299	1.165	1.073	1.000	0.929	0.852

$e^{\circ}_0 = 50$ into the tables with e°_0 of 20, 30, 40, 60, and 70 in each family. Note that in all families except South (where β is quite large at high mortality levels) the parameters needed to transform from one mortality level to another are almost identical.

These examples show that the selection of a standard life table affects the detailed form of the survival curve in a life table fitted to the estimated mortality experience of a population by a linear logit transformation. The standard life table to be used in Africa, in other words, should ideally incorporate typical features (if such exist) of African age patterns of mortality.

Brass evolved the "African standard" mortality schedule given in Table 3.11 to reflect features that are at least apparently common in Africa. Up to age 10 or 20 the $p(a)$ curve in this table closely resembles a North model table with an e°_0 of about 46 years; but after age 20 the "standard" survival curve falls much more sharply than a North model table with the same child mortality, and indeed faster than a South, East, or West model table with the same child mortality. This feature matches a widespread characteristic of mortality by age as reported in African surveys for the pre-survey year, and is consistent with a tendency for reported African age distributions to taper rapidly through the 30's to the 50's. Whether these common features are a characteristic bias in African data or a characteristic feature of African mortality is a matter of conjecture.

Table 3.11. Proportion surviving, $p_s(a)$, and corresponding logits at specified ages of the African standard life table

Exact age in years a	$p_s(a)$	Logit $p_s(a)$
1	0.8802	0.9970
2	0.8335	0.8052
3	0.8101	0.7252
4	0.7964	0.6819
5	0.7863	0.6615
10	0.7502	0.5498
15	0.7362	0.5131
20	0.7130	0.4551
25	0.6826	0.3829
30	0.6525	0.3150
35	0.6223	0.2496
40	0.5898	0.1817
45	0.5535	0.1073
50	0.5106	0.0212
55	0.4585	−0.0832
60	0.3965	−0.2100
65	0.3210	−0.3746
70	0.2380	−0.5818
75	0.1500	−0.8673
80	0.0760	−1.2490
85	0.0310	−1.7211

Procedure for Using the Logit Transformation of the "African Standard" Life Table

The Brass model life table procedure is usually applied to mortality data derived from a demographic survey—data including the reported number of children ever born and the number surviving, classified by age of mother, and the reported number of deaths occurring in the pre-survey year classified by age, and usually by sex. With little error (in view of the general quality of the information) the population at risk can be considered to be the population enumerated in the survey, and age-specific mortality rates can be calculated for five- or ten-year age groups. These age-specific mortality rates (m_x values) can then be converted to life-table proportions dying (q_x values) by standard techniques, for example, the Reed-Merrell method.[21] These two sources of information give two alternative sets of proportions surviving to ages up to 5 or perhaps 10 years. The values of $p(2)$ and $p(3)$ are the most reliable inferences from the data on survivors among children ever born, and $p(5)$ may be a valid indication of current mortality risks up to age 5 if there has been no strong recent mortality trend and no tendency to omit dead children among those reported as born in the past five or ten years. At higher ages (10, 15, etc.) inferences about current mortality from data on children ever born are of ever decreasing reliability.

A comparison of $p(2)$, $p(3)$, and perhaps $p(5)$ estimated, on the one hand from the retrospective reports of children born and surviving and, on the other, from direct reports of deaths among children in the year before the survey generally shows much higher estimated mortality from the retrospective data. If we were prepared to assume an underreporting of mortality by the same degree at all ages (because, for example, of an error in "reference period") the ratio of $q(3)$ from retrospective data to $q(3)$ derived from deaths reported for the pre-survey year could be used as a correction factor to adjust the reported death rates at ages above 5. However, analysis quickly reveals that (in contrast to reported fertility) the age structure of reported mortality is often conspicuously distorted. There is a clear tendency to underreport mortality more among some age-sex groups than among others. Therefore the use of a simple correction-factor adjustment of mortality above childhood is not justified. Brass suggests making two $p(a)$ curves, each beginning with estimates of $p(2)$, $p(3)$, and $p(5)$ based on the reported survival of children ever born. The first $p(a)$ curve simply incorporates $_nq_x$ values obtained from reported mortality, and the second incorporates values based on reported mortality adjusted by the above-mentioned correction factor. Logits of these alternative $p(a)$ curves are plotted on one axis against logit $p_s(a)$ (the African standard) on the other. If either set of points falls approximately on a straight line, with a slope between 0.80 and 1.20, the line can be taken as the basis for constructing a model life table. Often a line intermediate between the two sets of points above age 5 fits best with the $p(a)$ values up to age 3. Brass suggests that when the reported adult mortality appears almost wholly non-credible or inconsistent, a model life table be constructed that fits $p(2)$ and $p(3)$ from the retrospective data, and has a

<hr>

[21] Lowell J. Reed and Margaret Merrell, "A short method for constructing an abridged life table," *American Journal of Hygiene*, Vol. 30, No. 2, September 1939.

value of β of unity in the logit transformation of the African standard table.

The Brass model life tables are thus a one-parameter family—formed by varying a in $p(a) = a + p_s(a)$—wherever there is insufficient evidence about adult mortality to justify a choice of β other than $\beta = 1$. The Coale-Demeny procedure would be to choose a West or North model table that comes closest to the $p(2)$ and $p(3)$ based on survival among children ever born, and accept the mortality rates at all ages above childhood in the chosen model table. The Brass procedure also includes acceptance of the childhood mortality estimated from retrospective data; in the absence of persuasive information about adult mortality, Brass uses a one-parameter set of model tables derived from his African standard; but when the adult mortality rates form a consistent pattern of "logits" with β not equal to 1.00, a modified model table of this family may be constructed.

Check of Estimated Mortality, Fertility, and Age Composition

The age composition of a closed population is determined by the recent history of its fertility and mortality. If the age schedules of both have been approximately constant, the population has the stable age composition. The principal determinant of the broad features of the age distribution—the mean age, the proportion under age 15, and the like—is the fertility history, so that the age distribution of a population with constant fertility rather closely resembles the stable, even if mortality has not been constant. The resemblance is especially close when the course of mortality has been one of gradual and continuous change. Indeed, even fertility changes, if slowly paced, result in an age composition not much removed from the stable population implicit in the fertility and mortality schedules prevailing at any moment.

Under the circumstances in which most African populations live, the normal expectation is that fertility has been more or less constant in the recent past, at current levels, because the customs that might affect fertility in African populations—age at marriage, mating customs outside of marriage, taboos on intercourse, folk practices of abortion and contraception—are not likely to be altered in the absence of social changes not yet evident in Africa. An exception to this generalization may occur in populations where fertility has been affected by pathological sterility resulting from infectious diseases. The spread of such diseases, and their successful control, may have caused major decreases or increases in the fertility of some African populations. In fact, the fertility of some populations—especially in some districts in the Congo—is below replacement at current estimated mortality levels, and would have been very much below replacement under the mortality risks early in this century, or late in the nineteenth. Hence it is implausible that the current low fertility of some populations could have persisted for as much as a century, and impossible that it could have extended into the remote past, unless we are prepared to postulate populations many times larger than at present one or two centuries ago. Hence we are led to suspect that where fertility is very low, the decline may have been recent enough to leave traces in the shape of the present age distribution.

It is also a fact that a population with a history of sharply changing mortality has an age distribution perceptibly different from one with the same present mortality and a history of no change, i.e., a stable population. According to our estimates, many African populations have levels of mortality that produce a rapid rate of increase—from 2 to 3 percent per year. If these rates had been long standing, the population of Africa would have been only about one-tenth or less of its present size a century ago, contrary to the impression of all students of African history. Again, it appears probable that many populations have experienced a decline in mortality recent enough to have left an impression —in this instance a relatively slight one—on the current age distribution.

In spite of these circumstances that would cause the age distribution to differ from the stable, the general form of the actual age distribution can be expected to resemble the age distribution of the stable population implied by current fertility and mortality. In fact it is a safe guess that the stable age distribution is closer to the actual age distribution than is the age distribution tabulated in a census or demographic survey of an African population, since the reported age distributions are based on rough estimates of the age of respondents who usually have little knowledge of age or date of birth.

It follows from the likely general resemblance of the true age distribution to the stable that a comparison of the stable population inherent in the estimated fertility and mortality schedules with the recorded age distribution will test their rough consistency. It is important to note just what aspects of mortality and fertility are tested by this comparison when the assumption of stability of the age distribution is accepted. Brass had found that stable populations formed by combining various of the Brass model life tables and various intrinsic rates of increase have very nearly the same cumulative proportions to ages 5, 10, 15, 25, 35, 45, 55, and 65 if the product of the birth rate and the proportion surviving to age 2 $[bp(2)]$ is the same—even though there is a wide range of values of b, and quite different growth and death rates. Comparisons of cumulative proportions in the regional model stable populations of Coale and Demeny also show that age distributions with the same $bp(2)$ are not very different within the same family of model tables. Hence if a comparison of the stable population implied by estimated fertility and mortality and the recorded population indicates good agreement, what has been confirmed is the consistency of the age distribution with the estimated birth rate and estimated level of child mortality. Since various levels of adult mortality would produce about the same general age structure—because the effect of higher adult mortality on $p(a)$ would be offset by its effect on r, the intrinsic rate of increase—the age distribution check fails to tell much about the estimated mortality above age 2. The recorded age distribution, especially in view of its typical distortions, thus provides no useful guidance in selecting a family of model life tables among the Coale-Demeny regional variants, or in determining the most appropriate among the various combinations of a and β (in the Brass logit transformation) that yield the estimated $p(2)$ or $p(3)$. Nor does the age distribution provide a good test of estimates of the crude death rate or the rate of natural increase.

The Brass Procedure of
Checking Stable and
Reported Age Distributions

The Brass method of estimating fertility yields an approximate age-specific fertility schedule, and the combination of his method of estimating child mortality and his model life table system yields an approximate age schedule of survival. These two can be combined by standard calculation procedures to obtain a stable population.[22] A comparison of the proportions in each five-year age interval in this stable population and in the enumerated population would never in Africa give an impression of uniform consistency, because the recorded age distributions are so erratic. Smoothing the recorded distribution by some graduating formula is a possibility, but the powerful smoothing required is likely to be unsatisfactory at the ends of the age distribution, or to involve arbitrary assumptions. Another method is to compare the two age distributions after cumulation to various ages. This method has the advantage of automatically removing the effect of all age misstatements except those that move a respondent's age across the boundary in question. Thus the reported proportion up to age 20 is affected only by the net transfer of persons from the below-20 range to the above-20 range or vice versa. Until one gains experience with interpreting comparisons of two cumulative age distributions, it is hard to judge what constitutes a good fit by looking at a table or a graph of the cumulated proportions. A comparison that is easier to understand is this: the difference in the cumulative proportions to each age in the reported and stable age distributions is converted into a statement of the incremental number of years of age needed to equalize the proportions. For example, a reported proportion of 40 percent under age 10 compared to 38 percent in the stable popu-

[22] D. V. Glass, *Population, Policies and Movements in Europe*, Oxford University Press, 1940, pp. 405-415.

lation based on estimated fertility and mortality would be explained if children up to 10.8 rather than 10.0 years of age on the average were reported as under 10. In Figure 3.7, the age differences needed to equalize the stable population calculated for the Republic of Guinea, 1955, with the reported population are shown, along with the age differences needed to convert the calculated stable into stables that would fit the most deviant points (high and low) in the observed cumulative distribution. If the positive and negative areas on the central curve are in rough balance, it can be said that the reported age distribution is consistent with the estimated fertility and childhood mortality levels; and the distance between the upper and lower curves indicates the extent to which

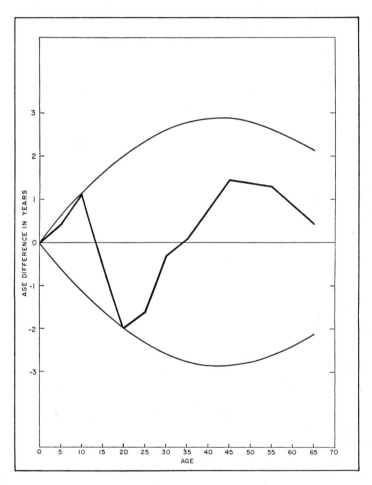

3.7. Republic of Guinea, 1955. Age differences required to make cumulative stable age distribution agree with the recorded distribution, and with alternative stable distributions that fit extreme points in the recorded distribution.

age misreporting has produced inconsistencies at different points in the cumulative distribution. It is essential to keep in mind in the interpretation of Figure 3.7 that the stable population was not chosen to fit the age distribution, but was based on estimates of fertility and mortality that are completely independent of the age distributions.

The conversion of a difference in the cumulative age distribution into an age difference is easily made by the following procedure:

(a) Let $C(a)$ be the cumulative proportion in the stable age distribution to age a, and $c(a)\,da$ be the proportion from age a to $a + da$.

(b) Then $dC(a)/da = c(a)$, and any discrepancy, $\Delta C(a)$, between the reported and stable distributions can be converted into an age difference by the approximate relation

$\Delta a = \Delta C(a)/c(a)$

$c(a)$ is readily calculated from standard formulae in stable population theory.

NOTE ON BRASS METHOD OF FERTILITY ESTIMATION

BY WILLIAM BRASS

Polynomial functions are often used to graduate observations because of the ease with which the mathematical manipulations can be performed. The use of a general polynomial without restrictions to describe distributions of specific fertilities is, however, cumbersome because several terms and, therefore, parameters are needed to obtain a good fit to the observations. The number of unknown parameters can be reduced by the imposition of restrictions, and the following function is satisfactory for the applications of graduation developed in this study:

$$f(a) = C\ (a\text{-}s)\ (s + 33 - a)^2$$
$$s \le a \le s + 33$$

where $f(a)$ is the specific fertility rate of women aged a years, s is the age of the start of the reproductive period, and C is a constant which varies with the level of fertility; $f(a)$ is taken as zero when a is outside the range s to $s + 33$ years.

The function is restricted to be zero at s and $s + 33$. Between these limits the shape is approximately that of empirical distributions with a sharp rise in rates following age s, a peak and then a more gradual fall to the end of reproduction; the mean and the mode are nearer the lower than the upper limit. The 33-year range of the function was chosen to make the variance (43.6) close to the average for observed distributions.

The two parameters which can be varied when the model is fitted to data for a population are C and s. The value of C, fixed by the level of fertility, does not enter into the applications here, which depend only on the shape of the curve, i.e., the relations between its parts. As s, the lower limit of the reproductive period, is increased, the curve is correspondingly displaced upward. In particular, the mean of the function is $s + 13.2$; for s equal to 15 years the mean of 28.2 is near the average for recorded distributions, and a variation of s from 13 to 18 covers the range of locations of observed data for nearly all populations. Relative distributions of specific fertilities from the model, in the standard five-year age groups, for a range of values of s and corresponding f_2/f_1 and $\bar{m}$ indices are illustrated in Table 3.A.1. In the calculation of the f_2/f_1 ratios, it was assumed (in accordance with common practice) that fertility of women before 15 years, although shown separately in the table, was included in the f_1 measure for the 15-20 age group.

Table 3.A.1. Model age-specific fertility rates, five-year age groups $[f(a) = C(a - s)(s + 33 - a)^2$; C chosen so that total fertility is 5.00]

Exact limits of age interval						
10-15	.020	.005	-	-	-	-
15-20	.179	.148	.111	.075	.044	.020
20-25	.262	.254	.242	.226	.205	.179
25-30	.249	.257	.263	.266	.265	.262
30-35	.179	.196	.211	.225	.238	.249
35-40	.090	.108	.126	.144	.162	.179
40-45	.021	.031	.044	.058	.074	.090
45-50	-	.001	.003	.006	.012	.021
f_1/f_2*	.764	.605	.460	.330	.213	.113
$\bar{m}$ (years)	26.2	27.2	28.2	29.2	30.2	31.2

* Computed from specific fertilities to more decimal places than shown in the table.

The cumulated fertility to exact age a, $F(a)$, is obtained as the integral of $f(x)$ from s to a. The f value for any age interval (c to d say) is $F(d) - F(c)$. Integration of $F(x)$ from c to d and division by $(d-c)$ gives the corresponding mean number of children ever born per woman in the group. The integrations and calculations are easily performed because of the simple polynomial form of $f(x)$. In this way f and F measures were computed for the standard five-year age groups for a series of locations of $f(x)$, with s and $\bar{m}$ spaced at one-year intervals over the range of variation for observed distributions. From these measures the k multiplying factors required to calculate the mean number of children ever born from the equation $F_i = \phi_i + k_i f_i$ were obtained. The factors are given in Table 3.A.2.

Table 3.A.2 gives indices for a one-parameter set of model fertility distributions specified alternatively by the values of $\bar{m}$ or f_1/f_2. For these distributions multiplication of an f_i (age-specific fertility rate) for an age interval by the appropriate tabulated factor gives exactly the *additional* mean children ever born from the start of the interval to women of these ages in the population. The sum of this and the cumulated f measures to the start of the interval gives the mean number of children ever born per woman for the age group. The multiplying factors will not, in general, be exact for observed fertility distributions but will give a

Table 3.A.2. Multiplying factors for estimating the average value over five-year age groups of cumulated fertility (F_i) according to the formula $F_i = \phi_i + k_i f_i$ (when f_i is for ages 15-20, 20-25, etc.)

Exact age of women								
15-20	.335	.680	1.030	1.390	1.760	2.130	2.460	2.745
20-25	2.025	2.170	2.265	2.330	2.380	2.420	2.455	2.485
25-30	2.420	2.455	2.485	2.510	2.535	2.560	2.580	2.605
30-35	2.560	2.580	2.605	2.625	2.650	2.675	2.700	2.730
35-40	2.675	2.700	2.730	2.760	2.800	2.845	2.895	2.960
40-45	2.845	2.895	2.960	3.040	3.145	3.285	3.470	3.720
45-50	3.195	3.455	3.720	3.980	4.240	4.495	4.750	5.000
f_1/f_2	.036	.113	.213	.330	.460	.605	.764	.939
$\bar{m}$ (years)	32.2	31.2	30.2	29.2	28.2	27.2	26.2	25.2

good approximation to the correct values. Since the accuracy of estimation for each age interval depends only on the agreement with the model over that interval, different distributions from the set could be fitted for each group of women. It has been found that in practice good results are obtained by using the observed f_1/f_2 ratio to determine the multiplying factors for the three youngest age groups and the mean $\bar{m}$ of the recorded specific fertility rates to fix the remainder.

Multiplying factors for deriving the mean number of children ever born per woman from specific fertility rates for age groups with a half-year displacement backward in time were calculated by the same procedure with the appropriate changes in the ranges of integration. These factors, which are for use when the current specific fertility rates are calculated from births in the past year, are shown in Table 3.1 of the text.

NOTE ON THE EFFECT OF AGE MISREPORTING

BY ETIENNE VAN DE WALLE

The aim of the present note is to show empirically some possible effects of age misreporting of the type encountered in African inquiries on a number of demographic measurements, namely those based on information concerning "current" and "retrospective" fertility; number of children born during a reference period—usually 12 months—preceding the inquiry; and number of children ever born and surviving. Underlying our discussion will be certain simplifying assumptions. The possible effect of underreporting on the female age distribution will be neglected. It will be assumed that the real age distribution can properly be described by a stable age distribution that can be fitted to the recorded population, and that difference between the stable population and the recorded one are due exclusively to transfers of women from one age class to the next, as a result of error in the estimation of ages. By making an assumption about the nature of the transfers, the number of transferred women and the direction of the transfers can be estimated by comparing the stable age distribution with the recorded one. The transferred women have a certain fertility and a certain parity. Implications of a number of hypotheses on the fertility and parity of these women will be investigated.

For illustrative purposes, we have selected the population of the Congo (Leopoldville). Table 3.B.1 gives the age distribution of the recorded and of the estimated stable population. The latter was obtained by selecting an appropriate level of mortality and by assuming that the age classes 0-9 are accurately reported. Only the female population is relevant to our discussion.

Effect of Age Misreporting
on the Recorded Fertility

It will be assumed throughout this paper that the nature of transfers is such that women are shifted only from one age class to the next, either backward or forward. The missing girls of the age class 10-14 will be found in the class 15-19, and so on. There may be transfers both ways, but we are only interested in the net result. Let 1, 2, and 3 be the three age classes involved in the age misreporting of an age class 2. (Some women are transferred from age class 1 to age class 2, and some in turn from age class 2 to 3—or possibly from age class 2 to 1 or from age class 3 to 2.)

Let f_1, f_2, and f_3 denote the average fertility (number of children born per woman during the past year) of the real age classes; n_1, n_2, and n_3,

Table 3.B.1. Age distribution of recorded and stable population of the Congo, in per thousand, for females

Age	Recorded	Stable	Cumulated Difference (stable-recorded)
0-9	296	296	0
10-14	82	114	-32
15-19	72	100	-60
20-24	83	87	-64
25-29	92	76	-48
30-34	106·	65	- 7
35-44	136	104	+25
45+	133	158	0
Total	1,000	1,000	

the number of women in each age class; n_{12} and n_{23}, the net number transferred from class 1 to 2 and from class 2 to 3; and f_{12} and f_{23}, the average fertility of those transferred. (In case of a downward transfer the sign of n_{12} and n_{23} will be negative.)

Then the fertility f_2' of the recorded age class is

$$f_2' = \frac{n_2 f_2 + n_{12} f_{12} - n_{23} f_{23}}{n_2 + n_{12} - n_{23}}$$

or

$$f_2' = f_2 \cdot \frac{n_2}{n_2 + n_{12} - n_{23}} + \frac{n_{13} f_{12} - n_{23} f_{23}}{n_2 + n_{12} - n_{23}}.$$

Thus the recorded fertility depends both on the number of women transferred from one age class to the other and on the fertility of the transferred women.

f_2 and f_2' would be equal whenever

$$n_{12} (f_{12} - f_2) = n_{23} (f_{23} - f_2)$$

This condition might be fulfilled in three cases:

(a) The women transferred to, and removed from, a given age class have the same (average) age-specific fertility rates as the ones in the real age class:

$$f_{12} = f_{23} = f_2$$

(b) The numbers of women transferred to, and removed from, an age class are equal, and both groups have the same age-specific fertility rates

$$n_{12} = n_{23} \text{ and } f_{12} = f_{23}$$

(c) The ratio of the number of women transferred to the number re-moved from an age group is the inverse of the ratio of the absolute differences between the age-specific fertility of these groups and that of the original age class:

$$\frac{n_{12}}{n_{23}} = \frac{f_{23} - f_2}{f_{12} - f_2}$$

None of these cases is however likely to happen consistently in the presence of age misreporting. Furthermore, even if one of the conditions is fulfilled for any given age group 2 so that $f_2' = f_2$, f_1' and f_3' would still be affected by the transfers. In other words, whenever age misreporting takes place, the series of age-specific fertility rates will be distorted.

We shall now proceed with a numerical example, using the recorded and stable age distributions given above in Table 3.B.1 and age-specific fertility rates not unlike those of the Cocos Keeling Islands.[1] However, fertility before age 15 and after age 45 is assumed to be zero.

Our assumptions about the nature of age misreporting in this example imply that out of the 114 girls aged 10 to 14 years, 82 have been recorded as aged 10 to 14 and 32 as aged 15 to 19 . . . and so on, as shown in Tables 3.B.2 and 3.B.3.

Several hypotheses will now be made as to the fertility of the transferred women, i.e., about f_{12} and f_{23}. Due to the lack of knowledge about the nature of age misreporting our assumptions will necessarily be arbi-

Table 3.B.2. Distribution in recorded age classes of women belonging to given age classes of the stable population; age-specific fertility and number of births in the stable population

Recorded ages	0-9	10-14	Stable ("real") Ages 15-19	20-24	25-29	30-34	35-44	45+	Total recorded
0-9	296								296
10-14		82							82
15-19		32	40						72
20-24			60	23					83
25-29				64	28				92
30-34					48	58			106
35-44						7	104	25	136
45+								133	133
Total stable	296	114	100	87	76	65	104	158	1,000
ASFR	0	0	.165	.365	.390	.320	.200	0	
Births to stable	0	0	16.50	31.76	29.64	20.80	20.80	0	119.50

[1] In fact, rates for different cohorts have been averaged. See T. E. Smith, "The Cocos-Keeling Islands: a Demographic Laboratory," *Population Studies*, Vol. 14, No. 2, Nov. 1966, p. 109.

Table 3.B.3. Comparison between the recorded and the stable population

Age group	Transferred from lower age group	to	Correctly reported in age group	Transferred from higher age group	to	Recorded population (1)+(3)+(4)	Stable population (2)+(3)+(5)
	(1)	(2)	(3)	(4)	(5)	(6)	(7)
0–4	–	–	296	–	–	296	296
10–14	–	–	82	–	32	82	114
15–19	32	–	40	–	60	72	100
20–24	60	–	23	–	64	83	87
25–29	64	–	28	–	48	92	76
30–34	48	–	58	–	7	106	65
35–44	7	–	104	25	–	136	104
45+	–	25	133	–	–	133	158

trary and will therefore be kept as simple as possible. Specifically the following three cases will be considered.

(1) The transferred women have a lower than average fertility. We assume, as an example, that their fertility is only half the original average fertility of the age group:

$$f_{12} = \tfrac{1}{2} f_1, \text{ and } f_{23} = \tfrac{1}{2} f_2$$

(2) They have the same fertility as the age class from which they are transferred:

$$f_{12} = f_1 \text{ and } f_{23} = f_2$$

(3) They have an above-average fertility. For example, we take that fertility to be one-fourth higher than that of the group from which the women are transferred

$$f_{12} = 1.25 \, f_1 \qquad f_{23} = 1.25 \, f_2$$

When we speak of the fertility of the transferred women, we mean the *current* fertility, or the average number of children born per woman during the previous year. There is only, for each individual woman, the alternative of having had one child, or not. A "higher than average fertility of the transferred women" means that women who had a child during the previous year have a greater probability of being shifted when their age is misrecorded. If the fact of having had a child during the last twelve months had no influence on age misreporting, it would be logical to assume that the transferred women had the average fertility of their age class. If women with a newborn child are more easily transferred than the others, then their fertility will be above average; if they are less easily transferred, their fertility will be below the average of the group. Other factors than current fertility are obviously operative in the transfer; one factor, parity, will be discussed later. Fertility is not operative in the transfer of women of the age classes 10-14 and 45+, but the marital status of the women may then be important.

The age-specific fertilities resulting from our hypotheses are given in Table 3.B.4. This table indicates that, whatever the fertility of the transferred women, the "recorded" fertilities are seriously altered in the presence of strong age misreporting.

Table 3.B.4. Age-specific fertility rates of the stable population and of the recorded population under three hypotheses concerning the fertility of the transferred women

Age	Stable	"Recorded" under hypothesis		
		(1) Lower fertility	(2) Average fertility	(3) Higher fertility
15-19	.165	.160	.092	.057
20-24	.365	.302	.220	.180
25-29	.390	.353	.373	.385
30-34	.320	.269	.352	.391
35-44	.200	.161	.169	.174

It will be observed that the above computations involve (a) a single pattern of reallocation of women aged 10 years and over between the different age classes as indicated in Tables 3.B.2 and 3.B.3 and (b) three patterns of reallocation of children to be imputed to the women in different age classes as implied by our three hypotheses. Since the total number of women allocated to the childbearing ages does not change from case to case and since the number of children imputed to these women remains the same throughout, the general fertility rate is identical in all the three examples. [It differs from that of the stable population only in so far as the reallocation under (a) crosses the limits of the childbearing ages.] The age distribution of the mothers is, however, modified under our hypotheses. Maximum fertility may obtain, not in the age class 25-29, as among the Cocos Islanders, but earlier or later. The mean age of childbearing will apparently change from 27.8 years in the stable population to 29.0 years under hypothesis 1, 30.1 years under hypothesis 2, and 30.7 years under hypothesis 3. The cumulated fertilities, including the total fertility are also markedly different under the three hypotheses, as shown in Table 3.B.5. (The cumulated fertilities F were obtained by simple linear interpolation:

$$F_{(17.5)} = 2.5f_{(15-19)}$$
$$F_{(22.5)} = 5f_{(15-19)} + 2.5f_{(20-24)}$$

etc.)

Up to this point, the analysis yields two results:

(1) Age misreporting affects the shape of the fertility curve in a way depending both on the number of women displaced from one age class to the next and on their fertility.

Table 3.B.5. Cumulated fertilities with original age-specific fertility and under hypotheses 1, 2, and 3

Age	Stable	"Recorded" under hypothesis		
		(1) Lower fertility	(2) Average fertility	(3) Higher fertili
17.5	.413	.400	.230	.143
22.5	1.713	1.555	1.010	.735
27.5	3.625	3.193	2.493	2.148
32.5	5.400	4.748	4.305	4.088
40	7.200	6.225	6.030	5.935
45+	8.200	7.030	6.875	6.805

(2) The cumulated fertilities, computed from the recorded age-specific fertility rates in the presence of age misreporting, are substantially different from the original figures.

Effect of Age Misreporting on the Recorded Parity

With the same notation as previously, we now turn to the effect of age misreporting of the recorded parity of the women in our population.

Let P_1, P_2, and P_3 be the average parities in the age classes considered; P_{12}, the average parity of those transferred from class 1 to 2: P_{23}, the average parity of those transferred from class 2 to 3. Then the "recorded" parity P_2' will be

$$P_2' = \frac{n_2 P_2 + n_{12}P_{12} - n_{23}P_{23}}{n_2 + n_{12} - n_{23}}$$

We refer the reader to the discussion of the cases where f_2' would be equal to f_2, the formula for computing P_2' being essentially similar to that used for computing f_2'. Because of the shape of the parity curve as a function of age, as compared to the fertility curve, it is even less likely that P_2' would be equal to P_2 than that f_2' would be equal to f_2.

Applying the above formula to the number of women transferred in Tables 3.B.2 and 3.B.3, we make a series of hypotheses concerning the parity of the transferred women, parallel to those made previously concerning the fertility.

(A) The parity of the transferred women is below the average of the age class. If P_0 is the parity of the age class 0 immediately preceding the age class 1, we take as an example

$$P_{12} = P_1 - \left(\frac{P_1 - P_0}{2}\right) \text{ and } P_{23} = P_2 - \left(\frac{P_2 - P_1}{2}\right)$$

(B) The transferred women have the same average parity as the age class from which they are transferred;

$$P_{12} = P_1 \text{ and } P_{23} = P_2$$

(C) They have a higher than average parity. For example:

$$P_{12} = P_1 + \left(\frac{P_1 - P_0}{4}\right) \quad \text{and} \quad P_{23} = P_2 + \left(\frac{P_2 - P_1}{4}\right)$$

The resulting "recorded" parities are given in Table 3.B.6.

Table 3.B.6. Parity of stable population and of recorded population under three hypotheses concerning the parity of the transferred women

| Age | Stable | "Recorded" parity under hypothesis | | |
		(A) Lower parity	(B) Average parity	(C) Higher parity
17.5	.413	.401	.230	.143
22.5	1.738	1.142	.781	.600
27.5	3.625	2.343	2.312	2.297
32.5	5.400	4.227	4.596	4.780
40	7.200	7.154	7.291	7.360

Effect of Age Misreporting on the "Recorded" Parity/Cumulated Fertility Ratios. (P/F)

We can now combine the three hypotheses made on the parity of the transferred women with the three hypotheses made on their fertility. This is done in the form of P/F ratios. They appear in Table 3.B.7.

Table 3.B.7. P/F ratios under a combination of hypotheses concerning the fertility and the parity of the transferred women

| | Ages | P/F ratio under hypothesis | | |
		(1) Lower fertility	(2) Average fertility	(3) Higher fertility
Combined with hypothesis (A) Lower parity	15–19	1.00	1.74	2.80
	20–24	0.73	1.13	1.55
	25–29	0.73	0.94	1.09
	30–34	0.89	0.98	1.03
	35–44	1.15	1.19	1.21
(B) Average parity	15–19	0.58	1.00	1.61
	20–24	0.50	0.77	1.06
	25–29	0.72	0.93	1.08
	30–34	0.97	1.07	1.12
	35–44	1.17	1.21	1.23
(C) Higher parity	15–19	0.36	0.62	1.00
	20–24	0.39	0.59	0.82
	25–29	0.72	0.92	1.07
	30–34	1.01	1.11	1.17
	35–44	1.18	1.22	1.24

Table 3.B.7 shows that age misreporting will normally distort the P/F ratios. It is not inconceivable that the recording of age is related to parity or/and current fertility. For the districts of the Congo, it is always found that the P/F ratio at age 15-19 is greater than at 20-24, which in turn exceeds the P/F ratio at age 25-29. This sequence may be due to a systematic pattern in age misreporting, perhaps related to parity or fertility. In our model, a pattern such as the upward transfer of women of average fertility but lower than average parity could bring about the recorded sequence. It is however not clear why women of below average parity would be attributed a higher age than they actually have. It is possible perhaps that childless women, whose age is more difficult to estimate, would be shifted towards a central age class. This is however entirely conjectural.

4

Summary of Estimates of
Fertility and Mortality

BY ANSLEY J. COALE

AND FRANK LORIMER

This chapter brings together in tabular and cartographic form the estimates of demographic variables contained in the case studies, supplemented by estimates made after a less detailed critical examination of
the censuses and surveys in which the basic data were collected. These
less detailed analyses are described in an appendix to the chapter.

Summary tables and charts have an almost irresistible tendency to
suppress the qualifications and uncertainties surrounding the figures presented. Nevertheless, a summary seems worthwhile because it brings to
light aspects of the estimates—such as similar levels of fertility in con-
tiguous populations, even though the estimates are based on different
systems of data—that are not evident in a piecemeal presentation of
results. Also a summary is potentially useful to readers with little or no
interest in other parts of the book.

It is the hope of the authors that several sorts of readers will find the
book useful. Perhaps the most valuable part in the long run will be the
methods of analysis and estimation that were developed and applied as
our research progressed. We hope that demographers and statisticians
will use, improve, and extend these methods in applications to other
populations in Africa and elsewhere. The methods are described in
Chapter 3 and in the case studies. These technical aspects of the book
will appeal primarily to a technical audience.

The case studies may also prove of value to persons with a broad
interest in a specific area; e.g., someone with a general interest in the
Congo may find the demographic information in the chapter on the Congo useful. The summary may be useful to persons with a broad interest
in tropical Africa, just as the case studies may be of interest to students
of particular countries.

Geographical Distribution of
the Population of Tropical Africa

To analyze or even to record in detail the territorial distribution of the
population of tropical Africa was not one of the principal purposes of

the research reported in this book. It seemed nevertheless worthwhile to construct maps showing the average density of the rural population and the distribution of the urban population to enhance the meaning and value of the map showing estimated fertility. Accordingly, Figures 4.1 and 4.2 were prepared, on the basis of data summarized in Table 4.1. It can be seen from this table that the population figures do not all pertain to the same date, but rather in each area to the date of a recent census or survey providing figures with the requisite geographical detail —dates ranging from 1952-53 for Nigeria to 1963 for Gambia and Sierra Leone. Countries that have not been covered by a census or extensive demographic survey are left blank (Ethiopia, French Somaliland, and Somalia). The differences in the dates when population counts were

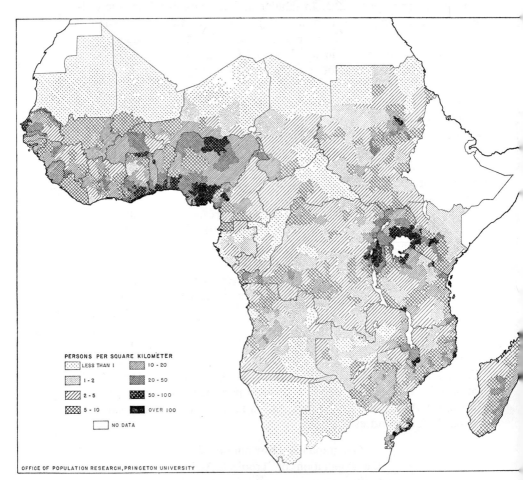

PERSONS PER SQUARE KILOMETER

LESS THAN 1   10 - 20

1 - 2   20 - 50

2 - 5   50 - 100

5 - 10   OVER 100

NO DATA

OFFICE OF POPULATION RESEARCH, PRINCETON UNIVERSITY

4.1. The density of indigenous population of tropical Africa by administrative subdivisions, according to recent censuses and surveys and exclusive of cities of 20,000 and more.

made has a negligible effect on the visual impression conveyed by the
population maps because of the broad range of densities included in
each density code. Since the ratio of the maximum to the minimum
density assigned the same code is 2 or 2.5 to 1, population differences
of 10 to 20 percent caused by differences in date of enumeration would
only rarely affect the code assigned. A population 20 percent smaller
in the same area would have about seven chances in ten of having the
same density code, assuming an even distribution of densities in each
interval. A more serious problem is the accuracy of the censuses or surveys, which may have been undercounts or overcounts. Unfortunately,
the largest national population in tropical Africa (that of Nigeria) has
been enumerated in censuses (1952-53 and 1963) that are obviously inconsistent, since they imply a wholly implausible average annual rate of

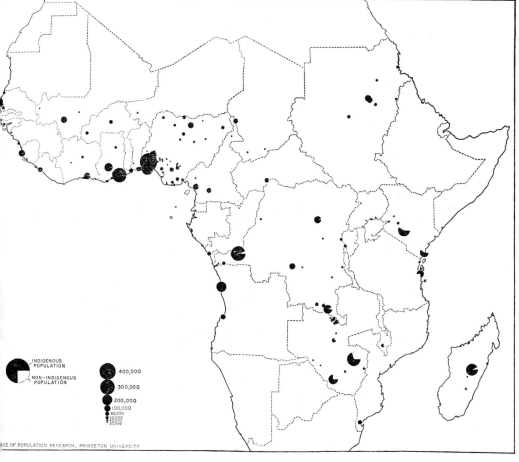

4.2. The population of tropical African cities of 20,000 and
more according to recent censuses and surveys.

Table 4.1. Population, area, and density of countries in tropical Africa according to censuses or surveys since 1950 (Data are for the same dates and from the same sources as in Figure 4.1)

Region	Country	Date of Census or survey	Population (thousands)	Area (thousands of km²)	Density (persons per km²)	Proportion of population in subdivisions with less than 2 per km²	Proportion of population in subdivisions with more than 50 per km² (including population resident in cities of 20,000 and more)
Northeast	Sudan	1955-56	10,263	2,506	4.1	7.9	8.7
West	Dahomey	1961	2,106	113	18.6	0	51.7
	Gambia	1963	315	10[2]	31.5	0	8.9
	Ghana	1960	6,727[1]	239	28.1	0	51.0
	Guinea	1954-55	2,436	246	9.9	0	1.7
	Ivory Coast	1955-60	2,885[1]	322	9.0	15.2	6.4
	Liberia	1962	1,016[1]	111	9.2	0	8.0
	Mali	1960-61	4,100[1]	1,202	3.4	12.4	0
	Mauritania	1957-58	640[1]	1,086	0.6	88.7	0
	Niger[3]	1959-60	2,888	1,267	2.3	10.6	1.0
	Nigeria[3]	1952-53	31,156	924	33.7	0	26.6
	Portuguese Guinea	1960	544[1]	36	15.1	0	10.6
	Senegal	1960-61	3,048	196	15.6	0	20.0
	Sierra Leone	1963	2,180	72	30.3	0	5.9
	Togo	1958-60	1,440	57	25.3	0	37.9
	Upper Volta	1960-61	4,393[1]	274	16.0	0	2.4
Central	Angola	1960	4,841	1,247	3.9	17.2	6.4
	Cameroon[4]	1960	4,100	475	8.6	5.2	17.3
	Central African Rep.	1959	1,227	617	2.0	5.4	6.5
	Chad	1958-60	2,693	1,284	2.1	4.2	3.8
	Congo (Brazzaville)	1960-61	834	342	2.4	11.1	24.4
	Congo, Democratic Rep. of	1955-57	12,777	2,345	5.4	6.1	8.1

[154]

Table 4.1 (continued)

Region	Country	Date of census or survey	Population (thousands)	Area (thousands of km²)	Density (persons per km²)	Proportion of population in subdivisions with less than 2 per km²	Proportion of population in subdivisions with more than 50 per km² (including population resident in cities of 20,000 and more)
Central (cont'd)							
	Equatorial Guinea						
	Fernando Po	1960	63	2.0	31.5	0	0
	Rio Muni	1960	183	26	7.0	0	14.7
	Gabon	1960-61	448	267	1.7	53.9	11.1
	Madagascar	1961	5,578	596[2]	9.4	.1.7	6.9
	Malawi	1956	2,570	962[2]	26.8	0	17.7
	Mozambique	1960	6,593[1]	778[2]	8.5	2.1	7.9
	Rhodesia	1962	3,618	389	9.3	1.0	12.5
	Zambia	1956	2,100	746	2.8	23.9	16.2
East	Burundi	1952-57	2,215	28	79.1	0	88.6
	Kenya	1962	8,366	583	14.3	5.5	58.7
	Rwanda	1952-57	2,634	26	101.3	0	91.7
	Tanzania						
	Tanganyika	1957	8,665	884[2]	9.8	2.4	15.2
	Zanzibar	1958	299	2.6[2]	115.0	0	100
	Uganda	1959	6,450	198[2]	32.6	0	49.8
South	Bechuanaland	1956	321[1]	575	0.56	100	0
	South West Africa	1960	428	824	0.52	34.6	3.3

[1]Total population rather than indigenous only.

[2]Excluding inland or open water.

[3]Including the provinces, Bamenda and Cameroons, which, effective 1 October 1961 joined the Republic of Cameroon.

[4]East Cameroon, formerly the French Cameroons, established 1 January 1960 as the Republic of Cameroon.

increase of nearly 6 percent, without substantial immigration. The density map is based on the 1952-53 census, since it provides the only available data with geographical detail. No detailed tabulations, geographical or otherwise, of the 1963 census have been released. There is a consensus among African demographers, expressed at conferences and in private correspondence, to the effect that the 1963 census was an overcount. There is also a general belief that the earlier census was incomplete. It is possible that the 1960 population of Nigeria (1960 is about the median date of censuses and surveys upon which the density map is based) was 50 or 60 percent larger than the 31 million recorded in 1952-53. If so, some (but by no means all) of the Nigerian provinces should have been one category higher in density than shown in Figure 4.1. Correspondingly, the Nigerian urban populations in Figure 4.2 would be larger, and possibly additional urban centers would appear. However, the overall visual impression would be only slightly altered. In the density map as drawn, the southernmost Nigerian provinces are seen as near the eastern end of a coastal area in West Africa of very high density that extends through several countries, and the northern part of the country appears as a more isolated pocket of only slightly less dense population. Higher population figures would in all probability simply accentuate these impressions.

These maps and figures are intended—to repeat—as a backdrop for the main aim of this chapter: a summary description of vital rates in those parts of tropical Africa for which we have made estimates.

Estimates of Birth Rates, Death Rates, Total Fertility, Child Survival, and Infant Mortality

Table 4.2 gives estimated values of certain measures of fertility and mortality for selected sub-national populations of tropical Africa. The first part of the table presents figures taken from the case studies contained in Chapters 6-10, and the second part gives estimates that were obtained by applying methods—generally those described in Chapter 3—similar to the techniques of estimation used in the case studies, but with a less exhaustive scrutiny of the survey or census than in these studies. These more cursory estimates are described in the appendix to this chapter. Figure 4.3 is a map showing in visual form the total fertility data of Table 4.2.[1]

The assembly of these estimates in a table and a map has the almost inevitable effect of betraying the cautionary warnings given by each author of the case studies, and also of lending an unwarranted appearance of certainty to the estimates based on less detailed analysis. The reader is therefore urged to use any estimate in part A of Table 4.2 only

[1] Figure 4.4 is a map showing the names of the areas for which fertility data are shown in Figure 4.3.

Table 4.2. Summary results of estimated fertility and mortality in tropical Africa

Part A: Estimates taken from case studies (Chapters 6-10)

Area	Year of Census or survey	Population (thousands)[1]	Births per thousand population	Deaths per thousand population	Total fertility	Proportion surviving to age 2 (l_2)	Infant Deaths per thousand live births
WEST AFRICA							
Dahomey	1961						
North		1,900	49	33	6.4	.719	206
South		600	47	32	6.0	.752	173
		1,300	50	33	6.6	.705	221
Guinea	1954-55	2,570	46	37	5.8	.688	223
Forest		760	45	42	5.6	.647	254
Fouta Djallon		970	47	34	5.9	.711	207
Maritime		500	44	31	5.7	.698	227
Upper Guinea		340	50	42	6.2	.694	203
Ivory Coast							
1st Agricultural Sector	1957-58	325	55	29	7.4	.751	176
Mali							
Mopti	1957-58	200	51	38	7.0	.574	354
Nigeria	1952-53	31,156					
Eastern Region	1953	7,968					
Bamenda		429	49	–	6.3	–	–
Cameroons		324	41	–	5.3	–	–
Calabar		1,540	57	–	7.5	–	–
Ogoja		1,082	50	–	6.5	–	–
Onitsha		1,768	51	–	6.7	–	–
Owerri		2,078	55	–	7.3	–	–
Rivers		747	54	–	7.1	–	–
Northern Region	1952	16,836					
Adamawa		1,181	50	–	6.5	–	–
Bauchi		1,424	46	–	5.9	–	–
Benue		1,468	46	–	5.9	–	–
Bornu		1,596	43	–	5.5	–	–
Ilorin		531	50	–	6.5	–	–

Table 4.2. Part A (continued)

	Year						
West Africa (cont'd)							
Nigeria (cont'd)							
Northern Region (cont'd)	1952						
Kabba		664	46	--	5.9	--	--
Kano		3,396	46	--	5.9	--	--
Katsina		1,483	43	--	5.5	--	--
Niger		716	44	--	5.7	--	--
Plateau		891	49	--	6.3	--	--
Sokoto		2,680	50	--	6.5	--	--
Zaria		805	50	--	6.5	--	--
Western Region	1952	6,352					
Abeokuta		630	50	--	6.5	--	--
Benin		901	55	--	7.3	--	--
Colony		505	44	--	5.7	--	--
Delta		591	49	--	6.3	--	--
Ibadan		1,650	66	--	9.1	--	--
Ijebu		348	47	--	6.1	--	--
Ondo		945	57	--	7.5	--	--
Oyo		783	58	--	7.7	--	--
Portugese Guinea	1950	544	37	31	4.8	.739	211
Senegal Valley							
Fouta Toro	1957	267	47	28	6.4	.717	224
Upper Volta	1960-61	4,300	49	36	6.5	.660	263
Mossi People		2,000	49	38	6.7	.629	292
Moslem People		700	47	32	6.1	.695	238
CENTRAL AFRICA							
Angola [2]	1940 and 1950	4,010	45	38	5.8	.652	273
Benguela		1,187	53	46	6.8	.654	275
Bie		702	39	41	5.0	.710	228
Huila		529	42	31	5.4	.787	166
Luanda		889	50	42	6.4	.591	329
Malange		703	44	41	5.6	.652	276
Central African Republic							
Central Oubangui	1959	400	34	33	4.3	.730	192

Table 4.2, Part A (continued)

Central Africa (cont'd)						
Democratic Republic	1955-57					
of the Cango		12,777	45	26	5.9	.792	173
Equateur		1,756	39	23	5.0	.801	168
Kasai		2,121	45	30	5.9	.744	204
Katanga		1,501	52	22	8.2	.841	146
Kivu		2,013	53	30	7.1	.774	197
Leopoldville		3,050	49	25	6.7	.800	164
Orientale		2,336	32	24	4.0	.833	157
Cameroon, North	1960	1,120	36	31	4.7	.705	223
Hill Pagans		290	41	37	5.3	.673	240
Moslems		330	27	27	3.6	.754	186
Plains Pagans		460	42	32	5.3	.688	240
NORTHEAST AFRICA						
Sudan	1955-56	10,263	49	21	6.3	-	-
Arabs		3,990	47	-	6.1	-	-
Beja People		646	44	-	5.7	-	-
Central Southerners		1,983	58	-	8.3	-	-
Eastern Southerners		549	60	-	7.9	-	-
Nuba People		573	44	-	5.7	-	-
Nubiyin People		330	47	-	6.1	-	-
Western Southerners		482	33	-	4.1	-	-
Westerners		1,359	46	-	5.9	-	-
EAST AFRICA						
Mozambique	1950	5,647	42	31	5.4	.729	212
Central		2,185	52	38	6.7	.679	254
North		1,400	39	32	5.0	.786	167
South		2,062	36	30	4.6	.743	201

Table 4.2 (continued)

Part B: Estimates based on analysis described in Appendix to Chapter 4

Area	Year of Census or survey	Population (thousands)[1]	Births per thousand population	Deaths per thousand population	Total fertility	Proportion surviving to age 2 (l_2)	Infant deaths per thousand live births
WEST AFRICA							
Gambia	1963	315	40	-	5.2	-	-
Ghana	1960	6,727	50	-	6.5	-	-
North		1,289	44	-	5.6	-	-
South		5,438	50	-	6.6	-	-
Liberia	1962	1,016	40		5.1	-	-
Niger	1960	2,611	50	-	6.8	.731	212
Stratum 1		150	28	-	3.7	.784	169
Stratum 2		529	49	-	6.3	.686	248
Stratum 3		389	54	-	7.4	.753	193
Stratum 4		408	50	-	7.1	.778	174
Stratum 5		351	52	-	7.7	.791	163
Stratum 6		785	52	-	7.1	.701	236
Senegal	1960-61	3,048	49	-	6.3	-	-
Togo	1961	1,537	56	-	7.3	-	-
CENTRAL AFRICA							
Gabon	1960-61	448	31	-	3.5	-	-
Rhodesia	1962	3,617	53	-	7.0	-	-
Zambia	1963	3,496	50	-	6.6	-	-

EAST AFRICA

Burundi	1952-57	2,215	46	22	6.4		↓
Kenya	1962	8,366	48	18	6.8	.831	132
Central		1,324	46	13	6.6	.878	98
Coast		741	40	20	5.4	.807	151
Eastern		1,558	47	15	6.8	.860	111
Nyanza		1,634	55	26	7.9	.754	193
Rift Valley		1,750	45	12	6.5	.889	89
Western		1,014	55	23	8.1	.782	170
Rwanda	1952-57	2,634	50	23	7.0	-	-
Tanzania	1957	8,665	46	26	6.4	-	-
Central		879	47	25	6.6	-	-
Eastern		1,040	43	27	5.7	-	-
Lake		2,229	48	31	6.9	-	-
Northern		759	48	17	6.9	-	-
Southern		1,008	42	23	5.5	-	-
Southern Highlands		1,024	52	25	7.4	-	-
Tanga		671	45	23	6.2	-	-
Western		1,053	44	27	5.9	-	-
Uganda	1959	6,450	44	22	6.0	-	-
Buganda (Rural)		1,834	38	18	5.2	-	-
Eastern		1,873	42	24	5.7	-	-
Northern		1,245	51	22	7.3	-	-
Western		1,498	46	22	6.4	-	-

[1]
The figures in this column are the approximate number of persons covered by the estimates in subsequent columns. Often the survey obtained data on fertility and mortality of the rural population only, or excluded certain defined segments of the total population. Hence these figures may be less than totals provided in the census or survey cited. When data are taken from a sample survey, the figures are the estimated number in the sample frame, not in the sample itself.

[2]Population in 1950, infant and child mortality from data in the 1940 census.

after reading Chapter 3 and the relevant case study, and to use estimates in part B only after considering Chapter 3 and the relevant parts of the appendix to this chapter. In addition, some general comments on the quality of the estimates may be helpful. First, it should be noted that estimates summarized from the detailed case studies (part A of Table 4.2) are not necessarily more reliable than those constructed after a less detailed examination of the basic data (part B). The case studies provide a better basis for judging reliability rather than necessarily more reliable estimates. Thus the fertility and mortality estimates for Kenya are probably less subject to error than those for Nigeria, the Sudan, or the Portuguese territories. *It cannot be emphasized too strongly that the estimates are very uneven in quality.*

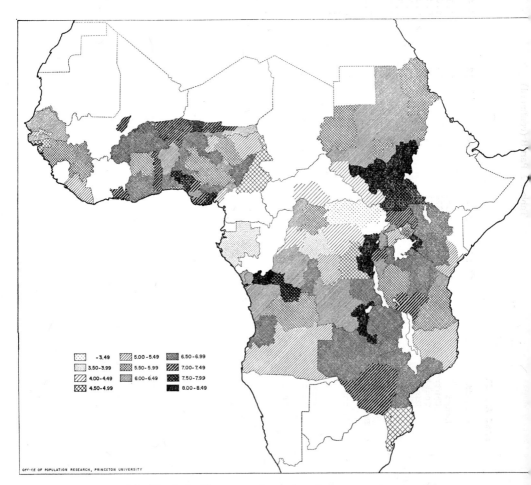

4.3. Total fertility rates for selected areas or peoples of tropical Africa.

In general the methods of estimation are more reliable in determining the approximate level of the birth rate than of the death rate. In fact the most we can claim for estimated mortality is that the figures given for the proportion surviving to age 2 in Table 4.2 can be accepted as a rather firm indication of the upper limit of survival to age 2 in the three to five years preceding the date of the census or survey. If there is a tendency for women to omit a higher proportion of dead children than surviving children in reporting those ever born (and this possibility seems quite plausible, especially in Africa), childhood mortality would tend always to be somewhat higher than indicated by these figures. Estimates of adult mortality and of the overall death rate are the least trustworthy of the figures we present. It was necessary to assume that

4.4. National boundaries and subdivisions of areas and peoples of tropical Africa for which total fertility rates are shown in Fig. 4.3.

[163]

the typical relationship between childhood and adult mortality rates found in other areas with good statistics prevailed in tropical Africa, or to make rough adjustments to figures (usually internally inconsistent) on deaths in the pre-survey year, or to estimate the crude death rate by subtracting an often untrustworthy estimate of the rate of natural increase from a merely approximate figure for the birth rate.

In any event, estimates of mortality, even when of acceptable quality, can be considered as characteristic only of the period to which the data are pertinent—usually the four- or five-year interval preceding the census or survey. This reservation must be kept clearly in mind when comparing mortality levels in different areas. The past two decades constitute a period of extremely rapid declines in mortality in many of the less developed countries of the world as low-cost but effective techniques of medicine and public health have been exported to these areas from the industrialized countries, often with the assistance of the World Health Organization or UNICEF. Some of the areas of tropical Africa have no doubt shared in this rapid change in mortality rate, which in other parts of the world has reached or exceeded changes in expectation of life at birth of one year each calendar year. Thus the difference between the estimated death rate of 26 per 1,000 in Tanzania and of 18 per 1,000 in Kenya is of dubious validity because of the differences in the basis of estimation; but even if the difference in mortality is accepted as valid, a large part could be caused by the five-year interval between the censuses from which the data were taken.

Although fertility is usually more amenable to estimation from survey or census data than mortality, and is less subject to recent fluctuation in most African populations, variations in the extent and quality of available information cause variations in the probable accuracy of fertility estimates. The most trustworthy estimates are those for the Congo, where in 29 districts there was very strong agreement between birth rates derived from the age distribution on the one hand and, on the other, from survey responses on births during the preceding year, after adjustment for the evident omission in some districts of children who had died. Moreover, birth rates derived from registered births also correlated very highly with the other estimates of fertility, as did (in a negative sense) the proportion childless among women in the central ages of childbearing.

The estimates of fertility in the territories of French expression analyzed by Brass (Chapter 7) are based on the number of births reported for the year before the survey, after adjustment to reconcile these birth data with the average parity given by younger women. There is reason to believe (see Chapter 3) that these adjustments can be distorted by misreporting. It is therefore of interest to compare these estimates with estimates that have a wholly independent basis: estimates derived from model stable populations selected to match the child survival (l_2) and the recorded proportion under age 15 of the population in question. The comparison of birth rates in the territories of French expression estimated on these two bases is shown in Figure 4.5. The agreement is far from perfect, although the existence of a high correlation is obvious. In

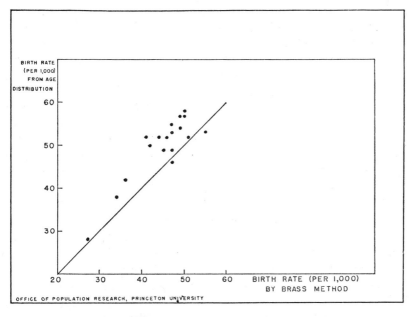

OFFICE OF POPULATION RESEARCH, PRINCETON UNIVERSITY

4.5. A comparison of birth rates (per thousand) derived by stable population methods from reported age distributions with those derived by the Brass method, for selected African populations.

these areas (but not in Uganda, Kenya, or the Congo, where a similar comparison is possible) the Brass method consistently tends to produce lower estimates (only two exceptions in 16 areas) of fertility than is obtained from stable populations with the given proportion under age 15. The broad distinction between high and low fertility areas is consistent in the two forms of estimation, but estimates based on model stable populations would often fall in the next higher fertility category on the map (Figure 4.3).[2]

[2] The alternative estimates of the birth rate and total fertility derived by the selection of a model stable population from the proportion under 15 (both sexes) and l_2 are as follows:

Area	b	T.F.	Area	b	T.F.
Dahomey	57	7.7	Guinea	52	6.8
North	53	7.3	Forest	49	6.2
South	—	—	(continued on page 166)		

The recency of the 1962 census of Kenya and the lack to date of published material on the sample survey that accompanied the census have prevented the detailed critical scrutiny and analysis that would be desirable; yet there is enough internal consistency in the retrospective data and the age distribution available to us in a preliminary unpublished version to provide substantial confidence in the levels of estimated fertility. The estimates for Tanzania are less reliable, being derived from age distributions that had been subjected to smoothing. The least reliable estimates are for Nigeria, the Portuguese territories, Ghana, Senegal, Gabon, Gambia, Liberia, Togo, Rhodesia, Zambia, and the Sudan.

Usually the reader can trust the relative levels of fertility within the sub-units of a nation or territory more than relative figures derived from two different data systems. On the other hand, the geographical pattern of fertility differences revealed in Figure 4.3 bolsters our belief that estimates of fertility derived from different data systems are for the most part approximately consistent. The source of this reassurance is a notable tendency for unusually high or low fertility to extend across international boundaries, notwithstanding the difference in the form of the data systems, and often in methods of estimation, in the two countries.

The most striking feature of the birth rates and total fertility figures given in Table 4.2 is the very large range, with birth rates varying from about 30 to about 60 per thousand and total fertility—the number of children that would be born during the lifetime of each woman experiencing the given fertility rates—ranging from about 3.5 to over 8.[3] A ridge of high fertility in East Africa extends from the southeastern Sudan down through parts of Uganda and Kenya, through Rwanda and Burundi and parts of Tanzania, and through the southern and eastern provinces of the Congo into Zambia, Southern Rhodesia, and the southern province of Mozambique. The provinces in this strip show a total fertility of 6.5 or higher. Somewhat lower fertility is found along the East African coast from the coastal province of Kenya to the northern part of Mozambique. The lowest fertility in tropical Africa is in a region extending, apparently, from the west coast in Gabon through north central and northwestern provinces of the Congo into the southwestern

Area	b	T.F.	Area	b	T.F.
Fouta Djallon	55	7.7	Mossi	58	7.8
Maritime	52	6.7	Western	46	5.9
Upper Guinea	57	7.7	CAR, Centre-		
Ivory Coast, 1st Agr.	53	7.1	Oubangui	38	4.8
Mali (Mopti)	52	6.8	Cameroon, North	42	5.4
Senegal V.			Hill Pagans	52	6.9
Fouta Toro	49	6.5	Moslems	28	3.7
Upper Volta	54	7.2	Plain Pagans	50	6.4

[3] As is apparent in Chapter 10, the highest fertility recorded in Table 4.2—for the province of Ibadan in Nigeria—is based (as are all Nigerian figures) on very uncertain evidence.

region of the Sudan. Unfortunately, we were not able to construct acceptable estimates for the Congo (Brazzaville), for the southern part of Cameroon, or for any but a small portion of the Central African Republic to confirm the continuity of this low fertility strip, but it is noteworthy that low fertility persists into at least some segments of the population in the northern part of Cameroon. The high fertility ridge mentioned earlier appears to have a spur extending to the coast of West Africa through the southern provinces of the Congo and the northern provinces of Angola. Another strip of exceptionally high fertility is found along the coast in West Africa from coastal Nigeria to the Ivory Coast, with a branch extending up through the western part of Nigeria into parts of Niger and Upper Volta.

As mentioned earlier, estimates of mortality in tropical Africa are less well founded and more dependent on the date of the census or survey than fertility estimates. The crude death rate probably ranges from no more than 15 per thousand in some provinces to more than 40 per thousand; infant mortality rates from less than 100 per thousand to over 300; and expectation of life at birth from less than 30 years to over 45. A fair generalization is that mortality in tropical Africa is among the highest in the world, although some provinces have already secured the advantages available in modern health techniques.

The variations in fertility recorded in Table 4.2 and Figure 4.3 should not be allowed to convey a false impression that the average fertility of tropical Africa is anything other than very high. The birth rate for all of the populations analyzed combined is about 49 per thousand, and average total fertility for tropical Africa is probably about 6½ children. Only Latin America from Mexico to Peru and Brazil has fertility approximately this high. These extremely high fertility rates are combined with mortality that also is among the highest in the world. The recent experience of other developing areas suggests that tropical Africa is in the early phase of rapidly accelerating population growth. In some areas, for example Kenya and the Sudan, the rate of natural increase has apparently already reached about 3 percent per year. In other words, tropical Africa is now beginning to encounter the whole range of new problems that other developing countries know very well—the barriers to social and economic progress that come with extremely rapid population increase.

NOTES ON AREAS FOR WHICH ESTIMATES
WERE MADE, BUT NOT SUBJECT TO A DETAILED STUDY

BY ANSLEY J. COALE AND
ETIENNE VAN DE WALLE

Estimates were made for 12 areas without as extensive study and analysis as was devoted to each of the case studies. In some instances there were not enough valid data to warrant more detailed analysis, and in others interesting information that might warrant such analysis arrived after the staff of the project had disbanded. This appendix contains brief notes on the data used and methods of analysis applied in making estimates for these populations.

RWANDA AND BURUNDI

The Data

In the area which was then Ruanda-Urundi, an uninterrupted series of demographic inquiries was taken yearly in the same sample between 1952 and 1957. This uncommon repetition of the same procedures at regular intervals provided a precise time reference for the asking of questions on vital events. From 1953 on, the interviewers asked about births "since the last inquiry" instead of the usual, more abstract "since 12 months." Similarly, the children recorded as aged less than one year were those born between two interviews. It is better to neglect the vital rates derived from the 1952 inquiry, since that feature was not present then.

It appears that the crude death rate was constantly underestimated; in Rwanda it declined from 19 per thousand in 1953 to 14 in 1957, and in Burundi from 25 in 1953 to 17 in 1957. Part of the decline appears to be genuine;[1] but the levels are suspiciously low, perhaps the result of a reluctance to declare deaths. In that case, very young children may be omitted most, and their omission would affect the birth rate as well. The latter is nevertheless high, and fluctuates moderately from year to year without precise trend. The average crude birth rate during the period 1953 to 1957 is 50 per thousand in Rwanda, and 46 per thousand in Burundi.

---

[1] There is some evidence of a decline in the fifties. According to official statistics given in the Annual Reports, the percentage of cases of infectious and parasitic disease decreases steadily from 38.5 percent of all diseases treated in hospitals in 1951, to 18.0 percent in 1960. On this proportion as an index of mortality, see J. Bourgeois-Pichat and Chia-Lin Pan, "Trends and determinants of mortality in underdeveloped areas," in Milbank Memorial Fund, *Trends and Differentials in Mortality*, 1955, p. 12.

The women were reported in broad age classes: under age 1, under puberty, from puberty to menopause, and over menopause. It is remarkable that the proportion in each class varies very little from year to year. On the average (period 1953 to 1957), the proportion of females aged under one year is 4.4 percent in Rwanda, and 4.0 percent in Burundi. The proportion under puberty is 45.7 percent in Rwanda, 41.9 in Burundi. Those aged under one year were born since the preceding inquiry. No precise age can be assigned to puberty or menopause; we may presume perhaps that puberty occurs on the average at the same age in Rwanda and Burundi, and that this age is close to 15 years, as in other populations.

At two dates, in the 1952 and the 1956 inquiries, a question was asked concerning the total number of children ever born to the women past menopause. The answers were remarkably consistent at the two dates, even for smaller political divisions. The average for the two inquiries together is 6.9 in Rwanda, and 6.4 in Burundi.

Analysis

The information on fertility derived from these three independent sources, i.e., the reported births of the years, the age distribution, and the answers of old women, are not incompatible. We require some information on either the mortality or the rate of increase to show this by reference to a stable population. But estimates of the rate of natural increase are no more trustworthy than those of the death rate. However, the growth of the sample population gives some valuable information. This growth is rather erratic from year to year and is much faster for males than for females. There may have been some migration and very likely, the disappearance of an initial distrust as to the interviewers' motives.[2] If so, the growth rate of the female sample population would be more reliable. Between 1952 and 1957, it reaches on the average 2.7 percent per year in Rwanda, and 2.4 percent in Burundi.

The consistency of this information on fertility and growth can now be tested in the framework of the stable North Model, Females.[3] The recorded birth rate (both sexes) may have been somewhat underestimated by the omission of early deaths, so we do not make any adjustment in order to estimate a female birth rate, which would normally be lower. The sample growth rate is used to approximate the quasi-stable

[2] The male age distribution was determined by questions on the payment of a poll tax. Perhaps not by chance, the highest growth occurs at the ages when the tax is not yet due (4.8 percent per year in Rwanda, 6.2 percent in Burundi, between 1954 and 1957) and at post-taxpaying ages (5.1 percent and 9.2 percent respectively). The breakdown by age of the sample population is available only in 1954 and 1957.

[3] Ansley J. Coale and Paul Demeny, *Regional Model Life Tables and Stable Populations*, Princeton University Press, 1966.

population's intrinsic rate of increase. Together, the two parameters give in Rwanda the following:

Total fertility[4]: 7.0 (as against 6.9 children ever born reported by old women);

Proportion aged under one year: 4.4 percent (as against 4.4 percent girls recorded under age 1);

Proportion under 15 years: 45.8 percent (as against 45.7 percent recorded under puberty).

And for Burundi:

Total fertility: 6.4 (as against 6.4);

Proportion under 1 year: 4.1 percent (as against 4.0);

Proportion under 15 years: 43.5 percent (as against 41.9).

Taking into consideration the approximations involved, the closeness of the fit is rather unbelievable in Rwanda; in Burundi, the only discrepancy is between the proportions under 15 years and puberty.

With the necessary caveat, one may thus accept the recorded birth rate. By subtraction of the sample growth rate, a crude death rate of 23 per thousand is obtained for Rwanda, and of 22 per thousand for Burundi. According to the same set of computations based on the quasi-stable population, the expectation of life at birth for females would be close to, and perhaps a little above, 40 years in both countries.

Sources

V. Neesen, "Quelques données démographiques sur la population du Ruanda-Urundi," *Zaire*, Dec. 1953, No. 10, pp. 1011ff.

Rapports soumis par le Gouvernement belge à l'Assemblée générale des Nations-Unies au sujet de l'Administration du Ruanda-Urundi, Brussels, 1952-1957, *passim*.

KENYA

The Data

A complete census of the population of Kenya was taken in 1962, accompanied by a sample survey covering 10 percent of the population. Chronological age was not asked in the census, but in the sample survey there were questions not only on age but on children ever born and children surviving (both tabulated by age of women) and on births and deaths during the preceding year. The results of the 1962 sample survey had not been published when the estimates for Kenya were prepared,

---

[4] Approximated by taking in the models twice the gross reproduction rate when the mean age of childbearing is 29 years. The average age at marriage (and therefore the mean age of childbearing) of Rwanda and Burundi is known to be rather late by African standards.

but through the kindness of the Government of Kenya, especially Mr. A. T. Brough, the Chief Statistician, and Mr. John Blacker, formerly the Chief Demographer, preliminary tabulations were made available to the Office of Population Research.

Method of Estimation

The comparison of cumulative fertility (based on births reported for the preceding year) and average parity gives a series of P/F ratios for almost every province that declines steeply and steadily with age. One can hardly attribute such a pattern to progressive omission of children ever born beginning with age 20 or 25, since substantial omission below age 30 is not found in other populations. Moreover, if the P/F ratios for women 20-25 are used as adjustment factors for the reported fertility rates, the result is estimated total fertility 8.4 or higher in every province but one, estimates that are inconsistent with recorded child survival rates and age distributions. It was judged that the P/F ratios were strongly affected by age misreporting of women in and adjacent to the childbearing span, and that the mechanical use of the Brass method of estimating fertility was not feasible. Instead, it was decided to estimate fertility on the basis of child survival (proportions surviving among children ever born to women in different age groups) and the age distribution of the population. Because of the strong presumption that mortality had declined in the years before 1962, the estimation of fertility from an early segment of the cumulated age distribution is preferable. The method of calculation was to derive values of l_2 from reported survival of children ever born to women 20-24, and then to find a model stable population (West female) with the given value of l_2, and the same proportion under age 15 as recorded for the given population (both sexes). Calculations were based on the proportion under 15 for males and females combined because in the Kenya survey as well as in other African data there is an evident tendency for overstatement of age of some girls 10-14, causing an understated proportion below 15 in the female population. On the other hand, the transfer of males across the age boundary 15 appears often to overstate the proportion below the boundary. In every region of Kenya, and indeed in almost every census of tropical Africa (see Tables 2.5 and 2.6, Chapter 2) the proportion under 15 is higher among males than females. The bias in one sex should offset the other to some degree.

Details of the Calculations

Child mortality. Data for estimation of l_1, l_2, l_3, and l_5 were available for the provinces shown in Table 4.A.1.

The level of mortality from province to province is remarkably consistent: the only change in ranking of the provinces is a shift in the or-

Table 4.A.1

			Province			
Age	Coast	Eastern	Central	Rift Valley	Western	Nyanza
1	.852	.883	.901	.905	.826	.793
2	.807	.860	.878	.889	.782	.754
3	.787	.836	.848	.863	.750	.714
5	.771	.813	.805	.844	.708	.670

der of l_5 as compared to l_1 through l_3, with Central and Eastern provinces interchanged. (The ranking at age 5 is maintained for l_{10}, l_{15}, l_{20}, and l_{25}, not shown in the table.)

The proportion estimated as surviving in each province generally falls more rapidly than in any of the model life tables from age 2 to 5, a surprising result in view of the expectation that older women would tend to omit more of the children who had died. On the other hand, this pattern would be consistent with a marked drop in infant and child mortality in recent years, which would imply that the older children had experienced higher death rates. The estimated level of mortality is generally low for Africa, and may be an understatement because, for example, of failure to report children who died very soon after birth. The values of l_2 seem usable maximum estimates.

Fertility data. The sample survey included questions on children ever born and on births in the year before the census. Under conditions of constant fertility, the sum of the reported age-specific fertility rates (TF) and the average number of children ever born to women 45-49 (P_7) should be about the same. The actual figures for the six provinces are shown in Table 4.A.2.

TABLE 4.A.2

			Province			
	Coast	Eastern	Central	Rift Valley	Western	Nyanza
Reported average parity, women 45-49	4.5	4.9	5.5	4.9	7.3	7.2
Sum of age-specific fertility	3.9	5.0	6.3	5.5	4.4	5.2

The two forms of data are each subject to the deficiencies found in other African surveys. For example, average parity is lower at 50-54 than at 45-49, and the reported fertility bears no consistent relation to parity. However, the steeply declining values of P/F (reported parity divided by average value of cumulative fertility for the same age interval) did not lend support to the automatic use of P_2/F_2 or P_3/F_3 as an adjustment factor to compensate for "reference-period error." Indeed, the use of P_2/F_2 leads to estimates of total fertility ranging from 8.4 to 8.9 for five of the six provinces—a level that seems implausible although far from physiologically impossible.

Fertility estimated from l_2 and the proportion under age 15. Proportions under age 15 in the six provinces were as shown in Table 4.A.3.

TABLE 4.A.3

Provinces

Coast	Eastern	Central	Rift Valley	Western	Nyanza
.396	.467	.466	.464	.491	.479

Model stable populations were found in the West family with these proportions under 15 and values of l_2 estimated from the proportion dead among children ever born to women 20-24. The tabulated value of the gross reproduction rate (mean age of fertility schedule 29 years) was multiplied by 2.03 to obtain estimates of total fertility. The mean age of reported fertility was above 29 in all provinces, and above 30 in four of the six, but it appeared that age misreporting inflated the rates at older ages. Had a higher mean age been used, the estimates of total fertility would have been slightly increased. The use of another family of model stable populations (North would have been a natural choice) would have added no more than 0.1 to 0.2 to the estimates of total fertility.

Brass-type adjustments for reference-period error in reported age-specific fertility rates. The fertility estimated from the age composition of the population and child mortality is higher than that estimated from reported births last year in every province, which suggests that women were using too short a reference period (less than a year) in reporting births. Because of the steady fall in the P/F ratios with age, it is possible to find an age (about age 30) where P/F gives an adjustment that for Kenya as a whole increases fertility to a level consistent with estimates based on age composition. Specifically, an adjustment based on ½ $(P_3/F_3 + P_4/F_4)$ produces the estimates shown on Table 4.A.4 as compared with those derived from l_2 and the proportion under 15.

Table 4.A.4

	Coast	Eastern	Central	Rift Valley	Western	Nyanza	Kenya
Total fertility from l_2 and proportion under 15	5.4	6.8	6.6	6.5	8.1	7.9	6.8
Total fertility from age-specific fertility rates multiplied by ½ $(P_3/F_3 + P_4/F_4)$	5.4	6.8	7.3	6.8	7.6	8.0	6.8

Source

Unpublished data from the 1962 Sample Census, hand copied in Nairobi through the courtesy of the Chief Statistician.

TANGANYIKA

The Data

A population census was conducted in Tanganyika (now part of Tanzania) in August 1957. It was followed by a sample survey based on a stratified, two-stage cluster design, intended to cover 5 percent of the population, or about 430,000 persons, but actually covering about 411,-000. The information obtained in the census was minimal, including only tribe, sex, and five age categories (under 1, 1-5, 6-15, 16-45, and over 45) on a form in which there was one line for each hut rather than for each individual. In the sample, where the enumerative form provided a line for each individual, the same age categories were used, but in addition there was a space to enter actual age if known. Questions on a number of additional topics were asked, including fertility and mortality. The fertility information included number of children ever born, the number surviving, and the number of births and deaths "since the last dry season." The crude birth and death rates from responses to these questions (assuming the interval to be a year) are shown in Table 4.A.5.

Method of Estimation

Mortality in childhood. The absence of detailed age information precludes the use of the Brass method of estimating survival to ages 1, 2, 3, 5, etc. Proportions dead among children ever born are tabulated for the small minority of women for whom detailed ages were recorded

Table 4.A.5

Region

	Cen-tral	East-ern	Lake	North-ern	South-ern	Southern Highlands	Tonga	West-ern	Tan-gan-yika
Birth rate	40	32	44	49	37	56	37	42	42
Death rate	29	21	26	19	23	22	27	18	23

in the sample survey, but this minority is clearly not representative of the whole population. It was therefore necessary to make use of the proportion dead among children ever born to women in the whole age range 16-45. Brass suggests that this proportion is approximately equal to the proportion dying from birth to age 10. Therefore l_{10}/l_0 was estimated from this proportion. The resulting estimates of l_{10}/l_0 are presented in Table 4.A.6.

Table 4.A.6

Cen-tral	East-ern	Lake	North-ern	South-ern	Southern Highlands	Tonga	West-ern	Tangan-yika
.687	.654	.625	.780	.700	.692	.703	.660	.674

Selection of a model stable population and estimation of fertility. The *African Census Report* for Tanganyika published in 1963 includes graduated ogives of male and female age distributions based on a visual fit to the age distributions by broad categories in both the sample survey and the complete count of 1957. The proportion under 15 in each region from these adjusted distributions and the estimated value of l_{10} were the basis for selecting a model stable population (West, female). The estimate of total fertility was taken as equal to the gross reproduction rate ($\bar{m} = 29$ years) in his stable population multiplied by 2.03. The parameters given in Table 4.3 are characteristics of stable populations chosen in this way.

Source

Tanganyika, *African Census Report 1957*, Government Printer, Dar es Salaam, 1963. Crude birth rates, Table 54; crude death rates, Table 62; proportions surviving among children ever born to women 16-45, Table 64; proportions under 15, Table 71.

UGANDA

The Data

The 1959 Census of Uganda had much in common with the 1957 Census of Tanganyika and is analyzed here along the same lines. It presented the same combination of a complete census and a sample survey, and used a similar questionnaire, with one significant difference: in Uganda, respondents were asked to report vital events over the last year, and not "since the last dry season." The age information also is similar for three of the four provinces. In Buganda Province, however, an attempt was made to obtain ages for all persons enumerated in the sample survey.

For the four provinces, the crude birth rates obtained by relating the number of births during the last year to the sample population, are shown in Table 4.A.7.

Table 4.A.7

	Province				
	Buganda	Eastern	Northern	Western	Uganda
Birth rate (per thousand)	36	40	50	45	42

The information concerning death was considered useless and discarded by the census officials.

Method of Estimation

For the three provinces where no detailed age distribution exists, estimates of l_{10}/l_0 are obtained from the proportion dead among children ever born to women aged 16-45: Eastern, 0.678; Northern, 0.706; Western, 0.716.

The crude birth rate and total fertilities of Table 4.A.8 are derived by the method described in the case of Tanganyika.

Table 4.A.8

	Eastern	Northern	Western
Birth rate (per thousand)	42	51	46
Total fertility	5.7	7.3	6.4

The estimates of the birth rate are close to those obtained directly. The same method produces estimates of the rate of natural increase in percent, which are given in Table 4.A.9 next to the average annual intercensal growth between the 1948 and the 1959 censuses. If the possibility of migration is taken into account, the agreement is rather good.

Table 4.A.9

	Eastern	Northern	Western
Natural increase	1.8	2.9	2.4
Intercensal growth	2.0	2.6	2.3

The age distribution for Buganda Province is heavily affected by immigration, and Buganda contains an important urban population. The age distribution of rural females of the Buganda tribe is smoother, and the estimates for the Province of Buganda in Table 4.2 are based on this age distribution. A stable population with the same proportion under age 35, and the estimated value of l_{10}/l_0 (0.775) indicated a crude birth rate of 38 per thousand, and a total fertility of 5.2.

The estimates given for the whole of Uganda are weighted averages of the values found for the Provinces.

Source

Uganda Protectorate, *Uganda Census 1959 African Population*, Statistics Branch, Ministry of Economic Affairs, Nairobi, 1961.

GABON

The Data

A complete census of the population of Gabon was taken in 1960-61, accompanied (for the indigenous population only) by a sample survey of about 10 percent of the population. The census covered standard demographic characteristics such as sex, age, and marital status, and the sample inquiry included data on births, deaths, and migrations. Among the questions asked were total number of children ever born, children surviving, and births and deaths occurring during the year before the survey. Only partial results were contained in the preliminary publication upon which our calculations were based. These partial tabulations included average parity of women by age, children born last year tabulated by age, and an age-sex distribution of the population. Unfortunately, the number of surviving children was not included in the preliminary report. Regional data were incomplete, so that the only estimates made were for the whole Republic.

Method of Estimation

Because of the absence at the time the analysis was made of data on child survival, there was no adequate basis for choosing a model stable population matching the ogive of the recorded age distribution. However, assuming child mortality about the same as in the Congo, the proportion under ages 15 (both sexes) or 35 (females) would indicate a total fertility under 4.0, confirming the low fertility estimate derived from births reported for the preceding year, adjusted so that cumulative fertility to ages 20-25 matched reported average parity. The birth rate based on reported fertility is 38 per thousand; total fertility is 4.2. The P/F ratio for women 20-24 is 0.822, indicating a tendency to use too long a reference period in reporting births. The adjusted birth rate and total fertility are 31 and 3.5 respectively.

The reported average parities in Gabon increase with age of women at ages beyond the childbearing span, despite obvious underreporting that normally increases with age. This tendency suggests that the low fertility as of 1960 was the result of a period of declining birth rates.

Source

République Gabonaise, Service de Statistique, France, Ministère de la Coopération, INSEE, *Recensement et enquête démographique 1960-61, Résultats provisoires, Ensemble du Gabon.*

NIGER

The Data

In 1960 the Republic of Niger was subject to a sample survey of its population. The sample was designed to cover all of the population except the town of Niamey, enumerated in a census in 1959, and certain northern extensive but sparsely populated subdivisions inhabited primarily by nomads. The two excluded segments had estimated populations of 30,000 and 234,000 respectively; the estimated number in the zone covered was 2,612,000. The sample included about 3 percent of this 2.6 million. Data are tabulated for six "strata" into which the southern part of the country was divided. The zone included in the survey stretches along the northern border of Nigeria; stratum one (150,000 persons) encompasses the easternmost part of this border area, extending from Lake Chad about one-third the length of the Nigerian border; stratum two (529,000 persons) occupies a narrow strip along the central third of the Nigerian border; strata three (389,000 persons) and four (408,-000) constitute additional narrow segments north of stratum two; stratum five (351,000) occupies a small segment of the border territory (about 10 percent of the Nigerian border with Niger just west of strata 2, 3, and 4); stratum six (785,000 persons) is the southwestern corner of Niger, bordering Nigeria (to the south and east), Dahomey (to the south), Upper Volta (to the west) and Mali (to the north).

The survey included questions on age, sex, number of children ever born to each woman and number of these surviving, and births and deaths during the preceding 12 months.

Methods of Estimation

Mortality in childhood. The published data provide the basis for estimating $_1q_0, _2q_0, \ldots, _{35}q_0$ by the Brass technique. Selected values are shown in Table 4.A.10.

Table 4.A.10

Stratum

	1	2	3	4	5	6	Total
$_2q_0$	.216	.314	.247	.222	.209	.299	.269
$_3q_0$	.229	.317	.270	.261	.223	.289	.278
$_5q_0$	.269	.323	.330	.293	.249	.344	.313
$_{10}q_0$	.347	.388	.295	.310	.276	.363	.339

In general, the progression shows implausibly low mortality above age 2 —a defect that is much worse for estimates of mortality above age 10 based on survival reported by women over 40. However, the mortality differences indicated by the estimated proportion dying before age 2 (based on responses of women 20-24) are consistently supported by the estimated proportions dying before age 3—the ranking of the strata is the same by either of these measures. In Table 4.3 the values of $_2q_0$ were accepted as valid.

Fertility. Total fertility can be obtained directly from responses about births during the year before the survey (Table 4.A.11).

Table 4.A.11

Stratum

1	2	3	4	5	6	Total
3.7	7.0	8.2	6.7	8.4	7.0	7.1

Another direct indication of total fertility is the average number of children ever born reported by women 45-49 (Table 4.A.12).

Table 4.A.12

Stratum

1	2	3	4	5	6	Total
4.1	5.4	6.1	6.1	5.5	6.3	5.8

But reported numbers of births in the preceding year are not reliable because of a possible misperception of the reference period, and parity is subject to understatement, especially by older women. The Brass method of estimation adjusts the reported number of births by the ratio of reported parity to cumulated fertility for women 20-24. The values of this adjustment (P_2/F_2) are shown in Table 4.A.13.

Table 4.A.13

| | | Stratum | | | | |
1	2	3	4	5	6	Total
.95	.84	.86	1.05	.91	1.11	.96

The adjusted values of total fertility are presented in Table 4.A.14.

Table 4.A.14

| | | Stratum | | | | |
1	2	3	4	5	6	Total
3.5	5.9	7.1	7.0	7.6	7.7	6.8

An alternative and independent set of fertility estimates can be obtained by selecting a model stable population having the same proportion under age 15 as each given population (both sexes), and the same value of l_2. The proportions under age 15 are given in Table 4.A.15.

Table 4.A.15

| | | Stratum | | | | |
1	2	3	4	5	6	Total
.298	.412	.471	.454	.476	.440	.438

The total fertility associated with each stable population was estimated by determining the gross reproduction rate with the mean age of the fertility schedule derived from births reported during the past year (with due allowance for the six months difference in age at time of birth and time of the survey) and multiplying this estimate of GRR by 2.03. The mean ages of the fertility schedules were as shown in Table 4.A.16.

Table 4.A.16

| | | Stratum | | | | |
1	2	3	4	5	6	Total
28.7	27.5	27.8	29.4	29.6	28.7	28.5

The fertility estimates derived in this way are presented in Table 4.A.17.

Table 4.A.17

| | Stratum | | | | | | |
	1	2	3	4	5	6	Total
Total fertility	3.7	6.3	7.4	7.1	7.7	7.1	6.8
Birth rate (per thousand)	28	49	54	50	52	52	50

The agreement between these estimates of total fertility and those obtained by the Brass method of estimation in striking. The estimates derived from the age distribution are the ones reproduced in Table 4.3. A final substantiation of their probable validity is the recorded proportions childless among women 30-34. Almost all women over 30 have been married; childlessness is almost certainly a sign of sterility. The proportions are shown in Table 4.A.18.

Table 4.A.18

		Stratum				
1	2	3	4	5	6	Total
.295	.155	.070	.084	.075	.079	.109

A comparison of these proportions with the estimates of total fertility shows stratum 1 with low fertility and a high proportion childless, stratum 2 with intermediate fertility and a moderate proportion childless, and the remaining strata with high fertility and a low proportion childless. In stratum 1 the proportions childless diminish with age past age 40, suggesting that childlessness has been increasing and fertility diminishing, and supplying an explanation for the fact that the estimate of total current fertility is below the average parity of women 45-49.

Source

République du Niger, Mission démographique du Niger—1960, France, Ministère de la Coopération, INSEE, *Étude démographique du Niger*, Part 2, *Données individuelles*.

GAMBIA, GHANA, LIBERIA, SENEGAL, RHODESIA, TOGO, ZAMBIA

The Data

For this group of countries, the only available direct observations of the populations relevant to the estimation of fertility at the time this chapter was written were recorded age distributions. For some of these populations more complete information has been collected, but not as yet published. Thus, the 1960 Census of Ghana was accompanied by a post-enumerative sample survey which included information on children ever born, surviving children, and on births and deaths during the year before the survey; but the results of this survey were not published in time for inclusion in this book.

The age distributions recorded for these populations had the usual distortions described in Chapter 2. The nature of these distortions—apparently including a typical understatement of the proportion of females and overstatement of the porportion of males under age 15—led to the use of the proportion of the total population under 15 as the basis of the fertility estimate.

Method of Estimation

The birth rate and total fertility of these populations were estimated by selecting a model stable population (West, female) with the same proportion under age 15 and a mortality level selected—on the basis of at best an informed guess—as approximately appropriate. Togo, Liberia, Gambia, and the Northern Province of Ghana were assumed to have an expectation of life at birth of 35 years, the rest of Ghana was assumed to have an $e°_0$ of 40 years, and Zambia and Rhodesia were assumed to have an $e°_0$ of 37.5 years—the same as estimated for Tanzania on the basis of data in the Census of 1957. Senegal was assumed to have a value of l_2 equal to that estimated for the Senegal Valley in 1957.

A separate estimate for the Northern Province of Ghana was made because it had a distinctly lower proportion of children than any of the other provinces (save Accra, where persons born outside the province constituted about a quarter of the residents).

The mean age of the fertility schedule assumed in estimating total fertility was 27 years—toward the low end of African experience. A higher estimate of the mean age of fertility would increase estimated total fertility.

Of course, the estimates both of birth rates and total fertility are influenced by the rather arbitrarily estimated level of mortality. For example, if $e°_0$ is really 30 when it is assumed equal to 35, the birth rate should be estimated as 48 rather than 45, and total fertility as 6.1 instead of 5.7 (corresponding estimates for $e°_0 = 40$ are a birth rate of 43 rather than 45, and total fertility of 5.5 instead of 5.7).

It goes without saying that these estimates are extremely rough, and may be repudiated by more satisfactory figures when better data become available.

Sources

Ghana, 1960 Population Census of Ghana, *Advance Report of Volumes III and IV*, Census Office, Accra, 1962.

Data for Gambia (1963), Liberia (1962), Rhodesia (1962) and Zambia taken from U. N. Department of Economic and Social Affairs, *Demographic Yearbook 1964*, Table 5.

Togo. Service de la Statistique, *Recensement général de la population du Togo 1958-60*. Parts 5 and 6.

Senegal. Verrière, Louis. *Où en est, où va la population du Sénégal*, Institut de Science Appliquée, Dakar, 1963.

5

Marriage in African
Censuses and Inquiries

BY ETIENNE VAN DE WALLE

This chapter is concerned with the analysis of data on marriage drawn from recent African censuses and sample inquiries. Data gathered by social anthropologists will not be surveyed here. They have assembled a great wealth of information on marital customs and on their role in the formation of kinship groups, in a wide variety of African cultures. In the process, they have dealt with subjects of demographic interest, such as the influence of marital customs on fertility,[1] the relation between kinship systems or social change and the stability of marriage,[2] etc. Yet they recognize, as stated by Ardener, the limitations of demographic information "on a circumscribed and small population, and based on investigations by workers trained outside demography proper, the results of which are not certainly extrapolable beyond the population."[3] A census, on the other hand, deals with various cultures at the same time, but it cannot adjust the questions asked to fit every particular custom. Reliance is often placed on ready-made methods tailored to Western traditions. Even if procedures are designed to take account of conditions in a particular country, census officials must use all-purpose categories which may have no meaning in some local cultures. The anthropologist can study marriage on the culture's own terms. He can undertake time-consuming inquiries in a small community, whereas the census interviewer must complete his daily quota of interviews and cannot tarry. Many defects in the census results arise from insufficient training and from overburdening of the interviewers. There are, however, some defects that care in interviewing cannot eliminate entirely, defects indeed that both the census taker and the anthropologist must accept. For instance, no expenditure of effort can ensure a reliable age dis-

---

[1] See among others, E. Ardener, *Divorce and Fertility*, Nigerian Social and Economic Studies, No. 3, Oxford University Press, 1962; V. R. Dorjahn, "The factor of polygamy in African demography . . . ," in W. R. Bascom and M. J. Herskovits, eds., *Continuity and Change in African Cultures*, University of Chicago Press, 1959.

[2] J. C. Mitchell, "Marriage stability and social structure in Bantu Africa," paper presented to the International Population Conference, New York, September 1961.

[3] *Op.cit.*, p. vi.

tribution of people who do not know their own ages. Similarly, answers to the most carefully worded questions bearing on a distant past—as, for example, on the number of previous marriages—are subject to recall lapses. The nature of these defects are often more clearly evident in census data, where random variations are swamped in big numbers, and where systematic biases can be observed and, in some cases, measured. Censuses and anthropological studies are essentially complementary. We shall center our attention directly on the investigation of data concerning marriage and kindred topics provided by censuses and sample demographic inquiries. One aim of the present study will be to assess what questions can meaningfully be asked on marriage in an inquiry that includes a much wider range of demographic questions.

Two general obstacles stand in the way of an efficient use of the recent African censuses and sample inquiries for the demographic study of marriage: (1) a lack of comparability of census definitions and (2) deficiencies in the tabulation of the collected data.

It is not possible to adapt census methods precisely to all variations in tribal culture. Nevertheless efforts by those responsible for various surveys to take such conditions into account so far as possible—and the lack of coordination in their efforts—seriously limit the comparability of the results obtained in different regions. Our analysis must, therefore, frequently be limited to the data for various districts within the same country. The data on marriage from inquiries in the Congo will often be found most useful for this purpose. Somewhat similar data are provided by several sources of French inspiration.[4] One must however constantly bear in mind that apparent differences in results for different regions may be due to differences in the methods by which they were obtained.

The second obstacle to the efficient use of the collected data is that they have usually not been published in sufficient detail to permit systematic development. For instance, there is very little information on marital status in relation to tribal affiliation, though this is a matter of great importance. If nuptiality data were available for the Fulani in Nigeria, Guinea, Senegal, and other countries where they are found, a comparison would be highly informative and might perhaps even be used to detect the effects of different survey methods. Similar data, if provided, could be used to measure variations in marital patterns within the same ethnic group in rural areas and under the influence of an urban environment.

Data on marriage have not been published for all the territories where we can study mortality and fertility. Results for a number of inquiries

[4] The census reports published in the English language do not usually include any information on marriage. Questions on this subject were included in the post-enumeration survey in Ghana, but its results are not yet available. The 1957 Tanganyika post-enumeration survey included a question on the number of wives, but no other information on marital status.

were as yet only published in a provisional form without tabulations on marriage. On the other hand, meaningful information may sometimes be available in regions where data on vital events are not exploitable. Apart from some urban studies or inquiries that contain very limited information, and to which we shall only make cursory allusions, Table 5.1 contains a list of all the material that we have used, with an indication of the approximate size of the interviewed population. This material is

Table 5.1. Data used in this study of marital status, by country and region, year of inquiry, and size of sample

Country or region	Coverage of population	Date of Inquiry	Number of persons enumerated (thousands)
Whole Countries			
Burundi	sample	1960	17
Congo	sample	1956-57	1,360
Dahomey	sample	1961	123
Guinea	sample	1954-55	300
Mozambique	full	1950	5,647
Niger	sample	1960	71
Portuguese Guinea	full	1950	502
Senegal	sample	1960-61	83
Regions			
Cameroon - Mbalmayo	full	1956	48
Central African Republic - Oubangui Center	sample	1959	42
Guinea - Konkouré	full	1957	28
Ivory Coast - Bongouanou	sample	1955-56	10
Mali - Central Niger Delta	sample	1957	23
Senegal and Mauritania- Fouta-Toro	sample	1957	34
Togo - Kabré Country	sample	1957	18

of a very heterogeneous nature and of uneven quality. Small samples adjoin national full-coverage censuses in our list. Our comparisons will have to take the characteristics of the data into account.

The chapter will have the following plan. We shall first discuss the problems of definition and measurement involved in the collection and presentation of marriage statistics in Africa. In the second section, we will present results obtained on several indices, defined and discussed in the first section, and we will consider their implications. A third section will be devoted to the special problem of urban-rural differentials in nuptiality. Finally, in the fourth section, we shall examine information on the relations of types of marriage and marital status to fertility.

Definitions and Methods
of Measurement

Concepts of Marriage
and Free Union

Although marriage has a definite meaning in most African cultures, it is difficult to define in general terms. Marriage is the opposite of celibacy, but must be distinguished from free and consensual unions as well. In fact, there exists a gradient of situations, ranging from celibacy (in which there may be considerable promiscuity), through free union, consensual union, and customary marriage, to religious and civil marriage. According to the United Nations' *Multilingual Demographic Dictionary*, "the term *consensual union* implies a socially recognized stable union."[5] *Free union* implies instability and is synonymous with concubinage; it is characterized by the absence of continuous cohabitation. The distinction between consensual and free union is meaningful from a demographic point of view, as the latter implies lesser exposure to risks of childbearing.[6]

We have avoided using the term "common law union" as a synonym for consensual union because "common law" is another word for custom, and in Africa customary marriage is the most frequently encountered type of fully legal marriage. Customary marriage is characterized by the performance of prescribed rites, and in many societies it includes the payment of bridewealth. In the words of Radcliffe-Brown,[7] "marriage is a developing process," and there are often several stages between preliminary rites (e.g., small gifts to the family of the betrothed or a first installment of the bridewealth) and full recognition of the couple as an independent social unit. There not only are thus several kinds of unions, but each type may pass through several stages before it is completed.

The multiplicity of marital categories, distinguished by variable conditions, poses a dilemma for the census taker. Will he try to establish

[5] United Nations, 1958, p. 31.

[6] See G. W. Roberts, "Some aspects of mating and fertility in the West Indies," in *Population Studies*, Vol. 8, No. 3, March 1955, p. 200. The term "keeper unions" is employed in this case.

[7] A. R. Radcliffe-Brown and Daryll Forde, eds., *African Systems of Kinship and Marriage*, International African Institute, London, 1950, p. 49.

all these distinctions by questions relating to the payment of bridewealth, the performance of a ritual, the length of cohabitation, and other topics? Will he distinguish free unions from prostitution, stable consensual unions from customary marriages, and so on? If he takes this approach, he must employ a battery of questions and tabulate marital status in several categories—an expensive and perhaps impractical procedure. On the other hand, if the census taker attempts a less detailed classification, the problem of what one includes under the general heading of marriage is still unsolved. Where, in the gradient of possible situations, will one draw the line between union and non-union, and if one distinguishes between several categories of unions, what will the criteria be? Whatever decision is taken, the criteria must be clearly indicated. Although ambiguous and unsatisfactory in theory, the simple dichotomy found in many censuses and sample inquiries between "married" and "single," may very well be the only practical solution in that type of investigation.

In the Guinea inquiry, persons were asked to report themselves as married, living in free union, or single, without explicit definitions of these types. A free union was interpreted in an economic report by the agency responsible for the demographic inquiry, as one "for which the customary ceremony of marriage has not been celebrated."[8] This definition, however, is not found anywhere in the written instructions to the interviewers, nor in the final report, and no question on a marriage rite was included in the form. An informal union that has endured through several years may, in the absence of conflict between the partners or their kin, be generally regarded as a regular marriage. It is, therefore, probable that only the most temporary unions have been recorded as free in Guinea and that all the others were lumped together under the heading "married." There are certain advantages in letting each person select the marital status appropriate to his situation, and the same procedure has subsequently been followed in all former French territories. However, this procedure naturally leads, as shown by the experience of Guinea, to the inclusion of all unions, except unstable temporary alliances, under the name of marriages.

There was one departure in the Guinea inquiry from this general principle. In the Forest Region, where it was thought that free unions were especially prevalent, the men were asked explicitly whether they had concubines.[9] This variation in procedure destroys the comparability of the results for different regions. We show in Table 5.2 the percentage of free unions among adult males and females in the four regions. The pro-

[8] Mission Démographique de Guinée 1954-55, *Études agricoles et économiques de quatre villages de Guinée Française. IV Guinée Forestière Village de Niehen*, Feb. 1957, p. 18.

[9] Enumerators were instructed to report extant free unions in which there was cohabitation at the time of the inquiry, or from which children had been begotten even if the couple was not usually living together.

Table 5.2. Percent of adults in free unions, by sex—regions of Guinea

	Males	Females
Forest	1.1	1.9
Fouta-Djallon	-	0.1
Maritime	*	0.2
Upper	*	0.2

portions of reported free unions are, however, surprisingly low in all regions, even in the Forest Region, where the special question about concubines was used. This indicates that all but the most unstable matches were reported as marriages. A negligible proportion of free unions turned up in almost every inquiry in which a question relating to them was included. It is very possible that whenever a large number of free unions was reported, this was the result of a different interpretation of the instructions on the subject of marriage. Most inquiries in the French series have left this question out altogether. In all subsequent discussions of Guinea, we shall make an abstraction of the few persons reported as living in free unions.

An illustration of apparent differences in the interpretation of instructions is afforded by the Census of Urban Centers in the Ivory Coast. Four centers of similar size, inhabited by populations of similar tribal origin, were surveyed at approximately the same time (1956-57) and using the same forms, but by different teams. The proportions of females reported as living in wedlock varies between 7 and 87 percent, and that recorded as living in free union between 1.0 and 66 percent (see Table 5.3).

It is most unlikely that there are real differences of this magnitude

Table 5.3. Percent of persons 15 years or over, married and in free unions, by sex—Ivory Coast centers

		Married	Free Unions	Totals
Abengourou	Males	7.0	40.3	47.3
	Females	6.6	66.4	73.0
Agboville	Males	47.0	0.2	47.2
	Females	81.6	1.1	82.7
Dimbokro	Males	14.9	40.1	55.0
	Females	19.6	52.8	72.4
Man	Males	48.9	0.2	49.1
	Females	86.7	1.0	87.7

among these cities in the relative incidence of unions by type. It is more reasonable to assume that a restrictive definition of marriage (perhaps limited to registered marriages) was used in Abengourou and Dimbokro.

The classification of the conjugal unions in the Congo 1956-57 Demographic Inquiry may be contrasted with that of Guinea. Instead of relying on the informant's interpretation of his own marital status, the organizers of the Congolese inquiry stressed the concept of legality. Their procedures were planned to conform to principles established by legislation, which were reflected to a large extent, though imperfectly, in local record systems. Customary law was recognized in legal theory, but subject to important modifications by official decree. The registration of marriages was required, with provision for a record of bridal payments. Furthermore, the name of the bride was inscribed on the identity document that every adult male was expected to have at hand at all times. In conducting the Demographic Inquiry, the interviewers generally examined these documents. The name of a wife in a man's identity booklet established a presumption as to the legality of the union. The absence of such an entry drew attention to possible irregularities in actual unions. The union of a man with a woman whose name was not in the booklet was generally classified as a consensual union (*union de fait*) if the couple had lived together for at least six months. If cohabitation had not lasted this span of time, the union was to be ignored completely in the reports by enumerators.

The concept of consensual union in the Congo is not without its ambiguities. As we shall see, many polygamous unions established by customary ritual but declared illegal by a law of Western inspiration were included in this category. Furthermore, the instructions required the inclusion among the consensual unions of a type they called "marriage on approval," (*mariage à l'essai*). This generally refers to unions during a probationary period between the first and the principal installments of the bridewealth. As the preliminary payments usually bring ritual recognition of rights and obligations by the man and woman and their kin, it would seem preferable for demographic purposes to treat these as customary unions (i.e., marriages) rather than as merely consensual unions. Thus, the concept of consensual union as defined in the Congo suffers from conflicts between traditional African and modern European principles, so that the results are difficult to interpret.

Married couples and consensual unions taken together in the Congo are roughly comparable to married couples in Guinea, though both figures lack precision. The Guinean "free unions" indicate temporary cohabitation and thus form a category that has no counterpart in the Congo because of the exclusion there of consensual unions of less than six months' duration.

[189]

Measurement of Proportion Married

We will assume here that marriage is well defined, and we will ignore any intermediary categories between celibacy and marriage. We will then consider the measurement of two aspects of marriage in the population: (1) the proportion married at the time of census and (2) the proportion ever-married, including widowed and divorced persons.

In Africa, the married (i.e., persons living in marital relation at a given time) represent, at least at the fecund ages, an overwhelming majority of the ever-married. Where marriage patterns are stable, the proportion of ever-married persons in a population with a given age and sex distribution is a function of two variables: (1) the proportion of all persons passing through life who ever marry and (2) the age of marriage. A measure of the proportion ever marrying is provided by subtracting from 1 the proportion single above 45 years of age (assuming that first marriages beyond that age can be ignored). Most adults marry in Africa. The age at marriage is therefore the most important variable that has to be studied when a definition of marriage has been agreed on. It is a significant element in a study of fertility. Furthermore, the age at marriage influences the forms of marriage practiced in a society, or is influenced by it. Polygyny, for instance, is made possible in part by the difference between the males and the females in age at marriage.

Registration data on marriages by ages of spouses are practically non-existent in Africa. An attempt has been made in several inquiries of the French tradition to obtain retrospective information on this subject.[10] However, one can hardly expect to obtain useful information in this way, in view of the great difficulty of getting reliable reports even on actual ages at the time of inquiry. The great obstacle in fact to any accurate measurement of the age at marriage lies in the prevalence of misstatements of age. It makes the computation of detailed nuptiality tables impossible. Can a single index such as mean age at marriage be derived from census data?

Hajnal has developed a method to compute the "singulate mean age at marriage" from the proportion single in successive age groups.[11] The method rests on the fact that the mean age at first marriage is equal to the mean duration of single life. The latter can be computed from the proportion of single persons at successive ages if there have been no changes of the age patterns of marriage in the recent past and if differential mortality and net migration rates by marital status may be considered negligible. Under such conditions, a cohort moving through life would have the same proportions single at successive ages as persons at the same ages in the present population.

[10] Dakar, Kabré Country, Centre-Oubangui.

[11] John Hajnal, "Age at marriage and proportion marrying," *Population Studies*, Vol. 7, No. 2, Nov. 1953, p. 111ff, in particular pp. 129-131.

If s_x is the proportion single at age x, and if all first marriages are assumed to have taken place by age 45, the singulate mean age at marriage is as follows:

$$\text{SMAM} = \sum_{x=0}^{45} \frac{s_x - 45s_{45}}{1 - s_{45}}$$

The use of five-year age classes instead of single years does not significantly alter the results.

This formula yields good results with European populations and has been used for India.[12] Its possible use in the African context must however be carefully evaluated.

The main difficulty stems from the unreliability of age reporting. Ages must often be estimated by the interviewer, and such estimation is subject to special biases in the case of women entering the childbearing ages. The use of historical calendars to assess age is likely to be less effective with women than with men. Women are less concerned with public events and often have even less experience in any sort of calculation than men. Furthermore, where virilocal rules prevail, past events in the husband's locality often lie outside the wife's frame of reference, and she may be isolated from kinsmen who could assist in recalling associations.

In the absence of reliable evidence, interviewers tend, almost inevitably, to be influenced by their assumptions about usual ages at marriage and maternity. Preconceptions of the "normal" age at marriage are not infrequent even among professional investigators.[13] Furthermore, most countries have legally determined minimum ages for marriage, usually 14 or 15, and censuses or inquiries do not consider earlier marriages. Under these circumstances, it may be expected that married women under the "normal" or legal age for marriage will be reported as older than others of the same age who are still single. Conversely, older single women may be rejuvenated. Estimates of age may furthermore be influenced by the number of previous births.

The existence of such bias is recognized by the authors of several reports, including those of the inquiries for Fouta Toro, Centre-Oubangui, and Southern Rhodesia. The Congo instructions included a specific recommendation to use an assumed age at marriage (between 15 and 18) and standard intervals between births (said to vary, according to customs, between two and three years) to estimate present ages. Similar rules of thumb were used in other inquiries because they are easy and convenient. The Oubangui Center report mentions it in these terms:

[12] Shri N. Agarwala, *Age at Marriage in India*, Allahabad, Kitab Mahal, 1962.
[13] For example: "As everywhere in Africa and in almost every case, as soon as a girl is nubile, i.e. on the average around fifteen years, her marriage is consummated." J. Brasseur "Étude de géographie régionale: Le village de Tenentou (Mali)," *Bulletin de l'IFAN*, ser. B, No. 3-4, Jan.-Apr. 1961, p. 625. There is no ground for such a generalization in the evidence that we shall set out in the second section of this chapter.

It can be stated that interviewers apply too rigidly the "two years rule" between successive births . . . the computation of the age of a woman having children becomes mere arithmetic: $14 + 2 \times$ number of children.[14]

Thus, in two neighboring countries, the indiscriminate use of a similar rule, but admitting different ages of marriage, and different intervals between births, could bring about systematic age misreporting of different magnitude.

The possible influence of marital and maternal histories on the estimates of ages must always be borne in mind in using the results of surveys in Africa. The preconceptions of enumerators about normal ages at marriage and about birth intervals may bias the results. If there are no explicit instructions, deviations of expectation from reality will vary among enumerators. If a particular pattern is provided, as in the Congo, enumerators will be tempted to bring all estimates into line with this pattern. Then, if that pattern is not really characteristic of the population under investigation, the whole age distribution may be distorted. Apart from other inconveniences (e.g., in the study of fertility or mortality patterns by age that do not concern us here), there is some circularity involved in deriving the mean age at marriage from the age distribution of the single women if interviewers have assumed that every girl was married at 18 years of age (or at whatever other age).

These considerations enforce caution in any application of Hajnal's method to African data. Nevertheless, if treated critically, the computation of the singulate mean age at marriage may be of some use in a number of African countries. The method can however only be used in a population in which the proportions married at specific ages have not been appreciably affected by migration. For this reason it cannot adequately measure urban-rural differentials in age of marriage.

Concepts of Divorce and Widowhood

As with marriage and celibacy, definitions of widowhood and divorce are beset with difficulties. Treatment in various African censuses and inquiries is far from uniform. With respect to divorce, a first question concerns types of union that are treated as susceptible to termination by divorce (or separation). One must then consider the criteria of divorce (or separation). The concept of divorce is obviously inapplicable to free unions, and even where these are recorded, as in Guinea, no attempt is made to take account of their termination. The dissolution of a consensual union however can be viewed as divorce. This was done in Guinea and in the Ghana Post-Enumeration Survey, but not in the Congo Demographic Inquiry. Unions not sanctioned by bridewealth can be dissolved more easily than regular customary marriages. If the former

[14] *Enquête démographique Centre-Oubangui, Méthodologie, Résultats provisoires*, p. 13.

are dissolved, the partners are thus considered as divorced in Guinea and in Ghana, but as single persons in the Congo.

How can a union be ended by divorce? Customary divorce normally prescribes refunding of the bridewealth, or some other rite that does not leave any doubt as to the rupture of the ties between the two kinship groups. Legal divorce supposes the intervention of a court. Census procedures differ with respect to these formal conditions. The Ghana P.E.S. of 1960 required a formal end by court or custom, but in Guinea divorce and separation were classed under the same heading. The Portuguese Guinea census of 1950 distinguished between "divorciado" and "separado acidalmente," but the latter was described merely as a common phenomenon in pagan populations and the distinction not otherwise made clear. It appears that the term "divorce" often covers an array of situations ranging from protracted grass-widowhood to divorce by court decision.

Definitions of widowhood are subject to similar uncertainties. A special source of difficulty is that in Africa the death of the husband often does not sever the ties between the two kinship groups involved, and that inheritance of the widows by a kin of a deceased man is standard practice in many tribes. The inheritance of a widow has as its primary function the continued use of her potential fertility by her late husband's lineage. It is therefore reasonable to include, as in the Congo, the inherited women among the wedded wives, provided there actually is cohabitation. Another set of rules was adopted in Guinea, with an eye to measurement of the phenomenon of inheritance. Inherited widows were recorded separately and are listed separately in the tables giving the marital status of the female population. However, only remarriages of this sort from which no children had been born were placed in this category. This procedure yields rather peculiar results in that the particular status of an inherited widow in Guinea is made to depend on factors like the duration and the fertility of the new union. Therefore in our treatment of the Guinea material, we shall include inherited widows in the general category of married women.

Measurement of Proportions Divorced and Widowed

The data most frequently available on the subject of widowhood and divorce are those which describe the current marital status of the informants at the time of the census or inquiry. It is possible to study them by broad age groups. For instance, the proportions of women divorced and widowed between ages 20 and 45 years and after 45 years tell something about the incidence of divorce and widowhood during the childbearing years and also thereafter. These data cannot however reveal much about the instability of marriage or the frequency of its disruption by the death of a partner because they are also affected by the frequency and timing of remarriages.

Questions on the total number of previous marriages have sometimes been included in demographic inquiries. In Guinea, for instance, women were asked the number of their marriages, including the extant one. No distinction was made between marriages ended by divorce and those ended by death of the husband. Men were not asked any similar question. The answers to these questions were not tabulated in detail. They have been tabulated however in other inquiries, e.g., Central Niger Delta and Fouta-Toro. Retrospective reports, especially by older persons, must always be used with caution.

Answers to the question on total number of marriages appear to be no exception. The series of marriages by age of the women usually reaches a maximum at the end of the childbearing period and then decreases in line with a pattern frequently found in reports on children ever born that is usually due mainly to lapse of recall among older women. The smaller numbers of marriages reported by the older women, though sometimes interpreted as showing an increasing instability of marriages in modern times, more probably reflect a similar bias. Where death rates are high, mortality among husbands is more important in accounting for the disruption of marriages than even high divorce rates. It is possible that the frequency of divorce has increased with Western contact, but related conditions have also tended to reduce mortality and hence widowhood. It seems that young women, say those aged 20-25 years, report widowhood and divorces with fair accuracy, because their number is small and these recent events are remembered vividly. As time goes by and husbands come and go, memory may be blurred with respect to the number and types of previous unions. Furthermore, inheritance of a widow may or may not be considered as the continuation of the previous match instead of as a new marriage.

The Concept of Polygyny

Polygyny is an important aspect of family relations in Africa. Although the primary concept is simple enough—a man being married to several wives—it is obscured by the effects of restrictive legislation in several African countries. In the Congo it became illegal to contract a new polygynous union after 1951. The legal definition of a polygynist becomes thus: a man who has several wives to whom he was married before 1951. However, the institution has not been eradicated. Polygynous unions formed since that time are still recognized in customary affairs. But customary law, where it conflicted with colonial law, was to be ignored in the Demographic Inquiry. So second and subsequent wives in plural marriages contracted after 1951 were, according to the instructions, to be aggregated with unions for which prescribed customary ritual had not been performed, and were to be recorded as living in consensual unions—*unions polygamiques de fait*. It is obvious that the instructions were not always followed on this point. For instance, one finds that 55 percent of the women aged 15-19 in polygynous union in the rural districts for which the information is available were inscribed as regularly married. If ages have been correctly reported, most of these women (who were then only 10-14 years old) were presumably single at the time of the 1951 edict and had entered polygynous households since that time. Consensual unions represent 8 percent of the monogamous unions and 12 percent of the polygynous ones. The frequency of consensual unions among polygynists is highly correlated by district with that among monogamists.

The distinction between polygynous unions formed prior to or after 1951 is not stressed in the published reports of the Congolese inquiry. Data on both types are usually presented under one heading. The gap between law and custom may nevertheless have brought about the underestimation of a social phenomenon which, though officially repudiated, has considerable importance.

We have dealt exclusively with the situation in the Congo, but similar difficulties are encountered in this sphere wherever new legislation is introduced which conflicts with customary practices.

Measurement of the Proportion of Polygynous Unions

Two different aspects of polygyny can be measured.

(a) *Its incidence.* A good measurement of the incidence is provided by the proportion (p) of polygynists among married males.

(b) *Its intensity.* The index used here is the average number (w) of wives per polygynist.

Data to compute these two ratios are not always available, and often one can merely obtain a measurement in which incidence and intensity are combined: the number (m) of married women per married man. The ratio of married females to married males is a reliable index of polygyny only for a population not appreciably affected by migration— or a population with temporary out- or inmigrants described by a purely *de jure* census.[15]

[15] The following results from two recent censuses of Mozambique show a sharp contrast:

Married women per 100 married men according to type of marriage:

	1940	1950
Customary marriage	120.2	123.2
Catholic marriage	118.1	100.4
Protestant marriage	111.2	99.8
Civil marriage	108.2	99.9
Other religions	110.2	119.9
Total	119.9	122.6

In both cases, the census required migrants to be recorded. The discrepancies suggested that only in 1950 were the absent males correctly reported. The excess of monogamously married males (i.e., those in Catholic, Protestant, and civil marriages) in 1940 would thus be explained.

The relation among the three indices of polygyny is as follows:

$$m = 1 + p \, (w - 1)$$

For instance, in the Congo as a whole, the number p of polygynists per married man was 0.166; the number w of wives per polygynist was 2.252, and the number m of married women per married man was 1.210. So an indirect estimate of one index (for example, m', an estimate of m) can be drawn from the other two:

$$m' = 1 + (0.166 \times 1.252)$$
$$= 1.208$$

This result is very close to the number obtained directly, 1.210. Abstracting from errors, if m' is different from m, it indicates a non-closed population.[16]

General Information on Marriage

We shall now deal with the application of the definitions and methodology outlined in the first section. The question of urban-rural differentials is reserved for separate treatment. Finally, a section will be devoted to the relationship between nuptiality and fertility.

Table 5.4 gives for selected age groups a general view of the marital status of various regions of Africa where a demographic census or sample inquiry has been taken. The data are tabulated for the age groups 20-44 and 45 and over. The age group 15-19 has been left out at this stage because its marital composition is overwhelmingly a function of age at marriage, a variable that we shall study at a later point. Comparable figures are also shown for the United States of America.

We have explained in the first section that the definitions used in the various countries are too dissimilar to afford more than rough international comparisons. Nevertheless, Table 5.4 enables one to get a general picture of marriage in tropical Africa, and to note certain apparent exceptions to the general pattern. Between ages 20 and 45 in a typical African region, over 25 percent of the males are single, 70 percent are in a conjugal union of some kind, and less than 5 percent are widowed or divorced. Among females, the corresponding proportions are usually under 5 percent, over 90 percent, and under 5 percent respectively. After age 45, the percentage of single males has fallen to less than 5; 85 percent are in a union, and the rest widowed or divorced. Among females the proportion single has become negligible; over 50 percent are still married, but nearly 50 percent widowed and divorced. Some countries diverge from this general pattern. Mbalmayo in Cameroon shows a

[16] In the Congo Inquiry, wives as well as husbands supplied information on the polygynous character of the union. Where, as in many inquiries of the French tradition, only the males are interviewed on the polygynous character of their union and on the number of their wives, the equality $m = m'$ is built into the data.

great number of single persons 20-44 years, and over 10 percent of the males never marry. Guinea on the contrary exhibits a pattern of very young and quasi-universal marriage. The differences in marital status between the population of the United States (as of March 1961) and the African populations are conspicuous only with respect to the females. There is a larger proportion of spinsters and a smaller proportion of widows in the United States.

In general, Table 5.4 brings out more similarities than differences. However the influence of differences in age at marriage has been largely eliminated by tabulating the data only from 20 years on. We do not know of an African population which does not share in an ideal of universal marriage. Proportions single and in conjugal union of some sort, and those divorced or widowed, do not usually differ greatly above age 20 from region to region. The highly variable factors are age at marriage, types of union, and stability of marriage.

We must underscore again that the figures in Table 5.4 are the product of different procedures and definitions and are subject to various degrees of bias and error. Some countries have however published marital data in sufficient detail to allow significant regional comparisons, with constant definitions and standards of data collection. Such detailed information is provided in Table 5.4 for the Congo, Guinea, and Mozambique. However the apparent variations are small, and the data do not lend themselves to precise analysis in a comparative treatment. There is only a 9 percent difference between the highest and the lowest proportions married among provinces of the Congo. The range is wider for divorce, but the figures are so small that random errors become important.

The southern districts of Mozambique (Lourenço Marques, Gaza, and Inhambane) have a high proportion of widows. This phenomenon may be somehow related to past migration; at any rate, the sex ratio above age 45 is only 47 males per 100 females, a most unusual ratio, and the proportion of widows exceeds by far that reported for other regions of Africa.

Proportion Single and Age at Marriage

One can state with fair accuracy that almost everyone gets married in tropical Africa. Many anthropologists have noted that celibacy is an unnatural state and that unmarried persons are cut off from full participation in the life of a society. The statement of Elizabeth Colson about the Plateau Tonga can be extended to large parts of Africa:

Marriage is . . . the doorway not only to the founding of a family and a household but also the goal which must be reached before an individual can acquire independent status within the community.[17]

[17] E. Colson, *Marriage and the Family among the Plateau Tonga of Northern Rhodesia*, Manchester University Press, 1958, p. 95.

Table 5.4. Marital status in regions of Africa, for age groups 20-44 and 45 and over, by sex

Males

	20-44					45 and over				
	Single	Married	Widowed	Divorced	Total	Single	Married	Widowed	Divorced	Total
Burundi	16.6	82.6		0.8	100.0	0.1	98.4	1.5		100.0
Cameroon										
Mbalmayo	40.6	56.4	1.4	1.5	99.9	11.1	80.8	6.1	2.0	100.0
Central African Republic										
Oubangui Center	11.1	78.9	3.3	6.7	100.0	1.3	81.4	10.0	7.3	100.0
Congo	20.0	75.0	1.6	3.3	100.0	2.2	86.0	7.5	4.3	100.0
Equateur	19.6	75.1	1.4	3.9	100.0	2.7	85.0	7.7	4.6	100.0
Kasai	19.7	75.4	1.7	3.2	100.0	1.5	89.4	5.9	3.2	100.0
Katanga	16.6	78.4	1.9	3.0	99.9	1.4	87.6	6.4	4.6	100.0
Kivu	16.1	79.4	1.5	3.0	100.0	2.0	84.3	9.9	3.8	100.0
Leopoldville	25.8	72.0	1.0	1.3	100.1	2.0	90.6	4.6	2.9	100.1
Orientale	19.2	73.1	2.2	5.5	100.0	3.2	80.9	9.9	6.1	100.1
Dahomey	24.4	70.6	1.3	3.7	100.0	3.3	82.1	7.7	6.9	100.0
Guinea	31.0	65.8	1.7	1.5	100.0	1.9	89.9	6.9	1.3	100.0
Forest	35.2	61.3	2.3	1.2	100.0	3.4	84.5	11.2	.9	100.0
Fouta Djallon	22.9	73.9	1.3	1.9	100.0	.4	94.1	4.2	1.2	99.9
Maritime	34.1	63.0	1.2	1.7	100.0	2.0	89.8	6.0	2.2	100.0
Upper	36.5	60.8	1.7	1.0	100.0	2.2	92.5	4.4	.9	100.0
Guinea										
Konkouré	31.5	67.1	0.6	0.8	100.0	2.6	93.6	3.0	0.9	100.1
Mali										
Central Niger Delta	34.8	63.2	1.1	1.0	100.1	.4	94.6	4.2	.8	100.0
Mozambique	21.2	75.8	1.4	1.7	100.1	3.5	88.6	6.4	1.6	100.1
Central	26.5	70.9	1.6	1.0	100.0	3.7	87.6	7.6	1.1	100.0
North	12.7	84.2	.9	2.2	100.0	2.8	90.6	4.8	1.9	100.1
South	26.0	70.6	1.6	1.8	100.0	4.4	86.4	7.5	1.7	100.0
Niger	9.0	87.7	0.9	2.4	100.0	0.2	92.9	5.5	1.4	100.0
Portuguese Guinea	35.4	60.9	1.5	2.1	99.9	3.4	84.3	9.2	3.1	99.9
Senegal	32.5	64.7	.5	2.2	99.9	1.6	89.1	5.5	3.8	100.0
Senegal and Mauritania										
Fouta-Toro	31.5	66.4	0.4	1.7	100.0	0.3	96.7	2.0	1.0	100.0
Togo										
Kabré country	-	-	-	-	-	-	-	-	-	-
United States of America (1961)	21.3	76.5	0.3	1.9	100.0	7.1	82.6	7.9	2.5	100.1

Table 5.4 (continued)

Females

	20-44					45 and over				
	Single	Married	Widowed	Divorced	Total	Single	Married	Widowed	Divorced	Total
Burundi	14.8	79.3	5.9		100.0	0.7	46.7	52.6		100.0
Cameroon Mbalmayo	13.2	76.4	9.4	0.9	99.9	2.0	40.1	56.9	1.0	100.0
Central African Republic										
Oubangui Center	3.1	87.2	6.0	3.6	99.9	–	45.8	45.3	8.9	100.0
Congo	1.6	88.5	4.8	5.1	100.0	0.6	53.0	41.2	5.2	100.0
Equateur	3.2	91.0	2.9	2.8	99.9	0.5	58.8	36.5	4.1	99.9
Kasai	1.6	88.8	6.4	3.2	100.0	0.4	48.2	48.0	3.5	100.1
Katanga	2.6	87.4	3.7	6.3	100.0	1.1	53.4	36.5	9.0	100.0
Kivu	1.3	91.4	5.2	2.0	99.9	0.7	53.3	42.8	3.2	100.0
Leopoldville	6.5	83.6	5.7	4.2	100.0	0.9	45.7	45.9	7.4	99.9
Orientale	2.3	90.2	3.9	3.6	100.0	0.4	59.2	35.8	4.6	100.0
Dahomey	1.5	94.5	2.8	1.2	100.0	0.4	55.9	41.3	2.4	100.0
Guinea	0.7	95.2	3.1	1.0	100.0	0.1	63.6	35.6	0.7	100.0
Forest	1.4	93.7	3.9	1.0	100.0	.2	56.3	43.0	.5	100.0
Fouta Djallon	.4	96.0	2.8	0.9	100.1	–	70.9	28.1	1.0	100.0
Maritime	.4	96.5	2.0	1.1	100.0	–	69.5	29.5	1.0	100.0
Upper	.8	94.1	4.1	1.0	100.0	–	51.7	48.3	–	100.0
Guinea Konkouré	.6	96.3	1.7	1.3	99.9	2.0	75.5	19.7	2.8	100.0
Mali										
Central Niger	1.1	94.0	3.3	1.5	99.9	.3	50.6	46.5	2.7	100.1
Delta	7.4	82.5	5.4	4.7	100.0	2.5	49.5	44.4	3.7	100.1
Mozambique										
Central	9.9	80.1	5.4	4.6	100.0	2.9	58.0	36.0	3.1	100.0
North	4.6	86.5	2.7	6.2	100.0	2.5	60.4	30.8	6.3	100.0
South	8.2	79.6	9.6	2.5	99.9	1.9	29.2	67.5	1.4	100.0
Niger*	0.5	93.8	3.9	1.7	99.9	–	34.0	62.6	3.4	100.0
Portuguese Guinea	3.0	92.8	2.1	2.1	100.0	0.6	60.4	37.3	1.6	99.9
Senegal and Mauritania	3.0	89.4	3.5	4.1	100.0	0.6	45.2	50.3	3.9	100.0
Senegal Fouta-Toro	1.4	90.8	3.4	4.4	100.0	0.1	41.1	53.7	5.1	100.0
Togo Kabré Country	1.0	93.3	5.2	0.5	100.0	0.1	47.5	50.4	2.0	100.0
United States	11.3	83.7	1.6	3.3	99.9	7.0	62.3	27.8	3.0	100.1

* Age groups are 20-49 and 50+.

As we saw in Table 5.4, Mbalmayo stands out as an exception in that 11 percent of its males aged more than 45 were reported as single. The highest percentage of single females above 45 (in Mozambique) is only 2.5.

Though consensus on the ideal of marriage is fairly unanimous, customs do not agree on the right age for marriage nor on related values such as the licit or illicit nature of premarital sexual relations. There are in these respects very significant differences among regions and tribes. The factors that determine the age at marriage are complex. The ways in which bridewealth may influence the ages of men and women at marriage and the supply of wives are obscure, although one frequently meets statements to the effect that high marriage payments delay the marriage of males and favor moral laxity and polygyny. There are also many stereotypes concerning the age at which girls should marry.

Table 5.5 gives for various African countries and for the provinces of the Congo the proportions single at successive ages. It would appear from the quoted figures that first marriages continue to occur until rather late ages. The apparent dispersion of ages at first marriage is greater than might be expected.

A summary measure of the proportion single at successive ages is provided by the mean age at marriage. We have already described the computation of the "singulate mean age at marriage," i.e., at first marriage. We called attention there to its sensitivity to the biases in age reporting that one expects in illiterate societies; this limitation must be kept constantly in mind. Table 5.7 shows the singulate mean age at marriage for the various regions for which the required data on proportions single are available. We shall first discuss the significance of the figures for females.

Not considering age- and marital-state-selective omission (or overreporting), two types of errors in the data could cause fictitious differences in singulate mean age of marriage: (a) errors in classification according to marital status and (b) errors in age reporting. The first type of error is limited to the classification as between single and ever-married. We are not overly concerned here with any looseness in the concept of marriage itself. Whatever the state on which the name of "marriage" is bestowed, it is meaningful to ask at what age that state is reached. And if we accept his definition of celibacy, an African will certainly better report whether he is single or not than his age. But we have in mind here, as an example of the first type of error, the case where girls under a certain age—15 years, for instance—would be systematically classified as single, even if they were married. In Guinea the interviewers were instructed to report marital status only if the girl was above 14 years of age. The floor was put at age 15 in the Congo and the Portuguese territories. Children's marriages occur in many parts of the area, and this might have resulted in the reporting of married girls of less than 14 in

Table 5.5. Proportion single in regions of Africa by age and sex

Males
(in per cent of population at each age)

Region	14	15-19	20-24	25-29	30-34	35-39	40-44	45-49
Burundi		91.2	44.2	15.9	3.2	2.2	0.7	0.4
Cameroon								
Mbalmayo		98.3	78.6	49.5	34.0	26.4	16.4	13.3
Congo								
Equateur		97.4	58.0	22.7	9.1		4.2	2.2*
Kasai		97.7	55.4	22.2	10.8		5.0	2.8
Katanga		98.0	61.9	25.1	9.2		3.6	1.6
Kivu		96.5	53.5	18.9	6.6		2.4	1.2
Leopoldville		93.9	45.7	15.1	5.9		3.0	1.7
Orientale		99.2	70.1	27.0	9.6		4.1	2.1
Dahomey		96.8	54.3	24.0	11.0		5.6	3.2
Guinea		94.7	65.0	28.9	11.2	6.4	4.2	4.9
Forest		99.1	75.3	41.1	17.4	8.6	4.8	3.3
Fouta Djallon		99.0	77.2	46.6	25.3	13.2	7.9	5.8
Maritime		98.6	64.8	26.6	8.6	3.6	2.0	0.5
Upper		100.0	83.7	46.2	19.4	9.1	4.9	2.7
		100.0	86.1	51.7	20.0	7.8	3.8	4.2
Guinea Konkouré		97.7	79.4	37.3	12.3	6.4	5.1	3.4
Mali								
Central Niger	100.0							
Delta		99.7	92.1	52.9	14.5	4.2	1.2	0.6
Mozambique		89.8	54.1	22.8	12.1	6.7	4.9	3.8
Central		93.2	64.5	28.0	14.7	7.7	5.5	4.1
North		78.9	34.6	13.9	8.0	4.8	3.7	3.2
South		95.0	61.2	28.6	14.9	8.5	6.0	4.6
Niger		89.2	19.2			1.9		0.7
Portuguese Guinea		97.9	79.2	49.0	23.0	11.0	7.4	4.5
Senegal and Mauritania								
Fouta-Toro		99.6	89.6	44.4	8.9	2.5	0.8	0.6
Togo								
Kabré Country	100.0	97.0	70.0	38.0	14.0	10.0	5.0	5.0

Table 5.5 (continued)

Females

(in per cent of population at each age)

Region	14	15-19	20-24	25-29	30-34	35-39	40-44	45-49
Burundi		82.2	36.1	14.5	6.5	2.9	2.2	1.4
Cameroon								
Mbalmayo		68.3	33.7	16.3	8.8	4.6	2.4	2.5
Congo								
Equateur		53.3	9.7	3.1	1.3		0.7	0.5*
Kasai		67.8	11.8	2.6	1.3		0.6	0.5
Katanga		44.8	5.3	1.7	0.8		0.4	0.3
Kivu		36.4	7.7	3.0	0.8		0.5	0.7
Leopoldville		37.7	3.6	0.9	0.6		0.4	0.5
Orientale		69.6	17.8	6.0	2.6		1.4	0.9
Dahomey		51.8	7.6	2.7	1.0	0.2	0.4	0.3
Guinea	80.8	33.3	3.7	1.2	0.9	0.2	0.4	0.6
Forest	86.8	18.0	1.8	0.8	0.3	0.6	**	**
Fouta Djallon	72.2	27.5	3.5	1.3	0.8	**	**	**
Maritime	81.3	10.5	0.8	0.4	0.3	**	**	-
Upper	96.0	13.4	0.8	0.8	**	**	**	-
Guinea Konkouré		18.1	1.2	0.3	0.8	-	1.0	0.7
Mali								
Central Niger	89.2	32.9	2.7	0.9	0.3	-		
Mozambique								
Delta		64.8	17.2	7.3	4.9	3.7	3.1	2.7
Center		73.5	23.9	9.3	6.5	4.3	3.7	3.1
North		43.3	9.2	4.5	3.4	2.9	2.8	2.6
South		74.2	19.0	8.6	5.3	4.1	2.9	2.3
Niger		18.9	0.8		0.1		0.1	
Portuguese Guinea		54.7	9.0	2.3	1.2	0.6	0.6	0.8
Senegal and Mauritania								
Fouta-Toro		31.0	4.0	1.2	0.6	-	0.6	-
Togo								
Kabré Country	97.0	35.0	2.0	1.0	**	**	-	-

* 45-54
** small numbers

one case, and less than 15 in the other, as single. However, errors in the reporting of marital status are probably not sufficiently important to affect the singulate mean age at marriage strongly. Concretely, 19 percent of the girls reported as 14 years of age in Guinea were married; these girls would quite probably have been reported as over age 15 in the neighboring Portuguese enclave or, for that matter, in Guinea itself had the minimum age of marriage been put at 15 years instead of 14.

It is clear that ages have usually been particularly misrecorded around the age of marriage in practically every African census or inquiry. There is, in general, a marked underreporting of females in their teens and an overreporting of females over 20. This point is illustrated in Table 5.6 and Figure 5.1 by a detailed year-by-year age distribution from 10 through 24, taken from the Guinea inquiry. It is contrasted in both table and graph with the deceptively regular curve of the proportion ever-married. A stable population with same birth and death rate as Guinea is plotted on the graph.

Table 5.6. Reported age distribution and reported percentage ever married, females 10-24—Guinea

Age	Population per 1,000	Percentage ever-married
10	10.2	0
11	16.0	0
12	16.0	0
13	13.3	0
14	12.5	19.2
15	10.3	41.3
16	16.6	71.0
17	17.7	85.1
18	22.6	90.3
19	27.8	95.1
20	8.2	96.3
21	23.5	97.4
22	21.0	98.9
23	19.0	98.0
24	20.3	99.3

Even if the upward shifting of young women were not influenced by their marital status, it would affect the singulate mean age at marriage. It is argued elsewhere in this volume that it is precisely marital status that causes a powerful bias in age reporting, and it is probable that overstatement of age is especially prevalent in the case of married girls. If so, the singulate mean age at marriage is even more affected. Its computation involves detailed age groups, whose sizes are considerably affected by misreporting of age. The simple overall dichotomy single–non-single should therefore provide a better measure of age at marriage. It can be translated into an age at marriage if we have an estimate of the age distribution. This estimate will typically be a stable population with the same fertility and mortality characteristics as the actual popula-

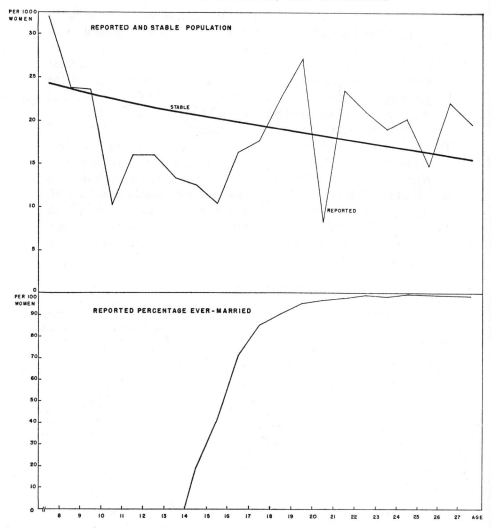

5.1. Reported and stable population from between 7 and 8 years to between 27 and 28 years, by single years of age, per 1,000 women (above). Reported percentage ever married per 100 women aged 14 through 27 to 28 (below)—Guinea.

tion. By linear interpolation on the stable model, one can determine the age at which the population, cumulated since birth, equals the proportion single. A small adjustment can (and in the following results will) be made for those in the population who never marry. This index, which we will designate by the expression "age at first marriage in the stable population," is largely free of bias due to errors of reporting of ages. It may have other defects, particularly in the case of males, if there is differential migration by marital state. We present in Table 5.7 both the singulate mean age at marriage and the "age at first marriage in the stable popu-

Table 5.7. Singulate mean age at marriage and age at first marriage in the stable
population, by sex—regions of Africa

	Singulate Mean Age at Marriage		Age at First Marriage in Stable Population	
	Males	Females	Males	Females
Burundi	22.9	22.1	23.6	19.4
Cameroon				
Mbalmayo	28.4	21.3		
Congo	24.3	18.3	21.3	16.0
Equateur	24.2	19.1	21.5	16.4
Kasai	24.7	17.6	21.4	14.6
Katanga	23.8	17.3	19.9	15.4
Kivu	23.1	17.2	20.4	16.4
Leopoldville	25.3	19.7	23.6	17.8
Orientale	24.2	18.1	20.9	16.8
Dahomey	24.9	16.9		17.1
Guinea	26.7	15.8		16.4
Forest	27.4	16.6		
Fouta Djallon	25.2	15.3		
Maritime	27.7	15.6		
Upper	27.7	16.6		
Guinea				
Konkouré	26.2	16.0		
Mali				
Central Niger Delta	28.1	16.8		
Mozambique	23.8	19.4		
Central	24.8	20.3		
North	21.4	17.6		
South	24.8	20.1		
Niger	23.1	15.2		
Portuguese Guinea	27.8	18.3		
Senegal and Mauritania				
Fouta-Toro	27.2	16.2		15.0
Togo				
Kabré Country	25.7	16.9		

lation" for different regions of Africa. There are significant differences
between these two figures. The singulate mean age at marriage tends to
be an overstatement. It would seem that Africans usually marry earlier
than most census data would lead us to believe. On the other hand, it
seems unwarranted to assume that every female marries at the time of
puberty. We have fairly well-documented evidence of rather late female
marriage in some regions, notably in Burundi.

We are able to get two more estimates of the mean age at marriage in
Burundi. In several sub-populations totaling 17,000 persons first marriages of inhabitants of the areas under observation were recorded as they
occurred. In this case, the ages of spouses had been estimated before the
marriage, and independently from it, with the help of calendars of local
events. Another estimate is derived from the baptism and marriage registers of an old Catholic mission,[18] using only records for spouses for
whom exact dates of birth and of first marriage are given. Continuous

[18] Buhonga, founded in 1898.

observation yields a mean age at marriage of 23 years for males and of 21 years for females. The marriage records give 21 and 20 respectively. The various measurements of age at marriage are without any doubt affected by various biases,[19] but they all point toward a relatively high age at marriage for the women.

Age at marriage in Africa thus varies rather widely from tribe to tribe. Possible implications of such differences in age at marriage for fertility will be investigated in the fourth section of this chapter.

Divorce and Widowhood

The reader is referred to Table 5.4 where data were presented on proportions of widowed and divorced persons at strategic ages. These proportions are usually small, at least during the reproductive years. As the death toll is known to be heavy, and the instability of marriage has been noted in several tribal societies, it is evident that rates of remarriage must generally be very high. The proportion widowed increases sharply at ages over 45 years, especially among women, because the rate of remarriage is then very small. Around 50 percent of all women over 45 are widows.

Tables 5.8 and 5.9 describe in more detail the evolution of the proportion widowed and divorced in several African regions. The most remarkable feature of these tables is that there is a continuous increase for both sexes in the proportion of widowed persons with age, but that the proportion divorced does not usually show any appreciable trend. Table 5.8 shows the very different increases in the proportions widowed by sex. Although the mortality of both wives and husbands increases apace with age, changes by age in the proportion of widowed persons of either sex at any given moment is highly dependent on the rate of remarriage. Men at all ages and women of reproductive age remarry rapidly. By contrast, remarriage of women over 40 is rather infrequent in most African populations.

We noted in the first section of this chapter that the Guinea inquiry made provision for a special category of married women, to wit, inherited widows who had not yet borne a child in their new situation. Although this procedure has serious disadvantages, it affords an insight into one type of remarriage process. The proportion of "inherited" women increases with age along with the proportion of widows to age 45. This apparent trend could merely reflect decreasing fertility with age, i.e., longer and longer delays between the time a woman is "inherited" and the birth of the next child. However, the evolution of the percentage of inherited widows after 45 is not affected by subsequent

[19] For instance, the use of mission records is fully justified only if (a) the religious ceremony coincides with the customary marriage and (b) the Christian population is representative of the total population. Neither of these conditions is fulfilled.

Table 5.8. Proportion widowed, by age and sex, in percent of each age—regions of Africa

Males:

	14	15-19	20-24	25-29	30-34	35-39	40-44	45-49	50-54	55+	60+
Cameroon											
Mbalmayo		0.1	*	0.5	0.8	2.3	3.4	4.3	4.0	8.6	
Congo											
Equateur		*	0.2	0.9	1.3	----	2.5	----	4.0	14.2	
Kasai		*	0.5	1.2	2.1	----	2.3	----	3.9	9.7	
Katanga			0.7	1.5	2.4	----	2.4	----	3.7	10.7	
Kivu		0.1	0.4	1.1	1.7	----	2.6	----	4.1	16.1	
Leopoldville		*	0.3	0.7	1.1	----	2.4	----	2.5	8.7	
Orientale		*	0.4	1.1	2.6	----	1.8	----	5.5	17.2	
Dahomey		0.2	0.3	1.0	1.3	1.7	2.8	3.1	4.2	----5.0----	13.2
Guinea		-	0.5	0.8	1.7	2.7	2.9	3.8		9.5	
Forest		-	0.4	1.7	2.1	3.7	3.7	6.8	7.6	15.2	
Fouta Djallon		-	0.4	0.8	1.8	2.0	2.0	1.6	2.1	6.2	
Maritime		-	0.7	*	1.4	1.9	2.5	2.7	3.9	8.4	
Upper		-	1.0	*	1.3	2.9	3.8	2.8	2.0	6.5	
Guinea Konkouré		-	0.3	0.8	0.8	0.5	0.9	1.4	2.2	4.0	
Mali Central Niger Delta		-	0.1	0.7	1.1	1.8	2.5	2.4	2.7	5.4	
Mozambique		0.1	0.5	0.9	1.4	1.8	2.5	3.1	4.2	10.2	
Central		0.1	0.4	1.1	1.8	2.3	3.1	3.8	4.8	11.7	
North		0.1	0.5	0.7	0.9	1.1	1.5	1.9	2.7	7.7	
South		0.1	0.4	1.0	1.7	2.4	3.3	4.0	5.7	13.3	
Niger	*										
Portuguese Guinea			----0.8----	0.7		----0.9----		----1.2----		----2.2----	9.1
Senegal and Mauritania											
Fouta-Toro			0.2	0.7	1.6	2.2	3.4	3.9	6.9	13.7	
Togo Kabré Country		-	*	1.0	3.0	2.0	5.0	5.0	10.0	-	

* small numbers

Table 5.8 (continued)

Females:

	14	15-19	20-24	25-29	30-34	35-39	40-44	45-49	50-54	55+	60+
Cameroon											
Mbalmayo		0.4	1.1	2.4	6.9	11.9	24.4	30.9	48.2	75.1	
		0.2	1.0	2.0	3.9				27.1	63.3	
Congo											
Equateur		0.1	0.8	1.5	2.6		9.6		19.8	60.8	
Kasaï		0.3	1.2	2.3	4.6		5.0		36.7	70.5	
Katanga		0.4	1.1	1.5	3.1		13.2		22.1	57.8	
Kivu		0.3	0.8	1.7	3.6		7.7		28.9	60.3	
Leopoldville		0.1	1.0	2.7	4.9		12.7		31.3	69.8	
Orientale		0.2	1.1	1.8	3.1		12.3		21.2	58.7	
Dahomey		0.2	0.6	1.3	2.5	4.1	9.8	17.6	33.6		67.0
Guinea		0.6	1.0	1.6	2.7	4.6	8.7	16.6	24.7	52.4	
Forest		1.1	1.5	2.0	3.5	5.1	11.1	20.0	31.4	64.7	
Fouta Djallon		0.6	1.0	0.6	2.3	4.1	7.3	11.9	17.9	41.1	
Maritime		0.4	0.8	0.8	2.1	3.1	5.1	10.3	16.1	46.7	
Upper		*	*	2.2	3.6	7.4	13.9	27.1	40.0	69.9	
Guinea											
Konkouré	0.8		1.3	1.3	1.3	2.2	3.5	5.2	8.8	30.9	
Mali											
Central Niger Delta		0.4	1.3	2.8	4.5	8.0	12.4	22.3	33.9	60.7	
Mozambique		0.4	0.6	1.3	3.4	4.7	11.1	19.3	30.1	64.9	
Central			1.6	3.1	5.1	7.8	11.5	19.7	27.4	50.4	
North		0.4	1.0	1.8	2.5	3.8	6.1	11.9	20.1	46.6	
South		0.4	1.3	4.2	7.5	14.6	23.5	39.8	57.3	82.8	
Niger					3.1						
Portuguese Guinea	0.4							1.5			
Senegal and Mauritania		0.2	0.8	1.1	2.0	2.7	5.1	10.5	22.2	62.3	
Fouta-Toro	0.4									45.4	78.1
Togo		0.6	0.6	1.0	2.7	5.9	11.1	20.4	42.4	72.2	
Kabré Country		0.3	0.8	1.0	3.9	7.5	16.8	27.7	34.8	65.5	

Table 5.9. Proportion divorced, by age and sex, in percent of each age—regions of Africa
Males:

	14	15-19	20-24	25-29	30-34	35-39	40-44	45-49	50-54	55+	60+
Cameroon											
Mbalmayo		0.1	0.5	0.8	1.3	2.2	2.7	1.8	2.2	2.0	
Congo	0.1		1.2	3.1	4.2		4.0	3.7		5.3	
Equateur		*	1.3	3.3	4.8		4.7	3.9		5.9	
Kasai		*	1.3	3.3	4.1		3.2	2.9		5.8	
Katanga		0.2	1.3	2.9	3.6		3.6	3.5		6.5	
Kivu		0.1	1.7	3.4	3.6		3.2	3.0		4.7	
Leopoldville		*	0.3	0.9	1.7		1.9	2.5		3.6	
Orientale		*	1.8	5.0	7.0		6.5	5.5		6.9	
Dahomey	0.3	*	1.5	2.5	4.1	4.6	6.6	6.8	----7.4----		6.5
Guinea		*	0.7	1.1	2.0	1.8	2.2	1.6	1.6	----1.0----	
Forest		*	0.4	1.4	1.1	1.5	1.6	1.0	1.7	0.6	
Fouta Djallon		*	1.1	1.9	2.3	1.6	2.5	1.6	1.4	1.0	
Maritime		*	0.7	*	2.8	2.6	3.3	2.7	2.6	1.9	
Upper		-	*	*	2.5	1.9	1.3	1.4	*	0.9	
Guinea											
Konkouré		-	-	0.6	1.4	0.6	1.9	0.9	1.1	0.8	
Mali											
Central Niger Delta											
Mozambique											
Central	0.1	0.1	0.9	1.8	2.0	1.8	1.4	1.2	0.8	0.6	
North		0.3	1.0	1.5	1.5	1.2	1.2	1.1	1.1	1.4	
South		0.1	0.8	2.4	2.4	2.1	1.9	1.9	1.8	1.1	
Niger	----0.8----		----3.2----			----1.9----		----1.7----		----1.0----	
Portuguese Guinea	0.1										1.8
Senegal and Mauritania											
Fouta-Toro			0.6	1.5	2.2	3.1	3.5	3.7	3.1	2.7	
Togo											
Kabré Country		*	*	1.0	2.0	3.0	2.0	2.0	2.0	0.7	-

* small numbers

[209]

Table 5.9 (continued)
Females:

	14	15-19	20-24	25-29	30-34	35-39	40-44	45-49	50-54	55+	60+
Cameroon											
Mbalmayo		0.2	0.6	0.7	1.0	1.0	1.3	0.9	1.1	1.0	
Congo		0.9	3.0	3.6	3.9	3.8			4.9	5.7	
Equateur		0.4	2.7	3.0	2.8	2.7			3.7	4.7	
Kasai		1.1	2.9	3.3	3.2	3.1			3.6	3.2	
Katanga		2.6	6.0	6.6	6.7	6.0			8.3	10.1	
Kivu		0.8	2.0	1.7	1.9	2.4			2.6	3.9	
Leopoldville		0.3	2.1	3.6	5.0	5.7			7.1	7.9	
Orientale		1.3	3.7	4.0	3.7	3.4			4.2	5.2	
Dahomey		0.3	0.7	0.9	1.1	1.7	2.0	1.9	‒‒2.7‒‒		2.5
Guinea		0.9	0.9	1.2	1.0	1.0	0.5	0.7	1.1	0.6	
Forest		1.5	1.2	1.0	1.2	0.9	0.5	0.5	1.0	0.4	
Fouta Djallon		0.9	0.8	1.2	0.6	0.9	0.8	1.0	1.4	0.8	
Maritime		0.6	0.8	1.6	1.6	1.0	*	1.0	1.8	0.7	
Upper		0.6	0.6	1.1	0.9	1.9	*	*	*	*	
Guinea Konkouré	‒‒1.7‒‒		2.2	1.3	1.0	0.7	0.8	1.0	2.4	3.8	
Mali Central Niger Delta		1.0	1.6	1.3	1.8	1.0	2.0	2.0	4.1	2.5	
Mozambique		0.9	3.5	5.1	5.1	5.0	4.9	5.1	4.3	2.7	
Central		0.6	3.2	4.8	5.1	5.0	4.6	4.5	3.6	2.0	
North		1.6	5.1	6.6	6.3	6.3	6.4	7.3	7.0	5.4	
South		0.4	1.7	2.8	2.7	2.9	2.7	2.9	1.8	0.8	
Niger	‒‒0.9‒‒		‒‒1.0‒‒		‒‒2.1‒‒		‒‒3.4‒‒		‒‒4.0‒‒		
Portuguese Guinea		1.1	2.6	2.3	1.8	1.8	2.0	2.0	1.9	1.3	2.8
Sanegal and Mauritania											
Fouta-Toro	‒‒4.0‒‒		5.5	3.0	4.6	4.4	5.1	7.4	7.4	3.3	
Togo Kabré Country		0.1	0.5	1.0	0.2	–	0.7	2.8	2.1	1.5	

childbirth. If no new remarriages of this type took place after age 45 the relative frequency of inherited widows would dwindle as the new husbands died and the women fell back into the category of widows. In fact, however, the proportion in this category rises, showing continued movement into this status (Table 5.10).

Table 5.10. Proportion of widows and inherited widows by age—Guinea

Ages	Widows as per cent of all women	Inherited widows as per cent of all women
15-19	0.6	0.2
20-24	1.0	0.9
25-29	1.6	2.0
30-34	2.7	3.8
35-39	4.6	5.4
40-44	8.7	10.4
45-49	16.6	11.2
50-54	24.7	15.2
55+	52.4	15.5

Marriage: Types of Conjugal Union

Conjugal union, as we saw earlier, can be classified in different ways. We shall give major attention here to contrasts (1) between marriage sanctioned by formal legislation or customary law and consensual union and (2) between monogamous and polygynous unions. As shown in Table 5.11 and Figure 5.2, referring to the whole Congo, there is a decline in consensual unions and a rise in marriages with age. There is

Table 5.11. Percentage of spouses in monogamous marriage, monogamous consensual union, and polygynous union, by sex and age—the Congo

	Ages in years						
	15-19	20-24	25-29	30-34	35-44	44-54	55+
Husbands by type of union							
Monogamous union							
Marriage	73.5	78.1	83.5	82.5	76.6	69.5	71.8
Consensual union	25.1	19.4	11.2	7.0	4.9	3.6	2.9
Polygynous union	1.4	2.5	5.3	10.5	18.5	26.9	25.3
Total	100.0	100.0	100.0	100.0	100.0	100.0	100.0
Wives by type of union							
Monogamous union							
Marriage	71.0	72.9	68.8	62.8	57.2	54.3	59.8
Consensual union	16.2	9.2	5.5	4.1	3.3	2.8	2.4
Polygynous union	12.8	18.0	25.7	33.1	39.5	42.9	37.8
Total	100.0	100.1	100.0	100.0	100.0	100.0	100.0

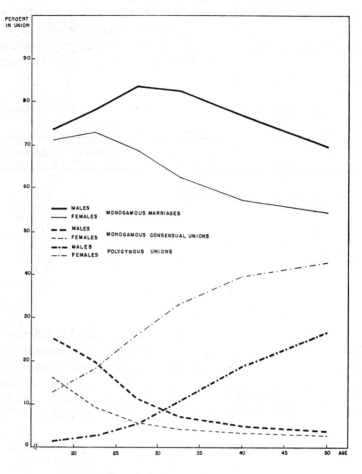

5.2. Types of union in percent of all unions, monogamous, monogamous consensual, and polygynous, by age and sex, for the Congo.

also a rise in polygynous unions as age increases. There is constant transfer among these categories. Consensual unions are depleted in favor of marriages, and monogamous unions in favor of polygynous.

Marriage vs. Consensual Union

Anthropological studies show that whereas most tribes accept conjugal union of some sort as a universal ideal, there is great variation throughout tropical Africa in cultural norms affecting formal marriages. The effects of such variation cannot generally be demonstrated at present from the results of demographic censuses and inquiries. As we have seen, most of the latter do not provide adequate data on consensual unions, due to a failure to apply any specific criteria. The Congolese data are exceptional in this respect. Consensual unions are explicitly defined and differentiated from customary legal unions in the Congo inquiry.

As there defined, the so-called *unions de fait* (consensual unions) include three types: (1) unions for which no bridewealth has been paid or ceremony held; (2) unions for which only a part of the bridewealth has been paid, only preliminary rites celebrated; and finally (3) unions for which all customary requirements were fulfilled but which are classified as illegal with respect to official legislation, notably recent polygynous unions. The first of these categories is presumably most important numerically, though the results at some points may be affected to an unknown degree by the other types also defined as consensual.

Table 5.11 shows a sharp decrease of the percentage of consensual unions with age in the Congo. The same conclusion must be drawn from Table 5.12, which gives the proportion of consensual unions by provinces, and from Figure 5.2, which shows the relative importance of marriages and consensual unions in the country as a whole. The younger the

Table 5.12. Consensual unions in percent of all monogamous unions, by age and sex—provinces of the Congo

	15-19	20-24	25-29	30-34	35-44	45-54	55+	Total
				Males				
Equateur	22.7	16.3	11.2	7.8	6.1	4.9	4.0	7.7
Kasai	23.6	18.7	10.0	6.7	4.7	4.0	3.4	6.6
Katanga	12.7	9.1	4.9	3.3	2.6	2.3	1.9	3.5
Kivu	14.6	9.3	5.0	4.0	3.2	3.3	2.7	4.5
Leopoldville	50.7	34.0	19.1	11.0	8.1	7.3	5.9	12.4
Orientale	45.2	27.7	15.6	11.3	8.2	6.0	4.6	10.6
Total Congo	25.4	19.9	11.9	7.8	6.0	5.0	3.9	8.1
				Females				
Equateur	19.5	11.6	7.7	6.3	5.4	4.8	3.9	7.6
Kasai	16.4	7.7	5.6	4.6	4.6	4.5	3.1	6.3
Katanga	8.2	4.0	3.1	2.9	2.5	2.1	2.5	3.5
Kivu	9.1	4.4	3.4	3.2	3.7	3.3	2.4	4.4
Leopoldville	34.0	19.4	10.5	8.1	6.5	7.2	6.1	12.5
Orientale	26.0	14.2	11.0	9.0	7.1	5.6	4.9	10.3
Total Congo	18.6	11.2	7.4	6.1	5.4	4.9	4.0	8.0

age, the greater the proportion of the unions that are consensual. The peak in the actual number of consensual unions is reached between 20 and 25 for females and 25 and 30 for males. The numbers, as well as the proportions of all unions that are consensual, decline steadily thereafter.

The steady decline of consensual unions with age shows clearly that they represent a transitional stage in conjugal status. There are, however, a few consensual unions after 55, which show that there is a small core of persons who never normalize their union or contract a full marriage. Another significant finding is that there are important differences among the provinces. This supports the suggestion offered above as to the importance of cultural conditions affecting the relative frequency of consensual unions.

Monogamous vs. Polygynous Unions

Table 5.13 (Regions of Africa) and Table 5.14 (Congo Provinces) give measures of the incidence (polygynists per 100 married men) and of the intensity (wives per 100 polygynists) of polygyny. They also show numbers of married women per 100 married men as a summary index.

In most of the countries for which there are data on the number of

Table 5.13. Measures of polygyny—African regions

	Incidence: polygynists per 100 married men p	Intensity: wives per 100 polygynists w	General index: married women per 100 married men m
Burundi	-	-	104
Cameroon			
Mbalmayo	12	(242)**	117
Central African Republic			
Oubangui Center	26	238+	132
Congo	17	225	121
Dahomey	31	(235)	142
Guinea*	38	251+	158
Forest	35	(246)	151
Fouta Djallon	41	(256)	164
Maritime	39	(244)	156
Upper	37	(251)	156
Guinea			
Konkoure	40	254+	162
Mali			
Central Niger Delta	23	215	127
Mozambique			123
Central	-	-	124
North	-	-	122
South	-	-	121
Niger	22	210	125
Portuguese Guinea	-	-	150
Senegal	27	(237)	137
Senegal and Mauritania			
Fouta-Toro	21	223	126
Sudan	16	-	-
Tanganyika	21	226+	127+
Togo			
Kabre country	-	-	150

Notes: - Indices computed from two other columns are in parentheses.
  - + indicates that the data on number of wives are given with the last category not detailed; 4 or more, 5 or more, etc.
  * Data for Guinea do not include inherited wives.
  ** The report gives the impossible figure of 57 wives per 100 polygynists.

Table 5.14. Measures of polygyny—Congo provinces

Province	Incidence	Intensity	General index: Reported	General index: Calculated
	p	w	m	m'
Equateur	19	225	123	124
Kasai	21	233	130	128
Katanga	12	215	115	114
Kivu	16	228	120	120
Leopoldville	14	224	110	117
Stanleyville	17	220	119	120
Total Congo	17	225	121	121

married women per 100 polygynists, these have been collected by interviewing the men only, so that the identity

$$m = 1 + p \, (w - 1)$$

(where m is the number of married women per married man, p is the
proportion of polygynists among married males, and w is the number
of wives per polygynist) is merely formal and can be used, as in Table
5.13, to derive one of the indices from the two others. In the Congo,
however, married women were asked whether they were wives of polygynists or of monogamists, and married men were asked the number of
wives. These two sets of data may be affected by different errors if husbands and wives are separated, as for example if the inquiry finds the
husband in a town and his wife or some or all of his wives in a village.
Where such conditions are prevalent the formula provides a check on the
internal consistency of the data. Despite the disturbing effect of interprovincial migration, the match is very good even within provinces (see
Table 5.14). The agreement appears to be perfect for the Congo as a
whole.

There is a significant correlation ($r = .86$) among the 26 districts between incidence and intensity. One might have expected that, due to
limitation in supply of potential wives, where there are many polygynists
there would be few wives per polygynist. The Congo data, however, indicate that where polygyny is practiced extensively there is both high
incidence and high intensity.

Tables 5.15 and 5.16 give for the Congo and Guinea the evolution
of polygyny with age for both sexes. (See also Figure 5.3.)

African men take supplementary wives as they grow older and more
affluent, and as they inherit the wives of deceased relatives. There is a
steady increase of polygyny with age in both the Congo and Guinea for
both sexes. The data indicate that polygyny is less prevalent in the
Congo than in Guinea at all ages, but that the rise with age is much
steeper in the Congo. When wives over 45 are compared with those aged

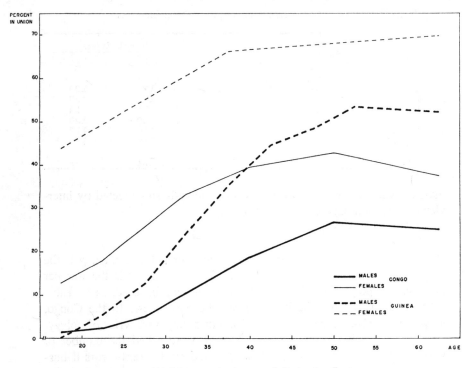

5.3. Polygynous unions in percent of all unions, by age and
sex, for the Congo and Guinea.

15-29 years, the percentage in polygynous unions doubles in the Congo
but increases only 40 percent in Guinea. We must, however, be cautious
about any inferences based on these data because of the possible effects
of the 1951 regulation both on the practice of polygyny and on the reporting of actual conjugal relations in the Congo. The steepness of the
apparent increase with age may be due, to an unknown extent, to a decline of polygyny in the younger cohorts or to bias in the reports. On

Table 5.15. Percentage of married persons in polygynous unions,
by sex and age—the Congo

Ages	Men	Women
15-19	1.4	12.7
20-24	2.6	18.0
25-29	5.3	25.7
30-34	10.5	33.1
35-44	18.5	39.5
45-54	26.9	42.9
55 and over	25.3	37.8
Total	16.6	31.0

Table 5.16. Percentage distribution of married persons by number of spouses, by sex and age—Guinea

Age	Married men with specified number of wives			Married women whose husbands have specified number of wives		
	1	2	3+	1	2	3+
14-19	100.0	*	..			
20-24	94.3	5.7	–	50.4	30.8	18.8
25-29	87.2	12.2	0.6			
30-34	75.7	20.3	4.0			
35-39	64.5	28.0	7.5	33.5	33.7	32.7
40-44	55.3	30.8	13.9			
45-49	51.6	30.6	17.8			
50-54	46.6	31.3	22.1	31.4	31.2	37.5
55 and over	47.7	29.2	23.1			

the other hand, the omission of inherited widows[20] from the count of polygynous couples introduces a bias in the Guinea data and tends to depress the recorded proportions.

The existence of plural marriages in a society in which almost all men are married presents an apparent paradox. This has led to considerable speculation about the presence of surplus women. Some strong polygynous tribes do draw additional wives from other tribes (see, for example, the study of a southern Nigerian village by Enid Charles and Daryll Forde).[21] This is a rather exceptional practice, and obviously impossible in a large, relatively closed population.[22] The problem is quite simply resolved by taking account of the age structure of populations and differences by sex in age at marriage. For example, if males and females were strictly identical in number at every age, the age patterns of marriage in Guinea would automatically yield a surplus of married women over married men. This is illustrated in Table 5.17 on the basis of a hypothetical stable population with the reported nuptiality of Guinea by sex and age.[23] These conditions yield a potential supply of 139 married women per 100 married men.

$$\frac{\text{Married females}}{100 \text{ Married males}} = \frac{5,258}{3,785} \times 100 = 139$$

[20] Inherited widows were classified as such only if the new union had not produced any child.

[21] Quoted in Frank Lorimer, *Culture and Human Fertility*, UNESCO, 1954, p. 98.

[22] For a general treatment of this topic, see V. R. Dorjahn, *The Factor of Polygyny in African Demography*.

[23] A stable population with a life table of the North family of models (Princeton Series) and the following characteristics: females, birth rate 44, death rate 34. These rates are presumed to be similar to those in Guinea.

Table 5.17. Numbers of married men and of married women in a hypothetical stable population (assuming equal numbers of males and females at each age) subject to Guinea's male and female nuptiality

Age	Population (each sex)	Per Cent Married		Number Married	
		Males	Females	Males	Females
0-13	3,597	-	-	-	-
14-19	1,167	.9	73.3	11	855
20-24	869	23.5	96.2	204	836
25-29	779	56.9	96.4	443	751
30-34	690	78.8	95.9	544	662
35-39	605	86.7	94.2	525	570
40-44	526	90.2	90.7	474	477
45-49	454	91.0	82.8	413	376
50-54	386	91.2	74.1	352	286
55-59	319	91.7	61.4	293	196
60-64	248	86.9	51.0	216	126
65-69	176	89.2	40.2	157	71
70+	184	83.4	28.3	153	52
Total	10,000			3,785	5,258

Table 5.17 (and Figure 5.4) show only in a general way how sex differences in marriage patterns produce a surplus of wives. The calculated number of wives per married man (1.39) is far below the actual ratio in Guinea if inherited widows are counted as wives (1.68). The difference is due to a combination of several factors, of which the two following are most important:

(1) Differential mortality by sex tends, despite a small excess of males at birth, to bring an excess of females among adults. This factor was ignored in our model for lack of data; we arbitrarily assumed equal numbers of males and females at each age. According to the reported results of the Guinea inquiry there were 122 females per 100 males among persons aged 14 years or over.

(2) Both the reported numbers of persons by age in Guinea and their reported distribution by marital status are affected by considerable bias, notably the inclusion of married females of less than 14 years in the adult population.

A high ratio of wives to husbands in a polygynous population is made possible, apart from differences in the total numbers of adult males and adult females, by the delayed marriage of males—especially in a population with sharply decreasing numbers of persons at successive ages. This may be partly offset (as shown in Figure 5.4) by an excess of married males at ages over 45 years resulting from the more frequent remarriage of males at advanced ages. The relation to polygyny of other factors, such as permanent celibacy of males, differences in rates of remarriage before age 45, and so on, usually have only secondary effects on sex ratios among married persons.

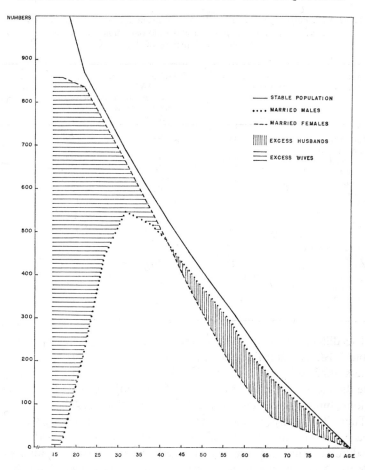

5.4. Surplus of wives in polygyny. Hypothetical stable population with Guinea's nuptiality.

The data now available from censuses and inquiries show certain general relations among (a) the number of married women per married man, (b) the differences in age at marriage, and (c) the percent of widowed and divorced among women over 45 years (see Table 5.18). Guinea, where polygyny is most intense, shows the greatest difference between males and females in mean age at marriage and the lowest percentage of widows and divorcees among women over age 45 years. Burundi, which stands out for its low polygyny, shows small difference in age at marriage and a high percentage of widowed and divorced women. Fouta-Toro has moderate polygyny together with a great difference in marriage age, but this discrepancy is compensated by a very high percentage of divorced and widowed women after the childbearing years.

Table 5.18. Polygyny, difference in singulate mean age of marriage between the sexes, and percentage divorced and widowed among women aged 45 and over—regions of Africa

Country or region	Married women per 100 married men m	Difference in SMAM between males and females (years)	Per cent widowed and divorced women 45 and over
Burundi	104	0.8	52.6
Cameroon Mbalmayo	117	7.1	57.9
Congo	121	6.0	46.2
Dahomey	142	8.0	43.7
Guinea	158	10.9	36.3
Guinea Konkouré	162	10.2	22.5
Mali Central Niger Delta	127	11.3	49.2
Mozambique	123	4.4	48.1
Niger	125	⁓	66.0
Portuguese Guinea	150	9.5	38.9
Senegal and Mauretania Fouta – Toro	126	11.0	58.8
Togo Kabré country	150	8.8	52.4

The difference in singulate mean ages at marriage has been used in Table 5.18, as a substitute for a measure of age at marriage that would be less affected by age misreporting. We have not yet been able to compute the mean ages at marriage in the stable population for these various regions, but present them for the Congo in Table 5.19.

There is a highly significant correlation ($r = .80$) among Congo districts[24] between number of married women per 100 married men and the difference in mean age at marriage between the sexes. Although one fails to register a significant correlation between polygyny and the pro-

Table 5.19. Polygyny, difference in mean age at marriage in stable population, between the sexes, and percentage divorced and widowed among women aged 45 and over—provinces of the Congo

	Married women 100 married men	Difference in age of marriage	Per cent Widowed + divorced 45 and over
Equateur	123	5.2	40.6
Kasai	130	6.7	51.5
Katanga	115	4.4	45.5
Kivu	120	4.0	44.6
Leopoldville	119	5.8	53.3
Orientale	119	4.2	40.4

[24] Only the 18 districts where no past decline in fertility was noticeable; i.e., those where the age distribution could be assimilated to a stable population for the computation of the mean age at first marriage in the stable population, as defined earlier in this section.

portion divorced and widowed among women aged 45 years and over, there is a significant negative correlation ($r = -.45$) between the number of married women per 100 married men and the proportion widowed and divorced among women 15-45 years old. This apparently reflects a slightly more rapid remarriage of fecund women in districts where polygyny is more important.

We must add a final word of caution. One would not be warranted in concluding from the evidence presented here that polygyny causes a difference between the sexes in age at marriage, or that polygyny condemns adult men to celibacy.[25] Moreover, sex differences in age at marriage, though a necessary condition for a high frequency of polygyny in a closed population, does not necessarily cause polygyny. Polygyny is merely one of a set of interrelated factors, including age at marriage of both men and women and remarriage rates of the widowed and divorced persons in the population, as well as social structure and cultural values. It is impossible to foresee how a change in one of these factors may affect the others.

Urban-Rural Nuptiality Differentials

The study of differences between rural Africa and its urban areas encounters one special type of problem: there is continuous interaction between the two types of community. Vital events (births, deaths for instance) which affect the urban population, occur in the villages, and vice versa. The study of marriage has to face this difficulty as well. Two aspects will be discussed here: first, the problems raised by the migration of married men unaccompanied by their wives; second, those raised by the features of the age distribution in towns that impede comparisons.

The Urban-Rural Continuum

Data from the general censuses and inquiries are often tabulated by type of community. There is, however, little agreement from one country to another on the division between "urban" and "rural" segments of the population. In the Congo, the rural population is that which has mainly agricultural occupations, while the predominantly non-agricultural population in localities of less than 2,000 inhabitants is classified as "mixed" and the remainder in larger towns, as urban. In Guinea, the urban centers are, "with the exception of Conakri and perhaps Kankan, essentially big villages, with strong rural ties and weak, or negligible industrial and commercial development."[26] In Togo, Lomé (65,000 inhabitants) and 7 townships (*communes urbaines*) of approximately ten thousand each, that were in some cases but clusters of villages, made up

[25] For a contrary opinion, see J. Binet, *Le mariage en Afrique noire*, Éditions du Cerf, Paris, 1959, p. 73 and p. 92.

[26] *Étude démographique par sondage en Guinée 1954-55*, p. 8.

the urban population. The effect of urbanization on nuptiality can hardly be expected to be the same in countries where such different definitions are applied.

It is generally impossible to use the results of special surveys in towns for urban-rural comparisons. This is especially difficult if, as is often the case in urban surveys, the population is not sharply defined as *de jure* or *de facto*. This distinction in studies of nuptiality cannot be neglected in regions where many men go to town temporarily and leave their wives behind in charge of their interests in the village. If the men are recorded as married in the towns, there will, in some cases, be a tendency to include reports on their wives even if these are not present. This may have happened in some of the urban centers of the Ivory Coast where a census was taken in 1956-57. Indeed, in three of these centers (Agboville, Dimbokro, and Man) each monogamist can be exactly matched with one present wife, each bigamist with two, and each polygynist of subsequent order with the required number of present wives. In the other centers of the Ivory Coast, where polygyny is recorded as less important, such matching is not possible.

Most censuses and inquiries in the towns, or where rural and urban regions are contrasted, have been taken on a *de facto* basis, or at least have relied heavily upon the notion of usual residence. The census of Mozambique has certain aspects of a *de jure* census. All the migrants who were out of the country at the time of the census were to be included. Within Mozambique, however, the towns have an excess of married males over married females, as expected in a *de facto* census. In Lourenço Marques, for instance, there are only 50 married women per 100 married men.

The ratio of married women to married men in a *de facto* census combines the effects of polygyny and of differential migration according to sex. Polygyny increases the ratio of wives to husbands; differential migration has the opposite effect in the towns. It would be interesting to isolate the two effects and to determine to what extent women accompany their husbands to the towns. This is only possible in a few countries. The censuses of Abidjan and Dakar give for each married woman the order of her husband's marriage with her, and for each man the number of his wives. To each bigamist correspond, if both wives live in town, one wife of first order and one wife of second order. By cumulating backward the number of men with at least 5 wives, at least 4, 3, 2, and 1 wife, and by comparing the total with the number of wives of 5th, 4th, 3rd, 2nd, and 1st order, one can obtain an indication of the extent to which polygynists of each order leave their wives in the rural regions. The results of this calculation are shown in Table 5.20. Results for Dakar are marred by the large proportion of married persons who

Table 5.20. Estimate of the deficit of wives living in the villages, derived from the number of wives of specified order and implied from the degree of polygyny of the husbands—Dakar and Abidjan

| Order | Number of wives of a specified order | | | | Deficit of wives in percent | |
| | Derived from degree of polygyny of husbands | | Derived from order of wives | | | |
	Dakar	Abidjan	Dakar	Abidjan	Dakar	Abidjar
1	30,399	21,024	28,327	20,063	7.3	4.8
2	5,327	3,269	4,655	2,799	14.4	16.8
3	897	472	794	415	13.0	13.7
4	165	101	176	89	-6.7*	13.5
5 and over	5	9	13	18	–	–
Total	36,793	24,875	33,765	23,384	8.3	6.4

* Excess of wives

did not give information on this subject. These results apparently suggest that in Abidjan over 6 percent of the wives are left outside of town, and that the percentage is lowest for wives of the first order, who are mostly wives of monogamists.

Another approach to this question is possible with data for the Congo. The number of monogamously married men and women is given by type of residence (rural, mixed, urban). For the Congo as a whole, there are 100.2 monogamously married females per 100 monogamously married males. This near equality supports confidence in the accuracy and completeness of the enumeration. In the absence of interprovincial migration and apart from the effect of sampling errors, the ratio per province should also be very near 100. The excess over 100 in the rural regions and the corresponding deficit in the mixed and urban regions indicate the extent of differential migration to the towns (see Table 5.21). In Leopoldville Township, for which there is specific information on this

Table 5.21. Number of monogamously married wives per 100 monogamous husbands, by province and by type of settlement—the Congo

Province*	Rural	Mixed	Urban	Total
Equateur	101	93	94	100
Kasai	103	97	98	102
Katanga	105	95	94	101
Kivu	103	91	98	100
Leopoldville	107	92	92	102

* Comparable information not available for Orientale Province.

subject, 12.7 percent of the married men (whether polygynists or monogamists) were recorded as not accompanied by wives. Of married women in the township 1.3 percent were not accompanied by a husband.

The differences by type of settlement, though considerable, are not as large as might be expected on the basis of some special urban studies in other African countries. For instance, grass widowers represented 28 percent of the married males in Livingstone in 1952-53.[27] In this connection it may be important to take account of special measures adopted by the government of the Congo to promote the movement of family units in the settlement of urban localities.

Effect of Urban-Rural Age Differences

The meaning of urban marriage statistics is generally obscured by the temporary separation of spouses associated with migration. Another upsetting factor is that of the different age structures of urban and rural populations. Towns teem with young people. Most marriage characteristics are, as we have seen, heavily dependent on age. Before one can prove that people behave differently in the towns than in the tribal environment, one must eliminate the effect of age. One way of doing this is to standardize the information to a selected age distribution. The results obtained in the Congo provinces, using the total national population as a standard, are shown in Table 5.22. The standardization generally reduces the differences in nuptiality among rural, mixed, and rural populations, although it does not produce any clear general pattern.

The percentage in wedlock is of course equal to one minus the per-

Table 5.22. Crude and standardized proportions males and females aged 20 and over who are in conjugal unions, by province and by type of settlement—provinces of the Congo

Sex and Provinces*		Crude			Standardized		
		Rural %	Mixed %	Urban %	Rural %	Mixed %	Urban %
Males							
	Equateur	78.8	76.2	76.7	77.6	76.9	77.3
	Kasai	80.3	80.7	77.6	78.4	80.3	81.5
	Katanga	80.5	81.1	83.9	79.1	83.1	84.4
	Kivu	82.1	76.6	78.3	83.1	77.7	79.9
	Leopoldville	81.7	75.6	63.3	81.1	82.4	71.5
Females							
	Equateur	80.3	91.4	81.6	82.7	85.7	79.8
	Kasai	78.3	91.4	84.0	78.4	83.1	73.1
	Katanga	75.6	92.3	90.0	77.1	86.3	80.7
	Kivu	81.0	92.8	83.4	81.8	84.1	78.1
	Leopoldville	71.4	93.7	85.0	72.3	85.4	78.4

* No similar information available for Orientale Province.

[27] Merran McCulloch, *A Social Survey of the African Population of Livingstone,* Rhodes-Livingstone Paper No. 26, p. 20.

centage single, divorced, and widowed. The percent of males who are single is exceptionally high in Leopoldville, the metropolis of the Congo, but it is not significantly different in other urban regions from the proportions in the rural areas. The proportions of females who are single by type of settlement do not differ systematically among regions. Neither do the proportions of widowed and divorced males, nor the proportion of widowed females as shown by more detailed statistics. However, the proportion of divorced persons among women is everywhere largest in the urban regions of the Congo. Results for different countries would presumably differ widely. In Togo, for instance, the proportion single is at all ages greater in townships than in villages (as it is in Leopoldville). On the other hand, non-married women are normally not permitted in towns of Northern Rhodesia; in Livingstone (1952), married females represented 96 percent of those aged 15 and over.[28]

Moreover, the absence of marked quantitative differences in marital status by type of community in the Congo conceals important qualitative differences in social relations. The most striking differences in marital status between urban and rural regions in the Congo appear in the proportions of consensual and polygynous unions. Rather surprisingly, the incidence of consensual unions is less in towns than in rural areas, despite the presumed laxity of the urban mores and the instability of urban marriage (see Table 5.23). Standardization by age increases

Table 5.23. Percentage of monogamous unions that are consensual, by type of settlement—provinces of the Congo

Province*	Males			Females		
	Rural	Mixed	Urban	Rural	Mixed	Urban
Equateur	6.7	11.0	5.5	6.7	11.0	5.6
Kasai	6.9	6.5	3.4	6.5	6.5	3.3
Katanga	3.6	4.8	2.3	3.6	4.7	2.7
Kivu	4.2	6.0	3.5	4.0	6.0	3.6
Leopoldville	13.8	15.8	6.2	13.6	17.0	6.1

* No similar information available for Orientale Province.

rather than decreases the difference. Apparently in the Congo social pressures toward the early formalization of marriage (perhaps including the effects of the system of family allowances) are stronger in towns than in rural communities. Marriages can be arranged in the towns with less cost or obligation to kin groups.[29] In particular, the practice of entering a consensual union as a first stage in married life may have declined under urban conditions.

[28] McCulloch, op.cit., p. 20.
[29] See P. Clement in Social Aspects of Industrialization and Urbanization in Africa South of the Sahara, UNESCO, Paris, 1956, pp. 417ff.

Polygyny as a recognized institution has all but disappeared in the towns of the Congo—presumably due both to economic conditions and to social and legal influences (see Table 5.24).

Table 5.24. Polygynists per 100 married males, by type of settlement: crude and standardized proportions—the Congo

Province*	Crude			Standardized		
	Rural	Mixed	Urban	Rural	Mixed	Urban
Equateur	22.5	10.7	4.9	21.4	12.5	5.3
Kasai	23.6	7.5	4.4	22.0	8.3	6.8
Katanga	16.7	9.4	2.2	15.6	10.9	2.9
Kivu	19.4	5.4	2.2	19.8	7.7	3.1
Leopoldville	19.1	4.6	2.1	17.8	6.4	2.8

* No similar information available for Orientale Province.

The situation in this respect is quite different in Guinea. Here the two standardized series are remarkably close, especially in view of the crudities of the data (Table 5.25). The so-called urban centers of Guinea still have an important agricultural component in which polygyny retains its social prestige.

Table 5.25. Polygynists per 100 married males, by type of settlement: crude and standardized proportions—Guinea

Regions	Crude		Standardized	
	Rural Areas	Urban Centers	Rural Areas	Urban Centers
Forest	34.5	35.9	34.3	38.1
Fouta-Djallon	41.1	40.0	41.6	41.3
Maritime	40.2	34.7	37.4	38.2
Upper	37.2	36.4	36.4	39.1

An extension of the treatment of this topic, as of other parts of this study, to include the results of various intensive investigations would reveal many significant differences in marriage patterns and in the effects of migration on conjugal status. Such an extension is, however, beyond the scope of this undertaking. We have attempted to show, mostly from the Congo material, what pitfalls are encountered in a study of marital status by type of settlement in the censuses and inquiries of the type examined in this chapter.

Marital Status and Fertility

The study of the relationship of marital status to fertility will be considered in two main directions. First, we will examine age-specific fertility rates by marital status, opposing illegitimate fertility to legitimate fertility, and comparing fertility in various types of legitimate unions: consensual union and marriage, monogamous and polygynous union. Second, the effect of the age at marriage on fertility will be investigated.

In the treatment of both points, it will be emphasized that apparent relations between marital status and fertility can either consist of the influence of marital state on fertility or of fertility on marital state. This ambiguity, though not limited to any world region, is especially important in Africa, where interest in marriage is to a considerable degree subordinate to interest in progeny.[30]

Age-Specific Fertility Rates by Marital State and Type of Union

The study of legitimate fertility is of great interest in demography. It isolates the fertility performance of women living under wedlock or in sufficiently stable unions, on the assumption that other women are not exposed, at least to the same degree, to the risks of conception.[31]

For demographic purposes, "strictly speaking, a legitimate child may be defined as one whose father and mother were married to one another at the time of conception."[32] In standard statistical practice, however, all births to a woman in wedlock or within a specified period after the dissolution of a stable union (e.g., 10 months) are normally classed as legitimate. No attempt is ordinarily made to distinguish births resulting from premarital conceptions. Legitimate births may in turn be distinguished as to those conceived or born (1) in a consensual union or a formal marriage or (2) in a monogamous or polygynous union.

Age-specific fertility rates by conjugal status are normally computed from two distinct sets of data: vital registration of births, classified according to marital status of the mother; and distribution of women by marital status as determined in a census. The situation is quite different if exclusive reliance must be placed on the results of a census or survey. The classification of births during the 12 months preceding a survey will be greatly affected by changes in marital status during the interval between births and the time of the survey. These changes could in theory be taken into account by relating the births to the marital status of the mothers at the time of confinement.

The most serious attempt to provide direct information from a large-scale inquiry on fertility by types of conjugal union in an African region was carried out in the Congo. We shall therefore give major attention here to the results of this undertaking. An attempt was made in this in-

---

[30] See Radcliffe-Brown's assertion: "An African marries in order to have children" in Radcliffe-Brown and D. Forde, eds., *op.cit.*, Introduction.

[31] This use of "legitimate" is found in L. Henry, "Some data on natural fertility," *Eugenics Quarterly*, Vol. 8, No. 2, June 1961, pp. 81ff. "A more valid comparison can be made by restricting the study to legitimate birth rates, or the equivalent; that is, the fertility of women who have formed a union which is stable enough for them to be considered as exposed to the same risk as married women" (p. 82).

[32] *Multilingual Demographic Dictionary*, U.N., New York, 1958, p. 36.

quiry to classify births during the previous year as legitimate or illegitimate and to distinguish among the legitimate births between those resulting from consensual unions and those resulting from formal marriages, with further distinction between births to monogamous and to polygynous marriages.

The enumerators' instructions in the Congo on this point were as follows:

> Children born of a regular marriage will be considered as legitimate and inscribed in column 51 [of the form]. Children conceived in a consensual union will be written down in the same column, but their number will be bracketed: (1), (2), etc.
>
> Children born outside of a marriage relationship (to women single, widowed or divorced) will be considered as illegitimate and inscribed in column 52.
>
> Children born of a monogamous marriage will be inscribed in column 53, those born of a polygamous one in column 54.

In the first paragraph quoted above, the term "conceived" used in referring to consensual unions is equated with "born" with reference to regular unions, and it is assumed in the second paragraph that both of these categories exclude "children born outside of a marriage relationship." This is rather confusing. It may have been assumed that the time of conception was to be taken into account only in the case of births occurring after the dissolution of a marriage or consensual union, but if so this limitation is not stated clearly. There were no explicit instructions to the enumerators about ascertaining the marital status of a woman at confinement if different from that at time of survey. A clear distinction between time of conception, of confinement, and of survey may, notwithstanding the ambiguity of the instructions, have existed in the mind of the interviewers. The effects of these distinctions, if applied, would be apparent in a tabulation of births both by type (illegitimate, consensual, monogamous, etc.) and by the marital status of the mothers at the time of the survey, but no such tabulation is presented in the report. It is, therefore, possible that the published tables represent merely a tabulation of births during the previous year by marital status of the mothers at time of survey.[33] In that case the entries in columns 51 to 53, referred to in the instructions, were not actually exploited.

We shall now examine the data as presented, bearing in mind the problems of interpretation considered above. Apparent age-specific fertility rates by marital status are shown in Table 5.26. We shall first consider

[33] Mr. Romaniuk, though not responsible for the processing of the data and somewhat uncertain on this point, thinks that this may have been the case.

Table 5.26. Age-specific fertility rates per thousand women, by
conjugal status—the Congo

| Age | Single, Widows, Divorcees | Women in Monogamous Unions | | | Women in Polygynous Unions | Women in All Unions |
		Consensual Unions	Formal Marriages	Total		
15-19	35.6	184.4	285.2	266.5	204.7	258.6
20-24	158.2	207.0	299.6	289.2	249.1	282.0
25-29	119.2	150.7	263.4	255.0	206.3	242.4
30-34	73.0	83.9	200.8	193.7	144.4	177.4
35-44	26.8	33.4	104.6	100.8	71.7	89.2
45-54	3.5	8.2	25.0	24.2	18.9	21.4
15-44	61.7	143.9	217.2	210.9	140.7	190.5

the so-called illegitimate birth rates in the first column for single, widowed, and divorced women combined. (These categories are not tabulated separately.) The bulk of the non-married women at ages 15-19 to whom illegitimate children were reportedly born is made up of single women. The confusion between time of birth and time of survey has least effect on the "illegitimate" fertility rate at age 15-19, because women were *a fortiori* single at the time of the birth if they were so at the time of the inquiry. The reported rates at this age are probably below the true rates, but this has no effect on the differentials by provinces and districts. Table 5.27 shows that premarital fertility varies widely among Congo districts between the extreme values for Kwango in Leopoldville Province (illegitimate fertility rate: 8.6 per 1,000 unmarried women aged 15-19 years) and for Luapula-Moëro in Katanga (104.2).

Table 5.27. "Illegitimate" fertility rates per thousand women aged 15-19, and
minimal and maximal values among districts—provinces of the Congo

Province	Average value	Minimal value	Maximal value
Equateur	32.5	20.0	72.4
Kasai	24.0	11.8	33.1
Katanga	89.5	65.5	104.2
Kivu	45.6	25.1	66.3
Leopoldville	26.6	8.6	73.3
Orientale	37.4	16.0	54.5
Total	36.4	8.6	104.2

After age 25, however, the so-called illegitimate children are mainly born to women who are widowed or divorced. We have noted earlier that the marital status at the time of the survey is in principle irrelevant to the legitimacy of the child, and that the latter is determined by the time of conception or of birth. As widowhood and divorces are usually phases of short duration among women of childbearing age in the Congo, the risks of conceiving and giving birth to a truly illegitimate child around age 25 must be rather small—presumably less than is implied by the rates in the first column of Table 5.26. These figures could be explained by the confusion of time of survey and time of conception. If they are the result of a tabulation of births by marital status at time of the survey, they must include an unknown (presumably large) proportion of legitimate births.

The two next columns of Table 5.26 purport to afford a comparison between the fertility of monogamous consensual unions and formal marriages. The former is substantially lower. This difference does not imply *per se* that formal marriage is more conducive to fertility than consensual union. There is normally an attrition of the numbers of women in consensual unions by the formalization of conjugal relations between a first conception and a first birth (or shortly thereafter). Indeed, the consensual union is frequently a transitional stage before marriage, and it is quite reasonable to assume that the transition may be speeded up by the pregnancy or childbirth. Such change in conjugal status tends to raise the fertility rates for regular marriages and to lower those for consensual unions. (This effect is not dependent on a confusion between time of birth and time of survey, but would be intensified by such confusion.)

The same reasoning does not apply directly to the mutual relation of polygynous and monogamous fertility. If there is no systematic tendency to conceive a child while one is a polygynist's wife, but to give birth at a time when the husband would be counted as a monogamist (another wife having died), lower polygynous fertility rates can be viewed as showing real differential fertility. Furthermore, it seems that useful information can be obtained from a tabulation of births during the previous year in function of the monogamous or polygynous status of women at the time of the survey, because changes of status in this respect will not generally have a large effect on the results. (Such tabulations were made for Guinea and for the Central Niger Delta, and might well be extended to other inquiries.) The findings of the Congo inquiry, shown in Table 5.26, are therefore impressive. They indicate significantly higher fertility rates for monogamous wives at all ages.

This finding is echoed in the data for the Central Niger Delta but not confirmed by the information for Guinea (see Table 5.28). In the latter country, the differences in age-specific fertility rates are slight and somewhat erratic, though the general fertility rate is higher for women whose husbands have fewer wives, due to differences in the age distribution of women by type of marriage. This result is surprising because other Guinea data show a decline of fertility with increasing age of the husband. The mean age of a monogamist is 40, the mean age of a bigamist 45, and the mean age of a polygynist with more than two wives is 51

Table 5.28. Age-specific fertility rates per thousand wives, according to number of wives of the husband—Guinea

Age	Number of Wives of Husband:			
	1 Wife	2 Wives	3 Wives and more	All Wives
14–19	283	266	277	278
20–24	358	328	341	345
25–29	331	318	318	323
30–34	262	272	257	264
35–39	199	181	183	188
40–44	86	93	73	84
45–49	57	32	28	38
14–49	274	246	222	252

years. The computed total fertility of wives with husbands[34] aged 20 to 29 years is 8; aged 30 to 39, 7.5; 40 to 49, 7; and 50 to 59 years, 6.4. To reconcile this evidence with that presented in Table 5.28, one has to assume higher fertility at each age for polygynous husbands. We suggest a mechanism that may have fictitiously raised the computed fertility of women in polygynous households. The reader may remember that in this inquiry inherited widows were classified as wives only if they had borne a child within the present union. The marital fertility of this class of women was therefore overestimated. This would mainly affect the polygynous fertility rates if widows are usually inherited by men who are already married.

Influence of Fertility
on Marital Status

We will now deal with the important question of the possible influence of fertility (or infertility) on marital state. The following hypotheses merit investigation:

(A) Where the consensual union is a preliminary stage of marriage, women who have given birth to less children, or at longer intervals, than expected, tend to remain longer in this state.

(B) Subfecund women are increasingly subject to the risk that their husbands will take additional wives to improve their prospects for progeny.

(C) Subfecund women are more likely to be divorced and to have greater difficulty in remarrying if divorced or widowed.

If each of these hypotheses were true, the women concerned would tend with age to be increasingly selected with respect to conjugal status according to their fertility. It follows, on Hypothesis A, that the ratio of

[34] The sum of the age-specific fertility rates of women married to men of the specified ages, expressed in children per woman.

the fertility of women in consensual union to that of women in formal marriage would decrease as the age of the women increases. A similar decrease would be expected, on Hypothesis B, in the ratio of the fertility of women in polygynous union to that of women in monogamous union. These two series of ratios for the Congo are set out in Table 5.29. Unfortunately, we cannot test Hypothesis C in this way because of the confusion, mentioned above, in the rates intended to measure illegitimacy.

Table 5.29. Comparison of age-specific fertility rates: (A) women in consensual unions and in formal marriages; (B) wives of polygynists and of monogamists—the Congo

| Women's Ages | Ratios of Fertility of | |
	(A) Consensual Unions to Marriages	(B) Polygynous to Monogamous Unions
15-19	.65	.77
20-24	.69	.86
25-29	.57	.81
30-34	.42	.75
35-44	.32	.71
45-54	.33	.78

The trend of Series A fits well with the first hypothesis stated above. On the other hand, though Series B indicates that polygynous fertility is less than monogamous fertility at all ages, the movement of the ratios with age in this column is irregular. The results do not provide a clear confirmation of Hypothesis B.

For a test of Hypothesis C on the possible influence of infertility on the chances of divorce and of remarriage, we must resort to data on the number of children ever born to women of a given age according to the number of marriages ever contracted. In Guinea (see Table 5.30), the latter shows a consistent negative relation to the former (excluding, of course, the case of women who have never married). This, however,

Table 5.30. Children ever born to women above age 50, according to total number of marriages ever contracted—Guinea

Number of marriages	Children ever born per woman
0	1.70
1	5.69
2	5.32
3	4.82
4	4.20
5 and over	4.05

leaves the nature of this relation an open question. Does marital instability cause low fertility, or is low fertility conducive to marital instability? Either or both these effects may be operative here.

Data from the Fouta-Toro inquiry on childless women (i.e., those who have never borne a child alive) classified by age and by number of marriages provide some further information on this subject (Table 5.31). Unfortunately, there are numerous irregularities in this table

Table 5.31. Percentages of women childless, by age and by number of marriages—Fouta-Toro

Age	Percent Childless Among Women Married Specified Number of Times					Percent Childless Among All Women
	0	1	2	3	4, over, and unknown number	
14-19	99.4	48.8	46.4	33.3	75.0	64.8
20-24	88.2	17.8	13.0	36.1	19.0	20.6
25-29	93.3	17.1	17.3	23.1	4.6	18.2
30-34	-	8.2	24.9	18.7	31.4	15.8
35-39	-	7.3	6.3	11.2	11.1	8.2
40-44	-	5.5	9.2	.15.3	21.2	10.2
45 and over	-	6.6	12.7	11.8	16.6	8.9
All Ages	95.4	16.1	14.3	16.5	17.9	19.9

(probably due, at least in part, to random fluctuations in a small sample). The results are, nevertheless, fairly consistent at ages over 30. It is unlikely that repeated marriage would have caused a significant increase in total sterility at these ages. These data support thus the hypothesis that childlessness was conducive to marital instability in this region (but not that it was an impediment to remarriage).

The only conclusions warranted on the basis of the fragmentary data reviewed in these paragraphs devoted to the influence of fertility (or infertility) on marital status, is that the available evidence supports some, though not all, of the hypotheses which we have considered, and that the whole subject requires further attention and more intensive investigation.

Age at Marriage and Fertility

We have up to this point discussed the relations between fertility and conjugal status. This section would not be complete without a discussion of the associations between age at marriage and levels of fertility. Available statistics do not allow sufficient insight in this matter, so that we will have to discuss the point on a more theoretical plane.

If all other things were equal, an earlier age at marriage for females would bring about a greater size of the completed family, because those who marry earlier than others are subjected to the risks of conception during a longer part of their fecund life. There are, however, social or physiological mechanisms that may reduce the subsequent fertility of women who marry early or enhance it for those who marry late.

Table 5.32. Singulate mean age of females at marriage, total fertility per woman, and crude birth rate—regions of Africa

Region (in order of mean age of marriage)	SMAM in years	Total fertility per woman	Crude birth rate per thousand
Guinea	15.8	5.9	46
Fouta-Toro	16.5	6.3	46
Dahomey	16.9	6.5	49
Portuguese Guinea	18.3	4.4	35
Congo	18.3	5.6	43
Mozambique	19.4	5.1	38
Burundi	22.1	6.7	49

Table 5.32 gives no clear support to the thesis that age at marriage is a major determinant of levels of fertility in Africa. Of the two countries on both ends of the range, the lower birth rate and the lower total fertility are found in Guinea where women marry on the average some six years earlier than in Burundi. The concentration of births during the married years must therefore be denser in Burundi, with shorter intervals between births, or fertility must be maintained well into later ages there than in Guinea. In fact, the specific fertility rates in Burundi, though inferior prior to age 25, appear superior thereafter, as shown in the lower part of Figure 5.5. Ratios of specific fertility rates at various ages to that at 20-24 years (taken as 100) are also plotted in Figure 5.5 to show patterns of fertility independently of differences in level. The fertility of the age group 15-19 is as expected, closely related to the proportion of married women at these ages. The shape of the curve after age 25 years shows the steepness of the decline of fertility with age.

The difficulty in evaluating the possible influence of age at marriage on fertility in Africa is increased by biases in age reporting associated with marital status. We resorted in the Congo to an index of age at marriage that would be independent from age errors, namely the age at marriage in the stable population, described previously. This index correlates positively with the crude birth rate and the total fertility by district. In other words, high fertility tends to be associated with later marriage. Several explanations for this surprising association might be suggested. High fertility results in a steep age distribution and in a higher proportion of the population in the young age classes than in a low-

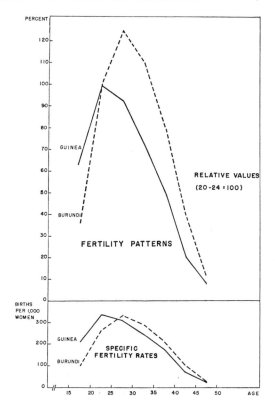

5.5. Fertility patterns and age-specific fertility rates, for
Guinea and Burundi.

fertility population. Therefore, proportionately more young women in
the marrying ages (i.e., grossly, 15 to 45 years) are to be matched with
proportionately less males in the marrying ages (i.e., 20 years and over)
in the high-fertility population. This may push up the age at marriage
of women. In other words, fertility may influence the age at marriage,
through the age distribution, and obscure an effect, in individual cases,
of early marriage on the final size of family. A psychological element,
the desire for offspring, may lead husbands of childless women to remarry younger women; and in regions of widespread sterility, this may
depress the age at marriage to a significant degree. Finally, the possibility
of a depressing effect on fertility of very early marriage cannot be dismissed.

The available evidence does not provide any clear answers to these
questions, and only fertility histories by age at marriage would do so.
As ages at marriage in tropical Africa are generally under 20 years for
females, that is, very soon after the beginning of the fecund period, this
may not go far to explain fertility differentials.

Conclusions and Suggestions

The subject of marriage in African censuses and inquiries is still under-developed and deserves further investigation. We will review here the main findings of this chapter, and at the same time make specific suggestions on possible avenues of inquiry.

I. The consensus seems general enough on the notions of "marriage" (broadly defined as conjugal union), "celibacy," "divorce" (including sometimes separation without legal sanction), and "widowhood." Questions on conjugal status are relatively easy to ask and to answer in a census or inquiry if they are limited to these simple categories. These questions elicit rather uniform results over age 20, because most, if not all, cultures in tropical Africa share in an ideal of general marriage—although widows and divorcees represent often up to 50 percent of all women past childbearing ages.

More variability is encountered whenever information is collected on the following subjects: (a) the types of conjugal unions; (b) polygyny; (c) age at marriage; and (d) stability of marriage.

(a) African customs vary widely with respect to marital systems. Furthermore, urbanization has affected the traditional ways of contracting marriage; new forms of marriage, such as civil and Christian marriage, have had their impact on the tribal societies. The complexity of the subject is such that the detailed classification of unions is probably beyond the reach of large representative inquiries or censuses. The following breakdown may, however, be of application in much of Africa: civil and Christian marriages; customary marriages; customary unions in the process of becoming fully institutionalized, although some element is still missing; and consensual unions. The border between consensual and incomplete customary unions, as well as between the latter and fully institutionalized customary marriages is often fuzzy. Criteria, such as the stage reached in bridewealth payment, or the residence of the couple, have to be determined in each case. The basic distinction, married vs. non-married, must always remain clear.

Consensual unions may be widespread in some African regions. They should be distinguished from free unions and more informal relationships. The most useful distinction for the study of fertility appears to be in terms of duration of cohabitation. It may serve no useful purpose to enumerate the very unstable free unions.

(b) Polygyny has been found to present a wide range of intensity and incidence. This institution is associated with the difference between the sexes in age at marriage. The surplus of wives created by the later age at marriage of the males is, however, partly compensated by the large proportion of women that remain widowed or divorced after their childbearing period is over.

(c) Age at marriage presents a surprising variety from one region to another. Measurement of the variable involves numerous problems in the presence of important biases which mar African age distributions and are probably themselves related to the assumption of a "normal" age for marriage by the enumerator when he tries to estimate ages. Measures of age at marriage were discussed and an index of age at marriage purporting to be immune from bias in age reporting was proposed.

(d) The proportion of divorced persons in a census gives only a residual, unsatisfactory index of the instability of conjugal unions after remarriage. This information has to be supplemented by data of the stock type, on the number of divorces. The following procedure is suggested—using the replies to two questions: (1) the total number of divorces experienced in the informant's life; (2) the number of divorces, if any, during the preceding year. Numbers of previous divorces reported in response to Question 1 by women at specified ages would be compared with the numbers of divorces per woman allegedly experienced in one year, cumulated to the same ages. One expects that the ratio of these two figures would be near unity at any early age (e.g., during the 20's) because the young women have been exposed to the risks of divorce only during a short time and must remember them well. If, then, this ratio at early ages is much above or below unity, the deviation can reasonably be attributed to an error in the reference period, i.e., the inclusion of events over a longer period than one year or limitation to a shorter period. The ratio thus obtained can then be used to correct the numbers of recent divorces reported at all ages, on the assumption that the error in reference period is constant, i.e., not affected by age. It must, however, be noted that the comparison here suggested may be seriously affected by chance variations except in the case of a very large sample or a population with a high frequency of divorce.

II. The study of the relationship of age at marriage and of marital status to fertility turned up mostly inconclusive results. The data analyzed give some indications of the influence of marital conditions on fertility (notably in the case of polygyny, which apparently tends to depress fertility) as well as of the influence of fertility on marital conditions (for instance, infertile women may stay longer in consensual unions and experience less stability in their unions). The analysis was, however, handicapped by the lack of a clear distinction between time of conception, time of confinement, and time of inquiry.

A question on duration of present marital status, suggested earlier to distinguish consensual from free unions and to determine the number of divorces during the past year, may serve in the computation of specific fertility rates by marital status. Answers to the question on duration would be classified as less than one year or more than one year. This would be supplemented by information on previous marital status. Births

[237]

during the last 12 months could thus be related to marital status one year before the survey. Informal unions of less than one year's duration would not enter in the computation of consensual fertility. Neither would births to a recently widowed woman be included in illegitimate fertility.

The relation between polygyny and fertility could similarly be investigated by asking a question on the duration of the present family form, provided (for instance) the following information is added: "Does your husband have other wives? For how long (less than one year, two and more)?" However, though the first of these two questions may always be included as a check in the study of polygyny, the second one is perhaps superfluous. It is probably sufficient to relate births to monogamy or polygyny at the time of survey to reveal a possible differential fertility.

III. This chapter should end by referring the reader once again to the rich anthropological material treating similar or related subjects, and stating that it was out of our frame of reference. We hope to have in a way facilitated the contact between census takers and social scientists by indicating some pitfalls of the subject as well as some very real successes in data collecting despite difficult circumstances.

PART II.

CASE STUDIES OF THE DEMOGRAPHY OF AREAS COVERED BY PARTICULAR KINDS OF CENSUSES OR SURVEYS

6

The Demography of the
Democratic Republic of the Congo

BY ANATOLE ROMANIUK

I. DEMOGRAPHIC DATA IN THE CONGO

The study of demography in the Congo is of particular interest because of the richness of the available data, allowing the pursuit of analysis along several complementary lines. The data will be used here with the primary objective of providing as far as possible some reliable estimates of basic demographic variables—fertility, mortality, and rate of population growth in the Congo.

In view of this volume's focus on the study of recent African census and survey results, no attempt has been made to pursue the study of past demographic trends in the Congo. Strictly speaking, the findings set forth here refer to the situation prevailing in the Congo at the time of the 1955-57 Demographic Inquiry. The post-independence period (after 1960) has been marked by civil upheaval and by dramatic deterioration of the economic situation and public health services. We are not yet in a position to measure the demographic consequences of these events, but it is possible that they have had marked impact on mortality, the most vulnerable demographic variable.

The body of this study has been organized into four sections (I-IV) followed by a brief summary, Section V. This section describes the Demographic Inquiry and related sources on Congolese population, and Sections II, III, and IV are concerned respectively with age distribution, mortality, and fertility. The interdependence among the estimates make the sequence of sections somewhat artificial and unsatisfactory. No section can really be complete until the others are presented. But it is necessary to break the circle of mutual interaction somewhere, and a sequence of sections each devoted to one of the traditional demographic measures has seemed as logical an organization as any.

The supply of Congolese demographic information for the 1950's is rather extraordinary by African standards. This supply of information is a result of (1) the evolution of a system of continuous population registration with a higher level of accuracy than has been attained in any other African country; (2) the rapid extension through most of the country of birth and death registration, approaching completeness in some regions by the close of the decade; and (3) the execution in the mid-1950's of a demographic inquiry through house-to-house interviews covering a large probabilistic sample of the whole population. The last of these undertakings provides the most comprehensive information and is therefore the major source of data on the basic demographic variables discussed here. These data from the Demographic Inquiry are in part dependent on the other undertakings mentioned above. The nature and characteristics of all three sources will be briefly reviewed here.

The Demographic Inquiry of 1955-57

Prior to the initiation of the 1955-57 inquiry, current reports on numbers of persons in the Congo were mainly summations of reports by local administrative officials, largely on the basis of the population registers maintained by AIMO, the governmental agency primarily concerned with labor supply and native affairs.[1] Additional information on the characteristics of the population was based on reports concerning particular areas, selected subjectively, often by considerations of convenience. Recognition of the inadequacy of these procedures led to the inauguration by AIMO, in cooperation with the Central Statistical Service, of a radically new program involving an extensive field operation by a staff divorced from administrative responsibilities, and to the adoption of new procedures. Primary responsibility for the development of this program was assigned to the present writer as Director of a newly formed Bureau of Demography.

The main results of the survey are presented in a series of eleven regional volumes and in a summary report, *Tableau Général de la Démographie Congolaise*, published by the Ministère du Plan et de la Coordination Economique, République du Congo, in 1961. Severe limitation in the number of properly qualified persons available for such an undertaking in 1955-57 made it advisable to sacrifice the principle of simultaneity, generally considered as one of the conditions of a correct census procedure. This sacrifice made it possible to use continuously during a three-year period about 100 selected and trained interviewers. They were divided into three teams with one European leader and one or two African supervisors. Each team worked successively through the sample areas within two provinces (Leopoldville and Equateur provinces; Orientale and Kivu provinces; Kasai and Katanga provinces). The interviewers gained experience in the course of their work. They interviewed 1.36 million persons in sample areas representative of a population of about 12.8 million (as of 1956) in a country of 2,343,930 square kilometers.

The continuous registration system provided a sampling frame for the inquiry. It included a list, by administrative areas, of the 50,000 villages in the Congo, with approximate figures on the number of per-

[1] AIMO: Service des Affaires Indigènes et de la Main d'Oeuvre.

sons in each village, or group of hamlets, or dispersed huts within geographical limits shown on reasonably satisfactory maps. In the case of urban agglomerations, there were lists of household dwellings or compounds, by wards, again with estimated figures on numbers of occupants. The housing units were generally numbered so that correspondence between lists and situations could, in most cases, be achieved without great difficulty.

The administrative structure of the Congo in 1956 comprised 6 provinces, 26 districts, and 138 territories.[2] Each territory was treated as a universe in the sampling design. Its population was initially divided into three strata: rural, mixed, and urban; these concepts will be defined presently. The sampling units in the rural and mixed segments were "localities," i.e., villages or comparable clusters. These were again strati-

6.1. Provinces and districts of the Congo, 1955-57.

[2] See maps, Figures 6.1 and 6.2.

OFFICE OF POPULATION RESEARCH, PRINCETON UNIVERSITY

6.2. Territories (administrative divisions of the districts) of the Congo, 1955-57.

fied in the rural segment (1) by tribe and (2) by size. The sampling units in the segment of mixed agglomerations were stratified (1) by socio-economic characteristics and (2) by size. Every tenth unit within each stratum was systematically selected. Sampling units in urban places were households or compounds. These were stratified, within each ward, by the listed number of occupants. Again, the selection of units within each stratum was systematic. Military and labor camps were included, but other institutional populations (schools, hospitals, and prisons) were not directly included in the sample.

A higher sampling ratio of 1 to 7 was adopted in non-rural strata in view of the greater heterogeneity of their populations. One of two alternative procedures was used in expanding the numbers reported for the samples to give corresponding estimates for the total population of each stratum. In urban places, where the sampling units were small and numerous, the expansion factor was the ratio of the total number of units in the stratum to the number of comparable units in the sample. In the mixed and rural segments the expansion factor was the ratio of the number of registered persons in the stratum to the number of registered persons in the sample (prior to the survey). The estimates for strata were summed to give estimates in absolute numbers for administrative divisions. The size of the sample population, in relation to the estimated total population, is shown in Table 6.1 for each district. The table indicates that the size of the district samples ranged from 18,800 to over 100,000, with a median close to 50,000 persons.

Table 6.1. Size of sample compared to the estimated population, by district and province—the Congo, *de facto* population

Province District	Time of the survey	Estimated population	Sample Numbers	Per cent of estimated population
Leopoldville Province		3,050,420	342,546	11.2
Leopoldville	May-July 1955	318,317	43,852	13.8
Lac Leopold II	Oct. 1957-Feb. 1958	271,330	37,901	14.0
Kwilu	Mar.-May 1956; Dec. 1957	1,143,456	116,376	10.1
Kwango	Feb. and June 1956; Oct.-Dec. 1956	466,054	52,595	11.3
Bas-Congo	Oct.-Jan. 1956	411,804	51.229	12.4
Cataractes	Aug.-Oct.1955	439,459	40,593	9.2
Equateur Province		1,756,190	194,546	11.1
Equateur	March-August 1957	302,162	32,666	10.8
Mongala	Aug.1956-Feb.1957	519,488	62,675	12.1
Ubangi	Oct.-Dec. 1956	539,060	59,243	11.0
Tshuapa	Feb.-April 1957	395,480	39,962	10.1
Orientale Province		2,335,585	222,670	9.5
Stanleyville	April-Aug.1957	634,948	63,599	10.0
Ituri	Oct.-Dec. 1957	651,044	53,066	8.2
Bas-Uele	Sept.1957-Jan.1958	467,632	45,824	9.8
Haut-Uele	Nov. 1957-Jan.1958	581,961	60,181	10.3
Kivu Province		2,012,508	200,895	10.0
Sud Kivu	Sept.1955-July 1956	831,353	86,930	10.5
Nord Kivu	Aug. 1956-Feb. 1957	734,633	71,063	9.7
Maniema	March-August 1956	446,522	42,902	9.6
Katanga Province		150,094	147,421	9.8
Elizabethville	October 1956	140,104	20,285	14.5
Tanganika	May – June 1957	396,938	36,983	9.3
Lualaba	Nov.1956-Jan.1957	320,463	26,636	8.3
Haut-Lomani	Jan. – June 1957	451,969	44,699	9.9
Luapula-Moero	Oct.1956-April 1957	191,620	18,818	9.8
Kasai Province		2,121,276	251,984	11.9
Lulua	April-Dec. 1955	654,486	76,977	11.8
Sankuru	Jan. - July 1956	493,549	58,960	11.9
Kabinda	July – Aug. 1956	480,379	60,248	12.5
Kasai	Feb. - July 1956	492,862	55,799	11.3

Table 6.1 (continued)

District, Province, and type of settlement	Time of the survey	Estimated population	Sample Numbers	Per cent of estimated population
Rural Strata		9,920,714	962,468	9.7
Mixed "		1,591,208	220,389	13.9
Urban "		1,265,151	177,205	14.1
Congo	May 1955-Feb. 1958	12,777,073	1,360,062	10.7

Note: 1) Unless otherwise stated, the tables presented in this and subsequent chapters are taken from the summary official report on the Demographic Survey (1955-57), "Tableau Général de la Démographie Congolaise," published by the "Ministère du Plan et de la Coordination Economique".

2) There are a few discrepancies between figures on total population published in different tables in the above mentioned official report. Thus for the Leopoldville province the published figures are 3,055,150 in Table 1 in Appendix and 3,045,535 in the summary tables 2, 6 and 7. For Equateur province the figures are respectively 1,765,190 and 1,756,190, and for Kivu province respectively 2,012,508 and 2,008,020. No adjustment was made on these figures; the sources of error are not clear.

Three schedules were used in the survey. Two of them are shown in the Appendix to this chapter. The third was entirely devoted to migration. Individual names contributing to a sample were entered on separate lines of the main schedule. Information was recorded for (1) all permanent residents, (2) all visitors present in the house on the night preceding the inquiry, and also (3) all absent residents. The information collected in the main form included, with other subjects not relevant here, the following topics:

Sex

Age: Year of age if known precisely, otherwise age class as follows: under 1; 1-4; quinquennial classes from 5 to 34 years; decennial classes from 35 to 54 years; 55 years and over.

Births in course of life (to each woman over 14 years old): live births; children still alive.

Births during the 12 months preceding the survey. Live births by sex; stillbirths; legitimate births (and, if legitimate, monogamous or polygynous); illegitimate births; infants alive at time of inquiry.

A separate schedule was used to record deaths within the locality or the household (in cities) during the 12 months preceding the inquiry, and related information including sex and age. A third schedule was used for obtaining information on outmigration from villages during a five-year period previous to the inquiry.

A unique feature of the Congo inquiry was an extensive use of supporting documents. Prior to entering a locality, or urban household, the interviewers had to obtain preliminary information on its characteristics, including the expected number of inhabitants, from the population registers. Also, for villages and mixed communities, they abstracted from the official registers lists of recorded births and deaths during the previous 18 months, with related information concerning these events. During the interview the enumerators were instructed to examine any relevant documents, such as identity booklets or certificates, and, in cities, house or compound registers of occupants.

An African village is in many respects a community without privacy. All members are familiar with the other members. Moreover its traditional structure involves respect for the authority of chiefs and elders, who, under colonial conditions, had close working relations with administrative officials. These factors provided considerable help in executing the inquiry. The chiefs were informed in advance about the nature of the survey and were asked to extend their cooperation. They did so almost universally.

The head of family was interviewed first, and then the other persons in order of seniority. Various members of the family, elders accompanying the enumerators, and visiting neighbors cooperated frequently and assisted in the recall of events and made statements about family relations. The only serious opposition encountered was a resistance in some localities to talk about death or to mention names of deceased persons. The resistance on this score was so strong in one district (Ituri) that it was deemed advisable to omit questions on this subject in some of its villages.

Undoubtedly the results were sometimes damaged by subterfuge or evasion. But, in the main, defects in the data can be attributed simply to ignorance, misunderstanding, or ordinary errors in reporting and recording. Unfortunately, an initial plan for a systematic series of check interviews and complete records of observed errors was not carried through. For the most part, therefore, the data can be evaluated only on the basis of internal evidence with respect to their consistency, or with results obtained from other sources.

The Continuous Registration
of Inhabitants and the Registration
of Births and Deaths

According to regulation codified by legislation in 1933, every adult had to be registered in the local administrative division (*circonscription*) of his residence. Parents were responsible for the registration of children. The system was designed to provide a continuous registration of inhabitants as they entered or left a given administrative area through birth, death, or change of residence. A card was established for the newborn and taken away in case of death; the card of a person who changed his residence was in principle sent to the office of *circumscription* where the person established his new residence. The primary purpose of the system was the administrative control of population, including collection of taxes, but it was also used as a source of demographic information. From this source the administration published annual reports on the total population, with distinction among "children," "men," and "women."

Theoretically, this registration system reflected at any given moment the status of each administrative division with respect to its population. In practice, however, the registers were incomplete; cards that were no longer valid tended to accumulate with time, due to failures in reporting changes of residence or deaths. The published estimates of population combined the use of this source with direct enumeration, in particular in cities with highly mobile populations such as Leopoldville. As shown in Table 6.2, the administrative estimates were extremely close to the figure of population derived from the 1955-57 Demographic Inquiry. The population registers served as a sampling frame. A further gain for the inquiry was the fact that population registers in local offices were complemented by individual identity booklets issued mostly to adult males. Most householders in the Congo, even if illiterate and living in mud huts, were keeping identity booklets, which contained records such as tax payments, vaccinations, names of other members of the family and frequently their ages or birthdays.

The legal obligation to register births and deaths within a month after their occurrence was introduced in certain parts of the Congo as early as 1940 and was gradually extended to other regions. By 1955 this requirement was applicable to areas containing 92 percent of the population. Trends in numbers of registered births and deaths, and in the percentage of the population subjected to legal obligation in this respect, are shown in Table 6.3 for the period of 1953-58.

An interesting feature of this table is the relative constancy in numbers of registered deaths as compared with the marked increase in numbers of registered births—3 percent increase in the former as compared with 44 percent in the latter in a five-year period during which the estimated population increased 13 percent. To some extent, improving mortality conditions were balancing improvements in the coverage of registration. There also was more interest in recording births than in recording deaths. Almost all confinements in the cities and an important fraction of those in rural areas were taking place in maternity hospitals.[3] Since for these births the certificate was prepared by the hospital staff at the time of de-

---

[3] The medical report for 1956, for example, states that among an estimated total of 444,000 births there were 210,000 confinements in hospitals; a proportion that is surprisingly high, even allowing for possible errors in these estimates.

Table 6.2. Ratio of *de jure* estimates and administrative estimates (1956) to *de facto* estimates from the 1955-57 Demographic Inquiry in the Congo

	De Jure Estimates De Facto Estimates			Total Population	Administrative Estimates De Facto	Administrative Estimates De Jure
	Rural	Mixed	Urban			
Leopoldville Province	1.035	1.022	1.041	1.035	.991	.958
Leopoldville	1.017		1.046	1.045	1.096	1.048
Lac Leopold II	1.045	1.010	1.048	1.041	1.035	.995
Kwilu	1.038	1.014	.989	1.034	.951	.920
Kwango	1.046	1.137	1.121	1.049	.966	.921
Bas-Congo	1.013	1.024	1.037	1.020	.990	.970
Cataractes	1.024	1.008	1.051	1.023	1.021	.998
Equateur Province	1.025	1.005	1.032	1.022	.981	.960
Equateur	1.011	1.002	1.051	1.014	1.017	1.003
Mongala	1.030	.998	.993	1.022	.968	.947
Ubangi	1.032	.997	1.041	1.027	.958	.933
Tshuapa	1.021	1.023	1.044	1.022	1.003	.981
Orientale Province	1.033	1.020	1.015	1.030	1.005	.976
Stanleyville					.996	
Ituri					.981	
Bas-Uele					1.020	
Haut-Uele	1.037	1.019	1.007	1.033	1.030	.997
Kivu Province	1.030	1.027	1.000	1.028	1.050	1.021
Sud-Kivu	1.027	1.028	.987	1.026	1.014	.989
Nord-Kivu	1.038	1.029	1.024	1.036	1.111	1.072
Maniema	1.018	1.025	.999	1.019	1.015	.996
Katanga Province	1.057	1.021	1.022	1.045	1.040	.996
Elisabethville			1.025	1.025	1.118	1.091
Tanganika	1.048	1.041	.990	1.038	1.021	.984
Lualaba	1.053	1.002	1.029	1.036	1.049	1.012
Haut-Lomani	1.073	1.018	1.027	1.065	1.019	.957
Luapula-Moero	1.040	1.027	1.061	1.040	1.058	1.017
Kasai Province	1.012	.994	.994	1.010	.978	.968
Lulua	.992	.943	1.051	.994	.976	.982
Sankuru	1.006	.963	.830	1.000	.964	.963
Kabinda	1.042	.997	1.000	1.038	.990	.954
Kasai	1.015	1.042	.926	1.013	.983	.970
Congo	1.030	1.017	1.025	1.028	1.005	.978

livery and later presented by the parents at the Office of Birth Registration, a high proportion of hospital deliveries stimulated more complete registration and increased the accuracy of the recorded data, especially as regards the date of birth. A second factor favoring complete registration was the family allowance allotted to all employed persons, both in private enterprise and in governmental service, provided legal proof of a birth was given.

On the other hand, the size of the country and the low density of population in many regions hampered the development of an efficient network of vital registration offices. In 1955 there were 1,906 registration offices,

Table 6.3. Number of registered births and deaths and percentage of the population subject to compulsory registration of vital events, by year—the Congo and provinces, 1953-58

Province	1953	1954	1955	1956	1957	1958
			YEARS			
	NUMBER OF BIRTHS					
Leopoldville	114,690	118,133	127,028	132,856	139,755	143,916
Equateur	47,444	51,109	53,292	56,001	63,225	62,459
Orientale	29,336	34,870	38,373	48,685	57,604	59,297
Kivu	33,777	71,886	78,086	83,821	93,646	98,409
Katanga	71,702	26,865	45,475	55,594	63,556	65,754
Kasai	60,833	68,877	70,032	77,822	77,892	83,613
Congo	357,782	371,740	412,286	454,779	495,678	513,448
	NUMBER OF DEATHS					
Leopoldville	44,287	42,057	40,386	39,290	40,540	39,459
Equateur	26,485	26,899	27,272	25,142	24,210	24,404
Orientale	17,879	21,280	21,507	26,925	28,304	26,626
Kivu	13,182	29,537	26,610	26,471	30,708	32,291
Katanga	30,216	11,966	13,653	14,453	16,267	14,825
Kasai	27,129	29,989	29,956	27,998	27,123	26,514
Congo	159,178	161,728	159,384	160,279	167,152	164,119
	Percentage of Population Subject to Compulsory Registration of Births & Deaths					
Leopoldville	97.6	98.5	99.0	99.4	99.7	100.0
Equateur	67.0	95.0	95.0	99.7	100.0	100.0
Orientale	67.2	74.8	79.6	90.8	90.5	86.3
Kivu	87.2	89.3	89.9	91.1	91.7	95.5
Katanga	72.0	75.1	88.7	87.8	91.2	93.8
Kasai	99.9	100.0	100.0	100.0	100.0	99.9
Congo	83.9	89.5	91.8	95.2	95.7	95.9

an average of one office for each 6,700 persons, but only of one office per 475 square miles. An attempt was made to establish auxiliary offices in remote regions and a system of itinerant registration whereby a clerk visited outlying villages and hamlets periodically to register newborn infants and deaths.

A comparison of numbers of births and deaths indicated by the Demographic Inquiry of 1955-57 with numbers of registered events at this time suggests that some 80 percent of the births but only about one-half of the deaths were being registered, with considerable variation in the figures from region to region.

Inquiry Estimates Versus Current Administrative Estimates

The series of annual population estimates, which we shall refer to as "administrative estimates," is based mainly on the continuous population registration described earlier. We noted that this system was highly developed in the Congo, to a level approaching completion in the post-war period. It remained subject to errors, but in the opinion of officials responsible for its operation, errors due to the retention in local files of the names of persons who had died or taken residence elsewhere posed as serious a problem as omissions or delayed entries. The figures obtained by a compilation of local records might, therefore, have been either somewhat too high or too low, but were probably not far removed from reality. The figure for the total population of the Congo, or a large division such as a province, in a given year was a summation of the reports on all constituent local areas received during that year. In some cases, especially if the reports were based on the results of field checks or surveys, there may have been some lag in their transmission and compilation. However the series during the postwar period shows an orderly progression generally consistent with available information on fertility, mortality, and population movements.

The inquiry estimates, though largely independent of the registration system, are not wholly so. Since the registration system was used as the basis of the sampling design for the surveys, the omission of any units (villages or urban compounds) in the registers would have entailed comparable error in the inquiry.

The surveys for the Demographic Inquiry were taken at various dates, centered on midyear 1956. The inquiry estimates and the administrative estimate for the whole Congo are as follows:

Administrative estimate:	12,844,000
Inquiry *de facto*:	12,769,000
Inquiry *de jure*:	13,135,000

Some deviations between administrative estimates and survey estimates can be ascribed to sampling errors and to differences in the timing
of the surveys. The errors due to timing may be quite large in the case
of rapidly growing urban centers, and still larger with respect to the
fluctuating population of industrial localities. These might be responsible
in large part for the extreme deviations from the administrative figures
of the inquiry estimates of the mixed segments of Katanga Province
(ratio 78/100) and of Kasai Province (ratio 167/100)—though, of
course, these results could be due to gross errors in one or the other of
set of estimates.

A comparison of these two sets of estimates for the 137 territories
(the third-order political divisions, many of which include both rural
elements and some urban or mixed segments) shows that in more than
half the cases, the inquiry *de facto* estimates and the administrative estimates differ by less than 5 percent, and the deviations of less than 10
percent are fairly equally divided in the direction of the difference (see
Table 6.4). However, in 15 percent of the cases the differences exceed

Table 6.4. Distribution of territories by relative values of inquiry *de facto* estimates
(F) and administrative estimates (AS)

Per cent Deviation	F < AS	F > AS	All deviations
0-4	38	33	71
5-9	22	23	.45
10-19	11	4	15
20+	5	1	6
All degrees	76	61	137

10 percent, and for these territories relative deficiencies in inquiry estimates as compared with the administrative figures (16 cases) seem to
be more frequent than relative excesses (5 cases), which may or may
not be significant.

The detailed comparison of the inquiry estimates by provinces and
districts have been presented in Table 6.2. The deviations shown in this
table, in so far as they are not due to sampling errors or differences in
timing, may of course be due to errors in either the inquiry estimates
or the administrative figures. The nature of these deviations does not
seem to be illuminated by any clear pattern in their distribution.

The comparison of the inquiry estimates with the administrative
figures, based mainly on the registration, gives no evidence of any gross
or consistent bias in either series. The significance of this finding with

respect to the credibility of both series will be somewhat reinforced in subsequent chapters by their apparent consistency in other respects— e.g., in comparing variations in populations of "children" and "adults" according to the registration system with data on proportions of children and the relative frequencies of births from the inquiry.

We shall proceed on the assumption that, with respect to the number and distribution of Africans in the Congo at the time of the inquiry, the estimates that it provides are affected only by relatively small errors. This cannot be affirmed beyond any reasonable doubt, but so far as we know there is no evidence to the contrary. Moreover, this assumption is in general supported by the comparison of the inquiry estimates with those based mainly on the continuous population registers. The possibilities of some differential underestimation of classes by sex and age will be considered in Section II.

Size and Distribution of the Population

On the basis of the Demographic Inquiry conducted during 1955-57, the *de facto* population of the Congo is estimated at 12,777,000 persons. This figure represents the sum of the population estimates of the various parts of the Congo resulting from the inquiry and was calculated for the time around midyear 1956. The figures for particular areas, especially rapidly growing cities, are affected by the timing of the surveys—as for example Elisabethville and Leopoldville, for which the surveys were separated by an interval of 16 months. However it is assumed that differences in timing do not appreciably affect the estimated total population or its broad regional distribution.

The distribution of the estimated *de facto* population by provinces and districts and by type of settlement is shown in Table 6.5. Variations in density among political divisions are also shown in this table. The density pattern is shown in greater detail in Figure 6.3, with territories as units and a distinction when this is significant between cities and the rest of the territory.

The estimated *de jure* population of the Congo was 13,135,000 persons, giving a difference of 358,000 or 2.7 percent of the *de facto* figure. The two estimates have a large common factor, namely persons classified as present residents of the areas in which they were enumerated, which makes up some 90 percent or more of each final figure. The differences therefore are wholly the result of differences between the estimated number of visitors (included in the *de facto* figure) and of absent residents (included in the *de jure* figure). It can be shown that the discrepancy is not mainly due to the presence or absence of international migrants, but that the estimated number of absent residents for the whole Congo is probably at least 50 percent above the estimated number of visitors—an indication of underestimation of the *de facto* population.

Table 6.5. Estimated *de facto* population according to 1955-57 inquiry—the Congo, provinces, districts, and type of settlement. (Area and density in square kilometers)

Province District	Estimated Numbers (thousands)			Total (a)	In per cent			Area in square kilometers (b)	Ratio total population to territory (a)/(b)
	Rural	Mixed	Urban		Rural	Mixed	Urban		
Leopoldville Province	2278	294	478	3050	74.7	9.6	15.7	357.7	8.5
Leopoldville	16		302	318	5.1		94.9		
Lac Leopold II	209	33	29 (1)	271	77.0	12.2	10.8	127.2	2.1
Kwilu	987	117	40	1143	86.3	10.2	3.5	78.4	1.5
Kwango	447	17	2	466	96.0	3.6	.5	93.3	5.0
Bas-Congo	257	70	84	412	62.5	17.1	20.5	14.4	2.9
Cataractes	362	57	20	439	82.4	13.1	4.6	44.2	9.9
Equateur Province	1368	312	76	1756	77.9	17.8	4.4	402.1	
Equateur	224	45	34	302	74.0	14.8	11.2	102.7	2.9
Mongala	383	114	22	519	73.8	21.9	4.3	101.5	5.1
Ubangi	450	73	16	539	83.5	13.5	3.0	64.9	8.3
Tshuapa	311	81	4	395	78.6	20.4	1.0	133.0	3.0
Orientale Province	1807	370	158	2336	77.4	15.9	6.8	503.2	4.6
Stanleyville	423	132	81	635	66.6	20.7	12.7	199.6	3.2
Ituri	529	111	12	651	81.3	17.0	1.7	65.7	10.0
Bas-Uele	379	63	25	468	81.0	13.6	5.4	148.3	3.2
Haut-Uele	477	64	41	582	81.9	11.1	7.0	89.7	6.5
Kivu Province	1601	339	72	2013	79.6	16.9	3.6	259.0	7.8
Sud-Kivu	692	109	31	831	83.1	13.2	3.7	64.7	1.3
Nord-Kivu	615	102	18	735	83.8	13.9	2.4	62.0	1.2
Maniema	295	128	23	447	66.0	28.7	5.3	132.3	3.4
Katanga Province	975	148	378	1501	65.0	9.9	25.2	496.7	3.0
Elisabethville			140	140			100.0		
Tanganika	294	40	63	397	74.0	10.0	15.9	135.0	2.9
Lualaba	146	46	129	320	45.4	14.4	40.2	88.7	3.6
Haut-Lomani	380	42	30	452	84.0	9.4	6.6	163.3	2.8
Luapula-Moero	156	20	16	192	81.5	10.3	8.2	109.0	1.8

Table 6.5 (continued)

Kasai Province	1890	128	103	2121	89.1	6.0	4.9	323.1	6.6
Lulua	580	26	49	654	88.6	4.0	7.5	48.1	1.4
Sankuru	455	30	9	494	92.1	6.1	1.8	117.6	4.2
Kabinda	430	27	23	480	89.5	5.7	4.8	61.8	7.8
Kasai	426	44	23	493	86.4	9.0	4.6	95.6	5.2
Congo	9921	1591	1265	12777	77.6	12.5	9.9	2341.9	5.5

(1) The units of estimation were categories of population by type of settlement within territories. Totals for larger divisions of the Congo were obtained by summation of estimates by territories. These totals are slightly different from those obtained directly by the summation of estimates by type of settlement.

Most cities outside the territorial structure were treated as comparable to territories; Leopoldville and Elisabethville are comparable to districts. The figures for the urban population of Katanga Province include an estimated 63,515 persons (obtained from the registration system) in four urban places where the inquiry was omitted for administrative reasons. These places are: center of Kongolo (4,594) in Tanganika; Centers Shinkologwe, Kambowe and Kolwezi suburban with a total population of 46,769 in Lualaba and military camps of Kamina (12,152) in Haut-Lomani.

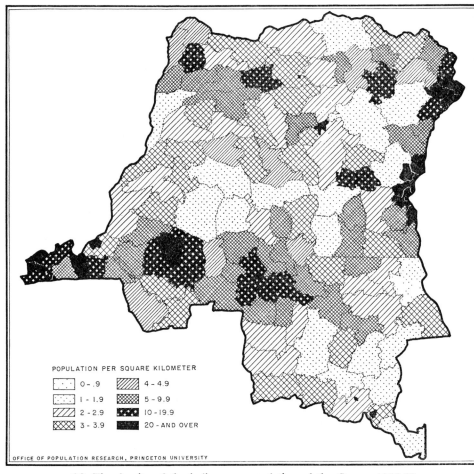

POPULATION PER SQUARE KILOMETER

0 - .9		4 - 4.9	
1 - 1.9		5 - 9.9	
2 - 2.9		10 - 19.9	
3 - 3.9		20 - AND OVER	

OFFICE OF POPULATION RESEARCH, PRINCETON UNIVERSITY

6.3. The density of the indigenous population of the Congo, 1955-57.

Three types of settlement were distinguished within each territory: rural, mixed, and urban. The rural category is restricted to villages, or clusters, with less than 2,000 inhabitants, in which the main occupation of the labor force was agricultural. Agglomerations with more than 2,000 persons were considered urban. The so-called mixed communities are mostly aggregations of less than 2,000 persons in industrial, commercial, or administrative centers or in labor camps. Settlements of laborers and their dependents on European plantations were also treated as mixed localities, regardless of size—the one exception to treatment of size as a primary criterion in the classification of localities. The threefold division by type of settlement used in the inquiry was designed to fit the two residential categories recognized in the administrative system of the Congo: (1) the "customary" (*coutumière*) population in rural localities administered under a system adapted to traditional tribal structures and customary law, and (2) the "non-customary" (*extra-coutumière*) population outside such localities, i.e., persons living in urban centers and mixed settlements.

The division of the non-rural population into urban and mixed strata is important because these segments of the population differ significantly in many respects. For example, in the mixed localities only 28 percent of all persons over 10 years of age had ever received instructions in school as compared with 50 percent of those in urban places—the comparable figure for the rural segment being 18 percent. Though heterogeneous in economic characteristics, for their occupational make-up is comprised of industry and agriculture, the mixed communities tend to be more homogeneous than the urban places in tribal composition, because most of their residents come from the proximate hinterland. Their populations include large mobile elements and may fluctuate in size in response to seasonal movement of workers to and from small semi-industrial and agricultural enterprises. The mixed population constitutes a segment that is in many respects intermediate between the rural and urban strata, but distinct from both in other respects.

Ten percent of the population was classified as urban and 12.5 as mixed (see Table 6.5). The relative importance of the urban population is greatest in the Katanga Province (25 percent) due to its mining complex and the associated network of cities (Elisabethville, Jadotville, Kolwezi, etc.) in the southern part of the province. Half of the population of the Lualaba District is non-rural. However, the largest urban population, in absolute numbers, is in Leopoldville Province. The city of Leopoldville, political and administrative capital of the Congo and an important commercial center, has about 350,000 of the 478,000 urban residents in this province. The Bas-Congo District also has important urban elements. The rest of the province is largely rural.

Equateur, Orientale, and Kivu provinces have relatively few persons in cities but quite large mixed populations. European farms and connected industries are especially important in these regions. Kasai is a province in which neither industrial nor large-scale agricultural activities are highly developed. Due to the lack of employment opportunities at home, the population of this province is characterized by quite heavy out-migration toward the industrial centers of Katanga Province.

II. THE AGE AND SEX DISTRIBUTION OF THE CONGOLESE POPULATION

The Basic Data

Analysis of demographic variables requires knowledge, or at least reasonable estimates, of the sex and age composition of the population under consideration. The information on ages in the Congo, as elsewhere in Africa, is incomplete and inaccurate. This poses a major problem. However, different measures of vital trends vary in their requirements for specificity and precision in the information on ages, and there are ways of overcoming some limitations in this field. Critical investigation of the information on the sex and age composition is, in any case, a fundamental aspect of all demographic analysis. If the reported composition of a population is seriously erroneous, the scope and nature of the errors must be rigorously examined, and an attempt must be made to estimate its actual composition, at least in broad outlines and within reasonable limits.

The Demographic Inquiry of 1955-57 provides information on the distribution of the Congolese population by sex and age classes. Persons enumerated in the sample survey were distributed by sex among eleven age classes as follow: under 1 year; 1-4 years; quinquennial classes for the ages 5 through 34; two decennial classes (35-44, 45-54); and a broad terminal class, 55 years and over. Published information is given on the sex and age distribution (on the basis of the sampling results) for the *de facto* population of the Congo as a whole, for its major political divisions (provinces and districts), for segments by type of settlement (rural, mixed, urban), and also for smaller territorial and social units with which we are not concerned here. The reported age distributions of males and of females are shown separately for the Congo and its major political divisions in Tables 6.6 and 6.7.

We shall assume *tentatively* that the actual age distribution of the population of the Congo as a whole and, to a lesser degree, of the populations of many of its component areas at the time of the inquiry, were largely determined by previous trends in fertility and mortality similar in level and pattern to those in force at that time. We recognize that this assumption, especially if applied to political divisions of the country, is subject to serious reservations. There is reason to believe that fertility has not been constant in some parts of the Congo during the last half century. The sex and age distribution of regions of the Congo has been seriously affected by migration. Comparison between observed and expected age distribution at advanced ages is especially fallible. It is, however, convenient to compare reported age distributions to hypothetical ones based on stable population assumptions.

The hypothetical age distribution was selected from among the set of stable population models produced by the Office of Population Research.[4] At least two indices related to the age distribution and an assumption about the age pattern of mortality are necessary to enable us to select a proper model fitting the actual age distribution of a given population.

[4] Ansley J. Coale and Paul Demeny, *Regional Model Life Tables and Stable Populations*, Princeton University Press, 1966. (See the discussion of these tables in Chapter 3, pp. 124 ff.

Table 6.6. Males: Age distribution per 100, Demographic Inquiry 1955-57—the Congo, provinces, and districts

	0-1	1-4	5-9	10-14	15-19	20-24	25-29	30-34	35-44	45-54	55+	Population (thousands)
Leopoldville Province	4.4	14.5	13.8	12.1	8.6	7.7	8.6	7.0	11.1	8.3	4.1	1,481
Leopoldville	4.5	12.1	9.7	6.5	7.2	13.1	16.0	10.4	11.9	6.2	2.4	191
Lac Leopold II	3.4	13.9	14.2	12.7	7.3	6.9	7.6	7.2	11.1	6.9	5.8	131
Kwilu	4.4	14.0	14.0	13.2	9.2	7.1	7.7	6.7	11.7	8.8	3.3	536
Kwango	4.5	15.5	15.7	13.9	8.5	5.4	6.1	5.6	10.5	8.9	5.3	215
Bas-Congo	4.2	14.9	11.9	10.1	9.1	9.8	10.5	7.8	10.4	7.1	4.1	202
Cataractes	4.1	15.3	16.5	14.3	8.8	5.4	5.4	5.4	10.2	8.9	5.9	206
Equateur Province	3.6	11.6	12.0	10.1	6.5	7.5	8.4	8.3	14.8	11.3	6.1	855
Equateur	3.3	10.4	10.0	9.1	6.2	5.6	8.0	7.5	16.0	14.3	9.5	147
Mongala	3.8	12.8	12.9	10.6	6.4	7.2	8.3	8.2	13.8	11.1	5.0	253
Ubangi	4.1	13.5	14.5	11.5	7.3	8.1	7.7	8.0	13.2	8.4	3.7	260
Tshuapa	3.0	8.4	9.1	8.4	5.6	8.4	9.6	9.4	17.2	12.7	8.1	195
Orientale Province	2.9	9.5	11.3	10.1	4.9	7.1	8.6	9.1	16.1	12.6	7.7	1,154
Stanleyville	3.2	10.5	12.0	9.0	5.8	9.6	10.8	8.7	15.5	10.3	6.0	318
Ituri	3.9	12.4	14.9	12.8	4.9	5.3	6.8	8.1	12.3	12.5	6.5	323
Bas-Uele	1.8	6.4	8.7	8.4	5.1	6.3	7.9	10.4	19.4	15.7	9.8	225
Haut-Uele	2.3	7.7	10.2	9.1	4.9	7.0	9.0	9.7	18.3	12.6	9.2	286
Kivu Province	4.4	14.9	14.4	11.3	6.5	7.8	8.4	7.7	10.8	7.2	6.7	985
Sud-Kivu	4.9	15.3	14.6	10.9	7.2	7.2	8.3	7.8	10.2	7.2	6.4	404
Nord-Kivu	4.4	17.0	16.2	12.6	6.4	8.3	7.7	6.3	9.5	6.0	5.5	359
Maniema	3.2	10.8	10.9	9.7	5.3	8.2	9.8	9.8	14.1	9.0	9.3	222
Katanga Province	4.8	15.0	13.1	10.1	4.7	6.3	8.8	8.6	11.8	10.3	6.3	700
Elizabethville	5.5	17.4	12.9	8.3	4.8	7.7	13.0	11.3	12.8	5.6	.6	75
Tanganyika	5.0	15.1	13.6	10.4	5.0	6.4	8.2	7.6	11.0	6.1	6.1	188
Lualaba	4.3	14.5	12.3	9.8	4.3	6.5	9.6	9.9	14.0	10.0	4.9	137
Haut-Lomani	4.5	13.8	12.3	10.2	4.9	6.0	8.0	8.1	11.5	11.5	9.1	210
Luapula-Moero	5.5	16.5	15.5	11.4	4.6	5.3	7.3	7.9	10.0	9.2	6.7	90
Kasai Province	4.4	12.7	13.2	11.7	6.3	5.6	8.4	8.2	12.0	11.5	5.9	1,007
Lulua	4.3	12.7	13.2	12.1	7.9	6.0	8.6	7.3	11.7	11.5	5.1	313
Sankuru	4.3	12.1	11.8	10.8	5.2	5.6	8.7	9.2	12.9	11.8	7.7	236
Kabinda	4.8	13.8	15.1	11.9	5.7	5.2	7.6	7.7	10.9	11.6	5.7	224
Kasai	4.5	12.5	13.0	12.1	6.0	5.3	8.6	8.8	12.6	11.3	5.5	233
Congo	4.1	12.9	13.0	11.0	6.5	7.1	8.5	8.1	12.7	10.1	6.0	6,182

Table 6.7. Females: Age distribution per 100, Demographic Inquiry 1955-57—the Congo, provinces, and districts

	0-1	1-4	5-9	10-14	15-19	20-24	25-29	30-34	35-44	45-54	55+	Population (thousands)
Leopoldville Province:	4.2	13.8	13.6	9.9	8.1	8.6	9.3	9.2	11.4	7.3	4.5	1,588
Leopoldville	5.9	16.8	14.5	7.6	8.4	13.1	12.8	7.9	7.8	3.4	1.7	142
Lac Leopold II	4.3	13.1	13.3	8.7	6.1	8.1	8.8	8.8	13.6	9.2	6.0	140
Kwilu	4.1	13.0	13.3	10.1	7.6	8.2	9.2	9.5	12.7	8.1	4.2	613
Kwango	4.3	13.6	14.4	10.6	7.4	7.7	9.1	8.8	10.9	7.9	5.2	251
Bas-Congo	4.0	14.4	12.3	9.0	9.6	10.3	10.1	9.3	9.4	6.3	5.1	210
Cataractes	3.6	14.3	14.4	11.4	9.9	6.8	7.4	9.6	11.1	6.6	4.8	233
Equateur Province	3.6	10.2	11.9	7.1	6.3	8.0	9.8	9.9	16.4	9.9	6.9	901
Equateur	3.1	10.0	9.3	5.5	5.2	7.5	9.1	9.5	18.3	13.2	9.1	155
Mongala	3.8	12.0	13.4	7.8	6.6	7.6	9.6	9.5	15.4	8.8	5.4	267
Ubangi	3.9	12.9	13.9	8.1	7.2	8.1	9.3	9.7	14.6	7.4	5.0	279
Tshuapa	3.0	8.1	8.8	5.6	5.5	8.1	10.8	10.6	18.1	12.0	9.4	201
Orientale Province	3.0	10.0	11.3	7.4	7.1	8.2	8.9	11.9	17.1	9.2	5.8	1,182
Stanleyville	3.3	10.9	10.7	6.9	8.9	11.1	9.7	10.8	15.0	7.4	5.3	316
Ituri	4.3	13.3	15.2	10.5	8.7	6.4	7.3	10.6	15.1	7.3	3.3	328
Bas-Uele	2.0	6.7	8.4	5.2	6.2	7.0	9.2	14.1	21.4	12.0	7.9	242
Haut-Uele	2.1	8.1	10.0	6.4	6.6	8.2	9.4	12.9	18.0	10.8	7.5	296
Kivu Province	4.4	14.9	14.3	8.8	8.7	9.3	8.7	9.3	10.4	6.2	5.0	1,028
Sud-Kivu	5.0	15.7	14.5	8.6	8.2	9.1	9.3	10.0	9.6	5.9	4.0	427
Nord-Kivu	4.3	16.5	16.3	10.3	9.8	9.3	7.0	7.2	9.6	5.3	4.4	376
Maniema	3.3	10.8	10.5	6.6	8.1	9.6	10.3	11.6	13.2	8.4	7.6	224
Katanga Province	4.6	14.9	13.0	7.4	6.9	8.1	9.0	11.2	12.4	7.4	5.0	739
Elizabethville	5.7	20.2	15.9	7.2	9.0	10.8	11.5	11.2	6.3	1.9	.3	65
Tanganyika	4.8	14.4	13.0	8.0	6.6	7.9	8.1	10.9	13.8	8.0	4.5	206
Lualaba	4.2	14.6	12.8	6.8	7.1	8.7	9.8	13.4	12.1	6.2	4.2	137
Haut-Lomani	4.1	13.4	11.6	6.9	6.2	7.1	8.8	10.0	13.9	9.7	7.3	230
Luapula-Moero	5.0	16.3	14.7	8.1	7.7	8.4	8.9	9.5	10.2	6.3	4.9	101
Kasai Province	4.0	12.5	12.4	7.6	5.4	7.4	9.7	12.5	14.6	9.2	4.6	1,114
Lulua	4.0	12.7	12.9	8.3	7.0	8.1	8.8	11.5	14.3	8.1	4.4	341
Sankuru	3.8	11.7	11.2	7.1	4.5	7.0	10.4	13.5	15.9	9.6	5.3	257
Kabinda	4.3	13.3	12.9	7.3	5.2	6.9	9.4	12.4	13.8	10.0	4.4	256
Kasai	3.9	12.4	12.7	7.5	4.6	7.2	10.4	13.0	14.5	9.4	4.4	260
Congo	4.0	12.7	12.8	8.2	7.2	8.3	9.2	10.6	13.6	8.2	5.2	6,551

The selection of the models for the Congo and its political divisions— districts and provinces—is based on the following two parameters: (1) the estimated proportion of children who die within the first five years, as the index of mortality level, and (2) the observed (reported) proportion of children under five years of age.

The problems related to the estimation of mortality in the Congo are discussed extensively in Section III. As concerns the age pattern of mortality, the analysis carried out in that chapter leads to the conclusion that the North family of tables seems most consistent with the evidence at our disposal about mortality conditions in the Congo. But the divergence of the results obtained by using alternative series of life table models from those obtained by using the North models is relatively narrow, except in the terminal age class, compared with the wide divergences of the reported distributions from the selected stable distributions. In other words, the patterns of incongruity between observed and expected relations among age classes on all these hypotheses are very similar. The four families of model life tables at our disposal do not, of course, exhaust all possibilities. The age pattern of mortality in the Congo may lie outside the range of these tables. Nevertheless, the degree of agreement in results obtained with the alternative hypotheses at our disposal supports our assumption that the observed deviations from the expected distribution are generally significant. In the remainder of this section, we shall use the North family of life tables as a basis, usually without reference to alternative hypotheses.

Compared to the other age segments, the reports on ages under 10 for females and under 15 for males seem to be acceptable for the completeness of the enumeration of children as well as for their classification in the proper age groups. It follows from the figures in Table 6.8 that there is a relatively good agreement between the reported proportion of children of both sexes in different age groups under 10 and the expected (stable) proportion, as based on the reported birth rate (42.7) and estimated expectancy of life at birth for the Congo (38.5 years).

In general, the reported proportion somewhat exceeds the stable proportion. This excess, although relatively small, is due to the fact that the

Table 6.8. Reported and stable proportions (percent) under 10, by sex and five-year age groups, for birth rate 42.7 and life expectancy at birth 38.5—the Congo

Age	Males		Females		Both Sexes		
	Reported	Stable	Reported	Stable	Reported	Stable	Reported/Stable
0	4.1	3.8	3.9	3.7	4.0	3.8	1.05
1-4	12.9	12.5	12.8	12.3	12.9	12.4	1.04
5-9	13.0	13.0	12.8	12.8	12.9	12.9	1.00
0-9	30.0	29.2	29.6	28.8	29.8	29.1	1.02

birth rate as reported is actually somewhat understated (by 6 percent) as compared to the estimated birth rate (45 per 1,000).

The relatively high agreement between the reported and the stable child proportions, based on the reported vital rates, is observed not only for the Congo as a whole but also for the regions. Moreover the internal consistency is high between particular age groups under age 10 for the whole Congo as well as for its components, considering each sex separately as well as both sexes together. This tends to demonstrate that the reports on age of children are relatively good and are consistent with various reasonable and accepted hypotheses on the true age distribution of the Congolese populations.

In the Congo, which is unique in this respect, the births of many of the younger children had been officially registered. The estimated ratio of registered to total births in the whole country was 70 percent in 1950 (five years before the beginning of the inquiry) and reached 84 percent in 1956. The birth dates of many of these children were inscribed in the father's identity booklet or in some other document in his possession. The existence of precise information on the ages of some children facilitated estimates of the ages of others in the same household or village.

There were, of course, errors in the enumeration and classification of children, and presumably overestimates and underestimates of children's ages did not exactly compensate each other. But the figures, especially for children under 5, seem to be reasonably reliable. We shall proceed on the assumption that they are substantially true.

We now present stable population distributions for the Congo and its regions based on the reported proportion under age 5 and on the estimated $q(5)$ for respective provinces or districts. Table 6.9 shows the stable population distribution for males and females as compared to the reported age distribution for the Congo. The ratio of the reported to the stable proportion (R/S) constitutes the index of deviation of the former from the latter in a given age group.

Tables 6.10 and 6.11 respectively present the age distribution for males and females for provinces and the districts, while Tables 6.12 and 6.13 give the ratio of reported (R) to stable (S) proportion in each age group for the indicated political divisions.

The Nature of Deviations Between the Reported and the Stable Age Distribution

The deviations for the Congo as a whole (see Figure 6.4) can be summarized briefly as follows: The male age classes are understated between ages 15 and 24, overstated between 25 and 54, and understated after

Table 6.9. Reported (R) and stable (S) age distributions in numbers (thousands) and percent—the Congo

age	MALE Reported (R) N	%	Stable (S) N	%	R/S	FEMALE Reported (R) N	%	Stable (S) N	%	R/S
0-4	1,051	17.0	1,051	17.0	1.00	1,099	16.8	1,101	16.8	1.00
5-9	803	13.0	841	13.6	.96	838	12.8	845	12.9	.99
10-14	681	11.0	723	11.7	.94	538	8.2	747	11.4	.72
15-19	403	6.5	637	10.3	.63	471	7.2	662	10.1	.71
20-24	437	7.1	544	8.8	.81	543	8.3	576	8.8	.94
25-29	527	8.5	470	7.6	1.12	603	9.2	498	7.6	1.21
30-34	499	8.1	402	6.5	1.25	693	10.6	432	6.6	1.61
35-44	786	12.7	631	10.2	1.25	891	13.6	675	10.3	1.32
45-54	622	10.1	433	7.0	1.44	534	8.2	504	7.7	1.06
55+	372	6.0	451	7.3	.82	341	5.2	511	7.8	.67
Total	6,182	100.0	6,182	100.0		6,551	100.1	6,551	100.0	

Table 6.10. Male stable age distribution, percent—the Congo, provinces, and districts

	0-4	5-9	10-14	15-19	20-24	25-29	30-34	35-44	45-54	55+	
Leopoldville Province	18.9	14.6	12.2	10.6	9.0	7.4	6.3	9.3	6.0	5.8	100.1
Leopoldville	–	–	–	–	–	–	–	–	–	–	–
Lac Leopold II	17.3	13.8	11.8	10.0	9.0	7.5	6.5	9.8	6.7	7.6	100.0
Kwilu	18.4	14.3	12.2	10.4	9.0	7.5	6.3	9.6	6.4	6.0	100.1
Kwango	20.0	14.7	12.5	10.8	9.0	7.3	6.1	9.0	5.8	5.1	100.2
Bas-Congo	19.1	14.8	11.9	10.4	9.1	7.3	6.1	9.4	6.1	5.7	99.8
Cataractes	19.4	14.8	12.3	10.6	9.0	7.2	6.4	9.1	5.8	5.4	100.0
Equateur Province	15.2	12.3	11.0	10.0	8.8	7.9	6.7	11.2	8.2	8.9	100.2
Equateur	13.7	11.8	10.7	9.5	8.6	7.8	6.5	11.5	8.8	11.2	100.1
Mongala	16.6	13.1	11.5	10.0	9.0	7.8	6.4	10.5	7.3	7.8	100.0
Ubangi	17.6	13.8	11.8	10.5	9.0	7.8	6.4	9.8	6.8	6.8	100.0
Tshuapa	11.4	9.8	9.4	8.8	8.4	7.8	7.0	13.0	10.6	13.8	100.1
Orientale Province	12.4	10.3	9.8	9.0	8.6	7.7	7.2	12.6	9.9	12.4	99.9
Stanleyville	13.7	11.5	10.2	9.6	8.8	7.8	7.0	11.4	8.9	10.9	99.8
Ituri	16.1	13.0	11.3	10.0	9.0	7.8	6.8	11.1	8.1	7.7	99.9
Bas-Uele	8.2	7.5	7.8	7.8	7.8	7.5	7.5	13.8	13.3	18.8	100.0
Haut-Uele	10.0	9.2	8.6	8.4	8.0	7.7	7.2	13.3	11.5	16.1	100.0
Kivu Province	19.3	14.5	12.3	10.5	9.1	7.3	6.0	9.3	5.7	5.9	99.9
Sud-Kivu	20.2	14.3	12.2	10.5	8.8	7.2	6.5	9.3	5.8	5.1	99.9
Nord-Kivu	21.4	16.0	13.0	10.8	8.8	7.2	5.4	8.3	5.0	4.4	100.2
Maniema	14.0	11.8	10.3	9.8	8.8	7.8	6.9	11.7	8.7	10.1	99.9
Katanga Province	19.8	15.2	12.6	10.5	8.8	7.4	6.0	8.8	5.6	5.3	100.0
Elizabethville	22.9	17.3	13.4	11.2	8.8	6.6	4.9	7.3	4.1	3.4	99.9
Tanganyika	20.1	15.5	12.8	10.8	8.8	7.0	5.8	8.6	5.4	5.2	100.0
Lualaba	18.8	15.0	12.5	10.8	8.8	7.3	5.6	9.2	5.8	6.0	99.8
Haut-Lomani	18.3	14.3	12.2	10.5	9.0	7.3	6.2	9.7	6.3	6.3	100.1
Luapula-Moero	22.0	16.3	13.2	10.8	8.8	7.0	5.4	7.8	4.8	3.8	99.9
Kasai Province	17.1	13.5	11.6	10.4	9.0	7.6	6.5	10.1	7.0	7.2	100.0
Lulua	17.0	12.9	11.3	10.2	8.9	7.7	6.6	10.9	7.5	7.0	99.9
Sankuru	16.4	13.2	11.4	10.2	9.0	7.8	6.5	10.5	7.4	7.4	99.8
Kabinda	18.6	14.5	12.3	10.5	9.0	7.5	6.3	9.3	6.1	6.0	100.1
Kasai	17.0	12.8	11.2	10.2	8.9	7.5	6.6	10.9	7.8	6.9	99.8
Congo	17.0	13.6	11.7	10.3	8.8	7.6	6.5	10.2	7.0	7.3	100.0

Table 6.11. Female stable age distribution, percent—the Congo, provinces, and districts

	0-4	5-9	10-14	15-19	20-24	25-29	30-34	35-44	45-54	55+	Total
Leopoldville Province	18.0	13.8	11.8	10.3	8.8	7.4	6.5	9.6	6.7	6.8	99.8
Leopoldville	22.7	7.2	17.2	13.5	10.7	8.7	7.5	5.2	3.6	3.7	100.0
Lac Leopold II	17.4	13.7	11.8	10.2	8.8	7.5	6.4	9.8	7.0	7.5	100.4
Kwilu	17.1	14.3	11.3	10.2	8.8	7.5	6.8	10.1	7.2	7.3	100.5
Kwango	17.9	13.5	11.6	10.1	9.0	7.8	6.4	10.1	7.0	7.0	100.3
Bas-Congo	18.4	14.0	12.0	10.4	8.8	7.5	6.4	9.4	6.5	6.5	99.9
Cataractes	17.9	13.7	11.8	10.3	8.8	7.3	6.4	9.7	6.8	7.1	99.9
Equateur Province	13.8	11.3	10.3	9.5	8.5	7.8	6.8	11.5	9.1	11.2	99.8
Equateur	13.1	11.2	11.2	9.4	8.5	7.5	6.8	11.4	8.7	12.9	100.0
Mongala	15.8	12.7	11.2	9.8	8.8	7.9	6.9	7.1	10.7	8.8	99.8
Ubangi	16.8	13.2	11.5	10.0	8.8	7.6	6.6	10.2	7.4	7.8	99.9
Tshuapa	11.1	9.8	9.0	8.6	8.1	7.5	7.0	12.7	10.8	15.6	100.2
Orientale Province	13.0	10.8	10.1	9.1	8.3	7.6	6.9	11.8	9.6	12.7	99.9
Stanleyville	14.2	11.8	9.8	9.8	8.8	7.8	6.8	11.2	8.6	11.2	100.0
Ituri	17.6	13.7	11.8	10.2	8.8	7.5	6.4	9.7	6.8	7.6	100.1
Bas-Uele	8.7	7.8	7.5	7.5	7.6	7.3	7.2	13.5	12.3	20.4	99.8
Haut-Uele	10.2	8.8	8.6	8.2	9.8	7.5	7.2	12.8	11.2	15.8	100.1
Kivu Province	19.3	14.3	12.2	10.5	9.0	7.8	6.4	9.4	6.2	5.2	100.3
Sud-Kivu	20.7	14.8	12.2	10.4	8.6	7.4	6.0	8.8	5.7	5.2	99.9
Nord-Kivu	20.8	15.4	12.7	10.5	8.9	7.2	5.8	8.3	5.4	4.9	99.8
Maniema	14.1	11.6	10.4	9.7	8.8	7.6	6.8	11.3	8.8	10.8	99.8
Katanga Province	19.5	15.2	12.4	10.5	8.8	7.3	6.0	8.8	5.8	5.5	99.8
Elizabethville	25.9	17.6	14.0	10.5	8.0	7.0	5.8	5.8	2.8	3.0	100.4
Tanganyika	19.2	14.9	12.3	10.5	9.0	7.5	5.9	8.8	5.9	5.8	99.8
Lualaba	18.8	14.9	12.3	10.5	9.0	7.5	5.8	8.8	5.8	6.3	99.7
Haut-Lomani	17.5	13.6	11.2	10.3	8.9	7.6	5.8	9.8	6.8	7.3	99.8
Luapula-Moero	21.3	15.8	12.9	10.5	8.9	7.0	5.9	7.8	4.9	4.9	99.9
Kasai Province	16.5	13.0	11.4	10.0	8.8	7.5	6.6	10.6	7.4	8.2	100.0
Lulua	16.7	12.6	11.0	9.8	8.8	7.8	6.8	10.5	7.8	8.2	100.0
Sankuru	15.5	12.5	11.0	9.8	8.8	7.8	6.8	10.5	8.0	9.4	100.1
Kabinda	17.6	13.6	11.6	10.2	8.7	7.6	6.4	9.8	6.8	7.6	99.9
Kasaf	16.3	12.2	10.7	9.8	8.7	7.8	6.8	11.1	8.1	8.9	100.1
Congo	16.8	12.9	11.4	10.1	8.8	7.6	6.6	10.3	7.7	7.8	99.9

Table 6.12. Ratio of the reported (R) to stable (S) male age distribution—the Congo, provinces, and districts

	0-4	5-9	10-14	15-19	20-24	25-29	30-34	35-44	45-54	55+
Leopoldville Province	1.00	.95	.99	.81	.86	1.16	1.11	1.19	1.38	.71
Leopoldville	1.00	–	–	–	–	–	–	–	–	–
Lac Leopold II	1.00	1.03	1.08	.73	.77	1.01	1.11	1.13	1.33	.76
Kwilu	1.00	.98	1.11	.88	.79	1.03	1.06	1.22	1.38	.55
Kwango	1.00	1.07	.85	.79	.60	.84	.93	1.17	1.53	1.04
Bas-Congo	1.00	.81	1.16	.88	1.07	1.44	1.28	1.11	1.16	.72
Cataractes	1.00	1.11		.83	.60	.75	.84	1.12	1.53	1.09
Equateur Province	1.00	.98	.92	.65	.85	1.06	1.24	1.32	1.37	.69
Equateur	1.00	.85	.85	.65	.65	1.03	1.15	1.39	1.63	.85
Mongala	1.00	.98	.92	.64	.80	1.06	1.28	1.31	1.52	.64
Ubangi	1.00	1.05	.97	.70	.90	1.03	1.25	1.35	1.24	.54
Tshuapa	1.00	.93	.89	.64	1.00	1.23	1.34	1.32	1.20	.59
Orientale Province	1.00	1.10	1.03	.54	.83	1.12	1.26	1.28	1.27	.62
Stanleyville	1.00	.93	.88	.60	1.09	.72	1.24	1.36	1.16	.55
Ituri	1.00	1.15	1.13	.49	.59	.87	1.19	1.11	1.54	.84
Bas-Uele	1.00	1.16	1.08	.65	.81	1.05	1.39	1.41	1.18	.52
Haut-Uele	1.00	1.11	1.06	.55	.88	1.17	1.35	1.38	1.10	.57
Kivu Province	1.00	.99	.92	.62	.86	1.15	1.28	1.16	1.26	1.14
Sud-Kivu	1.00	1.02	.89	.69	.82	1.15	1.20	1.10	1.24	1.25
Nord-Kivu	1.00	1.01	.97	.59	.94	1.10	1.17	1.14	1.20	1.25
Maniema	1.00	.92	.94	.54	.93	1.26	1.42	1.21	1.03	.92
Katanga Province	1.00	.86	.80	.45	.72	1.19	1.43	1.34	1.84	1.19
Elizabethville	1.00	.75	.62	.43	.88	.97	2.31	1.75	1.37	0.18
Tanganyika	1.00	.88	.81	.46	.73	1.17	1.31	1.28	2.13	1.17
Lualaba	1.00	.82	.78	.40	.74	1.32	1.77	1.52	1.72	.82
Haut-Lomani	1.00	.86	.84	.47	.67	1.09	1.31	1.19	1.83	1.44
Luapula-Moero	1.00	.95	.86	.43	.60	1.04	1.46	1.28	1.92	1.76
Kasai Province	1.00	.98	1.01	.61	.62	1.11	1.26	1.19	1.64	.82
Lulua	1.00	1.00	1.07	.77	.67	1.12	1.11	1.07	1.53	.73
Sankuru	1.00	.89	.95	.51	.62	1.12	1.42	1.23	1.59	1.04
Kabinda	1.00	1.04	.97	.54	.57	1.01	1.22	1.17	1.90	.95
Kasai	1.00	1.02	1.08	.59	.60	1.15	1.33	1.16	1.45	.80
Congo	1.00	.96	.94	.63	.81	1.12	1.25	1.25	1.44	.83

Table 6.13. Ratio of reported (R) to stable (S) female age distribution—the Congo, provinces, and districts

	0-4	5-9	10-14	15-19	20-24	25-29	30-34	35-44	45-54	55+
Leopoldville Province	1.00	.99	.84	.79	.98	1.26	1.42	1.19	1.09	.66
Leopoldville	1.00	2.01	.44	.62	1.22	1.47	1.05	1.50	.94	.46
Lac Leopold II	1.00	.97	.74	.60	.92	1.17	1.38	1.39	1.31	.80
Kwilu	1.00	.93	.89	.74	.93	1.23	1.40	1.26	1.12	.58
Kwango	1.00	1.07	.91	.73	.86	1.17	1.38	1.08	1.13	.74
Bas-Congo	1.00	.88	.75	.92	1.17	1.35	1.45	1.00	.97	.78
Cataractes	1.00	1.05	.97	.96	.77	1.01	1.50	1.14	.97	.67
Equateur Province	1.00	1.05	.69	.66	.94	1.26	1.46	1.43	1.09	.62
Equateur	1.00	.83	.50	.55	.88	1.21	1.40	1.60	1.52	.70
Mongala	1.00	1.06	.70	.67	.86	1.22	1.38	2.17	.82	.61
Ubangi	1.00	1.05	.70	.72	.92	1.22	1.47	1.43	1.00	.64
Tshuapa	1.00	.90	.62	.64	1.00	1.44	1.51	1.43	1.11	.60
Orientale Province	1.00	1.13	.73	.78	.99	1.17	1.72	1.45	.96	.46
Stanleyville	1.00	.91	.70	.91	1.26	1.24	1.59	1.34	.86	.47
Ituri	1.00	1.11	.89	.66	.73	.97	1.66	1.56	1.07	.43
Bas-Uele	1.00	1.08	.69	.83	.92	1.26	1.96	1.58	.98	.39
Haut-Uele	1.00	1.00	.74	.80	.84	1.25	1.79	1.41	.96	.47
Kivu Province	1.00	1.00	.72	.83	1.03	1.12	1.45	1.11	1.00	.96
Sud-Kivu	1.00	.98	.70	.79	1.06	1.26	1.67	1.09	1.04	.77
Nord-Kivu	1.00	1.06	.81	.93	1.04	.97	1.24	1.16	.98	.90
Maniema	1.00	.91	.63	.84	1.09	1.36	1.70	1.17	.95	.70
Katanga Province	1.00	.86	.60	.66	.92	1.23	1.87	1.41	1.28	.91
Elizabethville	1.00	.90	.51	.86	1.35	1.64	1.93	1.09	.68	1.00
Tanganyika	1.00	.87	.65	.63	.88	1.08	1.85	1.57	1.36	.78
Lualaba	1.00	.86	.55	.68	.96	1.31	2.31	1.38	1.07	.67
Haut-Lomani	1.00	.85	.62	.60	.80	1.16	1.60	1.42	1.43	1.00
Luapula-Moero	1.00	.93	.63	.73	.94	1.27	1.61	1.31	1.29	1.00
Kasai Province	1.00	.95	.67	.54	.84	1.29	1.89	1.38	1.24	.56
Lulua	1.00	1.02	.75	.71	.92	1.13	1.69	1.36	1.04	.54
Sankuru	1.00	.90	.64	.46	.80	1.33	1.99	1.51	1.20	.56
Kabinda	1.00	.95	.63	.51	.79	1.24	1.94	1.41	1.47	.58
Kasai	1.00	1.04	.70	.47	.83	1.33	1.91	1.31	1.16	.49
Congo	1.00	.99	.72	.71	.94	1.21	1.61	1.32	1.06	.67

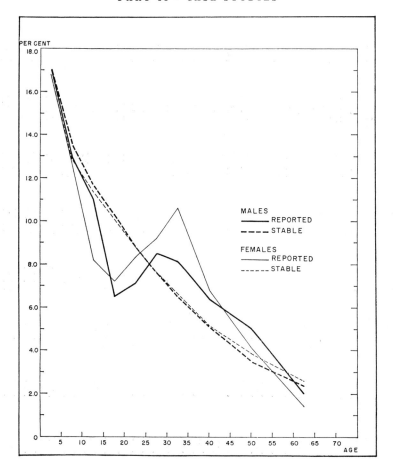

6.4. Reported and stable age distributions, for males and
females separately, the Congo.

55. The deficit starts earlier for females; there is a clear excess in the
age classes 20 to 44, reaching a peak between 30 and 34, with a ratio
of reported population to stable of 1.61—the highest of the series. Ages
45 and over are deficient. The provincial pattern is in general similar
to that of the entire Congo.

Three main factors have probably produced a distorting effect on the
observed age composition in the Congo and in its particular regions:
(a) age-selective migration, (b) erroneous enumeration (age-selective
omissions, possibly some double count), and (c) age misreporting. The
changing fertility and mortality have also probably caused some deviation of the reported from the stable distribution, but this aspect will be
examined here only incidentally.

The Effects of Migration

As far as the total Congo is concerned, migration can have only a relatively small effect on the age distribution. According to our estimate, there are about 300,000 to 350,000 persons (or about 3 percent of the total population) who resided in the Congo at the time of survey but who were born in other African countries. The total number of outmigrants probably does not exceed 50,000. About half of the immigrants were natives of Rwanda and settled in the Congo (Kivu) with their families. Hence, their effect on the age distribution can be of only minor importance. The immigration from other neighboring countries is age and sex selective to a larger extent, but in view of its small size relative to the total population, it has no appreciable effect on the age distribution of the total Congolese population.

Internal migration in some regions might produce a more considerable effect on age distribution. Migration in the Congo takes the form mainly of an exodus from rural areas toward the urban and industrial settlements, and involves more adults in working ages than children or elderly persons, as well as more men than women. Table 6.14 and Figure 6.5, which reproduce the age structure of the rural and urban populations, show the excess of the proportions in the adult ages in the latter as compared to the former. The adult (over age 15) sex ratio (males per female) is 0.81 in the rural, 1.25 in the mixed, and 1.30 in the urban communities, the national average being equal to 0.90.

But only in a few districts is it apparent from the data that there is a distorting effect due to migration. The two purely urban districts—Leopoldville and Elisabethville—are quite heavily affected. Lualaba (Katanga) and Bas Congo (Leopoldville Province) also have an important urban population and have received a relatively important inmigration from outside. On the other hand, districts such as Cataractes, Kabinda, and Kwango are known for their heavy outmigration toward the urban areas outside their own territory. The figures in Table 6.15 show how the sex ratio and proportion in adult age deviate from the national average in those districts where the inmigration happens to be important and in those which are known for relatively important outmigration.

Most of the districts of the Congo have not shown a migratory movement sufficient to produce a significant alteration of their age structure. A high proportion of their urban and mixed population is native from the same district.

Migration undoubtedly has affected the sex and age composition of populations in all parts of the Congo to varying degrees in particular age groups, but in many cases its impact has been only slight.

Table 6.14. Rural, mixed, and urban population by age, percent—the Congo

Age	RURAL			MIXED			URBAN		
	M	F	Both	M	F	Both	M	F	Both
0-4	7.85	8.27	16.12	9.26	9.59	18.85	10.26	10.36	20.62
5-9	6.42	6.65	13.07	5.80	6.27	12.07	6.08	6.41	12.49
10-14	5.66	4.47	10.13	4.22	3.35	7.57	4.27	3.38	7.65
15-19	3.20	3.63	6.83	2.83	3.92	6.75	3.34	3.94	7.28
20-24	2.78	3.85	6.63	5.80	5.83	11.63	5.64	5.63	11.27
25-29	3.27	4.47	7.74	7.08	5.87	12.95	7.42	5.49	12.91
30-34	3.31	5.60	8.91	6.39	5.22	11.61	5.67	4.43	10.10
35-44	5.81	7.77	13.58	7.91	4.56	12.47	6.81	3.86	10.67
45-54	5.30	4.95	10.25	3.41	1.39	4.80	3.46	1.68	5.14
55+	3.50	3.24	6.74	.69	.61	1.30	1.11	.77	1.88
Total	47.10	52.90	100.0	53.39	46.61	100.0	54.06	45.95	100.1
Numbers	4,682,000	5,256,000		844,000	737,000		656,000	558,000	

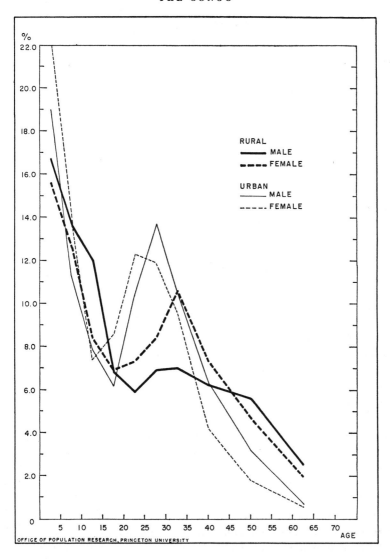

6.5. Rural and urban age distributions, males and females
separately, by five-year age groups through 34 years and by
ten-year groups to 55 years, the Congo.

The Effects of Selective Underenumeration

Differences by sex and age in the completeness of enumeration may
have exerted a certain influence in causing apparent deviations in the
reported age distributions of males and females from any stable population pattern. Unfortunately, however, it is difficult to evaluate or measure the possible effects.

Table 6.15. Percent urban, adult sex ratio (males per female), and proportions male and female aged 15-45—the Congo and migration districts

Districts of in-migration:	% of urban to total population	Adult sex ratio	Proportion Aged 15-45	
			Males	Females
Leopoldville	95	1.62	58.6	50.0
Elisabethville	100	1.25	49.6	48.8
Lualaba	45	.96	44.3	51.1
Bas Congo	20	.94	47.6	48.7
Districts of out-migration:				
Cataractes	5	.79	35.2	44.8
Kabinda	5	.77	37.1	47.7
Kwango	.5	.76	36.1	43.9
National average	10	.90	42.9	48.9

The possibility of differential underenumeration of some elements in the population is suggested by the discrepancy between the *de jure* and the *de facto* estimates of population. There is an inherent difficulty of complete enumeration of persons temporarily absent in fields or on highways (subject to enumeration as "present") and of persons recently settled in new localities, especially under African conditions. The complete omission of persons in certain institutions outside the *territoire* in which they resided must have occurred.

In addition to these difficulties, it is possible that some parents purposely sent young unmarried girls away before the arrival of the enumerators. Some enumerators reported a suspicion that this had happened in some villages. Moreover, and probably more important, young men approaching the age at which they become subject to taxation as "adults," normally at 18 years, may have tried to elude all official associations— thus, if possible, avoiding registration in other localities if away from home, and evading the survey enumerators. Such evasion may have been more prevalent among unemployed as compared with employed men, and among unmarried as compared with those who had established their status as "adults" by marriage and the assumption of responsibility for children. These observations are obviously purely qualitative.

There is, nevertheless, statistical evidence to the effect that the enumeration of married men and women was relatively complete, though this evidence, by its nature, refers only to those in monogamous marriages. According to the survey, in major subdivisions numbers of monogamously married husbands and wives in the *de facto* population are practically equal. For the whole Congo, the reported number of husbands with only one wife was 1,955,000 and that of wives in monogamous marriages was 1,961,000. The difference is trivial in view of the many possibilities of error, including sampling variance. This suggests that if there was some underestimation of the *de facto* population, as contrasted with the *de jure* population, the deficiency must have been chiefly among the younger unmarried persons.

Some further indication on this score is provided by Tables 6.16 and 6.17. The first table presents the distribution of present residents (PR), absent residents (AR), and visitors (V) by age and sex for Katanga Province, the only province for which these data were tabulated in such detail. It is significant, however, that the largest excess of absent residents over visitors coincides precisely with the critical ages within which one would suspect—as we pointed out above—the most frequent underreporting, that is, 10 to 14 for girls and 15 to 19 for boys. Table 6.17 provides the ratio of absent residents to the *de facto* population for some other districts and leads to a similar speculation. There are some differences among these districts in the magnitude of the ratio and the age at which it reaches its maximum. Nevertheless, a pattern of absenteeism which concentrates at the critical ages is obvious from this table. Although the excess of absent residents is too small to be held solely responsible for the apparent deficit observed among the adolescents and young adults, it does suggest the possibility of some correlation between the frequency of absences and the frequency of underenumeration.

Although persons at older ages are more stable and less motivated to evade the survey than are younger persons, the possibility of certain omissions among these persons should not be excluded *a priori*. Among certain tribes a custom still seems to prevail according to which the old persons approaching death have a tendency to settle in huts at the periphery of the village, and some old persons may have been overlooked for this reason.

Table 6.16. Proportions of present residents (PR). absent residents (AR), and visitors (V) in the enumerated population, by sex and age—Katanga Province

Age	Males			Females			AR-V	
	PR	AR	V	PR	AR	V	Males	Females
0	88.29	6.20	5.50	88.61	5.72	5.67	0.7	0.1
1-4	87.45	7.50	5.04	87.00	8.23	4.81	2.5	3.4
5-9	85.86	10.01	4.14	82.21	12.43	5.36	6.8	7.1
10-14	76.95	17.52	5.53	80.12	14.36	5.52	12.0	8.8
15-19	70.07	23.79	6.14	83.47	8.64	7.89	17.6	0.8
20-24	88.93	6.91	4.15	85.27	7.78	6.95	2.7	0.8
25-29	89.20	6.7	3.30	85.72	8.47	5.81	3.4	2.7
30-34	90.44	6.80	2.76	87.50	7.66	4.84	4.0	2.8
35-44	91.82	5.74	2.45	90.76	6.04	3.20	5.3	2.8
45-54	93.80	4.34	1.86	91.83	4.99	3.18	2.5	1.8
+55	95.00	3.36	1.65	95.55	2.34	2.10	1.7	0.2
All ages	87.24	8.89	3.86	86.52	8.34	5.02	5.0	2.7

Table 6.17. Absent residents per 100 of *de facto* population, by age, in specified areas

Age	Katanga Province	Equateur District	Kasai District	South Kivu District
0	6.34	7.92	6.67	2.58
1-4	8.55	8.11	5.93	3.99
5-9	12.69	9.49	10.07	5.59
10-14	19.29	7.55	12.68	13.07
15-19	18.02	14.13	12.29	19.30
20-24	8.00	10.45	8.97	9.58
25-29	8.26	10.13	7.03	6.86
30-34	7.87	8.19	5.03	5.19
35-44	6.27	7.53	4.73	4.67
45-54	4.84	4.72	3.92	2.89
+55	2.98	3.52	2.38	2.45
Total	9.43	8.03	7.13	7.00

To conclude, some plausible considerations and some evidence of uncertain significance give rise to a rather strong suspicion of some differential underenumeration by age, but to demonstrate that this occurred would require the near impossible: a measure of its incidence and magnitude.

Age Classification

Most of those interviewed in the inquiry were illiterate and unfamiliar with any abstract scheme of dating events or reckoning ages. They were, of course, deeply concerned with the successive stages of human experience, social grouping, and questions of seniority, but these do not require reference to calendars or the statement of ages in years. It was usually impossible to evoke a reliable reply to a direct question on this subject. And there were usually few or no records of year of birth or of age in years for persons over about ten years of age at the time of the inquiry. The interviewers were, therefore, forced to rely largely on indirect methods of age classification.

Since the interviewers were not required to obtain a precise statement or estimate of ages in single years but simply to assign each person from 5 to 55 years old to a quinquennial or decennial class, with a division into two classes of children under 5, but no division among "aged persons" 55 years or over, the method may have favored some laxity in the mind of interviewers, though the results are not conspicuously more irregular than those frequently obtained in replies to questions on ages by single years. The analysis of errors in the Congo material is, in any case, handicapped by the lack of such specific data.

In order to give some consistency to the evaluation of age, the enumerator was instructed to refer to certain criteria. A reference point in estimating the age of adult men was provided by the presumption that men are liable to the annual payment of taxes from 18 years until they are incapacitated by illness or old age. During the last two decades prior to the inquiry, though not before, annual tax payments were generally recorded in the identity booklets that all men are required to keep in their possession. These books contained other information, such as names and ages of children, relevant to the estimation of ages. In fact, in the years immediately preceding the inquiry there was an increasing tendency toward recording the estimated date of birth, or age at some point, in these books. The enumerators were authorized and expected to review documents concerning tax payments, though they sometimes refrained from doing so to avoid suspicion or embarrassment. Moreover, the records were frequently incomplete, especially in books used to replace deteriorated or lost records. The existence and use of such records restrained errors in the estimation of men's ages within somewhat narrower limits than in the case of females, but obviously did not prevent a strong tendency toward convergence in central age classes—involving the up-aging of young men under 25 years and the down-aging of older men from the terminal group into one of the decennial classes, i.e., 45-54 or perhaps in some cases 34-44 years.

As in other African surveys, the enumerators were instructed to attempt to relate some previous phase or event in a person's experience to some historical event, such as the First or Second World War, known to the enumerator. They were also told to take account of the relative ages of various persons in the same household or village and estimate thus the age of persons with unknown age by reference to the persons with known age. Both of these techniques were rather more applicable to men than to women, both because the labor experience of men was more frequently associated with public events than the affairs of women's lives and because the women had often passed their early years in other villages and with other associates.

Clues to the approximate ages of women were provided by their familial status, marriages, and maternity. The enumerators were explicitly asked to take these conditions into account. The estimate of mother's age could be made by reference to the known or estimated age of her children, assuming her age at marriage, in absence of other evidence, as being 17.[5] The number of children and some estimate of the interval between the successive births was also sometimes used to estimate a mother's age. This approach could frequently have led to a systematic upward or downward bias in age estimates.

[5] According to estimates made elsewhere in this volume, the age at marriage varies from 14.7 (Kasai province) to 17.8 (Leopoldville), with an average for the Congo of 16.5.

In spite of the instruction to refer to some "objective" basis for age evaluation, it would be presumptuous to claim that this was always done in a proper manner. The procedures outlined above are time consuming. Frequently the enumerator contented himself with accepting the age indicated in the booklet, or judged the age impressionistically from physical appearance, or some other casual reference. The extensive numbers both of males and of females in the central age classes may reflect to some degree a certain "age heaping," a tendency on the part both of the respondents and of the enumerators to assume that, in case of doubt, the "safest" course was to assign persons to some "ordinary" central class, from 30 through 54 years for men, and from 25 through 44 years for women, with pronounced preference in their case for the class 30-34 years.

It is difficult to evaluate the respective shares taken by various causes of distortion of the age distribution, and to distinguish them from the effects of underenumeration or from the marks left on the age distribution by changing fertility. For instance, given the methods recommended to estimate women's ages, one would expect a tendency to attribute a higher age to the married young women as compared to single girls (in fact of the same age). This might be particularly true for married girls under age 15, both because the survey concerning marital status was in principle limited to the persons over 15 years of age and because of the opinion that girls in the Congo marry at an average of 17 years. Also, the up-aging of a woman with many grown children would be likely to occur more frequently than the up-aging of the women of the same age having only few small children, etc. These hypotheses however are difficult to test. In Table 6.18 we present a set of correlation coefficients computed by district[6] between the ratio of reported population to computed stable population at successive age classes and (1) the mean age at marriage; (2) the birth rate. The estimate of the mean age at marriage has been derived from the proportion single in the population.[7]

If we restrict the discussion first to females, there is a relatively high correlation (.74) between the mean age at marriage and the R/S index for age 10-14. On the other hand, the association between the mean age at marriage and the age misreporting index (R/S) for females over 20 yields a significant negative correlation ($-.61$). In other words, the deficit tends (for the 10-14 age group) to be high in the districts where marriages occur at earlier ages; conversely, in districts with low age at marriage there is a stronger excess of reported to stable proportions after age 20. Thus, it might be assumed that one factor in the observed distortion of the female distribution around the 15-19 age level is a tend-

---

[6] Excluding the urban districts of Leopoldville and Elisabethville, not amenable to stable population analysis.

[7] The method is described in Chapter 5.

Table 6.18. Coefficients of correlation obtained between the R/S ratios in each
age group vs. mean age at first marriage and estimated birth rate

Age for which the ratios R/S are correlated	R/S vs. mean age at marriage		R/S vs. estimated birth rate	
	Females	Males	Females	Males
10-14	.74	–	.28	–
15-19	.48	.76	.01	.06
10-19	.69	.84	.15	.08
20-24	-.12	.05	-.04	-.33
25-29	-.53	-.30	-.37	-.05
30-34	-.60	-.68	-.18	-.23
35-44	-.15	-.14	-.39	-.59
45-55	-.40	-.22	.10	.41
+55	-.09	-.47	.59	.66
+45	-.12	-.39	.56	.65
15-44	-.43	.06	-.73	-.64
20-44	-.64	.02	-.61	-.59
+20	-.61	-.86	.25	-.02

ency to assign young married women (15-19) with one or more children to the age class over 20 years.

The high correlation between age misreporting and estimated age at marriage does not imply that the overstatement of the age of young married persons is the only source of age misreporting. In some districts the deficit at age 10-14 is nearly half the females in this age group, and it should not be concluded that all of the deficit consists of married girls whose ages were overstated. There is, in addition, a likely tendency to overestimate the age of a girl under 15 who has passed puberty, even if she is single. The higher correlations in Table 6.18 between age misreporting and mean age at marriage among males than females at ages 10-19 is puzzling, because enumerators were instructed to estimate female ages on the basis of marital status, but not male.

Explaining correlations between birth rate and ratio of reported to stable population by a tendency to report women in regions of high fertility as older would similarly not account for the possibility of time trends in fertility and of their effects on the age distribution. Indeed, when fertility is declining, the estimated stable proportion in age group 15-44 tends to be lower as compared to the actual proportion. It appears that the excess in reported to stable proportion happens to be larger precisely in the districts where the fertility underwent a downward trend in past decades.

None of the attempted interpretations of the correlations between such demographic variables as fertility and age at marriage, on the one hand, and R/S ratios, on the other hand, offers a satisfactory explanation for the real or apparent deficit within certain age groups and overreporting within other age groups in all districts.

Sex Ratio

The sex ratios by ages reflect to a large extent the differential under-enumeration and age misreporting by sex. They are presented in Table 6.19 as an illustration of the preceding sections. There are, however, two types of data on the sex ratio that may have particular significance. The sex ratio at birth in the Congo was reported as 97.8 boys per 100 girls. The sex ratio of the total population was 94.4 males per 100 females. These ratios are low by international standards, and might indicate a systematic undercount of the males, or some other defects. A discussion is thus in order.

Sex Ratio at Birth

A low recorded sex ratio at birth could be the result of sampling errors, of sex-selective underreporting or misreporting of the age of children of either sex, or of the systematic omission of one category of children in which the male sex is dominant (such as children dead in infancy).

In dealing with small populations, the instability of sex ratios is intensified by sheer random sampling errors as magnified by a "doubling effect"—an error in the proportion male affects both the numerator and the denominator of the ratio. Were the true sex ratio (males per female) equal to 1.03, random fluctuation would produce ratios, in 95 percent of the repeated observations, within 1.013 and 1.047 for 58,000 observed births. In other terms, the low sex ratio (0.978) observed in the Congo implies 95 percent confidence limits of 0.960 to 1.005.

There is no evidence for the Congo that female children are preferred to male children so that they would tend to be recorded more completely as happens in other cultures. There also is no clear evidence in the Congo statistics of a systematic misreporting of age of children which would result in an excess of males as compared to females under one year of age. In fact, the low sex ratio at birth is consistent with a low sex ratio in the age groups 0 to 1, 1 to 4, and 5 to 9 years, reported in all districts. One would expect a lower sex ratio—should the low sex ratio be attributed to a sex differential misclassification in one or another direction—in the districts with a lower proportion of birth registration, but there is no significant correlation between the two.

To a small extent, the deviation of the observed sex ratio from the expected one (1.03 to 1.06) can be explained by the undercount of the children who have died shortly after their birth. As will be shown later (see Sections III and IV) the reported death rate under age 1 is only 104 per thousand live births, while the estimated infant death rate amounts to 164. It is very likely that most (perhaps 80 or even 90 percent) of those omitted deaths are children born during the last year.

Table b.19. Sex ratio (males per female) by age according to the 1955-57 inquiry—the
Congo (rural, mixed, and urban) and provinces and districts

	0-1	1-4	5-9	10-14	15-19	20-24	25-29	30-34	35-44	45-54	55+	Total	+15 MF
Leopoldville Province	.961	.961	.944	1.143	.991	.835	.858	.715	.908	1.057	.863	.933	.886
Leopoldville	1.011	.968	.903	1.145	1.165	1.349	1.671	1.770	2.034	2.440	1.889	1.344	1.638
Lac Leopold II	.955	.991	.997	1.367	1.122	.794	.814	.774	.762	.903	.902	.936	.847
Kwilu	.943	.940	.922	1.139	1.062	.753	.728	.614	.805	.950	.687	.874	.788
Kwango	.906	.979	.939	1.124	.981	.600	.580	.549	.823	.964	.877	.859	.757
Bas-Congo	1.000	.994	.934	1.083	.916	.919	1.001	.817	1.062	1.084	.773	.965	.944
Cataractes	1.000	.944	1.008	1.108	.786	.698	.645	.494	.810	1.193	1.087	.885	.785
Equateur Province	.972	.994	.964	1.361	.978	.900	.822	.800	.865	1.079	.851	.949	.894
Equateur	1.020	.985	1.024	1.534	1.144	.714	.841	.751	.834	1.034	.998	.953	.891
Mongala	.943	1.012	.910	1.274	.920	.889	.820	.809	.850	1.193	.870	.946	.901
Ubangi	.973	.976	.972	1.326	.954	.926	.777	.768	.848	1.057	.701	.933	.861
Tshuapa	.982	1.004	1.002	1.462	.991	1.009	.866	.863	.925	1.025	.838	.971	.927
Orientale Province	.931	.927	.981	1.305	.707	.843	.951	.747	.916	1.336	1.283	.976	.948
Stanleyville	.969	.971	1.006	1.306	.653	.864	1.118	.815	1.040	1.397	1.141	1.006	.983
Ituri	.884	.908	.966	1.197	.718	.820	.911	.756	.799	1.682	1.939	.986	.978
Bas-Uele	.846	.891	.970	1.516	.762	.842	.797	.687	.847	1.220	1.153	.931	.894
Haut-Uele	1.040	.924	.988	1.362	.728	.833	.926	.730	.982	1.137	1.183	.969	.935
Kivu Province	.953	.956	.962	1.230	.710	.805	.929	.795	.994	1.108	1.299	.959	.917
Sud-Kivu	.926	.917	.952	1.205	.828	.742	.840	.742	.997	1.163	1.503	.945	.913
Nord-Kivu	.990	.985	.950	1.167	.626	.853	1.056	.841	.938	1.094	1.183	.956	.914
Maniema	.953	.988	1.021	1.457	.653	.844	.939	.836	1.058	1.049	1.205	.988	.940
Katanga Province	1.004	.955	.954	1.302	1.066	.736	.924	.731	.902	1.311	1.190	.947	.897
Elisabethville	1.103	.979	.925	1.312	.606	.809	1.286	1.149	2.312	3.395	2.753	1.138	1.247
Tanganyika	.962	.956	.954	1.197	.691	.740	.929	.634	.723	1.329	1.231	.912	.851
Lualaba	1.008	.999	.957	1.448	.598	.749	.977	.745	1.154	1.610	1.181	1.003	.963
Haut-Lomani	1.019	.940	.966	1.343	.723	.777	.833	.681	.757	1.084	1.142	.915	.848
Lupaula-Moero	.978	.903	.948	1.263	.540	.566	.736	.740	.876	1.295	1.228	.894	.816
Kasai Province	1.011	.919	.957	1.391	1.048	.683	.785	.590	.744	1.135	1.166	.904	.826
Lulua	.986	.917	.922	1.329	1.036	.679	.893	.580	.752	1.308	1.068	.918	.857
Sankuru	1.059	.950	.973	1.390	1.050	.735	.770	.626	.747	1.123	1.332	.920	.847
Kabinda	.971	.908	1.025	1.434	.968	.658	.711	.544	.693	1.014	1.144	.877	.769
Kasai	1.041	.904	.921	1.440	1.162	.623	.746	.609	.778	1.078	1.118	.899	.820
Congo	.978	.952	.950	1.265	.855	.806	.874	.720	.882	1.165	1.086	.944	.895
Rural	.956	.947	.965	1.266	.879	.725	.733	.591	.749	1.070	1.081	.891	.812
Mixed	1.002	.965	.924	1.261	.722	.995	1.206	1.225	1.735	2.448	1.120	1.145	1.245
Urban	1.013	.984	.947	1.261	.847	1.002	1.350	1.280	1.764	2.053	1.428	1.176	1.295

Many of them are probably first-month deaths. According to the available information for different countries, the sex ratio of children who died within one month varies mostly from 1.10 to 1.35, generally in an opposite direction from the level of mortality.[8]

An adjustment of the sex ratios for these children dead in infancy would shift the sex ratio at birth to a minor extent: from 0.98 to 1.00 in the hypothesis of a sex ratio of omitted births of 1.30 boys per girl.

The most reliable surveys taken in the Congo all indicate a low sex ratio at birth (see Table 6.20). The most reliable information is that provided by birth registration in Leopoldville City for a period of six years, covering 69,000 reported births. In this city where confinements usually take place in maternity hospitals, infant mortality is relatively low and the registration of births and deaths is nearly complete, omissions probably being somewhat more frequent in the cases of infants

Table 6.20. Sex ratio at birth in various surveys

Source of information	Male Birth / Female Birth	Number of observed births
Demographic survey (1955/57)	.978	about 60,000
" " 1952	1.057	" 14,000
" " 1937	.975	" 18,759
" " 1936	1.030	18,657
Medical survey in Equateur Prov. 1956	.987	34,572
" " FOREAMI Kwango 1937-1954[1]	.987 av. for 18 years[1]	ab. 420,000 (1954)
" " " Bas Congo 1936	.968	
Survey among governmental employees (1958)	1.006	630
According to birth registration:		
Niangara Territory 1947-56 (Rural)	1.048	8,836 (period of 9 years
Leopoldville City 1952	1.011	9,028
1953	.978	10,361
1954	1.000	11,331
1955	.959	12,382
1956	.999	13,271
1957	1.025	12,624(incomplete)
Average 1952to 1957	.995	68,917(5 yr. period)
Elisabethville City 1957	1.003	87,692
Coquilhatville City 1950-54	1.110	2,577

[1] FOREAMI Kwango: Maximum value 1.015 (1943), minimum value .968 (1948 and 1954)

[8] For the Congo the sex ratio of children reported as having died under age 1 during the year preceding the survey amounts to 1.09.

who died shortly after birth. Yet the sex ratio appears to be low, close to unity. The same is true for another large Congolese city, Elisabeth-ville. A sex ratio of 1.00 and 1.02 was observed in the maternity hospitals in the Kwango district (Congo), respectively, for live births and all confinements including stillbirths.

General Sex Ratio

For the whole Congo the survey reports 94.4 males for 100 females of all ages. At first sight one is inclined to consider such a ratio as too low. There are some indications supporting the hypothesis that in the Congo the enumeration of males was somewhat less complete than that of females. Generally there is more motivation for evading the survey (non-payment of tax, clandestine workers, etc.) among the males than among the females. But nothing conclusive can be advanced on this score, for the sex ratio in a closed population depends first of all on the sex ratio at birth, which we were not able to determine. It depends also on the relative schedule of the male and female mortality by age and, to a minor degree, on the rate of natural increase.

Pravin Visaria has found extensive variations in different populations in sex differentials in mortality.[9] The model life tables prepared at Princeton incorporate the differentials found, on the average, in the populations upon which they are based. A North model stable population with the estimated birth rate and rate of increase of the Congo and a sex ratio at birth of 1.03 would have a sex ratio of about 0.969. With a sex ratio at birth of 1.00, the model stable population would have a sex ratio of 0.941, and with the recorded sex ratio at birth in the Congo (0.978) the sex ratio of the model stable population would be 0.920. Thus the recorded sex ratio of the Congolese population (0.944) would be expected on the basis of a low sex ratio at birth and "normal" sex differences in mortality.

Conclusion

This section on age distribution can be concluded with the following observations:

1. The reported age distributions of both males and females obtained in the 1955-57 Demographic Inquiry in the Congo are seriously disturbed by various sorts of error. It can reasonably be assumed that the hypothetical stable distributions described above, though subject to many reservations, provide a closer approximation to reality than the reported distributions—except in areas most strongly affected by migration, notably Leopoldville and Elisabethville cities.

[9] Pravin B. Visaria, "The sex ratio of the population of India," unpublished doctoral dissertation, Princeton University, 1963.

2. The reported proportions of the population in childhood ages, especially in the class 0-4 years, can be accepted as reasonably accurate.

3. There was probably an appreciable amount of selective under-enumeration of young adults, especially males.

4. The sex and age distribution in some localities, most conspicuously in Leopoldville City, was appreciably affected by migration. Although the sex and age composition of some districts were quite strongly affected by migration, the composition of the provincial populations and that of most districts were less subject to these effects.

5. There was a tendency toward overestimation of the ages of females with real ages in the range 10-39 years, and also, though less marked, of males within the range 15-44 years.

6. Marital status and fertility were probably significant factors, among others, in distorting the age distribution of females, and apparently also that of males—with a tendency toward differential overestimation of the ages of married women in their teens and of mothers in their teens and 20's, and perhaps also of the young married men and fathers.

7. There seems to have been a general tendency to assign persons, both males and females, really aged 55 or over to a lower age class. However, comparisons between reported and stable proportions in this terminal age class are especially vulnerable to errors of estimation.

8. The sex ratio at birth appears to be lower than is normally the rule in countries with accurate statistics.

These characteristics of the age and sex distribution have important implications for the analysis of the mortality and fertility of the Congolese population.

III. MORTALITY IN THE CONGO

The Available Information

The main body of data on mortality is provided by the Demographic Inquiry of 1955-57. It consists of two types of information: (1) reports on deaths during the 12 months preceding the survey and (2) the number of children ever born alive, the number still living, and, by inference, the number deceased, reported by women in successive age classes.

There are also reports on deaths based on vital registration records. A complete set of these reports is at our disposal only for the year 1956. These cannot be used as a basis for measurement of mortality because of obvious underregistration. The registration records were nevertheless, as we shall see, useful in analyzing the material from the 1955-57 inquiry. The registration data for a few areas (notably Leopoldville) can also be used to throw light on recent trends in mortality.

Data on Deaths During the Previous 12 Months

A separate schedule[10] was used in the 1955-57 inquiry to record reports on deaths during the previous 12 months in each rural or mixed locality and in each urban household covered by the survey. Deaths were recorded by sex and age class: under 1; 1 through 4; quinquennial age groups from 5 through 34; decennial age groups from 35 through 54; and 55 and over. The information was collected on a *de facto* basis. The enumerators were instructed to record all deaths to persons present as residents or visitors in the sample unit at the time of their death, and also deaths to residents of these sampling units that occurred in hospitals and institutions not included in the sample but located within the same territory. They were expected to exclude deaths in other localities to absent residents.

The enumerators were instructed to inquire of each family concerning the members who had died within the year, and to examine documents in the possession of the family, such as the identity booklet, that might contain information about deceased members. In addition, the chief and notables of a village were asked about the deaths that had occurred, with special emphasis on persons without surviving relatives in the village. The interviewers were directed to visit any hospital, mission, or medical post in the vicinity and to copy the names of the deceased residents of the village. They were also expected to look for other evidence of recent deaths, such as an abandoned hut or a new grave.

Information on deaths from the vital registration system was used in rural areas by the survey takers to check the responses obtained in the household interviews, particularly with respect to the time of a death. For each village in the sample the enumerator was provided with a list of registered deaths in order of occurrence. The list indicated the name, sex, age (if known), or at least whether child, adult, or aged person, and the name of the parents of each deceased person. The list was extended to cover the previous 18 months rather than the more limited period for which deaths were entered in the schedule. This was done in order to provide a check as to whether or not a reported death had occurred within the specified 12-month period.

A considerable proportion of the deaths in most districts were registered. Registration was useful not only in checking registered deaths to see if they were reported in the survey, but also in estimating by comparison the time of other deaths that were not registered. The list of births during the previous 18 months, drawn from the vital registers, was also useful in this way. Thus the time of a reported death could frequently be fixed with reference to a registered birth in the same fam-

[10] Formulaire No. 2, see Appendix.

ily or elsewhere in the same village. Finally, to ensure close attention to the timing of these events, the enumerators were required to enter the month of the occurrence of each reported death. It can be assumed that these safeguards must have increased substantially the accuracy in discriminating between events within or prior to the reference period. The attention given to this phase of the inquiry undoubtedly also tended to promote completeness in reporting.

Some categories of deaths may have escaped detection despite the controls and checks, in particular the three following:

(1) It was difficult to obtain reliable information on infants who died soon after birth. In such cases it is likely that neither the birth nor the death was registered or recorded in the father's identity booklet. These events were matters of little concern to persons outside the immediate family, and even members of the family might forget, or choose to ignore them in the course of an interview.

(2) The safeguards mentioned above were largely lacking, or ineffective, in urban centers and mixed settlements. It was not possible to provide the enumerators with lists of registered vital events for each of the sample urban households, and the vital registers in mixed settlements were frequently very defective. Moreover, in view of the high mobility of the urban population and even more that of the population in small industrial or other mixed settlements, the attempt to obtain a *de facto* record of vital events during the preceding 12 months through retrospective inquiries was inherently subject to serious defect.

(3) Inquiries about death encountered serious resistance in some regions, due to traditional inhibitions or aversion to the mention of death or the names of dead persons. The resistance was so strong in parts of Ituri District that the inquiry on this subject was suppressed in some villages. Therefore there is no estimate of the number of deaths during the year prior to the inquiry in that district. Resistance was also encountered in some other communities, but was mitigated by the tact of the enumerators and the cooperation of the village notables.

The estimated numbers of deaths by districts and provinces and the corresponding rates are shown in Table 6.21—along with numbers of registered deaths in 1956 in the same areas.

Specific death rates by age obtained from these reports are available only for the whole country, for its rural, urban, and mixed segments, for one province (Kasai), and for the combined population of the Bas Congo and Cataractes districts of Leopoldville Province. These are shown in Table 6.22.

Table 6.21. Number of deaths (a) officially registered in 1956 and (b) estimated in the 1955-57 inquiry, the ratio of (a) to (b), and death rates according to the inquiry—the Congo, provinces, and districts

Provinces Districts	Official Registration 1956 (a)	Survey Estimates (1956/57) (b)	(a)/(b)	Death rates per 1000 persons
Leopoldville Province	41,240 (1)	55,643	.73	18
Leopoldville	3,176	3,229	.98	10
Lac Leopold II	3,902	5,155	.76	19
Kwilu	16,819	22,946	.73	20
Kwango	8,549	10,253	.83	22
Bas-Congo	4,872	6,589	.74	16
Cataractes	3,922	7,471	.52	17
Equateur Province	25,809	33,147	.78	19
Equateur	3,989	4,835	.83	16
Mongala	6,552	8,831	.74	17
Ubangi	8,205	10,781	.76	20
Tshuapa	7,063	8,700	.81	22
Orientale Province	19,619 (2)	34,220 (2)	.57	21 (2)
Stanleyville	4,709	12,064	.39	19
Ituri	(7,333)	— (2)	—	—
Bas-Uele	6,542	9,353	.70	20
Haut-Uele	8,368	12,803	.65	22
Kivu Province	26,875	39,933	.67	20
Sud-Kivu	11,231	16,627	.66	20
Nord-Kivu	10,664	16,162	.66	22
Maniema	4,980	7,144	.70	16
Katanga Province	15,030	27,865	.52	19
Elisabethville	1,140 (3)	1,681	— (3)	12
Tanganyika	4,420	7,474	.59	19
Lualaba	2,688	5,202	.52	19
Haut-Lomani	4,979	9,676	.51	22
Luapula-Moero	1,803	3,832	.47	20
Kasai Province	27,998	52,378	.53	25
Lulua	9,032	17,671	.51	27
Sankuru	6,408	9,871	.65	20
Kabinda	6,285	11,529	.55	24
Kasai	6,273	13,307	.47	27
Congo	156,571 (2)	243,186 (2)	.64	20 (2)

Table 6.21. (notes)

NOTES (1) The registration figure for Leopoldville (where the demographic survey was made in 1955) is for the year 1955. Incidentally, the number of registered deaths reported for the Leopoldville city (Suburban territory excluded) for 1954 is 3,249.

(2) Data not available for Ituri District. This district is excluded from provincial and national totals.

(3) The indicated figure for Elisabethville is for 1957, and refers only to the central city (122,400 inhabitants out of about 160,000 inhabitants in Greater Elisabethville). Source: La population Africaine à Elisabethville à la fin de 1957, J. Benoit, CEPSI, Elisabethville. The registration figure is, therefore, not comparable to the survey estimate, which is for Greater Elisabethville.

Table 6.22. Death rates (per 1,000 population) by age and sex—the Congo, rural, mixed, and urban populations; Kasai Province; and the districts of Cataractes and Bas Congo combined

	Sex	Under 1	1-4	5-9	10-14	15-19	20-24	25-29	30-34	35-44	45-54	55+	All Ages
Congo	M	110	32	11	6	6	8	8	11	15	27	51	21
	F	98	28	9	5	6	9	9	12	16	24	43	19
	M&F	104	30	10	5	6	9	8	12	15	25	47	20
Rural Population	M&F	113	34	11	6	7	10	11	15	18	28	48	23
Mixed Population	M&F	87	21	6	3	2	7	3	3	4	7	27	11
Urban Population	M&F	66	13	3	2	3	4	3	3	4	13	28	9
Kasai Province	M	129	33	17	11	10	10	12	16	18	34	68	27
	F	117	30	13	7	10	11	12	13	19	27	60	23
	M&F	123	32	15	9	10	11	12	14	19	31	65	25
Bas Congo & Cataractes Districts	M&F	87	25	7	3	4	7	5	8	10	20	40	16

Children Surviving among the
Children Ever Born to Women
Classified by Age

Each woman aged 15 years or over was asked about the number of children she had borne alive in the course of her life. The main questionnaire[11] had one column reserved for recording the number of children ever born alive and another column for those still living. In the case of women who had borne three or more children the enumerator was instructed to prepare a list of births by order, with names of children, present ages, and place of residence if living, or notation of death, taking account of information in identity booklets or other documents. This procedure was intended to improve the quality of the information offered by older women with many children. Information on stillbirths was recorded as a separate item in the reports on births during the previous 12 months, but not in the reports on children ever born. These were, however, explicitly limited to children born alive.

The information on proportions of children who had died among those ever born alive by age of mother at the time of the survey, obtained in this way, was used to provide estimates of the probability of death between birth and specified age a, $q(a)$; $q(a)$ in life table terms would be noted $_aq_o$. The method of estimation is that developed by W. Brass for this purpose. The basic data and the derived probabilities are shown in Tables 6.23-6.26.

Mortality Analysis, an Introduction

The treatment of each major aspect of the demography of the Congo is, in varying degrees, dependent on the treatment of other aspects and in turn contributes information of importance to the analysis of other issues.

Therefore the emphasis given to various features of mortality in this section has the goal of strengthening other estimates (for example, estimates of fertility) as well as estimating mortality itself. Considerations of this sort call for sifting the evidence on *age patterns* of mortality. The age pattern of mortality affects estimates of the birth rate from the age distribution and adjustments to the age distribution itself.

Both of the principal sets of data on mortality bear on both these issues. Their apparent implications are mutually consistent in some respects, inconsistent in others. At various points some data from each type of inquiry on this subject are more credible than others. We must, therefore, examine successively the evidence on each of these major issues and analyze the implications of concurrent and conflicting data in

[11] Formulaire 1, see Appendix.

Table 6.23. Proportions of children who have died among those ever born, by age of mother at time of survey (per 1,000)—the Congo, provinces, and districts

Provinces Districts	15–19	20–24	25–29	30–34	35–44	45–54	+55
Leopoldville Province	151	192	253	302	345	408	484
Leopoldville	89	103	150	200	240	275	475
Lac Leopold II	127	181	217	233	295	333	439
Kwilu	167	200	272	314	352	410	479
Kwango	199	243	301	343	381	437	489
Bas-Congo	183	213	256	299	338	421	520
Cataractes	155	203	252	303	351	424	483
Equateur Province	127	192	238	272	306	345	434
Equateur	101	118	138	184	243	306	417
Mongala	147	204	254	279	325	363	453
Ubangi	138	230	268	300	323	356	442
Tshuapa	107	152	214	260	286	330	416
Orientale Province	133	174	188	210	245	295	343
Stanleyville	141	191	220	262	313	353	419
Ituri	(63)	116	(138)	(164)	(188)	(261)	(212)
Bas-Uele	215	225	234	250	289	329	387
Haut-Uele	094	161	165	184	210	248	301
Kivu Province	168	230	291	334	367	406	453
Sud-Kivu	204	286	360	412	467	497	556
Nord-Kivu	130	163	190	219	248	288	334
Maniema	189	249	278	312	361	412	467
Katanga Province	134	166	193	236	268	318	362
Elisabethville	114	143	149	197	256	321	549
Tanganyika	147	143	198	228	252	317	356
Lualaba	137	161	195	226	282	340	386
Haut-Lomani	133	182	207	260	270	313	372
Luapula-Moero	132	207	195	246	291	309	322
Kasai Province	227	260	300	344	398	447	502
Lulua	251	295	326	378	427	468	510
Sankuru	170	205	262	312	354	405	461
Kabinda	193	202	241	278	347	413	465
Kasai	270	311	352	392	440	486	557
Congo	161	208	256	299	338	387	446

the light of their origins and possible sources of error. It will be necessary to suspend judgment in examining the apparent implications of any set of data on a particular problem until other available evidence on the same subject can be taken into account. It will then be in order to formulate "operative estimates," i.e., the estimates that command the greatest confidence and which will, therefore, be used in the analysis of information on other subjects.

Before turning to levels of mortality, we shall discuss indications on patterns derived both from current deaths and from retrospective reports of mothers.

Table 6.24. Estimated probability of death before age a, $q(a)$, derived from reports by mothers—the Congo, provinces, and districts

Provinces Districts	1	2	3	Age (a) 5	15	25	35
Leopoldville Province	.157	.200	.255	.306	.358	.432	.513
Leopoldville	.297	.098	.144	.198	.243	.282	.488
Lac Leopold II	.122	.181	.214	.231	.300	.344	.453
Kwilu	.178	.211	.277	.312	.359	.425	.496
Kwango	.220	.260	.309	.348	.395	.462	.517
Bas-Congo	.182	.217	.255	.297	.343	.434	.536
Cataractes	.174	.219	.260	.306	.363	.447	.509
Equateur Province	.130	.199	.238	.276	.316	.365	.460
Equateur	.094	.116	.135	.180	.243	.310	.422
Mongala	.155	.214	.258	.278	.331	.376	.469
Ubangi	.147	.242	.273	.298	.328	.367	.455
Tshuapa	.104	.153	.212	.256	.287	.336	.423
Orientale Province	.118	.167	.181	.205	.244	.298	.346
Stanleyville	.123	.180	.210	.250	.305	.348	.413
Ituri	-	-	-	-	-	-	-
Bas-Uele	.194	.217	.227	.245	.289	.334	.393
Haut-Uele	.087	.158	.161	.176	.204	.244	.296
Kivu Province	.158	.226	.285	.330.	.370	.417	.464
Sud-Kivu	.202	.291	.359	.408	.472	.510	.571
Nord-Kivu	.122	.161	.187	.216	.249	.294	.341
Maniema	.167	.238	.267	.298	.351	.406	.460
Katanga Province	.120	.159	.186	.230	.266	.358	.365
Elisabethville	.099	.135	.142	.193	.257	.326	.558
Tanganyika	.131	.137	.190	.224	.253	.322	.362
Lualaba	.121	.154	.187	.219	.279	.341	.387
Haut-Lomani	.117	.173	.198	.255	.270	.317	.376
Luapula-Moero	.124	.205	.192	.245	.296	.320	.333
Kasai Province	.213	.256	.294	.341	.402	.459	.537
Lulua	.237	.292	.321	.372	.429	.477	.520
Sankuru	.163	.205	.259	.306	.355	.412	.468
Kabinda	.176	.196	.234	.272	.347	.418	.471
Kasai	.258	.310	.347	.387	.444	.498	.571
Congo	.153	.208	.253	.297	.343	.400	.459

Mortality Patterns: Empirical Evidence

The two types of mortality information available both present distortions that can be best discussed in comparison with a standard pattern of mortality. The selection of this standard among the four models of the Office of Population Research[12] will be based on a discussion of the little information that can be derived on the subject from both types of data collected in the Demographic Inquiry.

[12] Coale and Demeny, *op.cit.*

Table 6.25. Proportions of children who have died among those ever born, by age of mother at time of survey (per 1,000)—the Congo and provinces, by type of settlement

Provinces	15-19	20-24	Age of mother 25-29	30-34	35-44	45-54	55+
Rural							
Leopoldville	160	219	272	315	354	412	485
Equateur	127	203	248	277	306	342	430
Orientale	160	203	211	234	269	304	360
Kivu	169	233	292	340	368	402	450
Katanga	144	180	211	250	275	317	361
Kasai	238	267	307	349	401	448	502
Congo	172	224	270	310	343	388	445
Mixed							
Leopoldville	199	175	249	279	322	421	497
Equateur	135	170	217	254	306	362	480
Orientale	139	162	195	232	313	347	420
Kivu	174	229	250	307	353	481	496
Katanga	125	176	194	229	229	300	395
Kasai	195	239	282	317	371	435	484
Congo	162	195	233	274	318	395	464
Urban							
Leopoldville	113	124	179	217	251	316	473
Equateur	110	161	199	242	292	414	537
Orientale	099	173	195	238	285	388	463
Kivu	134	191	237	273	362	430	563
Katanga	120	134	155	198	248	339	400
Kasai	180	212	205	268	314	447	581
Congo	123	148	201	221	267	362	491

Reports on Deaths During the Previous Year

The question of age patterns of mortality in this instance is obscured by two factors in particular (1) the omission of infant deaths from the reports, and (2) the uncertainty of the reporting of ages of deceased persons. Since the first of these factors bears heavily on the question of the level of mortality in the Congo, we will devote a part of the section on mortality level to its discussion. The misreporting of ages at death is at the center of the problem of mortality patterns.

Great difficulty was frequently encountered in obtaining information on the ages of deceased persons at their death. Even when deaths were registered, such information was frequently omitted—except where the exact age was known, as in the case of children whose births had been registered. It was, therefore, usually necessary to estimate the probable age of deceased persons by reference to the relation to some known event

Table 6.26. Probability of death before age a, $q(a)$, derived from reports by mothers—the Congo and provinces, by type of settlement

Type of Settlement and Province	Age (a)						
	1	2	3	5	15	25	35
Rural							
Leopoldville	.163	.226	.273	.319	.366	.434	.511
Equateur	.131	.211	.250	.281	.318	.362	.456
Orientale	.145	.198	.206	.230	.282	.310	.367
Kivu	.161	.232	.289	.338	.376	.416	.466
Katanga	.130	.174	.203	.245	.275	.396	.451
Kasai	.226	.266	.303	.347	.409	.463	.520
Congo	.167	.226	.269	.310	.351	.404	.462
Mixed							
Leopoldville	.192	.176	.247	.279	.329	.437	.517
Equateur	.132	.172	.216	.255	.313	.378	.501
Orientale	.118	.151	.184	.223	.305	.342	.414
Kivu	.155	.220	.240	.299	.351	.490	.506
Katanga	.111	.170	.186	.222	.227	.300	.395
Kasai	.180	.234	.275	.314	.374	.446	.496
Congo	.146	.188	.225	.269	.318	.399	.468
Urban							
Leopoldville	.101	.119	.173	.212	.251	.320	.478
Equateur	.104	.159	.195	.240	.295	.424	.549
Orientale	.084	.161	.184	.228	.278	.382	.456
Kivu	.114	.179	.224	.261	.353	.421	.552
Katanga	.105	.126	.148	.191	.243	.337	.398
Kasai	.154	.198	.194	.257	.306	.438	.569
Congo	.107	.140	.192	.213	.263	.360	.489

that could be dated or, more simply, by reference to some living person whose estimated age had already been recorded in the main schedule before entries were made on the special schedule for recording deaths during the previous year. These methods are similar to those used to estimate the age of living persons. The reporting and classification by age of living children was relatively accurate, and we seem warranted in supposing that this may also be true with respect to deaths. On the hypothesis that the divisions by age (1) of living persons and (2) of deaths *below* and *above* 5 years are accurate, the mortality rate for those over this age is not influenced by any errors in age classification. Omission of very young children can be accounted for by eliminating all deaths during the first year of life. Ratios of $_4m_1$ to m_{5+} (the death rate for all those over 5 years) are thus the best index available on mortality pat-

[291]

terns. These ratios for the whole Congo are 2.21 for males and 2.16 for females. With the same mortality rate above age 5 as the Congo and a growth rate of 2 percent per year, the ratio $_4m_1/m_{5+}$ takes up the following values according to the four series of model life tables developed at the Office of Population Research.

	Males	Females
North	2.33	2.18
West	2.22	2.16
South	3.35	3.26
East	2.64	2.43

For females, the figures on the North and West hypotheses and that observed for the Congo are all practically identical. For males, the observed value is practically the same as that on the West hypotheses and differs from the result obtained using the North series by only a small margin (0.12). The expected values on the other two hypotheses are farther away.

Child Mortality from Reports by Mothers on Children Born and Children Living

Insight into the most appropriate standard of mortality will be gained in this instance by comparing series of observed $q(a)$ values with the "expected" relations among these values characteristic of the mortality patterns represented by the four families of life table models at our disposal. It is convenient for this purpose to select a particular kind of $q(a)$ and to compare its observed values with the corresponding values implied by other observed $q(a)$'s and different sets of model life tables. We shall use the estimated $q(5)$ values derived from different child mortality at successive ages in this way.

We shall compare the hypothetical values $q'(5)$ obtained by finding the particular life table, within each of the four families of models, that has the same $q(a)$ value: $q(1)$, $q(15)$, $q(25)$, $q(35)$, as that observed in the Congo or in some part thereof, and then reading off the $q(5)$ value in that table—or, if necessary, obtaining the required value by interpolation between two adjacent tables. A comparison of observed and hypothetical values for the Congo as a whole, on the basis of different $q(a)$ values (as observed) and different sets of model life tables is presented later in Table 6.30.

We find that the ratio of the observed $q(5)$ to the estimated $q'(5)$ implied by the observed $q(1)$ is higher than expected on the basis of any of the mortality patterns represented in the models. This finding could be the result of any or all of the following conditions.

(1) The estimate of $q(1)$ may have a downward bias, or the estimate of $q(5)$ an upward bias, relative to each other.

(2) Post-infant child mortality may really be unusually high in the Congo in relation to infant mortality.[13]

(3) The high ratio of $q(5)$ (based on reports by women aged 30-34 years) to $q(1)$ (based on reports by women 15-20) could reflect a real decline of child mortality in the Congo during the decade prior to the survey. It is quite certain that mortality had declined appreciably in the Congo, especially in the urban centers. The reports by the younger women on children born and surviving are heavily weighted with the results of recent experience, but among the older women a high proportion of the children born to them passed their infancy (when risk of death is greatest) at times rather far removed from the time of the survey. Therefore if child mortality has really declined in recent years, the reports by the older women are subject to two different influences: (a) real differences in mortality between the period covered by their reports and that represented in the reports by younger women and (b) a progressive tendency to forget or ignore the births and deaths of infants who lived only a few weeks or months at an earlier stage in the lives of these women. An apparent constancy in levels of mortality indicated by values $q(a)$ derived from reports by older women might, therefore, reflect a balancing of these two influences—though presumably the series for different areas would probably reflect a predominance of one or the other of them, if they exist. One cannot, therefore, place much reliance on relations among the higher $q(a)$ values as indicative of the true age pattern of mortality in the Congo.

All of the conditions mentioned above as possible influences on the $q(5)/q(1)$ ratios in the Congo may be real. The $q(a)$'s derived from reports by women are also subject to errors of estimation, especially in view of the known prevalence of errors in age classification. It is, however, extremely difficult to know how such errors may affect particular $q(a)$'s. Thus, the evidence that one standard pattern of mortality is more adequate than another is not very strong.

The results presented in Table 6.27 show that, for the Congo as a whole, the expected $q'(5)$ on the basis of $q(1)$ using either the North or the South family of model life tables is much nearer the observed $q(5)$ (87 percent) than the corresponding value on the basis of the other two series: West (77 percent) and East (71 percent).

[13] This hypothesis is strongly supported by medical opinion in the Congo. Weaning involves serious risks where improper food, prepared under unsanitary conditions, replaces mother's milk. Children at this age may be weakened by intestinal worms and be frequently exposed during cool nights to the risk of pneumonia. See, among others: K. Kivits, *Pathologie et mortalité de l'enfance indigène au Mayumbe*, Institut Royal Colonial Belge, 1951; P. G. Janssens, *La mortalité infantile aux mines de Kilo*, idem. 1952: R. van Netsen, *L'enfance noire au Congo belge*, 1941.

Table 6.27. Observed $q(5)$ and hypothetical $q'(5)$ values on the basis of specified $q(a)$ and alternative models—the Congo

Congo

Observed q(5)	Hypothetical Values, q'(5)				
	Specified model	q(1)	Specified q(a)'s q(15)	q(25)	q(35)
.297	North.	.258	.280	.278	.290
	South	.257	.305	.316	.224
	West	.229	.300	.304	.299
	East	.210	.309	.325	.335
Relative Values (q(5) = 100)					
100	North	.87	.94	.94	.98
	South	.87	1.03	1.06	.75
	West	.77	1.01	1.02	1.01
	East	.71	1.04	1.09	1.13

A similar comparison is presented in Table 6.28 for each province. Here one finds that the hypothetical $q'(5)$ derived from the observed $q(1)$ on the basis of the North family of model life tables approaches the observed $q(5)$ most closely in four of the six provinces, though equaled in this respect by values obtained using the South series in two cases. The hypothetical values obtained by using the West and East models are more remote in all cases.

We shall henceforward use the North pattern of mortality as a standard, although the evidence that it fits the findings better than another pattern is rather tenuous.

Mortality Patterns:
Comparison of Reported Deaths and
Deaths in the Stable Model

Reported numbers of deaths and numbers of living persons in the population over 1 year of age by sex and age classes are shown in Table 6.29. Comparable values are shown here for a stable population with the mortality pattern represented in the North family of model life tables and a growth rate of 2 percent per year, with approximately the same death rate for males over 1 year of age as that reported in the results of the inquiry. The female stable population associated with this selected male model in the series is also used, although it implies a level of female mortality somewhat higher than that reported. The specific death rates implied by the reported numbers of deaths and of living per-

Table 6.28. Observed $q(5)$ and hypothetical $q'(5)$ on the basis of specified $q(a)$
and alternative models—provinces of the Congo

| Specified Model | Reported q(5) | Hypothetical Values, q'(5) | | | |
| | | Specified q(a)'s | | | |
		q(1)	q(15)	q(25)	q(35)
		Leopoldville	Province		
North	.306	.265	..294	.303	.335
South	.306	.265	.318	.344	.368
West	.306	.235	.314	.332	.343
East	.306	.212	.325	.354	.382
		Equateur	Province		
North	.276	.220	.258	.250	.290
South	.276	.211	.283	.288	.325
West	.276	.194	.277	.275	.300
East	.276	.175	.287	.295	.336
		Orientale	Province		
North	.205	.199	.197	.200	.206
South	.205	.186	.217	.235	.240
West	.205	.178	.213	.221	.215
East	.205	.158	.219	.237	.241
		Kivu	Provinc		
North	.330	.267	.303	.290	.293
South	.330	.268	.330	.330	.328
West	.330	.236	.325	.319	.303
East	.330	.214	.336	.341	.339
		Katanga	Province		
North	.230	.203	.215	.245	.219
South	.230	.190	.237	.282	.254
West	.230	.178	.232	.270	.229
East	.230	.161	.238	.289	.258
		Kasai	Provinc		
North	.341	.354	.330	.323	.364
South	.341	.376	.359	.368	.387
West	.341	.317	.356	.356	.363
East	.341	.291	.365	.380	.404

sons are also shown. The ratio of the reported age distribution of deaths to that of deaths in the stable population is shown in Figure 6.6 in conjunction with the ratio of the reported to the stable age distribution.

The gross features of Figure 6.6 can be summarized briefly as follows:

The distribution of deaths by age, both for males and for females, deviates widely from any expected distribution on the basis of the standard pattern. It is apparent that the data on the ages of deceased persons are distorted by gross errors.

Apparent distortions in the reported ages of persons at death parallel to a surprising degree apparent distortions in the reported ages of living persons, but the distortions are larger in the reported ages at death.

Table 6.29. Age-specific death rates; age distribution of deaths and of population—
population over age 1, by sex—the Congo

	MALE					
	Death Rate		Age Dist. of Deaths		Deaths	Populatic
Age	Reported (R)	Stable (S)	Reported (R)	Stable (S)	R/S	R/S
	(1)	(2)	(3)	(4)	(5)	(6)
1-4	.032	.034	25.17	26.81	.94	-
5-9	.011	.011	8.69	8.96	.97	.96
10-14	.006	.006	4.02	3.98	1.01	.94
15-19	.006	.006	2.38	3.95	.60	.63
20-24	.008	.009	3.44	4.90	.70	.81
25-29	.008	.010	4.15	4.46	.93	1.12
30-34	.011	.011	5.40	4.10	1.32	1.25
35-44	.015	.013	11.59	8.08	1.43	1.25
45-54	.027	.019	16.51	8.42	1.96	1.44
+55	.051	.057	18.66	26.35	.71	.82
TOTAL			100.01	100.01		

Death Rate per 1000
for Persons
Aged Over
1 Year

     17.15   17.18

The resultant sex- and age-specific death rates (obtained by relating reported deaths to enumerated persons) form a more reasonable pattern than might at first be expected in view of the extent of the aberrations in age reporting for deaths and for the base population. The specific rates resulting from the observed numbers of persons and of deaths are shown in Figure 6.7, along with the corresponding rates in the population model defined above. There is close agreement between observed and hypothetical values at early ages (e.g., 1-4 and 5-9 years), where age reporting is most accurate. At ages 30-54 years among males and 20-54 years among females the reported rates exceed the model rates, and the divergences in this direction are wide for males aged 45-54 and for females aged 35-54. On the other hand, the reported rates for persons over 55 years of both sexes are well below those expected on the stated hypothesis. Similar patterns appear in a sub-population (Kasai Province) for which we have similar information on deaths by sex and by age (see Figure 6.8).

Table 6.29 (continued)

		FEMALE			
Death Rate		Age Dist. of Deaths		Deaths	Population
Reported (R)	Stable (S)	Reported (R)	Stable (S)	R/S	R/S
(7)	(8)	(9) s	(10)	(11)	(12)
.028	.033	24.28	26.58	.91	–
.009	.011	7.78	9.17	.85	.99
.005	.006	2.78	4.21	.66	.72
.006	.006	2.91	3.92	.74	.71
.009	.007	5.04	3.98	1.27	.94
.009	.008	5.60	4.03	1.39	1.21
.012	.009	8.58	4.06	2.11	1.61
.016	.011	14.70	7.78	1.89	1.32
.024	.015	13.23	7.14	1.85	1.06
.043	.051	15.11	29.13	.52	.67
		100.01	100.00		
15.41	16.05				

We now turn to the mortality information derived from reports of mothers on the proportion of children surviving. Life tables for Scandinavian countries have been used to complete the North life table models to give $q(2)$ and $q(3)$ values not presented in the original tables. This enables us to bring the whole array of observed $q(a)$ values into systematic relationship. Estimated $q'(5)$ values are presented in Table 6.30 for the Congo and its provinces and districts on the basis of (1) all observed $q(a)$'s from $q(1)$ through $q(35)$ and (2) the North life table models. Figure 6.9 relates the derived $q(5)$ values to the observed ones by districts.

The series for the Congo as a whole, from $q(1)$ through $q(5)$, shows a quite orderly progression compatible with the hypothesis of a decline in child mortality during the years preceding the survey. The later values —$q(15)$ and following—derived from reports by mothers over 35 years of age are more irregular, as expected for reasons already stated. Some of the values for particular areas are erratic, showing the effects of errors

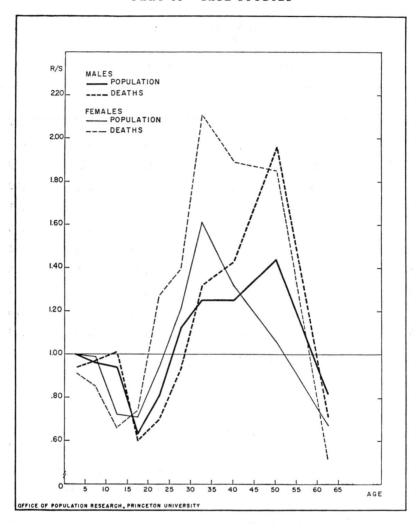

6.6. Ratios of reported age distribution to stable age distribution and of reported deaths to stable population deaths, by sex and age groups, for the Congo.

in the data or in estimation, fluctuations due to small numbers, or perhaps the effects of local epidemics. The series for several areas show especially consistent trends, but whether they reflect unusual conditions in reporting or in health is uncertain.

The sharp decline in Leopoldville District from $q(5)$ (198) to the corresponding values (167 and 131) implied by $q(3)$ and $q(1)$ is significant—though the still lower value (115) derived from $q(2)$ seems erratic. This decline can be attributed to the joint effect of two factors: (1) increase of medical services to mothers and children in Leopold-

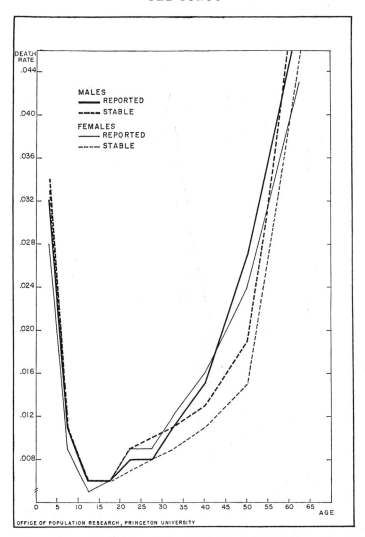

6.7. Reported death rates and comparable stable population
death rates, by sex and age groups, for the Congo.

ville and (2) higher mortality in the rural districts where many of the
children of inmigrant women in its rapidly growing population were
born and lived as infants—the proportion, in Leopoldville, of rural-
born infants rises with rise in age of the women interviewed. In Elisabethville a comparable drop appears between $q(5)$ and $q(3)$, but the
figures are relatively constant above and below this break.

The decline from the observed $q(5)$ to the estimated $q'(5)$ implied
by $q(1)$ on the basis of the North family of models is greater in the

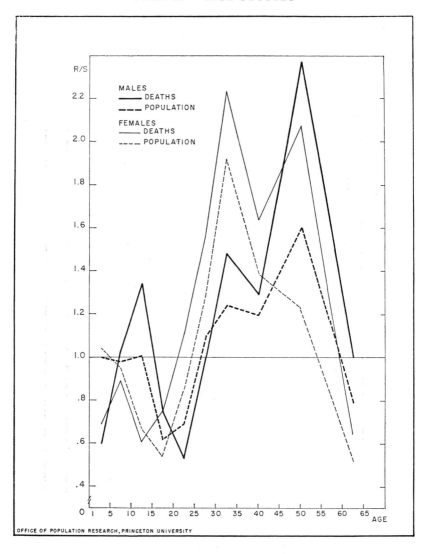

6.8. Ratios of reported to stable population deaths and reported to stable population, by sex and age groups, for Kasai Province.

whole urban population of the Congo (the latter value being 84.5 percent of the former) than in its rural and mixed segments (where the corresponding percentages are 91.0 and 91.4 respectively), though the movement above $q(5)$ is erratic. Estimated $q'(5)$ values for segments of the national and provincial populations by type of settlement are shown in Table 6.31. The movement of the q values in several of these series,

	Reported q(5)	Specified q(a)					
		q(1)	q(2)	q(3)	q(15)	q(25)	q(35)
Leopoldville Province	.306	.265	.262	.296	.294	.303	.335
Leopoldville	.198	.131	.115	.167	.197	.190	.310
Lac Leopold II	.231	.206	.237	.248	.240	.234	.284
Kwilu	.312	.300	.277	.320	.295	.294	.312
Kwango	.348	.364	.340	.357	.325	.327	.340
Bas-Congo	.297	.305	.285	.296	.280	.304	.363
Cataractes	.306	.294	.288	.301	.298	.313	.331
Equateur Province	.276	.220	.260	.276	.258	.250	.290
Equateur	.180	.158	.150	.156	.196	.210	.260
Mongala	.278	.262	.281	.299	.270	.259	.297
Ubangi	.298	.248	.317	.315	.267	.252	.285
Tshuapa	.256	.175	.200	.246	.233	.228	.261
Orientale Province	.205	.199	.218	.210	.197	.200	.206
Stanleyville	.250	.208	.235	.243	.248	.236	.253
Ituri	-	-	-	-	-	-	-
Bas-Uele	.245	.324	.285	.263	.235	.226	.240
Haut-Uele	.176	.145	.206	.186	.164	.164	.172
Kivu Province	.330	.267	.297	.329	.303	.290	.293
Sud-Kivu	.408	.336	.381	.420	.390	.372	.405
Nord-Kivu	.216	.206	.210	.217	.202	.199	.202
Maniema	.298	.282	.312	.309	.288	.283	.290
Katanga Province	.230	.203	.208	.215	.215	.245	.219
Elisabethville	.193	.166	.176	.164	.208	.221	.289
Tanganyika	.224	.221	.179	.220	.205	.218	.217
Lualaba	.219	.204	.201	.217	.226	.231	.234
Haut-Lomani	.255	.198	.226	.229	.219	.215	.226
Luapula-Moero	.245	.210	.269	.222	.240	.217	.197
Kasai Province	.341	.354	.336	.340	.330	.323	.364
Lulua	.372	.390	.382	.371	.350	.342	.345
Sankuru	.306	.275	.269	.300	.291	.287	.296
Kabinda	.272	.299	.257	.271	.283	.292	.298
Kasai	.387	.417	.406	.400	.366	.362	.405
Congo	.297	.258	.273	.293	.280	.278	.290

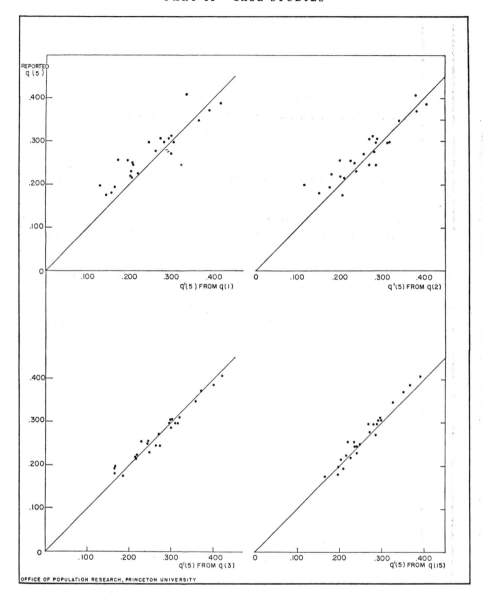

6.9. Values of $q(5)$ reported from Congo districts related
to $q'(5)$ values derived from similarly reported $q(1)$, $q(2)$,
$q(3)$, and $q(15)$, and the North model stable population.

especially in the relatively small urban segments of some provincial
populations (e.g., Orientale Province) and in the mixed segment of
Leopoldville Province seems quite erratic. This may be due in part to
sampling errors.

[302]

Table 6.31. Estimated $q'(5)$ values on basis of reported $q(a)$ values and North model—rural, mixed, and urban population of the Congo and of provinces

	Reported q(5)[1]	Specified q(a)					
		q(1)	q(2)	q(3)	q(15)	q(25)	q(35)
Rural population							
Leopoldville	.319	.275	.297	.315	.300	.305	.333
Equateur	.281	.221	.277	.290	.259	.304	.286
Orientale	.230	.245	.260	.239	.229	.212	.220
Kivu	.338	.272	.304	.334	.308	.291	.295
Katanga	.245	.220	.228	.235	.223	.275	.282
Kasai	.347	.373	.348	.349	.334	.327	.345
CONGO	.310	.282	.297	.311	.288	.282	.293
Mixed population							
Leopoldville	.279	.320	.230	.286	.268	.306	.340
Equateur	.255	.222	.225	.250	.256	.261	.320
Orientale	.223	.199	.197	.213	.248	.232	.254
Kivu	.299	.260	.289	.278	.287	.354	.326
Katanga	.222	.186	.223	.215	.182	.204	.240
Kasai	.314	.303	.305	.318	.307	.312	.316
CONGO	.269	.246	.246	.260	.259	.279	.297
Urban population							
Leopoldville	.212	.169	.155	.200	.203	.216	.303
Equateur	.240	.174	.208	.226	.240	.297	.379
Orientale	.228	.140	.210	.213	.226	.267	.286
Kivu	.261	.193	.234	.260	.287	.295	.382
Katanga	.191	.176	.164	.171	.197	.228	.242
Kasai	.257	.260	.260	.224	.249	.306	.404
CONGO	.213	.180	.182	.222	.213	.246	.310

[1] Observed q(5) values.

Indices of Mortality Levels

An assumption about the mortality pattern had to be made in order to bring different kinds of evidence into an analytic system and to explore their mutual implications. This assumption is that the North set of model life tables and stable populations suits the Congo demographic characteristics better than any available alternative pattern. It is undoubtedly subject to unknown margins of error, especially in application to component parts of the Congo population.

Attention is first directed here to a comparison between the indicated *infant mortality* [ratio of the number of reported deaths of infants under 1 year of age to the reported number of births in the same year, or $q(1)$] and the indicated *post-infant mortality* (ratio of the reported number of deaths at all ages over 1 year to the estimated *de facto* population over exact age 1 year, or m_{1+}). These values for the whole Congo are, respectively, 104 and 16.3 per thousand population.

The latter value (16.3 per thousand) seems a plausible level of mortality. It implies a crude death rate of 23 per thousand persons in the total population if the ratio of infant mortality to mortality at later ages in the Congo is equal to that found in the North family of life tables.[14]

On the other hand, the infant mortality rate indicated by reports on births and on deaths to infants under 1 year of age during the previous year appears too low to be credible. In the frame of the North model, an infant mortality rate of 154 per thousand births (as against an observed infant mortality rate of 104) is expected in conjunction with the observed mortality rate of all those over age 1 and the age distribution as indicated by the proportion of the population aged 0 to 4 years.[15]

Post-infant death rates (m_{1+}) by districts and estimated $q'(1)$'s derived from these observed post-infant rates and from corresponding relations at the same level in the North family of life table models are compared in Table 6.32 with the reported infant mortality rates obtained directly from accounts of births and infant deaths during the previous year. The sharp contrast between these rates is a general phenomenon. In all cases the reported $q(1)$'s obtained directly from reports on infant deaths fall below those derived from the post-infant rates and the selected set of life table models.

The most reasonable interpretation of this disparity is a simple one, namely that infant deaths, many of which occurred shortly after birth, were less completely reported than deaths of children over a year old

---

[14] Evidence to be considered later indicates that the crude death rate in the Congo must in fact be somewhat higher than 23 per thousand.

[15] If another model than North were used, an even larger discrepancy between observed and implied rates would obtain—an infant mortality of 175, 192, and 264 respectively with models South, West, and East.

Table 6.32. Reported post-infant mortality, estimated infant mortality on this basis, and reported infant mortality—the Congo, provinces, and districts

	Post-Infant Death Rate m_{1+}	Infant Mortality Rates	
		Derived from Post-Infant Rates $q'(1)$	Obtained Directly[3] $q(1)$
Leopoldville Province	13.8	132	103
Leopoldville	7.7	70	50
Lac Leopold II	14.8	140	104
Kwilu	15.7	152	112
Kwango	15.9	155	142
Bas Congo	12.7	121	80
Cataractes	13.2	126	96
Equateur Province	15.7	138	100
Equateur	13.9	110	75
Mongala	13.7	124	95
Ubangi	14.8	139	131
Tshuapa	20.8	165	61
Orientale Province[1]	17.9[1]	147	86
Stanleyville	16.5	141	88
Ituri[2]	-	-	-
Bas Uele	20.6	130	94
Haut Uele	20.7	153	77
Kivu Province	15.7	154	105
Sud Kivu	14.5	144	118
Nord Kivu	17.7	174	102
Maniema	14.1	115	71
Katanga Province	14.8	144	98
Elisabethville	6.5	65	101
Tanganika	14.3	139	99
Lualaba	13.7	126	89
Haut Lomani	18.5	178	96
Luapula Moero	14.9	149	105
Kasai Province	20.7	196	117
Lulua	22.1	214	134
Sankuru	18.0	166	68
Kabinda	19.4	187	114
Kasai	21.3	202	145
Congo[1]	16.3	154	104

[1] Ituri District not included.

[2] Not given.

[3] Reported infant deaths (under 1 year) per 100 reported births occurred during the year preceding the survey.

and adults. Such differential omission of infant deaths has often been noted in other surveys.

It is impossible to rely on an index of mortality (such as the observed crude death rate) which would be biased by this incomplete reporting. Alternative indices have biases of their own. For instance, reports on children surviving are to an unknown extent subject to recall lapses, presumably increasing in function of the mothers' ages. An estimate can be accepted only when it has been shown to be reasonably consistent with the other evidence. These limitations restrict our principal sources of information to (1) post-infant death rates (m_{1+}) i.e., reported deaths to persons over 1 year old relative to the total population aged 1 year and over and (2) the $q(1)$, $q(2)$, $q(3)$, and $q(5)$ values.

Our task in comparing these different sources of information is complicated by several problems of a general nature:

(1) A kind of data that yields the most reliable evidence concerning the level of mortality in some segments of the population may be less reliable than data of a different kind for other segments of the population.

(2) Different types of data on mortality provided by the inquiry refer to different time periods. The reports on deaths by sex and age refer to events during the year preceding the surveys (which were themselves spread through about two years). The reports by women refer to specified mean intervals of various lengths and represent events scattered through much longer periods prior to the surveys, periods which apparently were characterized by somewhat different levels of mortality. Because we must place heavy reliance on the $q(a)$'s, we cannot ascribe the resultant estimates to any precisely defined period. We shall, however, attempt to keep the reference period as narrow as possible.

(3) Along with the ambiguity of the "reference period" in using the $q(a)$'s, there is also ambiguity in the "reference areas" in the case of data collected from women in rapidly growing cities largely composed of migrants from rural areas where conditions of living are quite different. This complication may seriously affect the significance of observed $q(a)$'s for urban and mixed areas.

These reservations have to be kept in mind when we proceed to transform the available indices of mortality into the implied $q(5)$ value in the North model.

The use of these indices in estimating other mortality values is as follows. The combination of several $q(a)$ values is made by locating each observed value in a model life table conforming to the North family—using supplemental tables to locate intermediate values [$q(2)$ and $q(3)$]—and by finding the value of $q(5)$ in that table. This is interpreted as the $q'(5)$ values implied by each observed $q(1)$, $q(2)$, or $q(3)$. The implied $q'(5)$ values for any population obtained in this way are then arranged to give an estimated $q(5)$ implied by the selected indices in combination. A comparable value of $q(5)$ is also derived from post-infant mortality at the level of mortality implied by the observed m_{1+} and the observed proportion of the population under age 5. The results are shown in Table 6.33 for the Congo as a whole, together with the corresponding crude death rate. Table 6.35 shows various estimates of $q(5)$ for the districts and provinces of the Congo.

Table 6.33. Alternative indices of mortality (first estimates)—the Congo

Basis of Estimate		Estimated $q(5)$	Corresponding Death Rates
Post-Infant Death Rate (m_{1+}) [1]		.260	22.8
	$q(1)$	.258	22.5
	$q(2)$	.273	23.8
	$q(3)$	.293	25.6
	$q(5)$ [2]	.297	26.0

[1] Reported deaths during previous year at ages over one year related to population of same ages.

[2] Direct estimate.

Note that the DR based on BR (estimated) - r' (average rate of increase of population during 1950-58 based on registration figures) is 22.9 per thousand.

The Death Rate thus calculated becomes 24.0 when districts of North and South Kivu, which have received an important immigration from outside, are excluded.

The correlation coefficients r of $q(1)$ with $q(2)$, $q(3)$, and $q(5)$ are above .9 in all cases. On the other hand, the correlation between the combined index of mortality from reports by mothers and the index derived from the current reports on deaths is .56. This suggests that the two sets of data are more independent than one might have supposed.

Table 6.33 suggests at first sight that differences in the estimated values might be due in part to differences in the time intervals to which different indices refer and the effect of changes in mortality over time.

Another aspect of the divergence between these indices is revealed by obtaining comparable estimates separately for divisions of the population by type of settlement (see Table 6.34).[16] It is immediately evident that the differences by type of community in levels of mortality implied by the post-infant mortality rates are much larger than those implied by the child mortality. The differences should in theory be smaller on the basis of the former index than on the latter, because the design of the

[16] No adjustment is attempted here for the difference in age distribution by type of settlement, which affects death rates; the apparent differences persist, though in modified force, if such adjustments are made.

Table 6.34. Preliminary estimates of crude death rates—rural, mixed, and urban population of the Congo[1]

Basis	Rural	Mixed	Urban
Post-Infant Death Rate (m_{1+})	26.2	13.3	12.5
q(1)	24.5	21.7	16.4
q(2)	25.9	22.3	16.5
q(3)	27.1	23.0	19.3
q(4)	27.0	23.5	19.1

[1] Calculated on same basis as Table 6.33; unadjusted for differences in age distribution.

special inquiry on deaths was strictly *de facto* whereas the retrospective reports by mothers in mixed and urban areas included births and deaths of children in rural areas where mortality is generally higher. The most important reason for the wide divergence in this respect may be that the reports on deaths during the previous year in mixed and urban areas were less complete than similar reports in rural communities. Members of the mobile population of industrial centers could not in all cases have known about all deaths in the same compounds or neighborhoods during the previous year. Moreover, the fact that the enumerators in these areas did not have information from the civil registers at their disposal, as did the enumerators in rural areas, may explain part of the difference between mortality estimates in Table 6.33 and casts grave doubt on the reliability of any index of mortality in urban and mixed areas based on reported deaths during the previous year. We shall therefore study the mortality in these areas exclusively by means of the proportion of children surviving. It seems expedient to limit the basis of estimation to q(1) and q(2). Indeed it is likely that mortality has changed most rapidly in these localities and that the use of an index with more extended time reference intensifies the influence of rural experience on the results.

It is apparent from Table 6.35 that the mortality values derived from the q values are generally higher than those implied by the post-infant mortality rates not only in the two purely urban districts (Leopoldville and Elisabethville) but also in most predominantly rural districts. There are, however, some notable exceptions, such as Orientale and Katanga provinces.

Not barring the possibility of sampling errors and of unusual fluctuations of mortality in the preceding year, the estimates based on current

Table 6.35. Estimated $q(5)$ values based on (A) post-infant death rates and (B) average of $q(5)$'s derived from $q(1)$, $q(2)$, and $q(3)$; reported $q(5)$'s—provinces and districts of the Congo

	$q(5)$ derived from m_1+ (A)	Average of $q'(5)$ derived from $q(1)$ $q(2)$, and $q(3)$ (B)	Reported $q(5)$
Leopoldville Province	.223	.274	.306
Leopoldville	.111	.138	.198
Lac Leopold II	.236	.230	.231
Kwilu	.256	.299	.312
Kwango	.262	.354	.348
Bas-Congo	.205	.295	.297
Cataractes	.213	.294	.306
Equateur Province	.235	.252	.276
Equateur	.185	.155	.180
Mongala	.210	.281	.278
Ubangi	.235	.293	.298
Tshuapa	.279	.207	.256
Orientale Province	.248	.209	.205
Stanleyville	.243	.229	.250
Ituri	--	--	--
Bas-Uele	.220	.291	.245
Haut-Uele	.258	.179	.176
Kivu Province	.260	.298	.330
Sud-Kivu	.244	.379	.408
Nord-Kivu	.293	.211	.216
Maniema	.194	.301	.298
Katanga Province	.243	.209	.230
Elisabethville	.100	.169	.193
Tanganika	.235	.207	.224
Lualaba	.213	.207	.219
Haut-Lomani	.300	.218	.255
Luapula-Moero	.251	.234	.245
Kasai Province	.327	.343	.341
Lulua	.355	.381	.372
Sankuru	.280	.281	.306
Kabinda	.314	.276	.272
Kasai	.336	.407	.387
Congo	.260	.275	.297

reports could be inflated by overreporting, for instance as the result of an erroneous extension of the 12-month reference period. It will be shown in the section on fertility that there was little extension of the reference period in reporting births. It is true that the reporting of births was more adequately protected in this respect by the use of registration records than the reporting of deaths because the registration of births was more complete. On the other hand, considerable underreporting of deaths might be expected on *a priori* grounds in view of the well-established tendency in this direction in many other surveys. Underreporting could have resulted from (1) a reluctance to mention deaths or carelessness or ignorance on the part of those making the reports; (2) erroneous exclusion of deaths of visitors; or (3) the failure to include all institutions, for instance some hospitals and prisons, in the sampling design. It is, therefore, likely that estimates of the level of mortality on the basis of reported deaths tend in most cases to be too low rather than too high, though this cannot be affirmed with assurance.

There is, on the other hand, specific evidence in support of the hypothesis that in certain areas women frequently failed to report children who had died in infancy. This type of bias led us to reject the observed infant mortality rates, and it may well affect the reports by mothers on children ever born and surviving as well.[17]

On the whole there appears to be a greater tendency toward understatement of a mortality index than toward overstatement. Thus, in the rural population of the areas mentioned above (where levels indicated by the $q(a)$'s are inferior to those indicated by numbers of reported deaths during the previous year) the risk of error in using post-infant mortality rates as the basis of estimation appears less than the risk involved in relying on the child q values. This observation applies to the rural parts of Katanga and Orientale Provinces and Equateur, Tshuapa, and Lac Leopold Districts—comprising about 25 percent of the total population of the Congo.[18]

The observations selected as a basis for estimating levels of mortality are, therefore, as follows: (1) for the population of urban and mixed localities: $q(1)$ and $q(2)$ (combined); (2) for the rural population in areas where the mortality level implied by m_{1+} is superior to that implied by child mortality: m_{1+}; (3) for all other rural areas: $q(1)$, $q(2)$, and $q(3)$ (combined).

Different selections or combinations of indices which might also be defended as reasonable would necessarily give somewhat different results, but the results on any reasonable alternatives would not be radically different. The results obtained on the proposed basis are presented below.

Results

Table 6.36 presents final estimates of various mortality indices for the Congo and for types of settlement. Death rates and other functions given in this table were obtained by assuming that their relations with

[17] The Congo parity / fertility ratios (described elsewhere) at age 20 to 24 years correlate by districts ($r = .59$) with the ratio of mortality quotients based respectively on the proportion of children surviving and on the post-infant mortality. This strongly suggests that in areas of low q values, the parity / fertility ratios were deflated by non-reporting of dead infants.

[18] In preparing estimates on the provincial and national levels, the m_{1+} values are applied only to rural populations of these divisions. In dealing with the districts as units, this is not feasible and the m_{1+} values are used in estimating the general death rates of each district (except Elisabethville) within the areas listed.

Table 6.36. Estimated mortality values for rural, urban, and mixed populations
and for the whole Congo

	Death Rate	$q(1)$	$q(5)$	Expectation of Life at Birth ($\overset{o}{e}_0$)
Rural[1]	28.3	.195	.325	34.5
Mixed[2]	20.5	.142	.238	42.8
Urban[2]	15.8	.106	.178	49.8
Congo[3]	26.1	.177	.299	37.2

[1] Estimates based on $q(1)$, $q(2)$ and $q(3)$, or m_{1+} in the case of specified districts which the $q(a)$ values appear to give underestimates of mortality.

[2] Estimates based on $q(1)$ and $q(2)$.

[3] Weighted averages.

the most reliable index of mortality (selected as indicated in the previous section) are the same as those in the North stable population model with the same proportion under 5 years of age as that found in the actual population. The estimated values for sub-populations by type of settlement are obtained by applying the age-specific death rates in the selected model to the reported age distribution of each sub-population (rural, mixed, urban). Estimates for the total population of the Congo are taken as the weighted averages (by size of population) of the values for these population segments.

The estimated crude death rate of the Congolese population obtained in this way is 26 deaths per year per thousand population. The period to which this rate refers cannot be precisely defined. Most of the events which it represents were scattered with varying intensity from about 1950 to about 1956, with a probable center in the upper half of this range. The estimated rate for the whole Congo is at least a reasonable figure. A population growth rate in the vicinity of 2 percent per year was implied in the 1950's by the official estimates of population based on continuous registration. Evidence presented in Section IV indicates a birth rate in the vicinity of 45 per thousand (leaving its precise location for later consideration). These indications in conjunction lead us to expect a death rate in the vicinity of 25 per thousand, the figure obtained here independently.

The differences shown here among rural, mixed, and urban death rates can also be accepted as significant, though the precise figures for these components are probably subject to larger degrees of error than the combined estimate for the total population.

Comparable estimates (obtained on a somewhat different basis)[19] for provinces and districts are shown in Table 6.37. These figures are vulnerable both to local variations in the completeness and accuracy of the basic data and to errors of estimation. But, again, the array as a

Table 6.37, Estimated mortality values by provinces and districts of the Congo

	Death Rate	q(1)	q(5)	$\overset{o}{e}_o$
Leopoldville Province (1)	24.8	.164	.282	38.8
Leopoldville (2)	11.6	.078	.128	57.0
Lac Leopold II (3)	20.5	.142	.236	43.5
Kwilu (4)	26.2	.178	.299	37.0
Kwango (4)	32.3	.212	.354	32.5
Bas-Congo (4)	26.1	.175	.295	37.5
Cataractes (4)	25.9	.174	.294	37.8
Equateur Province (1)	23.1	.168	.268	40.0
Equateur (3)	17.1	.110	.185	49.5
Mongala (4)	19.3	.166	.281	39.0
Ubangi (4)	25.5	.174	.293	37.8
Tshuapa (3)	24.9	.167	.279	39.0
Orientale Province (1)	23.6	.157	.262	40.8
Stanleyville (3)	21.2	.144	.243	42.8
Ituri --	-	-	-	-
Bas-Uele (4)	27.8	.173	.291	37.8
Haut-Uele (3)	24.1	.153	.258	41.3
Kivu Province (1)	29.7	.197	.329	34.6
Sud-Kivu (4)	38.3	.230	.379	30.8
Nord-Kivu (3)	27.0	.173	.293	38.0
Maniema (4)	26.0	.178	.301	37.0
Katanga Province (1)	21.8	.146	.247	42.5
Elisabethville (2)	15.9	.104	.171	50.8
Tanganika (3)	20.8	.138	.235	43.8
Lualaba (3)	18.6	.127	.213	46.2
Haut-Lomani (3)	26.4	.179	.300	37.0
Luapula-Moero (3)	23.3	.150	.251	42.0
Kasai Province (1)	30.0	.204	.340	33.8
Lulua (4)	34.1	.232	.381	30.8
Sankuru (4)	24.3	.166	.281	39.0
Kabinda (4)	24.1	.164	.276	39.3
Kasai (4)	37.0	.250	.408	29.2
Congo (5)	25.5[6]	.173	.291	38.0

[1]Weighted average by districts

[2]Based on q(1) and q(2)

[3]Based on post infant mortality, m_{1+}

[4]Based on q(1), q(2) and q(3)

[5]Weighted averaged by province.

[6]See explanation in the text about the difference in crude death rate between this table and Table 6.36

[19] In this series, districts are treated as units—without separate estimates for the urban, mixed, and rural components.

whole is undoubtedly significant in the sense of showing wide variations in levels of mortality in different parts of the country. The crude death rate shown here for the whole Congo, obtained as a weighted average of these estimates (25.5), is somewhat below that shown in the previous table (26.1). The latter figure reflects the implications of the basic data on our stated hypotheses somewhat more accurately than the average of the figures for the political divisions. The true value may, of course, lie outside the narrow range defined by these averages.

IV. FERTILITY IN THE CONGO

Questions on fertility received major attention in the 1955-57 Demographic Inquiry. Direct information was obtained in the main schedule both on births during the previous 12 months by age of woman and on children ever born and children living, also by age of woman. Indirect evidence on fertility is also provided by the enumeration of children classified by age. The information on these topics is fortified by the use in the inquiry of information from other sources: the vital registration system and the continuous population registers and related identity booklets.

The results show a surprising regional variation in levels of fertility —estimated crude birth rates by district that range from about 25 to about 60 births per thousand persons. Wide variation in fertility has also been found in some other African countries. Thus the Congo findings are not unique in this respect, but the new documentation on this subject for the Congo is impressive.

The Data

Registered and Reported Births

The registration of births and of deaths had been extended as a legal obligation to 95 percent of the population of the Congo at the time of the inquiry. In fact, when the number of registered births in 1956 is related to the total population estimated from the inquiry we get a rate of 38 per thousand, as compared with 42.7 births directly reported per thousand persons in the inquiry itself. The latter figure, as we shall see, requires some upward adjustment. Even so, it appears that some four-fifths of all births were being registered at this time, a remarkable achievement under African conditions. Table 6.38 compares registered births and the births estimated within the survey framework.

The registration of births, though incomplete, was used to improve the quality of data recorded in the surveys. In all rural areas the enumerator was required, before entering a selected village, to draw from the birth register (in the *circonscription* office) a list of all births in this

Table 6.38. Numbers and rates of births (a) according to the 1955-57 inquiry and (b) according to vital registration statistics, 1956—the Congo, provinces, and districts

| | Survey | | | |
	Number of births	Birth rate	Registered births	Registered Reported
Leopoldville Province	143,183	46.65	132,844	.928
Leopoldville	17,351	52.17	15,155(1)	.873
Lac Leopold II	12,023	44.31	11,435	.951
Kwilu	51,842	45.15	48,212	.930
Kwango	22,420	48.11	21,386	.954
Bas-Congo	19,768	48.00	19,594	.991
Cataractes	19,779	45.01	17,062	.863
Equateur Province	67,487	38.43	56,378	.835
Equateur	10,190	33.72	8,464	.831
Mongala	21,294	40.99	18,130	.851
Ubangi	23,936	44.40	20,054	.838
Tshuapa	12,067	30.51	9,730	.806
Orientale Province	71,836	30.76	49,119	.684
Stanleyville	21,573	33.98	10,241	.475
Ituri	27,806	42.71	21,721	.781
Bas-Uele	8,951	19.14	7,397	.826
Haut-Uele	13,506	23.21	9,760	.723
Kivu Province	95,026	47.22	83,821	.882
Sud-Kivu	43,443	52.26	37,195	.856
Nord-Kivu	36,290	49.40	34,820	.959
Maniema	15,293	34.25	11,806	.772
Katanga Province	72,234(2)	50.21	52,366(3)	.725
Elisabethville	8,193	58.48	8,189	1.000
Tanganyika	21,332	54.23	11,014(3)	.516
Lualaba	12,077	44.13	11,754(3)	.973
Haut-Lomani	19,898	45.24	15,463(3)	.777
Luapula-Moero	10,734	56.02	5,946	.554
Kasai Province	94,209	44.41	78,022	.828
Lulua	28,183	43.06	23,733	.842
Sankuru	20,532	41.60	17,098	.833
Kabinda	23,153	48.20	19,707	.851
Kasai	22,341	45.33	17,484	.783
Congo	543,975	42.72	452,550	.832

(1) The difference between the estimated number of births and the number of registered births in Leopoldville may be due in a large part to the fact that the children under age 1 born outside of Leopoldville are generally not included in the registration figure.

(2) The total number of estimated births refers to the total population of the Congo (12,734,000). This figure does not include the births (roughly estimated at about 3000 units) occurring in the parts of Katanga province not covered by the survey with a total population of 63,515 persons.

(3) The figures on the registered births are taken from an official unpublished document. It seems that the registered births for the areas of Katanga (see note above) not covered by the survey are not included in the figures given here. Indeed, the total number of registered births for Katanga (see Table 5.3) is 55,594 (1956) instead of 52,366 given here.

village during the previous 18 months, with the names of the infants and their parents and the dates of the registrations. The enumerator was also required in the course of the interview to check the identity booklets or other household records in which the names and usually the birth dates or ages of all children are normally entered. These procedures were designed (1) to increase the completeness of the reports and (2) to sharpen the discrimination between events within the previous 12 months and events prior to this "reference period." It was not practical to prepare lists of registered events for use in urban households or in many of the mixed localities. However, practically all families in these areas, as well as most of those in rural areas, were able to show identity booklets and in some cases birth registration or medical certificates (the possession of such information was a matter of concern to the families of employed persons as a basis for claiming child allowance benefits). As shown in Table 6.38, the registration of births was incomplete. In some rural localities a large proportion, and perhaps in some remote places all, of the births may have passed without registration. However, the existence of even a few recorded events in a village facilitated the dating of other events and increased the ability of the enumerators to evaluate the statements of respondents in this respect.

Questions concerning births during the previous 12 months and concerning children ever born were asked of all females past puberty, whether or not ever married, except some of the very aged. These questions were explicitly limited to live births. A question was asked concerning stillbirths during the previous year, but stillbirths were recorded in a separate column and were not included in the tabulation of live births. The specific inquiry on stillbirths tended to distinguish these events clearly and to obviate their inclusion in reports on live births. Although these questions on fertility were specifically addressed to women, other interested persons were usually present during the interviews and could cooperate in framing the replies.

Two possible sources of error in reports on births during the previous year require special attention: (1) In some rural areas, where the vital registration system was inadequately developed, the checks obtained from this source must have been relatively ineffective. (2) In the case of infants who died soon after birth, it is likely that sometimes, perhaps often, neither the birth nor the death was registered. Moreover, the mothers and their associates may also have sometimes ignored or suppressed information on such events in replying to the survey questions.

The survey reports on births during the previous year provide direct and important data on fertility. Nevertheless, these data must be tested in relation to other types of information on this subject.

Age-specific fertility rates are provided by the reports on births by age of mother in conjunction with numbers of women classified by age (see Table 6.39). By cumulating the age-specific fertility rates of women, one obtains the cumulative fertility at the end year for each age group, as presented in Table 6.40. It should be noted that in fact the cumulative values do not refer to the exact end of the year of age but to the midpoint of the last year of each successive age group. This is so because the women were an average of about 6 months younger when the reported births occurred.

Children Ever Born to Women Classified by Age

Together with the question on births occurring in the 12 months before the interview, a question was addressed to all women concerning the number of children ever born to them.

Table 6.39. Age-specific fertility rates (f) and general fertility rates, according to the Demographic Inquiry, for the preceding year—the Congo, provinces, and districts

	f_1 (ages 15–19)	f_2 (ages 20–24)	f_3 (ages 25–29)	f_4 (ages 30–34)	f_5 (ages 35–44)	f_6 (ages 45–55)	General Fertili Rate (ages 15–44)
Leopoldville Province	.094	.280	.270	.213	.107	.019	.192
Leopoldville	.195	.300	.287	.236	.131	.028	.244
Lac Leopold II	.150	.269	.240	.196	.103	.027	.189
Kwilu	.079	.282	.259	.199	.094	.012	.179
Kwango	.065	.274	.285	.230	.134	.034	.203
Bas-Congo	.118	.281	.264	.187	.095	.019	.194
Cataractes	.057	.265	.297	.255	.123	.017	.189
Equateur Province	.089	.249	.219	.160	.072	.011	.150
Equateur	.131	.219	.190	.132	.063	.010	.133
Mongala	.079	.258	.244	.181	.084	.016	.164
Ubangi	.086	.299	.256	.188	.088	.011	.176
Tshuapa	.080	.191	.166	.118	.049	.008	.113
Orientale Province	.134	.201	.147	.103	.048	.012	.114
Stanleyville	.192	.196	.144	.086	.035	.011	.123
Ituri	.092	.318	.243	.203	.108	.037	.184
Bas-Uele	.102	.115	.098	.059	.023	.003	.064
Haut-Uele	.123	.168	.108	.065	.026	.006	.083
Kivu Province	.182	.290	.261	.182	.086	.018	.198
Sud-Kivu	.167	.316	.298	.199	.100	.034	.211
Nord-Kivu	.190	.314	.303	.234	.105	.018	.226
Maniema	.194	.201	.152	.102	.043	.002	.129
Katanga Province	.210	.306	.251	.186	.105	.022	.205
Elisabethville	.244	.338	.276	.229	.138	.017	.256
Tanganyika	.230	.324	.254	.212	.126	.021	.219
Lualaba	.202	.275	.209	.152	.068	.016	.173
Haut-Lomani	.194	.282	.248	.161	.095	.020	.184
Luapula-Moero	.189	.331	.296	.225	.131	.042	.238
Kasai Province	.144	.268	.234	.170	.080	.015	.170
Lulua	.134	.268	.222	.175	.074	.016	.166
Sankuru	.117	.268	.226	.149	.067	.015	.156
Kabinda	.191	.290	.252	.179	.094	.015	.189
Kasai	.137	.249	.238	.177	.087	.016	.173
Congo	.137	.265	.232	.168	.080	.016	.171

As in the attempt to establish the number of births to each woman during the year previous to the interview, there was a special procedure to be followed by the interviewer to obtain as accurate as possible a history of the fertility of each woman, to minimize errors caused by a lapse of memory or by the reluctance (widespread in Africa) to mention children who have died.

Here again, the interviewer had to check the report of a woman with the entries in her or her husband's identity booklet and with the birth certificates of her children. To minimize the understatements of numbers of children ever born, the enumerator was required to establish for each woman who had given birth to more than three children an exhaustive list, giving for each child ever born its order of birth, age, whether still alive or dead, present residence, and marital status.

Table 6.40. Cumulative fertility (ϕ_i) to various ages based on the age-specific fertility rates according to the Demographic Inquiry—the Congo, provinces, and districts

	ϕ_2 (to age 19.5)	ϕ_3 (to age 24.5)	ϕ_4 (to age 29.5)	ϕ_5 (to age 34.5)	ϕ_6 (to age 44.5)	ϕ_7 to age 54.5)
Leopoldville Province	.470	1.870	3.220	4.285	5.355	5.545
Leopoldville	.975	2.475	3.910	5.090	6.400	6.680
Lac Leopold II	.750	2.095	3.295	4.275	5.305	5.575
Kwilu	.395	1.805	3.100	4.095	5.035	5.155
Kwango	.325	1.695	3.120	4.270	5.610	5.950
Bas-Congo	.590	1.995	3.315	4.250	5.200	5.390
Cataractes	.285	1.610	3.095	4.370	5.600	5.770
Equateur Province	.445	1.690	2.785	3.585	4.305	4.415
Equateur	.655	1.750	2.700	3.360	3.990	4.090
Mongala	.395	1.685	2.905	3.810	4.650	4.810
Ubangi	.430	1.925	3.195	4.135	5.015	5.125
Tshuapa	.400	1.355	2.185	2.775	3.265	3.345
Orientale Province	.670	1.675	2.410	2.925	3.405	3.525
Stanleyville	.960	1.940	2.660	3.090	3.440	3.550
Ituri	.460	2.050	3.265	4.280	5.360	5.730
Bas-Uele	.510	1.085	1.575	1.870	2.100	2.130
Haut-Uele	.615	1.455	1.995	2.320	2.580	2.640
Kivu Province	.910	2.360	3.665	4.575	5.435	5.615
Sud-Kivu	.835	2.415	3.905	4.900	5.900	6.240
Nord-Kivu	.950	2.520	4.035	5.205	6.255	6.435
Maniema	.970	1.975	2.735	3.245	3.675	3.695
Katanga Province	1.050	2.580	3.835	4.765	5.815	6.035
Elisabethville	1.220	2.910	4.200	5.435	6.815	6.985
Tanganyika	1.150	2.770	4.040	5.100	6.360	6.570
Lualaba	1.010	2.385	3.430	4.190	4.870	5.030
Haut-Lomani	.970	2.380	3.620	4.425	5.375	5.575
Luapula-Moero	.945	2.600	4.080	5.205	6.515	6.935
Kasai Province	.720	2.060	3.230	4.080	4.880	5.030
Lulua	.670	2.010	3.120	3.995	4.735	4.895
Sankuru	.585	1.925	3.055	3.800	4.470	4.620
Kabinda	.955	2.405	3.665	4.560	5.500	5.650
Kasai	.685	1.930	3.120	4.005	4.875	5.035
Congo	.685	2.010	3.170	4.010	4.810	4.970

Attention of the enumerators was drawn to the existence of adopted children, open to confusion with the mother's own children, given the system of filiation in African society. These children normally appear in the identity booklet with the qualification "adopted."

The data on numbers of children ever born were tabulated by age of mother. The results are shown in Table 6.41.

Table 6.41. Average number of children ever born (P) by age of mother—the Congo, provinces, and districts

	Ages of Women						
	15-19	20-24	25-29	30-34	35-44	45-55	+55
Leopoldville Province	.206	1.331	2.671	4.041	5.066	5.192	4.895
Leopoldville	.48	1.47	2.55	3.42	3.74	2.93	2.86
Lac Leopold II	.30	1.32	2.37	3.03	4.04	4.26	4.15
Kwilu	.16	1.26	2.54	3.87	4.88	5.00	4.68
Kwango	.13	1.27	2.76	4.16	5.19	5.39	4.83
Bas-Congo	.27	1.45	2.83	4.14	5.28	5.67	5.43
Cataractes	.12	1.31	3.14	5.14	6.63	6.66	5.94
Equateur Province	.169	1.055	1.890	2.665	3.265	3.506	3.754
Equateur	.25	.97	1.46	1.97	2.37	2.50	3.14
Mongala	.16	1.20	2.20	2.99	3.64	4.19	4.53
Ubangi	.15	1.18	2.27	3.31	4.30	4.56	4.68
Tshuapa	.16	.75	1.33	1.94	2.38	2.79	2.94
Orientale Province	.352	1.228	1.632	2.068	2.540	2.722	2.818
Stanleyville	.54	1.47	1.93	2.35	2.96	3.13	3.36
Ituri	.19	1.15	1.88	2.88	3.50	3.68	2.80
Bas-Uele	.31	1.00	1.23	1.45	1.77	2.09	2.75
Haut-Uele	.30	1.10	1.41	1.63	2.01	2.27	2.64
Kivu Province	.522	2.019	3.315	4.330	4.878	4.423	3.220
Sud-Kivu	.39	2.07	3.61	5.09	6.03	6.15	6.23
Nord-Kivu	.56	2.21	3.60	4.75	5.34	4.86	3.41
Maniema	.57	1.66	2.30	2.92	3.11	3.46	2.82
Katanga Province	.542	1.657	2.459	3.292	3.829	3.702	3.385
Elisabethville	.72	1.93	2.80	3.71	4.09	3.92	3.68
Tanganyika	.55	1.67	2.50	3.37	4.00	3.61	3.26
Lualaba	.54	1.59	2.26	3.06	3.57	3.68	3.73
Haut-Lomani	.50	1.45	2.26	2.96	3.34	3.33	3.01
Luapula-Moero	.47	1.88	2.85	4.10	5.19	5.22	4.50
Kasai Province	.360	1.440	2.316	3.237	3.984	4.163	4.186
Lulua	.39	1.59	2.49	3.54	4.49	4.88	4.90
Sankuru	.28	1.24	1.97	2.72	2.31	3.59	3.60
Kabinda	.44	1.50	2.38	3.33	3.82	3.65	3.42
Kasai	.31	1.35	2.40	3.32	4.21	4.47	4.69
Congo	.345	1.450	2,386	3.252	3.850	3.969	3.748

Proportions of Children in the Population

The crude birth rate of any population can be estimated from (1) the proportion of young children in the population, (2) the survival rates from birth to the specified age class during the period of exposure to risk of death, and (3) the rate of increase (or decrease) of the population between the midpoint of the period during which these children were born and the time of the enumeration—the last being subject to certain disturbing factors, mainly factors associated with migration. In some cases, the effects of migration may seriously disturb the results. Therefore, this procedure will not be applied to the rapidly changing populations of Leopoldville and Elisabethville. It can, however, be assumed that disturbing factors of this sort are nearly negligible in most other districts.

The validity of any estimate of the birth rate obtained in this way is strongly dependent on the accuracy of the reported proportion of persons within each specified child age class. As shown in Section II, the results of the 1955-57 inquiry in the Congo are unusually reliable in this respect.

The proportions of persons under 5 years of age in the population of the Congo and its component parts are shown in Table 6.42.

A rough index of the age structure of component parts of the Congo also can be obtained from the threefold classification as "men," "women," and "children" in the continuous population registers. On the assumption that similar criteria are applied in different parts of the Congo in distinguishing between adults and children, one would expect a strong positive correlation between proportions of "children" by districts in the current estimates and proportions of persons classified in the inquiry as under 5 years, or under 10 years. Table 6.42 presents the proportion of children to total population and to total adult women, as based on the registration data.

The Analysis of Fertility Data

Responses to the question about the number of children born in the year preceding the survey and the administrative register of births both give direct measures of the birth rate in each district and province of the Congo. For those parts of the Congo not substantially affected by migration, birth rates can be estimated from reported age distribution either by reconstruction of the assumed past of young children with estimates of recent growth, or by the equivalent use of stable age analysis. However, Congolese demographic data, even though derived from a well-designed and carefully conducted demographic survey, must be viewed with some skepticism, as must all African demographic data. One must always bear in mind that the respondents are, for the most part, illiterate, and that data obtained through interviews are always subject to recall lapse, misunderstanding of the questions, ignorance of the required categorization, and other biases. Specifically, we are led to expect the following kinds of defects in the data described in the preceding pages:

Table 6.42. Proportions (per 1,000) under age 1, 1-4, and 5-9, to total population, according to the Demographic Inquiry, and proportion of children to total population and ratio of children to women, as provided by the continuous registration— the Congo, provinces, and districts

	-1	1-4	5-9	0-4	0-9	children per 1,000[1] persons all ages	Number children per 1,0 women
Leopoldville Province	43	140	137	183	324	482	1731
Leopoldville	51	141	118	192	310	444	1968
Lac Leopold II	43	135	137	178	315	450	1487
Kwilu	43	134	136	177	314	473	1582
Kwango	44	145	150	189	339	528	1942
Bas-Congo	41	147	122	187	309	457	1589
Cataractes	38	147	154	186	300	533	2086
Equateur Province	36	113	119	149	268	397	1235
Equateur	32	102	97	134	231	323	826
Mongala	38	124	131	162	293	434	1469
Ubangi	40	132	142	172	362	473	1725
Tshuapa	30	83	89	113	202	309	849
Orientale Province	30	98	113	127	240	357	1120
Stanleyville	32	107	107	139	246	356	1145
Ituri	41	127	150	169	319	478	1862
Bas-Uele	19	66	85	85	170	272	719
Haut-Uele	22	79	101	101	202	300	864
Kivu Province	44	149	143	192	335	474	1740
Sud-Kivu	50	155	145	205	350	491	1854
Nord-Kivu	44	168	163	211	374	522	2094
Maniema	33	108	107	141	248	358	1089
Katanga Province	47	150	131	197	328	440	1538
Elisabethville	56	187	143	243	387	456	1860
Tanganyika	49	147	133	196	329	444	1519
Lualaba	43	146	125	188	314	434	1615
Haut-Lomani	43	136	119	179	298	419	1356
Luapula-Moero	53	164	151	217	368	475	1706
Kasai Province	42	126	128	168	296	434	1420
Lulua	41	127	129	168	297	458	1558
Sankuru	40	119	115	159	274	384	1166
Kabinda	45	136	139	181	320	454	1502
Kasai	41	124	128	166	294	430	1433
Congo	40	129	129	169	298	433	

[1] Based on the figures provided by continuous registration (average for the years 1955 through 1957)

(1) Events reported as having occurred in the preceding year are subject to an erroneous interpretation of the reference period. Thus the respondent may report only events occurring in the last six to eight months or, on the other hand, may tend to include events occurring within a year and a half rather than within just 12 months. Misinterpretations of this sort appear to have occurred in many African surveys. Errors of this type, though not eliminated, were reduced in the data for

the Congo—as compared with information for most African countries —by the use of the unusual body of registration records.

(2) Reported parity of women (i.e., reported number of children ever born) is subject to progressive understatement as age and parity advance. Evidence of this is found in the fall-off in average parity beginning at age 40, 45, or 50 in areas in which there is no basis for expecting a decline in average parity with age. Understatements, increasing with age, concerning the number of children ever born are a well-known feature of survey and census data from many parts of the world. As we shall see, Congolese data also show this defect.

(3) Information on births and deaths of children who died early in infancy tend to be omitted from surveys and registers. Such omissions are problematical aspects of demographic data collection in many parts of the world. It appears to be hard to establish in the mind of a respondent the importance of reporting the birth and death or, indeed, the prior existence of a child whose life was very brief. These events also tend to escape systems of registration.

(4) Another possible deficiency is the systematic omission of deaths at any age—and hence of children who have died—due to a reluctance in some African tribes to mention death itself or a person who has died.

(5) Many Africans including Congolese have no knowledge of their age. More often than not, the enumerator must estimate the age of each person, guided by various clues including size and apparent maturity of children, marital status of adults, the parity of women, and general physical appearance. Estimates of this sort produce characteristic biases in the reported age distribution and reduce the validity, or at least the precision, of estimates of fertility based on analysis of the age distribution.

In view of these biases affecting the basic data, it is desirable to assess the estimates of fertility measures on several alternative methods of estimation. We have selected the following three methods which take account of the particular nature of the information available on fertility for the Congo:

(1) The correction of the reported birth rate for underreporting of children having been born and having died during the 12 months preceding the survey.

(2) The derivation of the birth rate from a combination of the proportion of the most accurately reported age group (under age 5) and an estimate of mortality.

(3) The method devised by W. Brass whereby cumulative fertility rates, derived from the reports on births for the 12 months preceding the survey, are confronted with the average parity by age of mother in such a way as to adjust the reported crude birth rate.

We shall describe these techniques in more detail subsequently and present the results that they have generated.

Birth Rates Based on Reported Numbers
of Births During the Previous
Year, Adjusted for
Underreporting of Deceased Infants

Table 6.38 above showed crude birth rates obtained directly from the number of births reported in the inquiry for the previous 12 months for various parts of the Congo. Deficiencies in these reported births have been discussed above and attributed in part to underreporting of those births that were followed by deaths within the same year. Also, the discussion in the previous section showed that the reported numbers of deaths of infants under 1 year of age during the year reported must have been deficient by varying degrees in different districts. Of those children dying in the year preceding the inquiry before reaching 1 year of age, only those who were also born during that year form a part of the births on which our birth rate is based and thus require our attention. An estimate of such possibly omitted births and deaths must be made so that a corrected birth rate can be calculated.

On the basis of extensive information for other countries, Logan has found that the proportion of children who have been exposed during a 12-month period to the risk of dying within one year after birth varies between 0.55 and 0.80 of the total infant deaths occurring in a single calendar year. This proportion, known as the separation factor s, tends to increase as the infant mortality rate decreases.[20] Thus for an infant mortality such as the 165 estimated for the Congo, the separation factor according to Logan's function would be 0.57.

The available Congolese data indicate that the proportion of children whose births and deaths are included in the year preceding the survey to the total of infant deaths under age 1 during the same period is 0.62.[21] There are, however, many unknown errors in the basic data on which this proportion is based. One of these is the possible excess in the proportion of living children under age 1 resulting from 0 entries, code zero having been attributed to the under-1-year age group. Moreover, since the omitted children are mostly those having died shortly after birth, the proportion of children having been born and having died

[20] Logan, W. P. D., "The measurement of infant mortality," *Population Bulletin of the United Nations*, No. 3, October 1953.

[21] $s = D'/D = (B-L)/D = 0.62$ (whole Congo)
where D and D' are, respectively, all infant deaths of age under 1 year which occurred during the 12 months preceding the survey and children *born and died* during the 12 months preceding the survey; B is the number of births reported for the 12 months preceding the survey; and L represents number of children aged under 1 year.

during the 12 months preceding the survey who have been omitted is likely to be larger than indicated by the separation factor s.

The estimated proportions of infants born alive who died within the first year of life in various parts of the Congo were presented in the previous section (Table 6.37) as well as the corresponding proportions taken directly from the reports on births and infant deaths during the 12 months prior to the surveys (Table 6.32). For the Congo as a whole, the figures are 0.173 and 0.104 respectively.

The correction of the birth rate b' for underreporting of children having been born and having died during the same year can be obtained by the following formula:

$$b' = b + [b'q_e(1)s' - bq_r(1)s']$$
$$= b\left[\frac{1 - q_r(1)s'}{1 - q_e(1)s'}\right]$$

where b' and b are, respectively, corrected and reported birth rate; $q_e(1)$ and $q_n(1)$ are, respectively, the estimated and reported infant mortality rates; and s' is the proportion of omitted children having been born and having died under age 1 during the 12 months preceding the survey to the total of omitted children having died under age 1 during the 12 months preceding the survey, or the separation factor among omitted children.

We have estimated the factor s' at 0.9. This is a rough and somewhat arbitrary estimate. But the error it might introduce in the corrected birth rate is of a small magnitude as shown in the following example assuming various possible values of s':

s'	birth rate per 1,000
1.0	46.26
0.9	45.83
0.8	45.43
0.7	45.04

The adjusted rates obtained in this way are shown in comparison with the original values in Table 6.45. Before discussing these results we shall proceed with another line of inquiry.

Birth Rates Based on the Proportion
of the Population under Five Years of Age

The supplemental values needed to obtain an estimated crude birth rate from the proportion of children classified in a specified age class relative to the total population are (1) an estimate of the ratio of living children at this age to births during the period in which they were born and (2) an estimate of the rate of population growth during this period.

This elaborate calculation can be avoided by using the stable population model giving the relationship between the proportion in an age group and the birth rate for a given mortality level.

As shown in Section II, the proportions of persons classified as under 1 year, under 5 years, and under 10 years of age in the Congo fit equally well the expected proportions in a stable population model appropriate to apparent vital trends in the Congo. Thus, we would obtain similar estimated birth rates by using any of these age classes (under 1, 0-4, 0-9) as a basis. It seems advisable to use a broader, presumably more reliable base than the single-year age class. There are two reasons for preferring the class 0-4 years rather than 0-9 years for this purpose: (1) It brings the implied reference period during which the children concerned were born nearer to the time of the surveys. (2) A higher proportion of the births of children under 5 years had been registered, so that estimation of their ages is more accurate than in the broader class born at various times during the entire decade prior to the survey.[22] We shall therefore select the age class 0-4 years for this purpose.

Estimates of ratios of survivors aged 0-4 years to births during the previous five years ($_5L_0/5\,l_0$) are implicit in the mortality values presented in Section III. These, it may be noted, are based mainly on reports by mothers concerning the survival of children during an ill-defined but somewhat similar period prior to the surveys. These mortality values were used in conjunction with observed proportions under 5 years to give stable population values with implicit rates of natural increase. Even though these hypothetical rates of increase may differ appreciably from actual trends in some districts, the estimation of crude birth rates from observed proportions of children by the application of stable population values will not be greatly distorted *except* in areas where the child population itself has been strongly affected in recent years by migration, notably in Leopoldville and Elisabethville and perhaps generally in the urban and mixed segments of the whole population. Although many rural areas have been affected by out-movements of children with their parents, the relative influence of these movements on the estimated birth rates is generally less important.

The estimated crude birth rate for the whole Congo obtained in this way is 45.2 per thousand. The corresponding rates for districts and provinces are shown in Table 6.45.

The correspondence among districts between (A) birth rates based on proportions of children under 5 years and (B) birth rates based on reported births adjusted for underreporting of the births of deceased infants is impressive. The coefficient of correlation between these series

[22] Use of the age class 0-9 years would give, on the procedure described here, an estimated birth rate about 0.7 per thousand points below that obtained by use of the 0-4 class (about 44.4 rather than 45.2 per thousand).

is .96, and the birth rate for the total Congo is, respectively, 45.2 or 46.0 per thousand. The two series have a common element in the esti- mated child survival or infant mortality values used in their derivation. However, only the child survival values are used in Series A, whereas the adjustment factor in Series B is the difference between the esti- mated and the "observed" infant mortality rates. Moreover, there is a correlation of .94 between the rates based on reported proportions under 5 years and the unadjusted rates based directly on numbers of reported births. The two sets of data from which these indices are derived are in large part quite independent. In view of the correspondence between these largely independent estimates of variations in levels of fertility among different areas within the Congo, it is safe to conclude that in general the indicated variations are real. Another rough but independent indication of fertility is the proportion of "children" in 1956 in the cur- rent population estimates based on the continuous registration system; the proportion of "children" thus obtained is highly correlated both with the birth rate derived from the proportions 0-4 years according to the inquiry ($r = .92$) and with the birth rate derived from reported births during the previous year adjusted for underreporting ($r = .85$).

Mean Parity of Women by
Age Class in Comparison
with Cumulated Specific Fertility Rates

The treatment of this important topic is more troublesome and the results are more ambiguous than those described in the previous dis- cussion.

For the Congo as a whole, slightly less than 4 live births on the aver- age were reported by women near or past the menopause—only 3.97 children by women classed as 45-54 years old and only 3.75 children by those classed as 55 years or over (see Table 6.41 above). On the other hand the sum of the age-specific fertility rates obtained directly from reported births during the previous year, in conjunction with numbers of enumerated women classified by age, is 4.97.[23] (See Table 6.40.) If the births of deceased children are adjusted for underreporting on the assumptions stated above, using 0.9 as the value of s', the latter figure is raised to 5.35. Even this figure is probably seriously deflated by the gross overestimation of numbers of women classified as 15 to 45 years old—the broad age class that comprises the denominators of the age- specific fertility rates (*see* treatment of the age and sex composition of the Congolese population, Section II). If it were possible to adjust the age-specific fertility rates (corrected for underreporting of deceased chil- dren) to take account also of the erroneous age classifications of women,

[23] The reported figure is, of course, 5 times the sum of the five-year age-specific rates.

the sum of these adjusted rates would probably indicate more than 5.9 live births per woman.[24]

If we can assume (1) that women classed either as 45-54 years or 55 and over include only negligible proportions of much younger women, (2) that they are otherwise representative of Congolese women at or beyond the end of the childbearing period, and (3) that fertility in the Congo as a whole was not much lower when these older women were at their most fertile ages than it has been in recent years—all of which (with the possible exception of the last item) appear to be fairly safe assumptions—then it is obvious that the older women grossly underreported (by more than 25 percent) the children borne by them.

We found evidence (Section III) that even the younger women in some districts omitted some non-surviving children; alternative estimates of child mortality (derived from post-infant death rates) were substituted for the $q(a)$ values obtained directly from reports by mothers in these districts. This evidence could be used to provide some upward adjustment of the mean parity values indicated by the reports on children ever born. However, the adjustment would be inadequate. Moreover, the basis for such adjustment becomes dubious at later ages.

Retrospective reports by older women on numbers of children ever born, as obtained in various inquiries in different parts of Africa, often appear deficient. A comparison of reports on this subject by younger women with cumulated age-specific fertility rates (see Table 6.43) can be a useful means of detecting and estimating a bias in the "current" fertility rates that can be attributed to misinterpretations of the prescribed "reference period" (usually 12 months). Such an error, due to the inclusion of births over a longer interval or their limitation to a shorter interval than that prescribed, would presumably characterize, in more or less equal degree, the reports by women in all age classes. Examination of a series of parity-fertility ratios (P_i/F_i) showing the relations at particular ages of mean parity values (obtained from retrospective reports on children ever born alive) to cumulated fertility rates to the same ages (obtained from "current" reports on births during the previous year) may warrant the selection of the P/F ratio in a particular age interval (e.g., 20-24) as an index of bias in the whole series of specific fertility rates. The fertility rates, adjusted on the basis of this ratio, may then be used to provide reasonable estimates of total fertility and birth rates, free from the bias of error in the "reference period."[25]

The sequence of P/F values (see Table 6.44) in some of the districts of the Congo does not follow the pattern expected from the assumptions underlying the Brass method of estimating fertility. The level of P/F

[24] The basis for this statement will be explained at a later point in this section.
[25] This technique, developed by W. Brass, is described in Chapter 3.

Table 6.43. Average value of cumulative age-specific fertility (F) in each age group
—the Congo, provinces, and districts

	15-19	20-24	Ages of Women 25-29	30-34	35-44	45-54
Leopoldville Province	.185	1.266	2.683	3.888	4.904	5.487
Leopoldville	.531	1.856	3.354	4.656	-	-
Lac Leopold II	.380	1.534	2,827	3.911	4.830	5.561
Kwilu	.143	1.189	2.582	3.725	4.680	5.145
Kwango	.109	1.090	2.547	3.836	5.006	6.021
Bas-Congo	.259	1.398	2.794	3.903	4.792	5.378
Cataractes	.092	1.022	2.497	3.886	5.103	5.757
Equateur Province	.180	1.155	2.350	3.289	4.004	4.384
Equateur	.344	1.295	2.330	3.118	3.727	4.083
Mongala	.149	1.125	2.418	3.473	4.295	4.799
Ubangi	.157	1.273	2.693	3.787	4.665	5.114
Tshuapa	.175	0.949	1.857	2.558	3.063	3.343
Orientale Province	.369	1.261	2.125	2.738	3.201	3.477
Stanleyville	.617	1.547	2.386	2.936	3.267	3.545
Ituri	.169	1.356	2.779	3.896	4.907	5.439
Bas-Uele	.316	0.852	1.388	1.764	2.001	2.117
Haut-Uele	.353	1.111	1.787	2.204	2.462	2.636
Kivu Province	.488	1.760	3.158	4.241	5.073	-
Sud-Kivu	.411	1.753	3.322	4.533	5.912	6.573
Nord-Kivu	.502	1.868	3.446	4.774	5.810	6.423
Maniema	.620	1.571	2.446	3.063	3.509	3.694
Katanga Province	.585	1.951	3.349	4.424	5.966	-
Elisabethville	.695	2.217	3.757	4.924	-	-
Tanganyika	.650	2.105	3.549	4.710	5.822	6.551
Lualaba	.580	1.822	3.027	3.914	4.561	5.022
Haut-Lomani	.541	1.800	3.140	4.130	4.958	5.564
Luapula-Moero	.484	1,911	3.503	4.787	5.873	5.914
Kasai Province	.358	1.500	2.773	3.766	4.540	4.974
Lulua	.321	1.447	2.685	3.673	4.409	4.886
Sankuru	.262	1.357	2.610	3.526	4.178	4.610
Kabinda	.523	1.807	3.177	4.232	5.106	5.640
Kasai	.344	1.410	2.655	3.678	4.505	5.026
Congo	.33	1.46	2.72	3.70	4.44	4.89

for ages 25-29 is almost always very much lower than at 20-24, and a much higher level of "forgetting" at 25-29 does not seem plausible. In a number of districts P/F rises with age, rather than declining or remaining constant, as would be expected if reported parity is increasingly deficient for older respondents. Moreover, the pattern of age misreporting in at least some districts could hardly fail to distort the P/F ratios to an extent that would make their use for adjustment of fertility estimates questionable. (See the appendix to Chapter 3.)

In spite of the questionable sequence of P/F ratios, birth rates adjusted by P/F ratios for women 20-24 (given in Table 6.45) are more

Table 6.44. Ratio of average parity (*P*) to the average cumulative fertility rate (*F*)
in each age group—the Congo, provinces, districts

	15-19	20-24	Ages of Women 25-29	30-34	35-44	45-54
Leopoldville Province	1.114	1.051	.996	1.039	1.034	.946
Leopoldville	.904	.792	.760	.735	–	–
Lac Leopold II	.789	.860	.838	.775	.836	.766
Kwilu	1.119	1.060	.984	1.039	1.043	.972
Kwango	1.193	1.165	1.084	1.084	1.037	.895
Bas-Congo	1.042	1.037	1.013	1.061	1.102	1.054
Cataractes	1.304	1.282	1.258	1.323	1.299	1.157
Equateur Province	.939	.913	.804	.810	.816	.800
Equateur	.727	.749	.627	.632	.636	.612
Mongala	1.074	1.067	.910	.861	.847	.873
Ubangi	.955	.927	.843	.874	.922	.892
Tshuapa	.914	.790	.716	.758	.777	.835
Orientale Province	.954	.974	.768	.755	.794	.780
Stanleyville	.875	.950	.809	.800	.906	.883
Ituri	1.124	.848	.677	.739	.713	.677
Bas-Uele	.981	1.174	.886	.822	.885	.987
Haut-Uele	.850	.990	.789	.740	.816	.861
Kivu Province	1.070	1.147	1.050	1.021	.962	–
Sud-Kivu	.949	1.181	1.087	1.123	1.020	.936
Nord-Kivu	1.116	1.183	1.045	.995	.919	.757
Maniema	.919	1.057	.940	.953	.886	.937
Katanga Province	.926	.849	.734	.744	.713	.620
Elisabethville	1.036	.871	.745	.753	–	–
Tanganyika	.846	.793	.704	.715	.687	.551
Lualaba	.931	.873	.747	.782	.783	.733
Haut-Lomani	.924	.806	.720	.717	.674	.598
Luapula-Moero	.971	.984	.814	.856	.884	.883
Kasai Province	1.006	.960	.835	.860	.877	.838
Lulua	1.215	1.099	.927	.964	1.018	.999
Sankuru	1.069	.914	.755	.771	.792	.779
Kabinda	.841	.830	.749	.787	.748	.647
Kasai	.901	.957	.904	.903	.935	.889
Congo	1.033	.997	.878	.879	.867	.810

highly correlated with age distribution measures and the proportion of
women 25-34 who are childless than unadjusted birth rates (see Table
6.46).

Relative Frequency of Childlessness

The incidence of childlessness varies to a remarkable degree in the
districts of the Congo—from less than 4 percent in Kwango to nearly 50
percent in Bas-Uele among women 30-34 years of age (Table 6.47).
This wide range takes on added interest when the proportions childless
are compared with estimates of fertility based on births reported for the
preceding year, or on the age distribution, since the correlation with
these estimates of fertility is very high (Table 6.46).

Table 6.45. Crude birth rates (BR) as reported and estimated by various methods, and some other indices related to fertility—the Congo, provinces, and districts

	Reported BR	Adjusted BR By P/F	BR Adjusted for Under-reporting of Dead Children	BR Derived from Proportion under 5	Proportion of Children Based on the Population Registration	Proportion Childless Women Aged 25-34 (All)
Leopoldville Province	46.7	49.0	49.7	49.0	48.2	11.5
Leopoldville	52.2	41.3	53.6	45.0	44.4	16.3
Lac Leopold II	44.3	38.1	46.0	45.9	45.0	18.7
Kwilu	45.2	47.9	48.4	47.6	47.3	13.1
Kwango	48.1	56.1	51.8	53.8	52.8	5.3
Bas-Congo	48.0	49.8	52.9	47.7	45.7	11.5
Cataractes	45.0	57.7	48.7	50.2	53.3	6.7
Equateur Province	38.4	35.1	41.2	38.8	39.7	29.5
Equateur	33.7	25.3	34.9	32.5	32.3	38.9
Mongala	41.0	43.7	44.1	42.6	43.4	24.0
Ubangi	44.4	41.2	46.4	45.9	47.3	19.1
Tshuapa	30.5	24.1	33.9	28.6	30.9	42.3
Orientale Province	30.8	30.0	33.1	32.2	35.7	38.5
Stanleyville	34.0	32.3	36.0	35.3	35.6	34.4
Ituri	42.7	36.2		44.1	47.8	22.7
Bas-Uele	19.1	22.5	20.7	21.4	27.2	49.8
Haut-Uele	23.2	23.0	25.0	24.7	30.0	47.2
Kivu Province	47.2	54.2	51.9	53.4	47.4	11.6
Sud-Kivu	52.3	61.7	58.9	60.4	49.1	6.5
Nord-Kivu	49.4	58.4	53.1	57.9	52.2	5.2
Maniema	34.3	36.2	38.2	37.2	35.8	27.2
Katanga Province	50.2	42.6	52.7	51.9	44.0	20.6
Elisabethville	58.5	50.9	58.7	–	45.6	16.5
Tanganyika	54.2	43.0	56.4	50.9	44.4	22.7
Lualaba	44.1	38.5	45.8	47.8	43.4	23.2
Haut-Lomani	45.2	36.5	49.2	48.3	41.9	22.8
Luapula-Moero	56.0	55.1	58.6	58.0	47.5	14.3
Kasai Province	44.4	42.6	48.7	45.2	43.4	22.5
Lulua	43.1	47.3	47.9	48.5	45.8	19.6
Sankuru	41.6	38.0	45.9	41.7	38.4	29.4
Kabinda	48.2	40.0	50.7	48.3	45.4	22.1
Kasai	45.3	43.4	50.8	49.1	43.0	19.2
Congo	42.7	42.6	45.8	45.2	43.3	22.2

Table 6.46. Coefficients of correlation between various fertility measures

	Reported BR	Adjusted BR by P/F	BR Corrected for Under-Reporting of Children Born and Died during the Year	BR Derived from Proportion under 5	Proportion Children Registered	Childless Women Aged 25-34 Years
	1	2	3	4	5	6
Reported BR (42.74)	–	.803*	.988*	.939	.827	−.845
Adjusted BR by P/F (44.29)	.803*	–	.844*	.914	.899	−.945
BR corrected for under-reporting of Children Born and Died during the Year (46.06)	.988*	.844*	–	.957	.848	−.878
BR Derived from Proportion under 5 (45.22)	.939	.914	.957	–	.916	−.933
Proportion Children (Continuous Registration)	.827	.899	.848	.916	–	−.960
Childless Women Aged 25-34 Years	−.845	−.945	−.878	−.933	−.960	–

* These parameters lack complete independence.

A high incidence of childlessness in some districts of the Congo is strong presumptive evidence of the existence of pathological sterility, because almost every woman has married by the time she reaches the central childbearing ages, and because Congolese society places a high value on fertility. In other words, almost every woman is exposed to sexual relations, and the practice of any effective form of birth control must be extremely rare, especially for women who have borne no children.

It seems unlikely that Congolese women would exaggerate the incidence of childlessness, since it is commonly viewed as a source of dishonor and chagrin. Some women whose children had all died might possibly report themselves as childless through a misunderstanding or a

Table 6.47. Proportions (per 100) of women who are childless, by age, according
to the Demographic Inquiry—the Congo, provinces, and districts

	15-19	20-24	25-29	30-34	35-44	45-54	55+	15+
				Ages of Women				
Leopoldville Province	82.61	26.16	12.40	10.53	9.64	9.46	8.74	22.69
Leopoldville	63.86	22.24	14.07	18.60	21.79	35.72	31.37	25.88
Lac Leopold II	72.61	24.61	19.42	18.02	16.60	17.79	17.55	24.22
Kwilu	85.88	26.86	14.08	12.03	10.25	8.86	7.98	22.70
Kwango	87.92	25.49	6.80	3.74	2.73	3.41	4.66	17.98
Bas-Congo	76.61	22.66	11.39	11.12	11.45	9.00	7.53	23.35
Cataractes	90.32	35.16	8.71	4.65	3.36	4.29	4.93	23.73
Equateur Province	84.78	37.19	29.67	29.20	29.82	28.61	20.67	34.64
Equateur	78.26	42.71	39.06	38.69	40.70	40.02	27.81	41.37
Mongala	85.52	32.07	22.72	25.36	27.06	26.48	17.05	31.91
Ubangi	86.39	27.74	19.38	18.77	17.34	14.64	11.71	26.55
Tshuapa	85.41	52.77	44.05	40.49	38.43	32.98	24.68	41.67
Orientale Province	72.14	38.94	38.85	38.12	35.33	30.30	24.17	38.93
Stanleyville	59.29	33.51	34.41	34.31	28.64	23.27	20.38	33.90
Ituri	83.64	34.80	25.10	20.23	22.25	19.96	20.78	30.50
Bas-Uele	75.43	48.12	50.66	48.95	44.67	37.29	25.49	45.82
Haut-Uele	75.18	43.99	46.19	48.15	44.41	36.90	27.54	45.17
Kivu Province	65.86	15.61	11.96	11.27	11.53	11.34	14.75	11.93
Sud-Kivu	67.33	14.65	7.07	5.94	5.61	4.58	3.91	16.12
Nord-Kivu	69.11	9.60	5.28	5.06	5.62	8.30	5.98	18.32
Maniema	56.47	27.13	27.91	26.50	27.00	23.48	34.27	30.91
Katanga Province	60.94	23.35	20.12	22.09	21.40	23.16	21.78	–
Elisabethville	47.15	16.60	15.25	17.69	20.93	20.58	35.63	22.70
Tanganyika	65.87	25.20	22.34	22.98	22.25	27.37	24.01	28.42
Lualaba	59.16	25.21	24.07	22.30	20.18	17.83	13.07	25.78
Haut-Lomani	61.77	25.44	20.11	25.42	24.37	25.76	25.37	28.01
Luapula-Moero	63.48	18.84	14.23	14.28	12.02	10.92	14.87	20.96
Kasai Province	71.42	28.81	22.77	22.22	20.85	19.97	16.89	–
Lulua	73.11	26.56	21.25	18.05	14.72	12.74	10.29	23.53
Sankuru	73.91	33.02	28.69	29.83	29.32	25.68	23.28	32.00
Kabinda	64.13	26.96	21.53	22.73	23.68	26.25	22.24	27.27
Kasai	70.79	29.83	19.71	18.79	16.92	15.72	12.77	22.97
Congo	74.01	28.12	22.12	22.37	22.26	20.51	17.55	28.40

reluctance to refer to the dead, but wide prevalence of such a practice is not consistent with the progression of reported proportions childless from age 30-34 to 45-54.

In short, the high negative correlation of childlessness with estimates of fertility by district serves as a further validation of the estimates, and at the same time suggests a partial explanation of the wide range of estimated fertility levels—the prevalence in some districts of pathological sterility. Where many women are sterile in the sense of giving birth to no children, one would expect that many others might suffer fecundity impairment at parity one, two, or higher. The existence of a high frequency of sterility in some ethnic groups in the Congo is well known, notably among the Mongo-Nkundo people living mainly in Equateur Province and among the Azande in Orientale Province. It has been observed in many official and medical surveys and has been the subject of much speculation and inquiry. The same phenomenon appears in data from the census of the Sudan on the Azande population living in the Sudan across the border from Orientale Province.

Other Measures of Fertility:
General Fertility Rate and
Gross Reproduction Rate

In appraising fertility, demographers prefer and for some purposes require age-specific fertility rates and various functions of these rates, such as the total fertility rate (i.e., the sum of the age-specific rates) and the gross reproduction rate (i.e., the sum of the specific rates, daughters only). Lacking such detailed information they may use the "general fertility rate," defined as births per thousand women aged 15-44 years. Unfortunately all fertility measures relative to women of childbearing age in the Congo are distorted by age misreporting, which takes a form that seriously inflates the proportion of the population consisting of women 15-44. This distortion affects both the age-specific fertility rates (plus such derivative measures as total fertility) and the general fertility rate. Only crude birth rates based on estimated births and estimates of the *total* population are free of this distortion.

In Section II we used the stable age distribution for the Congo and its districts to estimate the magnitude and direction of distortion in the reported age distribution. We showed that, as far as the childbearing ages are concerned, there was a marked tendency to move the women from the adjacent age groups to the central age group 15 to 45, generating an excess of about 12 percent for the whole Congo in this central age group. The direct effect of this inflation is to produce an accordingly depressed estimate of the general fertility rate and total fertility.

The general fertility rate was estimated by dividing the estimated crude birth rate by the proportion *in the stable population* of women 15-44.[26]

This adjustment is fairly rough, for it does not take account of the possible effect of age-selective migration on the age distribution in particular districts. Nor is the age distribution a stable one, especially in the districts having experienced a declining fertility in the past. Nevertheless, the effect of these complicating factors probably is not important enough to offset the value of compensation for the considerable inflation in the childbearing age span.

The regional corrected general fertility rate is presented in Table 6.48.

[26] More precisely, the proportion of women 15-44 in the stable female population was used in conjunction with the recorded ratio of females to total population.

Table 6.48. Estimates of general fertility rate and of total fertility based on birth rates derived from proportion under age 5—the Congo, provinces, and districts

	BR' (1)	Adjusted General Fertility Rate GFR' (15-44) (2)	Gross Repro- duction Rate (GRR)' (3)	Total Fertility TF' (4)	Mean Age of Fertility Distribution $\overline{m}$
Leopoldville Province	49.00	227.56	3.32	6.74	28.00
Leopoldville	53.50	274.76	3.70	7.51	26.81
Lac Leopold II	45.85	207.88	3.02	6.13	27.53
Kwilu	47.62	205.80	3.09	6.27	27.76
Kwango	53.84	230.37	3.89	7.90	29.04
Bas-Congo	47.69	220.54	3.15	6.39	27.46
Cataractes	50.15	222.19	3.96	8.04	29.40
Equateur Province	38.76	173.21	2.48	5.03	27.26
Equateur	32.50	145.71	2.07	4.20	26.52
Mongala	42.58	204.57	2.78	5.64	27.81
Ubangi	45.93	205.99	3.00	6.09	27.43
Tshuapa	28.63	128.68	1.82	3.69	26.89
Orientale Province	32.18	145.33	1.99	4.04	26.00
Stanleyville	35.30	159.53	2.13	4.32	24.81
Ituri	44.11	205.71	-	-	29.20
Bas-Uele	21.44	96.15	1.42	2.88	25.14
Haut-Uele	24.65	106.81	1.57	3.19	24.91
Kivu Province	53.42	243.53	3.51	7.13	26.61
Sud-Kivu	60.43	284.83	4.18	8.49	27.11
Nord-Kivu	57.88	278.67	3.95	8.02	27.02
Maniema	37.21	167.81	2.22	4.51	24.83
Katanga Province	51.86	243.64	4.04	8.20	26.68
Elisabethville	58.70	338.13	4.10	8.32	26.79
Tanganyika	50.86	232.96	3.31	6.72	26.88
Lualaba	47.80	229.78	3.02	6.13	25.83
Haut-Lomani	48.26	213.07	3.15	6.39	26.59
Luapula-Moero	57.96	274.13	4.09	8.31	27.63
Kasai Province	45.24	197.93	2.89	5.87	26.85
Lulua	48.50	212.97	3.12	6.33	26.92
Sankuru	41.71	183.09	2.56	5.20	26.81
Kabinda	48.26	211.88	3.10	6.29	26.57
Kasai	49.09	210.72	3.20	6.50	27.19
Congo	45.22	202.75	2.91	5.91	27.02

(1) BR' based on the proportion under age 5 except for Leopoldville and Elisabethville for which the BR corrected for underreporting of deceased children is used.

(2) $GFR' = GFR \times \dfrac{BR'}{BR} \times \dfrac{R}{S}$ (15-44)

Where GFR is the reported general fertility rate, BR' and BR are respectively estimated and reported birth rates and R and S are respectively the reported and estimated (stable distribution) proportion for the age span 15-44 years.

(3) Derived by means of the models north (OPR) supplying the relationship between BR and GRR for a given mean of fertility distribution, $\overline{m}$.

(4) GRR x 2.03, where 1.03 is sex ratio at birth.

Total fertility can be estimated by recourse to model stable populations, since they give the relationship between the estimated (stable) birth rate and the gross reproduction rate. The use of the model tables requires knowledge of the mean age of the fertility distribution. This was calculated on the basis of the reported (nonadjusted) age-specific fertility rates (see Table 6.39). The total fertility is obtained from the gross reproduction rate by taking account of the sex ratio at birth. But here again we encounter a difficulty. The sex ratio of the reported births for the Congo appears too low, only 98 males per 100 females, while a sex ratio of 103 to 107 is generally observed in the countries with adequate statistics.

There is evidence however (see Section II) which indicates that the sex ratio among Negro populations (USA, Caribbean countries) is in the lower end of this range, about 103. In the absence of sufficient evidence to support any precise operation, we have simply adopted the sex ratio as being equal to 103, and multiplied the gross reproduction rates by 2.03 to get total fertility.

Thus we obtained 5.91 as the total fertility for the whole Congo as against 4.97 derived from the direct cumulation of reported age-specific rates. This is an appreciable correction (19 percent).

Because of the considerable age misreporting and its probable significant effects on the individual age-specific rates, one has to be cautious in accepting the mean age of the fertility distribution, $\bar{m}$, presented in Table 6.48. Unfortunately there is no way of achieving an adjustment of the individual age-specific rates by any procedure devised for adjustment of the gross childbearing rates at ages 15-44. An adjustment by the ratio of reported to stable proportion in each individual age group would lead to an implausible pattern of age-specific fertility. In fact, the mean age of the fertility distribution $\bar{m}$, based on the unadjusted age-specific fertility rates, seems to provide an acceptable indication of the age pattern of fertility in the Congo and particular districts. We find a significant negative correlation ($-.72$) between the proportion of married women in the 15 to 19 age group and the mean age of the fertility distribution. In other words, the higher the proportion of females married young (or the lower the age at marriage), the younger the age pattern of fertility.

Final Appraisal

Various rates and indices when assembled show what is, for Africa, a remarkable standard of consistency with respect to the level of fertility as well as with respect to its regional variation. They all tell essentially the same story. Two estimates of the birth rate are particularly notable for their consistency: (1) the estimates derived from reports by women during the previous year, adjusted for underreporting of the births of deceased children and (2) the series based on proportions of persons under 5 years of age in each population. There is little basis for preference between these two.

The possible effects of migration on the latter series make the former preferred for rapidly growing centers, notably Leopoldville and Elisabethville, and as a basis of comparison between levels of fertility in the rural, mixed, and urban segments of the population.

Otherwise, preference will be given here to the latter series (based on the proportions of children under age 5). In the first place, this avoids dependence on any arbitrary factor, whereas the alternative series involves some estimate, which is necessarily arbitrary, of the proportion of the omitted births of children dying in infancy that occurred within the reference period. Moreover, the time reference implicit in using proportions of children under 5 years in the estimation of birth rates (namely, the five years prior to the survey) provides a somewhat firmer basis for estimation of general levels than the experience of a single year. This time period also fits that implicit in the use of child $q(a)$ values better than the year prior to the survey. Finally, we suspect that, in spite of the reliance on estimates of child mortality required on this procedure, it is rather less vulnerable to any sort of serious bias than the reports on births during the previous year.

CONCLUSION OF STUDY OF THE POPULATION OF THE CONGO

The substantive results of our study of the Congo can be summarized as follows:

1. The total Congolese population in 1956 was probably close to 13,000,000 inhabitants. The credibility of this estimate is enhanced by the fact that both the Demographic Inquiry (1955-57) and the continuous registration (1956), two largely independent sources of information, lead to very similar results concerning the size of the population in the Congo and its regional distribution.

In the period considered here (around 1956), 78 percent of the population was rural (residing in traditional villages), 10 percent was urban (nonagricultural in cities of more than 2,000 inhabitants), and 12 percent was mixed (in small commercial, administrative, and industrial conglomerations of less than 2,000 persons).

2. The crude death rate of the Congo is estimated at 26 deaths per thousand persons; this corresponds to an expectancy of life at birth $(e°_0)$ of 39.5 years. From various statistics considered in this study one can infer with great likelihood that the average death rate in the Congo around 1956 was not below 20 per thousand and not above 30, with a rate close to 25 as the most plausible estimate.

Rates in the vicinity of 25 per thousand are obtained from three largely independent sources: the post-infant deaths, reported for the year preceding the demographic survey; the children surviving among the children ever born to each mother, reported by the Demographic Inquiry; and the death rate, based on the difference between the estimate of birth rate (inquiry) and the rate of increase derived from the annual figures on the population (continuous registration), for a period of eight years (after rectification for possible effect of migration).

Among the most conspicuous negative aspects of the analysis is the finding that the infant mortality is invariably underestimated as far as the current reports on mortality are concerned. Therefore, it was necessary to derive the infant death rate from the combined resources offered by the post-infant mortality based on the data on the deaths which had occurred during the 12 last months preceding the survey, and by the $q(a)$ values based on the children surviving among the children ever born to women by age. The estimated infant mortality rate estimated on this basis amounts to 165 deaths under age of 1 year per thousand births for the whole Congo.

With respect to the age pattern of mortality, available indications are that a relatively low infant mortality is associated with a relatively high child mortality (ages 1-4). If this is so, then it would bring the Congolese mortality age pattern into accordance with the mortality pattern inherent in the North model, based on the life tables available for the Scandinavian countries. However, more and better data are needed to reach certitude in this matter.

In view of the approximative character of the basic information, little can be inferred from the analysis with respect to the regional variation of mortality. It is likely that the errors involved in the data are larger than the regional differences in mortality. It does not seem, however, that the regional variations, with probably few exceptions, are very important in the Congo in view of the fact that the medical assistance was relatively equally spread over the country.

By contrast, the rural-urban difference in mortality is considerable and consistent with the actual health conditions having prevailed in these communities at the end of the colonial regime. The death rate is estimated at about 28 per thousand for the rural populations, 16 for the urban, and about 20 for the mixed. These rates correspond to an expectancy of life at birth of 35, 50, and 44 years.

3. Perhaps the most valuable product of this study is the set of estimated measures of fertility. The average crude birth rate for the Congo is estimated at 45 births per thousand persons. This estimate is supported by various lines of evidence: reported births corrected for underreporting of dead children; birth rate derived from the proportion under age 5; and birth rate based on parity, that is, children ever born

to a woman. It is unlikely that in a country where sterility is so unusually high (over 20 percent of the women past the age of menopause being childless) the true birth rate could be far above the estimated rate (45 per thousand). Nor can it be much below this point, for a rate close to 40 (in 1958) is obtained from the figure provided by the official birth registration, in spite of the fact that there was still a considerable underregistration of births.

There is a surprising range between the highest and lowest fertility among the districts. On the one hand, there are districts (North and South Kivu, Kwango, Cataractes, etc.) where the birth rate exceeds 50 and approaches an exceptionally high rate of 60 per thousand. On the other hand, there are populations, especially in the central and northeastern parts of the country (districts of Equateur, Tshuapa, Maniema, Stanleyville) with the unusually low fertility of 25-35. Bas- and Haut-Uele districts exhibit a rate of only 20-25 per thousand.

There was no attempt made in this study to establish the underlying reasons for these striking differences in fertility rates among regions. However, childlessness appears to be the main immediate cause responsible for the low fertility observed in certain regions.

Indeed there is a high correlation (see Table 6.47) between the estimated birth rate and childless women. The high fertility districts are mostly those where the sterility is low (under 10 per thousand women aged over 45) and the low fertility districts are those with a high sterility rate (35 to 50 percent of the women). It is not within the scope of this study to deal with the problems and causes of this unusually high sterility. There can be no doubt that the sterility is involuntary and physiological. Venereal diseases were indicated as being responsible for this pathological childlessness.[27]

Although the urban-rural difference in fertility has not been thoroughly examined in this study, it suffices to mention that there is a higher natality among the urban as compared to rural communities. The adjusted birth rate is 44 for rural and 52 for urban areas. This difference is partly attributable to the more favorable age structure of the urban population, partly to a higher proportion of urban married women, especially in younger age classes. Whether there are genuine differences in the fecundity between the rural and urban areas resulting from better health conditions or from some psychological stimulus to procreate more, or from absence of certain customs inhibiting fertility, in those two communities is an open question subject to further investigation.

[27] A. Romaniuk, *Aspect démographique de la stérilité des femmes congolaises*, Institut de Recherches Economiques et Sociales, Studia Universitatis, Lovanium, Editions de l'Université Leopoldville, 1961. Also "Fécondité et stérilité des femmes congolaises," paper presented by A. Romaniuk at the World Population Meeting in New York 1961.

4. Rate of natural increase—the final concern of this study—amounts to 1.9 percent per year. At this rate, the population has a tendency to double its number about every 37 years.

It is worthwhile mentioning that the examination of a series of annual figures of population for a period of eight years (the continuous registration records for 1950 to 1958) yields an average actual rate of annual increase of 2.03 per hundred. The excess of the latter as compared to the former might be due partly to immigration from outside which has prevailed over outmigration during the period. If correction is made for the effect of the net migration, the rate of natural increase becomes very close for the two sources.

The regional variation in the estimated growth rate is largely the result of estimated regional differences in fertility. The low-fertility regions exhibit a low or even a negative rate of increase (Uele), while the rate is between 2 and 3 per hundred in the high-fertility districts. Among the two components of the natural growth rate estimate, the death rate is less reliable than the birth rate. Thus in some districts, as Equateur, Lac Leopold II, and Luapula-Moero, the death rate seems to be underestimated and, hence, the rate of increase overestimated. The impression of an understatement of growth rate in these districts is supported by the growth rate (not discussed in this study) based on the figures on population abstracted from continuous registration, for the period 1950-58.

Table 6.49 presents the final basic demographic measures for the Congo and its political divisions for the period covered by the Demographic Inquiry (1955-57).

Table 6.49. Summary table of demographic indices based on the results provided by the Demographic Inquiry 1955-57 in the Congo

	Total Population (De Facto) (thousands)	Birth Rate	Death Rate	Rate of Natural Increase
Leopoldville Province	3,050	49.0	24.8	24.2
Leopoldville	318	53.5	11.6	41.9
Lac Leopold II	271	45.9	20.5	25.4
Kwilu	1,143	47.6	26.2	21.4
Kwango	466	53.8	32.3	21.5
Bas-Congo	412	47.7	26.1	21.6
Cataractes	439	50.2	25.9	24.3
Equateur Province	1,756	38.8	23.1	15.7
Equateur	302	32.5	17.1	15.4
Mongala	519	42.6	19.3	23.3
Ubangi	539	45.9	25.5	20.4
Tshuapa	395	28.6	24.9	3.7
Orientale Province	2,336	32.2	23.6	8.6
Stanleyville	635	35.3	21.2	14.1
Ituri	651	44.1	-	-
Bas-Uele	468	21.4	27.8	-6.4
Haut-Uele	582	24.7	24.1	.6
Kivu Province	2,013	53.4	29.7	23.7
Sud-Kivu	831	60.4	38.3	22.1
Nord-Kivu	735	57.9	27.0	30.9
Maniema	446	37.2	26.0	11.2
Katanga Province	1,501	51.9	21.8	30.1
Elisabethville	140	58.7	15.9	42.8
Tanganyika	397	50.9	20.8	30.1
Lualaba	320	47.8	18.6	29.2
Haut-Lomani	452	48.3	26.4	21.9
Luapula-Moero	192	58.0	23.3	34.7
Kasai Province	2,121	45.2	30.0	15.2
Lulua	654	48.5	34.1	14.4
Sankuru	494	41.7	24.3	17.4
Kabinda	480	48.3	24.1	24.2
Kasai	493	49.1	37.0	12.1
Congo	12,777	45.2	26.1	19.1

FORMULAIRE N° I

1	Numéro d'ordre		
2	Maison ou hutte n°		
3	Nom et prénoms		
4	Tribu		
5	Masculin	Sexe	
6	Féminin		
7	Lieu de naissance		
8	— de 1	Durée de séjour	
9	1 - 5		
10	+ de 5		
11	Age connu avec exactitude		
12	M	0 - 1	AGE
13	F		
14	M	1 - 4	
15	F		
16	M	5 - 9	
17	F		
18	M	10 - 14	
19	F		
20	M	15 - 19	
21	F		
22	M	20 - 24	
23	F		
24	M	25 - 29	
25	F		
26	M	30 - 34	
27	F		
28	M	35 - 44	
29	F		
30	M	45 - 54	
31	F		
32	M	+ de 55	
33	F		

34	Monogame	H	Mariés — ETAT MATRIMONIAL
35	Bi- ou polygame		
36	Epouse de monogame	F	
37	Epouse de polygame		
38	Homme		Divorcés
39	Ancienne épouse de monogame	F	
40	Ancienne épouse de polygame		
41	Homme		Veufs
42	Ancienne épouse de monogame	H	
43	Ancienne épouse de polygame		
44	Homme	Célibataires	
45	Femme		
46	Naissances vivantes		Naissances au cours de l'existence de la mère — NAISSANCES
47	Enfants encore en vie		
48	Garçons		Naissances au cours des 12 mois qui ont précédé le sondage
49	Filles		
50	Mort-nés		
51	Naissances légitimes		
52	Naissances illégitimes		
53	Naissances monogamiques		
54	Naissances polygamiques		
55	Enfants encore en vie		
56	Religion		INSTRUCTION ET LANGUES
57	Langue parlée au foyer		
58	Français		Autres langues parlées
59	Lingala		
60	Kikongo		
61	Tshiluba		
62	Kiswahili		
63	Aptitude à lire et à écrire dans une langue quelconque		
64	Incomplet	Primaire	Degré d'instruction
65	Complet		
67	Incomplet	Post-primaire	
68	Complet		
68	(Personnes travaillant pour leur propre compte)	Population active	OCCUPATION
69	SALARIES (Personnes travaillant pour compte d'autrui)		
70	Personnes n'exerçant aucune activité lucrative	Population inactive	
71	CHOMEURS		

Divers

FORMULAIRE N° 2

(DÉCÈS)

Province : _____

District : _____

Territoire : _____

C. I. ou Centre : _____

Village : _____

Date _____

Nom de l'enquêteur : _____

PARCELLE N°	NOM DU DEFUNT	AGE DE LA PERSONNE DÉCÉDÉE																						TOTAL	
		0 - 1		1 - 4		5 - 9		10 - 14		15 - 19		20 - 24		25 - 29		30 - 34		35 - 44		45 - 54		+ 55			
		M	F	M	F	M	F	M	F	M	F	M	F	M	F	M	F	M	F	M	F	M	F	M	F
		1	2	3	4	5	6	7	8	9	10	11	12	13	14	15	16	17	18	19	20	21	22	23	24

7

The Demography of French-Speaking Territories Covered by Special Sample Inquiries: Upper Volta, Dahomey, Guinea, North Cameroon, and Other Areas

BY WILLIAM BRASS

Introduction

In the past ten years a number of demographic sample inquiries have been carried out in African territories formerly administered by France. The data obtained are extensive by African standards and of a particularly useful kind. These surveys were conducted with similar aims and procedures and controlled by statisticians and demographers drawing on a common body of experience. As a consequence the records have been collected and tabulated in the different areas in much the same form. In addition, as will be shown in detail later, there are characteristic errors in the recording and typical inconsistencies among the measures derived from the observations.

The similarities of these features make it convenient to treat the studies of these territories as an integral whole. Thus, there are many points in the analysis which hold for all or most of the inquiries. This chapter will, therefore, consist of an opening section in which the general nature of the materials, methods, and results will be discussed, followed by studies of the particular areas in detail with special reference to findings which are exceptional or anomalous.

The records analyzed were from sample inquiries covering the countries of Guinea (1954-55); Upper Volta (1960-61); Dahomey (1961); and parts of territories, namely the Northern section of the Republic of Cameroon (1960); Centre-Oubangui in the Central African Republic (1959); the Fouta-Toro region of the middle valley of the River Senegal, which is partly in Senegal and partly in Mauritania (1957); a small sector of the Ivory Coast (1957-58); the area on the River Niger around Mopti in Mali (1958). The results of these surveys have been published in varying degrees. In particular a very full and detailed report of the methods and statistics of the Guinea inquiry is available, but only partial and less complete accounts of the Upper Volta and Dahomey studies. It has, however, been possible to extract the basic information required for the present analysis, although in a few instances by indirect calculation from derived tables rather than from the raw data. Because of this some of the measures used here may be slightly different from the values which would have been obtained from the actual reported numbers, but the effect on the results is minimal.

Descriptions of the organization and field procedures for collecting the data are given in the survey reports. In the studies following only a relatively small section of the records collected will be utilized. This is partly because the aim is to estimate basic demographic measures of fertility, mortality, and growth as accurately as possible and partly because of the gaps in the information in these areas for which only partial results have been published. Full accounts of the survey methods and materials will not be given, therefore, but only a brief indication of those aspects which are directly relevant to the analyses of the observations.

It should be mentioned in particular that no attempt is made to examine the extensive information on nuptiality, including polygyny, in this section. These topics are examined in Chapter 5. Also there is no account of rural-urban differentials, although there are materials for such study. Because of the complex patterns of migration between rural areas and towns it is very difficult to apply the techniques for checking the accuracy of the recording to data for these environments separately.

The Records Analyzed

All the surveys were sample inquiries in which the fundamental unit was the household. Representative clusters of these were selected by stratified random sampling; the clusters were usually villages, but in some cases where these were not of a convenient size a frame of groups of households was constructed. Each of the sample households was visited by an enumerator who entered on a schedule both collective information, e.g., of births and deaths, and details of individuals in the family of a standard type—sex, age, marital status, occupation, etc. The enumerators did not just passively record the data as reported but attempted to check, wherever possible, that the questions were understood and the answers reasonable.

The primary data for the estimation of fertility and mortality are of two kinds, denoted by the terms "current" and "retrospective." The current information was obtained from questions about deaths in the past year by age of deceased and about births by age of mother. The retrospective material consists of reports by mothers, divided by age group, on the total number of children born to them and those still alive at the time of the survey. For most of the areas the retrospective data on numbers of children ever born and numbers surviving are not given separately for males and females, although current mortality is divided by sex. Presumably these data will all be tabulated by sex in the final reports. Although the lack of this division makes it necessary to introduce some rather arbitrary adjustments in the examination of age distributions by quasi-stable population techniques, any additional error is small. Furthermore, there are advantages in the amalgamation of the data for males and females in much of the material studied because of the reduction in sample variation. Age distributions by sex have been tabulated in all the areas for the intervals under 1 year, 1 to 4, 5 to 9, and thereafter in the standard five- or ten-year groups.

Tabulations are given for most areas of the distributions of women by age group and number of children born to them. This material is important in itself, particularly for the study of childlessness where fertility is low. It can also throw some light on the possibility of certain types of misrecording, e.g., misallocation of women for whom information on childbearing was not received to the group with no births. However, the true variability in such distributions can be very considerable, and such data alone can reveal large errors only. If information on the order of births occurring in the last 12 months is also tabulated, comparisons of the two sets of results can be a very powerful means of illuminating the sources of error and arriving at accurate estimates. Such tabulations have as yet been published only for Guinea. Their analysis is helpful in determining the features of misreporting in that inquiry.

Wherever possible the indices used in these studies have been computed from the raw data on numbers even if similar measures are presented in published reports. The indices given here therefore sometimes differ slightly from those published even when there is no adjustment of the observations. For example, the probabilities of dying are derived from the age-specific mortality rates by formulae which are slightly different from those used for the calculations in the official reports. In addition there are a few cases where corrections have been made to obvious misprints or errors in the published data. All of these changes are minor. Although there would have been little or no difference in the final estimates if the published measures had been used throughout (in a few instances they are necessarily adopted because actual numbers are not given), it was judged better to preserve consistency among the calculations for different populations and with the theoretical models on which the analysis is based.

The sampling errors of the derived indices depend, in the main, on the variations in the measurements among the clusters of households which are the primary units. It would only be possible to calculate such sampling errors if information on the data collected were available in considerable detail, and the computations would be very laborious. Since the observations are also affected by bias, due to reporting errors, which in many instances is clearly much larger than any possible sampling variation, it is doubtful whether these laborious computations would be justified. It is not easy even to guess at the order of the sampling errors of different measurements. It is clear, however, that these could be very substantial for indices based on numbers which are only a small proportion of the total sample size (e.g., the deaths in an age group in the year preceding the inquiry, used in the calculations of the current age-specific mortality rates). These remarks have special force in the consideration of the characteristics of the regional or tribal sub-groups of the population which are examined for Upper Volta, Dahomey, Guinea, and North Cameroon. The sample errors for some of the component indices must be high there.

Because of the errors it is necessary to be cautious about drawing any conclusions from an individual measurement for a small sub-section of the data. Only if there is evidence of consistent patterns or trends, preferably in a number of regions, can deductions be made with fair confidence. Although the argument is put forward primarily in terms of sampling variation, it is reinforced by the possibility that the effects of erratic fluctuations in demographic events, e.g., births and deaths, from year to year could be considerable. Again it is by no means unlikely that when reporting errors are high, individual aberrations of particular measurements will occur as well as more widespread distortions.

Organization of Account

The analysis has been organized in five sections: the account for Upper Volta is presented in section A; for Dahomey in section B; for Guinea in section C; for North Cameroon in section D, and for Centre-Oubangui, Fouta-Toro, the Ivory Coast, and Mopti areas in section E. Each section is arranged in four sub-sections, which deal with fertility, mortality, reproduction, and age distribution, respectively. In each of these sub-sections the details of the applications of the techniques developed in Chapter 3 are described, the methodological features of the results common to the different sets of data discussed, and conclusions drawn about the nature of the reporting errors and the value of the estimates of demographic measures. At all stages the relevance of the characteristics of indices of one type to the accuracy of observations of a different kind is kept in mind. In particular, however, the last sub-section is mainly concerned with the use of age-distribution records to check the validity of the estimates of fertility, mortality, and reproduction. The substantive results are not discussed here but in the overall review in Chapter 4. For convenience, similar sets of tables have been prepared for each case study; the tables giving corresponding statistics are specified by the same number, i.e., the second number in the heading (the first is the chapter number), which will be used for reference.

Fertility

In each section the age-specific fertility rates calculated from the births reported in the preceding year are given in Tables 7.1 (i.e., 7.1.A, 7.1.B, etc.). From these with the aid of the measures of the location of the fertility distribution in Tables 7.2, cumulated births per woman (F) were constructed as described in Chapter 3, and compared with the observed retrospective values for corresponding age groups (P) by means of the P/F ratios. In all cases the correction to allow for the fact that the women were half a year younger on the average at the birth of their children was applied. The ratios are shown in Tables 7.3. With the notable exceptions of Guinea and the Hill Pagan group in North Cameroon there is reasonably good agreement between the cumulated fertility and retrospective parity for the younger women (in effect for age groups 20-24 and 25-29 since the procedure is unreliable at ages 15-19). Apart from the areas indicated the discrepancy does not exceed 10 percent. Nor is the disagreement necessarily always or entirely due to misreporting, since birth fluctuations could easily cause small genuine differences in the values compared. In all cases of appreciable discrepancy the P/F ratios are less than 1.00, suggesting that too many births were noted as occurring in the preceding year. The most plausible explanation is that the average reference period within which events were reported was longer than a year (in parts of Guinea by as much as one-third). The possibility that the net error was decreased because a too long reference period was offset by omissions of current births is not excluded.

The P/F ratios fall with age in most of the populations, although there are erratic fluctuations, particularly for regions or tribes. This is to be expected because of sampling and periodic variations even if there are no distortions due to misreporting. The size of the fall ranges from slight to a 25 percent decrease for the oldest age groups of women, but in many cases it is of the order of 10 percent. The most obvious explanation of the tendency is that some of the children of the older women were not reported. It accounts for the form of the ratios satisfactorily and is plausible in the light of experience in other surveys. Although some part of the trend in particular areas might be due to increasing fertility, and age errors may have exaggerated the effect, neither of these possibilities explains convincingly both the pattern and consistency of the results. The variation in the size of the decrease with age will be considered further in the detailed case studies. In the regions where the P/F ratios rise substantially with age (North Cameroon and Centre-Oubangui), the older women reported larger average families than did those at the end of the reproductive period, and the estimates of current birth rates are low. There is a strong presumption that fertility has fallen, and other supporting evidence for this will be given later.

Correction factors were derived from the P/F ratios for the younger women as described in Chapter 3. They are used to adjust the current rates to consistency with the retrospective reports of children by these women. It is not necessarily implied either that the recorded births in the past year were wrong or that the fall in the P/F ratios with age was due to omissions. Sample fluctuations and trends could play a part, but the aim is to obtain the best estimate from the observations as a whole. In general the correction factor was taken as the value of the P/F ratio at 20-24 years. In a few of the series of data the P/F ratio drops sharply between the age groups 20-24 and 25-29 years (sometimes from slightly above 1.00 for the first group), and thereafter there is little or no decrease. The sharp drop for these young mothers is unlikely to be due to differential forgetting, which would have to be large since there is no evidence of such an extreme effect at later years. The high P/F ratios at ages 20-24 years are taken to be spurious; it can be shown that the effect could easily arise from errors in age recording, particularly if these were influenced by the number of children born to the women. The correction factor is then taken to be between the ratios at 20-24 and 25-29 years. Of course there is an arbitrary element in the procedure. More elaborate methods of estimation by fitting trends to the P/F ratios could easily be devised, but the changes in the derived correction factors would be slight and any improvement in accuracy hard to confirm. Because of the difficulty of establishing reliably the level of fertility of the younger women from the retrospective reports, the estimated correction factor could have an appreciable error even if the assumptions were completely valid.

The percentages of women who reported no children and the children ever born per mother are given in Tables 7.4. Although there are no very striking features, some evidence to support the previous conclusions can be extracted. In North Cameroon and Centre-Oubangui the proportions childless are lower for the older women than for those near the end of the reproductive period, consistent with the suggestion that fertility has fallen there. The pattern is particularly notable because in the other regions there is very little indication of variations in the proportions childless with age after 30 or 35 years. In these the fall in the P/F ratios for the older women is clearly not due to the exaggeration of the numbers with no children. There is some slight backing for the validity of the correction factors, because their application leads to improved consistency in the relations of birth rates to the percentages childless. Thus, in Guinea, the Upper region becomes appreciably the most fertile after adjustment, contrary to the reported current rates, and the percentage childless at the end of the reproductive period (3-4 percent) is the lowest recorded; the birth rate for the Ivory Coast is reduced from very high to high, and a moderate proportion (9 percent) of the older women had no live births.

The reported numbers of births were multiplied by the correction factors to give adjusted totals. In many of the regions the size of the male population was affected by migration, e.g., from rural to urban areas and seasonal labor movements. In order to nullify such influences and obtain more stable measures, adjusted female birth rates were calculated and are shown in Tables 7.2. It was assumed that the corrected births were in the ratio 103 male to 100 female; the derived female births were then expressed as a rate to the total female population. A fixed sex ratio was used rather than the recorded value for current births because (a) the latter has a high sampling variation and (b) differential errors in reporting by sex are not unlikely. There is some evidence that the sex ratio at birth may be low in Africa; the value chosen is in good agreement with the combined statistics from all the inquiries analyzed (including some divisions of the retrospective data by sex) and also with a long series of hospital records from the Congo (Leopoldville). The correction factors were applied to births rather than the current total fertility ratios because the latter are sensitive to errors in the reporting of ages of women in the reproductive period. Such errors are evident and will be discussed later.

Mortality

From the retrospective reports of the proportions of children dead by age of mother, life table survivorship ratios l_x at particular ages were estimated by the methods of Chapter 3. The results are presented in Tables 7.5. The current specific death rates by age group were calculated from the deaths reported in the preceding year; the corresponding probabilities of dying and the l_x values were derived by standard methods and are shown in Tables 7.6. At ages above 5 years the relations of probabilities of dying to the specific rates were taken from the Reed-Merrel tables. At under 1 year and 1 to 4 years the formulae adopted were:

$$1q_0 = \frac{1m_0}{1 + 0.7 \, 1m_0} \, 1m_0; \quad 4q_1 = \frac{4 \, 4m_1}{1 + 2.7 \, 4m_1} \, 4m_1$$

where q and m denote probabilities of dying and specific rates respectively. These formulae were calculated from the mortality pattern of the African "standard" life table of the model system used in the analysis. The assumption of other relations between probabilities of dying and specific rates for calculation purposes (such as adopted in the published reports on the inquiries) would have given slightly different results but not have appreciably affected the conclusions or estimates.

To assess the accuracy of the reports of mortality and graduate the observations the functional life table model system was applied. The logit of l_x will be denoted by $Y(a)$, where $Y(a) = \frac{1}{2}\log_e[q(a)/p(a)]$, or logit $p(a)$ and the corresponding measure for the African standard life table by $Y_s(a)$ where $Y_s(a) = \frac{1}{2}\log_e[q_s(a)/p_s(a)]$, or logit $p_s(a)$ [see equation (8) of Chapter 3]. It is assumed that on this scale the relation of any life table with the standard is approximately linear with slope β. For convenience the equation is written in the form $Y(a) - Y(2) = \beta[Y_s(a) - Y_s(2)]$. Thus the survivorship ratio at age 2 years is selected to represent infant mortality, and β measures the steepness, relative to the standard, with which death rates increase with age from childhood onward. The proportion of infants dying by age 2 is taken as the index of child mortality rather than more conventional measures for a number of reasons. It is derived from the retrospective reports of children dead to the age groups of mothers (20-24 years) whose experience is most recent and reliable (numbers for mothers aged 15-19 are too small); the relationship to death rates at later ages is more consistent from population to population for mortality under 2 years than under 1; the proportion surviving to age 2 is a good guide for the selection of an age distribution in stable population models.

The "linearization" by the use of the logit scale and an appropriate standard life table is, of course, very approximate, but it highlights erratic fluctuations and large deviations from the norm. The slope β indicates tendencies only, and its use for graduation is particularly speculative at the higher ages. Nevertheless, the observations are so doubtful that only very broad effects can be discerned. The logit scale is particularly useful in comparing the survivorship ratios estimated from the retrospective and current data because the values from the two methods are not always at corresponding ages and interpolation is necessary. These comparisons are given in Figure 7.1 of each section. For graphical illustration it is more illuminating to work with the difference of the logits, $h(a) = Y(a) - Y_s(a)$; the assumed equation is then $h(a) = Y(2) - Y_s(2) + (\beta-1)[Y(a) - Y_s(a)]$. When $\beta = 1.00$, the "central" value, the graph of $h(a)$ is a straight line parallel to the age axis.

The consistency of the points on the graphs, from both current and retrospective reports, varies greatly among regions. Little weight can be attached to the level at 1 year of age because these estimates are suspect; the current values have clearly been affected by omissions of deaths perhaps to a greater extent than at later years; the retrospective measures suffer from the difficulties of determining the mean length of exposure to risk for births to women under 20 years. Nevertheless the $h(a)$ values at ages 1 to 10 years show little tendency to deviate systematically from constant levels, although these are different for the two sets of measures. In other words, they conform to the mortality pattern of the African standard life table with the death rate at 1 to 4 years relatively high compared with that under 1. The use of a standard life table that is based on the average experience of all countries with acceptable data, rather than the North set of regional models of the Coale-Demeny system,[1] gives much more distorted $h(a)$ values. For reasons which are discussed below the survivorship ratios at ages beyond childhood obtained from the retrospective data are not acceptable, but the points on the graph derived from current mortality do not suggest that the fitting of a straight line trend is unreasonable. In several areas (Upper Volta, Dahomey, North Cameroon) the $h(a)$ points are approximately parallel to the age axis, indicating a value of β close to 1.00, but in others (Guinea, Mopti) the slope is considerable.

In general the childhood mortality of the current life tables is substantially lower than that implied by the retrospective reports of the proportion of children dead. The difference exists at the earliest ages, and there is no evidence that it increases with age. Although it is possible to conceive that such a result could follow from a sudden decrease in child mortality just prior to the survey, plus some error in age recording of current deaths at the very early years, the suggestion seems very implausible; the same pattern appears in data collected at different periods from populations in diverse stages of economic and social development. Nor is it reasonable to attribute the differential to mistakes in age reporting. The mortalities estimated from the retrospective observations are very insensitive to errors in the ages of the mothers. In order to bring the current rates of childhood mortality into line with the retrospective ones, an increase in some instances (South Dahomey and the Plain Pagans in North Cameroon) as much as 50 percent of those reported would be needed. Since the number of deaths in the age groups from 5 years to adulthood are relatively small, it is difficult to see how these extra deaths could be accounted for by a wrong age scale alone. The effect could only occur if reported ages at death had little relation to the true values. If this were so, the whole pattern of the life table would be destroyed, which is not in accord with the comparisons of Figures 7.1. It is true that in some areas the specific death rates recorded at ages 5 to young adulthood are high (particularly in Guinea), but this is not so in other regions where a large differential between current and retrospective childhood mortality exists.

The argument for a genuine difference in the reporting of the number of childhood deaths in the two types of record is overwhelming. The cause could be either an overstatement of retrospective deaths, an understatement of current ones, or both. It is difficult to believe that more retrospective deaths than occurred were reported, except possibly by the inclusion of stillbirths as deaths, and these would presumably be

[1] Ansley J. Coale and Paul Demeny, *Regional Model Life Tables and Stable Populations*, Princeton University Press, 1966. See also Chapter 3, pp. 124 ff.

counted as live births also. If such errors happened it seems likely that stillbirths would equally be included with the current events and the differential nullified. The most satisfactory explanation is that the deaths of children in the past year are underreported. It is possible that the omissions are partly compensated by the inclusion of stillbirths with child deaths, but it would be unwise to make any adjustment for this for the reasons discussed below.

Although there is no case for rejecting the patterns of early mortality shown by the observations on the internal evidence, an extreme division of the deaths under 5 years between the 0-1 and 1-4 age groups is implied. In general the $h(a)$ value at 1 year is less than those at later ages of childhood, and the mortality under 1 lower relative to the incidence in the next age group compared with the African standard life table. Despite the reservations about the validity of the measures, the possibility that some deaths of very young children have been omitted in both the current and retrospective reports cannot be ignored. There is no method of checking on the omission of early deaths by internal comparisons. However, the mortality patterns make it very unlikely that any appreciable overestimation could occur, on balance, due to the inclusion of stillbirths with the deaths. To correct for such an error it would be necessary to reduce the deaths under 1 year. Any such correction of practical importance would lead to the deaths in this group being a smaller proportion of the total under 5 years than for any set of reliable data of other populations.

To summarize, the level of mortality from the retrospective reports is accepted as the best estimate that can be made. It seems likely on the basis of general experience that some deaths (and the corresponding births) of children surviving a very short time will have been omitted (perhaps offset by inclusions of stillbirths), but the basis for making an adjustment or the certainty that one is required is lacking. The estimates of child mortality may plausibly be taken as lower limits. Since they are universally high (the proportion of children dead by age 5 varies from 30 to 50 percent, with most values in the range 35-40 percent), the scope for error is reduced.

To graduate the survivorship ratios at early ages, calculated from the retrospective observations, the logit differences $h(a)$ at 2, 3, and 5 years were used (the value at 1 year was omitted as unreliable). The mean of the three values was taken as the estimate of the difference $h(2)$ at age 2 and fitted values of $Y(2)$ and l_2 thus obtained. An approximate first estimate of l_5 was found by applying the same difference. The proportional increase in the reported current deaths under 5 years required to bring the corresponding survivorship ratio into agreement with this value of l_5 was then calculated. The resulting percentage corrections and the estimated l_2 levels are given in Tables 7.7.

The corrections lie between 20 and 50 percent except for Guinea, the Hill Pagans in North Cameroon, and Mopti. The reasons for the different results in the first two of these will be discussed in connection with adult mortality. In Mopti current deaths under 5 years were 13 percent higher than implied by the retrospective estimates, but the evidence suggests that special conditions caused a large increase in child mortality in the year preceding the survey. Certainly the reported incidence is enormous, with 57 percent of the children dead by age 5. The official report suggests that the epidemics of meningitis and chicken-pox may have been the cause. The statistics for Mopti are a good example of the limitations of taking the death rates in one year as representative of the level of mortality in a population. Some of the differences between current and retrospective measures may be due to periodical fluctuations in mortality, although many deaths of children of the younger mothers are common to the two sets of data.

The estimation of mortality after childhood raises even more difficult problems. The retrospective reports give survivorship ratios up to 35 years at most. In nearly all areas the estimated ratios imply exceedingly low (sometimes zero) mortality in early adulthood, because the proportions of children surviving, in general, show little change after the mothers are about 50 years old. The hypothesis that mortality had increased with time and that consequently fewer children of the women just over 50 survived to corresponding ages than those of older mothers is hardly tenable. It would be straining coincidence to accept that there would be no other evidence of such a change and that it should have happened to about the same extent under very different conditions.

The obvious explanation is that the older women have omitted more dead children from the reports. The corresponding trend for total births has already been established. It is tempting to carry the argument a stage further and make the tentative assumption that only dead children were forgotten, i.e., that the numbers of living children were correctly stated at all ages of mothers. Although the hypothesis leads to measures in satisfactory accord with the evidence for some populations, in others the agreement is not as good. It raises as many problems as are solved, and the situation is clearly more complicated. The possibility cannot entirely be ruled out that the progressive elimination of mothers in the poorer environments by differential death rates means that the children of the older women still living have had a mortality experience less severe than the average. More consideration will be given to the question of differential omissions in the detailed studies of particular populations.

Since the survival rates of children reported by the older mothers are too high but it is not possible to say where the effect becomes important, little guidance on the patterns of mortality at ages after childhood can be obtained from the retrospective reports. One difficulty with the current data is that it has already been established that a proportion of the deaths of children have been omitted. The problem is to decide whether the underreporting extends to all ages and if so to what degree. Life tables which are not obviously unacceptable can be calculated on the alternative hypotheses that on the one hand no deaths beyond early childhood were left out and that on the other reporting was equally bad at all ages. *A priori* it is possible to make out quite a strong case for either of these alternatives. Omissions of the reported deaths of children during the past year are too great in most areas to be confined only to those who died in the first few months of life. There are thus grounds for believing that the memory lapse may be connected with a time scale error which would extend to deaths at all ages. On the other hand, it seems likely that the deaths of adults, the influential and important section of the population, would be better recorded than those of children who were not old enough to be regarded as full members of the community. In addition, if some of the discrepancy between the current and retrospective childhood mortality levels were due to misreports of ages at death, the assumption that the derived correction could be extended equally to adults would give too low estimates of survivorship levels.

Since it is difficult *a priori* to weight the plausibility of the two alternatives, life tables were fitted to the observations on both assumptions by the use of the model functional system and the African standard. For each the same level of childhood mortality as measured by the fitted l_2 from the retrospective reports was accepted. To determine suitable life tables of the system it was therefore only necessary to choose a value of β, since the selection of a β and the acceptance of l_2 determines α (see Chapter 3). This was done as follows, starting in each case from the approximate first estimate of l_5 found, in the way explained above, to correspond with the fitted l_2. For the "low correction" the reported current age-specific death rates over five years were used to derive preliminary values of l_x at higher ages, given the l_5 values; "high-correction" values of l_x were found in similar ways, but with all age-specific rates adjusted by the percentage increase required to bring reported current childhood mortality up to the retrospective levels. For each set of measures the mean of the logits of l_x at 20, 30, 40, 50, and 60 years was calculated (denoted by $\overline{Y}$). β was then taken as the slope of the straight line relationship with the African standard on the logit scale, which passed through the points $\overline{Y}(2)$ and Y. The estimation formula was, therefore,

$$\beta = [\overline{Y} - Y(2)]/[\overline{Y}_s - Y_s(2)] = 1.532[\overline{Y} - Y(2)]$$

The approximate first estimate of l_5 was obtained on the assumption that β was equal to 1.00 between the years 2 and 5; the values of l_5

in the high- and low-correction life tables will, in general, differ from the first estimate, but only slightly. Although the method of fitting is rather arbitrary, little difference is found in the results if other techniques are used as long as small weight is given to the reported survivors at high ages. As has been pointed out earlier, the observations of the deaths of the older people are likely to be even more unreliable than those at younger ages. The common value of l_2 and the two slopes, β, define life tables which can reasonably be regarded as limits for the broad patterns of mortality implied by the data. Probably the truth lies somewhere between the two extremes. Although the limiting schedules are used to show the effect of the different assumptions about adult mortality on the other demographic measures, only one full life table is calculated, namely that for a β midway between the two extremes.

The method for finding high- and low-correction factors and corresponding life tables described above was satisfactory in most of the areas, but there were notable exceptions. One of these was Mopti, where, as explained previously, the reported current childhood mortality was very high, probably because of epidemics in the year preceding the survey. Since the current adult mortality was low there was no case for applying the negative correction factor, needed to adjust the childhood rates to the retrospective observations, at higher ages. The low-correction life table was estimated in the way described, and a very arbitrary high correction for adult mortality was obtained by transferring the deaths at under 5 years, subtracted from the current reports in the adjustment of childhood rates, to over 5 years. The assumption is that some part of the very extreme division of reported deaths between child and adult years might have been due to misreporting. Further discussion is contained in the case study.

In Guinea and its regions the differentials between reported current and retrospective childhood mortality are relatively small. Extremely high current death rates beyond childhood were recorded, particularly at ages 10 to 30 years, where the level is far above that for any other area. The pattern is reflected in the high values of β obtained when life tables from the model system are fitted to the observations. In the analysis of fertility it was shown that the P/F ratios for Guinea were low and the conclusion drawn that the births recorded were for a longer period than the preceding year. There seems a strong possibility that a similar lengthening of the reference period also occurred in the reporting of deaths but that it was offset, for young children at least, by omissions. Other evidence for such an effect exists (see case study). It is equally notable that (apart from Mopti) the only further population sub-group for which reported current and retrospective mortality are in close agreement is the Hill Pagans of North Cameroon, which provided the other low-fertility adjustment factor from the P/F ratios. Because of these considerations a low-correction life table was estimated for Guinea by assuming that current adult mortality was overstated by the same percentage as estimated for births. Apart from this, the principles of the adjustments to bring the current reports in line with the retrospective observations were unchanged; the high-correction life table is, therefore, the same whatever the assumption about the time-reference period. Although it might have been more consistent to apply the procedure outlined to the mortality observations in all the sub-groups where fertility adjustments were made, the effects would have been relatively small (except for the Hill Pagans in North Cameroon) compared with the accuracy of estimation. On the evidence such elaboration was not justified.

Tables 7.7 show reference measures for the low- and high-correction fitted life tables. The survivorship ratio at 27 years is given because the mean ages of the fertility schedules are close to 27 for all the populations. The ratio at 27 is then a rough guide to the proportion of women, on average, surviving to the reproductive years. Probabilities of dying and survivorship ratios for the life table with a β midway between the low and high values are given in Tables 7.8. The lines which represent the relations between the estimates and the African standard mortality pattern are traced on the logit scale in Figures 7.1. Despite the variations among populations, broad conclusions can be drawn by inspection of the graphs. With few exceptions (notably the high-correction tables in some regions of Guinea and the low-correction ones in Mopti) the divergences of the β values from 1.00 are moderate. The low-correction estimates agree better with the retrospective reports of children who died by women over the age of 35, but no weight can be laid on the comparison since the latter clearly understate mortality. In several of the populations the β values for the low-correction tables are well below 1.00, and the slope of the representative line brings it close to the points for the current observations at older ages. The fit is not plausible. The lines for high-correction estimates are not obviously an unreasonable description of the data, but the slopes are very steep in the Upper and Forest regions of Guinea. The medium life tables are as consistent with the observations as could be expected in view of the nature of the errors, and the characteristic β values are nowhere extreme, with the possible exception of the Upper region of Guinea. Although the medium estimates of adult mortality are accepted as the best available, the weakness of the information on which they are based is obvious; speculation has, inevitably, had too large a share in the process of reconstruction.

Separate tabulations of the retrospective reports of children dead for each sex have been published for few of the inquiries, and the results are not illuminating. Mortality measures calculated from current deaths are shown separately for males and females in Tables 7.9. In most of the populations differentials between male and female mortality are small. Only in the Ivory Coast and, to a lesser extent, Guinea and Mopti are the divergences of any size. For the studies of reproduction and age distribution, estimates of female mortality are required. In all population groups except the ones specified the female life tables were taken to be the same as constructed for the two sexes combined. In the Ivory Coast the probability of dying under age 2 was made 10 percent lower for females than for the two sexes together, and in Guinea and Mopti 5 percent lower. These percentages are approximately the observed advantages at 1 to 5 years. The β's estimated for both sexes combined are assumed to hold for female mortality patterns also. From the preceding discussion of the errors in current reports of deaths and the comments on the estimating procedure it will be clear that elaborate methods for distinguishing male and female mortality are not justified. The resulting inaccuracy is, moreover, small in comparison with other sources of error.

Reproduction and Natural Increase

If the stable female populations corresponding to the medium β life table (amended where necessary for a mortality differential by sex) and different rates of natural increase are calculated, the stable population from the series with a female birth rate equal to the estimate from the observations can be determined. In principle this was done for each population group, although in practice a number of procedures to reduce the labor of calculation, based on the insensitivity of the birth rates to the detailed patterns of mortality at adult ages, were used. The natural increase was that of the selected stable population series, and the death rate was obtained by subtracting the growth from the birth rate. The gross reproduction rate which would give the required number of births in the stable population was estimated by assuming that the specific fertility distribution followed the shape of the model system, with the mean obtained from the current data. The net reproduction rate was calculated in the standard way and the total fertility ratio derived on the assumption of 103 male for every 100 female births. The results (rounded off to avoid misleading apparent precision) are shown in Tables 7.10.

To complete the estimation of fertility measures, the age-specific rates calculated from current observations and presented in Tables 7.1 were adjusted in two ways. First, a rough correction was made to allow for the displacement of the rates, in terms of the ages of the women at the time of the inquiry, because the births had taken place on average half a year previously. The procedure for making the allowance is described in Chapter 3. Secondly, the rates were adjusted proportionately to make the corresponding total fertility ratio agree with the estimate. The corrected values are shown in Tables 7.11. Because of sample and age errors, as well as bias, these rates can only be regarded as a rough guide to the shape of the fertility distribution by age. No clear conclusion can be drawn about the relations between level and pattern of fertility in the different populations.

The method of arriving at demographic measures for the stable female population by the use of a corrected birth rate has disadvantages. The translation of the birth rate to a gross, and hence a net, reproduction index depends on the assumption that the relation between the numbers of women in the fertile age groups and total females is approximately the same in the population as in the specified stable model. The equation may be wrong not only because of errors in the estimated life table but as a result of changing fertility or mortality. In certain of the populations the evidence that fertility has been falling rapidly is strong; in the others the birth rates are high and there is little indication of change, but slight movements up or down are not ruled out. Mortality is everywhere severe; a substantial downward trend is thus precluded, and *a priori* an increase is unlikely. The assumption that the population age distributions approximate the stable form seems legitimate except for the cases in which fertility has clearly fallen. The alternative procedure of applying the correction factor from the P/F ratios directly to the current total fertility ratio is unsatisfactory because of the overstatement (in some cases substantial) of the proportion of women in the reproductive period. The approach through the corrected female birth rate is, therefore, used in all the case studies, but its implications are discussed further below in the examination of age distributions.

The intrinsic rates of natural increase given in Tables 7.10 are for stable populations with the estimated fertility and the mortality of the medium β life tables. The effects on death and growth rates of selecting the low- or high-correction adult mortality rather than the medium varies greatly from population to population. The greatest differences are in Guinea, where the mortality estimates are particularly speculative. For the Upper and Forest regions the range of the death and natural increase rates from the low- to the high-correction limits is 6 or 7 per thousand. Several of the differences in the other populations are 4 or 5 per thousand. The rates calculated by the use of the medium life table may, therefore, be in error by as much as 2 or 3 per thousand solely because of the difficulty in determining how well adult deaths have been reported. This source of error is of particular concern because there is no satisfactory way of checking the estimates of adult mortality by internal comparisons among the observations.

Age Distribution

Some checks of the techniques of analysis have been applied from general considerations of the consistency of measures and patterns. These have a definite although limited value in guiding decisions between clear-cut alternatives, but little for the drawing of reliable quantitative conclusions. The verification of the estimates of fertility and mortality by reference to the largely independent evidence on age distributions is of key importance in these studies. The checks are powerful only if it is reasonable to assume that the populations are effectively closed, i.e., not subject to appreciable migration, or if the results of migration can be allowed for. The assumption is not strictly valid for most of the populations examined, and the information on migration is not sufficiently complete or detailed to be used for adjusting the age distributions. (To do this properly is, in any case, a doubtful and complex matter.) However, migration of females between territories is very much smaller than that of males; there is evidence also that much of the female migration is of a family nature, with the children accompanying the mother. Movements of this kind have much smaller relative effects on the age distributions of the exporting or receiving countries than migration (permanent or temporary) of individuals, particularly young adults. In general, therefore, there are good reasons for believing that African female populations in substantial sized regions will be approximately closed or quasi-closed, i.e., with the same age distribution as a closed population. Most of the male populations are clearly very far from closed. The applications of stable age distribution theory will therefore be confined to female populations, although general comments about the male patterns will be made.

The age distributions reported are shown in percentage form in Tables 7.12. The variations in proportions from one age group to the next are very erratic, and it is clear from a glance that they must reflect errors in reports. The discrepancies are too large and systematic in the different populations to be explained by true fluctuations in births, deaths, and migration. Although it is not possible to establish with confidence the nature of the errors without other evidence, certain characteristics can be stated. The errors are generally in conformity with those found in other African censuses and surveys. See Chapter 2 for a discussion of typical patterns of age misreporting.

In all areas there is a large deficiency of females aged 10-14 years, and in most some understatement of the numbers at 15-19 also. As the obverse there are "bulges" in the proportions of females under 10 years and in the age range 20-29 (in some populations continuing into older groups). These patterns do not prove conclusively that the numbers of children and of women in the most fertile period are overstated but, combined with other features, make it very likely. For example, in the Ivory Coast the percentage reported as under 10 years (above 40 percent) is too great to be plausible and is inconsistent with the other evidence. For males also there is a large drop in numbers between the 5-9 and 10-14 age groups but, in general, no compensating bulge at higher years. The indications are, therefore, that relatively too many children were reported as under 10 years.

The comparison of the number of women observed in the age range 15-44 years (shown in Tables 7.12) with stable populations suggests some overstatement. The check is a powerful one because the proportions at these ages do not vary much with the level of mortality or natural increase. In the stable distributions computed from the African standard life table, the percentage in the 15-44 age range lies between 43 and 45 percent as the proportion under 15 years increases from 25 to 45 percent. Most of the observed values are greater than 45 percent, and within the broad age interval there is a concentration in the middle at 20-34 years. These characteristics of age reporting would lead to underestimates of total fertility if current births were accurately reported.

Little can be said about the adult male age distributions in detail because of the complications of migration, particularly temporary movements of labor. The percentages of both males and females at the higher ages are so affected by the pattern of mortality of the elderly and the demographic history of the distant past that they are unpromising material for study. Nevertheless, some points will be made in the more detailed comparisons below. It should be noted that in all populations but one the percentages of women at the higher ages (55 years and above) are lower than for men. Certainly there is no support for the idea of differential mortality in favor of females.

Stable age distributions corresponding to the estimated measures of Tables 7.10 were calculated. They are compared in Tables 7.13 with the observed values in terms of both the percentages in groups and the cumulated proportions under particular years of age. The latter measures are particularly useful for the study of systematic rather than erratic deviations. Before the examination of the agreement in detail it is important to state what a satisfactory fit implies. The broad shape of the age distribution is determined by the relation between the numbers of young children and of women in the reproductive period. Good agreement between the observed and stable distributions verifies that the estimate of fertility, reduced by the proportion of children dying in the early years of life, is about right. Although the estimates of fertility and of childhood mortality are not completely independent, certain aspects of them are. Much weight is given to the retrospective data on children born to the younger women in finding the P/F correction factor, and to the proportion of these children who have died, in calculating mortality. Consequently the reports by these women of the number of their living children have a major influence on the estimated stable population. Children who died very young could be omitted from records of both births and deaths without altering either the observed or fitted age distributions. On the other hand, the crucial assumption that the misreporting of current births is proportionately the same at all ages of women is independent of these considerations. The same is true of the technique for relating the proportion of children dead for an age group of mothers to the childhood mortality for a particular interval from birth. The age distribution comparisons are therefore a powerful check on the techniques for the estimation of both fertility and childhood mortality, with the reservation which has been noted.

Stable population comparisons supply no evidence, however, about the level of mortality in middle life and little about its pattern. If stable age distributions are calculated from the high- and low-correction life tables with appropriate adjustments of the natural increase to keep the estimated birth rate constant, they differ little. Still greater divergences in the mortality to the end of the reproductive period can be introduced with little change in the broad age pattern. Even if recording were very accurate it is doubtful whether such alternative schedules of adult mortality could be distinguished by the use of observed data; with the age errors in the data analyzed the attempt is hopeless. The course of mortality at higher ages does influence the age distribution at the upper end appreciably, but there are too many other possible disturbing factors to allow much weight to be laid on the evidence.

The differences in the proportions under various ages in the observed and stable distributions are not easy to interpret because of difficulties in grasping the scale. To illuminate the comparisons, Figure 7.2 has been constructed for each section. A line coincident with the x-axis would represent perfect agreement with the estimated stable distribution in the proportions under all ages. The y-axis gives deviations from agreement in years of age. Thus a point two years above the x-axis at age 10 stands for a percentage under 10 years which is equal to that under 12 years in the stable population; similarly a point two years below at age 10 represents the proportion under 8 years. The points plotted on the graph in accordance with the observed percentages under different ages thus show immediately the average error in years if the estimated stable distribution is accurate. These points have been joined by a dotted line to help the tracing of the pattern by eye but not, of course, to imply that errors at intermediate ages would follow this course.

On this system, stable age distributions other than the estimated one can be represented by lines on the graph. Two further alternative stable populations were constructed with the same medium life table as before but with values of the natural increase chosen with the largest possible deviations from the estimated rate r, positively and negatively, which lead to agreement with the observed proportions under some age. The extremes were confined to ages under 30 years. In practice the positive deviation corresponding to the observed proportion of females under 10 years and the negative value at 20 years were close to the extremes; in a few instances the levels at 5 and 25 years represented larger deviations than those at 10 and 20 respectively. The curves for these stable age distributions are traced on the graph. The deviations from the estimated natural increase, r, were calculated to the nearest unit per thousand, and the agreement with the observations at the relevant ages is therefore only approximate. In addition, the distributions at the higher ages are dependent on the death rates in this period of life, for which the estimates are speculative. Little account can therefore be taken of the comparisons at upper ages, and the calculations of deviations are very rough. They are shown on the graph, however, to indicate the continuance of trends. The differences along the y-axis between the points representing the observations and the corresponding values on a stable population curve measure roughly the errors in years of age which would exist if the latter was taken as the best fitting estimate.

Although there are considerable variations in the pattern of deviations, the x-axis tends to run through the middle of the observation points except in certain areas where there are special problems of changing fertility (North Cameroon) or non-typical current rates (Mopti). If the aim had been to select the stable population which minimized the observed deviations at ages up to the end of the reproductive period, the results would have been very close to those reached from the independent estimates of fertility and mortality. In general, therefore, agreement is as satisfactory as could have been hoped for in view of the limitations and deficiencies of the materials. The extreme stable populations traced on the graphs are a very implausible fit to the data since they imply very large errors in the proportions under certain ages and, in general, diverge systematically from the observations over long intervals. For example, in Upper Volta the choice of the upper extreme would mean that the numbers under 20 and 25 had been reported on average as under 24 and 29, respectively. With the choice of the lower extreme the error implied at age 10 would be nearly two and a half years and at some points above 40 more than four years. It is clear, however, from the graphs that the check, although it provides powerful evidence, allows an appreciable latitude of uncertainty. The range from the lower to the upper extreme stable population in terms of natural increase is in most areas 9-12 per thousand and in Ivory Coast as high as 18. With such erratic age data, movements in the stable population equivalent to several units per thousand of natural increase could be made and the goodness of fit would change little.

No one age can be specified such that the proportion of the population under it is in consistent agreement with the fitted stable age distribution for all the areas. Clearly, however, in these studies the use of the proportion under 5 or 10 years as a basic index in the estimation of fertility and mortality from age distributions would have given bad results. Greater accuracy is achieved by adopting as a measure the percentage under 30 or 35 years, partly because the effects of the large reporting errors of the 10-19 age group are dissipated by then and partly because the estimated stable population is less sensitive to deviations at these than at younger ages.

The conclusions about errors in the reported age distributions are confirmed by comparisons with the estimated stable populations and made more specific. In particular, the deficiency in numbers at 10 to 19 years is balanced by excesses both at under 10 and in the middle of the reproductive period. For operational purposes the finding applies whether the deficiency is due to the differential omission of females in the 10-19 age group or to age misstatements. It appears likely that the latter is the dominant effect and may be a consequence of the enumerators' desire to come to a clear-cut decision that a girl is a child or a marriageable adult rather than in the boundary adolescent class. In all populations there is an excess of observed over fitted percentages in the most fertile years, but the extent to which this is compensated in the reproductive range 15-44 years by overstatements of ages near the upper limit appears to vary.

Changes in β, the slope of mortality on the logit scale compared with the standard, have only a small influence on the broad age distribution. A life table with a high β, however, leads to stable populations with low proportions, relatively, of the elderly and vice versa. If the estimates of β have any validity there should be some evidence of such effects, at least in extreme cases. There are encouraging indications of such patterns. The fitted age distributions for North and South Dahomey are closely similar, but the higher β in the former region results in lower percentages at over 50 years, in accord with the observations. The high β levels in some of the sub-populations of Guinea are consistent with the low proportions over 55 years, e.g., in the Upper region. Again, the moderately low β's of Fouta-Toro and Mopti, and fairly high slope for the Ivory Coast, give better agreement with the observations at upper ages than if the standard level of 1.00 is adopted. Despite the limitations of the data there are strong suggestions that the estimates of adult mortality patterns have some validity and are not just an accidental outcome of errors in the reports of deaths and ages.

Although the techniques for estimating fertility and mortality give measures consistent with the age distributions, to verify them convincingly it is also necessary to show that more obvious unadjusted rates are not equally successful. The best attack is by the examination of populations in which the results from the two approaches are very different. More detailed investigations are contained in the case studies, but some instances which are particularly striking will be mentioned here. In Dahomey, the reported current birth rates for females (unadjusted) are

47 and 55 per thousand for the North and South regions respectively. The mortality rates calculated from deaths in the past year are almost the same in the two regions. If these measures were accepted the corresponding stable age distributions would differ greatly for the two populations. The techniques which were applied lead to higher corrections for overreporting of births and understatement of deaths in the previous year in the South than in the North. As a consequence the fitted age distributions are very similar for the two regions in accord with the observed values. Failure to apply the correction factor for births in South Dahomey would give an increase in growth rate of 5 per thousand, and the use of current instead of retrospective child mortality an equivalent further rise of 7 per thousand, completely inconsistent with the observed age distribution. The current female birth rate for the Forest area of Guinea was reported as 61 per thousand. A heavy correction factor for fertility of 0.73 was calculated, but current and retrospective mortality are in close agreement. If the fertility correction factor is not applied, a natural increase of 14 per thousand is obtained, 11 units greater than the estimate. As can be seen from Figure 7.2 stable age distribution with the former increase rate is far outside the course of the observations even at the most extreme deviations from the x-axis.

In North Cameroon and Centre-Oubangui the moderate levels of the estimated birth rates, the reports of larger family sizes by the older women, and the trends of the P/F ratios all suggest that fertility has been declining. The quantitative effects of such a trend on the estimates and the stable age distribution comparisons depend on the rapidity and pattern of change, which cannot be established. The average number of children born to the older women is too much affected by omissions (and possibly differentials in mortality by fertility rates) to give guidance of any accuracy. General conclusions can, however, be reached. As a result of the higher fertility of the past, the number of women in the reproductive period will be greater relative to the older women who were their mothers than is implied by the current rates. Thus the proportion of females in the higher age groups will be less than in the stable population corresponding to current fertility and mortality. The method of estimating reproduction from the birth rate on the assumption that the population is stable will give values which are inflated because too low a proportion of women are taken to be in the reproductive age range. As age increases the effect of the reduced number of older women on the comparison with the stable population becomes greater because they form a large proportion of the percentage remaining above the point of cumulation. As a result, it would be expected that the observed points on Figures 7.2 would deviate upward with age. This is exactly what happens for the North Cameroon and Centre-Oubangui populations.

A correction could be applied to the estimates by including an allowance for the "shortage" of older women, but there is no satisfactory basis for assessing its size. It must also be taken into account that changes or fluctuations in mortality levels (possibly far in the past) and discrepancies between the model and actual death rates of the elderly could also lead to appreciable differences in the number of old people in the fitted and observed populations. No adjustments were, therefore, made to the estimates. The comparisons in Figures 7.2, although far from consistent, do not suggest that the resulting error is large in relation to other causes of inaccuracy.

The order in which the studies of particular populations are presented was chosen in order that the principles and procedures of the analysis should be exhibited most clearly. Since the data from the Guinea inquiry are the earliest and most detailed it might have been more logical to start with these. However, the characteristics of the measures for Guinea are atypical, and special devices are used to arrive at estimates. An account of these problems and exceptions without the yardstick of a more straightforward analysis would be confusing. Since there is no very obvious order of presentation based on geographical, cultural, or ethnic considerations, priority has been given to convenience of exposition.

A. REPUBLIC OF UPPER VOLTA

The West African country of Upper Volta is situated on a plateau, south of the great bend in the middle reaches of the Niger River. Although the river largely encloses the territory except in the south, it does not touch it at any point. Upper Volta lies north of the coastal countries (from west to east) of Ivory Coast, Ghana, Togoland, and Dahomey. It has common boundaries with these and also with Mali in the northwest and Niger in the northeast. Until 1958 the country formed part of the overseas territories of France. The region is mainly covered by poor grasslands, although there are forest areas in the southwest. The inhabitants make a bare living from subsistence farming and little produce is exported. There are few urban centers and these are small.

The sample inquiry of October 1960 to March 1961 covered the whole country except the towns of Ouagadougou and Bobo-Dioulasso, which were taken to have between them about 100,000 inhabitants. The number of residents estimated from the sample was 4,300,000, with a confidence interval of plus or minus 150,000, giving a total population (including the towns) of 4,400,000 and a density of 16 per square kilometer. For convenience the results from the sample will be referred to as "for the country" despite the omission of the residents in the two towns. The main tribe is the Mossi, living in the moderately thickly populated east-central part of the country (35 persons per square kilometer). The Mossi and allied tribes number about two million and are the descendants of the people of a strong centralized state which covered this region from the middle ages onward. Several inter-allied tribes, numbering in total about 700,000, are grouped together under the heading "Western," from the region of the country where they live, which has a density of 15 persons per square kilometer. All the tribes in the two groups speak languages of the Nigritic family; the sub-families represented are Voltaic and Mande, for the Mossi and Western tribes respectively. The terminology is Murdock's[2] based on the classification of Greenberg.[3] In addition to these specified groups, there are a number of smaller tribes (e.g., Peul, Senufo, Lobi, Gurunsi, Gurmantche) which are not shown separately in the analysis because of the high sampling errors. It should be noted that although the sub-populations shown in the table are given the names of tribal groups, the results refer strictly to the sets of villages in which these tribes are a majority, and a small proportion of other Africans are included. The total number of persons for whom data were collected was about 90,000, and the sampling fraction over 2 percent.

Fertility

Table 7.1.A shows fertility rates in five-year age groups (which are properly located earlier by six-month intervals, at 14½ to 19½ rather than 15 to 20 years and so on) for the whole country and the tribal groups, calculated from the reported "current" births in the year preceding the survey and the corresponding total fertility ratios and birth rates. The means of the specific fertility distributions and the P_1/P_2 ratios

Table 7.1.A. Reported current birth and age-specific fertility rates—
Upper Volta and tribal groups

Age group of women in years*	Upper Volta	Tribal group Mossi	Western
15-19	.169	.144	.166
20-24	.308	.332	.292
25-29	.265	.278	.257
30-34	.220	.246	.190
35-39	.154	.177	.130
40-44	.084	.113	.054
45-49	.021	.031	.006
Total fertility	6.105	6.605	5.475
Birth rate per thousand	49.1	50.8	45.4

* The true age intervals for the rates are, on average, half a year younger than is shown.

[2] George P. Murdock, *Africa: Its Peoples and Their Cultural History*, McGraw-Hill, 1959.

[3] Joseph H. Greenberg, *Studies in African Linguistic Classification*, Compass Publishing Co., 1955.

Table 7.2.A. Estimated measures of fertility distributions—Upper Volta and tribal groups

Measure	Upper Volta	Tribal Group Mossi	Western
Mean $(\overline{m})$ in years	27.9	28.7	27.1
P_1/P_2	.19	.15	.19
Adjusted female birth rate per thousand	48.5	49.7	46.6

computed from the retrospective reports of numbers of children born per woman in the first two age groups are given in Table 7.2.A. These two measures are rough guides to the locations of the specific fertility distributions. The data show no unusual features. They indicate a high but not exceptional fertility, with only a moderately early start to child-bearing. The lower reported specific rates for women in the latter half of the reproductive period for the Western tribes as compared with the Mossi lead to a smaller total fertility ratio and a decreased mean for the distribution.

From the rates in Table 7.1.A, with the aid of the location measures of Table 7.2.A, average cumulated fertilities (F) for age groups were computed by the procedure described in Chapter 3. These are compared with the retrospective records of children ever born per woman (P) by means of the P/F ratios in Table 7.3.A. The percentage of women

Table 7.3.A. Cumulated fertility (F), reported parity (P), and P/F ratios—Upper Volta and tribal groups

Age group of women in years	F	P	P/F	F	P	P/F	F	P	P/F
15–19	0.42	0.32	0.76	0.32	0.24	0.75	0.42	0.31	0.74
20–24	1.74	1.66	0.95	1.68	1.60	0.95	1.68	1.61	0.96
25–29	3.19	3.13	0.98	3.22	3.13	0.97	3.07	3.00	0.98
30–34	4.40	4.11	0.93	4.54	4.34	0.96	4.17	3.67	0.88
35–39	5.31	4.81	0.91	5.57	5.11	0.92	4.96	4.00	0.81
40–44	5.88	5.14	0.87	6.28	5.59	0.89	5.37	4.32	0.80
45–49	6.10	5.34	0.88	6.59	5.70	0.86	5.47	4.53	0.83
50 and over	6.11	5.36	0.88	6.60	5.63	0.85	5.48	4.44	0.81

in each age group who were reported to have borne no live children and the total births per mother are shown in Table 7.4.A. The P/F

Table 7.4.A. Percentage of women childless and average parity of mothers—Upper Volta and tribal groups

Age group of women in years	Upper Volta Percent childless	Average parity of mothers	Tribal group Mossi Percent childless	Average parity of mothers	Western Percent childless	Average parity of mothers
15–19	73	1.21	79	1.17	73	1.15
20–24	16	1.97	14	1.87	15	1.90
25–29	7	3.37	5	3.29	12	3.42
30–34	7	4.41	4	4.52	12	4.19
35–39	6	5.14	4	5.33	12	4.56
40–49	6	5.60	4	5.87	12	5.04
50 and over	6	5.71	5	5.91	11	4.92

ratios are close to 1.00 for the women in the age groups 20-24 and 25-29 for the whole country and the two tribal divisions. At ages beyond 30 years the P/F ratios tend to fall. Although there are some variations, the size and pattern of the decrease are similar in the different series. At the end of the reproductive period the ratio is of the order of 0.85 and changes little for the older women. The latter feature is surprising, but there are many factors which cannot be assessed which could influence the values for the small proportions of women surviving to the late ages.

The evidence is convincing that births reported for the previous year are close to the true number. It seems equally valid to conclude that the decrease in the P/F ratios with age is due to the omission of births by the older women. The trend for the whole country (particularly the constancy at the older ages) might suggest that fertility was in fact increasing, but it is hard to accept that such a change could have occurred so consistently for the different tribal categories. It is easier to believe that the factors controlling child omissions, including the design of the inquiry schedule and the field procedures as well as psychological and cultural elements, determined the similarities. The overwhelming evidence of child omissions in other surveys of the same kind must also be given due weight.

There is no suggestion in Table 7.4.A that the fall in the P/F ratios with age could be due to the inclusion in the childless category of an increasing proportion of women for whom no information on children could be obtained. The percentage of women infertile shows no consistent change with age from about 25 years upward. Nearly all the mothers must have borne their first child by their early twenties. Very few Mossi women remained childless (only 4 percent), but infertility was quite substantial in the Western tribes (12 percent).

The P/F ratios do not establish the need for any correction of reported current births. Although the level is slightly below 1.00 for the younger women, the deviations could be due to age errors, approximations in the techniques, or a few omissions of retrospective births. The birth rates of the female population shown in Table 7.2.A have, therefore, been calculated from the data as collected except for the conventional assumption that there were 103 males born for every 100 females.

Mortality

The retrospective information on the proportions of children dead by age of mother and the derived life table survivorship ratios are shown in Table 7.5.A. The multiplying factors for converting the proportions into probabilities of dying from birth were obtained by the procedure described in Chapter 3. The location of the fertility distribution was estimated by the P_1/P_2 ratios for the first three age groups and by the means of the fertility schedules at later years. The most obvious features of the measures in the table are the heavy mortality exhibited, the relatively

Table 7.5.A. Percentage of children having died previous to the survey, by age of mother, and derived life table survivorship ratios *l*.—Upper Volta and tribal groups

Age group of mothers in years	Age of child survivor-ship	Upper Volta Per cent of children dead	l_x	Tribal Group Mossi Per cent of children dead	l_x	Western Per cent of children dead	l_x
15-19	1	23.1	.771	17.8	.816	15.9	.843
20-24	2	31.7	.678	34.2	.645	29.5	.700
25-29	3	39.6	.605	41.5	.581	36.9	.632
30-34	5	41.2	.586	44.4	.549	35.1	.649
35-39	10	45.2	.542	47.6	.512	40.7	.589
40-44	15	47.8	.527	48.8	.510	43.8	.568
45-49	20	49.4	.511	52.0	.478	46.7	.541
50-54	25	52.2	.476	54.7	.443	48.2	.518
55-59	30	51.3	.484	54.6	.444	49.5	.505
60-64	35	52.1	.478	54.4	.447	49.9	.503

high survivorship at 1 year compared with later ages of childhood, and the constancy in the percentages of children dead for mothers above 50. The last of these means that the survivorship ratios calculated at ages 25 to 35 years imply impossibly low death rates in this interval.

The age-specific death rates calculated from the events reported in the year preceding the survey and the resulting life table values (l_x) are given in Table 7.6.A for males and females together. Although mortalities are still high by contemporary world standards, the l_x values for children are appreciably above those found from the retrospective data. On the other hand, the gap narrows with increasing age, and the retrospective and current values for the whole country are about the same

Table 7.6.A. Life table measures from reported current deaths (both sexes)— Upper Volta and tribal groups. (*m*, age-specific death rate per 1,000; *q*, probability of dying in age group; *l*, proportion surviving to start of age group)

Age group in years	Upper Volta m	q	l	Tribal Group Mossi m	q	l	Western m	q	l
Under 1	205	.179	1.000	226	,195	1.000	181	.161	1.000
1- 4	58	.201	.821	69	.223	.805	56	.195	.839
5- 9	15	.072	.656	19	.091	.617	12	.058	.675
10-19	7	.064	.609	8	.077	.561	4	.039	.636
20-29	10	.098	.570	9	.087	.518	12	.114	.611
30-39	13	.119	.514	14	.132·	.473	9	.087	.542
40-49	18	.170	.453	19	.175	.410	17	.158.	.495
50-59	32	.282	.376	27	.241	.339	33	.287	.416
60-69	58	.456	.270	44	.366	.257	97	.648	.297
70 and over	99	1.000	.147	85	1.000	.163	164	1.000	.105
Death rate per thousand	30.5			33.0			29.7		

by 35 years. The age-specific rates of the Western tribes are erratic, but this is not surprising in view of the rather small number of events on which they are based.

The relations between the mortalities calculated from the retrospective and current data are examined in more detail in Figure 7.1.A by the use of the logit scale. The logit differences h from the African standard life table do not deviate systematically from a straight line for the current measures, showing that the linear parametric model gives a good representation of the mortality pattern. The h values calculated from the retrospective ratios drop with an impossible slope between ages 25 and 35 years; there is also an appreciable fall from 5 to 25 years, but it is impossible to distinguish how far this is a genuine feature of the mortality and to what extent it is caused by errors. Graphs for the tribal groups show much the same results, but the individual points are more erratic.

The comparisons have the typical characteristics discussed in the introductory section. The procedure given there for estimating low- and high-correction life tables of the parametric system, by calculating l_2 from the retrospective measures and two values of β on extreme assumptions about the misreporting of current deaths, is adopted. The results

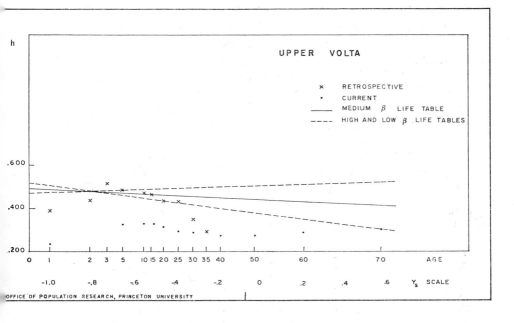

7.1.A. Proportion surviving to each age (l_x) in Upper Volta in life tables calculated from retrospective mortality data and current mortality data and fitted by linear logit transformations.

Table 7.7.A. Indices from estimated low- and high-correction life tables—Upper Volta and tribal groups

Estimated measures	Upper Volta		Tribal Group			
			Mossi		Western	
	Low	High	Low	High	Low	High
% correction to deaths	15	27	13	23	10	21
1(2)	.660	.660	.629	.629	.695	.695
1(27)	.470	.434	.436	.410	.519	.497
β	.87	1.03	.87	.99	.83	.93

are summarized in Table 7.7.A. The low and high percentage corrections are the proportions by which reported current deaths would have to be raised on the alternative assumptions that omissions occurred only for children under 5 years or were equally common at all ages, respectively. The adjustments are very similar in Upper Volta and the two tribal populations, with percentages over 20 percent to bring current and retrospective deaths at under 5 years into agreement. With the estimated values of l_2 and β's midway between the levels for the extreme mortality schedules, medium-correction life tables were constructed for the whole country and the two tribal divisions. These, which are presented in Table 7.8.A, are the best estimates, on the information from the inquiry, of the broad course of mortality in the populations. Straight lines representing the low-, medium-, and high-correction life tables on the logit scale of differences from the African standard are drawn on Figure 7.1.A. The low-correction line is not a convincing description of the trends in the observations if the conclusions about the nature of the errors in the reporting of current deaths have any validity; there is no evidence for choosing between the high- and medium-correction estimates, but the latter are the more conservative.

Table 7.8.A. Medium-correction life tables, males and females together—Upper Volta and tribal groups. (q, probability of dying in succeeding age interval; l, proportion surviving by age)

Age in years	Upper Volta		Tribal Group			
			Mossi		Western	
	q	l	q	l	q	l
0	.263	1.000	.292	1.000	.238	1.000
1	.197	.737	.209	.708	.167	.762
5	.081	.592	.084	.560	.068	.635
10	.083	.544	.086	.513	.068	.592
20	.132	.499	.136	.469	.112	.552
30	.139	.433	.143	.405	.118	.490
40	.185	.373	.184	.347	.157	.432
50	.283	.304	.279	.283	.242	.364
60	.440	.220	.441	.204	.402	.276
70	1.000	.122	1.000	.114	1.000	.165
β		.95		.93		.88

The levels of mortality of the Mossi, Western tribes, and Upper Volta as a whole are high, but there are no suggestions in the data that the patterns of death rates by age have unusual characteristics. The h values at age 1 are less than at 5 to 15 years for both retrospective and current observations. The differentials are not striking, however, and the implication that deaths under age 1 are a lower proportion of those in childhood than for the African standard can be given little weight; the estimates at age 1 are too unreliable. The medium-correction values of β are close to the "central" slope of 1.00, and the increases in death rates with age after childhood thus conform with the course in most populations.

If the medium values of l_x estimated for Upper Volta are compared with the values calculated directly from the retrospective reports of children born, it is seen that the former are about 10 percent lower than the latter at age 30 years (0.433 to 0.484). The 10 percent would account for most of the difference between the P/F ratios for the younger and older women shown in the fertility comparisons of Table 7.3.A. If it is taken that the living children were fully included in the retrospective reports by mothers but a proportion of the dead omitted, the true number of children born per woman in each age group can be estimated, on the assumption that the medium-correction mortality schedule was in operation. When this is done the new P/F ratios computed from the adjusted data show little consistent fall with increasing age group of women.

However, the investigation in detail raises serious difficulties. The steepest fall in the P/F ratios occurs between age groups 25-29 and 40-44 years, corresponding to mortality of children between 3 and 15 years or so; the differences between the survivorship ratios from the retrospective reports and the estimated life tables do not become notable until after 15 years. Again, although the assumption that omissions of children in the records of the older women were mainly of the dead would give a possible explanation of the discrepancies in the fertility data for the Mossi and Upper Volta as a whole, it would be of no help for the Western tribes: in this sub-population the fall in the P/F ratios is larger, but the estimated and retrospective survivorship ratios differ little. There are too many factors which cannot be assessed quantitatively to make the search for precise explanations of discrepancies productive. Sampling errors, fluctuations and changes in fertility and mortality, inadequacies of the models in detail, differential death rates, age misreporting, and many other features may influence the comparisons.

Retrospective data on children born and dead, separately for males and females, are not available. Current age-specific death rates for each sex have, however, been calculated. They show remarkably little evidence of systematic differences, although the fluctuations in some individual rates are large. Because of the relatively small samples and consequently high random errors no very useful accuracy can be achieved in the comparison of male and female death rates for the tribal divisions. Life tables for the two sexes have been derived from the current age-specific rates for Upper Volta as a whole and are shown in Table 7.9.A. The slight tendency for the l_x values of females to be lower than those of males at younger ages could easily be a sampling effect. There is no sound evidence upon which distinct mortality schedules could be constructed. The estimates of Tables 7.7.A and 7.8.A will be taken to hold for both sexes.

Table 7.9.A. Life table measures from reported current deaths by sex—Upper Volta. (*m*, age-specific death rate per 1,000; *q*, probability of dying in age group; *l*, proportion surviving to start of age group)

Age group in years	Male			Female		
	m	q	l	m	q	l
Under 1	204	.178	1.000	206	.180	1.000
1– 4	58	.201	.822	59	.204	.820
5– 9	14	.068	.657	15	.072	.653
10–19	6	.057	.612	7	.068	.606
20–29	11	.101	.577	11	.099	.565
30–39	12	.114	.519	13	.122	.509
40–49	20	.187	.460	17	.157	.447
50–59	34	.297	.374	31	.265	.377
60–69	48	.380	.263	74	.534	.277
70 and over	101	1.000	.163	98	1.000	.129
Death rate per thousand		30.1			30.9	

Reproduction and Natural Increase

Stable female age distributions were constructed with the medium-correction mortality schedules and natural increases which gave the adjusted birth rates of Table 7.2.A. The corresponding gross and net reproduction rates and estimates of total fertility were calculated approximately from the stable populations. To do this, model distributions of age-specific fertilities with locations determined by the means found from the current data were used. The resulting stable female population measures are given in Table 7.10.A and the fitted age distributions in Table 7.13.A. Although reported current births were accepted as accurate, the

Table 7.10.A. Estimated stable female population fertility and mortality measures —Upper Volta and tribal groups

Measure	Upper Volta	Tribal Group	
		Mossi	Western
Total fertility	6.5	6.7	6.1
Gross reproduction rate	3.20	3.30	3.00
Net reproduction rate	1.43	1.38	1.51
Rates per thousand:			
Birth rate	49	50	47
Death rate	36	38	32
Natural increase	13	12	15

total fertility estimated by this procedure is considerably higher than found directly from the observed specific rates for Upper Volta and the Western tribes. The discrepancies are explained by the differences between the reported and fitted age distributions as shown below.

	Percentage in age range 15-44 years		
	Upper Volta	Mossi	Western
Reported	46.4	44.8	46.9
Fitted	44.1	44.2	44.0

The estimated birth, death, and growth rates are very similar for Upper Volta and the two subdivisions but indicate slightly lower fertility and mortality among the Western tribes, leading to a rather larger natural increase. Although the differentials are small, they appear consistently in both current and retrospective observations and also in the age distributions. Despite the inaccuracies in the data and techniques, the evidence that the effects are real is convincing.

If the high- or low-correction life tables are used instead of the medium schedule, the estimates of natural increase are from 1 to 1½ units per thousand above or below the values shown, an appreciable but not forbidding margin of doubt. If the current reports were accepted without adjustment, the estimated birth rates would be the same but the death rates lower and the natural increases correspondingly higher. The change would have been about 6 per thousand for Upper Volta as a whole, giving a natural increase of 19 instead of the estimated 13 per thousand. The difference is of enormous practical importance, although it should be noted that the estimate refers to the current situation and is not a forecast for the future.

Table 7.11.A shows the age-specific fertility rates roughly adjusted to allow for the half-year displacement of the reported current rates from the standard age groups and to correspond with the estimated total fertility ratios. Because of the misreporting of ages of the women in the reproductive period, the rates for individual groups must certainly be distorted. There is no satisfactory basis for correcting the distortion

Table 7.11.A. Estimated age-specific fertility rates—Upper Volta and tribal groups

Age group of women in years	Upper Volta	Tribal Group	
		Mossi	Western
15-19	.205	.170	.210
20-24	.333	.344	.330
25-29	.279	.278	.281
30-34	.230	.244	.204
35-39	.156	.173	.138
40-44	.081	.107	.054
45-49	.016	.024	.003
Total fertility	6.5	6.7	6.1

which depends on the form of the age errors, and particularly for determining how these are related to the reports of fertility. The broad characteristics of the variations with age can nevertheless be seen, notably how the lower fertility of the Western tribes is due to decreased rates after age 30 rather than in the earlier childbearing period.

Age Distribution

The reported age distributions are shown in Table 7.12.A for both sexes, and the female proportions are compared with the fitted stable populations in Table 7.13.A. The latter comparisons are more vividly

Table 7.12.A. Percentage age distributions by sex—Upper Volta and tribal groups

Age group in years	Upper Volta Male	Female	Total	Mossi Male	Female	Total	Western Male	Female	Total
Under 1	4.2	4.2	4.2	4.4	4.2	4.3	3.5	4.3	3.9
1- 4	14.3	12.9	13.6	14.1	12.6	13.3	12.2	12.7	12.4
5- 9	16.2	14.3	15.3	16.3	14.4	15.4	14.7	13.4	14.0
10-14	9.9	7.5	8.7	10.4	7.8	9.1	8.4	7.6	8.0
15-19	8.3	7.3	7.8	8.9	6.9	7.9	7.1	6.4	6.8
20-24	6.9	9.8	8.4	6.4	9.4	7.9	7.5	9.3	8.4
25-29	7.7	9.8	8.7	7.4	9.4	8.4	8.2	9.8	9.0
30-34	5.9	7.3	6.6	5.8	7.3	6.6	6.9	7.5	7.2
35-39	6.4	7.4	6.9	5.8	7.2	6.5	7.4	8.0	7.7
40-44	4.4	4.8	4.6	4.0	4.6	4.3	5.7	5.9	5.8
45-54	7.6	7.3	7.4	7.3	7.5	7.4	9.3	8.0	8.7
55-64	4.6	4.3	4.5	4.4	4.8	4.6	5.6	4.6	5.1
65 and over	3.6	3.1	3.3	4.8	3.9	4.3	3.5	2.5	3.0
Total	100.0	100.0	100.0	100.0	100.0	100.0	100.0	100.0	100.0
Under 15	44.6	38.9	41.8	45.2	39.0	42.1	38.8	38.0	38.3
15-44	39.6	46.4	43.0	38.3	44.8	41.6	42.8	46.9	44.9
45 and over	15.8	14.7	15.2	16.5	16.2	16.3	18.4	15.1	16.8
Per cent male	50.2			49.7			52.0		

Table 7.13.A. Percentage female age distribution observed (O) and fitted (F)— Upper Volta and tribal groups

Age group in years	In Age Groups Upper Volta O	F	Mossi O	F	Western O	F	Cumulated to Lower Limit of Group Upper Volta O	F	Mossi O	F	Western O	F
0- 4	17.1	16.0	16.8	15.9	17.0	15.5	-	-	-	-	-	-
5- 9	14.3	12.7	14.4	12.4	13.4	12.6	17.1	16.0	16.8	15.9	17.0	15.5
10-14	7.5	11.2	7.8	11.1	7.6	11.2	31.4	28.7	31.2	28.3	30.4	28.1
15-19	7.3	10.1	6.9	10.0	6.4	9.9	38.9	39.9	39.0	39.4	38.0	39.3
20-24	9.8	8.7	9.4	8.8	9.3	8.8	46.2	50.0	45.9	49.4	44.4	49.2
25-29	9.8	7.6	9.4	7.7	9.8	7.7	56.0	58.7	55.3	58.2	53.7	58.0
30-34	7.3	6.7	7.3	6.7	7.5	6.7	65.8	66.3	64.7	65.9	63.5	65.7
35-39	7.4	5.9	7.2	5.9	8.0	5.8	73.1	73.0	72.0	72.6	71.0	72.4
40-44	4.8	5.1	4.6	5.1	5.9	5.1	80.5	78.9	79.2	78.5	79.0	78.2
45-54	7.3	7.8	7.5	7.9	8.0	7.9	85.3	84.0	83.8	83.6	84.9	83.3
55-64	4.3	4.9	4.8	5.1	4.6	5.1	92.6	91.8	91.3	91.5	92.9	91.2
65 and over	3.1	3.3	3.9	3.4	2.5	3.7	96.9	96.7	96.1	96.6	97.5	96.3
Total	100.0	100.0	100.0	100.0	100.0	100.0	100.0	100.0	100.0	100.0	100.0	100.0

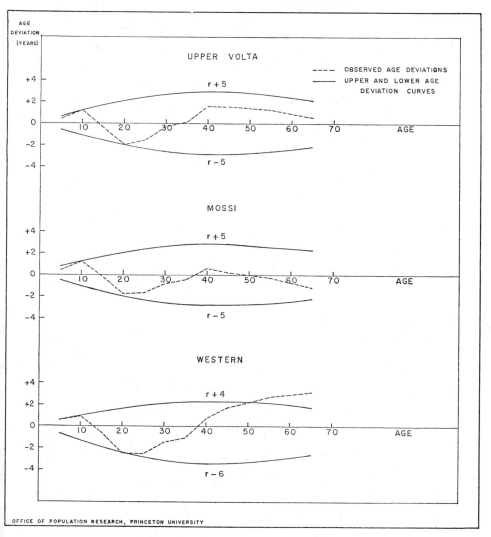

7.2.A. Age deviations, in years, between observed cumulative
age distributions, in Upper Volta, and stable age distributions
based on estimated fertility and mortality. For females.

presented in Figure 7.2.A in terms of the average erroneous deviations
in reported ages implied by the acceptance of the stable distributions as
correct. For Upper Volta and the two tribal divisions the x-axis runs as
nearly through the middle of the observed points as can practically be
determined. That the reported age distributions are consistent with the
estimates of fertility and mortality is clearly true. The similar agreement
for the different sub-populations gives great cogency to the arguments

[375]

on which the techniques of analysis are based and strengthens confidence in the accuracy of the results. The conclusion is, of course, only true if it is not possible to achieve equally good agreement by assumptions leading to substantially different demographic measures.

The general course of the fitted stable age distribution depends on the birth rate and estimated survivorship in early childhood (for concreteness on the level of l_2). The proportion surviving to age 2 was derived from the retrospective reports of the proportions dead among children of younger mothers. If, instead, the level from current rates were accepted the relative number of children surviving to age 2 in Upper Volta would be increased by about 10 percent. The effects on the comparisons of Figure 7.2.A would be roughly equivalent to keeping the mortality schedule the same but raising the birth rate by this percentage, i.e., by about 5 units per thousand, and hence the natural increase by the same absolute amount. The corresponding stable age distribution would then be represented by the extreme upper curve on the graph, which agrees with the observations in the proportions under 10 years of age, but implies that the numbers reported as under 20 were in fact under 16 and that later ages were all on average understated. Such distortions cannot be proved impossible but seem unlikely, and there is no evidence for them.

Furthermore, it would be necessary to explain why the retrospective reports included too high a proportion of dead children. Not only is this inherently unlikely, but unless living children were stated to be dead, it would follow that the total retrospective children per woman had been overstated and, to achieve consistency, the current births also. The actual fertility and mortality would both be lower than estimated and the resulting stable age distribution in better accord with the observations than would be the case if the current birth and death data were accurate. However, the adjustments would imply that too many dead children and the true number of live children were reported retrospectively but that for the previous year births were overstated but deaths about right. Such an occurrence is not plausible, and, although the necessary coincidence might happen in one inquiry, it is unlikely to be repeated in others.

Another possibility would be to accept the mortality level from the retrospective proportions of children dead as correct but to postulate that current births as well as deaths had been understated. Such an hypothesis would not be unreasonable in itself, but the other consequences are hard to justify. A further necessary assumption would be that the retrospective reports of children alive and dead were both too low by the same factor as current births. In addition, although the current deaths have to be raised by about 27 percent to reach agreement with the retrospective mortality levels, the adjustment for births would have to be much less. An increase of more than 10 percent would push the stable age distribution above the upper limit of deviations shown in Figure 7.2.A and imply that the proportions recorded as under any age were too low over the whole range. A percentage error in current deaths has a much smaller effect than one of the same size in births on the computed stable age distribution because the influence of mortality depends on the survivorship ratio in early childhood. In general the latter is considerably higher than the complementary probability of dying and is proportionately less affected by the discrepancy. The value of the age distribution checks is thus strengthened, because an accurate balancing of errors in current births and deaths (with the point of balance varying from population to population) is unlikely. The arbitrary nature of the corrections required if the level of mortality from the retrospective reports is accepted but fertility taken to be understated is clear.

These points have been discussed in some detail because they illustrate the power of the tests of consistency. The change in an assumption or measure in one aspect of the data has implications for the errors in others. Although it is possible to postulate patterns of misrecording which would give almost any demographic indices, a combination of special and more or less implausible characteristics is required. If the same assumptions and techniques lead to consistent results for a number of populations, the argument for their validity is reinforced. Of course, the methods are not precise, but they reduce the scope for substantial errors in estimation. The conclusion only holds where there are relatively independent cross-checks. Thus the possibility that some births and deaths of very young children were omitted from all reports cannot be closely investigated by internal checks.

The comparisons in Table 7.13.A and Figure 7.2.A do not suggest that the age distributions deviate from the stable form except perhaps among the Western tribes. The small proportion of the latter population at over 65 years might suggest that fertility (lower than in Upper Volta as a whole) had been falling, but such evidence is very uncertain. The errors in reported ages suggested by the fitted stable distributions are closely in line with the features discussed in the introduction to this section and in Chapter 2. The numbers at 10-19 years are greatly reduced by movements into the adjacent age groups. At the younger ages the overstatement extends to both the 5-9 and 0-4 age groups; within the reproductive period the reported ages are biased toward the middle of the range, with excess numbers at 20-39 years but the greatest effect at 25-29. Rather more of the deficiency at 10-14 years is accounted for by under- than overstating of ages. The overstatement plus a slight tendency for the numbers shown at above 45 years to be too low leads to the excess of women reported in the reproductive range already noted. Agreement between the observed and fitted proportions under each age is best at 35 years. For Upper Volta and the Mossi the percentages shown at the older ages in the stable populations are reasonably close to the observed values.

A large number of males in Upper Volta emigrate to work in neighboring countries for varied periods. It is not clear how the age distribution may have been affected by this and the exclusion of the two towns from the inquiry. There was a careful attempt to record all persons who were regarded as residents, whether present or not, but the results may be influenced by permanent movements, omissions of some absent residents, and wrong age reports for temporary migrants. For these reasons the stable age distribution comparisons are made in detail for females only, but a few comments will be made on the data for males.

Since the current death rates of males and females hardly differ, it was accepted that the estimated life tables for the two sexes together could be used for either. The corresponding stable age distributions are, therefore, the same for the two sexes, but, on the assumption that there were 103 males for every 100 female births, the total numbers would be about 3 percent higher for the former. The observed numbers were less than 1 percent higher. If this is taken to be due to differential emigration of adult males and a correction applied, the outcome would be an increase of a few percent in the proportion of children. There would then be close agreement between the observed and fitted percentages of males under 20 years, but the proportions reported under 15 years and, to an even greater extent, under 10 years would be much overstated. *A priori*, the suggestion that understatement of ages in the range 10-19 years may be much greater for males than for females is not implausible, because of the later puberty, marriage, and entry into adult responsibilities of the former.

Such a conclusion is given very strong support by the course of the male age distribution at ages beyond 20. Here are shown fitted and observed proportions under selected ages on the assumption that 7 percent of the males at each age in the interval 20-54 years (about 3 percent of the total numbers) were missing.

	Age in years						
	10	15	20	25	35	45	55
Observed, percent	34.7	44.6	52.9	59.8	73.4	84.2	91.8
Fitted, percent	29.6	41.2	51.6	59.9	73.6	84.1	91.5

The fit is remarkably close at ages above 20 years. In this range, in contrast to the statistics for females, there is no indication of massive transfers between age groups because of misstatements. A fitted distribution which reproduced the proportions under 10 and 15 years better would be in poor agreement with the data at all higher ages.

The techniques of analysis, based on clearly stated assumptions, have led to estimates of fertility and mortality which are consistent with the evidence from age distributions. Despite the limitations, which have been assessed, the measures can be accepted with more confidence than would, at first sight, have been justified in view of the deficiencies in the observations.

B. REPUBLIC OF DAHOMEY

The Republic of Dahomey lies on the Guinea coast. The southern region is a narrow strip, with an area of 30,000 square kilometers, between Nigeria in the east and Togo in the west. The northern region of 82,000 square kilometers broadens out toward the boundaries with Upper Volta and Niger. The southern part of the country is relatively thickly populated, with densities of 49 and 100 persons per square kilometer, overall and in the coastal districts, respectively. This is the area of influence of the former powerful kingdom of Dahomey, which was one of the main centers of the slave trade in the sixteenth to nineteenth centuries. Production of food crops reaches a good level, and a considerable export trade, mainly of palm oil, exists. Several important urban centers are situated on or near the coast, in particular Porto-Novo, the capital, Cotonou, and Ouidah. The northern section of the territory is poorer and thinly populated, with a density of less than 8 persons per square kilometer, although the mountain region adjoining Togo is more heavily settled.

The 1961 sample inquiry, which was carried out between May and September, covered the whole country except for small populations in the area of Tchi to the southwest and the town of Abomey, also in the southern region. With the inclusion of estimates for the areas omitted, the total population was 2.1 million. The analysis which follows, however, is confined to the numbers in the rural districts because the detailed statistics for the towns, necessary for the application of the techniques, are not available. Although the results for the rural populations have not been published in full, the data are sufficient for the investigation of the accuracy of recording of the basic observations of births, deaths, and age and for the estimation of vital rates. To avoid cumbersome phrasing, the locations of the rural populations will be referred to as north, south, and Dahomey without qualifications.

The rural population estimated from the 1961 sample inquiry was 1.9 million, comprising 1.3 million in the south region and 0.6 million in the north. The south is inhabited largely by the Fon tribe with a number of subdivisions and allied groups, speaking languages of the Twi branch of the Kwa sub-family of the Nigritic stock.[4] In the north there is a mixture of tribes which are ethnically and culturally very similar. These belong to the Voltaic sub-family of the Nigritic linguistic stock and are closely related to the tribes of Upper Volta.

The sampling fraction in the rural districts was approximately one in eighteen overall, and about 104,000 persons were included in the inquiry; 25,000 of these were in the northern region. With such substantial sample sizes in the divisions for which data are presented, the "nuisance" effect of random errors is reduced. Many features of the analysis for Dahomey are so similar to the corresponding characteristics found in the study of Upper Volta that they can be noted very briefly. However, divergences between the results for the northern and southern regions provide a stringent test of the techniques for correcting errors in the reports of vital events and hence of the assumptions upon which the methods depend.

Fertility

The fertility measures for the north and south regions and Dahomey as a whole, calculated from the births reported for the year preceding the survey, are given in Table 7.1.B. The measures show no anomalous characteristics; the fertility reported was high for both regions but rather greater for the south than for the north. Retrospective births per woman are compared with the corresponding cumulated values, computed from the specific fertility rates with the aid of the observed means and P_1/P_2 values of Table 7.2.B by the P/F ratios in Table 7.3.B. As in Upper Volta the ratios are not far from 1.00 for the women aged 20-24 years but fall consistently with age group. Again the most convincing explanation of the decrease is the omission of children by the older women

Table 7.1.B. Reported current birth and age-specific fertility rates—Dahomey and regions

Age group of women in years*	Dahomey	Region North	South
15-19	.207	.203	.210
20-24	.339	.289	.363
25-29	.311	.263	.331
30-34	.250	.216	.265
35-39	.167	.155	.171
40-44	.085	.080	.087
45-49	.027	.040	.022
Total fertility	6.93	6.23	7.24
Birth rate per thousand	54.6	46.7	58.3

*The true age intervals for the rates are, on average, half a year younger than is shown.

[4] Murdock, *op.cit.*

Table 7.2.B. Estimated measures of fertility distributions—Dahomey and regions

Measure	Dahomey	Region North	South
Mean (m̄) in years	27.7	27.9	27.6
P₁/P₂	.26	.28	.25
Adjusted female birth rate per thousand.	49.0	47.2	50.3

Table 7.3.B. Cumulated fertility (F), reported parity (P), and P/F ratios—Dahomey and regions

Age group of women in years	Dahomey			Region North			South		
	F	P	P/F	F	P	P/F	F	P	P/F
15-19	0.55	0.49	0.89	0.57	0.52	0.91	0.54	0.48	0.89
20-24	2.03	1.89	0.93	1.87	1.87	1.00	2.11	1.91	0.91
25-29	3.68	3.28	0.89	3.27	3.08	0.94	3.88	3.38	0.87
30-34	5.07	4.49	0.89	4.45	4.18	0.94	5.35	4.66	0.87
35-39	6.08	5.11	0.84	5.36	4.87	0.91	6.41	5.24	0.82
40-44	6.68	5.73	0.86	5.92	5.34	0.90	7.02	5.88	0.84
45-49	6.92	5.81	0.84	6.21	5.48	0.88	7.24	5.98	0.83
50-59	6.93	5.77	0.83	6.23	5.33	0.86	7.24	6.04	0.83

in the retrospective reports. The P/F ratio for the north region is 1.00 for the women aged 20-24, consistent with the trend beyond 30 years despite the sharp drop for the 25-29 group. The reported births will, therefore, be taken as accurate. In the south, however, the P/F ratio at 20-24 years is only 0.91, and there is no suggestion in the data that the level might be much too low because of sampling or age errors. It will be accepted that the births have been overrecorded and a correction factor of 0.91 applied. Similarly for Dahomey as a whole a correction factor of 0.93 is obtained. Although from the statistics available it was only possible to calculate P/F ratios at under 60 years of age, it may be noted that the decrease in the ratios is of the same order as for Upper Volta and is slight after the women reach 40 years or so.

Table 7.2.B gives the adjusted female birth rates obtained when the corrections for overrecording are applied, with the standard assumption about the size of the sex ratio at birth. The rates are still high. However, the differential between the two component regions is much smaller than was suggested by the crude data, partly because of the overrecording correction for the south and partly because of the effects of the proportions of females in the regions.

Information on number of childless women has not been published, thus there is no Table 7.4.B.

Mortality

The information on mortality is summarized in Tables 7.5.B and 7.6.B. The first of these gives the life table survivorship to various ages calculated from the retrospective reports of the proportion of children

Table 7.5.B. Percentage of children having died previous to the survey, by age of mother, and derived life table survivorship ratios l_x—Dahomey and regions

Age group of mother in years	Age of child survivor- ship	Dahomey Per cent of children dead	l_x	North Per cent of children dead	l_x	South Per cent of children dead	l_x
15–19	1	18.9	.823	14.4	.867	21.5	.798
20–24	2	27.5	.729	24.8	.757	28.9	.714
25–29	3	31.9	.687	28.4	.723	33.2	.674
30–34	5	35.8	.641	31.5	.683	37.5	.625
35–39	10	37.7	.619	32.3	.672	39.6	.600
40–44	15	42.2	.583	36.6	.637	44.0	.566
45–49	20	44.2	.564	36.9	.635	48.7	.521
50–59	30	45.4	.540	38.7	.605	47.6	.522

dead by age of mother; the multiplying factor procedure was used in these computations as for Upper Volta. Table 7.6.B shows the age-specific rates calculated from the deaths reported for the year preceding the survey and the derived life table q and l values. The life table l_x values for Dahomey as a whole, obtained from the retrospective and current reports, are compared in Figure 7.1.B in terms of the differences h on the logit scale from the African standard life table values at corresponding ages.

Again the general conclusions are much the same as in the analysis for Upper Volta. The child mortality suggested by the retrospective data is heavy; that from the current deaths is substantially lighter. The differences between the two sets of calculated l_x's decrease with age. By thirty years the l_x from the current data is only a little above that from the retrospective for Dahomey as a whole; for the north region it becomes, in fact, the lower of the two by this age. These features are clearly

Table 7.6.B. Life table measures from reported current deaths (both sexes)— Dahomey and regions. (m, age-specific death rate per 1,000; q, probability of dying in age group; l, proportion surviving to start of age group)

Age group in years	Dahomey m	q	l	North m	q	l	South m	q	l
Under 1	114	.105	1.000	100	.093	1.000	119	.110	1.000
1– 4	46	.164	.895	46	.164	.907	46	.164	.890
5– 9	10	.049	.748	13	.063	.758	9	.044	.744
10–19	10	.096	.712	12	.114	.711	9	.087	.711
20–29	13	.123	.643	14	.132	.630	13	.123	.649
30–39	11	.105	.564	12	.114	.546	10	.096	.570
40–49	16	.150	.505	18	.167	.484	14	.132	.515
50–59	26	.233	.429	31	.272	.403	24	.217	.447
60–69	42	.352	.329	48	.393	.294	39	.331	.350
70 and over	126	1.000	.213	164	1.000	.178	115	1.000	.234
Death rate per thousand	26.4			26.9			26.2		

Region

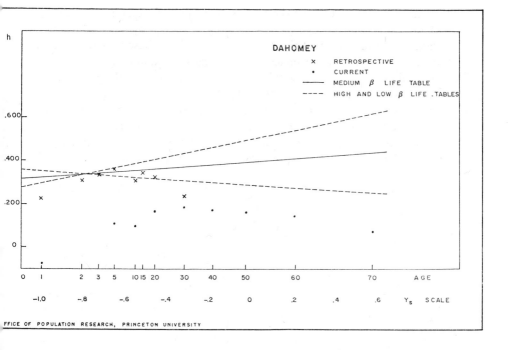

7.1.B. Proportion surviving to each age (l_x) in Dahomey in life tables calculated from retrospective mortality data and current mortality data and fitted by linear logit transformations.

exhibited, on the graph, by the large differences between the retrospective and current h values in childhood, which narrow in the early adult years. The reported mortalities between 1 and 5 years are high relative to those under 1 year, particularly for the current observations, as shown by the increase in the h values at early years of life. The discrepancy between the retrospective mortality pattern and that of the African standard is small, however, and, as has been pointed out, the estimates of the proportion surviving to age 1 are particularly unreliable. Since the current deaths in childhood in Dahomey show every sign of having been badly underreported, the extreme division between the under-1 and the 1-4 age groups may be due to even larger omissions of very young children. The h values from the current observations at ages after 5 years, although erratic, do not suggest a systematic deviation from linearity. The utility of the model mortality system, based on a linear relation between the logits of the survivorship ratios and those of the African standard life table, for the graduation of the information is therefore not obviously contradicted.

[383]

In accordance with the discussion in the introductory section to the chapter it is assumed that the child mortalities given by the retrospective data are correct but that the proportions surviving based on the reports of the older women are unacceptable because of differential exclusions of dead children, etc. Probabilities of dying at ages beyond 5 were calculated from the reports of current deaths, on the alternative postulates that there were no omissions and that omissions were proportionately the same as at under 5 years. Life tables of the parametric system were then fitted by the procedure described. The results are summarized in Table 7.7.B. Because of the large differences between the childhood

Table 7.7.B. Indices from estimated low- and high-correction life tables—Dahomey and regions

Estimated measures	Dahomey		Region North		South	
	Low	High	Low	High	Low	High
Per cent correction to deaths	23	48	15	35	27	54
1(2)	.719	.719	.752	.752	.705	.705
1(27)	.524	.465	.534	.485	.520	.462
β	.94	1.20	1.08	1.30	.88	1.14

mortalities derived from the current and retrospective information, the percentage corrections to the deaths are substantial (48 percent for Dahomey compared with 27 percent for Upper Volta). The ranges of the two estimates of β are correspondingly large, although no values which are unlikely, *a priori*, are arrived at, i.e., none is far from the levels commonly found for published life tables. The corrections to the deaths are much greater for the south than the north, since the estimated l_x's based on retrospective data are lower for the latter region although the current measures are about the same. The medium-correction life tables with the same estimated l_2 but β midway between the low and high values are shown in Table 7.8.B. On Figure 7.1.B are traced the straight lines for the low-, medium-, and high-correction estimated life tables. Despite the considerable deviation between the two extreme lines, no firm conclusion that the observations are fitted better by one or the other can be reached. The β levels of the high estimates, particularly for the north region, are however much above the standard value of 1.00, and the current h values increase sharply between 10 and 30 years. These features may indicate that adult deaths in the preceding year were better reported than those of children. On the other hand, with such large corrections for the omission of child deaths it seems unlikely that recording for adults was complete. Again, the medium estimates must be given preference.

Table 7.8.B. Medium-correction life tables, males and females together—Dahomey
and regions. (q, probability of dying in succeeding age interval; l, proportion
surviving at age)

Age in years	Dahomey		Region North		South	
	q	l	q	l	q	l
0	.206	1.000	.173	1.000	.221	1.000
1	.184	.794	.180	.827	.182	.779
5	.079	.648	.081	.678	.077	.637
10	.082	.597	.087	.623	.080	.588
20	.137	.548	.146	.569	.129	.541
30	.148	.473	.160	.486	.142	.470
40	.199	.403	.216	.408	.186	.404
50	.300	.323	.334	.320	.286	.329
60	.487	.226	.531	.213	.460	.235
70	1.000	.116	1.000	.100	1.000	.127
β	1.07		1.19		1.01	

Some backing for the choice can be obtained from an examination of
the retrospective reports of total children born. When total fertility for
the whole country is multiplied by the adjustment factor from the P/F
ratios of 0.93, the value 6.44 is obtained, which is almost the same as the
estimate derived from the adjusted female birth rate and the fitted
stable age distribution (see below). If it is assumed that the differences
between this total fertility and the live births reported per woman in
the older age groups are solely due to omissions of dead children, new
retrospective l_x values can be calculated. Proportions surviving from
birth of 0.510 and 0.483 at 20 and 30 years, respectively, are obtained.
Although these estimates are subject to considerable sampling and other
errors, it is noteworthy that they are at about the same level as the
corresponding ratios from the medium-correction life table. The life
table is then in harmony with the view that most of the omissions of
children ever borne by the older women are of children already dead.
On the other hand, the high-correction mortality schedules could only
be made consistent with the retrospective reports if fertility of the older
women had been higher than deduced or dead children were shown as
alive. Despite the crudeness of these comparisons (inevitable because
of the nature of the data), they suggest strongly that for Dahomey at
least current deaths were better reported from age 5 to 30 years or so
than for young children. It is important that the same conclusions hold
for the north and south regions separately, although the estimated proportion of total births omitted by the older women is much higher for
the former population.

Retrospective information for the sexes separately on live and dead
children has not been published, but life tables for males and females,
calculated from current data, are given in Table 7.9.B. As in Upper
Volta, there is remarkably little indication of any sex differential in mortality, and the estimates of Tables 7.7.B and 7.8.B will be taken to hold
for both males and females.

Table 7.9.B. Life table measures from reported current deaths by sex—Dahomey.
(*m*, age-specific death rate per 1,000; *q*, probability of dying in age group; *l*,
proportion surviving to start of age group)

Age group in years	Male m	q	l	Female m	q	l
Under 1	115	.106	1.000	113	.105	1.000
1- 4	47	.167	.894	45	.160	.895
5- 9	11	.054	.745	10	.049	.752
10-19	10	.096	.704	10	.096	.715
20-29	11	.105	.637	15	.141	.646
30-39	12	.114	.570	10	.096	.555
40-49	15	.141	.505	16	.150	.502
50-59	28	.249	.434	24	.217	.427
60-69	47	.386	.326	36	.310	.334
70 and over	112	1.000	.200	143	1.000	.231

Death rates

26.0

Reproduction and Natural Increase

The stable female age distributions with the medium-correction life tables, which gave the required adjusted birth rates, were calculated and are compared with the observations in Table 7.13.B. The corresponding gross and net reproduction rates and total fertility ratios, derived for locations of the age-specific fertility schedules fixed by the means for the current data, are listed in Table 7.10.B. The estimates of total fertility differ little from the values which would have been found if the correction factors for birth recording had been applied directly to the current age-specific rates. Effectively, therefore, the reported and fitted proportions of women in the reproductive period are the same, in contrast to the similar comparisons for Upper Volta.

The differences between the estimated vital rates of the two regions are slight. Although the south is taken to have a total fertility 10 percent higher than the north, the birth rate is only some 6 percent greater because of the divergent mortality patterns characterized by the levels of β. Differentials in mortality and natural increase rates are too small relative to the inaccuracies of the observations and methods of analysis to

Table 7.10.B. Estimated stable female population fertility and mortality measures
—Dahomey and regions

Measure	Dahomey	North	South
Total fertility	6.4	6.0	6.6
Gross reproduction rate	3.15	2.95	3.25
Net reproduction rate	1.54	1.49	1.59
Rates per thousand			
Birth rate	49	47	50
Death rate	33	32	33
Natural increase	16	15	17

be accepted as meaningful. The adoption of the low- and high-correction mortality schedules would have led to death rates about 2 per thousand below and above the medium estimates respectively, with the reverse changes in the levels of natural increase. As a result of the comparative techniques of analysis, current births were reduced to allow for over-recording and deaths raised to correct for omissions. Consequently, the estimated rate of growth is 16 per thousand compared with the reported value of 28 per thousand; the discrepancy for the north region, 17 as against 32 per thousand, is even greater. The differences in implications of the two sets of rates are vast, and the need for checks by the examination of other aspects of the data even more imperative.

The current specific rates were corrected, by the same percentages for each age group of women in a population, to sum to the estimated total fertility ratio and adjusted to allow for the half-year displacement. The derived rates, given in Table 7.11.B, do not indicate any notable sys-

Table 7.11.B. Estimated age-specific fertility rates—Dahomey and regions

Age group of women in years	Dahomey	Region	
		North	South
15–19	.216	.220	.217
20–24	.318	:281	.336
25–29	.285	.250	.298
30–34	.224	.203	.235
35–39	.146	.142	.147
40–44	.072	.071	.072
45–49	.019	.033	.015
Total fertility	6.4	6.0	6.6

tematic variations in pattern between the north and south regions. Differences are erratic, and it is not possible to disentangle true divergences from the nuisance effects of sampling and age reporting errors.

Age Distribution

The age distributions recorded are shown, separately by sex, in Table 7.12.B. The examination of the detailed characteristics is hindered by the lack of information by five-year groups at ages over 10, but the broad features can be discerned. The comparisons of observed and fitted female age distributions of Table 7.13.B are illustrated by Figure 7.2.B in the manner described in the introduction to the chapter. The good agreement of the stable distribution constructed from the fertility and mortality estimates with the age data for Dahomey as a whole is evident. Discrepancies at ages above 10 years are moderate and not systematically positive or negative. The points from about 15 to 45 years are not far from the x-axis, showing that the numbers of women in the

Table 7.12.B. Percentage age distributions by sex—Dahomey and regions

Age group in years	Dahomey Male	Dahomey Female	Dahomey Total	North Male	North Female	North Total	South Male	South Female	South Total
Under 1	5.3	5.4	5.4	4.7	5.1	4.9	5.6	5.6	5.6
1- 4	14.7	14.1	14.4	14.4	14.5	14.4	14.8	13.9	14.3
5- 9	17.7	15.7	16.7	18.0	16.5	17.3	17.6	15.3	16.4
10-19	16.9	15.4	16.1	17.1	16.6	16.8	16.9	14.9	15.8
20-29	12.9	18.4	15.7	13.8	19.3	16.5	12.4	18.0	15.4
30-39	11.7	12.8	12.3	11.7	12.1	11.9	11.8	13.1	12.4
40-49	8.6	8.1	8.3	8.7	7.2	7.9	8.5	8.5	8.5
50-59	5.7	5.1	5.4	5.8	4.5	5.2	5.7	5.4	5.5
60 and over	6.5	5.0	5.7	5.8	4.2	5.1	6.7	5.3	6.1
Total	100.0	100.0	100.0	100.0	100.0	100.0	100.0	100.0	100.0
Per cent male		49.0			51.3			48.0	

reproductive age groups do not differ much in the observed and fitted distributions. The same general conclusion was arrived at from the agreement between total fertility ratios estimated, respectively, from the direct application of the correction factors to the specific rates and from the relation between adjusted births and the stable population. Figure 7.2.B suggests that the proportions of the population under 5 and 10 years are greatly overstated. The alternative assumption that these proportions were accurate would imply large and systematic age errors at above 10 years, e.g., that on average the persons recorded as under 20 and 30 years were in fact below 15½ and 25½ years. Although the proposition that such misstatements are unlikely is not, by itself, irrefutable, it is reinforced by the interlocking of the age-distribution information with the independent estimates of fertility and mortality and also by the similarity of the comparisons for Dahomey and Upper Volta. The combined force of the evidence is powerful.

Table 7.13.B. Percentage female age distributions observed (O) and fitted (F)—
Dahomey and regions

Age group in years	In age groups Dahomey O	Dahomey F	North O	North F	South O	South F	Cumulated to lower limit of group Dahomey O	Dahomey F	North O	North F	South O	South F
0- 4	19.5	16.9	19.6	16.9	19.5	17.1	-	-	-	-	-	-
5- 9	15.7	13.4	16.5	13.5	15.3	13.5	19.5	16.9	19.6	16.9	19.5	17.1
10-19	15.4	22.1	16.6	22.4	14.9	22.0	35.2	30.3	36.1	30.4	34.8	30.6
20-29	18.4	16.7	19.3	16.9	18.0	16.6	50.6	52.4	52.7	52.8	49.7	52.6
30-39	12.8	12.2	12.1	12.3	13.1	12.2	69.0	69.1	72.0	69.7	67.7	69.2
40-49	8.1	8.9	7.2	8.7	8.5	8.6	81.8	81.3	84.1	82.0	80.8	81.4
50-59	5.1	5.6	4.5	5.5	5.4	5.6	89.9	90.2	91.3	90.7	89.3	90.0
60 and over	5.0	4.2	4.2	3.8	5.3	4.4	95.0	95.8	95.8	96.2	94.7	95.6
Total	100.0	100.0	100.0	100.0	100.0	100.0	100.0	100.0	100.0	100.0	100.0	100.0

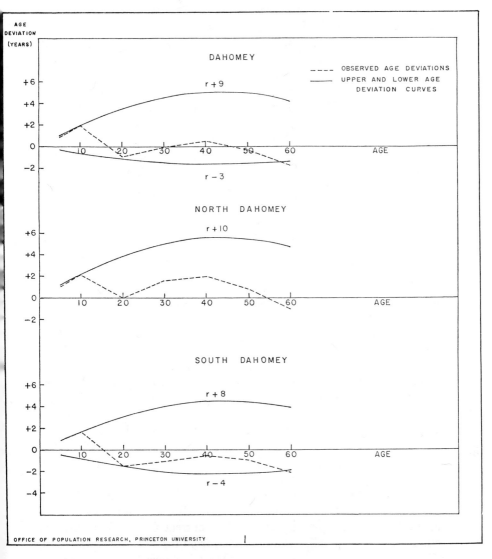

7.2.B. Age deviations, in years, between observed cumulative
age distributions, in Dahomey, and stable age distributions
based on estimated fertility and mortality. For females.

The general features of the agreement between observed and fitted
age distributions in the north and south regions are the same as for
Dahomey as a whole, but there are more signs of systematic discrepancies. Greater consistency in the fit would be achieved if changes corresponding to a rise of natural increase of about 2 units per thousand
in the north and the same reduction in the south were made. It is worth
noting that such changes would reinforce the effects of the corrections

already applied to reduce the reported north-south differential and would even reverse it. The basic assumption that age recording errors are the same in the north and south is weak, the size of the adjustments would be very arbitrary, and it is far from clear whether they should be applied to fertility or mortality. No further corrections have, therefore, been made to the estimated measures in Table 7.10.B, but for practical purposes birth, death, and growth rates in north and south Dahomey can be taken to be approximately the same as for the country as a whole.

The comparisons in Table 7.13.B and Figure 7.2.B are consistent with the assumption that the age distributions can be well represented by stable population models. The age errors have then a very similar pattern to that deduced for Upper Volta, with large deficiencies in numbers at 10 to 19 years balanced by excesses at under 10 and in the middle of the reproductive period. The latter discrepancy is, however, smaller in Dahomey. Again, agreement of the observed and fitted percentages under different ages is relatively most satisfactory at 30 or 40 years. At the upper ages the proportions in the stable populations are close to the reported percentages. It is particularly interesting that the fitted values for the north are lower than for the south, in conformity with the observations, because of the effect of the more extreme level of β in the former region. In fact the differential is greater in the observed than the stable distribution. Some support is, therefore, given to the method of using β as a guide to the course of mortality at ages beyond childhood.

The analysis procedures thus lead to consistent results for Dahomey, as for Upper Volta. It is again useful to consider the assumptions necessary to justify measures considerably different from those estimated. The examination is particularly interesting for the south region because the discrepancies between the current and retrospective sets of data on fertility and mortality were larger. If the current reports of childhood mortality are taken as correct for the region, the proportion surviving to age 5 years is 0.744. The division of the total births to women aged 30-34 years between children alive and dead on this basis is given below on the alternative assumptions that the level of current fertility reported was correct and that the adjustment obtained from the P/F ratios was valid. The values from the retrospective reports are shown for comparison.

	From current mortality		
	Reported fertility	Adjusted fertility	Retrospective report
Total births	5.42	4.93	4.66
Alive	4.03	3.67	2.91
Dead	1.39	1.26	1.75

Whatever the validity of the adjustment to fertility, in order to justify the use of the childhood mortality estimated from current data it would be necessary to explain why the women aged 30-34 years (and similarly for other ages) omitted a large number of live children from the retrospective reports but included too many dead ones. Alternatively, if it were argued that the reported fertility was too low in both the current and retrospective records, it would be necessary to postulate a total fertility ratio at least 25 percent higher than that reported, i.e., about 9.1, to avoid the assumption that too many dead children were recorded. The stable age distribution resulting from current mortality and such a fertility level is far outside the range of extremes traced in Figure 7.2.B, with even higher proportions of the population under 5 and 10 years than were reported. The postulate that deaths in the preceding year were accurately recorded leads to formidable difficulties of interpretation.

The check on the correction for fertility level in south Dahomey is not so searching because the factor at 0.91 only causes a 9 percent change. Nevertheless, the unadjusted female birth rate of 55 per thousand would determine a stable age distribution approaching the upper extreme in Figure 7.2.B. It has already been pointed out that better consistency among regions and with Upper Volta in the age distribution comparisons would be obtained by a fitted curve which deviated from the estimates in the opposite direction.

The most powerful evidence in favor of the methods for deriving fertility and mortality comes from the comparison of the results for the north and south regions. For the former there is no adjustment to current births, and the mortality correction is not much more than half that for the south. As a consequence the fertility ratio found for the south is only 10 percent higher as opposed to the reported 16 percent; the birth rate differential is further reduced by the estimated patterns of mortality in the two regions. Finally, the higher mortality correction in the south provides an estimated life table with lower survivorship ratios than for the north, although the current values show little differential. The combination of these effects results in stable age distributions for the two regions which are closely similar over most of the range, as can be seen from Table 7.13.B. The observed age distributions are also in fair agreement, but with rather higher percentages under corresponding ages in the north (which had the lower reported current fertility) than in the south. Either the methods of analysis are effective or a remarkable set of coincidences has occurred.

The comparison of the reported age distributions for males and females reveals much the same features in Dahomey as in Upper Volta. The percentages in the years of childhood are higher for males, but there is no suggestion of excess numbers at the middle adult ages (20-39 years). These sex differentials are not, however, as large as in Upper Volta. Since the estimated life tables for males and females are the same, the stable age distributions are also identical. Below are shown fitted and observed proportions under selected ages. Despite the higher percentages observed at the lower ages, there is fair agreement at 30 and 40 years.

	Age in years					
	10	20	30	40	50	60
Observed, percent	37.7	54.6	67.5	79.2	87.8	93.5
Fitted, percent	30.3	52.4	69.1	81.3	90.2	95.8

After 30 the fitted proportions are greater largely because of the substantial number of men stated to be over 60 years. More females than males were recorded in the inquiry, probably in part because of permanent or temporary emigration of the latter. If some correction is applied for this, the fitted and observed percentages under the given ages agree better at 10 and 20 years and also in old age, but worse in the middle years of life. It is clear that no improvement in fit at all ages can be achieved by varying the stable population measures, unless a very different pattern of mortality is assumed for adult males. Although this cannot be ruled out, it seems more likely that the high percentage of males over 60 is due to overstatements of ages or special circumstances in the past history of the population.

C. REPUBLIC OF GUINEA

The sampling inquiry in the Republic of Guinea, which covered the whole country, took place between October 1954 and April 1955, when the territory was a French possession. It was the earliest large-scale survey of its kind undertaken in the French-speaking African territories. The planning and field work were organized with great care, and a detailed report of the methodology and results has been published. In several ways, the analysis of the data presents difficulties and reveals unusual features. These are not, in general, specific to the Guinea inquiry but rather exaggerations of characteristics which are also apparent in some of the other surveys. The experience gained from the pioneer Guinea project has been used profitably to reduce errors in the succeeding studies. Because of these features the estimation of measures raises some awkward and special problems. The discussion of the Guinea results was, therefore, postponed until after the studies of the more consistent Upper Volta and Dahomey data. Although the statistics for Guinea are more detailed than for the other countries, the analysis is confined in the main to the types of information which were available from all the inquiries examined. The extra detail has only been used for a few additional checks.

Guinea lies on the extreme west of the "bulge" of Africa. It has a short coastline of 300 kilometers between Portuguese Guinea and Sierra Leone but, in the main, stretches inland north of the latter territory and Liberia to the Ivory Coast at its eastern limits. The northern boundary is formed by Senegal and Mali. The area is approximately 250,000 square kilometers in extent. Guinea, with its mountains and high rainfall, is a major watershed, the source of the Gambia and Niger rivers and tributaries of these and the Senegal. The country is divided into four regions. These are Maritime, the hot and humid alluvial costal plain; Fouta-Djallon, adjacent to Senegal, a less humid mountain area; Upper Guinea, a savannah country next to and similar to the Sudan; Forest, north of Liberia, mainly consisting of forested mountains. The Maritime region is the most developed, with a considerable port at Conakry and a major modern industry in the mining of bauxite. Export crops such as coffee and palm nuts are of increasing importance for the Forest region. Fouta-Djallon is an area of scattered villages with extensive cattle grazing. Most of the inhabitants of Upper Guinea live in the river valleys in widely separated villages. The territory as a whole has a large industrial and agricultural potential. The inquiry gave a total *de facto* population of 2.57 million, of whom 0.50, 0.97, 0.34, and 0.76 million were in Maritime, Fouta-Djallon, Upper, and Forest regions respectively. The overall density was just over 10 persons per square kilometer. In addition it was estimated that some 80,000 people were absent more or less temporarily from the territory but resident there. About 300,000 persons were included in the sample, i.e., about 12 percent of the population. Because of these substantial numbers the sampling variation would be expected to be low. A more critical consideration of the effects of recording errors can, therefore, be made.

The country is inhabited by a mixture of tribes, although these nearly all fall into well-defined groups. All the groups have languages of the Nigritic family; the main sub-families represented are Mande and Atlantic. The Mande tribes are the major component of the populations of Maritime (mainly Susu) and Upper Guinea (Malinke and allied tribes); the Atlantic groups are the Peul (Fulani) of Fouta-Djallon and the mixed tribes of the Forest region; there are, however, also tribes of the Atlantic subdivision on the coast of Maritime and Malinke in the Forest region. Although some of the data from the inquiry were tabulated by tribal groups, the detail is not sufficient for the full analysis applied in these studies; only results by regions are therefore given. No separate study is made of differentials between rural and urban inhabitants.

Fertility

Table 7.1.C gives the basic indices of fertility derived from the reports of births in the year preceding the survey. The measures for the four regions are very similar, with a total fertility in the neighborhood

Table 7.1.C. Reported current birth and age-specific fertility rates—Guinea and regions

Age group of women in years*	Guinea	Maritime	Fouta-Djallon	Upper	Forest
15–19	.241	.276	.253	.205	.213
20–24	.335	.321	.342	.334	.335
25–29	.310	.296	.304	.329	.320
30–34	.246	.201	.252	.244	.271
35–39	.171	.157	.166	.181	.181
40–44	.069	.076	.060	.068	.076
45–49	.028	.027	.022	.025	.034
Total fertility	7.000	6.770	6.995	6.930	7.150
Birth rate per thousand	61.7	59.5	62.7	57.9	63.6

* The true age intervals for the rates are, on average, half a year younger than is shown.

of 7.0 and a birth rate varying a little around 62 per thousand. The specific fertility rates for the 15-19 age group of women and the means of the distributions (shown in Table 7.2.C) suggest a slightly later start to childbearing in Upper and Forest than in the other two regions.

Table 7.2.C. Estimated measures of fertility distributions—Guinea and regions

Measure	Guinea	Maritime	Fouta-Djallon	Upper	Forest
Mean ($\bar{m}$) in years	27.3	26.9	27.0	27.6	27.8
P_1/P_2	.31	.35	.32	.26	.28
Adjusted female birth rate per thousand	46.4	44.4	46.9	50.0	44.5

Comparison of the reported parity (or retrospective births) per woman with the corresponding values, constructed from the specific fertility rates by the use of the observed means and P_1/P_2 ratios of Table 7.2.C are shown in Table 7.3.C. The percentages of women in each age group who were recorded as never having borne a child and the retrospective total live births per mother are in Table 7.4.C. There are several surprising features in the tables. One is the low level of the P/F ratios for the younger women, which range from 0.70 to just over 0.80, except in the Upper region where they are about 0.90. In addition the ratios show little tendency to fall with age of women, except in the early years of the reproductive period, contrary to the trends in Upper Volta and Dahomey. In fact there is a slight but consistent rise with age from about 40 years in all regions. The pattern could be due to differential survival of women or to a fall in fertility (perhaps associated with the extensive migration which has occurred). Both effects might be in operation. A provisional interpretation is that there was some tendency for women

Table 7.3.C. Cumulated fertility (F), reported parity (P), and P/F ratios—Guinea and regions

Age Group of Women in Years	Guinea F	Guinea P	Guinea P/F	Region Maritime F	Maritime P	Maritime P/F	Fouta-Djallon F	Fouta-Djallon P	Fouta-Djallon P/F	Upper F	Upper P	Upper P/F	Forest F	Forest P	Forest P/F
15-19	0.69	0.54	0.78	0.84	0.63	0.75	0.73	0.60	0.82	0.54	0.47	0.87	0.58	0.42	0.72
20-24	2.19	1.75	0.80	2.33	1.79	0.77	2.28	1.86	0.82	2.00	1.83	0.92	2.05	1.50	0.73
25-29	3.83	2.86	0.75	3.90	2.84	0.73	3.91	2.97	0.76	3.70	3.04	0.82	3.72	2.60	0.70
30-34	5.20	3.89	0.75	5.10	3.81	0.75	5.29	3.93	0.74	5.11	4.48	0.88	5.19	3.65	0.70
35-39	6.22	4.48	0.72	5.99	4.39	0.73	6.30	4.45	0.71	6.16	5.10	0.83	6.29	4.37	0.69
40-44	6.77	5.01	0.74	6.54	5.07	0.78	6.81	4.78	0.70	6.71	5.88	0.88	6.87	4.93	0.72
45-49	6.99	5.29	0.76	6.76	5.36	0.79	6.99	4.96	0.71	6.92	6.26	0.90	7.14	5.16	0.72
50-59	7.00	5.36	0.77	6.77	5.11	0.75	7.00	4.96	0.71	6.93	6.29	0.91	7.15	5.41	0.76
60 and over	7.00	5.57	0.80	6.77	5.73	0.85	7.00	5.13	0.73	6.93	6.61	0.95	7.15	5.58	0.78

Table 7.4.C. Percentage of women childless and average parity of mothers—Guinea and regions

Age Group of Women in Years	Guinea Per cent childless	Guinea Average parity of mothers	Maritime Per cent childless	Maritime Average parity of mothers	Fouta-Djallon Per cent childless	Fouta-Djallon Average parity of mothers	Upper Per cent childless	Upper Average parity of mothers	Forest Per cent childless	Forest Average parity of mothers
15-19	56	1.24	50	1.27	54	1.29	60	1.18	63	1.13
20-24	15	2.06	15	2.12	15	2.18	13	2.11	16	1.79
25-29	9	3.15	11	3.19	8	3.22	8	3.32	10	2.89
30-34	7	4.20	10	4.23	7	4.23	4	4.69	7	3.92
35-39	7	4.80	9	4.81	7	4.78	5	5.39	6	4.63
40-49	6	5.48	8	5.63	7	5.25	3	6.25	5	5.30
50 and over	5	5.76	7	5.87	7	5.41	2	6.56	3	5.68

to omit live births in reporting with increasing age, particularly in Fouta-Djallon, but that there were offsetting factors at later years. The indices in Table 7.4.C give some confirmation for these anomalous features but throw little further light on them. The proportions of older women infertile are relatively low in all regions and very low in Upper Guinea. Only a small percentage of mothers have their first birth after the age of 25 years. Both the proportions fertile and the live births per mother are higher for women over 50 than for those approaching the end of the reproductive period, in conformity with the real or apparent higher fertility of the past.

The evidence from the P/F ratios for the younger women suggests that in the various regions 10 percent to 40 percent too many births were reported for the year preceding the survey. The existence of such large discrepancies must be checked by all means possible. For Guinea the information on the number of the births which were recorded as of parity one can be used for the purpose. If age-specific first birth rates could be calculated and cumulated to give a measure analogous to the total fertility for all births, the resulting index would be a current estimate of $P(1+)$, the proportion of women who become mothers. Since the breakdown by age of mother is not given for Guinea, indirect procedures are necessary. The ratio of first births to the average number of women per year in the age interval 15-24 was taken as the first approximation. (It will be noted that the percentages of childless women by age suggested that very few first births occurred after 25 years.) These ratios give too high estimates, partly because the majority of the births occur in the early part of the interval, where there are more women per year, and partly because of the typical age recording errors, which lead to an understatement of the average number in the range. By the use of the stable populations derived later and the distribution of age at first birth suggested by the retrospective reports, a rough correction to the ratios of 7 percent was derived. Moderate variations in the stable populations and distributions of age at first birth affect the percentage correction very little, and more elaborate methods of estimating $P(1+)$ by the use of demographic models give results very close to those obtained by the cruder procedure.

The table below shows the estimates of $P(1+)$ found for the regions by the method. Since they give measures for the proportion of women becoming mothers of well over 1.00, the first births reported in the year preceding the survey are clearly too high. An indication of the corrections needed for overreporting can be obtained by dividing the proportions of women in the age group 30-39 years recorded as being mothers, M, by the corresponding estimates of $P(1+)$. It seems unlikely that these corrections will be much biased by omissions of births from reports. Only data on whether younger women have become mothers are used, and the proportions recorded as remaining childless are small. The corrections are compared with the P/F ratios for the age group 20-24 years from Table 7.3.C.

Indices of Overreporting of Children in Preceding Year

Region	$P(1+)$	$M/P(1+)$	P_2/F_2	Ratio: children under 1 to children 1-4 years
Guinea	1.32	0.71	0.80	0.38
Maritime	1.31	0.69	0.77	0.37
Fouta-Djallon	1.24	0.75	0.82	0.37
Upper	1.19	0.81	0.92	0.35
Forest	1.62	0.58	0.73	0.41

The corrections estimated from the $M/P(1+)$ values are even greater than those found from the P/F ratios but the regional variations among the two sets correspond closely, with the smallest percentage for Forest and the highest for Upper. Part of the differences between the two series of corrections may be due to the approximations in the calculation of $P(1+)$ and sample errors in the relatively small numbers of first births reported for the current period. It seems likely, however, that some of the discrepancy reflects a genuine differential between the reporting of first and later births.

The very high ratios, in the last column, of the infants under 1 year to those 1-4 years suggests strongly that the bias in reporting births is linked to the estimation of child ages. The regional variations are in broad agreement with those of the other two sets of measures. In Guinea more than twice as many children were reported as under 1 year compared with those over 1 but under 2 years of age. This extreme difference is clearly another aspect of the general tendency to underestimate ages of children. It is possible that the underestimation at very early ages is linked with an equation of the under-1's with unweaned children when the average age of weaning is much above 12 months. The studies of the inquiries in Upper Volta, North Dahomey, and other territories have shown, however, that it is possible to record the live births in the year preceding a survey with good accuracy.

The adjustment factors for overreporting of live births in the preceding year were taken as the P/F ratios at 20-24 years of age. The female birth rates of Table 7.2.C were then estimated on the assumption that 103 males were born per 100 females. These derived rates are not only much lower than the observed values, but in a different order of size by regions. In particular, the rate for the Upper region becomes much the highest instead of the lowest, and the Forest population changes from being apparently the most fertile to almost the least.

Mortality

The retrospective observations of the percentage of children dead by age of mother and the life table survivorship ratios derived by the multiplying factor technique are shown in Table 7.5.C. Age-specific death rates calculated from reported current deaths and corresponding life table measures are given in Table 7.6.C. Figure 7.1.C compares the survivorship ratios obtained from the two sets of data by the use of the differences h at various ages between the logits of the estimated and model African standard life table values.

The mortality exhibited by the retrospective reports is high, particularly in the Forest region. Unlike the results for Upper Volta and Dahomey, childhood death rates calculated from the current reports differ little from the retrospective estimates except in Upper Guinea. In the latter region the differential is of the order found in Upper Volta. Again, with the partial exception of the Forest region, a heavy death rate between 1 and 4 years relative to the infant mortality is shown in both the retrospective and current reports. The logit model based on the African standard is in good agreement with the recorded rates in childhood, as can clearly be seen from Figure 7.1.C. The survivorship ratios estimated from the retrospective reports by the older women decrease very slowly with age. The effect is particularly notable after the 50-54 age group of women in Maritime, Upper Guinea, and the country as a whole. Conversely, there is a very rapid fall in the current survivorship ratios because of the high reported specific death rates at 10 to 50 years. As a consequence of these contrary trends the current and retrospective values of h diverge sharply from age 10 after being at about the same level in childhood.

As in the previous studies it is clear that the mortality implied by the slow decrease with age in the survivorship ratios, estimated from retrospective reports by the older women, is much too low. Presumably the discrepancy is due to the differential omission of dead children, despite the lack of evidence in the retrospective reports of live births of such a trend. However, the possibility of changes over time in either fertility or mortality cannot be ruled out. On the other hand, in contrast to the observations for Upper Volta and Dahomey, the current reported death rates at ages 10 to 40 years are implausibly high, as illustrated by the steep increase in the h values of Figure 7.1.C. The reported rates in the age interval are much above the comparable measures in the United Nations or Coale-Demeny model life tables. In the logit model system a β of about 1.50 would be required to reproduce the rates at the estimated high level of mortality. Although such a β value is not inconceivable, it is outside the range normally occurring with data of acceptable accuracy.

Table 7.5.C. Percentage of children having died previous to the survey, by age of mother, and derived life table survivorship ratios l_x—Guinea and regions

Age group of mother in years	Age of child survivorship	Guinea Per cent of children dead	l_x	Maritime Per cent of children dead	l_x	Fouta-Djallon Per cent of children dead	l_x	Upper Per cent of children dead	l_x	Forest Per cent of children dead	l_x
15-19	1	25.3	.772	22.4	.803	24.9	.777	19.7	.816	32.5	.701
20-24	2	31.6	.694	29.9	.715	31.1	.701	28.4	.720	35.0	.658
25-29	3	36.4	.648	35.0	.665	33.5	.677	36.1	.646	41.4	.596
30-34	5	38.5	.617	39.7	.607	34.9	.654	39.2	.608	42.4	.575
35-39	10	41.0	.588	40.1	.599	37.8	.622	39.8	.598	44.9	.546
40-44	15	43.0	.578	42.0	.591	39.9	.611	43.9	.567	47.2	.533
45-49	20	44.4	.565	44.9	.564	40.4	.607	44.7	.560	48.0	.526
50-54	25	47.1	.532	48.2	.524	43.5	.570	50.3	.498	49.0	.509
55-59	30	48.3	.519	47.6	.530	44.6	.558	49.5	.505	52.1	.477
60-64	35	49.8	.506	49.7	.510	46.7	.539	48.1	.520	54.7	.452

Table 7.6.C. Life table measures from reported current deaths (both sexes)—Guinea and regions. (m, age-specific death rate per 1,000; q, probability of dying in age group; l, proportion surviving to start of age group)

Age Group in Years	Guinea m	q	l	Maritime m	q	l	Fouta-Djallon m	q	l	Upper m	q	l	Forest m	q	l
Under 1	251	.213	1.000	249	.212	1.000	231	.199	1.000	202	.177	1.000	307	.253	1.000
1- 4	52	.182	.787	64	.218	.788	47	.164	.801	49	.173	.823	54	.189	.747
5- 9	13	.063	.644	13	.063	.616	12	.058	.670	10	.049	.681	17	.082	.606
10-19	19	.175	.603	16	.150	.577	16	.150	.631	21	.192	.647	24	.217	.556
20-29	20	.184	.498	16	.150	.491	20	.184	.536	23	.209	.523	21	.192	.435
30-39	23	.209	.406	21	.192	.417	19	.175	.438	31	.272	.414	25	.225	.352
40-49	27	.241	.321	16	.150	.337	25	.225	.361	30	.264	.301	30	.264	.273
50-59	37	.317	.244	33	.287	.287	33	.287	.280	51	.412	.222	39	.331	.201
60-69	66	.501	.166	65	.495	.204	63	.484	.199	76	.553	.130	69	.514	.134
70 and over	125	1.000	.083	116	1.000	.103	126	1.000	.103	161	1.000	.058	111	1.000	.065
Death rate per thousand	40.0			38.1			37.4			39.3			44.9		

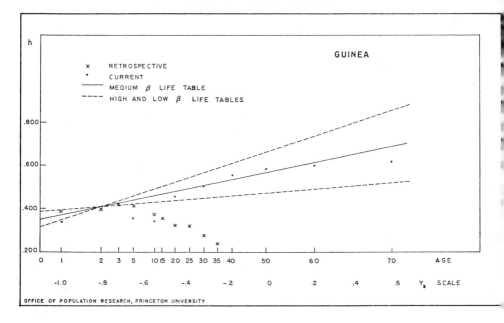

7.1.C. Proportion surviving to each age (l_x) in Guinea in life
tables calculated from retrospective mortality data and current mortality data and fitted by linear logit transformations.

The analysis of the observations from Guinea differs from those of the
other inquiries in showing (a) the existence of a large exaggeration of
the time reference period in the recording of current births, (b) reported
current and retrospective mortality of children at about the same level
rather than a deficit for the former, (c) excessively high current death
rates at ages after early childhood. These discrepancies in the characteristics of reported mortality can be plausibly explained by the assumption
that for Guinea the current time reference period was exaggerated for
deaths as well as for births, compensated in childhood by omissions.
Some support for the hypothesis is given by the considerable differential
between the mortalities up to 5 years estimated from the current and
retrospective data for the Upper region, in which the error in the time
reference period for births was much smaller than in the other areas.

As explained in the introductory section of the chapter, a different
method was adopted for the estimation of life tables for Guinea and
its regions from that used in the other studies, because of the discrepant
features in the records of deaths. Reported current deaths were first reduced by the correction factor for fertility derived from the P/F ratios,
on the assumption that the error in the time-reference period was the
same for the two types of vital event. The procedure thereafter, to derive the low-correction life table from the adjusted deaths, was exactly

the same as in the other studies. The probabilities of dying at ages beyond 5 years found from the adjusted deaths were spliced to the mortality up to that age estimated from the retrospective data. A life table of the logit model system was then fitted by the technique described. On the basis of the deaths adjusted for the time-reference period, a high-correction life table could have been calculated by the procedure used for the other populations. Because current and retrospective child mortality estimates were not very different for Guinea the results reached would be much the same as obtained by changing the adjusted deaths back to the original reported values. The high-correction life tables were, therefore, calculated from the observed current death rates at 5 years upward, rather than the more elaborately adjusted measures.

Selected indices of the high- and low-correction life tables are presented in Table 7.7.C. The terminology for specifying the two sets of measures is not as appropriate as in the other studies but is retained for convenience. Although the technique for estimating β reduces the effect of the heavy death rates at 10 to 40 years, the high-correction values of the parameter for the Upper and Forest regions still deviate greatly from the central level of 1.00. Probabilities of dying and survivorship ratios for medium-correction life tables, with the fixed l_2 estimate and β midway between the high and low values, are shown in Table 7.8.C. The straight lines representing the high-, medium-, and low-correction life tables, constructed from the model system for the whole of Guinea, are drawn on the logit scale in Figure 7.1.C. The high-correction line is so extreme and outside the range of the observed points as to be an implausible estimate. It is interesting to note, however, that the general course of mortality implied by the medium β life tables is very close to the reported current level, although the fitted and observed specific rates differ considerably in some age groups. Broadly speaking, therefore, the medium schedules are appropriate if the numbers of deaths recorded in the year preceding the survey were about right but their age distribution was distorted; this might be due to errors in the assessment of ages at death or overreporting in parts of the range and underreporting in others. It must be pointed out, however, that even the medium β life tables are

Table 7.7.C. Indices from estimated low- and high-correction life tables—Guinea and regions

Estimated measures	Guinea		Maritime		Fouta-Djallon		Upper		Forest	
	Low	High	Low	High	Low	High	Low	High	Low	High
Per cent correction to deaths	−6	9	−14	−5	−5	9	5	23	−9	12
l(2)	.688	.688	.698	.698	.711	.711	,694	.694	.647	.647
l(27)	.455	.402	.496	.464	.486	.439	.415	.353	.412	.342
β	1.08	1.32	.95	1.09	1.06	1.27	1.29	1.58	1.07	1.40

Table 7.8.C. Medium-correction life tables, males and females together—Guinea and regions. (*q*, probability of dying in succeeding age interval; *l*, proportion surviving at age)

Age in years	Guinea q	Guinea l	Maritime q	Maritime l	Fouta-Djallon q	Fouta-Djallon l	Upper q	Upper l	Forest q	Forest l
0	.223	1.000	.227	1.000	.207	1.000	.203	1.000	.254	1.000
1	.223	.777	.188	.773	.203	.793	.256	.797	.255	.746
5	.099	.604	.092	.628	.089	.632	.120	.593	.112	.556
10	.105	.544	.083	.578	.095	.576	.130	.522	.118	.494
20	.168	.487	.134	.530	.156	.521	.211	.454	.188	.436
30	.185	.405	.144	.459	.168	.440	.229	.358	.201	.354
40	.239	.330	.191	.393	.221	.366	.297	.276	.258	.283
50	.355	.251	.292	.318	.337	.285	.428	.194	.376	.210
60	.549	.162	.467	.225	.524	.189	.631	.111	.565	.131
70	1.000	.073	1.000	.120	1.000	.090	1.000	.041	1.000	.057
β	1.20		1.02		1.16		1.43		1.23	

difficult to reconcile with the retrospective data of children born and dead. If it is assumed that only dead children were omitted by the older women and the medium-correction mortality schedule was in operation, 6.92 births each on average should have been reported by the 55-59 years age group instead of the given 5.39. The final estimate of the total fertility at the time of the survey is 5.8. The discrepancy from 6.92 is large even if the possibility of falling fertility and other differentials is admitted. It seems much more likely, therefore, that the medium β death rates are over- rather than underestimates.

Both the current and retrospective data of deaths have been published by sex for Guinea. Life table measures for the whole, calculated for each sex from the reported current specific rates, are shown in Table 7.9.C. The indices suggest that childhood mortality of males was heavier than that of females. The calculated probabilities of dying by ages 1 and 5

Table 7.9.C. Life table measures from reported current deaths by sex—Guinea. (*m*, age-specific death rate per 1,000; *q*, probability of dying in age group; *l*, proportion surviving to start of age group)

Age Group in Years	Male m	Male q	Male l	Female m	Female q	Female l
Under 1	279	.233	1.000	227	.196	1.000
1- 4	56	.195	.767	48	.170	.804
5- 9	14	.068	.617	12	.058	.667
10-19	18	.167	.575	20	.184	.629
20-29	21	.192	.479	19	.175	.513
30-39	23	.209	.387	23	.209	.423
40-49	27	.241	.306	26	.233	.335
50-59	38	.324	.233	36	.310	.257
60-69	67	.506	.157	66	.501	.177
70 and over	132	1.000	.078	116	1.000	.088
Death rate per thousand		43.3			37.0	

years are, respectively, 16 percent and 13 percent lower for females. The differentials for the regions (not shown) are of much the same size. At ages after 5 the death rates tend to be higher for males also, but the differences are slight and not systematic. The pattern of the results from the retrospective reports is not entirely consistent with the current observations. The derived probabilities of dying by particular ages are shown for the two sexes.

	Probability of dying before age		
	2 years	3 years	5 years
Males	0.323	0.362	0.389
Females	0.289	0.342	0.377

These measures give an 11 percent lower female mortality up to age 2 but of only 3 percent up to 5 years. The corollary that female death rates were higher than male between 2 and 5 years is not consistent with the current evidence. One possible reason for the discrepancy might be vagueness in statements about the sex of dead children by the older women, resulting in a more equal reported division than the true breakdown. Another consequence of this could be a sex ratio of live births closer to 1.00 for the older women, and there is some indication of such a tendency. However, there are other possibilities, for example, differential reporting of numbers and ages by sex. Estimates of female mortality are required for the subsequent analysis. They were obtained by assuming that the probability of a female child dying before age 2 was 95 percent of the combined value for the two sexes. Life tables were estimated by making this adjustment to the l_2 levels in Table 7.7.C and constructing the corresponding parametric models with the medium β values of Table 7.8.C. The models are consistent with sex differentials in death rates up to 2 years of about the same size as exhibited by the retrospective data, but rather less than shown by the current reports. At later ages the current pattern is followed. Despite the arbitrary element in the estimates, the further error introduced into the stable population comparisons would seem to be small.

Reproduction and Natural Increase

Stable female age distributions were calculated with the mortality schedules derived from the medium-correction life tables and rates of natural increase which gave the adjusted birth rates of Table 7.2.C. They are compared with the observations in Table 7.13.C. The resulting vital rates are given in Table 7.10.C. Gross and net reproduction rates and total fertility ratios were calculated by the use of model distributions by age with means equal to those found from the reported current specific rates. In Guinea as a whole and in all regions except Upper, the estimated

Table 7.10.C. Estimated stable female population fertility and mortality measures
—Guinea and regions

Measure	Guinea	Maritime	Region Fouta-Djallon	Upper	Forest
Total fertility	5.8	5.7	5.9	6.2	5.6
Gross reproduction rate	2.85	2.80	2.90	3.05	2.75
Net reproduction rate	1.28	1.41	1.41	1.23	1.08
Rates per thousand					
Birth rate	46	44	47	50	45
Death rate	37	31	34	42	42
Natural increase	9	13	13	8	3

total fertility ratios are appreciably higher than would have been found if the correction factors for current births had been applied directly to the specific rates. The difference is due to the fact that, with the exception of Upper, the reported numbers of women in the childbearing range were larger than in the corresponding stable populations because of the characteristic crowding toward the central age groups.

The total fertility ratios by region exhibit much the same relations as the birth rates, although the level for Forest is now more clearly the lowest. As a consequence of this and the heavy mortality estimated for that region, the derived rate of natural increase is very low at only 3 per thousand per year. The other regions and Guinea are found to have modest growth rates of the order of 1 percent. The use of the low-correction life tables, which, as suggested above, may be closer to the true mortality patterns, would give natural increases 2 to 3 per thousand greater. The growth rate calculated from the reported births and deaths in the preceding year was 20 per thousand for the whole of Guinea, about 10 per thousand more than the value arrived at by the methods of analysis applied here. As for Dahomey, the discrepancy is large, but for different reasons; in Guinea it is mainly due to the reduction in estimated compared with reported fertility, but in Dahomey to the higher derived death rates.

The current specific fertility rates were corrected in proportion to give agreement with the estimated total fertility ratios and adjusted for the half-year displacement between ages at the survey and, on average, at the births. The results in Table 7.11.C show no regional differences in the distribution of rates by age sufficiently consistent to be accepted as genuine in view of the possible errors. It would appear that variations in the total fertility ratios are not associated with distinctly different age patterns in rates.

Age Distribution

The reported age distributions by sex are shown in Table 7.12.C. Comparisons, for females, of the observed proportions with those of the fitted stable age distributions are presented in Table 7.13.C. The per-

Table 7.11.C. Estimated age-specific fertility rates—Guinea and regions

Age group of women in years	Guinea	Maritime	Region Fouta-Djallon	Upper	Forest
15–19	.223	.257	.238	.208	.188
20–24	.280	.271	.291	.304	.266
25–29	.252	.244	.252	.291	.248
30–34	.199	.164	.207	.211	.207
35–39	.134	.127	.132	.154	.134
40–44	.053	.058	.044	.055	.054
45–49	.019	.019	.016	.017	.023
Total fertility	5.8	5.7	5.9	6.2	5.6

centages are given both by age group and cumulated from birth upward. The relationships between observed and fitted distributions are exhibited in Figure 7.2.C by the technique of comparison developed for the purpose. The agreement of the fitted with the observed age distributions for Guinea as a whole could hardly have been bettered, given the erratic nature of the data. The x-axis in Figure 7.2.C, which represents the stable population estimates, runs as nearly through the center of the observation points as is practicable to determine. Although the fits do not look quite as good for the regions, this is partly due to peculiarities in the observations, and deviations are nowhere large. The indications are that better agreement would be obtained if the estimates of natural increase were made slightly lower for Fouta-Djallon and Upper but higher for Maritime, either by modifying child mortality or, more plausibly, the total fertility ratios. The latter changes would tend to reduce the variations among regions without eliminating them. The assumption that the pattern of age reporting errors was exactly the same in all regions is, however, of doubtful validity and not supported by the differences in the shapes of the observed curves in Figure 7.2.C. The evidence is not sufficient to justify making the small adjustments which would be required.

The pattern of age reporting errors implied by the deviations of the observed from the fitted distributions is very similar, in its main features, to that found for Upper Volta and Dahomey. Again, there is a large relative deficiency in the number of females reported to be aged 10 to 19 years, compensated by excesses at under 10 and in the middle of the reproductive range. For Guinea the latter inflation is primarily in the 25-29 age group. An interesting feature, of relevance here, is that the enumerators were warned about the dangers of digit preference in the recording of ages. Presumably as a result, the numbers shown at ages ending with digit zero were very much less than at the adjacent single years. A correction for the effect would have reduced the excess numbers observed under 10 and at 25-29 years. In all regions except Upper

Table 7.12.C. Percentage age distributions by sex—Guinea and regions

Age group in years	Guinea			Maritime			Fouta-Djallon			Upper			Forest		
	Male	Female	Total	Male	Female	Total	Male	Female	Total	Male	Female	Total	Male	Female	Total
Under 1	5.2	4.9	5.0	4.7	5.0	4.9	5.5	4.8	5.1	5.2	4.8	5.0	5.0	5.0	5.0
1- 4	13.9	12.6	13.2	13.5	12.7	13.1	15.0	12.7	13.8	14.5	14.4	14.4	12.4	11.8	12.1
5- 9	17.2	14.5	15.8	17.7	15.0	16.3	18.3	14.9	16.5	17.6	15.7	16.6	15.5	13.2	14.3
10-14	9.4	6.8	8.0	9.0	6.7	7.8	10.5	7.4	8.8	10.3	7.8	9.0	7.9	5.7	6.8
15-19	8.3	9.5	8.9	7.8	9.3	8.6	7.7	10.0	8.9	9.0	8.9	9.0	8.9	9.3	9.1
20-24	6.1	9.2	7.7	6.1	9.5	7.8	5.9	9.1	7.7	6.2	8.9	7.6	6.4	9.2	7.8
25-29	7.0	10.0	8.6	7.5	10.0	8.8	5.8	9.4	7.7	7.3	10.1	8.7	8.1	10.5	9.3
30-34	5.2	6.8	6.0	5.9	7.4	6.7	5.5	6.6	6.1	4.9	6.1	5.5	5.3	6.8	6.0
35-39	6.4	7.3	6.9	6.3	7.6	7.0	5.5	6.5	6.1	6.3	6.0	6.1	7.4	8.7	8.1
40-44	4.8	4.7	4.8	5.0	4.6	4.8	4.4	4.8	4.6	4.8	4.0	4.4	5.3	4.9	5.1
45-54	7.9	7.0	7.5	7.8	6.1	6.9	7.3	6.7	7.0	7.4	7.5	7.5	8.9	7.9	8.4
55-64	4.9	3.7	4.3	4.5	3.4	3.9	5.1	3.8	4.4	4.0	3.6	3.8	5.2	4.0	4.6
65 and over	3.7	3.0	3.3	4.2	2.7	3.4	4.0	3.3	3.6	2.5	2.2	2.3	3.7	3.0	3.4
Total	100.0	100.0	100.0	100.0	100.0	100.0	100.0	100.0	100.0	100.0	100.0	100.0	100.0	100.0	100.0
Under 15	45.7	38.8	42.0	44.9	39.4	42.1	49.3	39.8	44.2	47.6	42.7	45.0	40.8	35.7	38.2
15-44	37.8	47.5	42.9	38.6	48.4	43.7	34.3	46.4	40.8	38.5	44.0	41.4	41.4	49.4	45.4
45 and over	16.5	13.7	15.1	16.5	12.2	14.2	16.4	13.8	15.0	13.9	13.3	13.6	17.8	14.9	16.4
Per cent male		47.6			49.1			46.0			47.6			48.6	

Table 7.13.C. Percentage female age distributions observed (O) and fitted (F)—
Guinea and regions

Age Group in Years	Guinea O	Guinea F	Maritime O	Maritime F	Fouta-Djallon O	Fouta-Djallon F	Upper O	Upper F	Forest O	Forest F
0- 4	17.5	15.9	17.7	15.7	17.5	16.5	19.2	17.3	16.8	14.9
5- 9	14.5	12.7	15.0	12.7	14.9	13.2	15.7	13.5	13.2	11.8
10-14	6.8	11.3	6.7	11.2	7.4	11.6	7.8	11.8	5.7	10.7
15-19	9.5	10.2	9.3	10.1	10.0	10.4	8.9	10.7	9.3	10.0
20-24	9.2	9.1	9.5	8.9	9.1	9.1	8.9	9.3	9.2	9.0
25-29	10.0	7.9	10.0	7.8	9.4	7.8	10.1	7.9	10.5	8.0
30-34	6.8	6.9	7.4	6.8	6.6	6.7	6.1	6.8	6.8	7.2
35-39	7.3	6.0	7.6	5.9	6.5	5.8	6.0	5.7	8.7	6.3
40-44	4.7	5.1	4.6	5.1	4.8	4.9	4.0	4.8	4.9	5.5
45-54	7.0	7.8	6.1	7.8	6.7	7.3	7.5	6.9	7.9	8.6
55-64	3.7	4.6	3.4	4.9	3.8	4.4	3.6	3.7	4.0	5.2
65 and over	3.0	2.5	2.7	3.1	3.3	2.3	2.2	1.6	3.0	2.8
Total	100.0	100.0	100.0	100.0	100.0	100.0	100.0	100.0	100.0	100.0

Exact Age in Years	Per Cent Under Age									
5	17.5	15.9	17.7	15.7	17.5	16.5	19.2	17.3	16.8	14.9
10	32.0	28.6	32.7	28.4	32.4	29.7	34.9	30.8	30.0	26.7
15	38.8	39.9	39.4	39.6	39.8	41.3	42.7	42.6	35.7	37.4
20	48.3	50.1	48.7	49.7	49.8	51.7	51.6	53.3	45.0	47.4
25	57.5	59.2	58.2	58.6	58.9	60.8	60.5	62.6	54.2	56.4
30	67.5	67.1	68.2	66.4	68.3	68.6	70.6	70.5	64.7	64.4
35	74.3	74.0	75.6	73.2	74.9	75.3	76.7	77.3	71.5	71.6
40	81.6	80.0	83.2	79.1	81.4	81.1	82.7	83.0	80.2	77.9
45	86.3	85.1	87.8	84.2	86.2	86.0	86.7	87.8	85.1	83.4
55	93.3	92.9	93.9	92.0	92.9	93.3	94.2	94.7	93.0	92.0
65	97.0	97.5	97.3	96.9	96.7	97.7	97.8	98.4	97.0	97.2

the observed points at 15 years in Figure 7.2.C are a little below the axis and those at 45 years above it, showing that too high a proportion of the women were recorded in the age interval. The comparisons suggest that the effect was as much due to the ages of women over 45 being underestimated as to overstatements at the lower end of the range. Theoretical and reported proportions at under 30 and 35 years are close except in the Maritime region. The observed and fitted percentages at the older ages (55 years and over, say) are in reasonable agreement. There is thus some evidence that the high values of β estimated for Guinea and the Upper and Forest regions reflect genuine characteristics of mortality patterns. The adoption of the central value, 1.00, for β would have produced poorer fits. The drawing of firm conclusions is hindered, however, by the indications from the P/F ratios that fertility in Guinea may have been higher in the past. If it was, the effect on the age distribution would be a reduction in the numbers at the later years of life relative to the stable population based on current measures. The size of the deviation would depend on the rate and period of the change. The estimates of adult mortality must, therefore, still be treated with great caution.

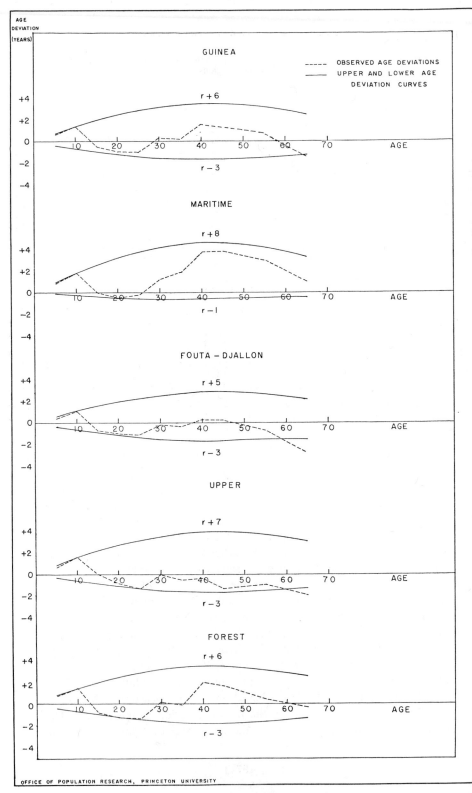

7.2.C. Age deviations, in years, between observed cumulative age distributions, in Guinea, and stable age distributions based on estimated fertility and mortality. For females.

The stable age distribution constructed from the estimates of fertility and mortality graduate the observations in a way which is consistent with expectations and also with the applications to other populations. Powerful support is, therefore, given to the method for correcting the reported current births. The adjustment factors were large and varied greatly among regions. The issue is not complicated by alternative mortality schedules, since the current and retrospective data lead to very similar estimates. The acceptance of the births reported in the previous year as accurate for the Forest region would give, with the medium-correction life table, a stable age distribution in which 34.8 percent, 47.3 percent, and 74.6 percent were under 10, 15, and 30 years, respectively, far removed from the observed proportions 30.0 percent, 35.7 percent, and 64.7 percent. It is worth noting also how the sizes of the adjustment factors for Upper (0.92) and Forest (0.73), which invert the apparent ordering by level of birth rate, are confirmed by the consistency of the observed age distributions with the corrected relations of the fertilities.

As in Upper Volta and Dahomey, the proportions of males reported to be in the child age groups are considerably higher than for females. Conversely there is no crowding of males toward the middle age range of 20-39 years, and the percentages under 30 are about the same for the two sexes. Considerably larger proportions of males than females were recorded at later ages, which is not consistent with the observed current mortality.

A stable male age distribution was constructed for Guinea with the differentials in mortality by sex arrived at above, i.e., a 10 percent higher probability that a male child will die by age 2, and a medium-correction β the same for both sexes. It was assumed that there were 103 males for every 100 female births. On this basis there would be about 5 percent fewer males than females in the total population. The deficit recorded was 1.22 million compared with 1.35 million, or nearly 10 percent. In the inquiry an attempt was made to obtain information on persons, considered to be residents, who were absent. A total of 77,000 was reported in this category, of whom the majority (56,000) were males over 14 years of age. The addition of these to the enumerated totals would reduce the male deficit to about 5 percent. It is not possible to make allowance for more permanent emigration or immigration, but the evidence supports the view that temporary movements at least do not seriously distort the female age distribution.

Below are shown observed proportions of males under selected ages and the corresponding values from the estimated stable population.

	Age in years						
	10	15	25	35	45	55	65
Observed, percent	36.3	45.7	60.1	72.3	83.5	91.4	96.3
Fitted, percent	29.4	40.8	60.2	74.9	85.8	93.3	97.7

Adjustments for the residents reported to be absent at the inquiry would improve the agreement between the two distributions and bring them into good accord over the range 25-45 years. The discrepancies at under 15 and at the older ages would still be large, however. The results of the examination of the male age distribution are inconclusive. The analyses for Upper Volta and Dahomey suggested that ages of males were underestimated in adolescence and exaggerated at later adult years, but the deviations were not so large as found for Guinea. The possibility that the age structure has been much distorted by immigration of adult males cannot be ruled out.

D. NORTH CAMEROON

Between February and May 1960 a demographic sample inquiry was undertaken in the north sector of the Republic of Cameroon. The Republic had become independent of the French Government in January of 1960, but the parts of the former British Cameroons on the west which have been incorporated in the country were not added until the following year. The area included in the survey was the triangular northern tip stretching south from Lake Chad to the narrowed neck caused by a projection of the territory of Chad, which lies to the east. Although the area is only a small part of the total of Cameroon it contains about 30 percent of the population. There is little development of industry, and most of the inhabitants live by subsistence cultivation. Millet is the main food crop, some livestock is kept, and the diet is supplemented by fish. Cotton is grown as a cash crop. Two small towns, Maroua and Garoua, with a population between them of nearly 40,000, were included in the inquiry.

The sample units were mainly villages, with the larger of these subdivided to give convenient numbers of residents. The stratified random sample of 425 units contained 45,000 persons. The total population was estimated at 1.12 million. Separate analyses are made for three sub-groups, which include all the inhabitants except those in the towns. The "Moslem" group covers 330,000 people, in villages where the religion is dominant, of Arab and Fulani descent, although considerably mixed with Negro strains. The "Hill Pagans," who totalled 290,000, consist of tribes, classed by Murdock as Plateau Nigerians, mainly speaking languages of the Nigritic family. The "Plain Pagans" are a mixture of peoples, some of the same stock as the Plateau Nigerians and others belonging to the Chadic sub-family of the Hamitic linguistic class. Their estimated number was 460,000. The division into sub-groups is not of individuals but of villages in which the inhabitants fell predominantly within the categories described. Moslem and Plain Pagan living areas are not clearly separated geographically but are intermingled.

Although the characteristics of the analysis of the North Cameroon data are very much the same as exhibited by the preceding studies, there is one new aspect which is of particular interest, namely the convincing evidence of falling fertility. Particular attention will be paid to the effects of the trend on the techniques of analysis, and findings which duplicate results discussed previously will be treated briefly.

Fertility

The fertility indices derived from the births reported for the year before the survey are shown in Table 7.1.D. The striking feature is the

Table 7.1.D. Reported current birth and age-specific fertility rates—North Cameroon and population groups

Age Group of Women in Years*	North Cameroon	Population Group		
		Moslem	Plain Pagan	Hill Pagan
15-19+	.190	.147	.221	.200
20-24	.237	.150	.242	.347
25-29	.202	.141	.225	.262
30-34	.153	.095	.168	.207
35-39	.104	.062	.103	.181
40-44	.052	.024	.055	.104
45-49	.012	.006	.007	.035
Total fertility	4.750	3.125	5.105	6.680
Birth rate per thousand	42	29	44	57

* The true age intervals for the rates are, on average, half a year younger than is shown.
+ Estimated from rates given for women aged 14-19 years.

apparently low rates for the Moslem villages, compared with the moderate to high levels for the Pagan peoples. Comparisons of retrospective births per woman with the corresponding cumulated values, calculated from the current rates of Table 7.1.D are made in the specified way by the P/F ratios of Table 7.3.D. The ratios are very close to 1.00 for the women aged 20-29 years in the Moslem and Plain Pagan communities, suggesting that there was little time scale error, on average, in the re-

Table 7.2.D. Estimated measures of fertility distributions—North Cameroon and population groups

Measure	North Cameroon	Population Group		
		Moslem	Plain Pagan	Hill Pagan
Mean ($\bar{m}$) in years	26.7	26.0	26.4	28.0
P_1/P_2	.29	.34	.27	.26
Adjusted female birth rate per thousand	36.3	27.1	41.7	41.3

Table 7.3.D. Cumulated fertility (F), reported parity (P), and P/F ratios—North
Cameroon and population groups

Age group of women in years	North Cameroon			Moslem			Population Group Plain Pagan			Hill Pagan		
	F	P	P/F	F	P	P/F	F	P	P/F	F	P	P/
15-19	0.57	0.44	0.77	0.47	0.40	0.85	0.69	0.49	0.71	0.52	0.39	0.
20-24	1.65	1.50	0.91	1.18	1.18	1.00	1.83	1.82	0.99	2.01	1.48	0.
25-29	2.76	2.60	0.94	1.92	1.90	0.99	3.01	3.08	1.02	3.53	2.91	0.
30-34	3.63	3.38	0.93	2.49	2.27	0.91	3.97	3.98	1.00	4.69	4.05	0.
35-39	4.26	4.23	0.99	2.87	3.07	1.07	4.62	5.04	1.09	5.67	4.82	0.
40-44	4.62	4.53	0.98	3.07	3.24	1.06	5.00	5.60	1.12	6.36	5.20	0.
45-49	4.75	4.65	0.98	3.12	3.59	1.15	5.10	5.25	1.03	6.66	5.62	0.
50-59	4.75	4.92	1.04	3.13	3.79	1.21	5.11	5.97	1.17	6.68	5.68	0.
60 and over	4.75	4.96	1.04	3.13	4.19	1.34	5.11	5.58	1.09	6.68	6.20	0.

porting of the preceding year's births. In contrast, the implication is that
something like one-third too many children were recorded as born in
the past year to the Hill Pagan women, if the retrospective births reported by the younger ones can be accepted as reasonably accurate. Such
a large discrepancy between the replies of sub-populations in one survey
did not appear in previous analyses; it emphasizes the complexity of
factors such as community culture, organization, and enumerator training upon which response errors depend. The pattern of falling P/F ratios
with increasing age of women, characteristic of other surveys and explained by differential omissions of children, does not occur in the
North Cameroon data. The ratios, in fact, rise consistently with age for
all groups. The most plausible explanation for this trend is that there
had been a genuine fall in fertility over many years before the survey.
The conclusion is reinforced by the estimated birth rate for the Moslems,
which is very low by African standards. It may be noted that the P/F
ratios suggest that the drop in fertility had been more rapid in this group
than in the others. In the light of the results from other areas it seems
likely that some differential omission of children occurred but is dis-
guised by the fertility changes. The apparent fall may, therefore, be less
than the true one.

The evidence on childlessness and births per mother in Table 7.4.D
also supports the view that fertility was decreasing and had reached a
low level in the Moslem villages. Reported mean parity is considerably
higher in all groups for women over 50 years compared with those at
ages toward the end of the reproductive period. Percentages childless
are less for the older women. The level at 25-34 years of about 10 percent for the Plain and Hill Pagans is moderate, although above the 5
percent or so common in African communities of high fertility; but
among the Moslems the very high proportion of one-third of women
were recorded as childless in this age range.

Table 7.4.D. Percentage of women childless and average parity of mothers—North Cameroon and population groups

Group Women years	Cameroon. Per cent childless	Cameroon Average parity of mothers	Moslem Per cent childless	Moslem Average parity of mothers	Plain Pagan Per cent childless	Plain Pagan Average parity of mothers	Hill Pagan Per cent childless	Hill Pagan Average parity of mothers
5-19	73	1.6	76	1.7	70	1.6	74	1.5
0-24	27	2.1	41	2.0	19	2.2	19	1.8
5-29	20	3.2	35	2.9	11	3.5	12	3.3
0-34	19	4.2	32	3.3	12	4.5	8	4.4
5-39	17	5.1	25	4.1	13	5.8	8	5.2
0-49	13	5.3	20	4.3	9	6.0	6	5.7
and over	11	5.6	16	4.8	7	6.2	4	6.1

The level of reporting of current births was accepted for Moslems and Plain Pagans but corrected by the P/F ratio at 20-24 years for the Hill Pagans. The trend of the ratios suggests that the latter adjustment may be slightly too large, but it was thought preferable not to make a small and partly arbitrary modification. With the standard assumption that 103 males were born per 100 females the adjusted female birth rates of Table 7.2.D are obtained. The rates for the Plain and Hill Pagans are approximately equal and represent a moderately high fertility, 50 percent above that of the Moslems.

Mortality

The retrospective data on the proportions of children dead by age of mother and the derived life table survivorship ratios are presented in Table 7.5.D. Table 7.6.D shows the basic mortality indices calculated

Table 7.5.D. Percentage of children having died previous to the survey, by age of mother, and derived life table survivorship ratios l_x—North Cameroon and population groups

Age group of mothers in years	Age of child survivorship	North Cameroon Per cent of children dead	North Cameroon l_x	Moslem Per cent of children dead	Moslem l_x	Plain Pagan Per cent of children dead	Plain Pagan l_x	Hill Pagan Per cent of children dead	Hill Pagan l_x
15-19	1	24	.781	20	.823	26	.759	26	.758
20-24	2	30	.708	26	.751	33	.676	32	.685
25-29	3	33	.679	30	.712	34	.668	36	.648
30-34	5	38	.625	30	.706	39	.616	42	.577
35-39	10	42	.582	35	.655	43	.573	46	.533
40-44	15	44	.573	39	.626	46	.555	46	.543
45-49	20	45	.564	37	.646	47	.546	51	.496
50-54	25	47	.538	42	.592	49	.520	51	.486
55-59	30	48	.527	44	.572	48	.529	54	.456
60-64	35	49	.519	41	.602	51	.501	58	.418

Table 7.6.D. Life table measures from reported current deaths (both sexes)—
North Cameroon and population groups. (m, age-specific death rate per 1,000;
q, probability of dying in age group; l, proportion surviving to start of age group)

Age group in years	North Cameroon m	q	l	Moslem m	q	l	Population Group Plain Pagan m	q	l	Hill Pagan m	q	l
Under 1	208	.182	1.000	191	.169	1.000	208	.182	1.000	221	.191	1.000
1- 4	43	.154	.818	24	.090	.831	31	.114	.818	79	.260	.809
5- 9	11	.054	.692	7	.034	.756	11	.054	.725	16	.077	.599
10-19	11	.105	.655	9	.087	.730	8	.077	.686	17	.158	.553
20-29	9	.087	.586	7	.068	.666	9	.087	.633	11	.105	.466
30-39	11	.105	.535	10	.096	.621	10	.096	.578	14	.132	.417
40-49	15	.141	.479	17	.158	.561	10	.096	.523	23	.209	.362
50-59	37	.317	.411	25	.225	.472	33	.287	.473	64	.490	.286
60-69	59	.461	.281	45	.373	.366	62	.478	.337	83	.587	.146
70 and over	107	1.000	.151	100	1.000	.229	127	1.000	.176	109	1.000	.060
Death rate per thousand	27			22			24			41		

from the deaths reported for the year preceding the inquiry. The measures from the two sources for North Cameroon as a whole are compared in Figure 7.1.D, which gives the differences h of the logits of survivorship ratios from the corresponding values of the African standard life table at the same ages.

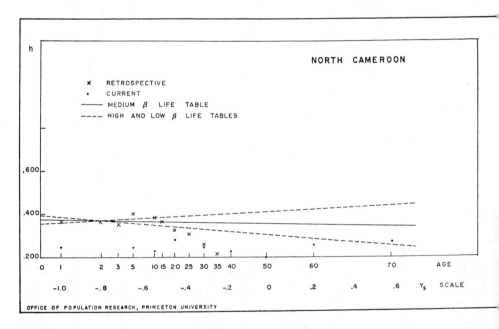

7.1.D. Proportion surviving to each age (l_x) in North Cameroon in life tables calculated from retrospective mortality data and current mortality data and fitted by linear logit transformations.

With one partial exception, the features of the analysis are in close accord with the findings for Upper Volta and Dahomey. Child mortality as shown by the retrospective reports is at much the same level as in these two countries and is greater than calculated from current deaths. The differences between the two sets of survivorship ratios decrease with age. The pattern is clearly seen in Figure 7.1.D, where the substantial difference between the retrospective and current h values at early years disappears by age 30. Neither the current points nor the retrospective ones up to age 15 deviate systematically from a straight line despite some fluctuations. It can again be concluded that the use of the logit mortality model system based on the African standard life table is satisfactory for graduating the data. It also seems valid to assume once more that the child mortalities derived from the retrospective reports are correct but that the survivorship ratios at later ages are in error because of differential omissions of dead children by the older women.

By the procedure described in the introduction to the chapter, the percentages of dead children under 5 years omitted in the current reports were calculated and are shown in Table 7.7.D. The estimated un-

Table 7.7.D. Indices from estimated low- and high-correction life tables—North Cameroon and population groups

Estimated measures	North Cameroon		Moslem		Population Group Plain Pagan		Hill Pagan	
	Low	High	Low	High	Low	High	Low	High
% correction to deaths	11	24	10	32·	25	51	–	–
l(2)	.705	.705	.754	.754	.688	.688	.673	.673
l(27)	.510	.481	.581	.545	.514	.462	.429	.429
β	0.92	1.05	0.88	1.04	0.82	1.05	1.12	1.12

derreporting for the Moslem and Plain Pagan villages is large (32 percent and 51 percent), as for Upper Volta and Dahomey, but for the Hill Pagan group it is negligible. (The survivorship ratios from the current data are slightly higher at both 1 and 5 years than the corresponding levels from the retrospective measures, but the differential virtually disappears when the latter are graduated in relation to the values at 2 and 3 years.) As for the regions of Guinea, therefore, current and retrospective mortality reports are in good agreement; notably also the overstatement of current births was estimated to be at about the same high level for the Hill Pagans and Guinea, in contrast to the other populations. It is hard to avoid the inference that a lengthening of the reference period above one year has offset omissions of dead children. No adjustments, similar to those in the Guinea analysis, for the possible effects on the current reports of adult deaths were made to the Hill Pagan data, however, because of the variation in patterns among the sub-populations.

Table 7.8.D. Medium-correction life tables, males and females together—North Cameroon and population groups. (q, probability of dying in succeeding age interval; l, proportion surviving at age)

| Age in years | North Cameroon | | Population Group | | | | | |
| | | | Moslem | | Plain Pagan | | Hill Pagan | |
	q	l	q	l	q	l	q	l
0	.223	1.000	.186	1.000	.240	1.000	.240	1.000
1	.179	.777	.146	.814	.180	.760	.220	.760
5	.074	.638	.062	.695	.074	.623	.094	.593
10	.076	.591	.064	.652	.076	.577	.099	.537
20	.125	.546	.108	.610	.122	.533	.159	.484
30	.136	.478	.118	.544	.132	.468	.170	.407
40	.179	.413	.158	.480	.172	.406	.225	.338
50	.274	.339	.250	.404	.265	.336	.332	.262
60	.447	.246	.419	.303	.433	.247	.520	.175
70	1.000	.136	1.000	.176	1.000	.140	1.000	.084
β	0.98		0.96		0.94		1.12	

By the procedures described, low- and high-correction life tables of the logit system were fitted to the data for North Cameroon and the component populations on the alternative assumptions that omissions of deaths beyond age 5 from the current reports were zero and proportionately the same as at under 5, respectively. The resulting indices are shown in Table 7.7.D. Survivorship ratios and probabilities of dying by age group for the medium-correction life table with a β midway between the estimated high and low estimates are shown in Table 7.8.D. The straight lines representing the three fitted model life tables are drawn on Figure 7.1.D. The β values for the models are all close to the central value of 1.00, and none is, therefore, implausible. The trend of the line for the low-correction life table is not, however, in good accord with the apparent path of the current points (or the retrospective below 15 years) and crosses it at the higher ages. Both the medium- and high-correction mortality patterns provide acceptable estimates, and the former, with β very close to 1.00, is the more cautious in guarding against extreme errors. It is interesting to note that the β obtained for the Hill Pagans is higher than for the other sub-populations (although far from extreme). If the estimating procedure adopted for Guinea had been applied, smaller low- and medium-correction β's would have resulted. The mortality estimates will be taken to apply to both males and females. The life table measures, calculated from the current data for each sex and presented in Table 7.9.D show little sign of any systematic differential.

Reproduction and Natural Increase

By the use of the medium-correction life tables and different levels of natural increase, stable female age distributions were constructed in which the birth rates were equal to the adjusted values of Table 7.2.D. Because of the cogent evidence that fertility had fallen over a period

Table 7.9.D. Life table measures from reported current deaths by sex—North Cameroon. (*m*, age-specific death rate per 1,000; *q*, probability of ·dying in age group; *l*, proportion surviving to start of age group)

Age group in years	Male			Female		
	m	q	l	m	q	l
Under 1	203	.178	1.000	214	.186	1.000
1- 4	45	.160	.822	42	.151	.814
5- 9	12	.058	.690	10	.049	.691
10-19	12	.114	.650	10	.096	.657
20-29	9	.087	.576	8	.077	.594
30-39	8	.077	.526	13	.123	.548
40-49	14	.132	.486	16	.150	.481
50-59	33	.287	.422	42	.352	.409
60-69	63	.484	.301	53	.424	.265
70 and over	84	1.000	.155	132	1.000	.153
Death rate per thousand		28			27	

prior to the survey, however, it is not valid to assume that the population age distributions have approximately a stable form. The procedure used in the other analyses for deriving the reproduction indices from the birth rate on that assumption, with the mean of the specific fertility distribution taken at the value calculated from the current data, is subject to error. In general, it would be expected to give too high an estimate, because the number of older persons in the population would be lower than in the stable model and hence the proportion in the reproductive age groups higher. In fact, this pattern of deviation from a stable distribution occurs in the data. The same types of discrepancy result, however, from errors in the recording of female ages, common in African population inquiries, in which there is a "heaping" of observations from the limits of the reproductive period toward the center. There seems no satisfactory way of estimating the relative effects of age error and fertility change in North Cameroon.

The alternative procedure is to adjust the total fertility ratios, calculated from the data on current births, directly by the correction factor deduced from the P/F ratios. The estimates thus obtained are likely to be too low because of overstatement of the number of women in the reproductive period. Below, the total fertility ratios derived by this method are compared with the values found on the stable population assumption.

	Population group			
Method of estimation	North Cameroon	Moslem	Plain Pagan	Hill Pagan
Stable population	4.7	3.6	5.3	5.3
Direct adjustment	4.3	3.1	5.1	5.0

The differences between the two measures for the Plain and Hill Pagans are relatively small, but the discrepancy for the Moslem group is substantial, in conformity with the other evidence that fertility had fallen more drastically in that community. Presumably the best estimates of the current total fertility ratios lie somewhere between the alternative values. For mortality at the level of the medium-correction life tables the implied differences in natural increase per thousand are 5 for the Moslems and 2 for the Pagan groups. It should be noted that the birth rates previously derived would remain valid for the populations *at the survey time*, although they would not be the same as the corresponding stable age distribution indices. There is not sufficient information about the pattern of fertility changes for a convincing method of adjustment to be applied. For consistency with the previous analyses the estimates of the total fertility ratio on the assumption that the populations are stable will be retained provisionally, but there will be further discussion of what the indices can be taken to represent.

Table 7.10.D gives these total fertility ratios and the corresponding gross and net reproduction, birth, death, and natural increase rates. Comments on fertility have already been made. The death rates are derived on the assumption that the medium-correction life tables are in operation and the population is stable. The lower proportion of older persons,

Table 7.10.D. Estimated stable female population fertility and mortality measures
—North Cameroon and population groups

| Measure | North Cameroon | Population Group | | |
		Moslem	Plain Pagan	Hill Paga
Total fertility	4.7	3.6	5.3	5.3
Gross reproduction rate	2.3	1.75	2.6	2.6
Net reproduction rate	1.15	1.00	1.29	1.13
Rates per thousand				
Birth rate	36	27	42	41
Death rate	31	27	32	37
Natural increase	5	0	10	4

relative to the stable age distribution, resulting from the falling fertility would make the corresponding current death rate somewhat lower. On the other hand, the mortality study indicated that the medium-correction measures were more likely to be under- than overestimates. The birth, death, and natural increase rates in the table can, therefore, be taken as a reasonable assessment of the current situation. The analysis implies, however, that the true stable population reproduction rates are lower and death rates higher. A continuance of the level of fertility and mortality would, therefore, lead to natural increase rates even smaller than shown and, for the Moslems, to a falling population. Although the estimates suggest a considerable differential between the Plain and Hill Pagans in death and natural increase rates, it may be surmised that the large error in the previous year reference period for the latter group has caused some exaggeration of the divergence.

Table 7.11.D gives the age-specific fertility rates, obtained by adjusting the measures calculated from reported current births for the half-year displacement and multiplying by the same factor for each age group to make the total fertility ratios agree with the estimated values of Table 7.10.D. Because of errors due to sampling and age misstatement little

Table 7.11.D. Estimated age-specific fertility rates—North Cameroon and population groups

Age group of women in years	North Cameroon	Moslem	Population Group Plain Pagan	Hill Pagan
15-19	.209	.186	.254	.181
20-24	.235	.174	.251	.277
25-29	.196	.159	.230	.202
30-34	.147	.105	.168	.161
35-39	.098	.067	.101	.139
40-44	.047	.024	.052	.077
45-49	.008	.005	.004	.023
Total fertility	4.7	3.6	5.3	5.3

weight can be put on the unsystematic differences between the Plain and Hill Pagan rates. The relative distribution of specific fertilities is much the same for the Moslems as for the other population sub-groups, although the level is one-third lower.

Age Distribution

The reported age distributions by sex are shown in Table 7.12.D. In Table 7.13.D the age patterns for females from the fitted stable populations are compared with the observations; a visual representation by the technique described in the introduction to the chapter is given in Figure 7.2.D. The evidence from the comparisons can only be assessed if an allowance is made for the effects of falling fertility on the age distributions. The resulting divergences from the stable form depend on the extent and time trend of the decrease, which, as will be clear from the preceding discussion, cannot be estimated with any hope of accuracy. Only a general consideration of tendencies will, therefore, be attempted. If fertility has been higher in the past, the ratio of old people to the succeeding generation of adults in the middle years will be lower than implied by the stable population corresponding to current rates. The true proportions under given ages will not differ much from the current stable values in the earlier part of life, but the divergence, in terms of equivalent fertility measures, will increase at later years. The effect expected in Figure 7.2.D is a bending of the path of observed points upward as

Table 7.12.D. Percentage age distributions by sex—North Cameroon and population groups

Age group in years	North Cameroon			Population Group								
				Moslem			Plain Pagan			Hill Pagan		
	Male	Female	Total	Male	Female	Total	Male	Female	Total	Male	Female	Total
Under 1	3.9	3.4	3.6	2.6	2.4	2.5	4.0	3.4	3.7	5.2	4.5	4.9
1–4	11.7	11.0	11.3	8.4	7.8	8.1	13.0	12.7	12.9	13.6	12.4	13.0
5–9	15.0	13.3	14.2	11.6	10.1	10.8	16.9	15.1	16.0	16.4	14.9	15.7
10–14	8.9	6.6	7.7	9.0	6.1	7.4	9.6	7.1	8.3	8.3	6.7	7.5
15–19	7.0	8.0	7.5	7.3	7.9	7.6	7.7	8.3	8.0	6.1	7.8	6.9
20–24	6.1	9.5	7.9	6.7	9.8	8.4	6.4	8.9	7.7	4.8	9.7	7.2
25–29	7.2	9.8	8.5	8.1	9.7	8.9	6.8	9.2	8.0	6.4	10.4	8.4
30–34	6.3	8.8	7.6	7.3	8.9	8.2	5.6	8.3	7.0	5.7	9.3	7.5
35–39	7.7	7.6	7.7	7.6	8.2	7.9	5.4	7.7	7.5	8.2	6.7	7.5
40–44	5.5	5.5	5.5	6.1	6.5	6.3	5.3	5.3	5.3	4.4	4.6	4.5
45–54	10.1	8.5	9.3	11.5	11.0	11.2	8.7	7.5	8.1	10.8	7.3	9.0
55–64	6.1	4.5	5.3	7.5	6.1	6.8	5.1	4.0	4.5	6.3	3.3	4.8
65 and over	4.5	3.5	3.9	6.3	5.5	5.9	3.5	2.5	3.0	3.8	2.3	3.1
Total	100.0	100.0	100.0	100.0	100.0	100.0	100.0	100.0	100.0	100.0	100.0	100.0
Under 15	39.5	34.3	36.8	31.6	26.4	28.8	43.5	38.3	40.9	43.5	38.6	41.1
15–44	39.8	49.2	44.7	43.1	51.0	47.3	39.2	47.7	43.5	35.6	48.5	42.0
45 and over	20.7	16.5	18.5	25.3	22.6	23.9	17.3	14.0	15.6	20.9	12.9	16.9
Per cent male		48.2			47.2			48.1			49.7	

Table 7.13.D. Percentage female age distribution observed (O) and fitted (F)—
North Cameroon and population groups

Age group in years	North Cameroon O	F	Moslem O	F	Plain Pagan O	F	Hill Pagan O	·F
0– 4	14.4	12.8	10.2	10.5	16.1	14.4	17.0	14.1
5– 9	13.3	10.8	10.1	9.3	15.1	11.8	14.9	11.5
10–14	6.6	10.0	6.1	8.9	7.1	10.7	6.7	10.5
15–19	8.0	9.3	7.9	8.6	8.3	9.7	7.8	9.7
20–24	9.5	8.6	9.8	8.2	8.9	8.7	9.7	8.9
25–29	9.8	7.9	9.7	7.7	9.2	7.8	10.4	8.0
30–34	8.8	7.2	8.9	7.3	8.3	6.9	9.3	7.1
35–39	7.6	6.5	8.2	6.9	7.7	6.2	6.7	6.4
40–44	5.5	5.8	6.5	6.4	5.3	5.4	4.6	5.6
45–54	8.5	9.6	11.0	11.1	7.5	8.6	7.3	9.0
55–64	4.5	6.7	6.1	8.3	4.0	5.7	3.3	5.7
65 and over	3.5	4.8	5.5	6.8	2.5	4.1	2.3	3.5
Total	100.0	100.0	100.0	100.0	100.0	100.0	100.0	100.0

Exact age in years			Per Cent Under Age					
5	14.4	12.8	10.2	10.5	16.1	14.4	17.0	14.1
10	27.7	23.6	20.3	19.8	31.2	26.2	31.9	25.6
15	34.3	33.6	26.4	28.7	38.3	36.9	38.6	36.1
20	42.3	42.9	34.3	37.3	46.6	46.6	46.4	45.8
25	51.8	51.5	44.1	45.5	55.5	55.3	56.1	54.7
30	61.6	59.4	53.8	53.2	64.7	63.1	66.5	62.7
35	70.4	66.6	62.7	60.5	73.0	70.0	75.8	69.8
40	78.0	73.1	70.9	67.4	80.7	76.2	82.5	76.2
45	83.5	78.9	77.4	73.8	86.0	81.6	87.1	81.8
55	92.0	88.5	88.4	84.9	93.5	90.2	94.4	90.8
65	96.5	95.2	94.5	93.2	97.5	95.9	97.7	96.5

age rises. A comparison of the graphs for North Cameroon with those for Upper Volta, Dahomey, and Guinea suggests that this is exactly what has happened. Adjustments downward, progressively increasing with age, to the observed points would result in a curve in close accord with the patterns revealed by the analyses for the other populations. The conclusions about the nature of the main errors in age reports would, therefore, also apply to the North Cameroon inquiry.

As explained previously, the estimates of reproduction and hence of natural increase are biased upward because of the failure to allow for the fall in fertility. Consequently, the tendency should be for the observed age deviations in Figure 7.2.D to be negative in the earlier part of the curve, where the divergence from the stable form has not a large effect. The observations for the Moslems are clearly consistent with expectation; a reduction of the total fertility estimate from 3.6 to about 3.4 and a lowering of natural increase by 2 per thousand would bring the fitted stable distribution line more nearly through the center of the observed points and the relationship into conformity with the results for

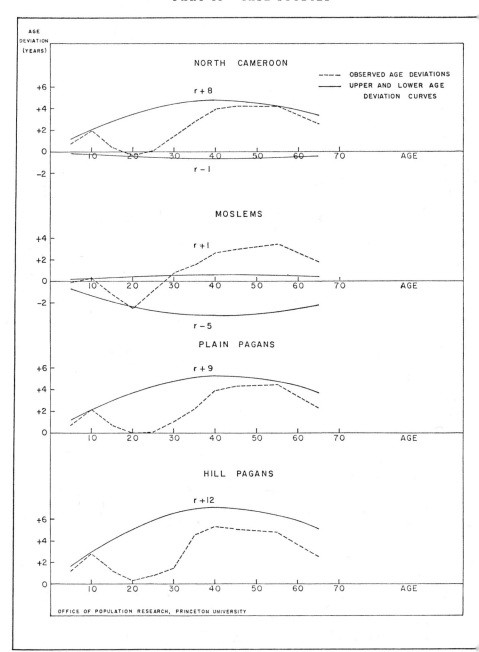

7.2.D. Age deviations, in years, between observed cumulative age distributions, in North Cameroon, and stable age distributions based on estimated fertility and mortality. For females.

the other surveys. In contrast, the graphs for the Plain and Hill Pagans suggest that the total fertility ratios may have been underestimated. The effects of bias due to a fall in fertility for these two sub-populations are likely to have been slight and could easily have been more than offset by small errors in the P/F ratio adjustment factors. The age distribution comparison graph for North Cameroon as a whole does not provide support for the view that the derived reproduction rates are too high but rather indicates that the level is about right when allowance is made for the "bending" of the curve of observed age deviations. Despite the difficulties and uncertainties of errors, due to the limitations of the assumption that the populations are stable, the cross-checks have shown a coherent pattern of relationships among measures, consistent with the other analyses. The margin of doubt is too great, however, for the attempt to apply refined adjustments for bias to be justified. The values in Table 7.10.D will be accepted tentatively as the best single estimates.

The sex differentials between the reported age distributions in the North Cameroon and other inquiries are similar. Relative to females there are higher percentages of males under 15 years and over 45. The lower proportion of males in the population (48.2 percent) suggests that absences of adults as migrant labor may have been common, since mortality rates were about the same for the two sexes. This, combined with the evidence of falling fertility, makes it difficult to examine how the reported male age distributions conform with the estimates of vital measures. It does not appear, however, that even after adjustment for migration there would be the deficit in the observed numbers at older ages, compared with the stable population, which is so notable for females. There may be overstatements of male ages at later years. Nevertheless, these characteristics give support to the view that the reduced percentage of older women is due in part to age errors and not solely to falling fertility.

E. OTHER AREAS

Centre-Oubangui, Fouta-Toro, Ivory Coast, Mopti

A number of other demographic sampling inquiries, similar in type to those examined, have been carried out in the territories of the former French West and Equatorial Africa. The areas and populations included have been limited and variable in size; commonly the demographic inquiry has formed part of a more extensive economic, agricultural, or medical survey. The data from four of these inquiries, where the tabulations necessary for the application of the techniques had been published, were analyzed. The results are presented in the tables of this section. In general, the findings about reporting errors and their adjustment are in accord with the conclusions already reached for the other populations.

More weight is added to certain features of the evidence, and a few further points arise. Despite the relative smallness of the populations for which vital indices are estimated, the measures are valuable because they provide reference points in wide regions of the map of Africa where demographic knowledge was scanty. Notes on the location and nature of each of the areas follow.

Centre-Oubangui

The French name for the district which covers about one-third of Ubangi, a zone of the Central African Republic, is retained. It is roughly a rectangle, 400-500 kilometers long, with a west-east base on the River Ubangi, a main tributary of the Congo, and a breadth to the north of 250-350 kilometers. The Republic of the Congo (Leopoldville) is the boundary on the south of the river. The country consists of savannah with clumps of trees and some tropical rain forest. The people live by subsistence farming, with ground nuts the chief crop, sesame and cassava subsidiary. There is also, however, a substantial cash crop, cotton, and recently some coffee has been grown.

The population of the area in the latter half of 1959, the time of the inquiry, was nearly 400,000. The people were mostly dispersed in small villages averaging about 120 persons each, but there is a substantial sized town in the middle of the district which had 40,000 inhabitants. The overall density was just over 3 persons per square kilometer, considerably lower than to the west where Bangui, the capital of the Central African Republic lies. About half the population belonged to the Banda tribe, others to the Mandjia, Nzakara, Langba, and smaller groups. These tribes, which speak languages of the eastern sub-family of the Nigritic stock, are very similar in characteristics and way of life.

The sample contained more than 300 villages and urban sections which, by subdivision and amalgamation were reorganized into 157 primary units of roughly equal size. More than 40,000 persons were in the sample units, giving a fraction of the total population of 10 percent.

Fouta-Toro

The Fouta-Toro area lies south of the middle reaches of the Senegal River, but the designation is used here for the smaller region, stretching along the river valley, which the demographic inquiry covered. The region runs for about 300 kilometers upstream from the town of Dagana, which is situated where the river turns to the south from an east-west flow. None of the villages sampled lies far from the river, but the part of the area to the north is now in the Republic of Mauritania and that to the south in the Republic of Senegal. The valley is a fertile strip with semi-desert country on both sides. The analysis is confined to the rural population, which has a subsistence economy based mainly on the cultivation of sorghum and millet; a proportion consists of semi-sedentary pastoralists.

The inquiry took place between April and November 1957. The total population of the defined region at that time was about 340,000, including 56,000 persons classed as Arabic. Since the demographic character of these Arabic people is distinctly different from that of the rest of the population they have been excluded. When the urban residents are also subtracted the number remaining is estimated to be 267,000. Because of the concentration of the inhabitants along the river valley, the figures of density in the geographical areas sampled have little meaning. Much the largest tribe in the region, containing about 70 percent of the population, was the Tukulor; there were substantial minorities of Peul and Wolof. All of these speak languages of the Atlantic sub-family of the Nigritic stock. Smaller numbers of Sarakole and Bambara (about 15,000 in total) who speak Mande languages, also of the Nigritic stock, were included. Sampling, with a fraction of one-tenth, was of complete smaller villages and parts of larger ones.

Ivory Coast: First Agricultural Sector

The district of the Ivory Coast in which the demographic inquiry was conducted lies on the coast around the modern and rapidly developing urban area of Abidjan and Grand Bassam, but these towns were excluded from the survey. The area covered was an irregular block stretching for some 240 kilometers along the coast and 100 kilometers inland. The southern part of the Ivory Coast is within the belt of tropical rain forest; there is a large production of timber and cash crops such as coffee and palm oil for export. Crops are grown by shifting cultivation in the rain forest, with yams the staple food; fish from the lagoons are an important supplement.

The inquiry was undertaken at various times between June 1956 and February 1958. The population was estimated to be 325,000, and the sample results relate to more than 26,000 of these, or approximately 8 percent. All the tribal groups can be classed as Lagoon peoples, with languages of the Twi branch of the Nigritic stock.

Mopti

The region of the inquiry, designated by the name of its main town, was at that time part of the French Sudan but is now in the Republic of Mali. It is situated southwest of Lake Debo in the triangle formed by the Niger, Bani, and Diaka rivers; the area is 17,000 square kilometers, with greatest lengths and breadths of about 200 kilometers and 100 kilometers. The triangle is in the flood plain of the river, and most of it is under water for part of the year. The villages are established on higher patches of ground. The inhabitants are subsistence cultivators, with rice and millet as the main crops; fishing is an important economic activity, and there is some grazing of livestock.

The population at the time of the inquiry in 1957-58 was about 200,000, giving a density of 12 persons per square kilometer. Of these 30,000 were living in small towns. The sample included 13,000 people, 6.5 percent of the total, with a rather larger fraction in the towns than in the rural areas. The sample units in the latter were primarily villages, with some adjustments to make sizes more equal. The tribal groups are basically Nuclear Mande, speaking languages of this sub-family of the Nigritic stock, although Arabic and Berber strains are intermixed and there are many Moslems.

Fertility

The birth rates and the age-specific fertilities, calculated from the reports of vital events in the year before the inquiry, are presented in Table 7.1.E. The data suggest that fertility in Fouta-Toro and Mopti was high

Table 7.1.E. Reported current birth and age-specific fertility rates—four areas

Age group of women in years*	Centre-Oubangui	Fouta-Toro	Ivory Coast:1	Mopti
15-19[+]	.106	.169	.243	.190
20-24	.247	.262	.353	.275
25-29	.194	.275	.338	.239
30-34	.139	.240	.224	.234
35-39	.082	.173	.177	.175
40-44	.028	.088	.092	.126
45-49	.015	.037	.057	.065
Total fertility	4.055	6.220	7.420	6.520
Birth rate per thousand	39	48	59	53

* The true age intervals for the rates are, on average, half a year younger than is shown.

[+] Estimated from rate given for 14-19 years.

and in the Ivory Coast sector very high; in Centre-Oubangui on the other hand the level was moderate, with specific rates beyond 30 years very much lower than in the other populations. The corresponding total children ever born per woman, found with the help of the measures in Table 7.2.E, are assessed in relation to the retrospective reports by the P/F ratios in Table 7.3.E. The ratios for all regions are reasonably close to 1.00 for the women aged 20-24 years. The deviations from unity could easily be explained by the effects of sampling variability, birth fluctuations, age misreporting, and graduation errors. There is, thus, little evidence of any time scale bias in the reports of events in the preceding

Table 7.2.E. Estimated measures of fertility distribution—four areas

Measure	Centre-Oubangui	Fouta-Toro	Ivory Coast: 1	Mopti
			Area	
Mean ($\overline{m}$) in years	26.9	28.6	27.8	29.2
P_1/P_2	–	.24	.31	.31
Adjusted female birth rate per thousand	34.4	46.6	54.5	50.5

year. The P/F ratios show a consistent downward trend with age in all the series except that for Centre-Oubangui, where there is a fall followed by a rise. The latter pattern combined with the lower fertility level in the region strongly suggests that the birth rate has decreased. The comparisons add to the weight of the evidence from the other surveys analyzed that the women as they grow older progressively omit more of their children from the reports, although the effects may be masked in communities with falling fertility.

The measures of infertility in Table 7.4.E are consistent with the conclusions above. Apart from the Centre-Oubangui population, the percentages of women childless are little above 10 percent by the age group 25-29 years and fall to 7-9 percent at later ages. In Centre-Oubangui the proportion infertile is higher, at 25 percent, for women aged 25-39 years but drops substantially to 15 percent at 50 years and over, in conformity with the proposition that fertility was greater in the past.

Although the P/F ratios for the younger women are sufficiently close to 1.00 for the existence of any bias in the recording of births in the previous year to be in doubt, they are rather low for the Ivory Coast sector and Centre-Oubangui. Consistent with the methods used in the analysis of observations from the other inquiries, correction factors were derived from the level of the ratios at 20-24 and 25-29 years. The factors

Table 7.3.E. Cumulated fertility (F), reported parity (P), and P/F ratios—four areas

Age group of women years	Centre-Oubangui			Fouta-Toro			Ivory Coast: 1			Mopti		
	F	P*	P/F	F	P	P/F	F	P	P/F	F	P	P/F
15-19	0.24	0.4		0.46	0.40	0.87	0.68	0.65	0.96	0.53	0.56	1.06
20-24	1.24	1.2	0.97	1.61	1.68	1.04	2.25	2.10	0.93	1.76	1.79	1.02
25-29	2.35	2.1	0.89	3.00	2.86	0.95	4.02	3.28	0.82	3.06	3.00	0.98
30-34	3.17	2.5	0.79	4.28	3.83	0.89	5.37	4.35	0.81	4.25	4.02	0.95
35-39	3.70	3.2	0.86	5.29	4.55	0.86	6.37	5.01	0.79	5.26	4.54	0.86
40-44	3.94	3.7	0.94	5.90	5.05	0.86	7.01	6.09	0.87	6.00	4.65	0.78
45-49	4.05	4.0	0.99	6.20	5.32	0.86	7.40	5.91	0.80	6.47	5.09	0.79
50-59	4.06	4.2	1.03	6.22	5.25	0.84	7.42	5.84	0.79	6.52	4.90	0.75
and over	4.06	4.3	1.06	6.22	5.27	0.85	7.42	5.83	0.79	6.52	4.73	0.73

* The published data only give retrospective children born to one decimal place. The P/F ratio at 15-19 years was omitted because of the large rounding error.

Table 7.4.E. Percentage of women childless and average parity of mothers—
four areas

Age Group of Women in Years	Centre-Oubangui		Fouta-Toro		Ivory Coast: 1		Mopti	
	Per cent childless	Average parity of mothers	Per cent childless	Average parity of mothers	Per cent childless	Average parity of mothers	Per cent childless	Average parity of mothers
15-19	71	1.3	68	1.3	50	1.3	63	1.
20-24	37	1.9	24	2.2	12	2.4	20	2.
25-29	26	2.8	12	3.3	10	3.6	12	3.
30-34	27	3.4	11	4.3	9	4.8	9	4.
35-39	25	4.3	8	4.9	11	5.6	8	4.
40-49	20	4.8	7	5.6	8	6.5	8	5.
50 and over	15	5.0	6	5.6	9	6.4	9	5.

were taken to be 0.95 and 0.90 for Centre-Oubangui and Ivory Coast, respectively; no correction was applied for Fouta-Toro and Mopti. Rather less weight was put on the exact P/F ratio for women aged 20-24 years than in the other studies because of the larger sampling errors for the present populations. The adjusted female birth rates, which result from applying the correction factors and the use of a standard sex ratio at birth, are given in Table 7.2.E.

Mortality

Life table survivorship ratios, estimated by the multiplication factor procedure from the retrospective reports of children dead by age of mother, are shown in Table 7.5.E; mortality measures, obtained by standard methods from the deaths recorded for the year preceding the survey, are in Table 7.6.E. Comparisons of survivorship ratios, in terms of differences from the African standard life table on the logit scale, are exhibited in Figure 7.1.E.

Table 7.5.E. Percentage of children having died previous to the survey, by age of mother, and derived life table survivorship ratios l_x—four areas

Age group of mothers in years	Age of child survivorship	Centre-Oubangui Per cent of children dead	l_x	Fouta-Toro Per cent of children dead	l_x	Ivory Coast:1 Per cent of children dead	l_x	Mopti Per cent of children dead	l_x
15-19	1	21	.803	19.5	.814	23.7	.786	36.5	.67
20-24	2	27	.733	28.0	.721	23.8	.770	45.3	.56
25-29	3	32	.686	31.5	.689	29.0	.720	46.7	.54
30-34	5	33	.673	35.5	.640	33.3	.666	49.3	.49
35-39	10	36	.640	39.0	.600	34.1	.655	46.9	.51
40-44	15	39	.620	42.0	.579	35.0	.654	48.8	.50
45-49	20	43	.582	43.5	.564	36.0	.644	48.9	.50
50-54	25	46	.546	44.0	.552	38.5	.614	47.6	.51
55-59	30	47	.535	45.5	.536	43.9	.559	51.7	.46
60-64	35	51	.497	45.5	.538	44.5	.555	50.9	.47

Table 7.6.E. Life table measures from reported current deaths (both sexes)—four areas. (*m*, age-specific death rate per 1,000; *q*, probability of dying in age group; *l*, proportion surviving to start of age group)

Age group in years	Centre-Oubangui			Fouta-Toro			Area Ivory Coast:1			Mopti		
	m	q	l	m	q	l	m	q	l	m	q	l
Under 1	219*	.190	1.000	190	.168	1.000	164	.147	1.000	369	.293	1.000
1- 4	32	.118	.810	46	.164	.832	37	.135	.853	133	.391	.707
5- 9	8	.039	.714	13	.063	.696	9	.044	.738	25	.118	.431
10-19	11	.105	.686	7	.068	.652	12	.114	.705	8	.077	.380
20-29	17	.158	.614	6	.059	.608	13	.123	.625	6	.059	.351
30-39	14	.132	.517	8	.077	.572	12	.114	.548	6	.059	.330
40-49	24	.217	.449	12	.114	.528	26	.233	.486	7	.068	.310
50-59	40	.338	.352	18	.167	.468	32	.280	.372	11	.105	.289
60-69	61	.473	.233	26	.233	.390	63	.484	.268	25	.225	.259
70 and over	94	1.000	.123	66	1.000	.299	122	1.000	.138	33	1.000	.201
Death rate per thousand	26			24			28			41		

* Estimated from the infant mortality rate.

The results for Mopti have special features. For the other three regions individual measurements are erratic, possibly because of high sampling errors, but the general patterns are similar to those found in most of the other inquiries studied. The differences of the logits of survivorship ratios from the corresponding African standard life table measures in child-hood give no systematic indication that the model is an unsuitable framework for graduation purposes. Child mortalities estimated from the retrospective reports are higher than the values from the current data. By age 35 years, however, the current survivorship ratios are as low or lower than the retrospective measures. The conclusions reached previously are supported, namely that deaths in the preceding year are, in general, understated and that as women grow older the proportion of dead children they fail to report increases steadily. The evidence is, therefore, satisfactory for the application of the life table estimation procedure, described in the introductory section to the chapter, based on the premise that the retrospective child mortalities are correct and alternative assumptions about errors in the current reports at later ages. The estimated mortality measures from the fitted life tables of the parametric system are given in Tables 7.7.E and 7.8.E, and the straight lines representing the low, medium, and high alternatives are drawn in Figure 7.1.E.

In all three regions the percentage corrections for the understatement of deaths in the previous year are moderate and the differentials between the alternative life tables relatively small. Because of this and the erratic individual measures, there is little scope for distinguishing among the merits of the different life tables. Inspection of Figure 7.1.E gives the

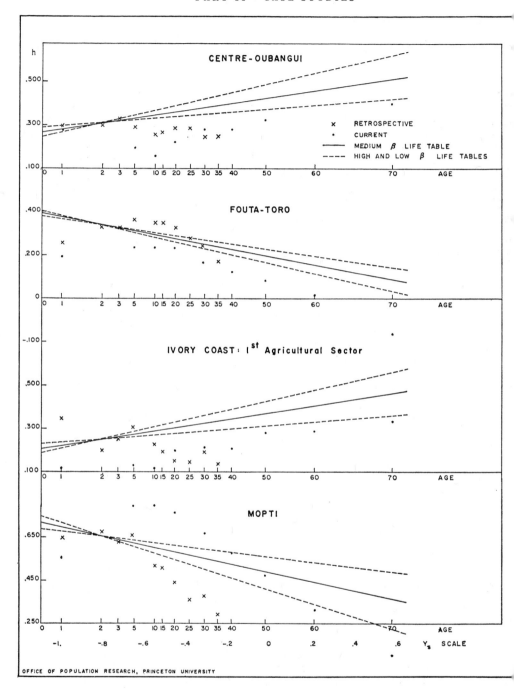

7.1.E. Proportion surviving to each age (l_x) in Centre-Oubangui, Fouta-Toro, Ivory Coast, and Mopti in life tables
calculated from retrospective mortality data and current
mortality data and fitted by linear logit transformations.

Table 7.7.E. Indices from estimated low- and high-correction life tables—four areas

	Area							
	Centre-Oubangui		Fouta-Toro		Ivory Coast:1		Mopti	
Estimated measures	Low	High	Low	High	Low	High	Low	High
% correction to deaths	9	22	11	19	12	23	-13	-
1(2)	.730	.730	.717	.717	.751	.751	.574	.574
1(27)	.505	.472	.557	.539	.533	.501	.420	.379
β	1.08	1.23	0.78	0.86	1.08	1.22	0.69	0.88

impression that the high β life tables may be too extreme for Centre-Oubangui and the Ivory Coast sector, but such a conclusion would carry little conviction. It seems preferable, on *a priori* grounds, to use the medium estimates if single life tables are required; there is no suggestion in the comparisons that such a course would be inconsistent with the combined evidence of the current and retrospective observations. If it is assumed that nearly all the children omitted in the reports of the older mothers were dead, the resulting estimates of mortality in early adulthood are not far from the medium β life table measures for Fouta-Toro and the Ivory Coast sector, although the comparisons can be only very rough because of error sensitivity. The procedure is not applicable to the Centre-Oubangui data because of the effects of fertility trends. The estimates of child mortality levels in the three regions are very similar, but the life table slope β, which is moderately high for Centre-Oubangui and the Ivory Coast sector, is low for Fouta-Toro. The latter area would therefore appear to have appreciably less severe adult mortality. These findings do not arise from idiosyncrasies of the graduating procedures but are a direct reflection of the reports of current deaths.

The consideration of mortality in Mopti has been omitted from the above paragraphs because of the atypical nature of the results. The

Table 7.8.E. Medium-correction life tables, males and females together—four areas.
(q, probability of dying in succeeding age interval: l, proportion surviving at age)

	Area							
	Centre-Oubangui		Fouta-Toro		Ivory Coast:1		Mopti	
Age in years	q	l	q	l	q	l	q	l
0	.192	1.000	.224	1.000	.176	1.000	.354	1.000
1	.189	.808	.146	.776	.176	.824	.205	.646
5	.084	.655	.057	.663	.078	.679	.078	.514
10	.088	.600	.059	.625	.083	.626	.078	.474
20	.146	.547	.097	.588	.139	.574	.123	.437
30	.161	.467	.102	.531	.154	.494	.126	.383
40	.214	.392	.136	.477	.206	.418	.161	.335
50	.325	.308	.214	.412	.319	.332	.242	.281
60	.519	.207	.361	.324	.513	.226	.385	.213
70	1.000	.100	1.000	.207	1.000	.110	1.000	.131
β		1.15		0.82		1.15		0.79

recorded current death rates in childhood are very high and at 1 to 4 years astonishingly so. Mortalities shown by the retrospective reports of children dead are also extremely severe, although at a slightly lower level than the current measures. Although there is no firm explanation for the exceptionally high child death rate, the opinion of the inquiry organizers was that it might be due to epidemic disease, particularly meningitis and measles. The conditions at the time of the survey would, then, not be representative of the average recent force of mortality in the area. Since the retrospective records cover a longer period, the effects of an epidemic on the derived measures, although still substantial, will be less than on the current values. There is still a strong case, therefore, for basing the child mortality estimates on the retrospective reports by age of mother, although it cannot be established, as in the other populations, that deaths in the previous year were understated.

In contrast to the statistics for children, the recorded current death rates of adults were low, below those for Fouta-Toro, on which comments have already been made. There is no satisfactory information on the likely level and pattern of adult mortality in populations with such high child death rates. The construction of a full life table must, therefore, be very speculative. The low β measures in Table 7.7.E were obtained by using the retrospective estimates up to age 5 and the current specific rates at later years; the observations were graduated by a parametric model in the usual way. The resulting life table is hardly acceptable because of the extremely low β value, but there seemed no logical method of deriving a high-correction mortality schedule. It should be noted that, in contrast to the Guinea inquiry, there was no suggestion from the P/F ratios for Mopti that the reference period for which vital events were reported was longer than a year. Arbitrarily, a life table was constructed with the child mortality calculated from the retrospective reports but with adult specific rates increased to establish agreement with the overall crude death rate observed. Graduation gave a high-correction life table, and the medium mortality schedule was inserted between the two limits as before. The medium β, although low, is not far from the values found for other areas, e.g., Fouta-Toro. It is clear, however, that although the medium-correction life table may give a fair representation of the mortality in Mopti in the year or two preceding the inquiry, it is not necessarily satisfactory as a component in the estimation of natural increase when the emphasis is on developments over a longer period in the past or the future. Reservations of this kind must be made for all the populations studied, but they are more serious when there are obvious discordant features as for Mopti.

Separate life tables for males and females, derived from the reports of deaths in the year preceding the inquiry, are shown in Table 7.9.E.

Table 7.9.E. Life table measures from reported current deaths by sex—four areas.
(m, age-specific death rate per 1,000; q, probability of dying in age group; l, proportion surviving to start of age group)

Area

Age group in years	Centre-Oubangui			Fouta-Toro			Ivory Coast:1			Mopti		
	m	q	l	m	q	l	m	q	l	m	q	l
						Male						
Under 1	227	.196	1.000	191	.169	1.000	187	.165	1.000	398	.311	1.000
1- 4	35	.128	.804	46	.164	.831	43	.154	.835	142	.411	.689
5- 9	8	.039	.701	12	.058	.695	11	.054	.706	31	.144	.406
10-19	11	.105	.674	7	.068	.654	12	.114	.668	9	.087	.347
20-29	14	.132	.603	8	.077	.610	13	.123	.592	7	.068	.317
30-39	13	.123	.523	9	.087	.563	11	.105	.519	3	.030	.296
40-49	28	.249	.459	12	.114	.514	24	.217	.465	7	.068	.287
50-59	44	.366	.345	20	.184	.455	32	.280	.364	12	.114	.267
60-69	75	.548	.219	27	.241	.372	56	.443	.262	31	.272	.237
70 and over	125	1.000	.099	84	1.000	.282	119	1.000	.146	39	1.000	.172

| Death rate per thousand | 29 | | | 25 | | | 30 | | | 46 | | |

						Female						
Under 1	210	.183	1.000	188	.166	1.000	144	.131	1.000	339	.274	1.000
1- 4	29	.108	.817	46	.164	.834	31	.114	.869	124	.372	.726
5-9	8	.039	.729	14	.068	.697	6	.030	.770	19	.091	.456
10-19	13	.123	.700	7	.068	.650	11	.105	.747	6	.059	.414
20-29	19	.175	.614	5	.049	.606	13	.123	.668	6	.059	.390
30-39	14	.132	.507	7	.068	.576	13	.123	.586	9	.087	.367
40-49	17	.158	.440	13	.123	.537	28	.249	.514	6	.059	.335
50-59	34	.295	.370	16	.150	.471	32	.280	.386	9	.087	.315
60-69	46	.379	.261	25	.225	.400	79	.568	.278	18	.167	.288
70 and over	52	1.000	.162	49	1.000	.310	127	1.000	.120	27	1.000	.240

| Death rate per thousand | 24 | | | 22 | | | 26 | | | 36 | | |

All suggest a somewhat higher mortality for males than females. In Centre-Oubangui and Fouta-Toro, however, the differential is nearly all concentrated at late ages, and there is little indication of a systematic female advantage before the end of the reproductive period. For these two populations the medium β life tables were taken to apply to both sexes. In the Ivory Coast sector and Mopti the reported child mortalities were considerably lower for females than for males.

Since the estimated underreporting of current child deaths relative to the retrospective measures was small in the Ivory Coast and not established for Mopti, it seemed reasonable to accept that there was a genuine sex differential. The proportions of female children dying before age 2 were taken to be 10 percent and 5 percent lower than the estimated levels for both sexes of Table 7.7.E for Centre-Oubangui and Mopti, respectively, in approximate conformity with the relations for the current rates. The life tables were extended at ages beyond 2 by the use of the medium β values. Although at late ages the reported current death rates for males continue to exceed those for females in Mopti, while in Centre-Oubangui there is a reversal of the differential, the evidence on adult mortality is too doubtful for further refinements in estimation to be justified.

Reproduction and Natural Increase

With the medium-correction life tables for females as a base, stable population age distributions which gave the adjusted birth rates were constructed. These are compared with the observed distributions in Table 7.13.E. The resulting gross and net reproduction rates and total fertility ratios are given in Table 7.10.E; the specific fertility distributions were taken to be located by age in accordance with the current measures. Because of the strong evidence that fertility had been decreasing in Centre-Oubangui for a long period prior to the inquiry, the method of estimating the reproduction rates via the stable population is not completely satisfactory, since the results will have an upward bias. It is, however, difficult to arrive at a quantity for the size of the bias. The question has been fully discussed in the study of the North Cameroon data.

Except in Centre-Oubangui the proportions of females in the reproductive period, 15-44 years say, from the fitted stable populations are only a little higher than the observed values. The estimates of the total fertility ratio are, therefore, not much above those which would have been obtained by the direct application of the correction factors to the current specific rates. Because the adjustments for errors in reports of ages and births have been modest in size, the total fertilities in Table 7.10.E do not differ greatly from the uncorrected ratios of Table 7.1.E, although the level in Mopti has been somewhat increased. The age-specific fertility rates of Table 7.11.E, obtained by raising the current measures by the fixed percentage required to give the estimated total fertility and adjusting for the half-year displacement, also show no changes of significance and demand no comment. The percentage corrections to recorded current deaths, deduced from comparisons with

Table 7.10.E. Estimated stable female population fertility and mortality measures
—four areas

Measure	Area			
	Centre-Oubangui	Fouta-Toro	Ivory Coast:1	Mopti
Total fertility	4.3	6.4	7.4	7.0
Gross reproduction rate	2.10	3.15	3.65	3.45
Net reproduction rate	1.03	1.71	1.99	1.46
Rates per thousand:				
Birth rate	34	47	54	51
Death rate	33	28	29	38
Natural increase	1	19	25	13

Table 7.11.E. Estimated age-specific fertility rates—four areas

Age group of women in years	Area			
	Centre-Oubangui	Fouta-Toro	Ivory Coast:1	Mopti
15–19	.131	.196	.273	.229
20–24	.266	.274	.357	.296
25–29	.201	.281	.330	.254
30–34	.141	.243	.215	.247
35–39	.081	.170	.169	.183
40–44	.026	.083	.086	.130
45–49	.014	.033	.050	.061
Total fertility	4.3	6.4	7.4	7.0

the retrospective reports of children surviving by age of mother, are relatively small. As a consequence, the replacement of the medium β life tables by the high- or low-correction schedules alters the estimated rates only slightly; the maximum change in the natural increase is not more than 1 1/2 points per thousand. The allowances for sex differentials in mortality in Mopti and the Ivory Coast sector raise the natural increase by 2 to 3 per thousand.

Age Distribution

The percentage age distributions by sex are given in Table 7.12.E. In Table 7.13.E the observations for females are compared with the fitted stable population age distributions; the points in Figure 7.2.E, drawn as described in the introduction to the chapter, illustrate the relationships. Broadly, the age deviations of the observations from the fitted values follow a similar course to the curves determined in previous analyses, with a peak at age 10, followed by a dip to a minimum at 20-25, and a rise again; the subsequent trend is less consistent. Despite the systematic pattern, the sizes and, in some cases, the directions of the deviations from the stable measures vary considerably among the populations.

For the Ivory Coast sector the fitted stable population could hardly be improved, since the axis line which represents it runs closely through the middle of the observed points. The only notable feature is the very large deviation, in terms of natural increase, at age 5. If estimates are made on the assumption that the constructed life table is satisfactory and the proportion of females under 5 years correct, the resulting birth rate and total fertility ratio are 67 per thousand and 9.2; the corresponding stable age distribution bears no resemblance to the observed pattern at ages beyond 5. It is important to note that in the Ivory Coast sector the proportions recorded as under 5 and 10 years were higher for females than for males, contrary to the usual finding in these inquiries of a substantial deficit. The convincing evidence that the proportion of females under 5 years—and hence of males also—was greatly

Table 7.12.E. Percentage age distributions by sex—four areas

Age group in years	Centre-Oubangui Male	Female	Total	Fouta-Toro Male	Female	Total	Ivory Coast: 1 Male	Female	Total	Mopti Male	Female	Total
Under 1	3.6	3.2	3.4	3.9	3.8	3.9	4.4	5.6	5.0	4.6	3.3	3.9
1– 4	11.3	10.6	10.9	14.6	13.6	14.1	16.2	18.5	17.3	11.2	10.8	11.0
5– 9	14.7	12.5	13.5	16.8	13.8	15.3	16.9	16.3	16.6	14.5	13.0	13.7
10–14	8.3	5.7	6.9	8.9	6.7	7.8	6.7	5.2	6.0	7.9	7.7	7.8
15–19	5.1	4.9	5.0	7.3	7.5	7.4	6.2	9.0	7.5	7.2	8.9	8.1
20–24	5.8	7.4	6.6	6.4	8.2	7.3	7.9	10.0	8.9	6.4	9.1	7.8
25–29	8.5	11.9	10.3	6.9	10.0	8.5	9.6	10.6	10.1	7.7	10.1	8.9
30–34	7.4	10.0	8.8	6.3	6.6	6.4	6.7	6.3	6.5	6.4	6.6	6.5
35–39	10.0	12.8	11.5	6.1	6.8	6.4	6.9	5.6	6.3	7.2	6.6	6.9
40–44	7.4	7.5	7.5	4.6	4.6	4.6	3.9	3.3	3.6	5.4	5.4	5.4
45–54	11.9	9.2	10.5	8.8	8.2	8.5	6.9	5.2	6.1	9.5	8.5	9.0
55–64	4.7	3.4	4.0	5.1	5.4	5.2	4.0	2.5	3.3	7.0	5.4	6.2
65 and over	1.3	0.9	1.1	4.3	4.8	4.6	3.7	1.9	2.8	5.0	4.6	4.8
Total	100.0	100.0	100.0	100.0	100.0	100.0	100.0	100.0	100.0	100.0	100.0	100.0
Under 15	37.9	32.0	34.7	44.2	37.9	41.1	44.2	45.6	44.9	38.2	34.8	36.4
15–44	44.2	54.5	49.7	37.6	43.7	40.6	41.2	44.8	42.9	40.3	46.7	43.6
45 and over	17.9	13.5	15.6	18.2	18.4	18.3	14.6	9.6	12.2	21.5	18.5	20.0
Per cent male	47.0			49.3			52.0			48.3		

Table 7.13.E. Percentage female age distribution observed (O) and fitted (F)—
four areas

Age group in years	Centre-Oubangui		Fouta-Toro		Ivory Coast: 1		Mopti	
	0	F	0	F	0	F	0	F
0- 4	13.8	12.4	17.4	16.1	24.1	19.5	14.1	15.3
5- 9	12.5	10.6	13.8	13.1	16.3	15.3	13.0	12.2
10-14	5.7	9.9	6.7	11.4	5.2	12.7	7.7	10.8
15-19	4.9	9.4	7.5	10.1	9.0	10.8	8.9	9.7
20-24	7.4	8.7	8.2	8.8	10.0	9.0	9.1	8.7
25-29	11.9	8.0	10.0	7.5	10.6	7.4	10.1	7.6
30-34	10.0	7.4	6.6	6.6	6.3	6.1	6.6	6.7
35-39	12.8	6.7	6.8	5.6	5.6	5.0	6.6	5.9
40-44	7.5	6.1	4.6	4.8	3.3	4.0	5.4	5.1
45-54	9.2	10.0	8.2	7.5	5.2	5.6	8.5	8.2
55-64	3.4	6.6	5.4	4.9	2.5	3.1	5.4	5.5
65 and over	0.9	4.2	4.8	3.6	1.9	1.5	4.6	4.3
Total	100.0	100.0	100.0	100.0	100.0	100.0	100.0	100.0

Exact age in years				Per Cent under Age				
5	13.8	12.4	17.4	16.1	24.1	19.5	14.1	15.3
10	26.3	23.0	31.2	29.2	40.4	34.8	27.1	27.5
15	32.0	32.9	37.9	40.6	45.6	47.5	34.8	38.3
20	36.9	42.3	45.4	50.7	54.6	58.3	43.7	48.0
25	44.3	51.0	53.6	59.5	64.6	67.3	52.8	56.7
30	56.2	59.0	63.6	67.0	75.2	74.7	62.9	64.3
35	66.2	66.4	70.2	73.6	81.5	80.8	69.5	71.0
40	79.0	73.1	77.0	79.2	87.1	85.8	76.1	76.9
45	86.5	79.2	81.6	84.0	90.4	89.8	81.5	82.0
55	95.7	89.2	89.8	91.5	95.6	95.4	90.0	90.2
65	99.1	95.8	95.2	96.4	98.1	98.5	95.4	95.7

exaggerated in the Ivory Coast sector adds weight to the conclusion that the ages of male children have been much understated in all the surveys studied in this chapter. That age recording errors in Centre-Oubangui were large can be seen from the comparisons in Table 7.13.E or Figure 7.2.E. Nevertheless, it is clear that the general nature of deviations of observed from fitted stable values, with extreme positive excesses at ages beyond 40 years, is consistent with the view that fertility has been falling steadily in the area. A slightly lower estimate of current fertility —and hence natural increase—would be in good accord with the observed age distribution, but the errors are too large for a satisfactory method of adjustment to be devised. No amendment has therefore been made. In a period of changing fertility there is little advantage in applying a speculative amendment to make the estimate slightly more up to date. It should be noted that the rates in Table 7.10.E are for stable populations; the actual birth and death rates in Centre-Oubangui would be different because of the reduced proportion of old people compared with the model.

The points on Figure 7.2.E representing the observed age distribution of Mopti relative to the fitted stable measures show a greater tendency to fall on a straight line than appears in the corresponding comparisons

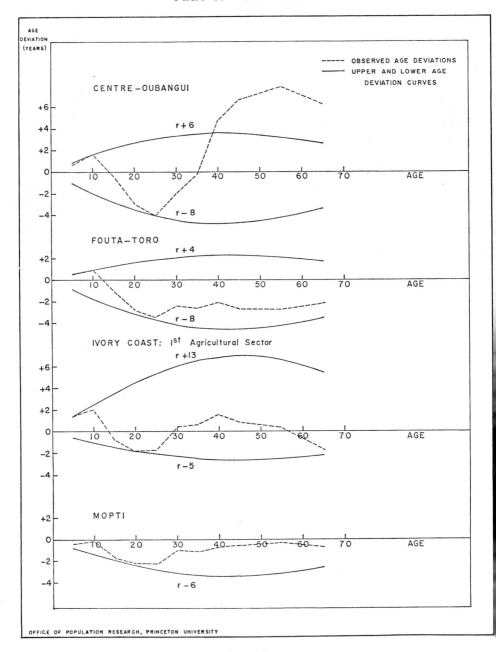

7.2.E. Age deviations, in years, between observed cumulative age distributions, in Centre-Oubangui, Fouta-Toro, Ivory Coast, and Mopti, and stable age distributions based on estimated fertility and mortality. For females.

for other populations. The deviations are all negative, however. In the analysis of mortality it was suggested that the current death rates, particularly in childhood, were higher than the estimates accepted but that the latter might better represent the "average" situation. The pattern in Figure 7.2.E is in accord with that view. A lower l_2 survivorship ratio would lead to better agreement between observed and stable points in the earlier part of life, but the age distribution at later years is in good accord with the index chosen. There is no suggestion, however, that the very heavy estimated mortality was too extreme, and, in fact, slightly more severe rates would have given improved consistency with the observed age distribution.

The comparisons for Fouta-Toro are not so satisfactory. The observed proportions under given ages are below the fitted values at 15 years of age and upward. The implication is that the fertility estimate should have been lower or the child mortality higher. An inspection of the respective analyses, however, reveals no grounds to justify such amendments. Other possibilities seem no more plausible, e.g., that fertility had been increasing or that relatively low mortality of adults had led to larger numbers than expected at later ages. In fact, the estimated β is already low; otherwise the discrepancies would have been worse. The relatively small rise in the graph of observed points after the minimum at age 25 leaves open the possibility of errors in recording rather different from those established for other inquiries. There seems no case for arbitrarily adjusting the estimates to give better agreement with the age distribution without some clue to the causes of the divergences.

The analyses of the data for these four populations have confirmed that the typical errors in female ages, revealed in the other studies, are present. These are understatements around age 10 and overstatements around 15, with some piling up toward the center of the reproductive period. The latter effect is more erratic, however, and the consistency of errors at later years has not been established. There is further evidence that the mortality characteristics described by the slope parameter β are not a product simply of chance and systematic errors but that the attempt to estimate their tendency is worthwhile. In all these populations the use of a model life table with β equal to 1.00, the central value, gives poorer agreement between the observed and fitted stable distributions. With the exception of the Ivory Coast sector, where the atypical finding has already been discussed, the male age distributions show excess proportions under 15 years compared with the female and deficits in the middle adult years. The differentials can be explained in a general way by immigration (less males than females were recorded in all the regions except the Ivory Coast sector) and factors in the age estimation. There is no information which could be used profitably to make the examination for these populations more incisive.

||||| 8 |||||

The Demography of the Portuguese
Territories: Angola, Mozambique, and
Portuguese Guinea

BY DON F. HEISEL

The mainland territories in Africa under Portuguese administration—
Angola, Mozambique, and Portuguese Guinea—provide a body of demographic data with more or less uniform characteristics. First, the Portuguese have relied entirely upon total enumeration; no sampling procedures have been employed. Second, for the two larger territories the
series of modern censuses began in 1940 and has been repeated decen-
nially since. (However, the results of the 1960 censuses were not available in time to be included in the present analysis.) Third, none of these
censuses includes reports of births or deaths within some specified period of immediately past time, and thus the evaluation of fertility and
mortality must be based solely on women's retrospective reports on
their lifetime experience.

The total "non-civilized"[1] populations recorded in the respective territories in 1950 are shown in Table 8.1. The rather large differences
in the sizes of the three populations are more than matched by differ-

Table 8.1. Total population, area, and average density of the mainland
territories under Portuguese administration as of 1950

	Angola	Mozambique	Portuguese Guinea
Population (thousands)	4,010	5,647	509
Area (km^2)	1,247	783	36
Average density (persons per km^2)	3.2	7.2	14.1

[1] Introductory notes to the 1950 census of Mozambique described the civilized
population as including all those of White, Mongolian, Indian, and Mixed race
and those of the Negro race who (1) speak Portuguese; (2) do not practice the
customs associated with an indigenous environment; (3) are employed in com-
merce or industry or have means of support.

The "non-civilized" population includes all those of the Negro race and their
descendants who cannot satisfy all three of the conditions set forth above.

ences in the areas of the territories. Thus, the average density of the three territories is far from uniform.

The three countries have different climatic and natural conditions, and they are separated by such distances that there has been scant contact between their indigenous populations. Indeed, the primary and nearly the sole factor tending to produce similarities among the three territories has been Portuguese administration and culture. From the point of view of population statistics, by far the most important uniformity in the three territories is the very similar census procedures employed. Recording took place at an assembly in each community rather than by a house-to-house canvass. Before the census taker arrived at a predesignated center for enumeration, the local populace was notified to present itself on the appointed day. Local authorities and local languages (using translators where necessary) were employed to facilitate both the advance notice and the actual census recording. The local areas of enumeration were established in such a way as to correspond as far as possible to local settlements.

The unit of enumeration was the individual; each person enumerated was given a token (*bilhete*) to be presented as evidence of enumeration in all contacts with persons of authority for a fixed period following the census. This served as an inducement to full cooperation in the census.

The majority of the enumerators were governmental functionaries who were simply assigned their census tasks along with their other duties as resident administrators. They were assisted by a large staff of auxiliary personnel and by the local indigenous authorities. The census agents received no special training for their task. (However, in Portuguese Guinea in 1950, members of the auxiliary staffs did receive a few days training prior to actual field operations.)

The time element in the census was approached with two goals in mind. First, the "statistical moment," the period during which enumeration took place, was to be made as short as possible. This was an important element of the rationale behind the use of assembly procedures in the field. Second, the censuses were timed to minimize disruptions of the populations' seasonal activities.

The three territories vary with respect to their classification of the population as either *de jure* (*de residencia habitual*) or *de facto* (*presente*). In Angola the latter category alone is employed. In Portuguese Guinea totals are given for both, with some 1.3 percent of the *de jure* population presumably temporarily out of the country. Detailed information is given only for the population present at the time of the census. In Mozambique the *de jure* category is used to refer to the total population. (That is, some persons who were outside of the territory at the time of the census were included in the tabulation of the population of the regions in which they normally reside.) However, it appears that all persons within Mozambique at the time of the census were recorded where they were found by enumerators.

A rough estimate based on the 1946 and 1951 censuses of native populations in the Republic (then the Union) of South Africa cites 153,000 males of Mozambique origin in the Republic. According to the 1950 census report of Mozambique, the gold mines of Johannesburg employed almost all of the 156,380 persons native to Mozambique who were working outside their mother country. The closeness of these figures derived from independent sources reflects the fact that this labor migration is contractual and is strictly controlled by the governments concerned.

Some unrecorded emigration apparently occurs in Angola, Portuguese Guinea, and Mozambique. But there is no evidence to suggest that this unrecorded migration is of such a magnitude as to seriously distort further analysis, especially since much of it is restricted to females, who migrate less frequently.

In particular, intercensal growth of female population between 1940 and 1950 may be presumed to reflect mostly the natural increase of the population and to be affected by migration only in a minor way. Intercensal growth rates can be obtained for Angola and Mozambique and their subdivisions. There are some small changes in administrative boundaries of both areas. The five provinces of Angola (Luanda or Congo, Malange, Benguela, Bie, and Huila) can be identified in both censuses.[2] The following regions and their names in both censuses serve for the analysis of Mozambique:

	1940	1950
South[3]	Sul do Save	Lourenço Marques, Inhambane, and Gaza
Central	Manica e Sofala and Zambezia	Quelimane, Tete, and Beira
North	Niassa	Lago, Cabo Delgado, and Nampula

Description of the Data on Age, Fertility and Mortality

The Portuguese censuses all have detailed age distributions, and this fact as well as the availability of relevant data on fertility and mortality is recorded in Table 8.2. The completely retrospective nature of this fertility and mortality data rather limits the possibility of internal checks

[2] A part of the Concelho de Cazengo with 5,000 inhabitants in 1940 went over from Luanda to Malange.

[3] The Circunscrição do Govuro, in 1940 part of Manica and Sofala Province with 26,000 inhabitants, but belonging geographically south of the Save River, was reintegrated with Inhambane in 1950.

Table 8.2. Data available for the analysis of vital rates—Portuguese African territories

| | Censuses of | | | | |
| Tabulations of | Angola | | Mozambique | | Portuguese Guinea |
	1940	1950	1940	1950	1950
1. Age					
a. single year					+
b. five year	+	+	+	+	
2. Fertility					
a. children ever born by age of mother	+	+	+	+	+
b. children ever born by sex by age of mother			+	+	
c. mothers by age by number of children born		+	+	+	d
3. Mortality					
a. surviving children by age of mother	+		+	+	+

d. married women only.

for consistency. Specific information on age, fertility, and mortality is given in the tables of Chapter 2 on systems of data. The present section will be devoted to a summary discussion of the nature of the Portuguese data. A later section will be devoted to their analysis.

Reported Age Distributions

The age distributions reported in the 1940 and 1950 censuses of Portuguese Africa are shown in Figure 8.1 (for males) and Figure 8.2 (for females), where their general similarities can easily be seen. But few generalizations about data on age distributions in Portuguese Africa hold with any accuracy for Mozambique in 1940. The most superficial glance comparing the Mozambique distribution with those from other Portuguese censuses shows that it has an extremely high proportion under ages 5 or 10, a marked "sawtoothing" of the proportions (especially among females), and a younger (i.e., 10-14 for females) depleted age group. The same peculiarities of the 1940 census are found in all three regions of Mozambique.

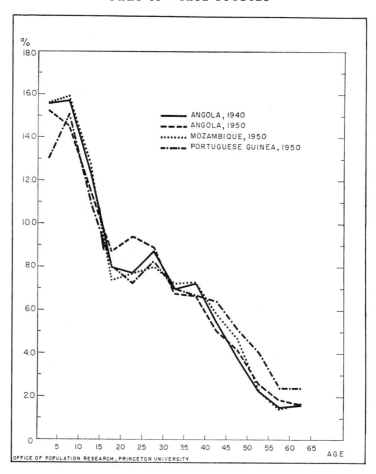

8.1. Reported male age distributions by five-year age groups:
Angola, 1940 and 1950; Mozambique, 1950; and Portuguese
Guinea, 1950.

The most plausible explanation of these peculiarities is that data by
single years of age have been regrouped for publication into unconventional intervals: Under 1, 1 to 5, 6 to 10, and so on. Since the data
generally have been interpreted as referring to standard groupings (under 1, 1 to 4, 5 to 9, etc.), we go to some length to justify our interpretation in an appendix to the present chapter. The change in age intervals introduces a complicated distortion into every distribution of
characteristics by age and necessitates special care in using the 1940
Mozambique data for comparison with the other Portuguese African
censuses. The following description of the data will be restricted to the

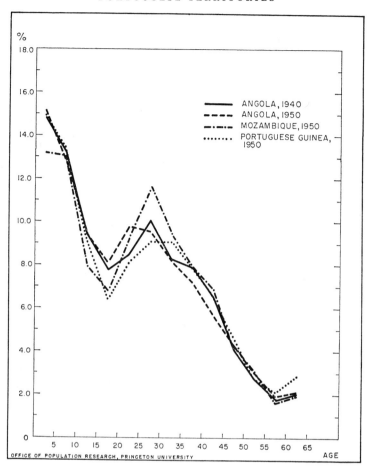

8.2. Reported female age distributions by five-year age groups: Angola, 1940 and 1950; Mozambique, 1950; and Portuguese Guinea, 1950.

1940 and 1950 Angola censuses and to the 1950 Mozambique and Guinea censuses.

Another apparent difficulty arises in Portuguese Guinea in that no infants—persons aged under 1—are reported. The numbers given as age 1 do not seem adequate to represent both infants and 1-year-olds. Whether this unconventional system is the result of procedures of enumeration or of editing cannot be determined. Therefore, what has been done is to accept the age distribution on the assumption that those reported in ages 1, 2, 3, and 4 make up the group conventionally reported as 0-4 (thus leaving unsolved the question of how they were apportioned into the single-year categories).

The age distributions of Portuguese censuses exhibit several note-worthy characteristics which must be considered in analyzing them. Especially notable among these is an apparent underenumeration in the 0-1 and the 0-4 years categories. A consistent shortage also occurs in the 15-19 age group, and less often at 20-24. There is an extremely rapid fall-off in the first four (or five) age groups followed by increases, which in turn give way to a sloping off through the mature years. In most cases there is a slight bulge in the 60-64 age group.

The consistency of this pattern in three widely separated territories and in successive censuses indicates that it is highly unlikely that it is to any great extent due to anything other than errors in age recording. The pattern is, of course, not unlike that reported for other African territories.

At a later stage of this discussion it will be necessary to take up some of the implications of this pattern of errors for the estimation of vital rates. For the present, a clear implication is that intercensal calculation of the survivorship of particular cohorts is impossible. There is simply an insufficient likelihood that at the end of a decade an individual respondent will report himself as ten years older than he did at the previous census.

It is noteworthy that in general the male age distributions do not show as great a bulge in the early adult years. Indeed in some of the regions (Southern and Central Mozambique) there is no such bulge at all. In every case except Portuguese Guinea and Benguela district in Angola in 1950 the proportion of males under age 5 was greater than that of females. In general, the males show a younger and less obviously distorted age distribution.

However, this somewhat less erratic appearance ought not lead to any real confidence that individual male ages are more accurately recorded than female ages. The actual age distributions of males and females differ because of selective migration and the effects of sex differentials in mortality; the reported distributions also differ because of errors of age reporting and differential omission by age. Since there is no adequate basis for determining how these various factors operate, it is not possible to account precisely for the fluctuations appearing in the distributions of the age-specific sex ratios shown in Figure 8.3 for Portuguese territories.

For persons in the age groups 50 and older in Mozambique quite distinctive patterns appear in the sex ratios. They fail to show the tendency to stabilize or rise which is found in Angola and Portuguese Guinea. It is possible that either excess male mortality or permanent male emigration is reflected in these figures.

A final characteristic of the sex ratios which calls for comment is the uniformly low values reported for children less than 5 years of age. In this instance it is difficult to see how migration could be a factor. Therefore, either male children's ages are reported as older than they actually are or female children's ages are reported as younger or there is a relative underestimation of male children. There was underenumeration of

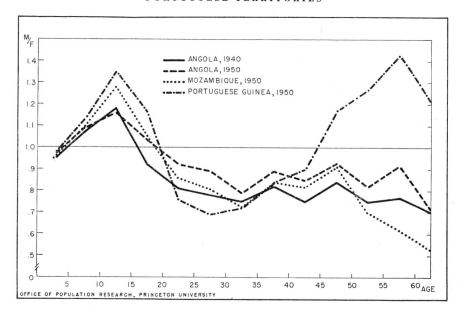

8.3. Age-specific sex ratios (males per female) by five-year
age groups: Angola, 1940 and 1950; Mozambique, 1950;
and Portuguese Guinea, 1950.

children of both sexes, and perhaps more males were omitted than females.

Reported Fertility

In this section the available direct evidence on fertility will be examined
for internal coherence and plausibility. As noted in Table 8.2, no reports of current fertility are available; retrospective reports alone can
be employed. In Table 2.12 (in Chapter 2) and Figure 8.4 the reports
of children ever born per woman by age are shown for each territory and
its sub-regions.[4] Table 8.3 shows the ratios converted to age-specific
fertility rates by means of the Brass multipliers.[5] Multiplied by the number of females in the relevant age groups, the resulting age-specific
fertility rates yield number of births and—in relation to the total population—birth rates of the order of 28 per thousand in Portuguese Guinea,
36 in Angola, and 34 in Mozambique. These figures constitute obvious
underestimates. For example, Guinea next to the Portuguese enclave
has an estimated rate of 45.[6]

---

[4] The 1950 Mozambique figures on children ever born include stillbirths. But
the effect of this inclusion is minimized by the general tendency to underreport
dead children; reported children ever born and surviving in this census are clearly
deficient in spite of inflation from stillbirths.
[5] W. Brass, "The graduation of fertility distributions by polynomial functions,"
Population Studies, Vol. 14, No. 2, p. 154.
[6] See Chapter 7.

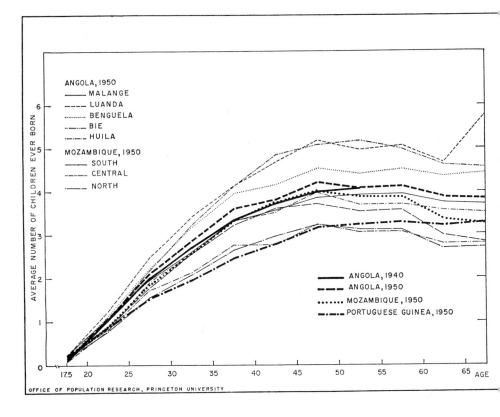

8.4. Average parity by age of woman: Angola, 1940 and
1950; Mozambique, 1950; Portuguese Guinea, 1950; and
subdivisions of Angola and Mozambique, 1950.

There is also internal evidence pointing toward underreporting of
children ever born. There is a common pattern of declining parity for
the years beyond the end of childbearing in all but two regions of the two
larger territories. Women aged 45 to 49 years (or less frequently 50 to
54) report the maximum number of children ever born; this maximum
is followed by an irregular decline as the age of the women increases.
It is most unlikely that this apparent decline reflects actual time trends
in fertility in all three Portuguese territories. The reported proportion of
childless women increases steadily with age. Among women aged 40
and over, it was 13 percent in Angola and 15 percent in Mozambique in
1940; among women aged 50 and over in 1950, it became 16 and 18
percent. Women who were once mothers cannot become childless ten
years later.

The fall-off of parity in the post-childbearing years probably reflects
an increased forgetting of children as mothers become older. The sex
ratio of children ever born increases steadily with age of mother ac-

Table 8.3. Age-specific fertility rates implied by reported parities*—Portuguese censuses in Africa

Ages of women	Angola 1940	Angola 1950	Country and year Mozambique 1950	Port. Guinea 1950
15-19	.102	.108	.093	.098
20-24	.204	.212	.180	.149
25-29	.179	.191	.177	.109
30-34	.124	.136	.148	.085
35-39	.097	.100	.116	.090
40-44	.075	.070	.072	.077
45-49	.022	.019	.017	.022
Total fertility	4.016	4.181	4.015	3.152

* Note: Age specific fertility rates were computed by using Brass multipliers. They reflect understatement of children ever born reports and should not be taken at their face value.

cording to the reporting, so that females appear to be more readily forgotten than males.[7] There is no reason to assume that the omissions are restricted to older mothers. The number of children ever born is probably seriously underreported at ages 45 to 49, although the highest parities are usually reached by women of these ages. Since the age distributions appear to be deficient in young children, it is possible that they were omitted from retrospective counts of births as well.

It might perhaps be ventured by way of conjecture that underestimation of children is particularly important because of procedures followed in the Portuguese censuses. When persons had not turned up to be enumerated at the required time, headmen, neighbors, or acquaintances would supply information. In such cases, recent births and children dead in infancy would be more exposed to omission. Children of older women who left home (in particular girls in areas where exogamy prevails) might similarly be left out.

Despite a general underestimation of parity, the pattern of variation of fertility by age among the territories and regions is consistent (see Figure 8.4). At least until the age classes over 50 are reached, the same regions show consistently low or high fertility at all ages. In consequence, the pattern of differential fertility is more or less the same when fertility is measured by the average parity achieved at various ages. Since the average parity of women 45 to 49 would very nearly equal total fertility, this measure of reported fertility is used in the remainder of this chapter. There is a wide range of variation in this index among the Portuguese territories.

[7] See Figures 2.12 (Chapter 2).

Mozambique and Angola are rather similar in their reported levels of fertility, while Portuguese Guinea is lower. Within the two larger territories considerable variation can be found. Within Mozambique, for example, fertility in the central region is 57 percent greater than in the northern. In Angola in 1950 the difference from lowest to highest fertility was 60 percent. Both the absolute and the relative levels of fertility indicated by children ever born at 45-49 will be scrutinized more critically below in conjunction with fertility estimated from the age distribution.

Reported Mortality

Table 8.2 shows that the data on reported mortality are even more restricted than on fertility. Again the reports are retrospective, and in Angola no data on mortality were published in 1950. However, survivorship values can be estimated for at least one date for each territory.

Table 2.21 (Chapter 2) shows the basic data on mortality: at each age of mother, the proportion of children ever born who have died. Table 8.4 shows (for Angola, Mozambique, and Guinea) these proportions converted by means of Brass's multiplying factors into estimates of survivorship from birth to various exact ages.[8] Note that in the conversion, l_1 is based on the reports of women aged 15-19, l_2 on the reports of women 20-24, and so forth. A striking characteristic of both of these tables is the sizeable difference in the general level of mortality between Angola (in 1940) and the other two territories (in 1950). For example, in Table 2.21 it may be seen that the proportions of those reported as

Table 8.4. Values of l_x implied in reported proportions of children surviving by age of women*—Portuguese censuses in Africa

Age x	Angola 1940	l_x Mozambique 1950	Port. Guinea 1950
1	.628	.737	.755
2	.652	.729	.739
3	.642	.734	.713
5	.627	.729	.728
10	.609	.719	.726
15	.580	.712	.690
20	.556	.680	.680
25	–	.638	–
30	–	.616	–
35	–	.599	–

* Note: l_x's (proportions surviving at exact age x) were computed by using Brass' multipliers. They reflect understatement of children surviving and should not be taken at face value.

[8] See Chapter 3.

born but not surviving in Angola are equal to or higher than those at any comparable age in any of the other territories or their component regions. Indeed, the same can be said of all of the regions of Angola with the exception of Huila and some of the younger age groups of Bie.

It is further notable that despite differences in the time period to which the values in Tables 2.21 and 8.4 refer and the geographic separation of the territories, fairly similar patterns in the progression of values by age can be seen.

A useful method of showing the possible magnitudes of distortion in the patterns of mortality values is to consider the observed values in the light of the pattern found in a variety of model life tables. For $q(a)$, which in life table terminology is $_aq_o$, where a is age, the question is asked: what value of $q(5)$ is implied by each of the four regional life tables in the Coale-Demeny[9] system if the reported value of $q(1)$ is taken as accurate? This deduced value of $q(5)$ can then be compared with the value actually observed. Estimates of $q(5)$ can also be made from $q(15)$ and $q(20)$ for all of the regional life tables and from $q(2)$ and $q(3)$ from the North table using relations within the North family in the age range 1-5. These estimates make possible comparisons of the level of mortality based on the reported mortality values over a quite extended span of ages. The results of this procedure are shown in Table 8.5 and in Figure 8.5. The progression of estimates of $q(5)$ derived from reported proportions of dead children falls as the age of the women reporting increases to age 30-34, and sometimes beyond. Such a sequence *could* indicate either a unique age pattern of mortality or rising mortality in the years before the census, but a much more probable explanation is that women omit a higher proportion of the children who have died than of those who have survived and that this form of faulty reporting increases with age of mother. This explanation implies that there is a downward bias in the estimates of child mortality and that the most reliable estimates can be derived from the reports of young mothers. The most acceptable estimate appears to be that of $q(2)$ based on the reported proportion of dead children among those ever born to women 20-24. The $q(1)$ estimate would be preferred were it not for the fact that estimates based on the youngest mothers (15-19) are inherently less reliable because of sensitivity to the precise shape of the fertility schedule. The proportion dead among the children ever born to women 20-24 will be used as an index of reported mortality in the further analysis.

The $q(2)$ values indicate a high level of mortality. They may in certain cases even exaggerate the mortality because the Brass conversion factors are selected on the basis of the shape of the fertility curve (as

9 Ansley J. Coale and Paul Demeny, *Regional Model Life Tables and Stable Populations*, Princeton University Press, 1966. See also Chapter 3, pp. 124 ff.

Table 8.5. Estimates of $q(5)$ implied by values of $q(a)$ derived from proportions of children surviving, in the four families of life tables, for $a = 1$, 15, and 20, and in the North model for $a = 2$ and 3—Portuguese censuses in Africa

		q(5) implied by reported q(a)		
a	Model	Angola 1940	Mozambique 1950	Port. Guinea 1950
1	North	.598	.441	.414
	East	.504	.367	.344
	South	.674	.485	.451
	West	.539	.398	.373
2	North	.472	.367	.353
3	North	.420	.312	.336
15	North	.345	.231	.250
	East	.378	.249	.273
	South	.371	.254	.273
	West	.368	.247	.268
20	North	.344	.241	.241
	East	.382	.266	.266
	South	.373	.267	.267
	West	.364	.256	.256
Reported value of q(5)		.373	.271	.272

reflected by the ratio of the two first age groups' parities). As the Portuguese parities have a slow start at age 15-19, the conversion factors are unduly high and compensate for an eventual underestimation of the dead children.

Analysis

The description of Portuguese censuses in the preceding section has revealed the following characteristics of the data:

(1) *Age distribution.* Except for the 1940 census of Mozambique, aberrant in its pattern of age classification, the Portuguese censuses of African territories all show rather consistent features in the midst of obvious bias. Distortion in the reporting of ages and omissions result in much uncertainty as to the actual range of ages covered by nominal age classes. For instance, the age class 0 to 14 years appears to be the combined result of underreporting of infants, misreporting of ages around puberty, and other biases.

(2) *Fertility.* There are distortions in the shape and uncertainties concerning the level of the fertility curve derived from retrospective reports on children ever born. Specifically, the latter certainly underestimate actual fertility. There is nevertheless a rather smooth gradation of fertility at successive age groups.

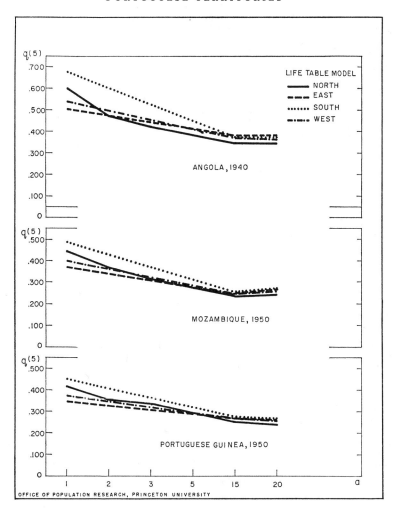

8.5. Values of $q(5)$ derived from reported proportions of children surviving to age a (where a is 1, 2, 3, 15, and 20): Angola, 1940; Mozambique, 1950; and Portuguese Guinea, 1950.

(3) *Mortality*. The progression of the survivorship ratios is regular, but too slow. Two levels of mortality are indicated by the data, a high level by the survivors to women aged 15 to 19 years—from which values of $q(1)$ are derived—and a low level by the survivors to women aged 30 to 34 years—from which values of $q(5)$ are derived. The underreporting of dead children is obvious.

(4) *Growth*. Since the methods and the quality of the 1940 and 1950 censuses appear to have been similar, intercensal growth rates for Angola and Mozambique are not implausible.

(5) *Migration*. The importance of migration cannot be precisely measured, but it appears to have been important at least among males in Mozambique. It is therefore desirable to restrict analysis of age distribution and intercensal growth to the female population.

It is within these limitations of the data that the analysis must proceed. It is clear from the summary description given above that errors are of such magnitude, and that the exact combination of various biases is to such an extent unknown, that there is *a priori* no hope of deriving completely accurate estimates of vital rates. It must however be pointed out that there exist empirical correlations between rather independent sets of information which show in spite of the biases that underlying differentials in vital rates are reflected in the data.

Two kinds of comparisons are of interest:

(1) Comparison of the same index calculated in two different censuses. Since we are concentrating here on differentials rather than on absolute levels, Mozambique in 1940 can be included in the comparison despite the non-comparability of its age classification.

(2) Comparison between different indices within the same census. Some variables *a priori* are expected to exhibit a higher degree of intercorrelation than others. For example, the age distribution must show the influence of fertility more than of any other force.

Table 8.6 shows various recorded values used in comparisons of variables for Portuguese areas at two different dates wherever possible:

(1) An index of age distribution, the proportion of females aged 0 to 14 years. Other indices of the age distribution were tested, and the proportion 0 to 14 appeared to give the most consistent results, perhaps because age 15 corresponds approximately to the point where women attain sexual and social maturity.[10] The proportion at age 15 in Mozambique (1940) has been assumed to be the same as in Portuguese Guinea, for which a detailed age distribution exists, and this proportion has been subtracted from the original census proportions aged 0 to 15 years.

(2) An index of reported fertility, the number of children born per woman aged between 45 and 49 years.

(3) An index of mortality, the proportion of dead children among those born to women aged 20 to 24 years.

(4) And finally, the annual intercensal growth rate of the female population. Border changes were taken into account. One other adjustment was made in the case of Luanda Province. The capital city, Luanda, was eliminated in order to compute the intercensal growth rate. The female population of the city had multiplied by 2.5 between 1940 and

[10] Reported age 15 may actually correspond to another true age, but the proportion of the females under that age will nevertheless give a reliable index of the age distribution.

Table 8.6. Selected reported indices: proportions of females aged 0 to 14, average parity of women aged 45 to 49, proportion dead of children ever born to women aged 20 to 24, and average annual intercensal increase of the female population— Portuguese censuses, 1940 and 1950

Region	Proportion females 0 to 14		Parity of women 45 to 49 (Children per woman)		Proportion dead of children ever born to women 20 to 24		Female annual increase
	Per cent				Per cent		Per cent
	1940	1950	1940	1950	1940	1950	1940-50
Angola	37.4	37.4	3.99	4.22	.312	-	.7
Luanda	39.4	39.7	4.83	5.18	.380	-	.8
Malange	36.1	35.3	3.68	3.87	.315	-	.3
Benguela	39.7	39.8	4.68	4.55	.309	-	.7
Bie	32.3	32.5	2.92	3.25	.265	-	-.2
Huila	38.2	37.2	3.62	3.98	.191	-	1.1
Mozambique	38.3*	37.2	3.59**	4.01	.221	.262	1.1
South	36.5*	34.1	2.99**	3.72	.164	.244	1.3
Central	42.3*	41.1	4.87**	5.08	.249	.312	1.4
North	35.4*	35.3	2.99**	3.24	.223	.210	.7
Port. Guinea	-	34.2	-	3.16	-	.273	-

Notes: * The population 0 to 15 in the 1940 census of Mozambique was diminished by a proportion equal to that of age 15 in the census of Portuguese Guinea.

** To women aged 46 to 50.

1950, no doubt in part as a result of migrations from outside the province.[11] No other city in the Portuguese territories underwent a similar growth in its female population.

Figure 8.6 (a and b) relates some of these indices two-by-two in the form of scatter diagrams, using the data from the subdivisions of the Portuguese territories. When age distribution and fertility indices are related (Figure 8.6a), they conform to expectations and demonstrate a generally linear relationship between the two variables. The other variables in combination fail to show as clear a pattern. There are two sets of mortality indices in Mozambique only, and at their face value there was a decline in the survivorship ratios between 1940 and 1950—which is somewhat unexpected and probably fallacious. The intercensal growth fails to show a consistent relationship with indices of either mortality or fertility. This was expected, since growth is the resultant of the combination of the two variables and also of migration. Growth shows a

[11] The elimination of Luanda city is not entirely satisfactory, since some of its growth was probably resulting from migration from inside the province; but this was probably compensated for the province by inmigration from other areas of Angola. The elimination of the capital reduces the growth rate of the province from 14 to 8 per thousand.

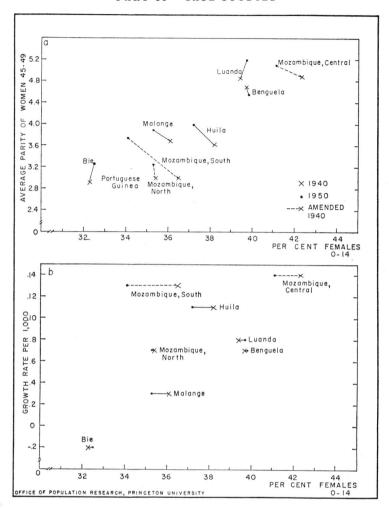

8.6. *a*: Scattergram of average parity of women aged 45-49
and percent females aged 0-14. *b*: Scattergram of average
annual intercensal increase of female population and percent
females aged 0-14.

somewhat more linear pattern when related to age distribution (Figure
8.6b). There exists a notable similarity of all indices at two different
dates.

In the absence of indications to the contrary, we may assume that
mortality and fertility have been stable in the past, and we may attempt
to derive intrinsic rates from the available information by using the
concept of the stable population. We shall proceed by successive hypotheses in order to derive estimates of the birth and death rate as compatible
as possible with the recorded data.

[456]

We now proceed to construct a set of final estimates of birth and death rates in the Portuguese territories and to make two kinds of tests of consistency of these estimates. The final estimates of birth and death rates are derived by stable population analysis from the age distributions and the intercensal rates of increase; the principal test of consistency is to confront the estimated birth rates with the average parity reported by women 45-49, and the estimated death rates with the proportion dead among children ever born to women 20-24. In addition, the estimates are compared with vital rates estimated for adjacent provinces analyzed in other chapters of this book.

In applying stable population analysis it is necessary to make an assumption about the age pattern of mortality. We shall conform to the choice made by the authors of other chapters in this book, who have shown a slight preference for the North series of model life tables developed at the Office of Population Research.

The birth rates estimated from the intercensal female growth rates in Angola and Mozambique, and from the female age distributions cumulated respectively to ages 1, 5, 10, 15, . . . , 35 are shown in Figure 8.7.

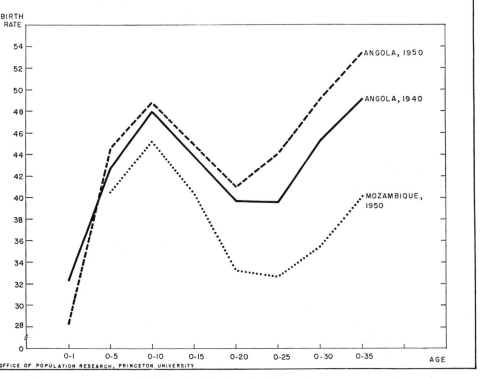

8.7. Birth rates implied by the cumulated female age distribution and the average intercensal growth rate, North model: Angola, 1940 and 1950, and Mozambique, 1950.

The pattern of varying estimates is a familiar one, in the light of experience with other African data and also data from censuses of other illiterate populations. It reflects net undercounts under age 1 and under 5, and undercounts at 10-14 and 15-19. The most plausible estimate of the birth rate is bounded by the high value at age 10 and the low value at age 20. We have somewhat arbitrarily accepted the birth rates derived from the proportion under 15 in preparing estimates for the various subdivisions. The resultant estimates of birth (and death) rates are shown in Table 8.7.

Table 8.7. Vital rates estimated by using the proportion females aged 0 to 14 and the intercensal rate of increase with the North model—Portuguese censuses, 1940 and 1950

Region	Birth rate per thousand		Death rate per thousand		Growth rate per thousand
	1940	1950	1940	1950	1940–50
Angola	45	45	38	38	7
Luanda	50	51	42	43	8
Malange	45	43	42	40	3
Benguela	·53	53	46	46	7
Bie	39	39	41	41	-2
Huila	43	40	32	29	11
Mozambique	44	40	33	29	11
South	37	31	24	18	13
Central	54	50	40	36	14
North	39	39	32	32	7

In Figure 8.8, the estimates based on intercensal growth plus the proportion under 15 are compared with the direct reports of fertility and mortality for each of the subdivisions. The closeness of the relationship is gratifying and lends credibility to the pattern of differentials (if not to the levels of mortality and fertility) among the eight Portuguese regions listed in Table 8.7. The similarity in birth rates between Luanda (50-51 per thousand) and neighboring Leopoldville Province in the Congo (49 per thousand) on the one hand, and between Malange (43-45 per thousand) and neighboring Kasai (45 per thousand), on the other hand, is reassuring.

Birth rates estimated in this way are more reliable than death rates, since they are relatively less sensitive to irregularities in the intercensal growth rate—those in particular that resulted from migration. For instance, the death rate estimated for Mozambique South (18 per thousand in 1950) probably reflects to a large extent population movements. This prompted us to attempt an alternative estimate of the death rate based on estimates of l_5 consistent (in the North model) with l_2 esti-

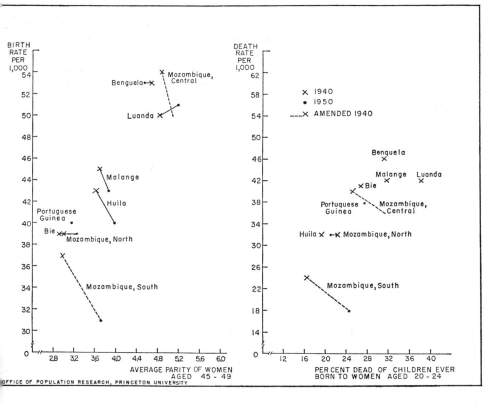

8.8. Relation of vital rates (estimated from the proportion
of females aged 0-14 and the growth rate) to reported indices
of fertility and mortality, by areas, Portuguese territories.

mated from the surviving children of women aged 20 to 24 years. The
procedure used to get these values has been explained previously in connection with Table 8.5 and Figure 8.5. The level of mortality implied
by these l_5 values and the proportion of the female population under
age 15 corresponds, in the frame of the North model, to a set of death
rates and, implicitly, to a set of growth rates (see Table 8.8). These
death rates are compared with the death rates derived from birth estimates minus intercensal growth rates (see Table 8.8) in Figure 8.9;
in the same figure the new set of growth estimates are related to the
intercensal growth rates. There is, once again, a clear relationship between the two sets of estimates.

Table 8.9 presents final estimates of various vital indices for the
Portuguese territories. Birth and death rates are the average of the 1940
and 1950 rates given in Table 8.7, with two exceptions. The first exception is South Mozambique, where population growth appears to have
been influenced by migration. The second exception is Portuguese

Table 8.8. Death rates and rates of natural increase estimated using the proportion females aged 0 to 14 and estimates of l_5 implied by $q(2)$ values derived from the proportion of children surviving to women aged 20 to 24—Portuguese territories of Africa

Region	l_5	Crude death rate per 1,000	Rate of natural increase per 1000
Angola 1940	.528	44	4
Luanda	.423	58	1
Malange	.517	45	2
Benguela	.485	50	5
Bie	.588	36	0
Huila	.662	29	12
Mozambique 1950	.633	32	10
South	.653	30	6
Central	.560	41	11
North	.737	23	12
Portuguese Guinea	.647	31	6

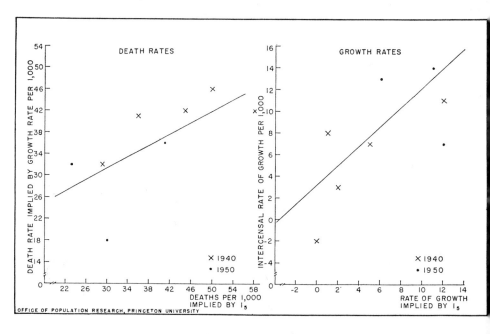

OFFICE OF POPULATION RESEARCH, PRINCETON UNIVERSITY

8.9.a. Comparison between death rates obtained from inter-censal growth and proportion of females aged 0-14 and death rates obtained from l_5 and proportion of females 0-14: Angola, 1940 and 1950, and Mozambique, 1940 and 1950.

8.9.b. Comparison between intercensal growth and growth implied by l_5 and proportion of females aged 0-14: Angola, 1940 and 1950, and Mozambique, 1940 and 1950.

Table 8.9. Final estimates of vital indices—Portuguese territories of Africa

Region	Crude birth rate	Crude death rate	$\overset{o}{e}_o$
Angola	45	38	27
Luanda	50	42	24
Malange	44	41	25
Benguela	53	46	23
Bie.	39	41	25
Huila	42	31	33
Mozambique	42	31	32
South	(36)	(30)	(32)
Central	52	38	28
North	39	32	31
Portuguese' Guinea	(37)	(31)	(32)

Guinea, where there was only one census. The estimates in these two instances are based on the age distribution and the mortality indicated by l_5; they are given in parentheses. The mortality thus implied for Portuguese Guinea is markedly below that of neighboring French Guinea, several years later (death rate of 38 per thousand). If, as we believe, this estimate for Portuguese Guinea understates the true mortality, the true birth rate may also be closer to the French Guinea estimate (46 per thousand). On the other hand, the second estimate for South Mozambique seems an improvement on the first. Table 8.9 also includes estimates of the expectation of life at birth consistent with the other measurements in the North model.

As the discussion in this chapter indicates, even the figures not qualified by parentheses are subject to much uncertainty. We would expect the estimated birth rates to lie no closer than within about 10 percent of the true figures, and the death rate estimates to be still more uncertain.

APPENDIX TO CHAPTER 8

THE TABULATION OF AGE IN THE
1940 CENSUS OF MOZAMBIQUE

The distribution of the population in age intervals and the age pattern of various population characteristics in Mozambique appear to be markedly different in 1940 and 1950. The changes recorded for the intercensal decade are not of a sort that could plausibly occur in the circumstances, in Mozambique, and the possibility of different patterns of error or bias in the two censuses is a natural alternative explanation.

The form in which the age data were reported in the volumes of the 1940 census at first suggested that the explanation might be quite simple. The age classes used in 1940 were:

> Ate 1 ano.
> De mais de 1 ate 5 anos.
> De mais de 5 ate 10 anos.

This would normally be translated as "up to 1 year (that is, up to the first birthday), from more than 1 up to 5 years (ages 1, 2, 3, and 4)," and so on. In other words, different phrasing for the more conventional 0-4, 5-9, . . . system. However, in 1950 in Mozambique, and in Angola in both 1940 and 1950, precisely this more conventional notation was used. The difference in terminology thus suggested that the categories used in Mozambique in 1940 were to be taken as: "Up *through* 1 (i.e., comprising ages 0 and 1), from more than 1 through 5 (ages 2, 3, 4, and 5)," and so on.

This explanation finds no support in the text accompanying the 1940 census figures, and the United Nations Yearbooks, in reproducing the census data, have not interpreted the age grouping in this way. Nevertheless, calculations and comparison presented in the remainder of this appendix establish beyond doubt that the simple explanation given in the preceding paragraph is the correct one. The principal calculation is a comparison between the age distribution of each sex in Mozambique in 1940 with the age distribution of Portuguese Guinea in 1950 (where single-year figures are available), when the Guinea population is grouped into age intervals of 0-5, 6-10, 11-15, etc., supplemented by a comparison between the 1950 Mozambique distribution and the Portuguese Guinea data grouped into intervals of 0-4, 5-9, 10-14, etc. In addition to this calculation, comparisons are made between reported marital status, average number of children ever born, and proportions of women having borne no children as functions of age in the 1940 and 1950 Mozambique censuses. It is seen that most of the apparent differences in age pattern of these characteristics in 1940 and 1950 are the combined result of (a) tabulations by age intervals of 0-5, 6-10, 11-15, etc. in 1940, and of 0-4, 5-9, 10-14, etc. in 1950 and (b) age heaping, with special preference for ages ending in 0 and 5.

Comparison of Mozambique Age Distributions with Approximately Grouped Single-Year Data from Portuguese Guinea

The tendency for age distributions in pre-industrial and pre-literate populations to remain approximately constant is well known. If it is assumed that the proportion at each age in Mozambique was *exactly* the same in 1940 and 1950, and if the 1940 census listed proportions at 0-5, 6-10, 11-15, etc., while the 1950 census listed proportions at 0-4, 5-9, etc., it is possible to estimate the proportions recorded at ages 0-4, 5, 6-9, 10, 11-14, 15, etc., in the two censuses. By cumulation of the data recorded in 1940, the proportions from 0 through ages 5, 10, 15, . . . etc. are obtained, and by cumulation of 1950 census data, the proportions through ages 4, 9, 14, etc. are obtained. By subtraction, the proportions at ages 5, 10, 15, etc. are estimated, on the assumption (to repeat) that the proportionate age distributions in 1940 and 1950 were identical. By another simple calculation, the proportions at 6-9, 11-14, 16-19, etc. can be estimated. In Figure 8.A.1 estimates derived in this way from the Mozambique censuses are compared with age distributions for the same age intervals obtained from the single-year data of Portuguese Guinea in 1950. The patterns of age heaping in the estimates obtained by differencing the two Mozambique censuses resembles the data recorded in Portuguese Guinea in a remarkable number of details—especially, of course, the indicated "heaping" on ages ending in 0 or 5, with greater male heaping than female in childhood, and greater female than male heaping among adults. A close scrutiny of Figure 8.A.1 leaves no room for doubt that the 1940 and 1950 age distributions in Mozambique were very similar, and that the 1940 tabulation was in intervals of 0 and 1, 2-5, 6-10, 11-15, etc.

Reported Marital Status, Children Ever Born, and Proportions Childless, by Age, in the 1940 and 1950 Censuses of Mozambique

The data in the 1940 Mozambique census, pertaining as they do to age intervals of 6-10, 11-15, 16-20, etc., might be expected to lag data pertaining to intervals of 5-9, 10-14, 15-19, etc. by about a year. However, as Figure 8.A.1 shows, a large proportion of the population is reported in ages divisible by 5, so that a large fraction of persons reported as

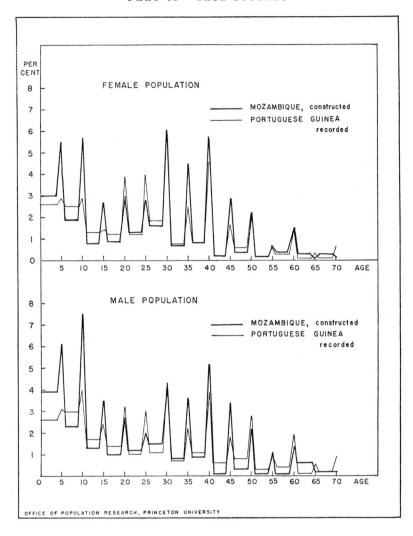

8.A.1. Proportion per single year of age, intervals alternating
one and four years in width, estimated for Mozambique,
.recorded for Portuguese Guinea.

20-24 are those reported as 20, and a large fraction of persons reported
as 21-25 are those reported as 25. When allowance is made for the effect
of age heaping, a lag of two years or more would be no surprise. In
Figure 8.A.2, characteristics that change more or less monotonically
with age are plotted. The data from 1940 are shown as if the tabulations
were for age intervals 5-9, 10-14, etc. Note in each instance that when

the characteristic is rapidly changing with age the line representing 1940 is displaced by as much as 2 to 2 1/2 years. In other words, the apparent differences in age pattern of nuptiality and fertility between 1940 and 1950 in Mozambique are mostly the result of the difference in tabulated age intervals.

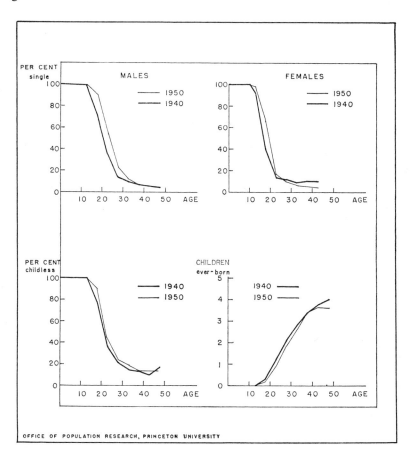

OFFICE OF POPULATION RESEARCH, PRINCETON UNIVERSITY

8.A.2. Top: Proportions single by five-year age intervals: Mozambique, 1940 and 1950. Bottom: Proportion of women childless (left) and average number of children ever born (right) by five-year age intervals of female population: Mozambique, 1940 and 1950.

9

The Demography of the Sudan:
An Analysis of the 1955/56 Census

BY PAUL DEMENY

The aim of this chapter is a description of the main demographic features—in particular fertility, mortality, and age distribution—of the population of the Republic of Sudan as reflected in the national census of 1955/56. Attention is limited to this body of data for the simple reason that up to today it constitutes virtually the only source of quantitative information on the Sudanese population. Numerical estimates relating to the period prior to 1956 were limited to the total population, usually broken down by major political subdivision. There is no reason to suppose these reliable, and no statistical checks can be performed to establish their accuracy to any reasonable approximation. Consistency among a sequence of estimates, such as suggested by a plausible time trend, may be due to the influence that any estimate, once advanced by an author or agency, tends to exert upon later estimators. At best such a time trend may serve as a basis for a cautious, qualitative statement. Thus it was argued[1] that the historical records show a high rate of growth. But it seems impossible to quantify such a statement save between very broad limits. A comparison of the total population figure as estimated by the 1955/56 census (10.263 million) with the latest previous official estimate relating to a time three and a half years earlier that set the population at 8.766 million[2] shows that there must be a substantial difference in the coverage of the two figures. Change in coverage and genuine population change in the Sudanese historical series are inseparably bound together. Another classic source of demographic information—continuous registration of births and deaths—is yet to be developed in Sudan.

The uniqueness of the 1955/56 census as a source of information is a major limitation in describing the demographic situation of that country.

---

[1] Karol J. Krotki, "The use of the quasi-stable population theory with census-collected vital events," *International Population Conference, New York 1961*, London, 1963, pp. 411-419. A more elaborate discussion of this topic, and the other topics treated in this title, can be found in Krotki's "Estimating vital rates from peculiar and inadequate age distributions (Sudanese experience)," unpublished doctoral dissertation, Princeton University, 1959.

[2] United Nations, *Demographic Yearbook 1954*, New York, 1954, p. 100.

First of all, any such description should contain many elements that are dynamic in character and that can be depicted with reference to periods instead of points of time, as is the case with births and deaths. There are great inherent difficulties in obtaining data of this sort from a census, even with respect to the period immediately preceding the census. Secondly, the applicability of standard analytical procedures to evaluate the quality of census information is severely limited. No comparison with information originating from another census, or any other independent source, is available. The only "outside" checks that can be performed consist in confronting patterns of data observed in the census with typical patterns established in other populations. Such comparisons, however, are bound to be inconclusive, in particular when the variability of "typical" patterns is large and there exists little or no basis for selecting some particular patterns as more applicable than others. Yet it will be necessary to use such comparisons extensively. Because of the paucity of demographic information collected by the Sudanese census, the powerful checks of internal consistency can also be applied only within very narrow limits. Under these circumstances our analysis will inevitably tend to assume the form of an exercise in conditional statements. The reader should keep constantly in mind, and often question, the premises upon which the conclusions are built. Throughout this chapter an effort will be made to indicate the ways these conclusions would have to be changed upon modification of the underlying assumptions.

Before turning to an examination of the data of the 1955/56 census the reader's attention should be called to two salient features in which that operation differed from a "census" as traditionally defined.[3] First, the enumeration was stretched out over a period of 14 months, and, second, it was carried out on a sample basis. Both features can be justified by the census takers' objective to use optimally the limited resources that were available for the operation. Concerning the first feature it is to be noted that in any given census area, of which there were 94 in the country, the enumeration took some two to six weeks, the first areas being enumerated in June 1955. Exact reference dates between two census areas thus may differ by as much as roughly one year. To minimize the obvious possibility of omission and/or double counting implicit in such a procedure a *de jure* population concept was adopted. As to the design of the sample, no description can, or need, be given in the present discussion. Suffice it to say that a carefully designed multistage sampling procedure was employed, with households as the smallest units, embracing about 10 percent of the total population.[4] Due to

[3] Our reference to this survey as a census is in conformity with the official Sudanese publications.

[4] Sampling was confined to the rural population. Persons living in areas of urban character—roughly an additional one-tenth of the total population—as well as some population of an institutional nature were enumerated fully.

sampling variability, figures relating to small subdivisions of the population should be treated with extra caution.

Since in this chapter our interest is directed entirely to the structure and dynamics of the population, the possible difficulty these features introduce in the interpretation of absolute population figures taken in isolation is irrelevant. Conceivably, however, various subdivisions of the population might have been unequally affected by errors, thus affecting the structure of the population and any measures that might be derived from that structure. No *a priori* statement is possible about the errors, if any, due to these sources. The possibility of their presence, however, should be kept in mind.

Many other features specific to the various phases and circumstances of the 1955/56 census could have possibly resulted in distortions.[5] But since the author had no part in the design and execution of the census, and does not even have firsthand knowledge of the Sudan, he cannot interpret, correct, or defend any peculiarities found in the results of the Sudanese census except by the analysis of the numerical results themselves. We shall now turn to this task.

The Data

Data by Provinces

The population categories of primary demographic interest provided by the Sudanese census are the following:

Sex.

Age (four classes for males: under age 1, 1-4, 5 to age of puberty, and past age of puberty; five classes for females: under 1, 1-4, 5 to puberty, past puberty but in the childbearing age, and past the childbearing age).

Number of children ever borne by females past the childbearing age (13 classes: parities increasing by a single child up to 10 children).

Marital status of males and females past puberty (2 classes: single and ever married; females past childbearing age do not constitute a separate category here).

Number of wives of married males (11 classes).

In addition, three questions were asked concerning vital events that took place during the 12 months that preceded the time of the census, namely the number of (live) births, the total number of deaths, and the number of infant deaths. This information is usually available by such subdivisions as territorial, tribal, urban-rural, and socio-economic. The

[5] For a description of the organizational background the reader is referred to the official publications of the Republic of Sudan, H.Q. Council of Ministers, Department of Statistics, in particular *Methods Report*, Vols. 1 and 2, and also the introductions of the final reports.

basic territorial subdivision is by nine provinces and, further, by the 94 census areas already mentioned. Table 9.1 presents—with the exception of data on age and marital status—the demographic information listed above, for the provinces and for the country as a whole. The parity distribution for women past childbearing age is summarized by its mean, labeled as completed family size.[6]

Unquestionably the most striking feature in Table 9.1 is the extremely high birth rates registered in Bahr el Ghazal and Upper Nile provinces and, to a lesser extent, in Equatoria. The associated rates of natural in-

Table 9.1. Population, sex ratios (males per 100 females), vital rates,[1] and completed family size, by provinces—the Sudan

Province	Population (males and females) 1,000	Males per 100 females	Birth rate	Death rate	Rate of natural increase	Infant death rate	Completed family size
Bahr el Ghazal	991	103.9	84.6	27.3	57.3	111.8	5.3
Blue Nile	2,070	106.1	45.7	14.7	31.0	72.2	4.9
Darfur	1,329	90.8	41.8	13.0	28.8	75.0	4.7
Equatoria	904	96.2	54.1	27.0	27.1	132.9	4.0
Kassala	941	114.8	42.6	17.5	25.1	82.0	4.4
Khartoum	505	117.5	40.7	14.9	25.8	71.4	4.5
Kordofan	1,762	101.5	50.0	15.5	34.5	76.0	4.4
Northern	873	93.7	43.0	12.1	30.9	66.7	5.1
Upper Nile	889	104.8	69.3	32.6	36.7	143.9	5.5
Sudan	10,263	102.2	51.7	18.5	33.2	93.6	4.7

1
Vital rates are expressed throughout this chapter in the usual manner: per 1,000 population, or, in case of the infant death rate, per 1,000 births. A small deviation from the conventional calculation is that end-year, instead of mid-year, population is used in the denominator. Due to this factor alone the rates as reported by the census publications and reproduced here are slightly overestimated. Accepting the reported data at face value the birth rate for the Sudan should be taken as approximately 51.7 (1 + $\frac{r}{2}$), r being the rate of increase per year per unit population. This would give a "correct" birth rate of 52.6. A similar correction for Bahr el Ghazal would increase the birth rate from 84.6 to 87.0, etc.

[6] Unless otherwise indicated all numerical data in this paper refer to statistics taken from the 1955/56 census of the Sudan and are quoted from *Final Report*, Vol. 1 of the census. Such data are presented here only to the minimum extent that is deemed necessary to render the paper readable without recourse to the basic source. One reason absolute figures are provided is to indicate the order of magnitude of the sample from which any statistics (e.g., percentage of females under 5 in a given province) have been derived. Absolute numbers have been rounded to the nearest thousand. Rates have been calculated from the unrounded figures. Figures that are results of some transformation of the data or are the author's estimates will be clearly so indicated throughout the paper, either explicitly or by context.

crease in the first two provinces are also unusual, despite the high death rates that were registered in these areas. Another observation one cannot fail to make is the apparent existence of great differences among provinces with respect to both fertility and mortality. Reference to Figure 9.1, which shows the provincial subdivision of Sudan, in conjunction with the table reveals this difference as a contrast between southern and northern provinces. This differential, of course, is just another as-

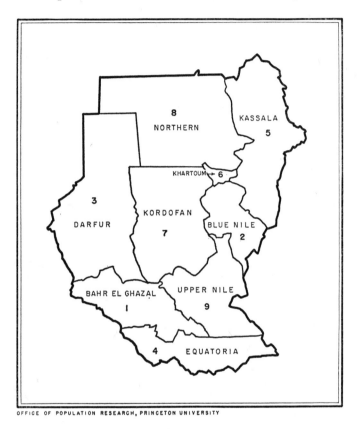

9.1. The provinces of the Republic of the Sudan.

pect of the first feature mentioned above: in the northern provinces the level of birth rates is more in conformity with what one tends to consider "normal," or "typical" for countries of Africa, thus offering a sharp contrast with the provinces of very high registered birth rates. Are those rates and differences apparent or real? To answer this question satisfactorily is the main challenge in any analysis of the 1955/56 census. To some the answer may seem to be only too obvious, since no birth rates of such magnitude are on the record anywhere for a population of substantial size. Yet it would be philistine to reject recorded data merely by arguing, perhaps in one disguise or in another, that they are obviously inconsistent with one's preconceptions. To go further, it would be pointless to gather demographic information in a census if one were prepared to accept only what were believed to be the correct answers to begin with. The difficulty of the analyst who tries to approach these figures with full respect, however, is that there is only scanty basis to prove or disprove any given statement implicit in the data. Paradoxically, this difficulty results in a certain simplicity as well; the number of analytical possibilities are limited, hence fairly obvious. Consider the data in Table 9.1. Two checks of consistency can be readily envisaged: one between the birth rate and the completed family size, and another between the rate of infant mortality and the crude death rate. A third check might try to establish the consistency of the recorded sex ratios with what we know about the variation in sex ratios at birth and male-female mortality differentials. Directly or indirectly each of these comparisons requires some knowledge of, or some explicit assumption concerning, the distribution of the population by age. This is so because, for example, birth rates and death rates measure average frequencies of events whose occurrence is strongly age-specific. Similarly the sex ratio of the population is affected by the age structure, since the sexes tend to have unequal chances of surviving to given ages. Also, a comparison between the birth rate—a measure of "current" fertility—and the completed family size—a measure of "past" performance—can serve as a check only if we know something about past trends of fertility. If such information is lacking, as in the case of the Sudan, the "current" age distribution may be sufficient to indicate whether such a comparison may be based, e.g., on the assumption of past constancy of fertility, since the shape of that distribution is fundamentally determined by past fertility.

Unfortunately, as was indicated above, the scope of the information on the Sudanese age distribution is severely limited. The customary definition of age—in terms of completed year-length intervals lived—is applied only to delineate those under age 1 and age 5. The benchmarks given for the population of age 5 and over—puberty and, for females, menopause—supply new data only at the price of posing difficult new problems of interpretation. Furthermore, it is clear that given the number of births and infant deaths the number of those under age 1 is determined within narrow limits, or, in other words, given any two of the following three pieces of data—birth rate, infant mortality rate, and the proportion of persons under age 1—availability of the third provides little new information, although it does shed some light on the reliability of reporting. Accordingly, the proportion of those age 0 in the various provinces shows essentially the same south-north differentials as the birth rates, somewhat modified by different infant mortality rates. On the other hand, the proportions under 5 and, insofar as age at puberty and menopause can be expected to vary within reasonably narrow limits, the proportions under puberty (and menopause) should provide evidence independent of the data presented in Table 9.1, not only concerning the age distribution itself (hence facilitating the checks listed above), but also concerning the fertility and, to a lesser extent, the mortality of the population. Thus we might examine, for example, the consistency of these pieces of evidence on the age distribution with each other, with the reported birth rate, or with the reported number of children ever born to women past the age of menopause, and so on.

Instead of working our way repetitiously through the various checks and comparisons outlined above, a simpler approach will in fact be followed. We shall try to fit the various pieces of evidence available into a comprehensive population model expressing the interrelationships of fertility, mortality, and age distribution under specified conditions. The model that naturally suggests itself is that of the stable population, incorporating the assumption of continued past constancy of fertility and mortality and of continued absence of migration. The selection of this model is justified by two lines of argument. One is simply the lack of direct evidence that would disprove its assumptions or that would replace these assumptions with more reasonable ones. Since the assumptions of the stable model are the simplest, resulting in relative computational simplicity and ease of interpretation, it is obviously preferable to possible alternatives. Secondly, some crucial aspects of the model, in particular the constancy of fertility, are tentatively supported partly by the analogy with populations that are in a phase of demographic development presumably comparable to that of the Sudan, and partly by a deductive argument. The latter is based on the impression provided by the recorded birth rates and by the general shape of the recorded age distribution, both of which tend to suggest that Sudanese fertility in general is "high," or "extremely high." Such levels *a fortiori* leave little or no scope for a hypothetical past decline. Since there is no reason to assume that fertility has been increasing in Sudan, constant past fertility remains the most acceptable hypothesis.

A similarly impressionistic look at the Sudanese mortality data indicates that if recorded mortality is accepted at face value there is considerable scope for assuming past improvements in mortality. Should a sudden substantial improvement have taken place in the period immediately preceding the census, the applicability of the stable model would be subject to strong qualifications. There is no evidence, however, that such a sudden change in mortality conditions did in fact occur: on the contrary, the strong probability of rather high rates of population growth for several decades preceding the census suggests that any improvement in mortality conditions during this period must have been gradual and relatively slow. Under such so-called quasi-stable conditions the stable age distribution determined by current mortality and the level of fertility is a very close approximation to the actual one.

We are on less firm ground concerning the absence of migration ideally required by stable population analysis. The 1955/56 census gives some indirect information on the extent of migration in the Sudan through its statistics on the place of birth. For the country as a whole discrepancies between province of residence and province of birth are relatively minor: some 6 percent of the total population was born at a place other than the place of residence at the time of the census. This proportion, however, is not uniform; it is small in some provinces, particularly in the south, but is quite substantial in such northern provinces as Blue Nile, Kassala, and Khartoum. In the latter province some 19 percent of females and 27 percent of males were born outside the province. A province of substantial outmigration, on the other hand, is Northern: some 12 percent of those born in this province and living in the Sudan now reside in another province. The potential disturbing effect of migration might be magnified by the age distribution of migrants, which is likely to be deviant from the average, although no breakdown of place of birth statistics by age has been published that could establish this point.

Data by Tribal Groups

Fortunately, the Sudanese statistics provide tabulations according to a criterion that, unlike residence, presumably remains unchanged through life, thus—apart from minor qualifications due to international migration and intermarriage—isolating populations that are closed by definition. This criterion is tribal affiliation or origin. Over 500 identified Sudanese tribes were classified for census purposes into some 50 tribal groups that in turn form eight main groups called "peoples." The workability of this criterion in the Sudan is supported by the fact that while only declared tribal allegiances were recorded, over 99 percent of the enumerated native population did in fact declare such an allegiance. Since persons classified as foreigners represent only some 2.5 percent of the total, the classification by people substantially covers the whole population of the Sudan. It was decided therefore to use the tribal classification to define the main demographic subdivisions to be used in our analysis.

This decision is supported by another consideration, only partly related to the applicability of stable techniques. An examination of the data by census districts reveals that to accept as units of analysis the areas delineated by the political boundaries of the provinces would in many cases represent an unfortunate choice. The heterogeneity of the population with respect to various demographic characteristics is apparently considerable even within the same provinces, a circumstance that, if real, would make the interpretation of the average values largely meaningless or, if unreal, would render the discovery of irregularities in the data exceedingly difficult. Instances of such apparent heterogeneity are found in the province of Equatoria which suggest very sharp contrasts between eastern and western areas; there is a cluster of adjacent census districts of distinctly different character from the rest of the districts in Kordofan Province; and a noticeable apparent fertility difference exists in western Bahr el Ghazal as contrasted with the eastern parts of that province. Conversely, provincial boundaries in some instances separate adjacent census districts of seemingly closely similar demographic characteristics. These difficulties might be lessened were the analysis to be carried out separately for census districts. This choice is prohibited in the present case by limitations of space; it would, in any case, present difficulties of another kind due to the large sampling errors in the statistics on the district level. A regrouping of the census districts into larger units but different from the provinces might be feasible, but there exists no obvious demographic criterion for such a regrouping and no obvious way to interpret the meaning of newly formed clusters of census districts. The case for rejecting the territorial classification in favor of the tribal one is thus strengthened: the tribal grouping does provide a criterion for a meaningful breakdown of the population. On the one hand, whether differences in the demographic makeup of the various Sudanese peoples do or do not exist is an important question *per se*. On the other hand, it is reasonable to assume that if any differentials do exist within the total population such differentials are at least partly related to tribal characteristics.

Table 9.2 shows the same statistics for the eight "peoples" of the Sudan that were given in Table 9.1 for the Sudanese provinces. Table 9.3 gives the data on age distribution by sex for the same tribal subdivisions. Those who declared no tribal affiliation (less than 1 percent of the population) and the foreigners living in Sudan (some 2.5 percent) are not shown separately but are included in the total. The listing of the peoples is in the same order as in the official Sudanese publications. The first four groups are of arabic, berberic, or arabicized, "northern" character. Far the largest among these is the Arab people; 39 percent of the population was classified as belonging to that people. The three smaller groups, the Nuba, Beja, and Nubiyin peoples together represent some 15 percent of the population. The last four groups are negroid peoples. Among them the Westerners are of non-indigenous origin and have distinctly different physical and cultural characteristics. About 13 percent of the population belongs to this group. Another 30 percent is classified as southerners, subdivided into three main groups. The largest among these are the Central Southerners, composed of tribes that racially are mainly Nilotic. The Eastern Southern tribes are Nilo-Hamitic; the Western Southerners are Sudanic people.

Table 9.2. Population, sex ratios, vital rates, and completed family size, by major
tribal subdivisions ("peoples")—the Sudan

People	Population (males and females) 1000	Males per 100 females	Birth rate	Death rate	Rate of natural increase	Infant death rate	Completed family size
Arab	3990	104.5	44.7	14.7	30.0	72.8	4.8
Nuba	573	98.2	60.0	17.2	42.8	79.5	4.3
Beja	646	110.8	39.1	14.9	24.2	62.8	4.6
Nubiyin	330	94.9	40.6	11.3	29.3	67.2	4.9
Central Southerners	1983	104.6	74.6	28.4	46.2	123.7	5.4
Eastern Southerners	549	97.6	69.3	25.3	44.0	135.5	5.5
Western Southerners	482	93.9	36.6	28.5	8.1	113.7	3.2
Westerners	1359	94.3	43.8	13.9	29.9	74.9	4.6
Sudan[1]	10263	102.2	51.7	18.5	33.2	93.6	4.7

[1]
Including 259 thousand foreigners and 94 thousand Sudanese not
classified by people.

While one of the attractions of the tribal classification, as was explained above, is precisely the fact that it eliminates the arbitrariness of
geographical subdivisions by bringing together all persons who share
an important common characteristic (tribal affiliation) regardless of
where they reside, it is of considerable interest to show the general geographical pattern of the new classification. This is possible since the
various Sudanese peoples are concentrated in areas that can be delineated
reasonably well by classifying the census districts according to the people that is predominant (largest in an absolute sense) in any given district. In fact, with relatively few exceptions, the census districts show
a high degree of tribal homogeneity. The areas thus obtained are pictured
in Figure 9.2. The Arab people are shown to occupy a large part of
the country, surrounded, as it were, by the various smaller tribal groups.[7]
A joint comparison of both figures and Tables 9.1 and 9.2 reveals some
interesting modifications of the general picture suggested by the vital
rates reported on the provincial basis. Among the northern provinces,

[7] Here, as in case of Figure 9.1, the reader should be aware of the fact that the
areas shown are in no way proportionate to the populations they represent.

Table 9.3. Distribution of the population according to age, by major tribal subdivisions (peoples) males and females, per 100 population of each sex*—the Sudan

People	Males					Females					
	0	1-4	5-P	P+	Total	0	1-4	5-P	P-M	M+	Total
Arab	4.04	14.80	28.28	52.87	100.00	4.40	16.20	22.77	43.96	12.67	100.00
Nuba	6.03	13.98	24.49	55.50	100.00	5.31	13.49	17.94	48.34	14.91	100.00
Beja	3.76	13.58	27.39	55.27	100.00	3.85	15.56	20.53	48.45	11.61	100.00
Nubiyin	3.94	14.87	30.84	50.35	100.00	3.67	15.38	22.61	44.09	14.24	100.00
Central Southerners	6.83	15.99	20.86	56.31	100.00	6.66	16.30	18.46	43.70	14.87	100.00
Eastern Southerners	6.19	17.68	25.02	51.11	100.00	6.44	18.52	20.41	41.45	13.18	100.00
Western Southerners	3.55	11.10	19.11	66.23	100.00	3.42	10.38	14.23	43.38	28.59	100.00
Westerners	4.24	14.38	26.00	55.39	100.00	4.09	14.21	21.33	45.50	14.87	100.00
Sudan	4.79	14.74	25.50	54.97	100.00	4.82	15.47	20.67	44.60	14.44	100.00

* Abbreviations used in the heading of the table: P = puberty, M = menopause.

9.2. Districts of the Republic of the Sudan grouped by major
peoples forming the predominant majority in each area.

Kordofan has the highest reported birth and growth rates: 50 and 34.5
per thousand respectively. It appears now that these rates are the
weighted averages of the rates for Arab and Nuba peoples, which apparently have rather different demographic characteristics: a reported
birth rate of 44.7 vs. 60.0; a growth rate of 30 vs. 42.8. The contrast
between north and south appears also in a somewhat different light.
Among the three southern provinces even the lowest reported birth rate
(that for Equatoria, 54.1) was higher than the birth rate reported for
any of the northern provinces. The tribal classification does suggest similar spectacular differences between north and south. At the same time it
delineates a group that consists of some half a million people, the Western Southerners, occupying a large area in the south and apparently
having the lowest birth rate in the whole country: 36.6. Their growth rate
is reported as 8.1, while none of the provincial growth rates is below
25.1. These examples seem to confirm that an analysis of the data by
tribal rather than territorial classification definitely promises to yield

more meaningful results. We shall therefore concentrate on such an analysis. This is the subject of the following section. An inconvenience of the tribal classification is that some of the groups are very large, as shown in Table 9.2. The possibility of finding smaller homogeneous groups within these larger populations, as well as the possibility of obtaining estimates on a territorial (provincial) basis, will be examined at a later point.

A Critique of the Data

Problems of Analysis

As was indicated above, we shall assume that the Sudanese population, and its various sub-groups, are approximately stable populations. The general strategy of the stable analysis consists in selecting pieces of data that are known to be reliable ones, constructing a stable population as determined by these data, and accepting the various parameters of that stable population model as estimates of the parameters of the actual population. Alternatively, when there is no *a priori* basis for putting more reliance on some pieces of data than on others, one might proceed with a series of *tâtonnements*, somewhat in the fashion a jigsaw puzzle is solved. As stable populations determined by various sets of data are constructed, some patterns of consistency will usually emerge, proving some kind of data "stronger" than others, thus indicating a certain type of stable population model as the best approximation of the actual population. The various estimates are then obtained from that model in the way just outlined. In practice the process of estimation is likely to be a mixture of these two approaches. General familiarity of the reader with the technical procedures applied in such analyses will be assumed throughout this paper. Only unusual choices or, more correctly, compromises in applying those techniques which are dictated by the peculiar nature of the Sudanese data will be discussed in some detail.

By definition the computation of a stable population requires the knowledge of a life table plus a rate of growth (or some characteristics that jointly with the life table imply that rate of growth, e.g., the birth rate, a table of fertility, or some index of the age distribution). However the availability of a reliable life table for a population presupposes the existence of statistics of a high quality. Stable estimating techniques are seldom used in such a situation. They are needed when only fragmentary mortality information is available. Such information is then used typically to select either a particular model life table or at least a family of model life tables showing a pattern of mortality with which the information concerning the given population is consistent. No obvious basis for any such procedure exists however in the Sudan, since, as was indicated above, the only mortality data available are the number of deaths—infants and others separately—that reportedly occurred in the

12 months that preceded the census. If we try to fit the various Sudanese data within a system of stable populations the results will differ according to the family of model life tables that underlies that particular system. Since the variability of the age pattern of human mortality is limited, such differences are normally contained within relatively narrow bounds, not affecting orders of magnitude. It is nevertheless mandatory to make the effects of alternative assumptions concerning the pattern of mortality on the various estimates explicit whenever there is no *a priori* basis for choosing a particular pattern, as is the case for the Sudan. We shall accomplish this by preparing in most instances two sets of stable estimates that differ only with respect to the assumption concerning the family of underlying model life tables.

The general principle of the procedure we shall employ is best illustrated by a simple example, illustrated diagrammatically in Figure 9.3.

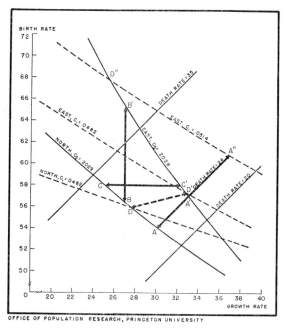

9.3. Stable estimation illustrated: combinations of birth and death rates associated with given proportions under age 1 and age 5, East and North stable populations and associated constructions.

Suppose we want to estimate the birth rate and the rate of increase in a female stable population that has a mortality pattern described by the North family of regional model life tables.[8] Suppose, furthermore, that in this population the proportion of persons under age 5 is 20.29 percent

[8] A. J. Coale and P. Demeny, *Regional Model Life Tables and Stable Populations*, Princeton University Press, 1966. See also Chapter 3, pp. 124 ff.

($c_5 = .2029$), the same as reported for the female population of the Sudan. There exists an infinitely large number of stable populations and hence pairs of birth rates and growth rates (and implied death rates) that satisfy these conditions: in Figure 9.3 the line marked "North, $c_5 = .2029$" shows a wide range of such pairs. Obviously the solution of our problem remains indeterminate until some additional information is supplied. Assume for example that we know that the death rate d in this population is 24 per thousand. We can draw a line showing the points where d is 24 (in this diagram it will be a line with a slope of 45 degrees), which provides the intersection point A, corresponding to the unique stable population satisfying the specified conditions (namely "$c_5 = .2029$" "$d = 24$" and "the mortality pattern is that of model North"). We can now read off the implied birth rate b: it is 54.1, while the growth rate r is 30.1. Assume now as a second example that the mortality pattern and c_5 are the same as before but instead of knowing the value of d, we know that r equals 27. The intersection point is now B. As a third example assume finally that instead of knowing d or r we know that b equals 58. This defines point C. The values for the unspecified vital rates at B and C are easily read off from the diagram.

Let us now modify our hypothesis concerning the pattern of mortality in our population, assuming that the model life table that correctly describes the actual pattern belongs to the East family. The same proportion under 5 as before now defines the line marked "East, $c_5 = .2029$," and the same assumptions specified above as to the value of the second independent measurement result in points A', B', and C' respectively. Inspection of the diagram reveals that the uncertainty introduced in our estimates due to the lack of information on the pattern of mortality is substantial, even assuming perfect stability and no error in the observations that serve as a basis of the estimates. Given, for example, the observations $c_5 = .2029$ and $r = 27$, the birth rate and the death rate are estimated as 56.4 and 29.4 (point B) or 65.3 and 38.3 (point B'), depending on whether the life table underlying the stable population is assumed to belong to the North or to the East family of model life tables. The reader should be able to read off the appropriate figures for the other two examples as well. The spread of the values of the estimates is indicated by the arrows, on Figure 9.3, connecting A to A', B to B', and C to C'. The numerical results depend of course on the particular values that were specified for the parameters and are merely indicative of orders of magnitude. Naturally insofar as the true pattern of mortality in the population in question is "within" the range indicated by models North and East, the actual errors introduced as a result of assuming either of these patterns as correct will be smaller than the spread of the values shown in Figure 9.3 would suggest. In fact, we have selected these two models after an examination of two additional patterns: those described by the regional model life table families West and South. Given the same proportion under 5, the lines corresponding to these models are between the lines for models North and East; the same is true for a line constructed on the basis of the United Nations model life tables. Whether the "true" mortality pattern of the Sudan is also within this range is a moot question. The possibility that Sudanese mortality is in some sense more "northern" than North or more "eastern" than East cannot be entirely discarded *a priori*. This is the reason that we shall use in our analysis stable population models based on sets of model life table families which constitute extremes—extremes in the limited sense that given the kind of data supplied by the Sudanese census they result in higher or lower estimates of various indices of fertility than estimates derived from alternative choices of stable population models available to us.

A new set of possible pairs of estimator-parameters is obtained if instead of using the proportions under age 5 we take the alternative choice for the index of the age distribution that is at our disposal in the Sudan: the proportion under age 1.[9] The recorded figure of c_1 for the female population of the whole country is 4.82 percent: isoquants for this value corresponding to both models North and East are drawn in Figure 9.3 by dashed lines. If observed values of any of the vital rates are paired with c_1, the derived estimates will differ from the estimates obtained with c_5, excepting the case when such values correspond to points D or D' —the intersection of the isoquants for c_1 and c_5. (The divergence between the alternative sets of estimates will depend on how far the points are located from D and D'.) These latter two points are of considerable interest since they suggest that estimates of the vital rates, or for that matter any other characteristics of the derived stable population, can be obtained merely by reference to two indices of the age distribution.[10] Unfortunately this is so only in a formal sense: to derive estimates with any reasonable precision would require very exact recording of ages, a condition obviously not satisfied by the Sudanese statistics.

This point brings up the important question of the differing degree of "resistance" to errors that characterize estimates derived from various pairs of estimators. If, *ceteris paribus*, the observed values of the estimators are different from their actual values, any estimates based on these

[9] Note that we use proportions *up to* a certain age (cumulated indices of the age distribution) in preference to an age interval, such as 1 to 4, or 5 to puberty, etc. Provided that we have no evidence concerning age-specific omissions in the census count, such cumulated values are more reliable as indices of the age distribution, since they depend only on the correct location of a single point (e.g., age 5) on the age scale, instead of requiring the estimation of two such points, that is, in the example, ages 1 and 5.

[10] The arrow connecting points D and D' is drawn with a broken line; intersections between isoquants of c_1 and c_5 in stable populations associated with other model life table families would not necessarily fall on that line, although are likely to be in the neighborhood of it.

observations can also be expected to be incorrect, unless the errors happen to be compensating. There are great differences however both with respect to the likelihood that an observation contains an error of a certain magnitude *and* with respect to the sensitivity of an estimate to errors in the parameters from which it has been derived. An inspection of Figure 9.3 shows for example that—given the availability of a reading on the age distribution, such as c_5, uncertainty about the pattern of mortality, and the objective of estimating the birth rate—a rough guess as to the value of the death rate would be far preferable to a rough guess of the rate of growth. In a similar fashion, the sensitivity of estimates of vital rates derived from two observations on the age distribution— such as c_1 and c_5—to errors in the values of these parameters can be experimentally established by reference to tabulated stable populations or to suitable diagrams representing such tabulations. As a simple example, contemplate a stable population of the East type, further characterized by the parameter values $c_1 = .0482$ and $c_5 = .2029$, hence by vital rates defined by point D'. Assume now that we are able to identify correctly the pattern of mortality and that we have a precise reading of c_5 but that in recording ages a one-month misstatement is committed by underestimating ages around age 1, i.e., classifying as of that age all those under 13 months. Assume for simplicity a rectangular distribution between ages 1 to 4 (this assumption will understate the implied distortion, mortality being non-zero at that age, and the population being a growing one) this error will result in inflating c_1 by $(c_5 - c_1)/48$. The reported value will therefore be $c_1 = .0514$. The isoquant drawn to correspond to this value intersects the isoquant for the appropriate c_5 at point D'' on Figure 9.3. Comparison of this point with D' shows that a hypothetical age misstatement error of by no means exceptional magnitude resulted in extremely poor estimates of the vital rates. Note that, e.g., combining an identically misstated c_1 value with an observed death rate (defining point A'') introduces a much smaller bias in such estimates. The extraordinary "mobility" of the intersection point between c_1 and c_5 isoquants can be understood from the following argument. Given the assumption of stability and the selection of a model pattern, the variability of the proportion under 1 and under 5 (or 1 to 4) is relatively limited, even if wide variation of growth rates and levels of mortality is allowed for. Thus to rationalize a relation between c_1 and c_5 as reflected by erroneous data may require drastic assumptions concerning the controlling factors, which, by definition, must carry the burden of adjustment: the rate of growth and the level of mortality. In fact recorded c_1 and c_5 values in the Sudanese census often imply values of these factors that are manifestly beyond the realm of possibilities, such as, e.g., expectations of life less than 15 or more than 80 years. Conversely, it follows from this reasoning that trying to derive a pattern of mortality by observing the behavior of the points of intersection between c_1 and c_5 isoquants, and accepting model life tables as valid provided they result in intersections around more plausible values than is the case with alternative sets, is likely to be a futile exercise.

The range of choices available to us is now considerably narrowed. More specifically, the strategy we will have to adopt should have among others the following features: (1) Stable populations are to be calculated[11] on the basis of both c_1 and c_5 (each paired with some other parameter). Using both these parameters will fully utilize the age information that is couched in terms of age in calendar years. (2) The estimates are to be prepared separately for both sexes; using data for either sex only, or using data merged for both sexes, would sacrifice part of the already scanty information. (3) The estimates are to be prepared on two alternative assumptions as to the pattern of mortality.

The first two of the above points reflect the fact that we can advance no reason for putting more confidence on data relating to either the location of age 1 or age 5 on the chronological scale, or on data relating to either of the sexes. A preference for one or the other, just as a preference for a particular pattern of mortality, might only emerge as part of the solution of the jigsaw puzzle itself. The solution of the puzzle should take place in the framework outlined above, utilizing to the fullest whatever information remains on age distribution (i.e., puberty and menopause) and the information on mortality, fertility, and marriage. Among the alternatives that offer themselves to the analyst at this point, the most efficient procedure, both analytically and from the point of view of least labor, is to use some index of the level of mortality jointly with the parameters c_1 and c_5 to determine first-approximation stable estimates. The consistency of these with other pieces of evidence can then be examined, possibly resulting in modifications of the initial estimates.

Mortality

In order to obtain a suitable index of mortality from the Sudanese data, the reported infant mortality figures were first scrutinized. Some impressionistic judgment on these figures can be obtained by checking the consistency of the reported number of persons under age 1, the number of births said to have occurred during the 12 months preceding the census, and the number of infants reported to have died during the same period. The difference between the first two figures supplies the number of infants who both died *and* were born during the reference year. The ratio of such infant deaths to all infant deaths is predictable within not too broad limits: save for extraordinary circumstances, such as a brief

---

[11] It should be clear for the reader that the expression "calculating a stable population" used in this sense actually means the simple procedure of locating a stable population on the basis of some specified criteria within a set of pre-computed stable populations.

but violent epidemic, it should be in the neighborhood of roughly 0.7, somewhat higher or lower depending on whether mortality is low or high. The ratios calculated for the various Sudanese peoples are as follows (in percent):

Arab	77.7	Central Southerners	77.5
Nuba	69.7	Eastern Southerners	65.6
Beja	42.8	Western Southerners	42.3
Nubiyin	94.3	Westerners	65.3

The figures for the Beja and for the Western Southerners stand out as impossibly low. It is not feasible to isolate the particular mechanism that is responsible for these ratios, but some weakness in the enumeration of deaths for these groups is clearly indicated. It might be noted that the lowest reported infant mortality in the Sudan is that of the Beja, while the Western Southerners report lower infant mortality than the rest of the Southerners. Both differentials are subject to suspicion. At the other end of the scale an impossibly high ratio is reported for the Nubiyin people. It is possible that this is due to some special error in questioning, e.g., to a tendency to ask first about the persons born during the past year and then to inquire about the number among these who have died. The omitted infant deaths may then in fact be classified as having occurred over age 1. There is no indication that this was indeed the case. A more plausible explanation for such a ratio is an actual reference period shorter than one year or, more generally, omission of infant deaths that increases with the time that has elapsed since the occurrence of the death. It is not claimed that other groups were not subject to the same errors. The ratio of 0.94 however suggests that in the case of the Nubiyin such an effect might have been particularly strong. Again, it should be noted that the Nubiyin report the lowest infant mortality rate except for the Beja and, more importantly, report a general death rate that is the lowest in the country by a substantial margin. One must question the validity of this differential.

As a second step in trying to detect possible errors in the available mortality data the consistency of the reported infant mortality with the reported general mortality over age 1 was examined. It was found that the reported infant mortalities [$q(1)$] reflect a lower level of mortality than is the case with the reported death rates over age 1 (m_{1+}) insofar, one must add, that the mortality pattern of the Sudanese population can be expected to lie in the range or in the neighborhood of reliable reported experience. As a matter of formal classification of possibilities, a given relative difference in these levels is explainable by one of the following assumptions: (1) both $q(1)$ and m_{1+} were overreported but m_{1+} was more so; (2) $q(1)$ was correctly reported, m_{1+} was overreported; (3) $q(1)$ was underreported, m_{1+} was overreported; (4) $q(1)$ was underreported, m_{1+} was correctly reported; (5) both $q(1)$ and m_{1+} were underreported but $q(1)$ was more so. No internal evidence exists on the basis of which one could choose among these hypotheses; such a choice must be a matter of deductive reasoning and conjecture. It might be observed, first of all, that given the population count the value of m_{1+} is directly influenced by the length of the reference period used by respondents in reporting deaths. In contrast, no such direct influence is at work on the values of $q(1)$, since this rate is calculated by relating figures both of which are based on the same reference period. Case (1) therefore implicitly assumes a most unlikely kind of *differential* reference error and can be confidently ruled out. Case (2) can be eliminated on a somewhat weaker but still convincing basis: first, it assumes that recall of infant deaths is not worse than recall of births, general experience to the contrary; second, it assumes perfect counting of deaths over age 1 within the 12-month period *plus* a very substantial reporting of such deaths as really occurred prior to that period or, alternatively, a less than full reporting of deaths more than compensated by an appropriately lengthened actual reference period. The latter argument can be invoked against accepting case (3) as well, although it is impossible to state flatly that the reported m_{1+} may not be to some extent overreported due to reference errors. On the grounds of sheer plausibility case (5) is the most likely one. As a compromise solution we shall assume that case (4) is the correct explanation, i.e., we shall adopt as the index of mortality the reported death rate over age 1.

Our task is now to derive an index of mortality from the reported death rate over age 1 on the basis of both mortality patterns North and East, an index that is expressed in a more conventional form, is not dependent on the age distribution, and also permits the analysis to be carried out separately for the sexes. To satisfy the latter requirement death rates over age 1, for males and females separately, were calculated from the reported average figures on the basis of the sex differentials of mortality incorporated in models North and East.[12] These death rates for each sex were then used jointly with the reported proportion under age 1 (c_1) for the appropriate sex to locate a stable population in both models North and East, and the same procedure was repeated, using c_5. The expectation of life underlying the stable populations thus determined was then read off. In each model and for each sex it turns

---

[12] This is a feasible procedure since given the average m_{1+} the dependence of the male and female values on the level of fertility (growth rate) is negligible within the models. The values read off from the tables for a wide range of growth rates are seldom as far apart as 2 per 10,000 within a given sex, thus the adopted middle estimates are in error by not more than 1 per 10,000 for each sex. This is trivial, hence the validity of this derivation need not be questioned in contrast to the validity of the underlying assumption, i.e., that sex differentials in the Sudan are correctly estimated by the sex differentials found in the models.

out that these e°_0 values differ little for practical purposes—in most cases by less than one year of expectation of life at birth—and the comparison of male and female figures shows that the relation of male and female life expectations incorporated by the underlying model patterns is also reproduced to a very close approximation. This phenomenon cannot be taken to indicate a significant consistency of reported c_1 and c_5 values for the two sexes. Rather the explanation is that over a wide range of fertility indicated by the reported c_1 and c_5 figures, the values of e°_0 implied by a given death rate over age 1 is much the same (if the level of mortality is medium to light). The age distribution, in other words, does not much affect the death rate. A numerical example might usefully illustrate this contention. Assuming that the female expectation of life is 35 years and the pattern of mortality is that of North, the variation of the death rate over age 1 will be contained within an interval of 5 per 10,000 population (specifically between 19.85 and 20.35), provided that the population is stable and has a growth rate that is between 20 and 49 per thousand—an interval equivalent in terms of the birth rate to a range of 48.6 to 83.7 and, in terms of the gross reproduction rate, to a range from slightly above 3 to over 6. The proportions under age 1 and under age 5 would vary in such populations from 4.18 to over 7 per hundred, and from 17.74 to over 28 per hundred respectively. These experimental facts are a consequence of the pattern of human mortality over age 1 at higher levels of general mortality, characterized by mortalities in early childhood that are high enough to affect adversely the average mortality over age 1 if weighted sufficiently strongly, as is also the case with old age mortality. Thus both very young and very old age distributions result in higher m_{1+} values than some age distributions of an intermediate type. This minimum value in the above example is associated with a growth rate of some 32 per thousand; it is located at higher growth rates (higher fertilities) when lower general levels of mortality are selected. Obviously, with lower mortality the "premium" on a younger age distribution increases. Furthermore, in a broad neighborhood of these minima the death rate over age 1 responds very weakly to changes in the age distribution. Now, the reported m_{1+} values and the reported c_1 and c_5 values place all our populations in the neighborhood of such minima, hence, given the pattern of mortality, under the Sudanese conditions the death rate over age 1 can be translated to a single value of the expectation of life with a high degree of precision. To avoid spurious exactness, however, the estimates for the female life expectation at birth were in practice rounded to the nearest year, and the equivalent male values were then determined from the models. From the previous discussion it should be clear that, while the estimates were obtained by using c_1 and c_5 values, even a substantial revision of these latter values would have resulted in essentially the same mortality estimates. The single exception is the Western Southerner group, since its reported c_1 and c_5 values are in a range that *is* significant in selecting the appropriate life tables. Should the reported c_1 and c_5 figures for the Western Southerners (already the lowest in the Sudan) be proved to be overestimated, this would imply that for them the estimate obtained by the procedure described above underestimated the expectation of life at birth.

Table 9.4 presents the estimates of expectation of life at birth for the peoples of the Sudan, for both sexes, under the two assumptions as to the pattern of mortality. The death rates over age 1 as calculated from the census statistics are also shown. For model North, the range of estimated female $e°_0$ values is from 31 years to 58 years; for model East, the range is from 25 to 53 years. These limiting values characterize the Western Southerners and the Nubiyin people respectively. As suggested above, the latter value is to be revised downward: it might be in the range of the figures for the other northern groups. The figure for the Western Southerners, on the other hand, may be an underestimate and may actually not be different from that for the other Southerners. These modifications would still leave us with at least the north-south mortality differential clearly established. Note that it is not possible to explain away this differential by assuming a longer reference period for the Southerners. Although we have rejected the reported infant mortality figures as underestimates it is important to observe that they do help to confirm the north-south differential, since this differential is shown by the infant mortality rates too, despite the fact that they are independent of

Table 9.4. Reported death rates over age 1 for both sexes and estimated expectations of life at birth for females and males under two different assumptions as to the age and sex pattern of mortality. (Estimates of $e°_0$ are based on the reported proportions of persons under ages 1 and 5 and on the reported death rate over age 1)—major tribal subdivisions (peoples) of the Sudan

People	Reported death rate over age 1 per 1,000	Estimated expectation of life at birth in years			
		Mortality pattern "North"		Mortality pattern "East"	
		Females	Males	Females	Males
Arab	11.9	51.0	47.6	45.0	42.0
Nuba	13.2	47.0	43.7	41.0	38.1
Beja	12.9	49.0	45.7	44.0	41.0
Nubiyin	9.0	58.0	54.5	53.0	49.6
Central Southerners	20.6	35.0	32.0	28.0	25.4
Eastern Southerners	17.0	40.0	36.9	33.0	30.3
Western Southerners	25.2	31.0	28.1	25.0	22.4
Westerners	11.1	52.0	48.6	47.0	43.9
Sudan	14.4	46.0	42.7	39.0	36.2

reference period errors.[13] As to the sex differences in mortality shown in Table 9.4, it is necessary to keep in mind that these differences originate in the models, not in the data. However, if the actual sex differences in mortality in the Sudan are unlike those of the models this would in no appreciable way affect the average estimates for the two sexes; it would merely push closer, or farther apart, the figures about this average. In attempting to interpret various pieces of demographic information later in this paper we must remember that part of any explanation might be a different relation of the mortalities of the two sexes.

Table 9.5 shows the infant mortality rates implied by the life expectations given in Table 9.4 and compares these estimated rates with the reported ones. According to these figures the omission of infant deaths must have been substantial. This conclusion emerges from either assumption on the mortality pattern, although accepting the North (or a "northern-type") pattern leads to a much less startling numerical proposition as to the extent of the omission than the East (or an "eastern-type") alternative. The drastic underreporting implied by the latter pattern is particularly remarkable in view of the fact that it is derived on the assumption of 100 percent reporting of death over age 1. It would indeed be surprising if such extremely strong *differential* underreporting did in fact occur in the Sudan. Concerning the differences between the

Table 9.5. Reported infant mortality rates for both sexes and averages of estimated male and female infant mortality rates. (Estimates correspond to expectations of life at birth shown in Table 9.4)—major tribal subdivisions (peoples) of the Sudan

People	Reported infant mortality rate	Estimated infant mortality rate		Reported infant mortality rate as per cent of estimated rate	
		"North"	"East"	"North"	"East"
Arab	72.8	110	197	55	37
Nuba	79.5	130	229	61	29
Beja	62.8	120	205	52	31
Nubiyin	67.2	80	141	84	48
Central Southerners	123.7	204	358	61	35
Eastern Southerners	135.5	170	303	80	45
Western Southerners	113.7	235	396	48	29
Westerners	74.9	106	182	71	41
Sudan	93.6	135	246	69	38

[13] It might be objected that if births are erroneously reported with a reference period of longer than one year this does not necessarily imply that the period error will be the same in reporting (infant) deaths; a "longer memory" for births than for deaths is more plausible to assume. If so this would further strengthen our argument, since an extended reference period that would presumably explain away the higher reported mortality over age 1 for the Southerners would then be expected to produce *lower* infant mortalities for the same groups.

various sub-groups, the good performance of the Nubiyin and the Eastern Southerners might be noted. If $e°_0$ for the former is to be revised downward as was argued above, the latter remains the only outstanding group. It is likely that this position is more apparent than real, suggesting that if the mortality of the Eastern and Central Southerners is substantially the same, the equalization is more likely to be carried out by an upward revision of the reported death rate over age 1 for the Eastern Southerners than by a downward revision of the same statistics reported for the Central Southerners. The exceedingly high suggested underreporting for the Western Southerners, and to a lesser extent for the Beja, is to be interpreted in the light of previous comments.

Age Distribution and Implied Vital Rates

Having arrived at estimates of the level of mortality for the various Sudanese peoples we are now able to compute the vital rates that would prevail in stable populations characterized by these mortalities and by the reported proportions of persons under age 1 or under age 5. The possible modifications of the relative magnitudes of the derived life expectations that we suggested above cannot be quantified; thus, for the sake of simplicity, we shall adopt as a working hypothesis a mortality for each people that is precisely the same as shown in Table 9.4. The resulting vital rates are given in Tables 9.6 and 9.7. These rates spell out the implications of all the information on age distribution that is available in conventional chronological terms. If this information is correct, these rates can be accepted as estimates of the real intensity of demographic phenomena for the peoples of the Sudan. Our remaining task can thus be conceived as an effort to confirm, reject, or modify various features of Tables 9.6 and 9.7.

First of all, among these features the effect of the revised infant mortality figures (implicit in the mortality levels underlying the stable populations) should be noted. This effect is best gauged by comparing the reported vital rates given in Table 9.2 with the rates derived from the reported proportions under age 1 shown in Table 9.6. It now becomes clear that given the assumption of correct age reporting of infants, not only the census death rates but the census birth rates as well are downward biased. The problem is not—as was posed earlier—to explain high birth rates such as 69 and 75 (reported for the Eastern and Central Southerners) but to explain rates substantially higher than these. Thus—to pick an extreme example—the average of the male and female rates for the Central Southerners under the East hypothesis of mortality is as high as 92 per thousand. The figures of Tables 9.6 and 9.7 could be further scrutinized with respect to the differences among the various peoples, with respect to the consistency of the results derived from c_1 and c_5, with respect to the consistency of male and female rates, and

Table 9.6. Rates of birth, death, and growth in male and female stable populations characterized by the levels of mortality and by the proportions of persons under age 1 as shown in Tables 9.4 and 9.3, for the peoples of the Sudan

People	Birth rate		Death rate		Growth rate	
	Males	Females	Males	Females	Males	Females
Mortality pattern "North"						
Arab	44.7	48.1	17.3	15.4	27.4	32.7
Nuba	70.2	59.2	21.5	18.9	48.7	40.3
Beja	41.8	42.3	18.8	16.7	23.0	25.6
Nubiyin	42.5	39.2	12.9	11.5	29.6	27.7
Central Southerners	82.5	78.7	38.0	33.6	44.5	45.1
Eastern Southerners	72.6	75.0	29.8	28.0	42.8	47.0
Western Southerners	43.3	40.5	36.0	32.4	7.3	8.1
Westerners	46.8	44.5	16.6	14.7	30.2	29.8
SUDAN	54.2	53.7	21.5	19.2	32.7	34.5
Mortality pattern "East"						
Arab	48.2	51.2	23.4	20.3	25.8	30.9
Nuba	74.7	62.9	30.5	25.3	44.2	37.6
Beja	45.1	44.8	23.0	20.6	22.1	24.2
Nubiyin	44.8	40.8	16.2	14.3	28.6	26.5
Central Southerners	95.6	88.3	55.9	48.0	39.7	40.3
Eastern Southerners	81.9	81.7	42.8	38.5	39.1	43.2
Western Southerners	50.9	45.9	46.1	40.9	4.8	5.0
Westerners	49.9	47.0	20.8	18.5	29.1	28.5
SUDAN	59.6	58.1	29.6	26.4	30.0	31.7

Table 9.7. Rates of birth, death, and growth in male and female stable populations characterized by the levels of mortality and by the proportions of persons under age 5 as shown in Tables 9.4 and 9.3, for the peoples of the Sudan

People	Birth rate		Death rate		Growth rate	
	Males	Females	Males	Females	Males	Females
Mortality pattern "North"						
Arab	47.4	52.6	17.3	15.5	30.1	37.1
Nuba	52.1	47.6	20.5	18.2	31.6	29.4
Beja	43.7	48.7	18.7	16.8	25.0	31.9
Nubiyin	45.0	45.6	12.8	11.2	32.2	34.4
Central Southerners	67.0	65.1	34.6	31.0	32.4	34.1
Eastern Southerners	67.3	68.9	28.9	26.3	38.4	42.6
Western Southerners	42.6	38.3	35.9	32.2	6.7	6.1
Westerners	46.5	44.8	16.6	14.7	29.9	30.1
SUDAN	51.0	52.1	21.3	19.1	29.7	33.0
Mortality pattern "East"						
Arab	52.8	56.1	22.8	20.7	30.0	35.4
Nuba	59.1	53.0	27.5	23.9	31.6	29.1
Beja	48.6	53.0	23.3	21.3	25.3	31.7
Nubiyin	48.9	48.3	16.3	14.3	32.6	34.0
Central Southerners	83.8	77.6	51.5	44.6	32.3	33.0
Eastern Southerners	80.7	79.5	44.4	37.9	38.3	41.6
Western Southerners	54.5	46.3	47.1	41.0	7.4	5.3
Westerners	50.9	48.3	20.9	17.5	30.0	30.8
SUDAN	58.9	59.2	29.5	26.6	29.4	32.6

with respect to the differences shown according to the assumed pattern of mortality. To do this fruitfully, however, some further implications of assuming the correct reporting of c_1 and c_5 should be spelled out. In particular we must examine the levels of fertility implied in the figures of Tables 9.6 and 9.7 as compared with the reported number of children ever borne by women past the childbearing age. We must also show the consequences of accepting the reported c_1 and c_5 values on the ages of puberty and menopause, and on the age at marriage. Finally, the bearing of the recorded sex ratios on the interpretation of Tables 9.6 and 9.7 must be discussed.

Fertility

The level of fertility in the female stable populations shown in Tables 9.6 and 9.7 is given in Table 9.8 in terms of gross reproduction rates, along with the reported number of female children per woman past childbearing age, approximated simply as half of the reported completed family size. Given stability, the latter figure should be roughly identical to the gross reproduction rate; it turns out, however, that the derived rates are substantially higher. Such discrepancies indicate beyond doubt that family size was underreported. Since the extent of the underreporting is not known, these data cannot serve as a check on the validity of the derived gross reproduction rates. Underreported retrospective data are not surprising: omissions are hardly avoidable in data collected from women of an advanced age about events a large proportion of which took place in the remote past. One might assume, however, that by and large relative fertility differences, or at least the order of ranking

Table 9.8. Approximate number of female children ever born per woman past childbearing age,[1] as reported by the census, and gross reproduction rates in female stable populations characterized by the levels of mortality as shown in Table 9.3, for the peoples of the Sudan. (Calculation of the gross reproduction rate assumes that the average age of maternity in the maternity function is 27 years)

People	Children per woman past child-bearing age	Gross reproduction rates supplied by:			
		reported c_1		reported c_5	
		"North"	"East"	"North"	"East"
Arab	2.40	3.21	3.36	3.59	3.76
Nuba	2.15	4.14	4.30	3.14	3.47
Beja	2.30	2.75	2.88	3.24	3.50
Nubiyin	2.45	2.57	2.64	3.05	3.20
Central Southerners	2.70	5.91	6.35	4.50	5.29
Eastern Southerners	2.75	5.56	5.92	4.98	5.69
Western Southerners	1.60	2.57	2.85	2.43	2.87
Westerners	2.30	2.93	3.06	2.96	3.15
SUDAN	2.35	3.63	3.85	3.50	3.94

[1] Reported number of children ever born per women past childbearing age divided by two.

with respect to fertility levels shown in such data, can still be accepted as valid. If so, the pattern of gross reproduction rates derived from the proportions under age 1 is revealed as rather erratic, while the pattern obtained from the reported c_5 figures is in reasonable conformity with the retrospective reports. In both series the Eastern and Central Southerners are shown to have the highest fertility, while the Western Southerners have the lowest. The relative differentials, however, are much more pronounced in the case of the derived figures, possibly suggesting substantial differentials in the extent of underreporting. Since the implied omissions are greater for peoples with high mortality and, in the case of the Central and Eastern Southerners, for peoples of concurrent high fertility, at least part of such differentials might indeed be explainable by invoking the possibly higher propensity to forget to report children when they are dead and, perhaps, when they are numerous. Differential mortality of mothers with respect to the number of children they bore—a possible minor explanation of the low reported numbers—must have been also more instrumental in the case of the Southerners. Still, one cannot fail to note that the extraordinarily high fertilities implied by the proportions of young children in the Central and Eastern Southerner groups are not borne out by the retrospective fertility reports.

It should be noted at this point that the gross reproduction rates shown in Table 9.8 were derived on the assumption that the mean of the maternity function $\bar{m}$ characteristic of Sudanese fertility is located at 27 years. This was an arbitrary assumption, since no data on age-specific fertility for the Sudan are at our disposal. It is not likely that the actual mean is lower than the one assumed, but in view of the high general level of fertility it may well be somewhat higher. Even if so, because of early marriage it could hardly be above 29 years. In the range of values prevailing in the Sudan this would necessitate an upward adjustment of the rates shown in Table 9.8. This adjustment would be higher for higher fertility figures and, given the level of fertility, higher when mortality is low. Depending on these factors the rates calculated for $\bar{m} = 27$ would have to be increased by some 4 to 11 percent if we assume that the correct mean was 29 years.

The above discussion shows that because of the large underreporting of children the retrospective fertility data are of limited usefulness. Some reflection upon the reasons why women fail to report all the children they have had suggests, however, that these causes must be operative to a very limited extent when only a few children were born and, in particular, when forgetting would move the reporting woman to the wrong side of the fundamental "no children"–"at least one child" dichotomy. Hence the proportion of childless women should be a relatively reliable piece of information even when the reported parity distribution of women in general is unacceptable. Limited as this information is, it nevertheless may provide some additional confirmation of suspected fertility differentials. Unfortunately the parity distributions of women have not been tabulated for tribal groups: they are available on a territorial basis only. However, in view of the high degree of tribal homogeneity on the census district level, a reasonable approximation of what must be the actual distribution for the main tribal groups can be obtained by regrouping the census districts according to the predominant tribal groups, that is, in the geographical pattern shown in Figure 9.2.[14] The result of the calculations with respect to the proportion reported to have had no children among women past childbearing age in the various peoples of Sudan is as follows:

Arab	9.0	Central Southerners	2.8
Nuba	9.3	Eastern Southerners	4.8
Beja	10.9	Western Southerners	30.5
Nubiyin	6.3	Westerners	9.4

The Central and Eastern Southerners stand out with very small proportions of childless women, a circumstance that is likely to indicate high fertility. The most prominent feature of the above series is, however, the extraordinarily high proportion of childless women reported for the Western Southerners, which tends to confirm that this tribal group is characterized by an exceptionally low level of childbearing. That the figure is not an outcome of some crude error in the enumeration or in the processing of the data (such as, e.g., classifying "no answer" as "no child") is indicated by the examination of the whole parity distribution. This shows that the Western Southerners have also the highest number of women reporting one or two children (12.3 and 10.5 percent respectively), and for all higher parities they register the lowest proportions among all main tribal groups. These latter proportions are, of course, depressed by necessity due to the high rate of childlessness and the apparent high number of women having only few children. In fact, an examination of the parity progression ratios (not shown in this paper) indicates that the behavior of those Western Southerner women who have had at least four children does not show any peculiar features: the probability of having an additional child above parity 3 is as high (or higher) than for the rest of the Southerners. This circumstance is most important, because it bars the possibility of some peculiar feature of the

[14] Identifying districts by their province or by the number assigned to them in the official Sudanese census reports, the exact pattern of regrouping we have adopted is as follows. Arabs: Blue Nile except 221; Khartoum; Kordofan except Nuba districts; Northern except Nubiyin districts; 313, 342, 343, 521, 531 and 541. Nuba: 731, 732, 733, 734, 751. Beja: 511, 512, 513, 542, 551. Nubiyin: 831, 851. Central Southerners: Bahr el Ghazal except 141; Upper Nile except 951; 221. Eastern Southerners: 411, 421, 441, 451, 951. Western Southerners: 141, 431, 461, 462. Westerners: Darfur except 313, 342, 343; 522.

pattern of forgetting in the Western Southerner group that would explain differentially the high proportion of low-parity women. One must conclude that a segment of this sub-population behaves "normally" with respect to childbearing (or at least used to behave so) whereas a large portion of the women actually bear no child or bear only one, two, or three children.

Ages at Puberty and Menopause

In our quest to interpret the plausibility of the vital rates derived from the reported proportions of infants and children under age 5 shown in Tables 9.6 and 9.7, we shall now show the implications of accepting these proportions—hence an implied stable age distribution—on the ages at puberty and menopause. This is feasible because both these events are inevitable consequences of aging (unlike, say, marriage), and age at both these events can be safely assumed as having low variance. Thus the age distribution within the interval in which puberty and menopause take place is nearly linear. It follows that, given the estimated age distribution of the whole population, if we find exact ages P and M so that the proportion under these ages will be the same as the proportions reported to be under the age of puberty and menopause, P and M will be a very good approximation of the age at which these events actually occur on the average. The results of such a calculation (assuming that North is the underlying pattern of mortality) are shown in Table 9.9.

The decision of the census takers not to attempt to establish ages in chronological terms for adults was dictated by the expected futility of any such attempt given the unfamiliarity of the population with chronological ages, well confirmed by many African censuses. In contrast, the notions of puberty and menopause were assumed to be generally understandable. Indeed, even if one cannot bar the possibility of systematic errors in such a classification, given the biological correlates of the classifying criteria, any such errors can be expected to be contained within not very broad limits. For interpreting this classification in the conventional chronological terms the crucial question is, of course, just how broad these limits are. Obviously, one must admit the possibility of some real differences with respect to average ages at puberty and menopause among the different sub-populations of the Sudan, given the differences in race, living conditions, and climate. The likely diversity of cultural factors that might be thought of as determining the subjective judgment of people as to what the biological correlates of puberty and menopause are, presents an even more important reason why one should expect differences among P's and M's. It follows that one cannot hope to determine from the Sudanese census data what the meaning of puberty and menopause actually is in chronological terms with any great precision: such determination would require a knowledge the lack of which led to the registration of age in non-chronological terms in the first place. We are thus led into a vicious circle.

Despite these pessimistic conclusions, the information collected on puberty and menopause in the Sudan is still very valuable. While we cannot say whether the average age at puberty is, say, 14 or 15 years (or conversely, if we derive 14 or 15 as such an age from certain premises we cannot say that one of these results confirms the premises more than the other), it is certainly possible to reject, say, age 11 or age 17 as the average age at puberty for women as utterly implausible. Similarly, one would not accept the assertion that the age of childbearing for women ends at, say, age 36 as an average, although one would not be prepared to argue that the actual age is 41 or 47. In other words, with all their cultural indeterminacy the notions of puberty and menopause can be held to contain a sufficiently strong biological element having limited variability. This enables us to conclude that certain premises are untenable provided that these premises are wrong to such an extent that they produce results clearly at variance with even the most liberal interpretation of the concepts of puberty and menopause. An inspection of Table 9.9 suggests that this is the case with all the three

Table 9.9. Average age at puberty for males (P_m) and average age at female puberty (P_f) and menopause (M) in North stable populations characterized by levels of mortality as shown in Table 9.4, and by proportions under age 1 (c_1) or under age 5 (c_5) as reported (shown in Table 9.3) for the peoples of the Sudan. (Average ages are derived from reported proportions under the age of puberty and under the age of menopause)

| People | P_m | P_f | M | P_m | P_f | M |
	implied by reported c_1			implied by reported c_5		
Arab	16.3	13.5	44.0	15.4	12.4	41.4
Nuba	9.9	9.1	36.0	13.6	11.7	42.2
Beja	16.4	13.8	49.4	15.7	12.1	45.0
Nubíyin	17.6	14.8	46.7	16.7	12.9	42.4
Central Southerners	9.5	8.9	31.4	11.7	10.8	36.5
Eastern Southerners	12.0	10.2	33.5	13.0	11.0	35.4
Western Southerners	13.5	11.0	37.7	13.7	11.6	38.1
Westerners	14.4	12.8	43.2	14.5	12.7	43.0
SUDAN	13.4	11.7	39.5	14.1	12.0	40.3

southern tribal groups regardless of whether the proportion under age 1 or the proportion under age 5 is accepted as correctly reported, and also with the Nuba people at least in the former case. In each instance absurdly low values of both puberty—whether male or female—and menopause are implied by the vital rates shown for these groups in Tables 9.6 and 9.7.

This is a result of major importance in the interpretation of Sudanese census data. It proves that at least for certain segments of the population the ages of young children were underestimated, hence the number of persons reported under ages 1 and 5 were spuriously inflated. There is no alternative hypothesis of sufficient plausibility that would explain the extreme low values of P and M shown in Table 9.9. Different premises concerning either the level or the pattern of mortality could not carry the burden of adjustment, and the assumption of underenumeration of pre-adolescent children and women of childbearing ages simultaneously with the full enumeration of small children would be far-fetched. As to the level of mortality, the adjustment resulting in higher ages at puberty and menopause would be an upward one. But the response of P and M to higher mortality is extremely sluggish. One numerical example will suffice to indicate the "gain" in assuming higher mortalities. The age at puberty derived from c_1 for the Eastern Southerners is 10.2 years; the age at menopause is 33.5 years. If the actual life expectation at birth was 5 years less than the one assumed in obtaining these figures, i.e., if it was 35 instead of 40, the derived P and M would have been 10.5 and 34.2 years. The reason is that the age distribution is affected in this case (made older) only slightly by a different (in this case higher) mortality. Note also that further and further downward adjustment of the assumed expectation of life will exact a higher and higher "price" in terms of the implied necessity of assuming increasingly higher levels of omission in the enumeration of deaths and in the counting of children ever born.

Adopting a different assumption concerning the pattern of mortality is equally powerless in rescuing the reported c_1 and c_5 figures for the tribal groups singled out above. If Table 9.9 is recalculated according to the East pattern of mortality, the results are in no case qualitatively different: the figures derived from c_5 are virtually identical, while the figures derived from c_1 are higher by less than 0.5 years, as an average, on the basis of the East mortality pattern for the women under the age of puberty and by less than 1 year for those below the age of menopause. Our conclusion pointing to the necessity of a rather drastic re-interpretation of the reported ages 1 and 5 at least for some of the peoples of Sudan remains unaffected. In fact the results just presented permit us to simplify greatly our discussion which was based up to this point on a parallel presentation of the pattern of mortality. We can now say that variations in that pattern are not capable of providing a rationalization of the peculiarities of the Sudanese data. On the level of precision permitted by these data, one can say that the differences in pattern boil down simply to differences in the assumption concerning infant mortality. Choosing the Northern, rather than the Eastern, pattern means that we posit a less drastic omission of infant deaths, as was shown in Table 9.5, and a somewhat less drastic omission of children ever born. In this limited sense North performs better than East, and we shall adopt it for purposes of further reference. We simply have to keep in mind that infant deaths might have been less adequately reported than implied by this pattern, in which case the birth and death rates were higher than we would conclude from North stable populations. But such higher rates, it should be emphasized, would in no case constitute a better rationalization of the raw census data; on the contrary, they would imply a higher level of errors in some features of the census without helping to explain other features to any extent. Note finally that the above results decisively confirm our earlier caution against trying to fathom the pattern of mortality by comparing the proportions under ages 1 and 5. We saw that irrespective of the assumed pattern it must be concluded that these ages were at least in some cases very erroneously estimated. If so, no similarity in the relative magnitudes of c_1 and c_5 as reported in the census and found in a system of model populations can possibly serve to identify a "proper" mortality pattern: the effect of age misreporting on these relative magnitudes must far overshadow any effects that would be introduced by different patterns of mortality.

Age at Marriage

There is some possibility of using the data on nuptiality, besides the proportions under the age of puberty and menopause, to shed some light on the validity of the reported proportions under ages 1 and 5. The differentiation between the basic "ever married" and "never married" (single) states can be expected to be a relatively strong feature of the Sudanese statistics. Given the age distribution of the population (or an estimate of it) and the proportion that ultimately gets married (in practice the proportion ever married at some more advanced age) the average age at (first) marriage can be approximated in precisely the same fashion as we have calculated the ages at puberty and menopause from reported proportions under these ages. Since we have no data on the proportion ultimately married, the procedure is not applicable to the male population, where that figure may not approach 100 percent; in any case the undoubtedly large variance of the age at marriage for males would make such an application somewhat problematical. On the other hand, for the women of Sudan, although probably with the notable exception of the Western Southerners, we may assume that marriage is universal. Such an assumption does introduce an upward bias in the derived mean age at marriage, but since we are merely looking here for some further confirmation of a suspected error (underestimation of exact ages 1 and 5) the presence of that bias will mean that our reasoning will be protected by an additional margin of safety. Once again, however, census tabulations for the proportions single are not available; thus we have to apply the same approximation as was carried out above with respect to the proportions childless; i.e., we calculate proportions single in the total female population in the clusters of census districts shown in Figure 9.2. The results are as follows (in percent):

Arab	42.9	Central Southerners	49.8
Nuba	43.2	Eastern Southerners	52.4
Beja	50.7	Western Southerners	34.9
Nubiyin	46.5	Westerners	43.1

The age at marriage to be derived from these figures is admittedly rather sensitive to errors that may be introduced by the approximation through territorial data. As an indirect check on the accuracy of the approximation, the proportions single in the male population were computed by the same method as for the females and compared with the actual percentages, which for the male population *are* available. The average of the absolute deviations between the two series was found to be 0.7 percentage points. Individually the approximation was satisfactory in each case with the exception of the Westerners, where the estimated proportion single falls short of the actual one by 2.2 percentage points. The corresponding adjustment for the females increases the figure for the Westerners from 43.1 to 44.9. The mean ages at (first) marriage for females derived from the above proportions single, jointly with the reported c_1 (first column) and c_5 (second column) according to the North stable populations, are as follows (in years):

Arab	15.8	14.6	Central Southerners	11.6	14.0
Nuba	10.6	14.0	Eastern Southerners	12.7	13.6
Beja	18.9	16.7	Western Southerners	14.3	15.0
Nubiyin	17.1	14.8	Westerners	15.0	14.9

There can be little doubt that accepting the reported c_1 and c_5 figures as correct once more leads to unacceptable conclusions in case of the Nuba people and for at least the Central and Eastern Southerner groups. Note that the figures given are estimates of the mean of an unknown distribution with presumably small, but by no means negligible, variance. Very roughly speaking, asserting that the mean is 13 implies that for every marriage contracted at age 15 there is a marriage contracted at age 11. There exist no similarly low estimates of age at marriage for any African populations. Our conclusions are further strengthened if we consider the upward bias in the figures for the Sudanese peoples that was mentioned above. Notice, finally, that this bias is probably exceptionally strong in case of the Western Southerners, where the proportion ultimately remaining single might be large, as suggested by the fact that over 30 percent of the women past childbearing age were reported as never having had children. The relatively more "reasonable" figures for the Western Southerners thus provide no support for the reported proportion of children under ages 1 and 5.

Sex Ratios

The reported sex ratios for the total population in each tribal group were shown in Table 9.2. Their divergent magnitudes are open to various interpretations, none of which can be satisfactorily proved to be the correct one. However the hypothesis that the reported sex ratios reflect precisely the actual balance of the sexes within each people can certainly be rejected. Whatever differences may exist in the sex ratios at birth—and it may well be that similar to other negroid populations, masculinity of sex ratios at birth is less pronounced among the southern Sudanese than is the case elsewhere—they could be responsible for only a small fraction of the reported variation. This leaves two factors—fertility and mortality differences among the various peoples—to carry the burden of the explanation. Neither of these factors is able to do so, at least if we assume for the moment that the relative mortalities of the sexes in the regional model life tables are adequately representative of the actual situation in the Sudan. In model stable populations approximating Sudanese demographic characteristics, higher fertility means higher masculinity ratios for the total population, given the level of mortality. Similarly, given the level of fertility, higher mortality means lower masculinity ratios. Both effects are very weak, however; they could explain only variations of perhaps 2 or 3 percentage points. Furthermore the differences in sex ratios in the Sudan are not correlated with the apparent fertility and mortality differences in the country in the indicated fashion. If we admit now the possibility that the relative intensity of male and female mortalities in the Sudan may be substantially different from the ones incorporated in the various families of model life tables, we certainly come into possession of a device that is capable of "explaining" any arbitrarily specified sex ratio. A difficulty in invoking this factor as an explanation of the recorded sex ratios in Sudan is the fact that the divergences that need to be posited point in opposite directions; we have to assume a relatively much higher female mortality for the Arabs, for the Beja, and for the Central Southerners than is "typical," and a relatively higher male mortality for the rest of the tribal groups. Such an assumption seems somewhat strained but, in view of the diversity of the Sudanese peoples, cannot be categorically rejected. By the same token neither can we bar the suspicion that at least a significant part of any peculiarities of the reported sex ratios in the Sudan are to be explained by errors in the enumeration, rather than by peculiarities of the actual demographic characteristics of the population.

Since the effect of international migration on the sex ratio can safely be ignored in the Sudan, only two types of enumeration errors can be invoked to explain an unlikely sex ratio for a given people. One is a sex differential in misclassification of people by tribe. For example if non-

Arab single adult males were sometimes classified as Arabs this would increase the masculinity of the Arab population and would have an opposite effect on the population from which the misclassified persons were drawn. The second type of error capable of explaining peculiarities of sex ratio is a sex differential in omitting (or, possibly, double-counting) persons in the census. Which of these errors or what mixture of these errors caused—in conjunction with any possible "real factors," i.e., sex ratios at birth and sex differential mortalities divergent from the "normal"—the recorded peculiarities of the Sudanese sex ratios it is impossible to discern. Nevertheless the higher than expected masculinity of the total population suggests that the first type of error alone would provide an insufficient explanation. It should be observed also that sex differential misclassification could hardly affect young children, yet we find marked irregularities in the sex ratios for the youngest age groups. The recorded sex ratios by age are shown in Table 9.10. (Note that sex

Table 9.10. Reported sex ratios (number of males per 100 females) at various ages, by major tribal subdivisions (peoples) of the Sudan

Peoples	Under age 1	Under age 5	Over age 5	All ages
Arab	96.0	95.6	106.8	104.5
Nuba	111.4	104.5	96.8	98.2
Beja	108.3	99.0	113.6	110.8
Nubiyin	101.8	93.7	95.2	94.9
Central Southerners	107.2	103.9	104.8	104.6
Eastern Southerners	93.8	93.3	99.0	97.6
Western Southerners	97.5	99.8	93.0	93.9
Westerners	97.7	95.9	93.9	94.3
SUDAN	101.3	98.3	103.1	102.2

ratios over and under puberty are ignored in this discussion since they might be more affected by unknown sex and tribal differences as to the age of attainment of puberty than by any other factors.) To explain these age-specific ratios, of course, a third type of enumeration error may be invoked, namely sex differentials in the estimation of the age limits "one" and "five." The presence of such errors in the census data is indeed unmistakable. The only series of sex ratios by age that conforms to the expected pattern is that of the Westerners. Some nine-tenths of the rest of the population (i.e., excepting the Nuba and the Western Southerners) has sex ratios under age 5 that are lower than those over age 5, contrary to what stable population models would suggest. Once again the hypothesis of unusual sex differences in mortality would be powerless to account for this finding, since not only the relative but, with the exceptions just mentioned, the absolute levels of the ratios under age 5 are low too. It would be clearly inadmissible to ascribe this to a (higher) tendency to omit very young boys, as opposed to girls, particularly in the cultural milieu of the northern peoples. The only remaining explanation is then that ages of young girls tended to be (relatively) underestimated; that is, apparently with the exception of the Nuba and the Central Southerners, if the limiting age "five" was correctly estimated for boys, the corresponding actual limiting age for girls must have been over age five. With the added exception of the Beja the same bias seems to have been instrumental in shaping the sex ratios of infants; "age one" must have meant generally a higher age for girls than was the case for boys. (The change in the direction of the bias for the Beja is probably more apparent than real: an argument to be presented later suggests that their high infantile masculinity ratio reflects a relatively higher omission of girl babies, thus masking a bias of age estimation that is probably the same as in the large majority of the population.) To appreciate these findings properly, we must recall our discussion in the previous section that showed that for the three Southerner groups and for the Nuba people there was a *general* underestimation of ages of very young children. Thus the detection of sex differentials within that general error is not surprising; nor is it particularly important, relatively speaking, in its effects on the estimation of vital rates.

Among the remaining four peoples, however, the estimated vital rates for the Arabs and for the Beja differ appreciably depending on whether they are derived from data for males or for females; hence the interpretation of the reported sex ratios must be an important facet of our analysis. The series for these two peoples are similar in a number of aspects. In particular both show high masculinity ratios over age 5; this remains true even if a suitable adjustment is performed in reallocating girls from the "under age 5" to the "above age 5" category (or, less likely, reallocating boys in the opposite sense) in order to "normalize" the sex ratio under age 5. The same can be said about the derived growth rates, which are higher for females than for males, as is shown in Tables 9.6 and 9.7, although under stable conditions the growth rates for the two sexes should be identical. To narrow the differences in the derived growth rates by assuming higher female mortality—which at the same time would tend to justify the high masculinity found over age 5—would, *pari passu*, result in a further relative increase of the female birth rate in the "wrong" direction, contrary to theoretical expectation and to recorded experience of other populations. A simpler and far more plausible explanation is that the female population over age 5 among the Arabs and the Beja was undercounted. An examination of the recorded age distribution and the derived ages at puberty and menopause suggests, furthermore, that such an undercount was limited to women past the age of puberty.

Naturally it would be presumptuous to advance a quantitative estimate of the possible magnitude of the omission. We have too many degrees of freedom in making feasible assumptions and one's conclusions differ accordingly. Nevertheless, in order to suggest the extent of divergence between the reported data and the model stable population that has been used heavily in this analysis (the North family), a numerical exercise might be illuminating. Let us take the case of the Arab people, where the imbalance of the sexes is pronounced, and let us suppose, as before, that the death rate over age 1 was correctly reported, and posit 1.05 as the sex ratio at birth. Concerning the correctness of age estimation and the fullness of enumeration assume now the following: (a) ages of males were correctly estimated both at age 1 and at age 5; (b) males over age 1 were enumerated fully; (c) females between age 1 and puberty were enumerated fully; (d) the extent of omission (if any) of female infants was the same as for male infants. In other words, these assumptions mean that we squeeze the reported figures into the frame of the model age distribution by admitting the possibility of (a) omission of infants, (b) an inaccurate estimate of the female ages 1 and 5, and (c) the possibility of omission of females over puberty. The conclusions that result from these premises are the following: (a) infants were undercounted by 7.4 percent; (b) the female age "one" means actually age 1.09, and the female age "five" means actually 5.47; (c) 6.2 percent of the females over puberty were omitted from the enumeration. When the reported data are adjusted accordingly, the implied average age at puberty is 15.3 years for males and 13.3 years for females. As to the vital rates, the birth rate for the two sexes in the "adjusted" population is 47.2; the death rate is 16.4, implying a growth rate of 30.8.

It can be seen that, given the stated premises, the pattern of biases that must be posited to reconcile the reported numbers and their age distribution with those implied by the model is by no means extreme. Moreover the conclusion about the nature of the biases is, once again, highly insensitive to plausible modifications of the model itself. Accepting the Eastern pattern of mortality as relevant to the Arab people, for example, the implied biases are not qualitatively modified (in fact a somewhat higher percentage of infants and women over puberty is now to be accounted for as "omitted"). On the other hand, assuming a sex ratio at birth higher than 1.05 implies a less pronounced omission of women, but since the latitude of such a correction (which also implies even higher sex differentials in estimating the ages of young children) is very limited, the indication of the direction of the bias is not altered. Lacking alternative plausible explanations of the relative shortage of male children and the relative shortage of adult women in the Arab and Beja peoples, and taking into account the fact that in general young ages seem to have been under- rather than overestimated in the Sudanese census, we must assume that at least for the Arabs and the Beja the reported male age distribution provides a better basis for estimating vital rates than is the case with the females.

Estimates of Vital Rates

Estimates by Tribal Groups

We are now in a position to attempt a reinterpretation of the vital rates we had previously derived from the information on the age distribution that was available in conventional terms. In the light of the various pieces of evidence surveyed above we can say that the statistics concerning four peoples—the Arab, the Beja, the Nubiyin, and the Westerners—do not fundamentally contradict the validity of the vital rates shown in Tables 9.6 and 9.7. For the remaining four peoples, i.e., for the three Southern peoples and the Nuba people, we have found incontrovertible evidence pointing to a substantial overestimation of the youngest age groups. Speaking in the broadest terms concerning the first group, our finding means that since infant mortality was underestimated the actual birth rates and death rates are higher than the reported ones. In the case of the second group, an upward adjustment of the reported death rate and of the birth rate due to omission of infant deaths is also necessary, but this adjustment must be far overbalanced by a revision of the birth rate in the opposite direction required by the detected reference period error. This adjustment still preserves the position of the Central and Eastern Southerners as peoples having a substantially higher fertility than the rest of the country. However, the claim of the Nuba people to the same position, or at least to a position intermediate between their northern and southern neighbors, is revealed as invalid. The fertility of the Nuba, in fact, must be lower than the fertility of the Arab people. The lowest fertility in the country—lowest by a substantial margin—is found in the Sudanic people (Western Southerners). These findings concerning the Southerners and the Nuba also imply that their growth rates were also substantially overestimated by the official statistics.

Beyond these broad generalizations it is difficult to discern more refined features of the Sudanese demographic picture. The numerical estimates offered in the following brief commentary concerning the various peoples of the country represent the author's best judgment concerning the vital rates, the level of fertility, and the interpretation of the various indices of the age distribution.

Westerners. The statistics concerning the Westerners have emerged from our analysis as remarkably consistent with the stable population model we have applied in the present study. Apart from the corrections concerning infant mortality, and also the number of children ever born to women past childbearing age, we have no basis whatever for questioning the validity of the reported figures. Both age 1 and age 5 must have been determined with remarkable accuracy, implying an age at puberty just under age 13 for females and approximately age 14.5 for males. The suggested average age at menopause is 43 years. Assuming a pattern of mortality similar to that of model North (hence assuming some 30 percent omission of infant deaths) and an accurate count of the non-infant deaths, a birth rate of some 46 per thousand and a death rate of some 16 per thousand result, implying a rate of growth of 30 per thousand. The gross reproduction rate is estimated as being just under 3.0.

The Arab, Beja, and Nubiyin peoples. Assumptions concerning mortality identical to those given for the Westerners give a death rate of 17 and 18 for the Arab and Beja population respectively. As we have argued earlier, death registration for the Nubiyin was patently deficient; we shall arbitrarily posit their death rate as not lower than that for the Arabs, i.e., 17 per thousand. The estimates for the birth rate resulting from these mortality assumptions and from the reported age distribution differ by several permillage points, depending on whether the reported proportions under age 1 or under age 5 are selected as the index of age distribution—a lower level of fertility being suggested by the proportion under age 1 than by the proportion under 5. This inconsistency might be formally rationalized as due either to an underestimation of age 5 (given correct estimation of age 1) or to an overestimation of age 1 (given correct estimation of age 5). Neither explanation is easily reconciled with the pattern of age reporting in the Sudan. Nevertheless, should we have to choose between them, the second alternative is obviously the less objectionable, since the levels of fertility indicated by the reported proportions under 1 are definitely too low, as evidenced by the implied male ages at puberty and (if we take into account the omission of females discussed in the previous section) by the implied female age at puberty and age at menopause. A much more plausible picture emerges, however, if the relatively low reported proportions of infants are explained not by age misstatement errors but by differential omission of infants in the census count. Such omissions not only adequately explain the inconsistency between the vital rates shown in Tables 9.6 and 9.7 but also contribute to the understanding of the behavior of the sex ratios under age 1, in particular among the Beja, and to the understanding of the particularly strong proportion of unreported infant deaths among the Arabs and the Beja.

It is worth pointing out at this juncture that there is no indication for any of the remaining five peoples of Sudan that they too have been affected by differential omission of children under age 1; at any rate, if such omissions did occur, they were more than adequately masked by overestimation of age 1 relative to other ages. This is a most interesting finding, since it means that the behavior of the northern (arabic or arabicized) peoples of the country with respect to the census was similar to the classic pattern (found in most non-African countries, and also in North Africa) while the rest of the country reported children in the fashion that has been observed virtually without exception in censuses taken in various countries of tropical Africa.

The above arguments suggest that an adjustment of age 0 is necessary to estimate vital rates for the three peoples under discussion. For practical purposes a slightly upward-adjusted version of the vital rates derived from the reported proportions under 5 gives the same results. It should finally be recalled that according to our discussion of the sex ratio, adjustment of the female population is also called for; again, for practical purposes, estimates based on the male population provide a satisfactory short cut. It follows that the birth rate for the Arabs and the Nubiyin should be roughly 47, implying a rate of growth of 30 per thousand. The corresponding figures for the Beja are apparently at the somewhat lower level of 44 and 26 per thousand respectively. Ages at puberty in these populations are between 15.4 and 16.2 for males and about 13.5 to 13.9 for females. Average age at menopause—at least for the Arabs and the Beja—cannot be fixed because of the uncertainty about the age pattern of the omission of adult females; it is, however, apparently in the low to mid-40's in all three populations. The gross reproduction rate is 3.0 for the Arabs and the Nubiyin; it is probably not higher than 2.8 for the Beja.

The Nuba people and the Southerners. The statistics reported for the Nuba and the three large southern tribal groups offer what is unquestionably the *pièce de résistance* in the analysis of the 1955/56 Sudanese census. Our previous discussion has established the presence of serious age reporting errors in the data recorded for these peoples. However the more difficult task of estimating the extent of these errors, hence the extent of the needed modifications in the reported vital rates, has not yet been faced. To arrive at some conclusion concerning this matter we shall reverse our earlier procedure: instead of showing the implication of reported proportions in the early childhood ages on the average age at puberty, we shall now show the implications of some posited average ages at female puberty, in conjunction with the reported proportion up to that age, on the vital rates and on the real meaning of what the average enumerator perceived to be "age one," "age five," age at male puberty, and age at menopause. Table 9.11 illustrates the method just described within the framework of North stable populations. For each people, two columns are given, corresponding to two arbitrarily specified average ages at puberty, viz., 12.5 and 13.5 years. No special significance is claimed for these particular ages beyond the suggestion that they are in a range within which the actual age at puberty must

Table 9.11. Stable population estimates of vital rates, gross reproduction rates, and real ages at "age 1," "age 5," and average ages at puberty and at menopause for selected peoples of the Sudan corresponding to proportions reported by the census as under age 1, under age 5, and under the age of puberty and menopause, as implied by two different assumptions as to the actual average at puberty for females (P_t), assuming mortality pattern North and levels of mortality as shown in Table 9.4

	Nuba		Central Southerners		Eastern Southerners		Western Southerners	
	P_f=12.5	P_f=13.5	P_f=12.5	P_f=13.5	P_f=12.5	P_f=13.5	P_f=12.5	P_f=13.5
Birth rate, females	42.8	39.3	56.4	51.9	60.8	56.9	35.4	32.5
Birth rate, males	44.9	41.4	60.2	55.5	64.0	60.0	38.8	35.8
Death rate, females	18.1	18.1	29.6	29.0	25.1	24.6	32.2	32.3
Death rate, males	20.2	20.2	33.4	32.6	28.3	27.8	35.6	35.6
Growth rate	24.7	21.2	26.8	22.9	35.7	32.3	3.2	.2
GRR (m̄=27)	2.78	2.54	3.73	3.38	4.18	3.84	2.25	2.08
"Age one", females	1.54	1.71	1.59	1.77	1.33	1.45	1.22	1.37
"Age one", males	1.75	1.93	1.58	1.74	1.20	1.32	1.18	1.31
"Age five", females	5.62	6.14	5.91	6.46	5.78	6.21	5.47	5.99
"Age five", males	5.88	6.40	5.68	6.20	5.30	5.70	5.56	6.07
Age at puberty, males	15.47	16.68	13.05	14.03	13.56	14.35	14.82	15.91
Age at menopause	44.96	47.27	40.29	42.56	38.95	40.77	39.72	41.55

be located. Analytical manipulation cannot possibly pinpoint that age with precision. The reader is encouraged to familiarize himself with the response of the various indices listed in the table to changes in the posited age at puberty by performing rough linear interpolations, and also by extrapolating to values of P_t under 12.5 and over 13.5 years. Clearly, the particular combination of ages at puberty and menopause on the one hand, and the implied misreporting of ages 1 and 5 on the other hand that one finds least implausible is largely a matter of subjective judgment. Yet there are limits to the tolerable movement in either direction. Since the conclusion of gross underestimating of ages in early childhood cannot be avoided, one's willingness to reduce the estimated errors at age 1 and 5 at the price of assuming less than, say, 12.5 years as age at puberty, or less than 40 years as age at menopause, will be limited. The first column for each of the four peoples shows vital rates that can be considered as maxima, perhaps with the exception of the Nuba. The latitude for movement in the opposite direction is also problematical beyond a certain point: it involves the assumption of higher than plausible ages at puberty and at menopause, as well as an increasingly poor opinion of the enumerators' ability to judge children's ages. Comparisons of such factors suggest that for the Nuba and for the Central Southerners the first-column estimates ($P_t = 12.5$) must be nearer to reality; for the two other groups the second columns ($P_t = 13.5$) are likely to come closer to the mark. The birth rate for the Nuba people is then 44, providing jointly with the death rate of 19 a growth of 25 per thousand. The corresponding figures for the Central Southerners are 58, 31, and 27 per thousand.

For the remaining two tribal groups the underlying mortalities are determined by assuming that reported deaths over age 1 can be taken at face value. It was suggested earlier that the estimated mortality of the Eastern Southerners is (relatively) too low and that of the Western Southerners (relatively) too high; the latter assertion will be further corroborated presently. In the light of this, and considering the general weakness of death reporting, the mortality differences indicated thus far among the Southerners are likely to be spurious. We shall therefore assume the absence of such differences and equate the level of Southern mortality with that estimated for the Central Southerners (female $e°_0 = 35$, model North). This implies a death rate of 31 for the Eastern Southerners and 32 for the Western Southerners. The adjusted birth rates associated with a posited $P_t = 13.5$ are 60 and 34, respectively; the gross reproduction rates are 3.9 and 2.0. The approximate values of the other two groups' gross reproduction rate and the interpretation of the various age classification criteria can be read off from the appropriate columns of Table 9.11. These figures indicate that the underestimation of the age of very young children was widespread, as evidenced by the high values of the implied real average ages at "age one" and "age five." Undoubtedly the size of the apparent errors is surprising. It is fair to point out, however, that biases of this nature and of this magnitude are by no means peculiar to the Sudanese census: very similar patterns have been found in several surveys conducted in sub-Saharan Africa, as reported elsewhere in this volume. Our estimates of the vital rates in Sudan can finally be summarized in Table 9.12.

Table 9.12.

People	Birth rate	Death rate	Growth rate
Arab	47	17	30
Nuba	44	19	25
Beja	44	18	26
Nubiyin	47	17	30
Central Southerners	58	31	27
Eastern Southerners	60	31	27
Western Southerners	34	32	2
Westerners	46	16	30
SUDAN	48.7	21.3	27.4

For the country as a whole the indicated rates were calculated as the population-weighted averages of the previously cited estimates for the eight Sudanese peoples. The same procedure gives the overall estimate of the gross reproduction rate as 3.1. These values differ noticeably from what would have been arrived at on the basis of examining the national figures only. This fact points out the possible distortion inherent in such a procedure when dealing with a heterogeneous population.

The various estimates presented above were expressed as single figures; naturally they should be interpreted as representing ranges of possibilities. The width of these ranges, as should be clear from the foregoing discussion, varies from people to people and according to the object of the estimate. To give numerical estimates for them would be arbitrary. Instead, only a few qualifying remarks will be advanced below.

Among the estimates of Sudanese fertility, population growth, and mortality, the last represents the weakest element. It is possible to establish beyond any doubt the presence of a sharp differential only between the Southerners and the rest of the Sudanese people. The absolute level of mortality in these two groups, and the existence of any real differences within these groups, must remain a matter of conjecture. To preserve as faithfully as possible features of the reported data we have assumed that by and large the deaths above age 1 were fully reported and have selected a model life table pattern that minimized the extent of the implied omission of infant deaths. On these grounds the life expectation at birth for both sexes is about 32-33 years for the Southerners and about 45-50 years for the rest of the population. The crude death rates that result from these mortality levels are 30-31 for the Southerners and 16-19 for non-Southerners—higher than the recorded rates shown in Table 9.2. Experience recorded outside the Sudan suggests that these death rates may still be too low. Unfortunately, however, we are not in a position to declare that they are minimum estimates. The overestimation of the reference period revealed in the birth records might have had an effect in the registration of deaths too, resulting in a compensation of possible omissions, the extent of which it is impossible to estimate. On the basis of the Sudanese data alone mortality levels might have been lower or, conceivably, higher than our estimates indicate. The same thing is true about the conjectured magnitude of the proportion of omitted infant deaths.

In contrast to mortality, the estimates of fertility—of birth rates and of gross reproduction rates—represent the strongest features of the census data, being derived from the reported age distribution and corroborated by various pieces of evidence such as completed family size, childlessness, and nuptiality. The recorded birth rates and our estimates differ substantially, as the figures in Table 9.13 indicate.

Table 9.13.

People	Estimated birth rate	Recorded birth rate	Deviation
Arab	47	44.7	+ 2.3
Nuba	44	60.0	−16.0
Beja	44	39.1	+ 4.9
Nubiyin	47	40.6	+ 6.4
Central Southerners	58	74.6	−16.6
Eastern Southerners	60	69.3	− 9.3
Western Southerners	34	36.6	− 2.6
Westerners	46	43.8	+ 2.2
SUDAN	48.7	51.7	− 3.0

Upward corrections represent mostly the effect of assuming higher than reported mortality, in particular, infant mortality. Downward revisions reflect the net balance of the same adjustment *plus* a correction for misreporting of ages. If our estimates of the death rates are in fact too low, the estimated birth rates also contain a downward bias, roughly half the absolute size of the bias in the death rate. A reverse bias is present if we have overestimated the death rate. No conceivable adjustment necessitated by these factors could, however, obliterate the main feature of the above table—the presence of three different levels of fertility in the Sudan. The smaller differences within the higher fertility group and within the middle level fertility group shown above should not be overly emphasized, although these differences are probably significant. It should be added finally that the reliability of the birth rates given above for the Southerners and the Nuba is relatively poor, due to their dependence on somewhat subjectively selected ages at puberty. At least for the Southerners, however, the indicated rates are likely to be too high rather than too low.

Our estimates concerning the rate of growth have no independent statistical basis: they were obtained simply as the difference between the estimated birth and death rates. Thus all the weaknesses of the latter figures that were discussed above have a bearing on the growth rate estimates as well. It should be realized, however, that by the logic of the stable population model any modification in either the value of the estimated death rate or in the value of the estimated birth rate would involve a modification of the other, and this modification would be necessarily in the same direction. This means that the estimated growth rate is somewhat cushioned against the impact of changes in its determinants as far as absolute variations are concerned. If, for example, our death rate estimates are too low, this, *ceteris paribus*, does imply that the estimated growth rates are too high, but the needed modification in that rate will amount to only roughly half the absolute amount of underestimation in death rates, due to a concomitant upward adjustment of the birth rate. Hence the growth rate figures are more reliable than the quality of either the estimated birth rates or the estimated death rates would suggest if taken separately. Unlike the latter, our growth estimates display a great degree of uniformity among the different peoples; with the exception of the Western Southerners, whose growth rate is apparently only slightly above zero, all the other rates cluster closely around the national average of 2.75 percent per year. It is unlikely that the actual growth rates are higher than these; on the other hand, the possibility that for some peoples the true rates of growth were actually somewhat lower due to higher than estimated mortality (that is only partly offset by higher birth rates) cannot be dismissed.

Estimates by Provinces

For reasons we have discussed earlier in this paper, our analysis of the Sudanese demography was carried through for tribal instead of territorial subdivisions of the population. In view of the wide use of territorial classifications it will not be without interest to show the levels of vital rates that our estimates imply for each of the nine provinces of the country. Birth, death, and growth rates for the provinces obtained as a weighted average according to the tribal distribution (foreigners excluded) within each province are shown in Table 9.14.

Table 9.14.

Province	Birth rate	Death rate	Growth rate
Bahr el Ghazal	56	31	25
Blue Nile	47	18	29
Darfur	46	17	29
Equatoria	49	31	18
Kassala	45	18	27
Khartoum	47	17	30
Kordofan	46	18	28
Northern	47	17	30
Upper Nile	58	31	27
Sudan	48.7	21.3	27.4

These figures are to be interpreted in the light of two assumptions implicit in their calculation, namely that (1) each main tribal group, taken as a whole, is homogeneous with respect to its fertility and mortality characteristics and (2) the age and sex distribution of persons that belong to the same main tribal group is the same in each province. The first assumption seems to be valid to a good approximation; a careful study of the data by more detailed tribal classifications—a study which cannot be described here—failed to delineate sizeable sub-groups, within peoples, whose demographic behavior is significantly different from the average for the whole people. (The only apparent exception to this rule is the Azande of the Western Southerners, mainly in Equatoria province, who show exceptionally low fertility.) The second assumption is obviously untenable, at least with respect to several northern provinces, although the extent of the variation cannot be estimated. This circumstance, it will be recalled, was precisely one of the reasons why the territorial analysis was rejected in the first place. Thus the figures may not give the actual picture correctly by territorial units, disturbed as that picture is by the "openness" of these populations. They show, instead, what might be called the ideal picture in each province; the level of vital rates that would result from the given tribal composition and from the typical tribal demographic behavior. This qualification must be kept in mind in any comparison of the provincial estimates of Table 9.14 with the reported vital rates shown in Table 9.1.

The Applicability of the Stable Model

A final note that needs to be added to this analysis concerns, once more, the applicability of the stable model to the closed tribal populations of Sudan. It was stated at the beginning of our discussion that the model can be expected to perform satisfactorily, although under conditions of declining mortality it is subject to some qualifications. In the light of the preceding analysis we can now state that no qualifications of any practical importance need to be made. This is so because in the case of each people whose current mortality seems to imply the possibility of rapid past declines of mortality we have estimated vital rates from proportions in the younger ages plus an estimate of current mortality—a combination of estimators that makes these estimates almost completely insensitive to a bias due to declining mortality.[15] For the Southerners and the Nuba the estimates were based on current mortality plus proportions under the age of about 12-13 years. The bias that these estimator parameters may introduce if mortality has been declining is still small, although not necessarily negligible. It is negligible, however, in view of the mortality conditions of the Southerners current at the time of the census, which leave an extremely limited scope, if any, for past mortality declines. The only people concerning which the need for an adjustment may not be categorically excluded is the Nuba; it is possible that the stable estimates of the birth rate for this group are somewhat downward biased, and may well be 2 or 3 permillage points higher than we have suggested.

Our defense of the stable model with respect to the assumption of constant *fertility* that underlies it was based on the current high level of fertility in the country. Subsequent analysis in this paper showed, however, that there is a people in Sudan, the Western Southerners, whose fertility level is far below what can be called "natural" or "normal" in a non-contraceptive population, hence the possibility that there has been a decline of fertility within this people in the not far remote past, or that such a decline is still currently in process, cannot be ruled out.[16] A systematic study of the biases that result from applying stable techniques for estimating demographic quantities in a population with a history of declining fertility still remains to be made. However, the direction and the possible extent of the bias in estimating vital rates in the specific

[15] On this topic see Paul Demeny, "Estimation of vital rates for populations in the process of destabilization." *Demography* (Chicago), Vol. 2, 1965, pp. 516-530.

[16] In fact according to all indications low fertility is by no means of recent origin. Cf. H. B. McD. Farrel, "Dearth of children among the Azande: a preliminary report," *Sudan Notes and Records*, Vol. 35, Part I, 1954, pp. 6-19.

case of the Western Southerners is easily dealt with. Both deductive reasoning and experimentation with stable models indicate that, given the estimating parameters of current mortality and an index of the age distribution, the stable estimate of the birth rate when fertility has been in fact declining will be upward biased; it will give a birth rate that is higher than the actual one (which latter, in turn, will be substantially higher than the intrinsic birth rate). The magnitude of the bias is a function of many variables, most importantly the speed and duration of the fertility decline and the particular index of age distribution used as the estimator parameter.

The latter in our case is the proportion under the age of puberty, say 12.5 years of age. Even assuming steady and continuing fertility decline from a past high level, under these circumstances the maximum upward bias in the estimated birth rate will not exceed 3 permillage points. The death rate might be overestimated by a comparable amount, leaving a growth rate that is essentially correct or very close to the mark. The stable estimate of the gross reproduction rate, like the birth rate, is upward biased. All in all, no major qualifications are required on this score either, and any qualifications would be limited to the Western Southerners only. Their low birth rates, or gross reproduction rates, remain confirmed or are even made somewhat lower. A more consequential result of this digression is, however, the realization that while the current growth rate of the Western Southerners is in all probability positive, the intrinsic growth rate of this population must be negative, provided that the current fertility level is the outcome of a process of decline that took place not earlier than the turn of the present century.

The Scope of the 1955/56 Census

The aim of this paper has been to present an examination of the demographic data collected by the 1955/56 census and not a critique of the census itself. It will be appropriate nevertheless to conclude our discussion with a few remarks concerning the census takers' decisions on the scope and nature of the data that was to be collected in this survey. The most crucial of these was undoubtedly the one renouncing an attempt to obtain a detailed classification of the population by age. In retrospect this decision seems to be misguided and must be deplored. Admittedly a more ambitious classification of people by age would have contributed little, if any, direct additional information on the actual age distribution beyond what we are actually supplied by the data as collected. The poor general knowledge of age in the population made virtually certain that the reported age distribution would be beset by major biases, hence no detailed feature of that distribution could have been used to estimate the actual one. But granting all this, it would be wrong to conclude that the work of collecting age data would therefore have been useless; such a conclusion would ignore the multifarious uses of age data in combination with other types of demographic information. Data on marriage, on the number of children born during the year preceding the census, and on the number of children ever born and surviving are all of extremely limited use if given only for a single or at most two broad age categories of the adult population, but they become illuminating if accompanied by a breakdown by age even if the breakdown itself is extremely rudimentary. Techniques, discussed at another place in this volume, were recently developed to extract information on mortality and fertility from such data. These techniques are not highly sensitive to errors of age classification and are not affected by reference period errors either. Thus, one might say that even the crudest classification dividing the women in the childbearing ages into three broad categories (say, "young," "middle-aged," and "older") would have greatly improved the possibilities for a meaningful analysis of the data. Such age classes would have been heavily overlapping, no doubt, but would have been certainly properly ordered and significantly different as to their mean age. For example, if information from these women on the number of children ever born and surviving would also have been obtained this would have greatly contributed to remedy the weakest aspect of the 1955/56 census: the lack of adequate data on infant and childhood mortality.

It might be objected that the above remarks boil down to saying that the scope of the inquiry should have been wider, always an easy proposal that disregards the financial constraints necessarily imposed on a census. This objection is at least in part unjustified; the refusal to aim at a more detailed age classification was not based on budgetary considerations but on a view that held such an attempt useless. But we can go beyond this. In fact, a strong case can be made to advocate a scope for demographic inquiries that is wider than that of the 1955/56 Sudanese census, precisely in the name of economy. There seems to be a critical mass of data below which the tools of statistical analysis become painfully inefficient. Under such circumstances any piece of additional evidence becomes most valuable, not necessarily because of its intrinsic value, but because of its potential usefulness for illuminating patterns and biases in the rest of the material. The census of 1955/56 did provide, despite all its defects, data of remarkable consistency, permitting a reasonable description of the main demographic features of the Sudanese population. The scope of the census, however, seems to have been less than optimal. It is to be hoped that a second, wider inquiry will soon fill out the white spots on the demographic map of the Sudan and answer questions that were left open in the present analysis.

10

Fertility in Nigeria*

BY ETIENNE VAN DE WALLE

The demography of Nigeria is little known, even by African standards. There is no information on fertility or mortality representative of substantial numbers of its people. Birth and death statistics are published regularly for Lagos, but they can hardly be held representative of vital rates in the country or even in the Western Region. They are based on registration which appears complete and reliable, but the base population to which these births and deaths are to be related to yield crude birth and death rates is far less reliably documented. Registration of births and deaths in other parts of the country is, as elsewhere in tropical Africa, non-existent or incomplete. The only inquiry ever planned on a representative sample, including questions on fertility and mortality, was a 1962 post-enumeration survey. To the best of our knowledge the plans were not carried out.

The first real census was taken in 1952-53, but it contained no direct information on mortality and fertility. The 1962 census was invalidated. It is too early to know what results from the 1963 census will be published, and how detailed they will be, but the confusion of political and demographic issues is likely to have robbed this census of much of its scientific value.

Nigeria is the most populous country in Africa by far. The 1963 census figure of 56 millions[1] may be an overestimate, but even if the real figure is no more than 40 or 45 millions, it is much larger than the estimated populations of other countries of tropical Africa; the Congo had 14 million people around 1960; the Sudan had 12 million, Tanzania 9 million, Kenya 8 million, Uganda and Ghana 7 million. Any attempt to project the population of tropical Africa[2] is thus impossible without having at least an idea about the fertility and mortality of a country which contains a fifth of the total population of this area.

The United Nations has published an estimate of the fertility of Ni-

---

* This chapter appeared in essentially its present form in *Population Studies*, Vol. 19, No. 1, July 1965.

[1] United Nations, *Demographic Yearbook, 1964*, United Nations, New York 1965, Table 4.

[2] The present writer has prepared such a projection for the U.N. Population Conference in Belgrade, 1965.

geria based on the age distribution given by the 1952-53 census.[3] According to that estimate the gross reproduction rate of Nigeria was 3.7, and the crude birth rate between 53 and 57.[4] These estimates were obtained by the "reverse survival method." This method consists in considering the population at a certain age (or within a certain age group) as the survivors of a number of births occurring at some precise period in the past, and in relating these births to the population estimated at that time to obtain the crude birth rate. The gross reproduction rate likewise can be obtained from the births and the age distribution under an hypothesis concerning fertility by age of mother. This reverse survival method requires an hypothesis on mortality to estimate the fertility, since a different estimate of mortality between birth and census would inevitably give a different number of births of which the living are the survivors, and another base population to which these births have to be related.

The present chapter attempts an answer to the following question: Taking the 1952-53 census, which constitutes the best source of demographic information on Nigeria to date, what useful information on vital trends may be derived from it?

In the absence of migration, the age distribution of a country is determined entirely by its past fertility and mortality. We shall consider at a later point the importance of mortality in shaping the age distribution. At this stage it is sufficient to state that fertility influences the age distribution in the most marked fashion and that a large proportion of young children reflects a high fertility in the recent past. Conversely, a low proportion of children is the result of low past fertility. Thus it is normal to look at the 1952-53 age distribution of Nigeria and its parts for information on the fertility of that country.[5]

The 1952-53 Age Distribution

The following age groups (based on age at last birthday) are given for each sex: under age 2, from 2 to 6 years, 7 to 14 years, 15 to 49 years, and 50 years of age and over. In Table 10.1 we give this age distribution in percentages for the provinces of Nigeria. It is also available for divisions and smaller administrative units.

These age classes are different from those used in most other countries. There may have been advantages to the adopted classification in a country where the estimation of age presents almost insuperable difficulties. For instance, a good case can be made for the use of an age class that

[3] Nigeria Department of Statistics, *Population Census of Nigeria, 1952-53*, Summary Table 3.

[4] United Nations, *Demographic Yearbook, 1963*, p. 487.

[5] Information has been collected from the following sources: Nigeria, Department of Statistics, *Population Census of Northern Nigeria, July 1952; Population Census of Western Nigeria, December 1952; Population Census of Eastern Nigeria, June 1953*, Lagos, The Census Superintendent.

Table 10.1. Age distribution in percentages for each sex—provinces of Nigeria, 1952-53 census

Provinces	Males						Females					
	Under 2 yrs.	2–6 yrs.	7–14 yrs.	15–49 yrs.	50 yrs. and over	Total	Under 2 yrs.	2–6 yrs.	7–14 yrs.	15–49 yrs.	50 yrs. and over	Total
	%	%	%	%	%	%	%	%	%	%	%	%
Adamawa	12·9	19·0	15·4	42·2	10·5	100·0	11·9	16·8	13·2	47·7	10·4	100·0
Bauchi	10·7	17·4	16·3	45·1	10·4	99·9	10·2	15·5	13·5	48·8	12·0	100·0
Benue	10·2	18·3	14·4	53·0	4·0	99·9	10·1	16·4	12·9	54·8	5·8	100·0
Bornu	11·2	17·2	13·2	47·3	11·1	100·0	10·7	15·1	11·5	51·2	11·6	100·1
Illorin	12·8	16·2	16·3	44·7	10·1	100·1	12·6	14·7	14·9	45·9	11·8	99·9
Kabba	10·3	17·8	16·7	48·6	6·6	100·0	10·3	16·4	12·9	52·1	8·4	100·1
Kano	11·2	16·8	17·2	45·5	9·3	100·0	10·8	14·9	13·1	51·1	10·2	100·1
Katsina	9·5	18·8	20·0	47·5	4·3	100·1	8·6	16·4	12·5	53·6	8·8	99·9
Niger	9·9	17·4	14·0	48·5	10·3	100·1	9·8	16·3	12·4	49·3	12·1	99·9
Plateau	10·0	18·6	13·8	50·4	7·2	100·0	10·2	18·3	12·1	51·0	8·3	99·9
Sokoto	11·5	18·7	17·4	42·3	10·2	100·1	11·0	17·0	13·6	47·1	11·3	100·0
Zaria	11·3	18·2	17·4	43·7	9·5	100·1	11·1	17·8	13·4	47·3	10·5	100·1
Bamenda	10·5	18·5	19·0	47·4	4·6	100·0	9·9	17·1	14·3	53·6	5·2	100·1
Cameroons	6·9	12·3	15·8	61·7	3·3	100·0	9·3	14·4	12·8	58·9	4·6	100·0
Calabar	10·4	20·0	19·7	45·6	4·4	100·1	10·7	19·5	15·5	49·3	5·1	100·1
Ogoja	9·3	17·7	19·5	49·1	4·4	100·0	9·6	17·1	15·2	53·2	4·9	100·0
Onitsha	9·6	17·6	19·1	48·9	4·9	100·1	9·5	17·4	16·2	51·7	5·3	100·1
Owerri	11·6	20·1	19·1	43·9	5·3	100·0	11·1	18·6	15·6	49·3	5·4	100·0
Rivers	9·4	17·9	18·5	49·2	4·9	99·9	10·2	17·9	15·7	51·2	4·9	99·9
Abeokuta	10·0	18·1	18·3	45·4	8·2	100·0	10·2	16·6	15·1	50·3	7·8	100·0
Benin	11·4	18·8	20·0	43·6	6·3	100·1	11·7	18·2	15·2	47·5	7·4	100·0
Colony	6·6	14·4	15·9	57·5	5·7	100·1	7·6	15·7	15·1	55·9	5·7	100·0
Delta	9·9	19·1	18·5	44·3	8·3	100·1	10·1	17·2	13·8	50·2	8·8	100·1
Ibadan	15·6	18·9	20·0	37·6	8·0	100·1	15·4	17·7	17·6	41·0	8·2	99·9
Ijebu	8·6	17·0	18·9	44·8	10·8	100·1	8·6	16·3	15·5	48·5	11·1	100·0
Ondo	11·7	17·9	19·3	44·2	7·0	100·1	12·1	17·2	16·4	46·9	7·3	99·9
Oyo	13·2	17·8	18·9	41·9	8·2	100·0	13·5	16·7	16·2	44·7	8·9	100·0

will include all infants before they are weaned. Similarly, one may recommend an age class including children of pre-school ages, an age class for those between school age and puberty, an age class covering fecund women, and so on. Clearly the divisions in the Nigerian age distribution correspond to this scheme. But there is no necessary equivalence between recognizable stages in human development and ages expressed in round digits. For instance, physical puberty or social maturity does not necessarily occur at exact age 15. Certainly the exact ages corresponding to recorded ages 2, 7, 15, or 50 years must have varied a great deal among individuals and perhaps among regions. Recorded ages may have corresponded to a different stage in life for men and women, as illustrated by sex ratios for the provinces in Table 10.2. Sex ratios (males per female) usually rise steeply from under unity for the age group under 2 years, to over 1.10 for the age group 7 to 14 years; they are mostly under 0.90 after age 15. The effect of selective underenumeration and migration should be taken into account in a detailed discussion of these figures. It cannot be said with certainty that the sex ratio under age 2 is incorrect, although it appears to be too low, and its fluctuation among

Table 10.2. Sex ratios (males per female) by age—provinces of Nigeria, 1952-53 census

Provinces	Ages					
	Under 2	2–6	7–14	15–49	50 and over	Total
Adamawa	1·00	1·05	1·08	0·82	0·93	0·93
Bauchi	1·00	1·07	1·15	0·88	0·83	0·95
Benue	0·97	1·07	1·07	0·93	0·67	0·96
Bornu	1·03	1·11	1·12	0·91	0·94	0·98
Illorin	0·96	1·04	1·03	0·92	0·81	0·95
Kabba	0·90	0·98	1·17	0·84	0·71	0·90
Kano	1·00	1·08	1·26	0·85	0·87	0·96
Katsina	1·04	1·08	1·50	0·84	0·46	0·95
Niger	0·98	1·04	1·09	0·96	0·83	0·97
Plateau	0·94	0·98	1·10	0·96	0·84	0·97
Sokoto	1·01	1·06	1·23	0·87	0·87	0·96
Zaria	0·97	0·97	1·24	0·88	0·87	0·95
Bamenda	0·96	0·98	1·20	0·80	0·81	0·91
Cameroons	0·94	1·07	1·54	1·31	0·89	1·25
Calabar	0·95	1·00	1·24	0·90	0·84	0·97
Ogoja	0·89	0·95	1·18	0·85	0·83	0·92
Onitsha	0·95	0·95	1·10	0·89	0·86	0·94
Owerri	0·93	0·96	1·09	0·79	0·87	0·89
Rivers	0·94	1·02	1·20	0·98	1·02	1·02
Abeokuta	0·95	1·05	1·17	0·87	1·02	0·97
Benin	0·93	0·99	1·27	0·88	0·82	0·96
Colony	0·94	0·99	1·14	1·11	1·08	1·08
Delta	0·92	1·04	1·24	0·82	0·88	0·93
Ibadan	1·03	1·09	1·16	0·93	1·00	1·02
Ijebu	0·92	0·96	1·13	0·85	0·89	0·92
Ondo	0·91	0·98	1·11	0·89	0·90	0·94
Oyo	0·95	1·03	1·13	0·90	0·89	0·97

provinces is difficult to accept.[6] After 2, the ages of boys appear to be recorded systematically as lower than those of girls of the same real age until age 15. This may be caused by slower physical development of boys, or by their desire to avoid taxation as long as possible by making false declarations. In turn, girls may have been declared to be older than they really were because of the use of social or physical criteria instead of objective ages in years.

Whatever the defects in the reporting of ages, it is clear that in the absence of vital registration the age data cannot be taken at their face value. A full census using large numbers of ill-prepared interviewers will fare worse in this respect than a sample survey addressed to a small percentage of the population. It may be interesting in this respect to refer to the British East African experience, where the full censuses, presumably less accurate, have uniformly yielded higher proportions of children than the sample surveys in selected areas taken to check and supplement them (for both sexes together). See Table 10.3.

[6] Sex ratios at birth close to or under unity have been found in most Central African surveys. Western populations with reliable statistics have sex ratios at birth around 1.06 males per female. But the American Negro, of Central African origin, has a distinctly lower ratio of 1.03.

Table 10.3. Proportions in certain childhood age intervals
—censuses of Tanganyika and Uganda

	Ages under one year (%)	1–5 years (%)	6–16 years (%)	Total under 16 (%)
Tanganyika 1948 Census[1]	5·2	17·4	22·3	44·9
„ 1948 Sample[1]	3·6	15·2	23·4	42·2
„ 1957 Census[2]	6·1	17·7	20·6	44·4
„ 1957 Sample[2]	3·8	17·2	22·6	43·6
Uganda 1959 Census[3]	5·7	18·2	19·6	43·5
„ 1959 Sample[2]	3·8	16·6	22·8	43·2

SOURCES: (1) Tanganyika, *African Census Report 1957*, The Government Printer, Dar-es-Salaam, 1963, p. 31.
(2) *Ibid.*, p. 29.
(3) Uganda, Statistical Branch, Ministry of Economic Affairs, *Uganda Census, 1959; African Population*, Entebbe, 1960.

In those cases at least, the haste and loss in quality inherent in a full enumeration appears to have resulted in an overstatement of the proportion of children.

It is thus obvious that the age distributions given for Nigerian provinces reflect not only past vital trends but also to a large extent the effect of misreporting of ages. Furthermore, there has been underenumeration of large portions of the population, the extent of which cannot be estimated. Although the omission of entire villages or complete households would perhaps not affect the age distribution to an important extent, it is not unlikely that underenumeration may have been concentrated on particular age and sex groups. What Mansell Prothero has to say of Northern Nigeria must be true of the entire country:

> The enumeration in 1952 aimed to include all, and the same importance was given to females as to males. This was not without its problems. There is the inclination among certain tribes to conceal the number of children, particularly the first born. Among Moslem communities there is the impossibility of checking the number of married women who are in "purdah."[7]

Finally, another upsetting factor was important: migration from and to certain areas of Nigeria. It probably affected young adult males most of all.

Fertility Information Derived from the Age Distributions

However important the biases that exist in the reporting of ages, it is still possible that they do not obscure the influence of fertility on the age

[7] R. Mansell Prothero, "The population census of Northern Nigeria, 1952: Problems and results," *Population Studies*, Vol. 10, No. 2, p. 173.

distribution. This influence will be reflected in the systematic tendency of successive childhood age groups to be large (or small) in the same provinces, and conversely of adult and old ages to represent a small (or large) part of the age distribution in the same areas. And indeed, as indicated in Table 10.4, there is a significant positive correlation between

Table 10.4. Correlation coefficients (r) between age classes, by sex—provinces and divisions of Nigeria

Age classes and sex	Provinces					Divisions				
	Under 2	2–6	7–14	15–49	50 and over	Under 2	2–6	7–14	15–49	50 and over
Males	**Males**					**Males**				
Under 2		0·54	0·16	−0·84	0·42		0·73	0·42	−0·86	0·37
2– 6	0·54		0·37	−0·71	0·05	0·73		0·55	−0·87	0·20
7–14	0·16	0·37		−0·42	−0·36	0·42	0·55		−0·64	−0·13
15–49	−0·84	−0·71	−0·42		−0·53	−0·86	−0·87	−0·64		−0·50
50 and over	0·42	0·05	−0·36	−0·53		0·37	0·20	−0·13	−0·50	
Females	**Females**					**Females**				
Under 2		0·21	0·40	−0·82	0·22		0·43	0·34	−0·81	0·15
2– 6	0·21		0·41	−0·32	−0·39	0·43		0·38	−0·54	−0·29
7–14	0·40	0·41		−0·46	−0·39	0·34	0·38		−0·48	−0·40
15–49	−0·82	−0·32	−0·46		−0·49	−0·81	−0·54	−0·48		−0·40
50 and over	0·22	−0·39	−0·39	−0·49		0·15	−0·29	−0·40	−0·40	
Males	**Females**					**Females**				
Under 2	0·94	0·21	0·28	−0·85	0·37	0·89	0·44	0·19	−0·83	0·35
2– 6	0·35	0·75	0·16	−0·49	0·03	0·45	0·70	0·08	−0·63	0·23
7–14	0·19	0·48	0·73	−0·28	−0·39	0·34	0·49	0·66	−0·52	−0·16
15–49	−0·70	−0·37	−0·36	0·90	−0·46	−0·64	−0·50	−0·23	0·85	−0·47
50 and over	0·30	−0·31	−0·21	−0·59	0·93	0·22	−0·23	−0·24	−0·49	0·94

the child age groups both at the provincial and at the division level. The highest correlation obtains between the group under 2 years old and that 2 to 6 years, but the correlation is significant among all segments of the child age groups for both sexes and between one sex and the other. There is also an inverse correlation between each of the three age groups under age 15 and the age group 15 to 49 years. Finally the age groups 15 to 49 years and 50 and over appear to be complementary (they correlate *negatively*), an indication of the type of bias which exists through transfers of persons from one of these two age classes to the other. Interestingly enough, similar inverse correlations do not obtain among the first three age classes, and the degree of inverse correlation between age groups 7 to 14 and 15 to 49 is less than that between ages 2 to 6 and, most of all, the group under 2 years old, on the one hand, and 15 to 49 on the other. This would be expected if the correlations express the respective influence of fertility on these age groups in various provincial populations.

It is now time to say more about the method followed here to derive fertility information, however partial and unreliable, from the age distribution. This consists in comparing ratios of reported age classes (child-adult ratios) with those in a series of stable population models. A stable population is one which has undergone constant fertility and mortality in the absence of migration for a large number of years. Provided its pattern of mortality is known or can be assumed, an actual population such as that of Nigeria may be surmised to have an age distribution very similar to that of a stable population with its present fertility and mortality levels provided it has not undergone fluctuations in fertility and/or very fast or catastrophic changes in mortality in the recent past.[8] These conditions are probably fairly well fulfilled in the case of Nigeria, except for migration. The effect of migration is minimized by considering primarily female age distributions.

The model is from the North tables,[9] which are life tables at successive levels of mortality, and a series of stable populations generated at these levels of mortality and for that pattern by various levels of the rate of population increase. For practical purposes, one assumes a likely level of mortality and then investigates what level of fertility within the model corresponds to the age group recorded in the census.

The age groups of the Nigerian census (under 2 years, 2-6, 7-14, 15-49, 50 years and over) may, as we have said, have presented convenient boundaries for interviewing purposes, but for purposes of analysis they are inconvenient compared with standard five-year age groups. Graduation methods designed to convert the age distribution into a more conventional one might constitute a screen between the collected data and the analysis and cannot be used for our purpose. The stable population models are presented in standard age groups—0-4, 5-9, 10-14 years, and so on. It is possible to compare the recorded age groups 0-14 and 15-49 without transformation of the data. We shall compare the reported age group 0-2 with half the age class 0-4 years in the model; the latter is slightly larger than the age group 0-2. Similarly, the reported age group 0-6 (at last birthday, or under exact age 7) is compared with the sum of the age group 0-4 and half the age group 5-9 years in the model; this total should also be larger than the proportion of the population under 7, and closer to that under 7½ years.

We shall systematically use ratios of the age groups under 2, under

---

[8] A more complete statement concerning the use of stable populations can be found in Ansley J. Coale, "Estimates of various demographic measures through the quasi-stable age distribution," in Milbank Memorial Fund, *Emerging Techniques in Population Research*, 1963.

[9] The choice of the North pattern of mortality is somewhat arbitrary, but conforms to other chapters in this book. For the models, see A. J. Coale and P. Demeny, *Regional Model Life Tables and Stable Populations*, Princeton University Press, 1966.

7, and under 15 to those over 15. The cumulation of age classes from 0 to 15 on seems advisable in order to reduce the effect of complementary bias and transfers between age classes. These child-adult ratios will be compared with the corresponding ratios in the model stable populations. Fertility will be measured in terms of gross reproduction rates, assuming the mean age of childbearing to be equal to 27 years.

It is necessary to reintroduce the effect of mortality on the age distribution. Table 10.5 indicates for both sexes the size of the child-adult

Table 10.5. Child-adult ratios* at selected levels of the female expectation of life at birth (e°_{0}) and of the gross reproduction rate with mean age of childbearing of 27 years, by sex—North model stable populations

e°_{0} and G.R.R. (27)	Ratio of specified age-class to adults over age 15 years					
	Males			Females		
	$\dfrac{(\text{o to 4})}{2}$	$\dfrac{(\text{o to 4})+(\text{o to 9})}{2}$	Under 15	$\dfrac{(\text{o to 4})}{2}$	$\dfrac{(\text{o to 4})+(\text{o to 9})}{2}$	Under 15
$e^{\circ}_{0}=25$						
G.R.R. (27)=20	0·080	0·224	0·411	0·074	0·207	0·381
25	0·115	0·299	0·534	0·100	0·278	0·499
30	0·136	0·373	0·653	0·127	0·350	0·616
35	0·165	0·448	0·771	0·155	0·423	0·730
40	0·194	0·523	0·886	0·183	0·496	0·844
$e^{\circ}_{0}=30$						
G.R.R. (27)=20	0·086	0·242	0·445	0·080	0·226	0·416
25	0·116	0·322	0·577	0·109	0·303	0·544
30	0·146	0·403	0·706	0·138	0·381	0·670
35	0·177	0·483	0·833	0·168	0·460	0·795
40	0·208	0·563	0·956	0·198	0·538	0·916
45	0·238	0·642	1·076	0·228	0·616	1·035
$e^{\circ}_{0}=35$						
G.R.R. (27)=20	0·091	0·258	0·474	0·085	0·242	0·447
25	0·122	0·342	0·614	0·118	0·330	0·610
30	0·154	0·427	0·750	0·147	0·408	0·717
35	0·187	0·513	0·885	0·178	0·491	0·849
40	0·219	0·597	1·015	0·210	0·574	0·978

* Ratios of half the age group o to 4, of the age group o to 4 plus half the age group 5 to 9, and of the age group under 15, to those of the same sex aged over 15 years.

ratios in the models for different levels of expectation of life at birth and different gross reproduction rates. The table shows that age distribution is much more sensitive to the effect of fertility than to that of mortality. It indicates within what range stable age distributions are found which have the same fertility but different expectations of life at birth, or which have the same expectation of life at birth but different fertility. For instance, to a range of 0.5 in the gross reproduction rate between 3.5 and

4,[10] for an expectation of life at birth of 25 years, corresponds a difference of the ratio of females under age 15 years to those over that age of between 0.730 and 0.844. About the same difference (0.730 to 0.849) corresponds to a range of 10 years in the expectation of life at birth—between 25 and 35 years—for an identical gross reproduction rate of 3.5. In other words, a range of 14 percent in gross reproduction rates accounts for the same difference in the age distribution as a range of 40 percent in the expectation of life at birth.

Since the sensitivity of the age distribution to mortality is markedly lower than to fertility, we are able to say something about differential fertility in Nigeria by assuming the mortality to be high but relatively homogeneous throughout the country. We could go no further if we did not make an assumption of the kind. It can be said without much danger of error that the expectation of life in the Nigerian provinces was somewhere between 25 and 35 years, 30 being a not unreasonable average for the period. One has to remember that the margin of error involved in assuming a uniform mortality throughout may very well be smaller than that due to various biases and errors which affect the data. It must also be conceded that we have not much hope of *a priori* determining the level of Nigerian fertility, but that meaningful differentials can possibly be derived from the age data in various provinces. Therefore the actual level of expectation of life in Nigeria is also of little importance to the reasoning, provided the variation in mortality conditions from region to region is not too considerable.

Results

For an assumed female expectation of life at birth of 30 years, the relationships set out in Table 10.5 between the child-adult ratios and the gross reproduction rates are used, by interpolation, to derive gross reproduction rates from the successive age classes given for Nigerian provinces (Table 10.6).

These results call for the following comments. First of all, comparisons among the columns of Table 14.6 confirm the relative consistency in ranking according to the various indices of fertility. The selection of one of the six indicators for plotting on a map has to be made in function of the previous discussion. The female age distribution is less affected than the male by migration; also, the larger the selected age group, the less will be the possibility of mistake and bias. Clearly, a mistake of a few months in the average estimation of age will carry more weight for the age class under age 2 than for that under age 15. A further consideration leads to the selection of females under 15. In girls, the latter age corresponds roughly to the age at puberty, although it may occur

[10] This is equivalent to a not very considerable range in completed family size: roughly between seven and eight children.

Table 10.6. Gross reproduction rates derived from ratios of
children under specified ages to adults aged over 15, by sex.
in Nigerian provinces according to the 1953-55 census

Province	Males			Females		
	Under 2	Under 7	Under 15	Under 2	Under 7	Under 15
Adamawa	4·6	4·3	3·8	4·1	3·7	3·2
Bauchi	3·8	3·7	3·4	3·5	3·3	2·9
Benue	3·5	3·6	3·2	3·5	3·4	2·9
Bornu	3·7	3·5	3·0	3·5	3·2	2·7
Illorin	4·4	3·8	3·5	4·3	3·6	3·2
Kabba	3·7	3·7	3·4	3·5	3·4	2·9
Kano	4·0	3·7	3·5	3·6	3·2	2·9
Katsina	3·6	3·9	3·9	3·0	3·1	2·7
Niger	3·4	3·4	3·0	3·4	3·3	2·8
Plateau	3·4	3·6	3·1	3·6	3·6	3·1
Sokoto	4·2	4·1	3·8	3·9	3·6	3·2
Zaria	4·1	3·9	3·7	3·9	3·8	3·2
Bamenda	3·9	4·0	3·9	3·5	3·5	3·1
Cameroons	2·4	2·3	2·4	3·1	3·0	2·6
Calabar	4·0	4·3	4·2	4·0	4·1	3·7
Ogojo	3·4	3·6	3·7	3·5	3·5	3·2
Onitsa	3·5	3·6	3·6	3·5	3·6	3·3
Owerri	4·5	4·5	4·3	4·1	4·0	3·6
Rivers	3·5	3·6	3·6	3·7	3·8	3·5
Abeokuta	3·7	3·8	3·6	3·6	3·5	3·2
Benin	4·3	4·3	4·2	4·3	4·0	3·6
Colony	2·3	2·6	2·5	2·6	3·0	2·8
Delta	3·7	3·9	3·8	3·6	3·5	3·1
Ibadan	6·2	5·2	4·6	5·9	4·9	4·5
Ijebu	3·1	3·4	3·4	4·6	3·2	3·0
Ondo	4·4	4·1	4·0	4·4	4·0	3·7
Oyo	4·9	4·4	4·2	4·9	4·2	3·8
Mean	3·9	3·8	3·6	3·8	3·6	3·2

on the average somewhat earlier or later in different human populations.[11]
On the other hand, in the absence of detailed knowledge on ages, the
distinction between women under and over age 15 must have relied upon
whether or not they had reached the adult stage, whether of physiological or of social maturity. Recorded age 15 may thus have corresponded
to an easily recognizable state. It is possible that there was some regional
variation in its occurrence, so that the overall confirmation given by the
other indices in Table 10.6 is welcome. It must be noted that with only
two exceptions (Cameroons and Colony) the estimate based on women
under age 15 is the lowest of the six estimates. In other African censuses
there is evidence of upward transfer of females across age 15—of probable understatement of the proportion under 15. This suggests that the
estimates chosen may be subject to a downward bias from this source,

[11] See, for instance, Raymond Pearl, *The Natural History of Population*, Oxford University Press, 1939. On p. 49 the author discusses the results of his analysis of the then existing literature and obtains a mean age at menarche in 142
studies, mostly European, of 15.17 years with a standard deviation of 0.9 years.

although in individual provinces, other biases, such as lower mortality or the effect of migration, may be greater.

Figure 10.1 indicates the distribution by provinces of the gross reproduction rate calculated on this particular scale. The area of highest

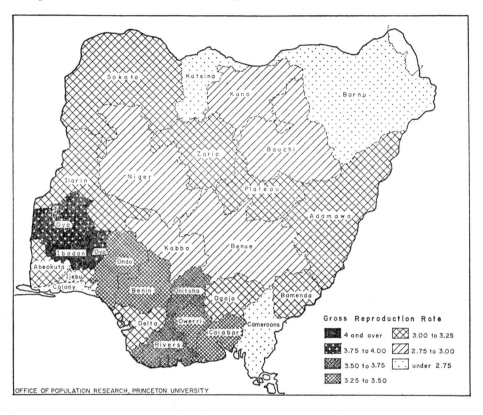

10.1. Estimates of gross reproduction rates in the provinces of Nigeria, 1952-53, based on the proportion of females under age 15. (North female stable populations, $e''_0 = 30$ years, $m = 27$ years).

fertility appears to be in Western Nigeria, particularly in the Yoruba region. The Eastern region includes one low-fertility area, Cameroons Province, with a gross reproduction rate under 3 according to our scale. Gross reproduction rates in Northern Nigeria offer the following pattern: two areas of low fertility (under 3)—Bornu-Bauchi-Kano-Katsina and Niger-Kabba-Benue—sandwiching a strip of higher fertility (between 3 and 3.25). It is interesting that the two provinces of lowest fertility, Cameroons and Bornu, have a common border area of distinctly low fertility in the adjacent country. Analysis of the North Cameroon inquiry by W. Brass has produced an estimated gross reproduction rate of

2.3.[12] A stratum of Niger also bordering on Bornu Province exhibits the lowest fertility in Niger, with a GRR of only about 1.8.[13] As for Cameroons Province, at least one demographic inquiry—that in not too distant Mbalmayo[14]—indicated low fertility. At the western border, estimates computed by Brass for Northern and Southern Dahomey indicate gross reproduction rates of 3.1 and 3.2, respectively. The southern part of Dahomey is indeed closer to the higher fertility area in Yorubaland. Outside indications thus partially confirm the distribution. Katsina's position as an area of low fertility is more doubtful, since it is not confirmed by the male child-adult ratios in Table 10.6. Mansell Prothero draws attention to the sex ratio in this and two other predominantly Muslim provinces and argues that large transfers of girls under 15 took place toward the upper part of the recorded age distribution.[15]

So much for the indications of differential fertility. As for actual levels of the gross reproduction rate, it may be argued that the chosen child-adult ratio may underestimate fertility. There is a tendency for the youngest age groups to indicate a higher fertility than the older ones. This would be even more obvious if the models had made it possible to use ages under 2 and under 7 years instead of age groups which are closer to ages under 2 1/2 and 7 1/2. Also, male age groups tend to indicate higher fertility levels than the corresponding female ones.

We showed that indications of level may be deceptive. At least the age group under 2 almost certainly constitutes an overestimate. The argument developed by Mansell Prothero according to which women, especially in predominantly Muslim areas, often marry before age 15 and are then "accorded adult status whatever their actual age may be"[16] is not implausible, but it would require large transfers of that sort, not compensated by the opposite transfer of unmarried girls of over 15, to affect the child-adult ratio much. For Nigeria as a whole, a computation based on the models shows that one would have to suppose that 37.5 percent of the age group 10-14 years had been transferred upward if one accepted the fertility implied by the child-adult ratio under age 2. In other words, practically every girl above age 13 would have to be married—a rather improbable situation.

However, before accepting a gross reproduction rate of 3.2 (mean of provincial gross reproduction rates based on the age group under 15) as a usable value for Nigeria as a whole, one must remember some of

[12] See Chapter 7.

[13] République Française, République du Niger, Mission Démographique du Niger, 1960, *Etude démographique du Niger*, 2ème Fascicule, *Données individuelles, Résultats définitifs*, Paris, Ministère de la Coopération, INSEE, Service de Coopération, 1963, Sect. 3. See also Chapter 4.

[14] Cameroun, Service de la Statistique Générale, *Résultats du recensement de la subdivision de Mbalmayo 1956, Population autochtone*, 1958.

[15] Prothero, *op. cit.*, pp. 173-174.

[16] *Ibid.*, p. 174.

the margins of error implied in the poor quality of the data and in the choice of assumptions. There may have been an undercount of children; the expectation of life at birth for Nigeria in 1952-53 may be overestimated. The choice of a mean age of childbearing of 27 years is based on the known prevalence of very young marriages in Nigeria; if mean age of childbearing were 29 years instead of 27, the national estimate of the gross reproduction rate would be 3.4 instead of 3.2, other things remaining equal. For all these reasons the latter value may well be a minimum estimate. The comparison with other areas of Africa tends to lend further credibility to a value of the gross reproduction rate of between 3.2 and 3.5, but this comparative argument has little value for a huge diversified country such as Nigeria.

Conclusion

The reader deserves some apologies for having been led through a forest of qualifications and reservations. The purpose was to demonstrate how little information exists on the population of Nigeria, and that no amount of ingenuity can yield reliable results where so little is available.

Is it possible to project the population of Nigeria under these circumstances? The very size of that population is uncertain after the last censuses, its mortality is unknown, and its fertility can only be guessed. Under these circumstances the answer is no. No sophisticated procedure upon which we could base even a mere guess about what this population would be 10, 15, or 25 years ahead is justified. Unfortunately this is still true of a large part of Africa.

Published Statistical Sources
Used in this Volume

ANGOLA

Colónia de Angola, Direcção dos Serviços de Economia, Repartição de Estatística Geral, *Censo Geral da População 1940*. Luanda, Imprensa Nacional. Especially: Vol. III, População presente, não civilizada, segundo a idade, o tipo somático e o sexo, por províncias, distritos, concelhos, circunscrições e postos administrativos, 1940. Vol. XI e XII, Constituição das famílias. Fecundidade e sobrevivência. Casais segundo a permanência na colónia, 1947.

Província de Angola, Repartição Tecnica de Estatística Geral, *II. Recenseamento Geral da População 1950*. Luanda, Imprensa Nacional. Especially Vol. IV, População nao civilizada, segundo as idades, a religião, os grupos étnicos, as mulheres que geraram filhos e a instrução, por Concelhos ou Circunscrições, 1955.

BURUNDI

V. Neesen, "Quelques données démographiques sur la population du Ruanda-Urundi," *Zaïre*, Dec. 1953, No. 10, pp. 1011ff.

Rapports soumis par le gouvernement belge à l'assemblée générale des Nations-Unies au sujet de l'administration du Ruanda-Urundi. Brussels, 1952-57.

CAMEROON

Cameroun, Service de la statistique générale, *Résultats du recensement de la subdivision de Mbalmayo 1956*. Population autochtone. 1958.

Cameroun, Service de la statistique et de la mécanographie, *Enquête démographique par sondage Nord-Cameroun*. Résultats provisoires de la mission socio-économique du Nord-Cameroun. Yaoundé, 1960.

CENTRAL AFRICAN REPUBLIC

République Centrafricaine, Mission socio-économique Centre-Oubangui; République Française, Secrétariat d'Etat aux relations avec les Etats de la communauté, *Enquête démographique Centre-Oubangui 1959. Méthodologie, résultats provisoires*. Paris, 1960.

CONGO (DEMOCRATIC REPUBLIC)

République du Congo, Bureau de la démographie, *Tableau général de la démographie congolaise. Enquête démographique par sondage 1955-1957. Analyse générale des résultats statistiques*. Léopoldville,

Ministère du plan et de la coordination économique, Service des statistiques, 1961.

The information by districts (except for Orientale Province) has been published in several volumes (*fascicules*) under the following auspices:

(a) Congo Belge, 2ᵉ Direction Générale, 1ᵉ Direction, A.I.M.O., *Enquêtes démographiques*

> Fascicule nº 1, Cité Léopoldville, 1957
> 2, Territoire Suburbain, 1957
> 3-4, Districts du Bas-Congo et des Cataractes, 1957
> 5, District de la Tshuapa, 1958
> 7, District du Maniema, 1959

(b) Congo Belge, Affaires économiques, Direction de la statistique, Bulletin mensuel des statistiques générales du Congo belge et du Ruanda-Urundi, Série spéciale nº 3, *Enquête démographique 1956/57*

> Fascicule b, Province de l'Equateur (except Tshuapa district), 1959
> e, Province du Katanga, 1960
> f, Province du Kasai, 1959

(c) République du Congo, Ministère du plan et de la coordination économique, Service des statistiques. Démographie, *Résultats de l'enquête démographique*

> Fascicule nº 11, Districts Lac Léopold II–Kwilu-Kwango, 1961
> nº 12, Districts Nord-et Sud-Kivu (no date)
> Fascicule e, followed: Katanga, 1961

DAHOMEY

Dahomey; France, Ministère de la coopération, I.N.S.E.E., Service de coopération, *Données de base sur la situation démographique au Dahomey en 1961*. Paris, 1962.

GABON

Gabon; France, Ministère de la coopération, I.N.S.E.E., Service de coopération, *Recensement et enquête démographiques 1960-61*. Résultats provisoires, ensemble du Gabon. Paris, 1963.

GHANA

Ghana, Census Office, *1960 Population Census of Ghana*. Advance report of Volumes III and IV. Accra, 1962.

GUINEA

Guinée; France, Ministère de la France d'outre-mer, Service des statistiques, *Etude démographique par sondage en Guinée 1954-55*. Résultats définitifs. Two volumes. Paris, no date.

Guinée; France, I.N.S.E.E., Service de coopération, *Enquête démographique de la région du Konkouré (Guinée 1957)*. Résultats définitifs. Paris, 1962.

IVORY COAST

Côte d'Ivoire, Service de la statistique et de la mécanographie; France, Ministère de la France d'outre-mer, Service des statistiques, *Etude démographique du 1ᵉʳ secteur agricole de la Côte d'Ivoire, 1957-58*. Résultats provisoires. Paris, 1958.

MALI

Soudan, Mission socio-économique du Sudan; France, Ministère de la France d'outre-mer, Service des statistiques, *Enquête démographique 1957-58*. Rapport provisoire No. 3. Paris, 1958.

Mali, Mission socio-économique 1956-58; France, Ministère de la coopération, I.N.S.E.E., Service de coopération, *Enquête démographique dans le Delta Central Nigérien*. Fascicule I, Résultats sommaires; Fascicule II, Résultats détaillés. Paris, no date.

MAURITANIA

Mauritanie, Sénégal, Mission socio-économique de la basse vallée du Sénégal; France, Ministère de la France d'outre-mer, Service des statistiques, *Enquête démographique 1957*. Résultats provisoires. Paris, 1957.

Mauritanie, Sénégal, Mission socio-économique du fleuve Sénégal, *La démographie du Fouta-Toro (Toucouleurs et Peulhs)*. Documents de travail. 1959.

Mauritanie, Sénégal; France, Ministère de la coopération. I.N.S.E.E., Service de coopération, *La Moyenne Vallée du Sénégal,* Prepared by J. Boutillier, P. Cantrelle, J. Causse, C. Laurent, and Th. N'Doye. 1962.

Note: The three publications cited present the same survey which refers also to a part of Senegal.

MOZAMBIQUE

Moçambique, Repartição Técnica de Estatística, *Censo da População em 1940*, Lourenço Marques, Imprensa Nacional de Moçambique. Especially: Volume II, População indígena. População total por sexos, idades e estado civil, segundo a sua distribução por divisões administrativas, 1943. Volume V. População indígena. Fecundidade, 1945.

Moçambique. Repartição Técnica de Estatística, *Recenseamento Geral da População em 1950*. Volume III, População não civilizada. Lourenço Marques, Imprensa Nacional de Moçambique, 1955.

NIGER

Niger, Mission démographique du Niger 1960; France, Ministère de la coopération, I.N.S.E.E., Service de coopération, *Etude démographique du Niger*, Fascicule II, Données individuelles. Résultats définitifs. Paris, 1963.

NIGERIA

Nigeria, Department of Statistics, *Population Census of the Eastern Region of Nigeria 1953.* Lagos, no date.

Idem. Population Census of the Northern Region of Nigeria 1952. Lagos, no date.

Idem. Population Census of the Western Region of Nigeria 1952. Lagos, 1956.

PORTUGUESE GUINEA

Provincia da Guiné. *Censo da População de 1950.* Volume II, População não civilizada. Lisbon, Tipografia Portuguesa, Lda., no date.

RHODESIA

Southern Rhodesia, Central African Statistical Office, *Report on the Demographic Sample Survey of the African Population of Southern Rhodesia.* Salisbury, 1951.

Federation of Rhodesia and Nyasaland, Central African Statistical Office, *The 1953-55 Demographic Sample Survey of the Indigenous African Population of Southern Rhodesia.* Salisbury, 1959.

RWANDA

Same sources as Burundi.

SENEGAL

Same sources as Mauritania (for the Senegal Valley).

SUDAN

The Republic of Sudan, H.Q. Council of Ministers, Department of Statistics, *First Population Census of Sudan 1955-56.* Final Report. Three volumes. Khartoum, 1961.

The Republic of Sudan, Ministry for Social Affairs, Population Census Office, *First Population Census of Sudan 1955/56.* Supplement to Interim Reports. Khartoum, 1956.

TANZANIA

Tanganyika, Central Statistical Bureau, *African Census Report*, 1957. Dar es Salaam, The Government Printer, 1963.

Zanzibar Protectorate. *Report on the Census of the Population of the Zanzibar Protectorate* (taken on the night of the 19th and 20th March 1958). Zanzibar, The Government Printer, 1960.

TOGO

Togo, Service de la statistique générale, Institut de recherche du Togo, *Etude démographique du pays Kabré 1957.* Paris, 1960.

République Togolaise, Service de la statistique générale, *Recensement*

fort >ML>

général de la population du Togo 1958-60. Especially: Fascicule n°
5 and 6. Lomé, no date.

UGANDA

Uganda Protectorate, Statistics Branch, Ministry of Economic Affairs,
Uganda Census 1959 African Population. Nairobi, 1961.

UPPER VOLTA

République de Haute Volta, Service de Statistique; France, Ministère
de la coopération, I.N.S.E.E., Service de coopération, *La situation
démographique en Haute Volta.* Résultats partiels de l'enquête démographique 1960-61. Paris, 1962.

ZAMBIA

Central African Statistical Office, *Report on the 1950 Demographic
Sample Survey of the African Population of Northern Rhodesia.* Salisbury, 1952.

GENERAL

United Nations, Department of Economic and Social Affairs, *Demographic Yearbook 1964.* New York, 1965.

Index

MAURITANIA

MALI

NIGER
(Strata)

SENEGAL

GAMBIA

UPPER VOLTA

PORTUGUESE
GUINEA

FOUTA
DJALLON

GUINEA

UPPER
GUINEA

FOREST

LIBERIA

IVORY COAST   GHANA

DAHOMEY

TOGO

First Agricultural
Sector

SOKOTO   KATSINA   KANO   BORNU

ZARIA   BAUCHI

NIGER   PLATEAU

NIGERIA   ADAMAWA

KABBA   BENUE   NORTH
CAMEROON

OYO

BENIN   ONITSHA

DELTA   OGOJA

CAMEROON

GABON

(UNINHABITED)

NUBIYIN

BEJA

WESTERNERS   ARAB   WESTERNERS

SUDAN
(Major Peoples)

NUBA

ARAB

CENTRAL

WESTERN   SOUTHERNERS

CENTRAL AFRICAN REPUBLIC

CENTRE

OUBANGUI

SOUTHERNERS   EASTERN
SOUTHERNERS

HAUT UELE

NORTHERN

EASTERN   NORTH

UBANGI   MONGALA   BAS UELE

ITURI   UGANDA   RIFT   EASTERN

KENYA   EAST

EQUATEUR   STANLEYVILLE   NORD   EASTERN   BUGANDA   CENTRAL

DEMOCRATIC
REPUBLIC   TSHUAPA

KIVU   WESTERN   WEST   RIFT
VALLEY

LAC LEOPOLD II   RWANDA

OF CONGO   MANIEMA   SUD KIVU   BURUNDI   LAKE   COAST

SANKURU

NORTHERN

CABINDA   BAS
(LUANDA   CONGO   CATARACTES   WESTERN   TANGA
ANGOLA)

KWILU   LULUA   TANZANIA

LUANDA   KWANGO   KABINDA   TANGANIKA   CENTRAL

SOUTHERN

MALANGE   HAUT LOMANI   HIGHLANDS   EASTERN

LUAPULA

BENGUELA   LUALABA   MOERA   SOUTHERN

ANGOLA   NORTH

BIE   MOZAMBIQUE

HUILA   ZAMBIA

CENTRAL

RHODESIA

SOUTH